MINUTES

OF THE

Sixth Biennial Convention

OF

The United Lutheran Church in America

ERIE, PENNSYLVANIA
October 9-16, 1928

THE UNITED LUTHERAN PUBLICATION HOUSE
PHILADELPHIA, PA.

THE UNITED LUTHERAN CHURCH IN AMERICA

CALENDAR, 1928-1930

OFFICERS

President—Rev. F. H. Knubel, D.D., LL.D.,
39 East 35th Street, New York City.

Secretary—Rev. M. G. G. Scherer, D.D.,
39 East 35th Street, New York City

Treasurer—Mr. E. Clarence Miller, LL.D.,
1508 Walnut Street, Philadelphia, Pa.

EXECUTIVE BOARD

Term Expires 1932

Rev. A. Charles R. Keiter, 940 Cumberland Street, Lebanon, Pa.
Rev. Charles D. Trexler, Fourth Avenue and 75th Street, Brooklyn, N. Y.
Rev. Abdel Ross Wentz, D.D., Ph.D., Gettysburg, Pa.
Hon. Wm. E. Hirt, Erie, Pa.
Hon. John F. Kramer, 3-5 Blymyer Building, Mansfield, Ohio.
George E. Neff, Esq., 29 S. Duke Street, York, Pa.

Term Expires 1930

Rev. Ellis B. Burgess, D.D., 73 Haldane Street, Crafton, Pa.
Rev. W. H. Greever D.D., Drawer 300, Columbia, S. C.
Rev. Arthur H. Smith, D.D., 259 Sandusky Street, Ashland, Ohio.
B. B. Miller, Esq., Salisbury, N. C.
Mr. John Greiner, Jr., 1 S. Centre Street, Pottsville, Pa.
Mr. Wm. H. Stackel, 93 Alliance Avenue, Rochester, N. Y.

Members Ex-Officio

Rev. F. H. Knubel, President.
Rev. M. G. G. Scherer, Secretary.
Mr. E. Clarence Miller, Treasurer.

Place of next Convention—Milwaukee, Wisconsin.

Minutes of the Sixth Biennial Convention of the United Lutheran Church in America

THE SERVICE—INTRODUCTORY

LUTHER MEMORIAL CHURCH
Erie, Pennsylvania
Tuesday, October 9, 1928, 8 P. M.

Preparatory to the Opening of the Sixth Biennial Convention of The United Lutheran Church in America, delegates-elect from the Constituent Synods, a large number of visitors and many members of the churches of the Convention City assembled to participate in The Service, at Luther Memorial Church, Erie, Pa., on Tuesday evening, October 9, 1928, at eight o'clock. The Secretary conducted The Service, including the Order for Public Confession, and the Reverends E. P. Pfatteicher, President of the Ministerium of Pennsylvania, and C. P. Swank, President of the East Pennsylvania Synod, had charge of the Administration of the Sacrament of the Altar.

The text of the Sermon, which was preached by the President, was "Gave Him to be the head over all things to the church" (Ephesians 1: 22): the theme, "Church Powerhouses."

FIRST MEETING

Morning Sssion

SUNDAY SCHOOL, CHAPEL, LUTHER MEMORIAL CHURH,
Erie, Pennsylvania,
Wednesday, October 10, 1928, 8:45.

Matins were conducted by the Rev. Samuel Trexler.

The President called the convention to order, and, after the use of the Order for the Opening of Synods, declared the Sixth Biennial Convention of The United Lutheran Church in America open for business. All business sessions were held in the Sunday school chapel.

5

The Rev. E M Gearhart, pastor of Luther Memorial Church, presented a block and gavel, the block being from the ruins of the Temple of Diana at Ephesus, and the gavel made from part of the keel of Perry's Flagship, The Niagara.

By general consent the report of the completed roll of delegates was deferred.

The roll, as finally established, follows:

ROLL OF DELEGATES BY SYNODS

1. Ministerium of Pennsylvania

Organized August 15, 1748

Clerical	Lay
Rev. E. P. Pfatteicher, Ph.D., D.D.	E. Clarence Miller. LL.D.
Rev. Prof. H. E. Jacobs, D.D., LL.D., S.T.D.	Mr. P. P. Hagan
	Hon. Claude T. Reno
Rev. Prof. C. M. Jacobs, D.D.	Mr. James M. Snyder
Rev. Prof. J. A. W. Haas, D.D., LL.D.	Mr. J. Milton Deck
	Mr. John F. Greiner
Rev. N. R. Melhorn, D.D., Litt.D.	Mr. W. M. Mearig
Rev. George Gebert, D.D.	Mr. A. Raymond Bard
Rev. Prof. H. Offermann, D.D.	Hon. F. M. Riter, LL.D.
Rev. W. L. Stough, D.D.	Capt. H. M. M. Richards, Litt.D.
Rev. F. M. Urich, D.D.	Mr. Grant Hultberg
Rev. J. H. Waidelich, D.D.	Mr. S. W. Deinniger
Rev. I. B. Kurtz, D.D.	Mr. D. F. Yost
Rev. A. B. MacIntosh, D.D.	Mr. Harry Hodges
Rev. P. A. Laury, D.D.	Mr. M. L. March
Rev. P. Geo. Sieger, D.D.	Mr. Chas. H. Esser
Rev. I. F Frankenfield	Mr. H. W. Cressman
Rev. J. Fred Kramlich	Mr. August Baur
Rev. J. C. Mattes, D.D.	Mr. James A. Schofer
Rev. E. F. Bachmann, D.D.	Mr. Robert Meyer
Rev. G. A. Kercher	F. V. Filbert, Esq.
Rev. G. H. Kinard	Mr. Chas. Albrecht
Rev. J. H. Harms, D.D.	Mr. R. D. Raeder
Rev. L. D. Ulrich	Mr. D. M. Reitz
Rev. A. Chas. R. Keiter	Mr. Frank H. Schmidt
Rev. J. J. Schindel, D.D.	Mr. Julius Gross
Rev. F. T. Esterly	Mr. Chas. A. Schell
Rev. J. C. Fisher, D.D.	Mr. J. H. Wisler
Rev. W. O. Laub	Mr. Lynn Neugard
Rev. H. F. Miller	Mr. Elmer Osenbach
Rev. O. Kleine	Geo. F. Seiberling, M.D.
Rev. H. W. Fitting	James F. Henninger, Esq.
Rev. W. Z. Artz	Mr. Ralph H. Schatz
Rev. W. A. Fluck	Mr. Henry F. Heuer
Rev. Prof. J. C. Seegers, D.D.	Mr. Herman A. Miller

Rev. E. R. Deibert
Rev. J. O. Leibensperger, D.D.
Rev. E. E. Fischer, D.D.
Rev. J. F. Ohl, Mus.D., D.D.

John L. Potteiger, Esq.
Mr. W. H. Hager

2. Ministerium of New York

Organized October 23, 1786

Clerical	*Lay*
Rev. H. Brezing	Dr. R. Moldenke
Rev. J. A. Weyl	Mr. J. Wagner
Rev. F. H. Bosch	Mr. W. Eck
Rev. A. H. Holthusen, D.D.	Mr. Frank A. Kalmbach
Rev. C. F. Dapp, D.D.	Mr. G. Bohrer
Rev. J. A. W. Kirsch	Mr. H. Weymann
Rev. H. C. Freimuth	Mr. O. Reisch
Rev. C. R. Tappert, D.D.	Mr. S. H. Horstmann
Rev. Fr. Noeldeke	Mr. H. D. Ungerer
Rev. G. A. Bierdemann, D.D.	Mr. L. Henrich a.
Rev. H. C. Wasmund	Mr. H. Beisler
Rev. M. Lorenz	Mr. Ch. Obenhack
Rev. W. Drach	Mr. W. Gaskell
Rev. H. Mackensen	Mr. George Zecher a.
Rev. C. Betz	Mr. E. Villnow a.

3. United Synod of North Carolina

* May 2, 1803

Clerical	*Lay*
Rev. J. L. Morgan, D.D.	Mr. W. K. Mauney
Rev. H. Brent Schaeffer, D.D.	Mr. J. V. Sutton
Rev. P. E. Monroe, D.D.	Hon. B. B. Miller
Rev. J. F. Crigler, D.D.	Prof. H. L. Mock
Rev. E. J. Sox, D.D.	Prof. G. F. McAllister a.
Rev. E. A. Shenk	Mr. H. E. Isenhour
Rev. G. H. Rhodes	Hon. B. Capps
Rev. Arthur M. Huffman, A.M.	Hon. A. L. Starr a.
Rev. L. D. Miller	Mr. Fred R. Shepherd

* Date of organization of the Evangelical Lutheran Synod and Ministerium of North Carolina which, on March 2, 1921, with the Evangelical Lutheran Tennessee Synod (organized July 17, 1820) merged into the United Evangelical Lutheran Synod of North Carolina under an amended charter of the former of the two synods which merged.

4. Maryland Synod

Organized October 11, 1820

Clerical	*Lay*
Rev. J. E. Byers, D.D.	Mr. Lester S. Birely
Rev. John B. Rupley	Prof. O. M. Fogle
Rev. William A. Wade, D.D.	Harry T. Domer, Litt.D.
Rev. O. F. Blackwelder	H. C. Poffenberger, Esq.

Rev. A. R. Wentz, Ph.D., D.D.
Rev. G. M. Diffenderfer, DD.
Rev. R. D. Clare, D.D.
Rev. Henry Manken, Jr.
Rev. Charles J. Hines
Rev. John G. Fleck

Mr. J. Henry Frick
Mr. Thomas P. Hickman
Mr. Charles E. Orth
Mr. Jesse W. Kolb
Mr. Walter C. LeGore
Mr. Austin M. Cooper

5. Synod of South Carolina

Organized January 14, 1824

Clerical	Lay
Rev. Charles J. Shealy	Mr. K. R. Kreps
Rev. P. D. Brown, D.D.	Mr. W. A. Rast
Rev. M. G. G. Scherer, D.D.	Prof. S. J. Derrick, LL.D.
Rev. J. C. Peery, D.D.	Mr. E. H. Schirmer
Rev. H. A. McCullough, D.D.	Prof. Jas. C. Kinard, LL.D.
Rev. W. H. Greever, D.D.	Prof. E. S. Dreher

6. Synod of West Pennsylvania

Organized September 5, 1825

Clerical	Lay
Rev. Henry Anstadt, D.D.	Mr. William H. Menges
Rev. L. A. Bush, D.D.	George E. Neff, Esq.
Rev. B. C. Ritz	Mr. E. H. Yohn
Rev. M. R. Hamsher	Hon. E. P. Miller
Rev. David S. Martin, D.D.	Mr. Alvin R. Nissly
Rev. George E. Bowersox	Mr. E. F. Fuller
Rev. S. H. Culler	Mr. Alexander Diehl
Rev. M. Coover, D.D., LL.D.	Mr. George W. Hafer
Rev. M. S. Sharp	Mr. George B. Hoover

7. Synod of Virginia

* August 10, 1829

Clerical	Lay
Rev. J. J. Scherer, Jr., D.D.	W. T. Stauffer, Esq.
Rev. C. A. Freed, D.D.	Mr. E. L. Keiser
Rev. C. M. Teufel	Mr. C. B. Patterson
Rev. C. W. Cassell	Mr. Harry E. Pugh
Rev. J. L. Sieber, D.D.	Mr. F. B. Walters
Rev. C. L. Miller, D.D.	Mr. A. D. Smith
Rev. R. H. Anderson	Hon. Otto V. Pence
Rev. L. W. Strickler	Mr. J. S. Dix

* Date of organization of the Evangelical Lutheran Synod and Ministerium of Virginia, which, on March 17, 1922, with the Evangelical Lutheran Synod and Ministerium of Southwestern Virginia (composed of the former Evangelical Lutheran Synod and Ministerium of Southwestern Virginia, organized September 20, 1842, and the Evangelical Lutheran Holston Synod, organized September 29, 1860), merged into the Lutheran Synod of Virginia.

8. Synod of New York

* October 26, 1830

Clerical	Lay
Rev. Charles W. Leitzell, D.D.	Mr. Fred H. Wefer
Rev. Arthur S. Hardy, D.D.	Mr. Henry Streibert
Rev. Andrew L. Dillenbeck, D.D.	Hon. A. E. Oberlander a.
Rev. Raymond Charles Deitz	H. C. Yeckel, M.D.
Rev. George Linn Kieffer, D.D.,	Hon. Harry M. Greenwald
Litt.D.	Mr. Frank Grumbach
Rev. William G. Boomhower	Mr. Karl Wolff
Rev. F. Hampton Berwager	Mr. A. S. Larson
Rev. Elmer J. Flanders	Mr. Alonzo Hayner
Rev. Henry H. Wahl	Mr. Alden Hart
Rev. Loren H. Grandy	Mr. H. K. Hess a.
Rev. George R. Swartz	Mr. Fred W. Bohney
Rev. Robert J. Van Deusen	Mr. Henry J. Wehle
Rev. Christian P. Jensen	Mr. W. P. Elson
Rev. Frederick Brezinski	

* Date of organization of the Hartwick Synod, which on October 7, 1908, merged with the Frankean Synod (organized 1837) and the New York and New Jersey Synod (organized 1871) forming the Synod of New York.

9. Ohio Synod

* November 7, 1836

Clerical	Lay
Rev. Paul W. Koller, D.D.	Hon. J. L. Zimmerman, LL.D.
Rev. E. W. Simon, D.D.	Mr. J. W. Kahler
Rev. H. A. Bosch	Mr. Paul R. Heymann
Rev. Alvin E. Bell, D.D.	Mr. A. W. Ulrici
Rev. W. J. Kratz, D.D.	Mr. C. J. Mitchell
Rev. H. C. TerVehn	Mr. Francis Seiberling
Rev. R. E. Tulloss, D.D., Ph.D.,	Mr. Harry B. Gerhardt
LL.D.	Mr. J. B. Wile a.
Rev. D. Bruce Young	Mr. Erle C. Greiner
Rev. W. M. Hackenberg, D.D.	Mr. W. H. Balch a.
Rev. A. M. Himes	Mr. D. W. Bates
Rev. H. E. Dunmire	Judge Henry Harter
Rev. C. D. Besch, D.D.	Mr. W. J. Gram
Rev. H. C. Getter	Mr. J. A. Armbruster
Rev. Harvey E. Crowell	C. G. Shatzer, Sc.D.
Rev. W. M. Brandt	Senator G. M. Kumler
Rev. E. G. Howard, D.D.	Mr. J. M. Longanbach
Rev. G. W. Miley	Mr. G. D. Lehman
Rev. E. E. Snyder	Mr. C. F. B. Repp
Rev. F. E. Strobel	

* Date of organization of East Ohio Synod which, on November 3, 1920, with the Synod of Miami (organized October 16, 1844), Wittenberg Synod (organized June 8, 1847) and the District Synod of Ohio (organized August 26, 1857) merged into the Synod of Ohio of the United Lutheran Church.

10. East Pennsylvania Synod
Organized May 2, 1842

Clerical	Lay
Rev. Calvin P. Swank, S.T.D.	Mr. Harvey Nagle
Rev. George A. Greiss, D.D.	Wm. H. Emhardt, Esq.
Rev. A. Pohlman, D.D., M.D.	Mr. E. G. Hoover
Rev. Carl C. Rasmussen, D.D.	Mr. J. Elsie Miller
Rev. Stanley Billheimer, D.D.	Mr. B. B. Slifer
Rev. S. W. Herman, D.D.	Mr. Croll Keller
Rev. Joseph D. Krout	Robt. T. Fox, Esq.
Rev. J. H. Musselman, D.D.	Mr. P. H. Fuhrman
Rev. Edwin Heyl Delk, D.D.	Mr. J. H. Brandt
Rev. U. E. Apple, D.D.	Mr. Alfred Bowman
Rev. David S. Hafer	Mr. Harry A. Fritch
Rev. C. G. Leatherman, D.D.	Mr. Wm. H. Wallace
Rev. Alfred T. Sutcliffe	Mr. Harold U. Landis
Rev. E. Allen Chamberlin	Mr. A. H. Durboraw

11. Alleghany Synod
Organized September 9, 1842

Clerical	Lay
Rev. E. L. Manges	Mr. C. L. Shaver
Rev. D. L. Shaffer	Mr. J. R. Detwiler
Rev. F. S. Schultz	Mr. H. S. Mann
Rev. H. C. Michael, D.D.	Mr. C. R. Bossler
Rev. M. J. Kline, D.D.	Mr. J. J. Gleichert
Rev. C. E. Naugle	G. G. Harman, M.D.
Rev. B. A. Peters	Mr. Harry Shaffer

12. Pittsburgh Synod
Organized January 15, 1845

Clerical	Lay
Rev. Ellis B. Burgess, D.D.	Mr. Charles Young
Rev. W. L. Price	Mr. Jesse Martsolf
Rev. J. C. F. Rupp	Mr. Albert W. Smith
Rev. Joshua H. Miller, Ph.D.	Mr. J. J. Houser
Rev. R. W. Yeany	Judge W. E. Hirt
Rev. H. H. Bagger	Mr. C. W. Herman Hess
Rev. J. F. Heckert	Mr. George F. Greiner
Rev. F. W. E. Bockelmann, D.D.	Mr. W. S. Kregar
Rev. R. F. Boethelt	Dr. H. C. Hoffman
Rev. P. H. R. Mullen	Mr. J. A. Hill
Rev. E. B. Boyer	Mr. J. V. Laver a.
Rev. J. E. F. Hassinger	Mr. Thomas M. Arnold
Rev. E. H. Daugherty	Mr. Raymond Goehring
Rev. M. R. Kunkelman	Mr. Samuel C. Pollak
Rev. E. L. Ritchie	Mr. John S. Lowry
Rev. T. L. Crouse, D.D.	Mr. C. H. Dills
Rev. G. A. Fry, D.D.	Judge J. W. King
Rev. C. D. Russell	Mr. Walter L. George
Rev. A. J. Holl, D.D.	Mr. Harry L. Kunkel
Rev. Henderson N. Miller, Ph.D.	Mr. George C. Beneke
Rev. John Aberly, D.D.	Mr. Harry W. Loos
Rev. J. G. Reinartz, D.D.	Mr. W. A. Weaver

13. Indiana Synod
October 28, 1848

Clerical	Lay
Rev. F. A. Dressel, D.D. a.	Mr. E. M. Haas
Rev. J. Earl Spaid	Mr. Oliver C. C. Fetta
Rev. Ira R. Ladd	Mr. A. G. Renau
Rev. J. C. Waltz	Mr. A. H. R. Hilbert
Rev. C. S. Powell	Mr. Charles E. Seng
Rev. W. P. Rilling, D.D.	Mr. Charles F. Deuser

* Date of organization of the Olive Branch Synod which, on June 24, 1920, with portions of the Chicago Synod (organized 1896), united to form the Indiana Synod of the United Lutheran Church in America.

14. Illinois Synod
September 8, 1851

Clerical	Lay
Rev. John M. Bramkamp, D.D.	Mr. C. J. Driever
Rev. W. A. Kiser	Mr. C. W. Howe
Rev. John F. Seibert, D.D.	Mr. C. G. Swanson
Rev. J. E. Hummon, D.D.	Mr. P. T. Lazarus a.
Rev. E. C. Harris, D.D.	Mr. Henry Berhenke
Rev. Roy G. Catlin, D.D.	Mr. Harry Currens
Rev. A. J. Beil	Mr. John P. Beckman
Rev. T. B. Uber, D.D.	Mr. Karl E. Lubke
Rev. J. J. Gent	Mr. Paulus List
Rev. Wm. J. Boatman	Mr. J. Phil Ruppel
Rev. Dwight P. Bair	Mr. H. W. Wibracht

* Date of organization of the Northern Illinois Synod which, on June 10, 1920, with the Southern Illinois (organized 1856), the Central Illinois (organized 1862), and portions of the Chicago (organized 1896) Synods, formed the Illinois Synod of the United Lutheran Church in America.

15. Texas Synod
Organized November 10, 1851

Clerical	Lay
Rev. M. A. Ritzen, B.D.	Mr. H. E. Diebel
Rev. F. F. Eberhardt, B.D.	Mr. C. C. Zirjacks

16. Susquehanna Synod of Central Pennsylvania
February 21, 1855

Clerical	Lay
Rev. G. R. Heim	L. A. Carl, M.D. a.
Rev. F. P. Manhart, D.D., LL.D.	Mr. J. L. Middlesworth a.
Rev. John Wagner, D.D.	Mr. J. Frank Dougherty
Rev. William J. Wagner	Mr. A. H. Stover
Rev. John S. English	Mr. John Kaup
Rev. J. M. Reimensnyder, D.D.,	Mr. Dan Smith. Jr.
LL.D.	Mr. C. R. Klepfer
Rev. Ammon W. Smith	Hon. Charles Steele
Rev. J. M. Rearick	

* Date of organization of the Synod of Central Pennsylvania which, on September 5, 1923, with the Susquehanna Synod (organized November 5, 1867) merged under the name of the Susquehanna Synod of Central Pennsylvania of the Evangelical Lutheran Church. The newly organized synod held its first session May 22, 1924.

17. Mississippi Synod

Organized July 25, 1855

Clerical	Lay
Rev. John W. Mangum	Mr. F. R. Epting

18. Synod of Iowa

Organized September 3, 1855

Clerical	Lay
Rev. A. B. Leamer, D.D.	Mr. John L. Berger
Rev. George G. Parker	Mr. Frank J. Heidt
Rev. F. Herbert Moehlman	Mr. F. C. Nus a.

19. Michigan Synod

* October 27, 1855

Clerical	Lay
Rev. A. H. Keck, D.D.	Mr. Ray W. Senusky a.
Rev. Paul H. Krauss	Mr. Gustave Sodt
Rev. R. J. White, D.D.	Mr. J. M. Landenberger
Rev. R. N. McMichael	Hon. E. K. Strong
Rev. A. K. Mumma	Mr. C. W. Kantz
Rev. J. N. Lentz	Mr. John W. Guard a.

* Date of organization of the Northern Indiana Synod which, on June 10, 1920, with portions of the Chicago Synod (organized 1896), formed the Michigan Synod of the United Lutheran Church in America.

20. Synod of Georgia and Adjacent States

Organized July 20, 1860

Clerical	Lay
Rev. W. E. Pugh	R. L. Gnann, D.D.S.
Rev. W. A. Reiser	Mr. D. F. Barthelmess
Rev. T. W. Shealy	Mr. W. A. Grovenstein

21. Synod of Canada

* July 21, 1861

Clerical	Lay
Rev. John H. Reble	Mr. A. L. Bitzer, B.A.
Rev. N. Willison, B.A., Litt.D.	Mr. John F. Casselman
Rev. H. Schorten, D.D.	Mr. Henry Pauli
Rev. Otto Stockmann	Mr. John Ziegler
Rev. John Schmieder	Mr. A. Ramsperger a.

* Date of organization of the Evangelical Lutheran Synod of Canada with which, on June 12, 1925, the Synod of Central Canada (organized November 11, 1908) united.

22. Synod of Kansas

Organized November 5, 1868

Clerical	Lay
Rev. E. E. Stauffer, D.D.	Mr. Louis T. Bang
Rev. G. N. Swihart, D.D.	Pres. Harrold W. Foght
Rev. J. A. McCulloch, D.D.	Mr. Leonard A. Swanson
Rev. D. L. McConnell	Mr. Carl W. Carlson

23. Synod of Nebraska

Organized September 1, 1871

Clerical	Lay
Rev. Wm. Ira Guss, D.D.	Mr. E. T. Tramp
Rev. O. D. Baltzly, Ph.D., D.D.,	H. Corbet, M.D.
LL.D.	Mr. Karl E. Vogel a.
Rev. H. F. Martin, Ph.D.	Joseph H. Miller, M.D.
Rev. O. W. Ebright	Mr. Arthur Sudman
Rev. J. C. Hershey	

24. Wartburg Synod

Organized 1875

Clerical	Lay
Rev. George Schulz, D.D.	Mr. Ervin Morack a.
Rev. R. B. Garten. D.D.	Mr. Chr. Hummel
Rev. A. Kaitschuk	Mr. A. H. Borman a.
Rev. P. C. Boysen	Mr. Martin Kottman
Rev. R. R. Belter	Mr. A. J. Ruppel

25. German Synod of Nebraska

Organized July 24, 1890

Clerical	Lay
Rev. C. Goede	Mr. A. Niemoth
Rev. F. C. Schuldt	Dr. W. H. Werkmeister a.
Rev. M. Koolen, D.D.	Mr. Christ Pfeiffer a.
Rev. G. K. Wiencke	Mr. Carl Loseke
Rev. K. Klinger	Mr. F. Reuter a.
Rev. F. Bahr, D.D.	Mr. W. H. Weiss
Rev. L. Hopp	Mr. F. W. Boxberger a.
Rev. J. Huebner	Mr. L. J. Sieckman a.

26. Synod of California

Organized April 2, 1891

Clerical	Lay
Rev. Edward P. Schueler, D.D.	Mr. Clarence B. Runkle
Rev. Edwin Moll	Mr. Wm. P. Greiner
Rev. Earnest A. Trabert	Mr. F. C. Noel
Rev. Samuel T. Himes, Ph.D.	Mr. S. F. Walck

27. Rocky Mountain Synod

Organized May 6, 1891

Clerical	Lay
Rev. Elmer W. Harner	Mr. A. E. Johnson
Rev. Robert B. Wolf	Mr. A. J. Jensen

28. Synod of the Northwest

Organized September 22, 1891

Clerical	Lay
Rev. R. H. Gerberding	Mr. J. K. Jensen
Rev. H. B. Reed, D.D.	Mr. J. W. Jouno
Rev. P. W. Roth, D.D.	Dr. F. C. Christiansen a.
Rev. A. A. Zinck, D.D.	Mr. Lief Henning a.
Rev. L. W. Steckel, D.D.	Mr. M. H. Veaux a.
Rev. H. K. Gebhart, D.D.	Hon. Andrew Holt a.
Rev. J. F. Fedders, D.D.	Mr. F. Peschau
Rev. P. L. Wetzler	Mr. O. H. Larson
Rev. P. R. Siebert, D.D.	Mr. R. C. Nelson

29. Manitoba Synod

Organized July 16, 1897

Clerical	Lay
Rev. Thos. Hartig	P. M. Bredt, Esq.
Rev. H. W. Harms	Mr. G. L. Maron

30. Pacific Synod

Organized September 26, 1901

Clerical	Lay
Rev. P. W. H. Frederick, D.D.	Mr. H. E. Turner
Rev. J. C. Kunzmann, D.D.	Mr. J. F. Olsen
Rev. L. B. Deck	Mr. D. W. Larsen

31. New York and New England Synod

Organized September 23, 1902

Clerical	Lay
Rev. Samuel Trexler, D.D.	Mr. Heiby W. Ungerer
Rev. Charles D. Trexler	Mr. Frederick Henrich
Rev. Augustus Steimle, D.D.	Mr. William H. Stackel
Rev. William M. Horn, D.D.	Mr. Robert F. Bowe
Rev. Paul E. Scherer, D.D.	Dr. Charles G. Schamu
Rev. Frederick R. Knubel	Mr. John H. Alfke
Rev. F. F. Fry, D.D.	Mr. G. A. W. Achenbach
Rev. Herbert T. Weiskotten, Ph.D.	Mr. William Richters

32.   Nova Scotia Synod

Organized July 10, 1903

Clerical	*Lay*
Rev. L. F. Hartzell	Mr. Douglas Conrad

33.   Synod of West Virginia

Organized April 17, 1912

Clerical	*Lay*
Rev. W. P. Cline, Jr.	Mr. J. C. Lynch
Rev. E. E. Campbell	Mr. J. F. Shafferman

34.   Slovak Lutheran "Zion" Synod

Organized June 10, 1919

Clerical	*Lay.*
Rev. Samuel Lichner, M.D.	Mr. George Sabo a.
Rev. Andrew Svasko	
Rev. Paul Faska	

35.   Synod of Florida

Organized September 24, 1928
Received October 16, 1928

(Associate Body)

The Evangelical Lutheran Church in the Andhra Country, India

Rev. Isaac Cannaday   Rev. A. F. A. Neudoerffer

a.   Absent.

The Revs. Isaac Cannaday and A. F. A. Neudoerffer, the two delegates of the Evangelical Lutheran Church in the Andhra Country, India, were presented by the Rev. L. B. Wolf and given a seat and voice in accordance with the resolution of the Richmond Convention.   Dr. Wolf also introduced the Rev. Dr. A. J. Stirewalt of Japan, who on motion, was given a seat and voice in the Convention. These missionaries bore the greetings of the Churches in the countries from which they severally come.

By common consent the President ruled that hereafter, following Robert's Rules of Order, no reports should be adopted as a whole.

On motion the reports of Boards and Committees as printed in the Bulletin were received.

The following program was adopted as the established order of business for the Convention:

PROGRAM OF THE CONVENTION

The offerings at all evening services will be applied to the deficit in the treasury of the Board of Foreign Missions.

TUESDAY, OCTOBER 9—Night, 8 o'clock.
The Service.   President's Sermon.   Sacrament of the Altar.

WEDNESDAY, OCTOBER 10—Morning, 8.45 to 12 o'clock,

1. Devotions.   (Matins will be used.   The Committee on Church Music will appoint those who are to conduct all devotions.)
2. Formal opening of the Convention.
3. Organization of the Convention—Roll.   Receipt of reports as printed in the Bulletin.   Order of Business.   Appointment of Special Committees.   General rules of procedure.
4. Amendments to by-laws read.
5. Approval of minutes of last convention.
6. Reports of the President and of the Secretary.
7. Election of the President and of the Secretary.
8. Treasurer's Report, with Audit.
9. Election of the Treasurer.
10. Report of the Executive Board.

Actions at this and succeeding sessions to be taken on the following items.   Any delegate may call up for consideration or question other items of the report, not included in the following.   These are given in the order in which they are found in the report.   Proposed Amendment to Constitution. Conference of Presidents (irregularities of retired clergymen). Conference of Presidents (minister's certificate of transfer). Apportionments (a ruling).   Licensure and ordination.   Pacific Synod (School of Religion).   Special days and seasons.   Presentation of causes to synods.   Regional representation on boards.   Cross appropriations.   Home mission agencies, authority to dissolve (b).   Rule concerning construction of by-laws (a ruling).   Foreign Mission Board—provision for deficit.   Presidents of synods as missionary superintendents

(d) and (e). National Lutheran Home for the Aged. Presence of chairmen at conventions. Luther League. Co-ordinations. Budget. Offerings. Lutheran Church House. Regulations of the National Lutheran Council. Lutheran World Convention—larger committee. World Conference on Faith and Order—Report of the Commission on Reports. Celebration of 1929 and 1930. 1930 and 1932 conventions.

(After the close of the morning session the chairmen of synodical delegations must secure ballots in the voting room for those elections which are to be held this afternoon. Each chairman will distribute the ballots to his delegation.)

WEDNESDAY, OCTOBER 10—Afternoon, 2 to 5 o'clock.
1. Reports of Nominating Committees as to members of the Executive Board, of the Commission of Adjudication, of the Church Paper Committee, and of the Executive Committee of the Laymen's Movement.
2. Continuation of action on the Executive Board's report.
(Immediately after the close of the session the election is to take place for membership on the Executive Board, the Commission of Adjudication, the Church Paper Committee, and the Executive Committee of the Laymen's Movement. Each delegate must deposit his own ballots, giving his name to the tellers. Polls will close at seven o'clock.)

WEDNESDAY, OCTOBER 10—Night, 8 o'clock.
Celebration of the Tenth Anniversary of the United Lutheran Church in America.
The Past—Address by Prof. H. E. Jacobs, D.D., LL.D., S.T.D.
The Present—Addresses by E. Clarence Miller, LL.D., and John L. Zimmerman, LL.D.
The Future—Address by Rev. M. G. G. Scherer, D.D.

THURSDAY, OCTOBER 11—Morning, 8.45 to 12 o'clock.
1. Devotions.
2. Minutes.
3. Report of tellers upon Wednesday afternoon's elections.
4. Action on amendments to by-laws.
5. Continuation of action on the Executive Board's report.

THURSDAY, OCTOBER 11—Afternoon, 2 to 5 o'clock.
1. Representatives and General Resolutions (as arranged by the Committee of Reference and Counsel for this place and for stated places on following days).

2. Continuation of action on the Executive Board's report.
3. At 3.30—Report of the Commission of Adjudication.
4. Report of the Laymen's Movement.
5. Report of the Church Paper Committee,
6. Report of the Committee on Memorials from Constituent Synods.

THURSDAY, OCTOBER 11—Evening, 6 o'clock.
Banquet arranged by the Laymen's Movement.

FRIDAY, OCTOBER 12—Morning, 8:45 to 12 o'clock.
1. Devotions.
2. Minutes.
3. Report of the Board of Foreign Missions.
4. Our India Mission—Report of President F. H. Knubel and Treasurer E. Clarence Miller.
(After the close of the morning session the chairmen of delegations must secure ballots for this afternoon's elections.)

FRIDAY. OCTOBER 12—Afternoon, 2 to 5 o'clock.
1. Representatives and General Resolutions.
2. Report of Nominating Committee for this afternoon's elections.
3. Report of the Board of American Missions.
(Immediately after the close of the session the election is to take place for membership on all boards and elective committees not included in the Wednesday elections. Polls will close at 7 o'clock.)

FRIDAY, OCTOBER 12—Night, 8 o'clock.
Program prepared by the Board of Foreign Missions.
Addresses by President Knubel and Treasurer Miller.

SATURDAY, OCTOBER 13—Morning, 8.45 to 12 o'clock.
1. Devotions.
2. Minutes.
3. Report of tellers upon Friday afternoon's elections.
4. Report of the Committee on Evangelism.
5. Report of the Committee on Lutheran Brotherhood. Hearing of the representative of the Brotherhood.
6. Report of the Committee on Women's Work. Hearing of the representative of the Women's Missionary Society.
7. Report of the Committee on Associations of Young People. Hearing of the representative of the Luther League of America.
8. Unfinished Business.

SATURDAY, OCTOBER 13—Afternoon, 2 to 5 o'clock.
1. Representatives and General Resolutions.
2. Report of the Board of Publication.
3. Report of the Committee on Common Service Book.
4. Report of the Committee on Church Music.
5. Report of the Committee on Church Architecture.
6. Report of the Committee on Statistics and Church Year Book (including the reports of the Statistical Secretary and of the editor of the Year Book).
7. Unfinished Business.

SATURDAY, OCTOBER 13—Night, 8 o'clock.
Program prepared by the Glee Club and the Dramatic Club of Thiel College.

SUNDAY, OCTOBER 14.
The Erie committee has arranged and will announce the preachers at all church services.

MONDAY, OCTOBER 15—Morning, 8.45 to 12 o'clock.
1. Devotions.
2. Minutes.
3. Report of the Board of Education, including survey of educational institutions.

MONDAY, OCTOBER 15—Afternoon, 2 to 5 o'clock.
1. Representatives and General Resolutions.
2. Report of the Commission on Theological Education.
3. Report of the Parish and Church School Board.
4. Report of the Commission on Science and Religion (with address by Dr. W. J. Showalter).
5. Report of the Committee on Moral and Social Welfare.
6. Report of the Necrologist.
(Immediately upon adjournment the Chamber of Commerce of Erie will provide an interesting automobile tour of Erie and surroundings.)

MONDAY, OCTOBER 15—Night, 8 o'clock.
Program prepared by the Board of American Missions.
A Living Dramatization of the Field.

TUESDAY, OCTOBER 16—Morning, 8.45 to 12 o'clock.
1. Devotions.
2. Minutes.

3. Report of the Board of Inner Missions, with Inner Mission institutions.
4. Report of the National Lutheran Home for the Aged.
5. Report of the Board of Deaconess Work.
6. Report of the Board of Ministerial Pensions and Relief.

TUESDAY, OCTOBER 16—Afternoon, 2 to 5 o'clock. Night, 8 o'clock. Also Wednesday, the 17th, as may be necessary to complete all business.

1. Representatives and General Resolutions.
2. Report of commissioners to the National Lutheran Council, including report on special publicity.
3. Report of the Executive Committee of the **Lutheran World Convention.**
4. Report of the Committee on German Interests.
5. Report of the Committee on Army and Navy Work.
6. Report of the representative to the American Bible Society.
7. Report of the Committee on Conference with Y. M. C. A.
8. Report of the Committee on President's Report.
9. Report of the Committee on Church and State.
10. Report of the Committee on Transportation.
11. Report of the Archivist.
12. Report of the Committee on Leave of Absence.
13. Report of the Lutheran Historical Society.
14. Report of the Lutheran Church Book and Literature Society.
15. Unfinished Business.
16. Printing of Minutes.
17. Final Minutes.
18. Formal close of the Convention.

The President appointed the following special committees:

COMMITTEE OF REFERENCE AND COUNSEL

This committee is appointed to consider all general resolutions before they are submitted to the Convention; to arrange with the President for the hearing of representatives sent to the Convention; generally to assist the President in the daily program.

Rev. H. Offermann
Rev. Henry Manken, Jr.
Rev. M. Coover
Rev. C. M. Teufel
Rev. C. D. Besch
Rev. George A. Greiss
Rev. O. D. Baltzly

Dr. R. Moldenke
H. C. Yeckel, M.D.
Judge J. W. King
Pres. Harold W. Foght
Mr. J. K. Jensen
Hon. Claude T. Reno
Mr. Francis Seiberling

Rev. Edwin Moll
Rev. P. W. Roth
Rev. H. A. McCullough

Mr. A. G. Renau
Mr. C. G. Swanson
Mr. Gustave Sodt
Mr. J. W. Jouno

COMMITTEE ON PRESIDENT'S REPORT

Rev. M. J. Kline
Rev. A. B. MacIntosh
Rev. J. A. Weyl
Rev. G. H. Rhodes
Rev. G. M. Diffenderfer
Rev. W. G. Boomhower
Rev. Herbert T. Weiskotten
Rev. E. E. Campbell
Wm. H. Emhardt, Esq.
Judge W. E. Hirt
Hon. E. K. Strong

Rev. E. W. Simon
Rev. Joshua H. Miller
Rev. F. Herbert Moehlman
Rev. A. K. Mumma
Rev. J. A. McCulloch
Rev. H. B. Reed
Mr. A. L. Bitzer
Mr. Heiby W. Ungerer
Mr. Charles Albrecht

COMMITTEE ON LEAVE OF ABSENCE

Rev. J. F. Fedders
Rev. W. L. Stough
Rev. W. Drach
Rev. P. D. Brown
Rev. David S. Martin
Rev. F. Brezinski
Rev. U. E. Apple
Rev. J. C. F. Rupp
Rev. J. E. Hummon
Rev. G. K. Wiencke

Rev. H. W. Harms
Mr. J. W. Kahler
Mr. E. M. Haas
Mr. H. E. Diebel
Mr. John L. Berger
Mr. E. T. Tramp
Mr. F. Peschau
Mr. H. E. Turner

COMMITTEE ON MEMORIALS FROM CONSTITUENT SYNODS

Rev. S. Billheimer
Rev. J. L. Sieber
Rev. Raymond C. Deitz
Rev. F. P. Manhart
Rev. John Schmieder
Rev. R. B. Garten
Rev. M. Koolen
Rev. P. E. Scherer
Rev. Robert B. Wolf
Rev. F. W. E. Bockelman
Rev. W. A. Reiser

Mr. W. K. Mauney
Judge Henry Harter
H. C. Poffenberger, Esq.
Hon. Harry M. Greenwald
Mr. Harvey Nagle
Mr. August Baur
Mr. F. A. Kalmbach
Mr. W. T. Stouffer

COMMITTEE TO NOMINATE EXECUTIVE COMMITTEE OF LAYMEN'S MOVEMENT

Rev. Arthur S. Hardy
Rev. M. A. Ritzen
Rev. J. M. Reimensnyder

Mr. J. F. Shafferman
Mr. Douglas Conrad
Mr. Charles E. Orth
Mr. Karl E. Lubke

COMMITTEE TO NOMINATE MEMBERS OF EXECUTIVE BOARD, COMMISSION OF ADJUDICATION, AND CHURCH PAPER COMMITTEE

Rev. G. A. Bierdemann
Rev. H. Schorten
Rev. H. Brent Schaeffer
Rev. R. D. Clare
Rev. J. C. Peery
Rev. F. Hampton Berwager
Rev. E. C. Harris
Mr. F. R. Epting
Mr. Albert W. Smith

Rev. Paul H. Krauss
Rev. L. B. Deck
Rev. O. Kleine
Mr. Frederick Henrich
Mr. A. E. Johnson
Mr. A. Niemoth
Mr. Leonard A. Swanson
Dr. H. C. Hoffman

COMMITTEE TO NOMINATE MEMBERS OF ALL OTHER BOARDS

Rev. C. A. Freed
Rev. M. R. Hamsher
Rev. S. W. Herman
Rev. Alvin E. Bell
Rev. H. C. Michael
Rev. G. A. Fry
Rev. J. Earl Spaid
Rev. George Schulz
Rev. F. M. Urich

Mr. P. M. Bredt
Mr. Clarence B. Runkle
Mr. Dan Smith, Jr.
Mr. J. A. Armbruster
Mr. Charles H. Esser

COMMITTEE ON DEVOTIONAL SERVICES

The Standing Committee on Church Music. Its duties are to name and secure men to conduct opening and closing devotions at the sessions of the Convention.

COMMITTEE OF TELLERS No. 1

To conduct the election of the President and of the Secretary, and also the Wednesday afternoon elections.

Mr. William H. Menges
Mr. D. F. Yost
Mr. J. Wagner
Mr. J. Henry Frick
Mr. K. R. Kreps
Mr. Croll Keller
Mr. Charles Young

R. L. Gnann, D.D.S.
Mr. J. C. Lynch
Mr. C. Obenhack
Mr. Thomas P. Hickman
Mr. E. G. Hoover

COMMITTEE OF TELLERS No. 2

To conduct the election of the Treasurer, and also the Friday afternoon elections.

Mr. Harry Hodges
Mr. F. V. Filbert
Prof. H. L. Mock
Mr. Alden Hart
Mr. Harold U. Landis
Mr. C. L. Shaver
Mr. Paulus List
Mr. J. Frank Dougherty

Mr. George F. Seiberling
Mr. W. A. Rast
Mr. E. L. Keiser
Mr. C. G. Shatzer
Mr. J. H. Brandt

Upon a suggestion of the President, it was moved and carried that resolutions of a general character be presented to the Convention through the Committee of Reference and Counsel.

Moved and carried, That in discussion the time of speakers be limited to five minutes.

It was moved and carried, That the privilege of the floor be granted to members of the Executive Board and to officers of other Boards when reports in which these Boards are directly interested are before the Convention.

The Secretary gave notice that at the next meeting the Executive Board would move the adoption of the following amendment to the By-laws:

"That Section 'V, 'A, be amended in the following particulars: Strike out Item 5, which reads, 'A Home Mission and Church Exension Board;' also strike out Item 9, which reads, 'A Commitee on Jewish Missions.'"

The Rev. S. W. Herman gave notice that at the next meeting he would move an amendment to Section V, B, Item 4 of the By-laws by the insertion of the words "unless he is an officer of the Board" immediately after the words "two successive terms." The item at present reads:

"No member of any Board shall be eligible for election for more tnan two successive terms; and no person shall be a member of more than two Boards at one and the same time."

The item as amended would read:

"No member of any Board shall be eligible for election for more than two successive terms, unless he is an officer of the Board; and no person shall be a member of more than two Boards at one and the same time."

The printed copy of the Minutes of the Richmond Convention, certified by the Secretary and President, was submitted and approved. The President thereupon declared it to be the official protocol of the proceedings of the Fifth Biennial Convention of The United Lutheran Church in America.

Pastor Gearhart then read a letter of greeting from his excellency John S. Fischer, Governor of Pennsylvania, and also one from the Right Rev. John C. Ward, Bishop of the Erie Diocese of the Protestant Episcopal Church.

The Hon. Joseph Crane Williams, Mayor of the City of Erie,

and Congressman Milton W. Shreve were present and addressed words of welcome to the Convention of the United Lutheran Church.

The Hon. Kenneth R. Kreps of South Carolina responded to these addresses of welcome.

The President submitted his report, which was referred to the proper committee.

PRESIDENT'S REPORT

Probably nothing done by the president during the past biennium was more important than the survey of the mission work in India, undertaken in company with the treasurer. The report sumbitted to this convention concerning that visit, therefore, covers in part the scope of this report. However, there are additional matters which need notation.

All regular committees and commissions were appointed for the biennium, as also the special commission on the relation of science and religion. Because of the death of E. K. Bell, D.D., a member of the Common Service Book Committee, Prof. H. D. Hoover, D.D., Ph.D., S.T.D., was appointed in his place. Mr. Charles A. Scheuringer was appointed as a member of the Committee on Church Architecture, in the place of Mr. J. A. Dempwolf, deceased. Rev. A. Steimle, D.D., represented us in a visit to the United Danish Evangelical Lutheran Church and Rev. J. M. Bramkamp. D.D., was our representative at a meeting of the Augustana Synod.

Although it does not fall directly within the sphere of this report, I cannot refrain from noting that by a resignation dated on Luther's Birthday, 1927, the Rev. George W. Sandt, D.D., LL.D., ceased to be a regular editor of *The Lutheran.* For thirty-one years his fluent pen, keen mind and warm heart have had an important part in guiding the life of the Church. It would be fitting that the convention recognize this service in connection with the report of the Committee on Church Papers or with this report.

An inquiry came to me, asking an official ruling as to the time when those elected to membership on boards and committees take office. It is important that such a ruling be placed on record. If elected men take office as soon as elected, boards will occasionally be left without officials until a regular meeting of these boards has been held. My ruling is, therefore, that those elected to boards and committees take office at the first regular meeting after the election. Until the time of such meeting the previous members continue in office. The convention is asked to approve this ruling.

It was originally my intention to summarize in this report of 1928 the story of our Church during its first decade. Something better has developed. An evening of this convention is to be devoted to a celebration of the tenth anniversary, with speakers who are peculiarly fitted for their special topics. This evident fact will alone prompt keen attention to their messages, so that the Church does not need any admonition to give them heed. Nevertheless, having knowledge of the intentions of at least some of them, I urge that we prayerfully prepare our hearts and minds for their words as to our past, our present, and then our critical future. None of them will be likely to include statistical information concerning the development of the ten years. The following facts have, therefore, been prepared by our statistical secretary, the Rev. G. L. Kieffer, D.D., Litt.D., the figures indicating the condition, first of 1918, then of 1928, and finally the amount of increase. Some desirable headings are of necessity omitted, because figures for 1918 were not in existence:

	1918	1928	Increase
Pastors	2,788	3,095	307
Congregations	3,734	3,877	143
Baptized Membership	1,066,921	1,329.260	262,339
Confirmed Membership	775,393	918,837	143,444
Sunday Schools	3,575	3,596	21
Officers and Teachers	53,837	64,059	10,222
Scholars	540,156	613,371	73,215
Members of Men's Societies	33,212	62,948	29,736
Members of Women's Societies	93.784	206,988	113,204
Members of Young People's Soc...	73,537	132,670	59,133
Valuation of Church Property	$54,924,257	$138,720,855	$83 796,598
Congregational Expenses	5,551,591	18,553,187	13,001,596
Total Benevolence	1,807,084	3.818,697	2,011,613

The By-Laws stipulate that this report shall summarize the general conditions in the Church. That requirement like the information as to the president's work is covered in part by the report on India. However, a statement therein as to India requires enlargement, I believe, in order to stress a condition which needs attention in the life of our Church here at home. It reads, "It seems necessary to recommend that definite effort be made to spread the spirit of Christian mercy into the congregations, so that the idea of serving love be given free play by the individual Christians in all their daily relations with their neighbors. This we found to be just as absent in India as is the case with American congregations. We can prove our faith by our serving love."

These biennial reports of the president have frequently referred to the classification of the Church's work as evangelistic, educational, and merciful We have all been conscious of our shortcomings in the evangelistic field, but at the same time have prayerfully devoted ourselves to remedy these lacks. In common with all American denominations we have also been opening our dull eyes to see the educational requirements of true Christian congregations and of the Church as a whole. The past biennium and the present convention in particular reveal many discussions and propositions for educational development. It is not fitting that the president aim to debate them here, since a chairman is practically excluded from such participation. Let it merely be said that we should rejoice in all possibilities of educational advance. This report asks single attention, as indicated above, to the third department of Church activity, to merciful work, particularly in the congregations. Here, also, we are derelict and, sad to say, not widely awake to our responsibilities. If we develop to realize that this also ought to be done, our congregations will begin to reveal a more rounded Christian life, while their evangelism and educational activity will also be intensified thereby. Before proceeding to the discussion, it is heartening to recognize that our Board of Publication has just issued Dr. F. U. Gift's study book, "The Ministry of Love." May it be widely used.

I.

The centre, the essence of the Christian message is grace, unmerited mercy, love. It is a love manifested above all in the forgiveness of the sinner for Christ's sake, but manifested also in the beauty of Christ's life as well as in the vicarious shame of His death. Even His miracles were testimonies of love only, not signs of power. Mere power can produce marvels, only love produces miracles.

That testimony as to Christianity's essence has not ceased. Christ still lives, and more strongly than in the first century. He continues to bear witness as then through His Word. He testifies now also, as then, through His works, His miracles, and the miracles are Christians. They are today His works of love, of mercy, of grace. If the essence of Christianity, mercy, is not clearly revealed in the lives of Christians, they are not creations of Christ. If Christ does not enter into us and renew us after His own likeness, His promises have failed. We are, however, His witnesses. His own testimony is repeated through us. It is a beautiful coat of many colors which our Father has made for us and which the apostle urges us to put on. Its hues, he says, are mercies, kindness, humbleness of mind, meekness, longsuffering, forgiveness. As though to bind it on us, we are to put on also charity, which is the bond of perfectness. This is the clothing of a Christian, seen by all. Nor is this Christlikeness merely an external garment of the Christian, for these things, according to the same apostle, exist also in our renewed minds and are fruits of the Spirit. As it is true of God that "He delighteth in mercy," so also that sentence increasingly describes the inner joy of a child of God. The life of the Christian must be, throughout, a manifest testimony as to the essence of Christianity. Like Jesus, he is to be a man who goes about doing good; wide awake to see the distresses of others and to help them; doing deeds of love even without thought of winning others to Jesus thereby; delighting in mercy.

This Christian love, were there the space to analyze it fully, is a very thorough thing. It sees men's whole needs, including the wrongs they suffer and their own deep wrongness; it puts a full cure at work; it has the strongest motive since it is done for Jesus' sake; and it would realize the highest ideal. It marks a life which is not brooding over its own miseries and does not evade care for the distresses of others, but willingly permits itself to become full of other men's troubles. All stress is necessary upon the fact that this mercy goes the full length in service in that it is ready personally to administer relief. It is not what has come commonly to be known as "Check Book Charity." All distress possesses loneliness and bitterness. Only the personal touch will heal the loneliness. Only the personal love will heal the bitterness. No help is really being offered and no relief is really being accomplished unless, somehow, the personal element enters in. "Though I bestow all my goods to feed the poor, and have not love, it profiteth me nothing."

The above states in brief the essential centre of Christianity, Christ's living and dying testimony to it, and the consequent necessity that the Christian's life testify truly of the same love and mercy. There follows, naturally, a responsibility upon the Church.

II.

The way of living above described must be definitely fostered by the Church, by the congregations, with the aim that it flourish in every Christian. The plans of all congregations must be shaped to accomplish that end. Only so will it be clear to the world that the Church cares for men in this life as well as the next, that the Church cares for men's bodies as well as their souls, that the Church feels a true concern for the community. Only in this way can the Church retain for herself the great and necessary sense of compassion, and express to the world the spirit of Christ. In other words every congregation must be manifestly and throughout its membership a great institution of serving love. The merciful institutions of which we are most proud must be not our orphans' and old people's homes, not our hospitals and asylums, but our congregations. Those former houses of mercy are great, but these latter ones will be greater.

In how far are our congregations so conceived and recognized today? How many of them have a special reputation in their communities for such service? How many of them have made the work of mercy actually a great third department of their service? How many of them are imbuing their members with an appreciation of such activity as a major factor in the life of the individual Christian? These questions are not asked in order to provoke direct answers, for we have a few such congregations, but with the prayerful hope that the Church may become genuinely concerned as to the work of mercy just as it has at last become concerned as to the work of education. We shall not become truly unselfish until our congregations are actively doing magnificent service in their communities which brings no return into their treasuries, and until our people's lives are overflowing with personal deeds of love in which money has no part. It is to be recognized by a congregation in planning for such work that the spirit of mercy cannot become fully an organized one. Where it truly exists, it will always include thousands of individual, daily, personal, often unknown acts. However, it can be fostered, taught, directed, inspired, and much of it can be organized within a congregation's plans.

It is not difficult to recognize some of the influences which keep the Church blinded to its responsibilities in this respect. The Church is in the world and its people once were of the world, so that the clinging ways of the world are not easily cast off. All men know vaguely that ours is a world of suffering—of poverty, disease, injustice, contention, misfortune, failure, pain. As a matter of fact, that suffering is doubtless a hundred times worse than any of us conceive it to be. There is a striking statement in Isaiah 53, as to the world's treatment of suffering. That chapter contains a picture of the typical Sufferer, and includes the words, "We hid as it were our faces from him." In other words, we do not wish to find out about it, to see it and know it fully as it is. We shut it away, put it into institutions, afraid of its contagion and afraid that the daily knowledge thereof would mar the superficial and reckless jollity of life. Even an old-world philosophy must be rejuvenated in Christian Science to persuade men that suffering is not a reality. Thus does the world hide its face. Such hypocricy must cease for the Christian. He cannot have a cheap happiness, but must learn the deeper joy. He realizes that suffering has a purpose, a future, and a God. The world, however, takes another step. Unable in the end to hide its face from some of the facts, and partly influenced in Christian lands by the mercifulness of Christianity, it strengthens the long-arm method of dealing with suffering. Still keeping it out of personal sight, welfare work is organized in ever stronger form, the government is led to towering expenditures, professional direction and oversight is provided, great foundations are established, even the public schools are enlisted. No doubt much of this is good and necessary for the conditions of modern society, and unquestionably trained workers are needed. All of it, however, is far from satisfactory to the ideal of Christian love, and falls far short of the inner necessity for a Christian that he *personally* manifest the essence of his Christianity. The Church cannot shift its responsibility to the shoulders of public welfare work. Even the world hears sometimes in its own journals that its welfare work fails in essential respects. In the single month of November, 1927, two noteworthy articles to this effect were seen in secular publications. One was headed "Check Book Charity" in the *New York Herald Tribune,* the other was "Christianity and Proselytism" in the *Atlantic Monthly.*

III.

One of the strong reasons for urging upon our Church this topic of merciful work in the congregations has been my conviction that we are at the threshold of the time when it will be agitated throughout our country. It is the next step which the growing American church will take in its recognition of the whole task of the Christian Church. A number of years ago great waves of missionary enthusiasm swept over America, and the Church's evangelistic responsibility became an accepted fact. More recently, as a second step, appreciation developed that the Church had sinfully ignored the necessity for genuine religious education, until today we find denominations, boards, and congregations in actual bewilderment before the responsibility of their educational work. Indeed all educational circles, even outside the Church, are discussing religious education. A congregation is inexcusably negligent now if it content itself merely with the old-time Sunday school and confirmation class. The third step will follow. The classification of the Church's work as evangelistic, educational and merciful still needs emphasis upon the third department. Unless the Church ceases to grow, mercy is coming next. May our Church be prepared for it.

The evidences that this development is coming are not wanting. Everywhere in Christendom the topic of social Christianity is being actively discussed. Many views are advocated, and deep differences of thought as to the responsibility of the Church are revealed. They were manifested as differences at the Universal Christian Conference on Life and Work, held in 1925 at Stockholm. (For a satisfactory summary of that Conference and its discussions the little book "Life and Work," by the Rev. Edward Shillito, is commended). Beneath the disagreements lies an inability to comprehend harmoniously the meaning of the Kingdom of God. Even deeper than this is the inability to comprehend and to define satisfactorily the Church, which is the doctrinal problem of this age, and which was a main subject before the World Conference on Faith and Order, held in 1927 at Lausanne. The Church is a social organization, the one abiding social organization, and without a comprehension thereof no true comprehension of social Christianity is possible. The Holy Spirit will guide us at last through the Word to a solution of present problems. The work of mercy, understood in its fullest sense, will then be clearly seen as essential to any true idea of social Christianity. The Church must embark upon such work more fully than hitherto, and it is conceivable that the solutions of the above mentioned problems will come only as the congregations actually undertake the task of mercy, thus doing God's will. The doing will clarify the knowing. To quote a text often used in similar connections, "If any man will do His will, he shall know of the doctrine."

There is another condition of the present time which calls upon the Church to press its privilege of merciful work. It takes us back to the opening sentence copied from the report on India. Whoever studies the teachings of the religions of the world, whoever faces them where their followers are most numerous, whoever realizes that the day is here when Christianity must confront these religions more definitely, more understandingly, and more truly than ever hitherto, will know that today, as in the first Christian centuries, the truth and the spirit and the works of mercy are essential Christianity and will prevail.

May that statement concerning our God, "He delighteth in mercy," ring over and over in our souls until we, His children, His Church, are "perfect, even as our Father which is in heaven is perfect."

The Secretary presented his report as follows:

REPORT OF THE SECRETARY

The Secretary reports that he has received memorials from the following Synods: Alleghany, Kansas, Ministerium of Pennsylvania, New York, Ohio, Pittsburgh, Susquehanna Synod of Central Pennsylvania. These memorials have been placed in the hands of the Committee on Proceedings of Constituent Synods.

A letter from Secretary George Drach, under date of August 2nd, reported that he had received the following communication through the Corresponding Secretary of our Mission in India:

"The delegates chosen to represent the Andhra Evangelical Lutheran Church at the Erie Convention have been communicated to me today by Mr. Samuel, Secretary of that body.
"The names are as follows:
"The Rev. Isaac Cannaday
"The Rev. A. F. A. Neudoerffer."

This Synod has been enrolled as an Associate Synod and the names of the delegates have been enrolled.

Respectfully submitted,
M. G. G. SCHERER, *Secretary*.

The Convention proceeded to the election of a President under the direction of Committee of Tellers No. 1.

Treasurer E. Clarence Miller presented his report as follows:

REPORT OF THE TREASURER OF THE UNITED LUTHERAN CHURCH

For the Fiscal Year Ending June 30, 1927

APPORTIONMENT AND SPECIALLY DESIGNATED FUNDS

Synod	Apportionment for Period	Paid on Apportionment	Paid on Specials
Ministerium of Pennsylvania	$376,231	$228,913.75	$19,298.44
Ministerium of New York	150,034	52,574.12	5,238.25
United Synod of North Carolina	46,917	28,265.65	2,065.94
Synod of Maryland	98,308	80,664.84	1,706.90
Synod of South Carolina	38,416	22,250.00	1,037.26
Synod of West Pennsylvania	88,702	72,752.00	19,079.01
Synod of Virginia	36,617	13,537.12	4,079.47
Synod of Ohio	147,536	127,000.00	16,544.85
Synod of East Pennsylvania	118,358	85,764.00	17,326.95
Alleghany Synod	67,173	58,401.00	20,609.99
Pittsburgh Synod	173,028	114,456.28	4,202.50
Indiana Synod	29,720	20,121.90	2,216.07
Illinois Synod	72,409	65,000.00	11,389.65
Texas Synod	5,986	2,946.97	381.18
Susquehanna Synod of Central Penna	75,822	60,338.50	3,709.00
Mississippi Synod	1,083	377.48	180.03
Synod of Iowa	18,452	8,450.00	472.12
Michigan Synod	35,196	18,326.94	641.00
Synod of Georgia	12,864	9,654.74	494.42
Synod of Canada	32,535	6,978.01	2,166.42
Synod of Kansas	19,780	12,151.83	125.00
Synod of Nebraska	29,071	21,093.52	1,936.20
Wartburg Synod	20,274	3,000.00	1,070.54
German Nebraska	16,113	2,450.00	62.56
Synod of California	14,319	9,592.65	92.75
Rocky Mountain Synod	6,286	3,428.37	462.71
Synod of the Northwest	57,757	29,196.84	3,308.87
Manitoba Synod	10,714	2,000.00	436.08
Pacific Synod	7,713	4,000.00	183.93
New York and New England Synod	82,553	54,000.00	6,920.18
Nova Scotia	4,600	1,440.10	757.68
New York Synod	82,335	42,956.00	2,794.77
West Virginia Synod	11,074	8,000.00	1,035.00
Slovak "Zion" Synod	12,024	564.61	422.51
Miscellaneous	....	330.00	5,356.46
Women's Missionary Society	....	....	271,942.87
	$2,000,000	$1,270,977.22	$429,747.56

Paid on Apportionment $1,270,977.22
Undistributed Balance on June 28, 1926................ 19,810.01

Total $1,290,787.23
Distributed in accordance with the basis of the
  United Lutheran Church Budget ....: 1,270,000.00

Undistributed Apportionment June 28, 1927............. $20,787.23

TREASURY OF THE UNITED LUTHERAN CHURCH

RECEIPTS

Proportion of Apportionment ....$	50,800.00
Board of American Missions—repayment.....................	5,142.04
Board of Publication for New York Office Bldg....	118,469.54
Interest to June 28, 1927......................................	1,705.94
	$176,117.52

EXPENDITURES

Salaries: President ....$	7,500.00
Secretary	5,958.34
Clerks	3,742.50
Traveling Expenses, President	315.65
Traveling Expenses, Secretary	56.41
General Expense	977.80
Printing and Stationery	494.13
Postage	313.05
Rent	2,702.00
Treasurer's Expense	156.15
Auditing Expense	400.00
Telephone	156.74
Executive Board	1,526.80
Common Service Book Committee	468.65
Necrology Committee	394.30
Statistical and Year Book Committee...................	849.77
Women's Work Committee...............................	175.71
Richmond Convention Expense...........................	20,474.55
Laymen's Movement Committee	41.30
Lutheran Brotherhood	23.00
Church Paper Committee	282.97
Committee of Adjudication	289.42
Church Music Committee	89.69
Committee on Moral and Social Welfare	270.11
Committee on Church Architecture	254.38
Committee on Evangelism	107.84
Publication of Minutes	4,522.68
Committee on Army and Navy Work....................	48.37
Young People's Assn. Committee.......................	5.00
Luther League	5,500.00
Federal Council of Churches	3,000.00
Publicity	1,500.00
Archivist	16.00
Committee on German Interests.......................	383.61
Commission on Theological Education	230.99
Committee on Transportation	13.20
World Committee on Faith and Order	2,560.19
New York Office Building	118,469.54
Joint Commission on Home Mission Boards..............	1,395.66
	$185,666.50

Balance	$ 9,548.98
Overdrawn, June 28, 1926	5,296.34
Overdrawn, June 28, 1927	$ 14,845.32

For the Fiscal Year Ending June 30, 1928

APPORTIONMENT AND SPECIALLY DESIGNATED FUNDS

Synod	Apportionment for Period	Paid on Apportionment	Paid on Specials
Ministerium of Pennsylvania	$452,900	$258,968.67	$255,443.02
Ministerium of New York	202,202	52,986.01	58,356.73
United Synod of North Carolina	52,177	28,154.00	13,874.33
Synod of Maryland	103,441	86,521.13	44,381.12
Synod of South Carolina	44,954	27,000.00	8,867.70
Synod of West Pennsylvania	115,346	83,010.00	61,387.01
Synod of Virginia	41,861	20,568.82	13,885.92
New York Synod	74,894	47,467.08	30,614.07
Synod of Ohio	152,341	130,000.00	59,256.01
Synod of East Pennsylvania	111,823	87,887.00	37,459.28
Alleghany Synod	71,779	54,780.00	27,843.00
Pittsburgh Synod	164,846	167,835.47	80,608.00
Indiana Synod	28,518	17,789.27	5,024.51
Illinois Synod	68,882	64,000.00	32,928.75
Texas Synod	9,611	3,300.42	95.55
Susquehanna Synod of Central Penna.	88,200	75,341.03	26,983.18
Mississippi Synod	886	742.15	786.42
Synod of Iowa	16,533	5,450.00	3,710.96
Michigan Synod	30,159	18,935.04	9,736.17
Synod of Georgia	11,525	9,354.38	7,081.28
Synod of Canada	37,527	5,903.55	1,689.23
Synod of Kansas	16,343	16,200.00	8,060.96
Synod of Nebraska	27,016	19,744.21	3,677.29
Wartburg Synod	27,502	3,500.00	6,881.33
German Nebraska	22,488	2,900.00	15,936.30
Synod of California	12,401	10,388.25	6,075.00
Rocky Mountain Synod	4,892	3,751.87	543.23
Synod of the Northwest	62,392	27,995.67	33,977.14
Manitoba Synod	13,266	2,250.00	1,056.55
Pacific Synod	6,692	5,013.00	2,507.66
New York and New England	79,358	60,000.00	64,666.96
Nova Scotia	4,158	1,791.59	1,508.12
West Virginia Synod	11,413	8,000.00	3,750.02
Slovak "Zion" Synod	17,890	350.00	1,147.47
Miscellaneous	....	235.00	2,318.64
Women's Missionary Society	....	....	355,284.55
	$2,186,216	$1,408,113.61	$1,287,403.46

Paid on Apportionment $1,408,113.61
Undistributed Balance of June 30, 1927................... 20,787.23

Total $1,428,900.84
Distributed in accordance with the basis of United
   Lutheran Church Budget 1,420,000.00

Undistributed Apportionment June 30, 1928............$ 8,900.84

TREASURY OF THE UNITED LUTHERAN CHURCH

RECEIPTS

Proportion of Apportionment	$56,800.00	
Pittsburgh Synod	10.00	
Interest on Bank Balances	2,365.34	
		$59,175.34

EXPENDITURES

Salaries: President	$ 7,500.00	
Secretary	6,000.00	
Clerks	4,012.50	
Traveling Expenses, President	1,099.00	
General Expense	514.96	
Postage	117.57	
Rent	3,611.20	
Treasurer's Expense	161.95	
Auditing Expense	450.00	
Telephone	164.43	
Executive Board	826.72	
Common Service Book Committee	843.59	
Necrology Committee	26.45	
Statistical and Year Book Committee	1,561.88	
Women's Work Committee	17.61	
Special Commissions	18.23	
Church Paper Committee	136.86	
Church Music Committee	3.92	
Committee on Moral and Social Welfare	382.24	
Committee on Church Architecture	504.99	
Committee on Science and Religion	283.22	
World Convention Expense	2,405.68	
Young People's Assn. Committee	209.40	
Luther League	6,000.00	
Federal Council of Churches	3,000.00	
Publicity	2,500.00	
Conference of Chaplains	9.87	
Committee on German Interests	179.37	
Commission on Theological Education	565.23	
Committee on Transportation	35.30	
World Committee on Faith and Order	241.52	
New York Office Building	3,398.50	
		$ 46,782.19
Balance		$ 12,393.15
Overdrawn, June 30, 1927		14,845.32
Overdrawn, June 30, 1928		$ 2,452.17

TREASURY OF THE UNITED LUTHERAN CHURCH

Summary of Cash Balances, June 30, 1928

Balance,	$8,900.84	
Balance, Sotter Trust	271.25	
Balance, General Bequests	700.00	
		$9,872.09

Overdrawn U. L. C. Treasury...$2,452.17
Overdrawn Pflaum Est. Income.. 106.67
Overdrawn Rev. Hafer Estate... 477.96
                                                            ———— 3,036.80

Balance on hand $6,835.29
    In hands of Treasurer...$6,335.29
    In hands of Secretary... 500.00
                                                            ————$6,835.29

RECAPITULATION OF APPORTIONMENT RECEIPTS

For the Fiscal Years ended July 31, 1919 to 1924, inclusive, the Eleven
  Months ended June 30, 1925, and the Fiscal Years ended June 30, 1926
                          to 1928, inclusive:

1919	$ 223,687 *
1920	877,995
1921	1,014,567
1922	1,026,672
1923	1,074,187
1924	1,167,115
1925	1,104,403 **
1926	1,258,381
1927	1,270,977
1928	1,408,113

* Partial year.
** Eleven months.

TREASURY OF THE UNITED LUTHERAN CHURCH
TRUST FUNDS
June 30, 1928

EMMA KIRMSE SOTTER TRUST
Income for Home Missions and Church Extension:
    $3,000 Altoona & Logan Valley 1st 4½'s.
      500 U. S. Liberty 4th 4¼'s.
    3,000 Appalachian Elec. Power 1st and Ref. 5's.
    3,000 Georgia Power Co. 1st and Ref. 5's.

W. P. HUFFMAN TRUST
Income one-third each to: Lutheran Orphans' Home at Salem, Va.
                          Home Missions.
                          Foreign Missions.
    $7,500 Hotel Huffry 1st Mortgage 6's.

M. S. HOTTENSTEIN TRUST
Income as determined by The United Lutheran Church.
    $1,000 Hotel Chelsea 1st Mortgage 6's.

CHRISTIAN PFLAUM, JR., TRUST
Income for Mission Purposes.
    $5,000 Times Square-46th St. Bldg. 1st 6's.

R. A. HAFER TRUST
Income: Three-fifths to Missions.
  Two-fifths to Education and Ministerial Pensions.
  40 Shares Northern Pacific R. R. Co.
  10 Shares Public Service Co. of N. J. 7 per cent pfd. stock.
Respectfully submitted,
E. CLARENCE MILLER, *Treasurer.*

We have audited the accounts of the Treasurer of the United Lutheran Church in America for the two years ended June 30, 1928, and we certify that, in our opinion, the foregoing statements of
  Apportionment and Specially Designated Funds,
    for the years ended June 30, 1927, and June 30, 1928,
  Receipts and Disbursements, General Fund,
    for the years ended June 30, 1927, and June 30, 1928,
  Summary of Cash Balances, June 30, 1928,
  Recapitulation of Apportionment Receipts,
    for the fiscal years ending July 31, 1919 to 1924, inclusive, the eleven months ended June 30, 1925, and the fiscal years ended June 30, 1926 to 1928, inclusive, and
  Trust Funds, June 30, 1928,
are in accordance with the books of account and are correct.
LYBRAND, ROSS BROS. & MONTGOMERY,
Accountants and Auditors.

On motion the report of the auditors was accepted.

The Convention proceeded to the election of a Treasurer under the direction of Committee of Tellers No. 2.

The Report of the Executive Board was taken up in due order.

REPORT OF THE EXECUTIVE BOARD

I. CONCERNING THE EXECUTIVE BOARD

The first item of our report must relate the fact that one of the members of the Board, elected for the first time at Richmond, namely, Hon. L. M Swink, was removed from office by death. He met with the Executive Board on December 16, 1926. At the next two meetings, February 10 and May 12, 1927, he was excused on account of illness. Six days after the latter meeting, on May 18, 1927, he was permitted to enter into rest. The following Minute, prepared by the Rev. Dr. W. H. Greever, was adopted by a rising vote at the meeting of the Board on September 22,

1927. By action of the Board a copy of the Minute was forwarded to Mrs. Swink at Winston-Salem, N. C.

Minute on the Death of the Hon. L. M. Swink

In the death of the Hon. L. M. Swink the Lutheran Church in the South and the whole United Lutheran Church lost an honored and valuable member and servant. Mr. Swink was a native of North Carolina and spent his entire life in his native state. By rare ability and industry he rose from obscurity to a position of notable prominence in both Church and State. He became one of the best known attorneys in North Carolina, with his home office in Winston-Salem. In many ways he was the leading member of the local congregation to which he belonged, and he gave willing and valuable service to his Synod as a member of its Executive Committee, as a member of the Board of Trustees of Lenoir-Rhyne College, and as a member of many important committees. When it became necessary to nominate a member as successor to Judge Efird in the Executive Board of the United Lutheran Church in America there was practical unanimity in the selection of Mr. Swink. What promised to be an outstanding service as a member of that Board was cut short by his death, May 18, 1927, following almost immediately upon his introduction to the Board.

The vacancy caused by the death of Mr. Swink was filled by the election of B. B. Miller, Esq., of Salisbury, N. C., whose term will expire in 1930.

The Rev. F. F. Fry, D.D., having accepted a call to become Executive Secretary of the Board of American Missions, presented his resignation to the Executive Board at the meeting on December 16, 1926. The resignation was accepted and a suitable resolution expressing appreciation of the services which had been rendered by Dr. Fry as a member of the Executive Board was passed. The vacancy was filled by the election of the Rev. Charles D. Trexler, Pastor of the Church of the Good Shepherd, Seventy-fifth Street and Fourth Avenue, Brooklyn, New York.

The following committees of the Executive Board were appointed by the president:

Committee on Constituent Synods

Rev. A. R. Wentz, D.D., Ph.D.   Rev. W. H. Greever, D.D.
                          Rev. A. C. R. Keiter

Committee on Boards and Committees

Rev. F. F. Fry, D.D.   Rev. E. B. Burgess, D.D
Rev. M. G. G. Scherer, D.D.   Rev. A. H. Smith, DD.
                          Mr. W. H Stackel

Finance Committee

E. Clarence Miller, LL.D.   Mr. George E. Neff
                          Mr. John Greiner, Jr.

Legal Committee

Mr. Robbin B. Wolf   Hon. J. F. Kramer

Hon. L. M. Swink

After the resignation of Dr. Fry the Committee on Boards and Committees was constituted as follows: E. B. Burgess, M. G. G. Scherer,
A. H. Smith, Charles D. Trexler, W. H. Stackel.

After the death of Mr. Swink and the election of Mr. Miller, the Legal
Committee was constituted as follows: Robbin B. Wolf, J. F. Kramer,
B. B. Miller.

The term of six members of the Executive Board expires at this con-
vention, namely: Rev. Charles D. Trexler, Rev. A. C. R. Keiter, Rev.
A. R. Wentz, Mr. Robbin B. Wolf, Mr. George E. Neff, Hon. John F.
Kramer. Of these all are eligible for re-election except Robbin B. Wolf,
Esq., who has served most acceptably two full terms, covering a period
of eight years.

The Board's nominations to fill vacancies are as follows: Rev. Charles
D. Trexler, Rev. A. C. R. Keiter, Rev. A. R. Wentz, Mr. George
E. Neff, Hon. John F. Kramer, Hon. William E. Hirt.

II. MATTERS REFERRED

1. **Minutes; Approval, Printing and Distribution:** (Min. 1926 Con.
   p. 645.)

The Executive Board approved the Minutes for the last session of the
Richmond Convention at its meeting held December 16, 1926, and ordered
4,000 copies of the Minutes of the Fifth Biennial Convention printed
and distributed. The work was done by our own Publication House and
the Minutes were ready for mailing on December 31, 1926. No complaints
were received concerning the condition in which the Minutes reached those
to whom they were mailed.

2. **Dissolution of Home Mission Agencies:** See IV, B, 2, of this report.
3. **East Jeypore Field in India:** See IV, B, 4, (c), of this report.
4. **Kentucky and Tennessee Synod:** See III, B, 1, of this report.
5. **Redistricting of Iowa Synod:** See III, B, 2, of this report.
6. **Uniformity in Dismissing and Receiving Ministers:** See III.
   A, 1, (b), of this report.
7. **World Conference on Faith and Order:** See XIII of this report.
8. **Committees, Representatives of, at Convention:** See IV, C, 1,
   of this report.
9. **Apportionment, 100%:** See VII, 1, of this report.

10. Licensure and Ordination, Uniformity in: See III, A, 3, of this report.

11. Three General Bodies, Continued Existence of:. (See Min. 1926 Con. pp. 105, 569.)

The question of the dissolution of the three general bodies was referred by the Executive Board to its Legal Committee. The Committee reported that for a number of reasons they were not ready to recommend the surrender of the charters of the three general bodies. Therefore, the Executive Board has taken no action and the matter stands as at the Richmond Convention.

12. Regional Representation on Boards: See IV, A, 3, of this report.

13. Proposed Amendment to Constitution: (See Min. 1926 Con. pp. 544.)

The proposed amendment of Article V, Section 1 of the Constitution of the United Lutheran Church, which was referred to the Executive Board by the Richmond Convention, was referred by the Board to its Committee on Constituent Synods. The method of accomplishing the proposed change was referred to the Legal Committee, which gave as its opinion that the proposed change is a change of basis and would therefore require an amendment to the Constitution in accordance with the provisions of Article XV, Section 2.

The following report of the Committee on Constituent Synods was approved by the Executive Board and is submitted to the convention as follows:

At the Convention of the United Lutheran Church in America, in Richmond, 1926, notice was given of a proposed change in the basis of representation as provided in Article V, Section 1 of the Constitution. The section referred to reads:

"Each Synod connected with the United Lutheran Church in America shall be entitled to representation at its conventions by one ordained minister and one layman for every ten pastoral charges or major fraction thereof, on its roll; provided, however, that each Synod shall be entitled to at least one ministerial and one lay delegate; and provided further that the delegates elected by the Synods to the last conventions of the general bodies to which they respectively belong held prior to the first convention hereunder, shall be and they are in the adoption hereof chosen by their respective Synods as their duly elected delegates to said first convention hereunder, irrespective of the basis of representation upon which they were chosen. The ratio of representation may be changed at any regular convention of the United Lutheran Church in America by a two-thirds vote, provided that notice of the proposed change has been given at the preceding regular convention."

The proposed change would strike out the words "for every ten pastoral charges" and would substitute "for every 2500 communicant members." (See Minutes, Richmond Convention, p. 544, paragraph 2. A study of the stenographer's notes from which the Minutes of the Convention were made and of the original copy of the resolution as written and signed by Rev. Theo. Posselt, indicates that the proposed substitute should close with the word "members" and should not include the words "or fraction thereof.") The Section would then read:

"Each Synod connected with the United Lutheran Church in America shall be entitled to representation at its Conventions by one ordained minister and one layman for every 2500 communicant members on its roll"—and so forth as above.

By action of the Convention this proposed change in basis of representation was referred to the Executive Board with instructions to report at the next convention.

With reference to this proposed change two questions arise: First, concerning its method; and, second, concerning its merit.

As to the method of accomplishing the proposed change the Legal Committee of the Executive Board has been asked to report.

As to the merit of the proposed change your Committee on Constituent Synods respectfully reports as follows:

I. The proposed basis of representation would be unwise because it would be less equitable as among synods, clergy, and laity, than the present basis.

II. The proposed basis of representation would be unwise because it would be out of harmony with the letter and the spirit of the Constitution of the United Lutheran Church in America.

I.

There are at least four possible bases of synodical representation in conventions of the United Lutheran Church in America:

1. The Synod, each Synod having the same number of delegates as every other Synod.
2. The clerical membership of the Synod, the clergy and laity having the same number of delegates, the number of each being determined by the number of clergymen on the roll of the Synod or in its pastorates.
3. The total membership of the Synod, baptized, confirmed or communing, the clergy and laity having the same number of delegates, the number of each being determined by the number of members reported by the parishes of the Synod.
4. The pastoral charges in the Synod, the clergy and laity having the same number of delegates, the number of each being determined by

the number of parishes embraced in the Synod and co-operating in its life.

1. The first basis alone would not secure a truly representative convention with delegates equitably proportioned among all the parts, interests and constituencies of the Church, because it would be obviously unjust to the larger Synods.

2. The second basis alone would not be equitable as between laity and clergy, nor would it be fair to the Synods with predominantly large congregations and parishes.

(a) It would not be equitable as between laity and clergy, because it would exalt the office of the ministry unduly in its relation to the government of the Church. It would undervalue the right of the Church, which is primarily the congregation of believers. The ministry does not make the Church, but the Church fills the divine office of the ministry. If, therefore, the Church in its conventions were constituted solely on the basis of the number of persons in its ministry there would be a logical reversing of the proper relationship between the Church and the ministry. This basis of representation would comport best with the hierarchical conception of the Church, the sacerdotal idea of the ministry, and the presbyterial order of church polity. It would contradict some of the implications of the Lutheran doctrine of the universal priesthood of believers. Then, too, in these days of enlarged benevolence and great increase in lay activities, this basis of representation as the sole basis, would not be suited either in theory or in practice to the needs of the Lutheran Church in America.

(b) Moreover, on this basis alone, the Synods with predominantly large parishes (i. e., the Synods with a relatively small ratio of ministers to lay membership) would have relatively less representation in convention as compared with the other Synods.

(c) Furthermore, Synods with an unusual number of clerical members retired or engaged in the general work of the Church would have a distinct advantage over other Synods, because the accident of a relatively large clerical roll would serve to increase the number of both clerical and lay delegates in convention of the Church.

3. The third basis alone, which is the one now proposed, would not be equitable as between clergy and laity, nor would it be fair to the Synods with predominantly small congregations and parishes.

(a) It would not be equitable as between clergy and laity, because it would undervalue the office of the ministry in its relation to the government of the Church and because it would neglect the rights of those who are charged with the oversight of the congregations in organized Christianity.

This basis of representation would be equitable as between clergy and laity only if all the clergy had exactly the same number of members in their congregations or parishes. In that case an equitable ratio of laity to clergy could be devised and then in convention the Church in all of its parts would be equitably represented as between ministers and members. But with the great divergence that actually exists in the size of our congregations this basis of representation in convention could not be made to operate with equity to all.

(b) Moreover, on this basis alone, the Synods with predominantly small parishes (i. e., the Synods with a relatively large ratio of ministers to lay membership) would have relatively less representation in convention as compared with the other Synods. Now the Synods with predominantly small parishes are the Synods on whose territory the Lutheran population is sparse, i. e., the home missionary Synods. These home missionary Synods are in need of assistance and encouragement from the other parts of the Church. They cover large territories, carry on work under peculiar difficulties, and have needs and problems that can be met only by the sympathetic co-operation of the larger and stronger Synods. If, therefore, the convention of the United Lutheran Church in America were constituted on the basis of lay membership alone, the delegates would come overwhelmingly from a few districts with problems and interests peculiar to those districts and foreign to other sections of the Church. Thus certain sections of the Church would be subject to relative neglect, and it would be more difficult for the United Lutheran Church to realize its fundamental purposes of "mutual assistance," "united effort," and "co-operation among all Lutherans." For the union in the United Lutheran Church in America is stated to be, *inter alia,* "for mutual assistance and encouragement and for "united efforts for the extension of the Kingdom of God at home and abroad," and "to cultivate co-operation among all Lutherans in the promotion of the general interests of the Church" (Constitution, United Lutheran Church in America, Article VI, Section 3).

This inequity and disproportion is clear from the following lists showing how differently the Richmond Convention would have been constituted if synodical representation had been computed on the basis that is now proposed.

Of the thirty-four Synods represented, seven would have been entitled to larger delegations, as follows:

1. Ministerium of Pennsylvania .... 112 instead of 74 (increase of 38)
2. Ministerium of New York .... 48 instead of 30 (increase of 18)

3. Maryland Synod .... 24 instead of 20 (increase of 4)
4. West Pennsylvania .... 28 instead of 18 (increase of 10)
5. Alleghany .... 18 instead of 14 (increase of 4)
6. Susquehanna .... 22 instead of 16 (increase of 6)
7. New York and New England .... 18 instead of 16 (increase of 2)

Of the thirty-four Synods represented, twenty-one would have been entitled to smaller delegations, as follows:

1. North Carolina .... 14 instead of 16 (decrease of 2)
2. South Carolina .... 10 instead of 12 (decrease of 2)
3. New York .... 20 instead of 28 (decrease of 8)
4. Ohio .... 36 instead of 38 (decrease of 2)
5. Pittsburgh .... 40 instead of 44 (decrease of 4)
6. Indiana .... 6 instead of 10 (decrease of 4)
7. Illinois .... 18 instead of 22 (decrease of 4)
8. Texas .... 2 instead of 4 (decrease of 2)
9. Iowa .... 4 instead of 6 (decrease of 2)
10. Michigan .... 8 instead of 10 (decrease of 2)
11. Georgia .... 2 instead of 4 (decrease of 2)
12. Kansas .... 4 instead of 8 (decrease of 4)
13. Nebraska .... 6 instead of 10 (decrease of 4)
14. Wartburg .... 6 instead of 10 (decrease of 4)
15. German Nebraska .... 8 instead of 16 (decrease of 8)
16. California .... 4 instead of 8 (decrease of 4)
17. Rocky Mountain .... 2 instead of 4 (decrease of 2)
18. Northwest .... 14 instead of 16 (decrease of 2)
19. Pacific .... 2 instead of 6 (decrease of 4)
20. West Virginia .... 2 instead of 4 (decrease of 2)
21. Slovak .... 4 instead of 6 (decrease of 2)

Of the thirty-four Synods represented, six would have been entitled to delegations of the same size as on the present basis, as follows:

1. Virginia 8
2. East Pennsylvania 28
3. Mississippi 2
4. Canada 12
5. Manitoba 4
6. Nova Scotia 2

The aggregate number of delegates in convention would have been increased by only eight, i. e., from 526 to 534. But the number of delegates would have been very differently distributed among the Synods, so that

Seven Synods now having an aggregate of 188 delegates and an average of 26.9 delegates each, would have increased their aggregate by 82 delegates and their average delegation by 11.7; and these seven Synods would have had an actual majority in the convention. Twenty-one Synods now having an aggregate of 282 delegates and an average of 13.4 delegates each, would have decreased their aggregate by 70 delegates and their average delegation by 3.3 delegates. Six Synods now having an aggregate of 56 delegates and an average of 9.3 delegates would have remained the same. It is evident, therefore, that on the proposed basis of representation, it would be predominantly the smaller Synods that would suffer decrease in representation. The result would be inequity of representation and disproportion of voice as between ability and need.

4. The fourth basis, which is the one now provided by the Constitution and which is a middle way between the second and the third, maintains a balance in convention among the interests that would be forwarded or retarded by one or the other of the bases already discussed.

When the convention of the Church is constituted on the basis of pastoral charges, the Synods with predominantly small congregations have more representation in relation to their lay membership than the larger Synods, i. e., the Synods with predominantly large congregations. Thus their peculiar needs and problems receive expression in the Church as a whole. At the same time the representation of the Synods with predominantly small parishes is so small that no combination of them could dominate any convention to the detriment of the Synods with predominantly large parishes.

Moreover, on this basis the Synods with predominantly small congregations have about the same representation in relation to the clergy enrolled as the larger Synods. This basis, therefore, is a more stable one than the second or third. It is less subject to fluctuation because of circumstances that vary among the Synods and congregations from biennium to biennium. It is less liable to pervert the statistics of the Church than the third basis. It is not influenced by the accident of an unusual number of vacant parishes nor by the presence of an unusual number of retired clergy or clergy in the general work of the Church, as would be the case on the second basis.

If it were proposed to make the legislative branch of the United Lutheran Church in America bicameral, then a combination of the first basis (an equal number for every Synod) and the third (total membership) would seem most equitable. In that case there woud be a parallel between the legislative branch of the United Lutheran Church in America and the legislative branch of the United States Government, and the Convention of the United Lutheran Church in America would express both the synodical organization of the Church and the individual membership in the Church as a whole (see Preamble of Constitution, 3rd paragraph, "We, members of Evangelical Lutheran congregations, etc."), just as the Federal Congress expresses both the State organization of the nation and the individual citizenship in the United States of America (see Preamble of Constitution, "We, the people, etc.") But so long as the conventions of the United Lutheran

Church in America consist of a single house, no such parallel can be drawn, and representation by pastoral charges commends itself from every practical point of view as affording the most even voice for all the parts and interests of the Church and yielding the most equitable representation as among Synods, clergy, and laity.

II.

The proposed change would be out of harmony with the Constitution of the United Lutheran Church in America, because

The Constitution sets forth as one of the "Principles of Organization" of the United Lutheran Church in America, that "Congregations are the primary bodies through which power committed by Christ to the Church is normally exercised" (Article III, Section 3). This means that the unit of organized Christianity is the congregation or parish, not the individual Christian or any number of individual Christians, not the clergyman nor any number of clergymen. With this "principle of organization" the proposed basis of representation in convention does not harmonize because it would make the individual (or an unorganized group of individuals) the unit.

For these reasons your committee recommends that the Executive Board report to the next convention of the United Lutheran Church in America that it deems the proposed change unwise.

14. **National Lutheran Council, Request for full payment of Budget:** See X, 1, of this report.

15. **Lutheran World Convention, Delegates to:** See XI, 3, of this report.

16. **Budget of Lutheran World Convention:** See XI, 1, of this report.

17. **Program and Budget for Lutheran World Convention:** See X, 2, of this report.

18. **Special Days and Seasons:** See IV, A, 1, of this report.

III. SYNODS

A. *In General*

1. **Conference of Presidents:** Owing to the fact that those who were in charge of the campaign for the Board of Ministerial Pensions and Relief desired a conference with the Presidents of Constituent Synods before launching their campaign, it was decided to hold the Conference of Presidents on November 1, 1927, instead of deferring it until January, 1928. The Presidents of all the Synods were in attendance the whole or a part of the time and there was a general consensus of opinion that this was the most profitable conference of its kind thus far held. Among the subjects discussed at the conference were "The Presentation of Causes at Synodical Meetings," "Methods for Congregational Mergers," and "Methods of

Synods in Dismissing and Receiving Ministers." (Min. 1926, p. 549). The conference requested the Executive Board (a) to undertake "a consideration of the irregularities of retired and inactive clergymen," and (b) to "appoint a committee to gather information from the Synods as to the methods used in dismissing and receiving ministers, the same to be used in forming an acceptable method for common use." The former of these requests was referred to a special committee consisting of the Rev. W. H. Greever, D.D., and the Rev. Charles D. Trexler. The report of this committee was approved by the Executive Board and is referred to the United Lutheran Church with the recommendation that it be forwarded with the approval of the Convention to the Constituent Synods.

(a) Your special Committee on Irregularities of Retired Clergymen submits the following for consideration as the declaration of this Board on the subject:

(1.) Every retired clergyman, or clergyman who is not serving under call from the Church, should be a member in good standing of some Lutheran congregation. This is a responsibility and an opportunity which every clergyman should recognize for his own benefit and also as an example for other church members and non-church members in the community in which he lives.

(2.) Every such clergyman should likewise hold such definite relationship to the Synod to which the congregation, of which he is a member, belongs, as may be specified under the constitution of that Synod, and he should thereby make himself obedient to all of the requirements of that Synod.

(3.) Whenever a pastor of a congregation is available, a retired clergyman or clergyman not serving under direct call of the Church, should perform ministerial acts only with the approval and authorization of the pastor in charge where such acts are sought. Every ministerial act performed under such conditions should be promptly and correctly entered upon the records of the congregation within which, or nearest to which, the act is performed. This applies even to clergymen who may be serving under call of the Church in positions other than the pastoral office.

(4.) Retired clergymen or clergymen serving in any other than a pastoral office should not be selected as lay representatives from any congregation, in order that the object of lay representation should be faithfully observed.
(See minutes first meeting, afternoon session.—Secretary.)

(b) **Uniformity in Dismissing and Receiving Ministers.** The other request was referred to the Committee on Constituent Synods. Upon report of this Committee the Executive Board adopted the following Certificate which it recommends for use among Constituent Synods:

Minister's Certificate of Transfer

THIS CERTIFIES, That the Reverend ....
is an ordained minister in good and regular standing of the Evangelical
Lutheran Synod of ...., and, called to
become .... of ...., is hereby
dismissed at his own request in order to unite with the Evangelical Lutheran
Synod of ...., to whose fellowship he is cordially commended. When regularly received by the latter
body, his membership in the Evangelical Lutheran Synod of ....
.... will cease. Given this ....
day of .... in the year of our Lord ....

....
President.

SEAL.

NOTE: When a pastor accepts a call to a parish in another Constituent
Synod of The United Lutheran Church in America, the Certificate of Transfer should be placed in the hands of the President of that Synod as soon as
the call is accepted.

Acknowledgment

This certifies that the Certificate of Transfer of the Reverend ....
....
...., recommended to the Evangelical Lutheran
Synod of .... by the Evangelical Lutheran Synod
of ...., has been received, and that he has been
regularly enrolled as a member this .... day of ....,
19.............

....
President.
....
Secretary.

SEAL.

2. Apportionments:

(a) According to the action of the Richmond Convention, as reported in
the Minutes, page 108, "communicant membership" alone was to be taken
as the basis of the apportionment. It having appeared that there was some
confusion as to the meaning of "communicant membership" in the action
referred to, the president ruled that the word "communicant" is to be understood in the same sense as the word "communing" in column eight of the
Parochial Report. The apportionment for the years 1928 and 1929 was pro-
rated among the Synods on the basis of "communing membership." In
the interest of an equitable apportionment all of the Constituent Synods

were requested to take such steps as might be necessary to secure accurate reports of communing members from all congregations, in strict harmony with the definition of communing members given in the Standard Parochial Blank where the "Communing Membership" is defined to mean the "Total number of present enrolled members who communed at least once during the year (counting no member more than once)."

(b) The budget of $2,200,000 voted at Richmond for the years 1928 and 1929 was apportioned among the Constituent Synods as follows:
For the year 1928:

	Communing Membership	Appor- tionment
Ministerium of Pennsylvania	137,025	$452,900
Ministerium of New York	61,176	202,202
United Synod of North Carolina	16,643	55,008
Synod of Maryland	31,296	103,441
Synod of South Carolina	13,601	44,954
Synod of West Pennsylvania	34,898	115,346
Synod of Virginia	12,665	41,861
Synod of Ohio	46,091	152,341
East Pennsylvania Synod	33,832	111,823
Alleghany	21,717	71,779
Pittsburgh Synod	49,874	164,846
Indiana Synod	8,628	28,518
Illinois Synod	20,840	68,882
Texas Synod	2,908	9,611
Susquehanna Synod of Central Pennsylvania	26,685	88,200
Mississippi Synod	268	886
Synod of Iowa	5,002	16,533
Michigan Synod	9,125	30,159
Synod of Georgia	5,278	17,446
Synod of Canada	11,354	37,527
Synod of Kansas	4,945	16,343
Synod of Nebraska	8,174	27,016
Wartburg Synod	8,321	27,502
German Nebraska Synod	6,804	22,488
Synod of California	3,752	12,401
Rocky Mountain Synod	1,480	4,892
Synod of the Northwest	18,877	62,392
Manitoba Synod	5,532	18,284
Pacific Synod	2,025	6,692
New York and New England Synod	24,010	79,358
Nova Scotia Synod	1,258	4,158
Synod of New York	22,659	74,894
Synod of West Virginia	3,453	11,413
Slovak "Zion" Synod	5,413	17,890
Total	665,609	$2,200,000

On the basis of revised figures for "Communing Membership," the apportionment of several of the Synods was reduced: for the North Carolina Synod, from $55,008 to $52,177; Synod of Georgia, from $17,446 to $11,525; Manitoba Synod, from $18,284 to $13,266.

For the year 1929:

	Communing Membership	Apportionment
Ministerium of Pennsylvania	140,733	$463,756
Ministerium of New York	49,299	162,455
United Synod of North Carolina	15,786	52,019
Synod of Maryland	31,500	103,803
Synod of South Carolina	13,031	42,942
West Pennsylvania Synod	35,408	116,679
Synod of Virginia	12,033	39,653
Synod of Ohio	47,688	157,146
East Pennsylvania Synod	33,988	112,000
Alleghany Synod	21,624	71,258
Pittsburgh Synod	50,122	165,167
Indiana Synod	8,768	28,893
Illinois Synod	24,353	80,249
Texas Synod	2,721	8,967
Susquehanna Synod of Central Pennsylvania	26,450	87,160
Mississippi Synod	256	843
Synod of Iowa	5,869	19,340
Michigan Synod	9,315	30,697
Synod of Georgia	3,685	12,129
Synod of Canada	12,776	42,101
Synod of Kansas	5,060	16,674
Synod of Nebraska	8,174	26,935
Wartburg Synod	8,732	28,774
German Nebraska Synod	6,500	21,419
Synod of California	4,005	13,198
Rocky Mountain Synod	1,566	5,161
Synod of the Northwest	21,516	70,902
Manitoba Synod	4,200	13,840
Pacific Synod	2,050	6,756
New York and New England Synod	25,810	85,052
Nova Scotia Synod	1,372	4,521
Synod of New York	23,977	79,011
Synod of West Virginia	3,253	10,721
Slovak "Zion" Synod	6,000	19,771
Total	667,620	$2,200,000

3. Licensure and Ordination: (See Min. 1926 Conv., p. 547).

Memorials concerning this subject were submitted to the Richmond Convention. These memorials were referred by the Convention to the Executive Board with the recommendation that a committee of five be appointed to make a careful study of the entire matter and report to the next convention of the United Lutheran Church. The committee appointed for this work consisted of the Rev. Dr. A. R. Wentz, a member of the Executive Board, and the following: The Rev. Drs. J. E. Byers, President of the Maryland Synod; John Wagner, President of the Susquehanna Synod of Central Pennsylvania; John W. Horine, Professor in the Theological Seminary at Columbia, S. C., and E. F. Krauss, Professor in the Chicago Theological Seminary.

The Report of the Committee, which was approved by the Executive Board for recommendation to the Convention, is as follows:

Report of Committee on Uniformity in Licensure and Ordination

The Committee appointed by the Executive Board, as required by the Richmond Convention, to "make a thorough study of the entire matter of uniformity in licensure and ordination," has made the study and reports as follows:

Whereas, the Lutheran doctrine of the ministry, based upon the Word of God and confirmed by the practice of the early Church, holds that the ministry is an office and not an order (Augsburg Confession, Article V), and requires that the minister be "regularly called" (Augsburg Confession, Article XIV), and

Whereas, the conditions that were held to justify the practice of licensure for the ministerial office in the Lutheran Church of America have passed away, and

Whereas, less than one-third of the constituent synods of the United Lutheran Church in America retain the practice of licensure, and much confusion has resulted from the lack of uniformity in this matter among the synods,

Therefore, be it Resolved,

(1) That the United Lutheran Church in America recommends to its constituent synods the discontinuance of the practice of licensure for the ministerial office.

(2) That the United Lutheran Church in America recommends to its constituent synods the practice of ordaining men to the ministry (a) only after they have been regularly called to the work of the ministry, and (b) by the synod on whose territory they have first accepted a call to the work of the ministry.

ABDEL ROSS WENTZ, *Chairman.*
J. EDWARD BYERS.
JOHN W. HORINE.
E. F. KRAUSS.
JOHN WAGNER.

(See minutes first meeting afternoon session and second meeting afternoon session.—Secretary.)

4. Model Constitution for Congregations, English and German:

Much time and labor have been devoted to the task of securing satisfactory model constitutions for the use of congregations in Synods connected with the United Lutheran Church. The Model Constitution for Congregations using the German language has been under consideration and the preparation of such a Constitution has been in the hands of the Executive Board's Committee on Constituent Synods in co-operation with the Committee on German Interests. The Constitution will be published as soon as the work has been satisfactorily completed. The Committee on Constituent Synods has revised the Model Constitution in English, offered some years ago by the Executive Board, and this revision has received the approval of the Board. This revised Constitution may now be had on application to the United Lutheran Publication House, 1228-34 Spruce Street, Philadelphia, Pa.

5. **Presidents of Synods as Missionary Superintendents:** See IV, B, 5, (d).

6. **Presentation of Causes at Synods:** See IV, A, 2.

B. *In Particular*

1. Kentucky and Tennessee Synod:

There was given to the Executive Board, at the Richmond Convention, power to authorize the formation of a new constituent synod to be known as the Kentucky and Tennessee Synod. (Minutes Richmond Convention, pp. 87, 569.) As no developments in reference to this matter have been reported to the Executive Board since the convention at Richmond, no action has been taken.

2. Iowa Synod: Question of redistricting with reference to support of institutions: (Min. 1926 Conv., p. 548).

Information received from the President of the Iowa Synod that this matter had been decided within the Synod itself, and that no change in the present arrangement is desired, made it unnecessary for the Executive Board to take action in regard to this matter.

3. Synod of Ohio, Petition from:

The Synod of Ohio in 1927 passed a resolution petitioning the United Lutheran Church to request the Common Service Book Committee to print the words between the staves of music in further editions of the Common Service Book. This resolution was forwarded to the Secretary of the United Lutheran Church. Inasmuch as the Common Service Book Committee had undertaken a revision of the Church's hymnal, the Executive Board, while providing that this petition should take the usual course of memorials, gave instruction that the Common Service Book Committee should be informed of its coming presentation at the Erie Convention. The instruction was carried out.

4. Pacific Synod:

(I) A statement concerning the proposed school of religion in the University of Oregon, together with a copy of the constitution, was forwarded to the Executive Board by the Rev. P. W. H. Frederick, President of the Pacific Synod, which had been invited to participate in the proposed school of religion by the appointment of two electors. Accompanying the statement was a copy of the action of the Pacific Synod authorizing the President to appoint two electors as requested, providing that the proposed participation by the Synod should be approved by the Executive Board of the United

Lutheran Church. The following statement and recommendation are submitted by the Executive Board:

We believe that important civic and religious principles are involved in this request and that careful consideration should be given to them. We therefore recommend that the Convention refer this request to the Board of Education in consultation with the Executive Board and give power to those Boards to answer the Pacific Synod.

(II) Two resolutions were received from the officers of the Pacific Synod. One of these resolutions came in two different forms; the first was sent by the Secretary of the Synod with the statement that it was a certified copy of a resolution passed by the Synod to be presented to the Executive Board of the United Lutheran Church in America; the other was sent by the President and Secretary of the Executive Committee of the Pacific Synod with a statement to the effect that it was a modification of the resolution already sent by the Secretary of the Synod.

(1) These two resolutions are submitted as follows:

(a) Resolved, that we memorialize the Executive Board of The United Lutheran Church in America to endeavor to effect an understanding with the authorities of the Augustana Synod, the Norwegian Lutheran Church, and any other Lutheran Bodies looking to the co-ordination of missionary effort on the territory of the Pacific Synod of The United Lutheran Church in America.

Signed: W. I. Eck, *Secretary.*

(b) Resolved, that the Executive Committee of the Pacific Synod memorialize the United Lutheran Church in America through the Executive Board to endeavor to effect an understanding with other Lutheran Bodies looking to the co-ordination of educational and missionary operations especially in the western portion of our Church and particularly upon the territory of the Pacific Synod.

Signed: P. W. H. Frederick, *President.*
W. I. Eck, *Secretary.*

(2) The following was also forwarded to the Secretary by the President and Secretary of the Executive Committee of the Pacific Synod. They are also President and Secretary of the Synod.

Resolved, that the Executive Committee of the Pacific Synod respectfully petition the United Lutheran Church in America to institute a forward movement for the endowment and equipment of the Pacific Theological Seminary in regard to faculty and buildings that shall enable it as soon as practicable to function in harmony with the standard set by the Commission on Theological Education and accepted by the United Lutheran Church.

Signed: P. W. H. Frederick, *President.*
W. I. Eck, *Secretary.*

The following action was taken by the Executive Board:

With regard to Resolution (1) (a) be it resolved, That the consideration of this resolution by the Executive Board be deferred until further information has been obtained.

With regard to Resolution (1) (b) and (2) be it resolved, That the Convention of the United Lutheran Chuch should not act upon a memorial or petition of the Executive Committee of a Constituent Synod unless the Synod has specifically empowered its Executive Committee to draft and present such memorial or petition.

Resolved, That the delegates of the Pacific Synod to this Convention be informed of these actions and instructed that any delegate or group of delegates to the Convention of The United Lutheran Church in America may present to the Convention any matter whatsoever either through the Convention's Committee of Reference and Counsel or directly on the floor of the Convention.

5. Florida Synod:

The Florida Synod of the United Lutheran Church in America was organized at Lakeland, Florida, September 24, 1928, by the thirteen congregations and their pastors formerly constituting the Florida Conference of the Evangelical Lutheran Synod and Ministerium of Georgia and Adjacent States. These congregations at regularly called meetings had authorized and instructed their pastors and lay delegates to join in the formation of the new synod. The Georgia Synod in January, 1928, had granted these congregations permission to withdraw and form a new synod. The Florida Synod was constituted by the adoption of a constitution and the election of the following officers: President, Rev. B. D. Wessinger; Vice President, Rev. T. K. Finck; Recording Secretary, Rev. J. H. Richard; Statistical Secretary, Mr. E. R. Sheldon; Treasurer, Mr. G. A. Schroeder. The new Synod states that in making application to be received as a constituent synod of The United Lutheran Church in America, it "subscribes to the Constitution and By-Laws of The United Lutheran Church in America."

The Constitution of the new Synod and the proceedings of its organization convention are found to be in complete accord with the Constitution and By-Laws of the United Lutheran Church in America. The Executive Board therefore recommends to the Convention that the Florida Synod be received as a Constituent Synod of The United Lutheran Church in America at the closing session of this Convention and enrolled as of that date.

IV. BOARDS AND COMMITTEES

A. *In General*

1. Special Days and Seasons:

All previous resolutions and arrangements concerning special days and seasons for the agencies of the Church, were referred by the Richmond Convention to the Executive Board (Min. 1926, pp. 197, 209, 411, 413) with full authority to prepare a revised schedule, such schedule to rescind all previous actions of this character.

After careful examination of the Minutes of the second and fifth biennial conventions of The United Lutheran Church in America, and after giving due consideration to the desires of the Church as well as her several Boards and other organizations, the Executive Board adopted a calendar for the United Lutheran Church, effective January 1, 1928.

Calendar of Special Days and Seasons

(1) Advent Season............................Board of Ministerial Pensions and Relief
(2) Epiphany Season...Board of Foreign Missions
(3) Septuagesima Sunday...Board of Deaconess Work
(4) Lenten Season..Board of American Missions
(5) Third Sunday in May..National Lutheran Council
(6) Month of June...Inner Mission Board
(7) Reformation Sunday—Day of Prayer for Colleges....Board of Education

In the use of these special days and seasons by the several Boards of the Church and the National Lutheran Council, the following rules shall govern:

(1) The Board of Ministerial Pensions and Relief is to make use of Advent Season to inform the Church of its work, take no offerings, but continue the privilege of soliciting individuals for the work of special relief.

(2) The Board of Foreign Missions is to make use of Epiphany Season in providing literature for the congregations, and furnishing envelopes for the gathering of offerings from the Sunday schools on Transfiguration Sunday.

(3) The Board of Deaconess Work is to make use of Septuagesima Sunday as recruiting day for the Deaconess work, but gather no special offerings.

(4) The Board of American Missions is to make use of Lent in providing literature for the congregations, and providing lenten-offering envelopes for the gathering of offerings from the Sunday schools on Easter Sunday.

(5) The National Lutheran Council is to use the first three weeks in May to inform the Church of the vital importance of the cause of World Service, and gather offerings from the congregations on the third Sunday in May.

(6) The Inner Mission Board is to use the month of June as the time to promote the cause of the Inner Mission throughout the entire Church; but the Constituent Synods shall have the right to gather offerings from the Sunday schools and congregations for the support of those institutions of mercy for which they are directly responsible.

(7) The Board of Education is to provide the congregations with suitable literature on the Day of Prayer for Colleges, and gather offerings from the Sunday schools for some definite object specified by the Board, except in such instances where Constituent Synods have arranged to use this Day of Prayer as the time to gather special offerings for the maintenance of educational institutions under their management and control.

(8) All these special offerings, marked special, shall be forwarded through the regular channels of congregational and synodical treasurers.

(9) Constituent Synods are requested to print this Calendar of Special Days and Seasons in their annual minutes.

2. Presentation of Causes to Synods:

At the request of the Conference of Secretaries the Executive Board took into consideration the question of amending the plan for the presentation of causes adopted by the Chicago Convention. This question was given careful consideration at the Conference of Presidents of Constituent Synods in November, 1927. The several elements entering into a successful presentation were debated revealing that the problem is not the same in all sections of the Church. The consensus of opinion was that the Chicago plan should be continued with modifications. Inasmuch as any such modifications should have the approval of the Church in Convention assembled, the Executive Board recommends to The United Lutheran Church in America the following amendments to the Chicago plan:

(a) That no less than two representatives be assigned to any Constituent Synod.

(b) That the schedules of representatives be so arranged that they may spend more time in personal conferences at all conventions.

(c) That the Secretary of the Conference of Secretaries correspond with the Presidents of all Constituent Synods two months in advance of conventions before making assignments.

(d) That the several Boards of the Church be requested to prepare concise statements of their work for the pamphlet of the Laymen's Movement, issued in connection with the Every Member Canvass, so that it can be distributed at the conventions of all the Constituent Synods, and made the basis of the presentations.

3. **Regional Representation on Boards:** (Min. 1926, p. 275).

The Executive Board was requested to take into consideration the advisability of introducing some form of regional representation of the various geographical sections of the United Lutheran Church on executive boards and committees.

The Executive Board submits the following for the consideration of the convention:

(a) A rule adopted by the Convention for the guidance of those making nominations, in order to be effective, must be binding also for the Convention.

(b) In the selection of members of boards and committees the chief consideration must be qualification for service.

(c) If the principle of regional representation be made the chief consideration and be enacted into a rule the Church would thereby limit its freedom to choose the best available men wherever they may be found.

(d) A rule prescribing regional representation would involve serious practical difficulties.

(e) The Executive Board believes that the provisions of the By-Laws concerning nominations (see By-Laws, V, B, Items 2 and 5) give freedom and ample opportunity for fair consideration of the principle of regional representation. There is nothing to prevent the suggestion of names to the Boards and Nominating Committees, and besides nominations may be made from the floor.

We therefore deem it inadvisable to introduce a rule prescribing the principle of regional representation.

4. **Cross Appropriations:**

The Board of Education having asked the Executive Board to lay down a general principle to govern Boards in the matter of cross-appropriation of funds the following was adopted:

That it is one of the co-ordination policies of the Executive Board not to favor cross-appropriations between the several Boards of the Church except as approved by the Executive Board.

5. A Caution to Boards and Committees:

In view of statements by the president concerning the frequency of miscellaneous religious conferences and the calls upon the agencies of the United Lutheran Church for participation therein, the Executive Board took action instructing the President to caution all Boards and Committees against too free participation in general conferences of administrative agencies and contribution of Church funds for such purposes.

B. *In Particular*

1. **Joint Commission Dissolved:** The Joint Commission on the Reorganization of Home Mission Agencies of the United Lutheran Church, having reported that an amendment to the Charter of "The Board of Home Missions and Church Extension of The United Lutheran Church in America" had been secured from the Court of Common Pleas of York County, Pa., changing the name to read "The Board of American Missions of The United Lutheran Church in America," and that the officers of the merging boards had been directed to turn over all records and documents to the new Board, the Executive Board approved the dissolution of the Joint Commission with expression of its appreciation of the efficient services rendered by the Commission. (See IV, B, 6, a.)

2. **Home Mission Agencies, Authority to Dissolve:** The United Lutheran Church having authorized the Executive Board at the Richmond Convention to dissolve the Home Mission Agencies which were merged into the Board of American Missions (see Minutes, pp. 90, 152), the matter was referred to the Legal Committee of the Executive Board. This Committee gave its opinion that the Board was without jurisdiction because these agencies are provided for in Section V, A, of the By-Laws, which By-Laws can be amended only as provided in Section VIII of the By-Laws.

(a) No other reason was found, however, why the Board of Home Missions and Church Extension and the Jewish Mission Committee might not be dissolved. The Executive Board therefore recommends to The United Lutheran Church in America that the By-Laws, Section V, A, as revised, be amended in the following particulars: Strike out Item 5, which reads, "A Home Mission and Church Extension Board;" also strike out Item 9, which reads, "A Committee on Jewish Missions." (See list of Boards and Elective Committees as revised by the Richmond Convention, Minutes, p. 645F.)

(b.) Information was secured from the Board of American Missions in accordance with which it was thought best that the dissolution of the Board of Northwestern Missions, the West Indies Mission Board and the Immigrants' Mission Board should not be immediately effected. The Secretary was thereupon instructed by the Executive Board to notify the Nominating Committee and the Boards concerned to make the usual nominations to fill vacancies in these three Boards. No provision has been made for nominations for a Board of Home Missions and Church Extension, nor for a Committee on Jewish Missions. The Executive Board recommends that the Board of American Missions be instructed to make whatever adjustments may be necessary for the dissolution of the three remaining Boards or Home Mission agencies. (See II, 2 of this report.)

3. **Ruling concerning construction of Section V, B, Item 4 of the By-Laws** as concerns the eligibility of members of merged Boards for membership in other Boards of the Church. In connection with the consideration of nominations by the West Indies Mission Board of members of the Board of American Missions to fill vacancies in the West Indies Mission Board, it was found that some of the nominees were already members of two or three Boards, provided each of the Boards merged into the Board of American Missions is to be classed as one of the Boards referred to in the By-Laws, Section V, B, 4. The President was thereupon requested by the Executive Board to rule on the question whether the Board of Northwestern Missions, the West Indies Mission Board, the Immigrants' Mission Board and the Committee on Jewish Missions are to be considered as included among the Boards mentioned in Section V, B, Item 4 of the By-Laws. The President ruled as follows:

"In view of the fact that these four Boards were, to all intents and purposes, merged into one common Board at the Convention of The United Lutheran Church in America held in Richmond, Va., a true construction of the Constitution (Article XIII, Section 2) would not regard these Boards as being included under the provision of Section V, B, Item 4, which states that 'no person shall be a member of more than two Boards at one and the same time.'"

4. **Foreign Mission Board:**

(a) **Special provision for the raising of its deficit:** The Board of Foreign Missions having in mind a special effort to raise the money necessary to pay off its deficit, requested favorable action by the Executive Board. The officers of the Executive Board were constituted a committee to confer with representatives of the Board of Foreign Missions in regard to this matter. On July 28, 1927, the Board of Foreign Missions took action which resulted from such conference. This action of the Board of Foreign Missions recorded an agreement reached between the officers of the United Lutheran Church and the Board of Foreign Missions as follows:

"1. That the Board of Foreign Missions request the Executive Board to permit the Epiphany Season appeal for two years to be made to congregations as well as Sunday schools in the interest of the reduction of the indebtedness of the Board of Foreign Missions.

"2. As a part of the financial policy of the United Lutheran Church the Board of Foreign Missions has the right and obligation to appeal to individuals for private contributions for the work of the Board.

"3. The Board of Foreign Missions shall arrange with the auditors for a six-year tabulation of its finances in detail for study by a committee of three laymen with a view to recommendations in the interest of producing a balanced budget."

This agreement was approved by the Executive Board on September 22, 1927.

(b) **Special Use of Epiphany Sunday in 1929-1930:**

On December 15, 1927, the following action was taken by the Executive Board:

"Inasmuch as the Foreign Mission Board seems to have taken steps whereby a balanced budget for that Board will result and inasmuch as its secretaries have been instructed to seek private gifts for at least one-half of the present deficit, the officers recommend that the Executive Board give consent to a special use by the Board of Foreign Missions of its Epiphany Sunday for the years 1929 and 1930. This special use involves the right for those two years that its appeal be addressed not merely to Sunday schools, but to the entire congregations."

(c) **East Jeypore Field in India:** Authority was given to the Executive Board (Min. 1926, pp. 173, 197) to decide concerning any plans of the Foreign Mission Board relative to the disposition of the East Jeypore Field in India. Action upon this matter was deferred in view of the proposed visit of President Knubel and Treasurer Miller to the India field. Since their return the Executive Board has approved the arrangements effected and reported by the Board of Foreign Missions in their Minutes of April 11th, May 31st, and September 26th, 27th, 1928.

(d) **Vacancies filled:** Upon nomination by the Board of Foreign Missions the following were elected to fill vacancies occurring in that Board: The Rev. J. L. Morgan, D.D., of Salisbury, N. C., in place of the Rev. Dr. M. J. Epting, deceased, term expiring 1930; the Rev. G. Albert Getty, D.D., of York, Pa., in place of the Rev. Dr. Ezra K. Bell, deceased, term expiring 1930.

5. **Board of American Missions:**

(a) **Charter Secured:** See IV, B, 1.

(b) **Documents of Boards merged into the Board of American Missions:** See IV, B, 1.

(c) **Organization:** It seems proper to record here that the Board of American Missions reported that it had met and organized in the Muhlenberg Building, Philadelphia, Pa., on December 28, 1926.

(d) **Presidents of Synods as Missionary Superintendents:** The Joint Commission on Reorganization of Boards asked a ruling of the Executive Board on the question of the eligibility to membership on the Board of American Missions of Presidents of Synods when acting as Synodical Missionary Superintendents. The Joint Commission cited Article III, Section 3 of the Constitution of the Board of American Missions as follows: "No Missionary Superintendent of any Constituent Synod of The United Lutheran Church in America, nor any Home Missionary of the Church, nor salaried officers in the employ of the Board, shall be eligible to membership in the Board."

The Executive Board gave the following opinion: That all **Acting** Missionary Superintendents of Constituent Synods of The United Lutheran Church in America are included in the term Missionary Superintendent as employed in Article III, Section 3 of the Constitution of the Board of American Missions. (See III, A, 5.)

(e) The Board of American Missions informed the Executive Board of the desire and purpose of certain Synods to create a dual salaried office, namely, that of the salaried President and Synodical Missionary Superintendent, the functions and duties of each office to be discharged by one and the same person. These Synods having overtured the Board to make an appropriation covering that part of the salary to be applied to the incumbent as Synodical Missionary Superintendent, the Board referred the propriety of such policy to the Executive Board for an opinion. The following action was taken: That the Executive Board is of the opinion that no Board of the United Lutheran Church should make an appropriation to the salary of the President of a Constituent Synod inasmuch as the duties of that office are of a general executive character and concern the vital interests of all Boards of the Church.

(f) With the consent of the President of The United Lutheran Church, an appeal has been sent out in the name of the Executive Secretary of the Board of American Missions for aid for the distressed Lutherans in the West Indies.

The Executive Board recommends the following:

Inasmuch as the heaviest losses suffered by Lutherans in the hurricane area have fallen upon those connected with The United Lutheran Church in America; and

Inasmuch as these losses in many instances will be hard to bear; therefore be it

Resolved, That we urge an immediate response by all our congregations to the appeal of the Board of American Missions for their relief.

(g) **Vacancies filled:** Upon nomination of the Board of American Missions, Mr. W. E. Black, of Milwaukee, Wis., was elected to fill the vacancy created in that Board by the death of Mr. J. B. Franke, term expiring 1932, and Mr. A. Raymond Bard, of Reading, Pa., was elected to fill the vacancy created by the resignation of Mr. C. J. Driever, term expiring 1930.

6. Board of Home Missions and Church Extension:

(a) To the Executive Board was referred by the Board of American Missions, the question of the status and membership of the Board of Home Missions and Church Extension of The United Lutheran Church in America. To this question the Executive Board replied as follows: "The Board of Home Missions and Church Extension of The United Lutheran Church in America" is now "The Board of American Missions of The United Lutheran Church in America;" and the lawful members of that Board are now those persons elected by the Richmond Convention of The United Lutheran Church in America in 1926 to serve as the Board of American Missions aforesaid. Consequently, all terms of former members in the Board of Home Missions and Church Extension have ceased. (See IV. B, 1.)

(b) **Proposed Amendment** providing for removal of this Board from the list of Boards and Committees. See IV, B, 2 (a).

7. Northwestern Mission Board:

(a) **Concerning the safekeeping of the documents of this Board:** The Board of Northwestern Missions having taken action requesting the New York Ministerium for permission to place documents of the Board in the archives of the Ministerium, the Executive Board directed the attention of the Board of Northwestern Missions to the action of the Executive Board, as authorized by the United Lutheran Church, naming the Krauth Memorial Library of the Philadelphia Seminary as the official depository of the archives of The United Lutheran Church in America. (Minutes U. L. C., 1920, p. 59.)

(b) **Vacancies filled:** In view of resignations of members of the Board of Northwestern Missions, the Board of American Missions submitted the following nominations to fill vacancies thus occurring:

Term Expiring 1932:
Rev. F. O. Evers and Mr. W. L. Glatfelter
in place of
Rev. E. Klotsche and Mr. William Eck, both resigned.

Term Expiring 1930:
Rev. Jacob Maurer, D.D., Rev. J. B. Markward, D.D., Mr. Grant Hultberg
in place of
Rev. C. S. Roberts, resigned, and Rev. H. Rembe, Sr., Mr. E. Muncke, both deceased.

Term Expiring 1928:
Rev. A. E. Bell, D.D., Rev. C. A. Freed, D.D., Rev. G. K. Rubrecht, D.D., Rev. J. C. Seegers, D.D., Rev. H. W. A. Hanson, D.D.
in place of
Rev. T. Hartig, Rev. Oscar Krauch, Rev. C. W. Knudten, Rev. O. C. D. Klaehn, Rev. C. R. Tappert, all resigned.

These were duly elected by the Executive Board at its meeting, May 17th, 1928.

8. West Indies Mission Board:

Vacancies filled: Vacancies which occurred in this Board through the resignation of members were filled upon nomination of the West Indies Mission Board by the election of the following persons:

Term Expiring 1932:

Rev. F. O. Evers and Mr. W. L. Glatfelter
          in place of
Dr. W. C. Schaeffer and Mr. J. Milton Deck, both resigned.

Term Expiring 1930:

Rev. J. B. Markward, D.D., Mr. Harry L. Snyder, Mr. Grant Hultberg
          in place of
Rev. B. F. Hankey, Mr. C. W. Fuhr, Mr. J. H. Brandt, all resigned.

Term Expiring 1928:

Rev. C. A. Freed, D.D., Rev. J. C. Seegers, D.D., Rev. A. E. Bell D.D., Rev. J. M. Francis, D.D., Mr. H. E. Young
          in place of
Dr. J. J. Scherer, Jr., Dr. W. M. Horn, Dr. S. N. Carpenter, Dr. F. U. Gift, Dr. M. S. Boyer, all resigned.

9. Committee on Jewish Missions:

(a) **Conference on Message to Jews:** Information came to the Executive Board that a Conference was to be held at Budapest and Warsaw in April, 1927, for the discussion of the presentation of the Christian message to the Jews and that arrangement could be made for the participation of one man representing the United Lutheran Church in America in that conference. This matter was referred to the Committee on Jewish Missions for favorable consideration.

(b) **Proposed Amendment** providing for removal of this Committee from the list of Boards and Committees. See IV, B, 2 (a).

10. Board of Education:

(a) On December 2nd, 1924, this Board, in response to a formal request of the Board of Foreign Missions, took the following action: that we pledge $3,000 per year, beginning August 1st, 1928, to cover salary and expenses of an American (or European) professor and an Indian Christian professor in the Andhra Christian College, the establishment of which was authorized by the Chicago Convention. Later, on December 6, 1927, the Board of Education reconsidered the foregoing action and decided to make an appropriation to Andhra College for two years and requesting the Executive Board to lay down a general principle to govern the Boards of the Church in the matter of the cross-appropriation of funds.

The Executive Board approved the emergency appropriation of $3,000 a year for two years by the Board of Education to Andhra Christian College, the same to be administered through the Board of Foreign Missions.

As regards the matter of cross-appropriations in general see action recorded at IV, A, 4.

(b) **Use of Reformation Sunday in 1927:** The Board of American Missions having, by special action, renounced its privilege of the use of Reformation Sunday in the year 1927 in favor of the Board of Education, approval was given by the Executive Board to this arrangement.

(c) **Instruction concerning aid to institutions:** The attention of the Board of Education having been called to the action of the Washington Convention approving the principle that institutions in large and prosperous synods or constituencies should derive their principal or total support from the synods or constituencies immediately concerned, and recommending that the Board of Education observe this principle and apply it as rapidly as possible in determining which institutions shall be aided and to what extent (Minutes, 1920, p. 74), the Board of Education indicated its obligation to carry out the instruction given at Washington and also the hope that, as a result of the survey now in process, they can more effectively put this rule into operation.

(d) **Vacancy filled:** Upon nomination of this Board Professor R. S. Saby, Ph.D., of Gettysburg, Pa., was elected to fill a vacancy created by the resignation of Mr. W. H. Stackel, term expiring 1930.

11. Inner Mission Board:

(a) Permission was granted this Board to approach the Presidents of other general Lutheran Bodies and seek their co-operation with us in immigrant work.

(b) **Vacancy filled:** Upon nomination of the Inner Mission Board, the Rev. John F. Fedders, of Milwaukee, Wis., was elected to fill a vacancy caused by the death of Dr. G. H. Gerberding, term expiring 1928.

12. Board of Publication:

(a) **Makes possible purchase of Lutheran Church House in New York:** See VIII.

(b) **Executive Board votes appreciation:** See VIII.

(c) **Board of Publication provides literature for use at Lausanne:** For the use of the delegates to the World Conference on Faith and Order at Lausanne, Switzerland, August, 1927, the Board of Publication issued five hundred reprints of the Smalcald Articles and shipped them together with a like number of copies of the Augsburg Confession and copies of Luther's Small Catechism to Lausanne. For this service the charge made was an amount sufficient only to cover the expenses. The Executive Board passed a motion of thanks for this service. See XIII, 1.

(d) **Vacancies filled:** Two vacancies having occurred in this Board through the deaths of Mr. George E. Schlegelmilch and Mr. D. F. Efird, the Board nominated Mr. Kenneth Baker, of Greenwood, S. C., and F. Wm. Cappelmann, Esq., of Columbia, S. C., to fill these vacancies respectively. The Executive Board elected the two nominees whose terms of office will expire in 1930.

13. Board of Ministerial Pensions and Relief:

(a) **Campaign:** The item of special interest in connection with the work of this Board during the biennium has been the campaign conducted under its auspices for four million dollars for ministerial pensions and relief. The campaign was wisely planned and ably managed as is evidenced by the successful issue. This Board will make full report of the results.

(b) **Vacancies filled:** Upon nomination of the Board of Ministerial Pensions and Relief, the Executive Board elected Mr. Paul F. Myers, of Washington, D. C., to take the place of Mr. Henry E. Passavant, resigned, term expiring 1932; Mr. J. L. Fisher, of Salisbury, N. C., to take the place of the Hon. George B. Cromer, resigned, term expiring 1928, and Mr. A. F. Sittloh, of Richmond, Ind., to take the place of Mr. J. B. Franke, deceased, term expiring 1932.

14. Parish and Church School Board:

After the Calendar of Special Days and Seasons (See IV, A, 1) had been adopted, the Parish and Church School Board renewed its request that the Executive Board grant them Rally Day, the last Sunday in September, to be used as Parish Education Day in the churches. After careful consideration the Committee on Boards and Committees reported as follows:

Your Committee recommends that in view of the large number of days and seasons which the churches are already requested to observe, we deem it unwise to amend the Calendar of Special Days and Seasons.

This recommendation was adopted by the Executive Board.

15. National Lutheran Home for the Aged:

The following agreement reached by a conference of officers of the National Lutheran Home for the Aged and of the officers of The United Lutheran Church in America was approved by the Executive Board and is submitted for the action of the Convention:

Statement of Agreement Reached at a Conference of Officers of the National Lutheran Home for the Aged and of Officers of the United Lutheran Church on June 23rd, 1927

At a meeting held in the Muhlenberg Building, Philadelphia, June 23rd, 1927, the officers of the Church considered at length with the officers of the National Lutheran Home for the Aged the affairs of the institution and its relationship to the United Lutheran Church in America. It is clear that the attorney for the institution is giving closest attention to the details of its title to its property and will continue to do so; that the moral and legal claim of the institution to direct relationship with the Church centres around the word "National" in the institution's title and the circumstances under which the institution came into existence; that such direct relationship with the Church is a distinct exception to the Church's policy concerning institutions of mercy; and that present plans to enlarge the institution will necessitate increased income for current expenses. In view of these facts the following statements are submitted for approval to the Executive Board of the United Lutheran Church in America and to the Board of the National

Lutheran Home for the Aged. If so approved they are to be submitted to the next convention of the United Lutheran Church in America:

1. The present direct relationship of the institution to the Church is recognized as a distinct and temporary exception to the policy of the Church concerning institutions of mercy.

2. The Church will continue for the present an apportionment of approximately the same amount as the institution now receives.

3. The institution will aim to secure the direct support of constituent synods of the Church. The Church requests particularly the following synods to give earnest consideration to the appeal: Maryland, West Pennsylvania, East Pennsylvania, Susquehanna of Central Pennsylvania, Alleghany, West Virginia.

4. The Church will elect the Board of the Institution in accordance with the present By-Laws of the institution.

5. This entire action is to be reviewed within the period of ten years. (See minutes first meeting, afternoon session.—Secretary.)

16. Laymen's Movement:

According to the provisions of the Constitution of the Laymen's Movement, Messrs. George E. Neff and John Greiner, Jr., of the Executive Board, were elected as members of the Administrative Committee of the Laymen's Movement.

C. Standing Committees

1. Presence of Chairmen at Conventions:

This matter was referred by the Richmond Convention to the Executive Board with power. (Min. 1926, pp. 95, 111.) The Board recommends that when the Chairman of a Standing Committee is not a delegate to a convention of The United Lutheran Church in America, the report of that committee shall be presented, if possible, by some other member of the committee who may be present. Exceptions to this arrangement may be authorized by the Executive Board.

2. Statistical and Church Year Book Committee:

The Executive Board elected the Rev. George Linn Kieffer, D.D., Litt.D., as Statistical Secretary of the United Lutheran Church, which office he has filled so efficiently from the beginning. Secretary Kieffer has also served as secretary of the Statistical and Church Year Book Committee.

3. Common Service Book Committee:

(a) The Report of the Common Service Book Committee will show what has been done with reference to the joint translation of Luther's Small Catechism in accordance with the action of the Richmond Convention. (See Minutes, 1926, pp. 95, 426.)

(b) By action of the Executive Board this Committee was informed of the petition from the Synod of Ohio relative to printing the words of hymns between the staves of music.

4. Committee on German Interests:

The Committee on German Interests at its own request was granted the privilege of holding a general German Conference at Ontario, Canada, in the fall of 1927.

5. **Committee on Publicity:** See X, 4, National Lutheran Council.

6. **Luther League:**

(a) An appropriation of $6,000 per annum was made to the Luther League for the fiscal years 1927 and 1928.

(b) Approval was given by the Executive Board to the request of the Luther League that it be permitted to raise $12,000 during the biennium for the Religious Education Building in Buenos Aires, S. A., to be known as Luther League Hall.

(c) The Executive Committee of the Luther League of Pennsylvania passed a resolution requesting the presidents of the several Lutheran Synods of Pennsylvania to appoint a representative from their respective Synods who should act in an advisory capacity to the Executive Committee in its State-wide work. Inasmuch as this action proposed the establishment of a new method of administration that would concern the whole Church, it was brought to the attention of the Executive Board and received its approval.

V. CO-ORDINATIONS

Upon petition of the Luther League of America, a conference with representatives of the Parish and Church School Board, the Women's Missionary Society and the Luther League of America, was held May 16th, 1928, for the purpose of considering the advisability of requesting the United Lutheran Church, through the Executive Board, to appoint a Commission on Parish Education. The action of the conference was approved by the Executive Board and is recommended for adoption by the Convention as follows:

That The United Lutheran Church in America be requested to direct the Parish and Church School Board to call in representatives of the Women's Missionary Society, the Luther League, and other agencies of the Church engaged in parish education, in order to make a survey and complete a comprehensive plan of parish education for the congregations of the United Lutheran Church, and report at the next biennial convention.

VI. INSTITUTIONS

1. **Feghtley Home:**

The Executive Board reports that the trusteeship of the Feghtley Home has been transferred from the General Synod to the Synod of Ohio of The United Lutheran Church in America and that the deed has been made over to the Synod of Ohio as trustee.

2. **Pacific Seminary:**

The matter of a special day for the presentation of the needs of the Pacific Theological Seminary was referred by the Richmond Convention to the Board of Education and the Executive Board. (Minutes, 1926, p. 413.)

The Board of Education at its meeting on December 7th, 1926, adopted the following: "That the Board of Education does not deem it wise to designate a special day for any institution but, if in the judgment of the Executive Board, the Pacific Seminary should receive a special offering during 1927, this Board suggests that the Seminary shall receive a proportion of the special offerings to be asked by the Board of Education on the Day of Prayer for Universities and Colleges."

Promptly thereafter the Executive Board took the following action: "Inasmuch as the Pacific Seminary has been commended to all churches of The United Lutheran Church in America (Minutes, 1920, p. 59f) the Executive Board is of opinion that the appeal of the Pacific Seminary should not be limited to participation in the offering of the Day of Prayer for universities and colleges."

VII. FINANCE

1. **The 100 per cent Apportionment for 1927:**

The action of the Richmond Convention (Min., 1926, pp. 98, 111) looking to the securing of a 100 per cent paid apportionment in 1927 was officially brought to the attention of the several Constituent Synods very soon after the appearance of the Minutes of the Convention. The Executive Board followed up this notification with an urgent appeal to the Synods and congregations to make the most earnest efforts to secure the full apportionment and this appeal was transmitted to the officers of the Synods and was also published in the columns of *The Lutheran*. The results of this effort to secure a 100 per cent apportionment are reflected in the report of the Treasurer.

2. **Recapitulation of Apportionment Receipts since the Organization of the United Lutheran Church:**

For the fiscal years ending July 31 or June 30:

1919	$ 223,687 (o)
1920	877,995
1921	1,014,567
1922	1,026,672
1923	1,074,187
1924	1,167,115
1925	1,104,403 (x)
1926	1,258,381
1927	1,270,647
1928	1,408,113

(o) Partial year.
(x) Eleven months.

3. **Apportionments for 1928 and 1929:** See III, A, 2 (b).

4. **Auditors:**

The firm of Lybrand, Ross Bros. & Montgomery was retained as auditors of Boards for the biennium.

5. Budget:

The budget for the years 1930 and 1931, approved by the Executive Board and recommended to the Convention, is as follows:

Board of	Amount	Percentage
Foreign Missions	$720,000	30.00
American Missions	912,000	38.00
Education	210,000	8.75
Parish and Church School	21,600	.90
Inner Missions	36,000	1.50
Ministerial Relief	282,000	11.75
Deaconess Work	50,400	2.10
National Home for the Aged	17,760	.74
Tabitha Home	12,000	.50
Lowman Home	2,880	.12
National Lutheran Council	27,600	1.15
American Bible Society	6,000	.25
United Lutheran Church Treasury	101,760	4.24
	$2,400,000	100.00

6. Mary Ellen Smith Trust:

Paul Van Reed Miller, Esq., our attorney in the case of the Mary Ellen Smith Trust reported that under the terms of the will, the United Lutheran Church would receive funds as follows: (a) $600, the annual interest to be applied toward the support of a boys' and girls' scholarship in the Telugu Mission. (b) $500, in payment of a legacy to the United Lutheran Church without any restriction on its use. (c) Check for $2,785.81, representing the residuary estate given to the United Lutheran Church for church extension purposes.

The following recommendations of the Finance Committee of the Executive Board were adopted:

Your Committee would recommend that if our counsel approves, the $600 be turned over to the Board of Foreign Missions, impressed with its trust, otherwise that it be held by the Treasurer of our Church under these terms.

That the bequest of $500 be placed in a General Bequest Account as having been received from Mary Ellen Smith, the income to be used as hereafter decided by the Executive Board.

That the amount of the residuary estate less the bill for professional services be turned over to the Board of American Missions for use as stipulated in the will.

7. Bohn-Gruver Litigation:

In the Bohn-Gruver litigation, reported by the Executive Board at the Richmond Convention (see Minutes, 1926, p. 106), there resulted an unfavorable decision. Our attorneys have advised an appeal from the adverse decision of the Trial Court, and in keeping with former authorization, the attorneys have been directed to proceed with the appeal.

8. Alta M. Smoots' Litigation:

In this case the Executive Board instructed the President of the General Synod to appoint the Hon. John F. Kramer as attorney to represent the General Synod in the litigation of Alta M. Smoots, *et al,* against the Synod of Ohio, *et al,* in the Court of Common Pleas of Licking County, Ohio. Mr. Kramer reported that a compromise had been reached in this case and the Executive Board approved the action of the officers of the General Synod and its attorney in compromising the case.

9. R. A. Hafer Bequest:

In the Will of the Rev. R. A. Hafer, a deceased pastor of The United Lutheran Church in America, a bequest of $5,000 was made as follows: "I give, devise and bequeath as a 'Rev R. A. Hafer Memorial Fund' the sum of dollars 'Five Thousand ($5,000)' in the form of forty (40) shares Northern Pacific Railroad Co., bearing 5 per cent interest, face value $100 per share, and also ten shares 7 per cent pref. Public Service Co. of New Jersey, to the 'United Lutheran Church in America,' only the interest of which sum is to be expended. The interest on three-fifth (3-5) thereof to be devoted to German and German-English Home Mission and Church Extension Work, including Foreign Missions; and the interest on two-fifth (2-5) thereof to be devoted to Education and Ministerial Pensions. Further particulars to be left to the discretion of the Executive Board of the United Lutheran Church in America." This bequest has been received.

10. Christian Pflaum, Jr., Bequest:

There was also received in this year, 1928, the Christian Pflaum, Jr. bequest of $5,000, the income to be used for mission purposes, which has been invested in $5,000 Times Square-46th Street Building, 1st 6's.

11. Offerings:

The Executive Board has provided that the offerings taken at this Convention shall be given to the Board of Foreign Missions

VIII. LUTHERAN CHURCH HOUSE

1. Arrangements for purchase:

The following action of the Executive Board, which was unanimously adopted, relates the story of the purchase of the property now known as the Lutheran Church House and also explains how the purchase was made possible:

Whereas, The United Lutheran Church in America at its Convention in the City of Chicago, Illinois, in October, 1924, did at one of its sessions, held in said city on October 29th, 1924, by unanimous action authorize and empower its Executive Board to secure, acquire and provide suitable quarters and offices for the general officers and Boards of said The United Lutheran Church in America; and

Whereas, the Executive Board under the above authorization finds it desirable and in the interests of the United Lutheran Church to secure and acquire a permanent headquarters building in the City of New York, State of New York, and for such headquarters' building has selected the property commonly known as 39 East 35th Street, in the City, County and State of New York; and

Whereas, the Board of Publication of The United Lutheran Church in America, a subordinate Board of the said The United Lutheran Church in America, has agreed to advance in the form of a loan or loans sufficient funds to the Executive Board of the aforesaid The United Lutheran Church in America, for the purpose of purchasing and fitting up the property known as 39 East 35th Street in the City of New York, for a United Lutheran Church Building; be it therefore

RESOLVED, That the Executive Board hereby authorizes and empowers the treasurer of The United Lutheran Church in America, Mr E. Clarence Miller, to borrow from the Board of Publication of The United Lutheran Church in America, sufficient funds, not to exceed $125,000, with which to purchase the aforementioned premises, subject to a first mortgage of $50,000, and with which to equip the aforesaid premises for the use of the Church; and

The Executive Board further authorizes and empowers its President, the Reverend Dr. F. H. Knubel, its Secretary, the Reverend Dr. M. G. G. Scherer, and its Treasurer, Mr. E. Clarence Miller, to act as its agents in the consummation and completion of the purchase of the aforesaid property, more particularly described as follows, to wit:

Beginning at a point on the northerly side of 35th Street, distant 100 feet westwardly from the westerly line of Park Avenue, thence running westwardly along the northerly side of 35th Street 29 feet; thence northwardly and parallel with Park Avenue and part of the way through a wall situate partly on the lot of land hereby described and partly on the lot of land adjoining on the west 98 feet and 9 inches to the center line of the block between 35th Street and 36th Street, thence easterly and along said center line of the block 29 feet; thence southwardly on a line parallel with Park Avenue 98 feet 9 inches to the northerly side of 35th Street at the point or place of beginning.

It should be stated that the original amount borrowed from the Board of Publication was found insufficient and that upon request of the Executive Board additional funds were secured from the Board of Publication for the completion of the work.

The Executive Board passed suitable resolutions expressing its high appreciation of this great service rendered the Church by the Board of Publication and recommends that the United Lutheran Church adopt a suitable resolution of thanks and appreciation.

2. Operation and Management:

President Knubel expressed his willingness to assume the responsibility of the operation of the Church House. This entailed the opening of a bank account. The Executive Board adopted the following: Resolved, That an account be opened in the Corn Exchange Bank, Grand Central Branch, under the name of "The Lutheran Church House," funds to be withdrawn by check signed by its treasurer, Frederick H. Knubel, only.

3. Dedication:

On December 15th, 1927, the Executive Board held its stated meeting in the new Church House at 39 East 35th Street, New York City. At 2.15 P. M., immediately preceding the afternoon session of the Executive Board, a service of dedication was held. Following the Order for the Dedication of a Church in the Common Service Book, President Dr. Knubel conducted the Service, reading the Invocation and leading in the Versicle and Psalm. Secretary Dr. Scherer read the Scripture passages, Ephesians 2:13-22 and I Corinthians 3:9-17. Dr. Knubel then led in a prayer specially prepared for the occasion and formally dedicated the Church House. Besides the members of the Executive Board there were present the personnel of the several departments occupying quarters in the Church House, several specially interested friends, among them, Dr. E. F. Eilert, President of the Board of Publication, who was present upon invitation as the representative of that Board.

IX. OFFICIAL VISITATION OF MISSIONS IN INDIA

1. It was announced to the meeting of the Executive Board on December 15th, 1927, that President Knubel and Treasurer E. Clarence Miller were contemplating a trip to India for a visitation especially of the United Lutheran Church mission operations in that land and that they would return by way of Jerusalem, where President Knubel would attend, as a member, the sessions of the International Missionary Council, March 24th to April 8th, 1928. In view of this contemplated visit the Executive Board commissioned Dr. Knubel and Dr. E. Clarence Miller as official visitors to the Church in India. An appropriation of $1,000 was made toward the expenses of the president in making this visitation.

2. **Ad interim arrangements during absence of the President and Treasurer.** The Executive Board made arrangements for the conduct of the business of the Church during the absence of the President and Treasurer as follows: (a) Resolved, That during the proposed absence of President Knubel on his visit to Jerusalem and India, the Secretary shall be charged with all rights and duties pertaining to the office of the President, and that where the signatures of two officers may be required for any lawful purpose, the Secretary, Dr. M. G. G. Scherer, shall sign as Acting-President and the Chairman of the Legal Committee, Mr. Robbin B. Wolf, shall sign as Acting-Secretary. (b) The request of Treasurer Miller, that on account of his expected absence he be permitteed to authorize his secretary-daughter, Mary R. Miller, and also (or) his former secretary-daughter, Doris M. Beardwood, to sign checks for him as Treasurer on the Fidelity-Philadelphia Trust Company and to endorse checks for deposit and do such other things as might be necessary in his financial operations as Treasurer, was granted.

3. Report of Visitors to the India Mission:

The report of President Knubel and Treasurer Miller, concerning the India Mission was ordered to be printed and distributed to all the pastors of The United Lutheran Church in America and to all delegates to this Convention. It was further provided that a special order be made on the program of the Convention for this report in the period assigned to the Board of Foreign Missions.

X. NATIONAL LUTHERAN COUNCIL

1. There was referred to the Executive Board a recommendation of the Commissioners to the National Lutheran Council that the Budget for the maintenance of the agency of the Council be assumed and that arrangements be made for its full payment. (See Minutes, 1926, p. 596.) The action of the Executive Board in regard to this recommendation was as follows: Inasmuch as the National Lutheran Council is on the budget of the United Lutheran Church, it shares with all other Boards in all apportionment income, and it is not possible for us to recommend any change in this method or basis.

2. **Budget of Lutheran World Convention:** There was also referred to the Executive Board by the Richmond Convention (Min., 1926, p. 567) a proposed program and budget for the continuance of the work of Christian mercy and conservation by the Lutheran World Convention for the year 1927. The Executive Committee of the Lutheran World Convention suggested that the raising of the American share of the sum of $75,000 for this work be referred to the National Lutheran Council. This suggestion was considered by the National Lutheran Council at its meeting in January, 1927, and the Council took action to the effect that, with the approval of the co-operating bodies, an appeal be made to secure the funds necessary for this work.

Inasmuch as the Calendar of Special Days and Seasons (See IV, A, 1) did not go into effect until January 1, 1928, the Executive Board authorized the appeal for World Service through the United Lutheran Church by a special resolution that the Council be permitted to use in 1927 the time assigned it in the Calendar.

3. **Regulations of the National Lutheran Council.** At the Richmond Convention a change in the regulations of the National Lutheran Council was approved. The United Lutheran Church, however, asked for the addition of one standing resolution which had previously been a part of the regulations.

Another of the bodies co-operating in the Council asked a further change. As a result the Council took action requesting the approval of the following changes in its regulations:

(1) That Article II, Division A, Item 2 of the Regulations, which formerly read "To represent the Lutheran Church in its attitude toward (a) national and state governments, etc.," be amended to read, *to represent Lutheran interests before.*

(a) That the following Standing Resolution be added to those already forming the Preamble, Regulations, and Standing Resolutions governing the Council:

"Any surplus remaining out of the contributions of any Body after deducting such Body's apportionment of expenditures, as provided for in Article XIV, shall, upon the dissolution or termination of the Council, be returned to the treasury of such Body."

These changes were tentatively approved by the Executive Board and are submitted to the Convention for final action.

4, **Publicity arrangements:** Arrangements were made with the National Lutheran Council for special publicity during the years 1927 and 1928 as formerly, at $3,000 per annum. With slight modification these arrangements have been continued with the Council for the coming biennium. It is understood that the cost of such special publicity shall not exceed approximately $6,000 for the biennium, including convention publicity; that about $4,000 may be expended in the year when the Convention takes place and about $2,000 in the second year. An exact statement of the expense is to be filed at regular periods by the National Lutheran Council.

XI. LUTHERAN WORLD CONVENTION

1. **Budget:** The Executive Board, in accordance with the action of the Richmond Convention (see Minutes, p. 567) made payments on the proportionate share of the United Lutheran Church to the provisional budget of the Lutheran World Convention for operating expenses as shown in the Treasurer's Report.

2. **Program and Budget for Continuance of Work of Mercy:** (See X, 2).

3. **Delegates to the Lutheran World Convention in 1929:** In accordance with authority given by the Richmond Convention (Min., 1926, p. 567) the Executive Board elected delegates to the Lutheran World Convention to be held at Copenhagen in 1929. The United Lutheran Church is entitled to ten delegates. The president is *ex-officio* a member of the delegation. The following were elected:

Principals	*Alternates*
Rev. E. B. Burgess, D.D.	Rev. F. P. Manhart, D.D.
Rev. C. M. Jacobs, D.D.	Rev. J. A. W. Haas, D.D., LL.D.
Rev. E. C. J. Kraeling	Rev. C. R. Tappert
E. Clarence Miller, LL.D	Hon. J. L. Zimmerman, LL.D.
Rev. J. A. Morehead, D.D., LL.D.	Rev. L. F. Gruber, D.D., LL.D.
Rev. J. J. Scherer, Jr., D.D.	Rev. J. W. Horine, D.D.
Rev. R. E. Tulloss, D.D., Ph.D.	Rev. P. W. Koller, D.D.
Rev. A. R. Wentz, D.D., Ph.D.	Rev. John Aberly, D.D.
Rev. N. Willison, Litt.D.	Rev. J. Maurer, D.D.

4. The following are nominated as members of the Larger Committee of the Lutheran World Convention: Revs. A. G. Voigt, Ellis B. Burgess, E. C. J. Kraeling and Dr. E. Clarence Miller.

XII. FEDERAL COUNCIL OF CHURCHES OF CHRIST IN AMERICA

The Rev. Drs. J. B. Markward, F. F. Fry and John F. Seibert were appointed as friendly visitors to the meeting of the Executive Committee of the Federal Council of Churches held in Cleveland, Ohio, January 23-24, 1928. Friendly visitors to the Quadrennial Meeting of the Federal Council of Churches which will be held in Rochester, New York, in December, were appointed as follows: Presidents H. Brezing, C. W. Leitzell and Samuel Trexler.

XIII. WORLD CONFERENCE ON FAITH AND ORDER

1. Continued authority concerning the relationship of The United Lutheran Church in America to the World Conference on Faith and Order having been given by the Richmond Convention (Min., 1926, p. 76) and no reasons having arisen why we should not participate in the proposed conference, delegates were elected to attend the conference as follows: Dr. M. G. G. Scherer, Convener; Dr. Holmes Dysinger, Dr. W. H. Greever, Dr. A. Steimle. The treasurer was authorized to provide a maximum of $600 to each appointed delegate to cover expenses.

At the request of the Executive Board, the Board of Publication (as noted at IV, B, 12, c) provided copies of the Augsburg Confession, the Smalcald Articles and Luther's Small Catechism for the use of the delegates.

2. **Report of Delegates:**

The delegates, upon their return, submitted the following report:

Report of the Delegates to the World Conference on Faith and Order
Lausanne, Switzerland, August 3-21, 1927

To the Executive Board of the United Lutheran Church:

The history of the movement culminating in this conference dates back to 1910, when the enthusiasm begotten of the Universal Missionary Conference in Edinburgh led Bishop Brent to suggest to the Protestant Episcopal Church in America, then assembled in General Convention, the appointment of a Commission to bring about a conference for the consideration of questions touching Faith and Order. This Commission was appointed and according to its instructions, invited all Christian Communions throughout the world which confess our Lord Jesus Christ as God and Saviour to unite in arranging for and conducting such a conference. The participating Churches were assured that acceptance of the invitation involved no surrender or compromise of any doctrine or position held by any Church.

A preliminary conference attended by members of commissions and other representatives of participating or invited Churches was held at Geneva, Switzerland in 1920 and appointed a Continuation Committee with a wide membership, ecclesiastically and geographically, which became the responsible agency for making the Conference an actuality. It likewise created a Subjects Committee which elaborated the Agenda prepared by the Continuation Committee. This material was placed in the hands of the delegates appointed for the Lausanne Conference some time before the convening of the Conference.

Your delegates sailed for Europe together on the S. S. Caronia July 16th and on the eight-day trip accross the ocean held daily consultations on the subjects proposed for discussion. Dr. Steimle was appointed to draft the report.

The city of Lausanne, beautiful of situation on the hills bordering Lake Geneva and ever cleanly and picturesque in its streets and buildings, showed a happy spirit of hospitality. It placed its University building at the disposal of the Conference for its sessions. It gave an official reception to the delegates at Hotel Beau Rivage, one of the splendid hostelries of Europe and tendered an excursion on Lake Geneva including inspection of Castle Chillon.

The Conference held its opening service on August 3rd in the stately cathedral crowning the heights of Lausanne. The cathedral was consecrated A. D. 1275 to "Our Lady", in the presence of Rudolph of Hapsburg, the first member of that family to be elected emperor of the Holy Roman Empire. The great Gothic structure has itself become a symbol of the changes in the Christian Church out of which this Conference grew. No altar was visible in the apse, its place taken by a simple table in front of the pulpit near the center of the edifice. On the table stood a cross and lay a large Bible.

The simple service, in French, was conducted by the pastor of the cathedral, the Rev. G. Secretan, in street attire, standing in the pulpit. Bishop Brent, Chairman of the Continuation Committee and later in the day elected President of the Conference, preached the sermon, in English, clad in purple cassock. Several thousand men and women filled the sanctuary, 435 delegates occupied the central seats. These represented over 70 Church Bodies, practically every Christian Communion except the Roman Catholic. The majority of them had been officially appointed by their respective Churches, the others had been coopted by the Continuation Committee or selected by a representative national committee, as in Germany, where the state and provincial churches had not taken action in the matter and the selections were made through the Evangelische Kirchenbund, an organization somewhat analogous to the Federal Council of Churches in America.

The delegates impressed one as thoroughly representative of their Churches. There were Patriarchs, Archbishops, Bishops, General Superintendents, Prelates, Presidents, Professors, Editors, Authors, Secretaries, Pastors, Missionaries, some laymen and eight women. The limited number of laymen included men like the Hon. Lord Sands, Judge of the Supreme Scottish Courts, Dr. Walter Simons, President of the Supreme Court of Germany, the Hon. Harold de Bildt, Swedish Minister to Egypt. Almost every race and color had contributed its quota to make up this ecumenical gathering—Anglo-Saxons, Germans, French, Scandinavians, Greeks, Hungarians, Czechoslovakians, Indians, Chinese, Japanese, Africans, representatives from the South Sea Islands.

The Conference began its labors with its first session immediately after the opening service and met twice every day. The rules adopted provided that "no statement shall be declared voted by the Conference unless it be accepted either unanimously or nemine contradicente." This procedure was strictly and impartially observed and reflected the assurances previously given that no delegate or Church represented would be committed by any action taken.

The first day's addresses were on the subject "The Call to Unity", preparatory to the discussions to be held on the six subjects of the Agenda, The Church's Message, the Nature of the Church, the Church's Common Confession of Faith, the Ministry of the Church, the Sacraments, the Unity of Christendom in Relation to Existing Churches. The opening address was given by Professor Werner Elert of the University of Erlangen in which he clearly, forcefully, yet irenically stated the position of our Church on the question of unity. Whereas the opening sermon had proceeded from John 17, Dr. Elert made John 18 his starting point: "Every one that is of the truth, heareth my voice." "Unity in Christ and unity in the truth are identical. . . . . If we are not one in the truth neither are we one in Christ. Therefore all who would unite themselves in Christ, must examine whether they are one in the truth." In crisp diction and ringing voice he expressed his convictions, culminating in three desires concerning the work of the Conference; 1st, that this Council (as he called it) may find the unity of Christians in the truth and express the truth with clearness without compromise with error; 2nd, that the larger unity which it strives for may not destroy the unities which now exist; 3rd, that differences in order and rites may not be a barrier to the affirmation of the unity in the truth which we seek.

Your delegates were highly gratified that the proceedings began with a significant utterance reflecting accurately what we believed to be the attitude of the Body we represented. It strengthened them in the conviction that the United Lutheran Church, born of a desire for unity and continuing to express such desire in its name, did not err in sending a delegation to a Conference of Christian Churches to which other Lutherans had likewise come to give testimony to their Church's deep yearning for unity in the truth.

The second, third and fourth days were given to the subjects scheduled for detailed discussion, the Church's Message, Nature and Confessions, one each day. Thereafter the Conference was divided into three commissions of about equal size for further consideration of the subjects presented and discussed in full Conference. The necessity of translating addresses into the other two of the three official languages, French, German, English, was cumbersome but unavoidable except for the two half-hour addresses on each subject which the appointed speakers had prepared long enough in advance to have printed copies in all three languages available at the hour of their delivery. The predilections of delegates were taken into consideration in constituting the commissions and your delegation distributed its membership so as to be represented on every commission. Dr. Dysinger represented us on the Commission on the Message of the Church, Drs. Scherer and Steimle on the Commission on the Nature of the Church and Dr. Greever on the Commission on the Confessions of the Church. The commissions, to stimulate thorough discussion, subdivided into groups of twenty-five, so that every delegate had ample opportunity of becoming vocal and stating his position. Three days were given to group and commission meetings after which the commissions reported their findings to the full Conference. For the second series of subjects, the Ministry of the Church, the Sacraments and the Unity of Christendom in Relation to Existing Churches, a like procedure took place. Our delegation was represented on each of the commissions on these subjects. In the presentation of the subject, the Ministry of the Church, before the full Conference, our Dr. M. G. G. Scherer delivered one of the two major addresses which met with great acceptance as voicing the convictions of a very large number of delegates in clearly reasoned manner and tempered speech. It was made available to our circles through the columns of *The Lutheran.*

As the Conference progressed, it became manifest that clearness was needed in respect to the exact meaning of a vote on the findings of the Conference which were to go forth to the world as the result of its labors. No one seemed to know just what adoption by the Conference of any statement of doctrine would signify. Tendencies showed themselves in the commission and group meetings for ambiguous formulations which could be interpreted in several ways. At this juncture our delegation under Dr. Scherer's leadership dispatched a letter to the President of the Conference, reciting our misgivings and stating our belief that the Conference should not adopt any formulation but receive the findings of the commissions for transmission to the Churches we represent. Dr. Scherer received a very gracious and sympathetic reply.

Discussion on these matters was general among the Lutheran delegates of whom there were about 70, representing the Lutheran churches of twelve countries. One of the plans in respect to this Conference evolved by your delegates in their consultations on board ship was an early meeting of the

Lutherans whom we should find at Lausanne. This was brought about on the evening of the first day of the Conference when fifty-eight Lutherans, fifty-three of them delegates, were assembled for dinner at the Hotel Cecil upon the invitation of your delegation. Thus was established at once a spirit of cordiality and friendship, and a common point of view was developed in regard to the work of the Conference. It likewise revealed a Lutheran strength and a consciousness that we saw eye to eye in laboring for the real unity of the Church in the spirit of our common heritage of the Reformation.

Through the helpfulness of your honorable Board and the Board of Publication, it was possible for us judiciously to distribute five hundred copies of the Augsburg Confession and the same number of copies of the Smalcald Articles among the delegates. They were placed on a table near the entrance to the University, fifty to seventy-five copies at a time, and when during the last week of the Conference the commission presided over by the Archbishop of Upsala sent for a number of copies for their use, it was found that the supply had been exhausted. Conversations with various members of the Conference revealed that the copies taken were also widely read.

The discussions among the Lutherans culminated in a meeting called by Archbishop Soederblom, at which forty-five were present and after prolonged discussion a committee of eight was appointed to draw up a statement setting forth the judgment of the Lutherans as to the action which the Conference should take regarding the reports of the commissions, and as to the form in which they should be submitted to the Churches. This committee met and drew up a statement in the three languages, which was handed by the Archbishop of Upsala to the President of the Conference on Monday evening, August 15th. It was read to the Conference on Wednesday morning, August 17th, and reads as follows:

"To the World Conference on Faith and Order:

"We members of this Conference who belong to the Evangelical Lutheran Communion, desire to lay before the Conference the following declaration: Our participation in this Conference proves more than any statement could do, how deeply we deplore the divisions in the Church and how profoundly we feel the need of unity among Christians. As Evangelical Lutherans we feel it to be our sacred duty to labor for the unity of the Church in faith and hope, and, especially in this day of dire need, in serving love to mankind. Of course, according to our Confessions it is not necessary to the unity of the Church that human traditions, rites or ceremonies should be everywhere alike, but this unity consists in the agreement concerning the doctrine of the Gospel and the administration of the Sacraments.

"To give accurate expression to the existing spiritual unity is, of course, possible only in the direction pointed out by the ecumenical creeds. It is a large task whose difficulty must not deter us, but which we dare not take lightly. The current discussions are, in large part, important and illuminating, and we desire that they may continue to the end of the Conference. But we question whether it is possible, and whether it comports with the dignity of this Conference and is worthy of Christendom to announce at once as finalities the formulations here made, on fundamental principles of faith and order.

"1. It is therefore our judgment that the Conference in its public proclamation should strongly express the great significance of this gathering, that deep spiritual unity which we recognize with gratitude to God, the serious will to unity which prevails, and the value and necessity of thorough and fraternal discussion and continuance of the labors here begun.

"2. Accordingly no final vote should be taken on the propositions formulated here. They should be added to the proclamation as material for further consideration.

"3. In order to secure a thorough and adequate consideration and to give the desired effect to the labors of this Conference the whole material should also be referred to a small commission composed of trusted representatives of the various groups, namely the Orthodox, the Evangelical Lutherans, the Reformed and the Presbyterians (Calvinists), the Anglicans, the Methodists, the Baptists, the Congregationalists, etc. This commission should be charged with the duty carefully to examine these propositions in the light of the discussions during this Conference and to set forth the points of agreement and difference in doctrine and practice.

"4. Commissions should also be appointed in the various communions in order to give thorough study to the propositions and report to the joint commission, which should submit the results of its labors to a future Conference.

"Lausanne, August 15th, 1927.
In behalf of a Meeting of Evangelical
Lutheran members of the Conference.

"LOUIS APPIA, *Inspecteur Ecclesiastique, Paris.*
PETER HOGNESTAD, *Bishop of Bjorgvin.* *
K. IRBE. *Bishop of Latvia.*
M. G. G. SHERER, *Secretary of The United Lutheran Church in America.*
D. DR. SCHOELL, *Praelat in Stuttgart.*
NATHAN SOEDERBLOM, *Archbishop of Upsala.*
A. STEIMLE, *Pastor, New York, United Lutheran Church in America.*
W. ZOELLNER, *D. General Superintendent, Muenster W.*
* The other Norwegian delegates desire a vote of the Conference on the other subjects, but not on the Church (Subject III), the Ministry (Sub. V.) or the Sacraments (Sub. VI.)."

This statement was read in English by Dr. Steimle of our delegation, by Pastor Appia in French and by Dr. Zoellner in German. The main proposal, that the reports should be "received" by the Conference and not "adopted", was accepted at once by the President of the Conference to be incorporated in the Preamble which he had been charged to write.

The Reports thus received by the Conference for transmission to the Churches are appended to this report. The report on the Message of the Church, the Gospel, was received unanimously. The delegates of the Orthodox Church participated in the discussions on the other subjects but abstained from voting on their reception. The report on the subject, the Unity of Christendom, was referred to the Continuation Committee and is not included in the series transmitted to the Churches for their consideration.

The Conference throughout was possessed by a spirit of seriousness, dealing with its grave problems with never a manifestation of levity. It approached its labors daily with a period of intercession and relieved the strain of its sessions with periods of silent prayer. It was always sane and self-possessed and was never swept off its feet by any outburst of oratory or wave of enthusiasm. It grappled with its problem bravely and brought clearness into it.

It was a necessary step on the long, hard road to Christian unity. It brought to visible expression the yearning of Christendom to be one. No one could listen to the passionate pleas of the representatives of mission fields without realizing that our divisions in Western Christendom are very confusing and are hindering the work of propagating the Gospel in non-Christian lands. But it brushed aside illusions harbored here and there concerning the method by which outward unity could be realized. It pointed the only way in which the Christian Church can ever hope for a solution of its problem of disunity, namely the calm, unhurried consideration of its fundamental tenets in a fraternal and non-controversial spirit, with the earnest hope and expectation of reaching such agreement in the unity of the Spirit as will prove to be the bond of peace, in the meanwhile giving itself earnestly to that common approach for the salvation of the world, which found unanimous approval by the Conference in its report on the Message of the Church.

Your delegates would recommend that the United Lutheran Church, through the Executive Board, appoint a commission of seven members to study the Reports herewith submitted and to consider any other report or reports that may be transmitted by the Continuation Committee, and to submit recommendations with regard to the future relationship of The United Lutheran Church to the World Conference on Faith and Order.

Respectfully submitted,

A. STEIMLE
HOLMES DYSINGER
W. H. GREEVER
M. G. G. SCHERER, *Chairman.*

3. Commission on Reports:

In accordance with the recommendation of the delegates, a commission of seven men was appointed to study the Reports and to submit recommendations with regard to the future relationship with the World Conference on Faith and Order: Dr. M. G. G. Scherer, Chairman, Dr. A. Steimle, Dr. Holmes Dysinger, Dr. W. H. Greever, Dr. J. A. W. Haas, Dr. Chas. M. Jacobs, Dr. John Aberly.

4. Report of the Commission on Reports:

The Commission above named met at Mt. Airy on April 11th, 1928 and reported to the Executive Board on May 17th. The report, as amended by the Executive Board, is recommended to the Convention as follows:

Report of Commission on Reports of the World Conference on Faith and Order

The papers put into our hands are the Reports of the World Conference on Faith and Order held at Lausanne, Switzerland, August 3-21, 1927.

Your Commission was charged with the duty of studying these Reports and submitting recommendations with regard to the future relationship of The United Lutheran Church in America to the World Conference on Faith and Order. The Conference itself received the Reports as containing subject matter for the consideration of the Churches and submits them to the Churches "for that deliberate consideration which could not be given in the brief" period of its sessions.

The Conference also adopted the following resolutions:

"That to all of those Churches which have sent delegates the findings of this Conference shall be sent through their official channels at as early a date as possible, asking those Churches to consider the findings and report back to the Continuation Committee the results of their deliberations, in view of which the Continuation Committee shall consider what steps need to be taken for another Conference.

"That the participating Churches be asked to continue their commissions or committees dealing with the subject of this Conference, both for educational purposes at home and in order to keep in touch with the Continuation Committee."

In studying these reports and making recommendations, your Commission has been guided by the official action of the United Lutheran Church contained in the Washington Declaration. In that Declaration the following statement is made:

"Our attitude toward any such organization or movement must be determined by a consideration of
"(a)   The purposes which it seeks to accomplish;
"(b)   The principles on which it rests;
"(c)   The effect which our participation will produce upon the independent position of our Church as a witness to the truth of the Gospel which we confess."

On the basis of this official statement of the United Lutheran Church the members of your Commission unanimously agree that there is nothing in the Reports which precludes the possibility of our further participation in the work of the Conference. Whether we may reasonably expect, however far away, results which would justify our continued participation can be decided only when we know what the Continuation Committee proposes to do with reference to the further study of the subjects which have been discussed, and with reference to the discussion of subjects which were not on the Lausanne program.

It is therefore recommended:

1.   That the United Lutheran Church appoint a Commission of five on the World Conference on Faith and Order whose duty it shall be to keep in touch with the Continuation Committee and to advise the United Lutheran Church of its plans and purposes.

2.   That the continuance of participation in the work of the Conference be dependent on the approval of these plans and purposes, and that the Executive Board of the United Lutheran Church be authorized to act *ad interim* upon any recommendation of this Commission with reference to the Conference.

3.   That this Commission be instructed to keep in touch with other Lutherans, especially those now related or hereafter to be related to the Conference on Faith and Order, and to frame its recommendations with a view to the maintenance and furtherance of Lutheran unity.

For the information of the Church the full text of the Reports of the Lausanne Conference is submitted.

PREAMBLE
Unanimously Adopted By the Full Conference
August 20, 1927

We, representatives of many Christian Communions throughout the world, united in the common confession of faith in Jesus Christ the Son of God, our Lord and Saviour, believing that the Spirit of God is with us, are assembled to consider the things wherein we agree and the things wherein we differ. We now receive the following series of reports as containing subject matter for the consideration of our respective Churches in their common search for unity.

This is a Conference summoned to consider matters of Faith and Order. It is emphatically *not* attempting to define conditions of future reunion. Its object is to register the apparent level of fundamental agreements within the Conference and the grave points of disagreement remaining; also to suggest certain lines of thought which

may in the future tend to a fuller measure of agreement.

Each subject on the agenda was first discussed in plenary session. It was then committed to one of the sections, of more than one hundred members each, into which the whole Conference was divided. The report, after full discussion in subsections, was finally drawn up and adopted unanimously or by a large majority vote by the section to which it had been committed. It was twice presented for further discussion to a plenary session of the Conference when it was referred to the Churches in its present form.

Though we recognize the reports to be neither exhaustive nor in all details satisfactory to every member of the Conference, we submit them to the Churches for that deliberate consideration which could not be given in the brief period of our sessions. We thank God and rejoice over agreements reached; upon our agreements we build. Where the reports record differences, we call upon the Christian world to an earnest reconsideration of the conflicting opinions now held, and a strenuous endeavor to reach the truth as it is in God's mind, which should be the foundation of the Church's unity.

I. THE CALL TO UNITY
Unanimously Adopted By the Full Conference
August 20, 1927

God wills unity. Our presence in this Conference bears testimony to our desire to bend our wills to His. However we may justify the beginnings of disunion, we lament its continuance and henceforth must labour, in penitence and faith, to build up our broken walls.

God's Spirit has been in the midst of us. It was He who called us hither. His presence has been manifest in our worship, our deliberations and our whole fellowship. He has discovered us to one another. He has enlarged our horizons, quickened our understanding, and enlivened our hope. We have dared and God has justified our daring. We can never be the same again. Our deep thankfulness must find expression in sustained endeavour to share the visions vouchsafed us here with those smaller home groups where our lot is cast.

More than half the world is waiting for the Gospel. At home and abroad sad multitudes are turning away in bewilderment from the Church because of its corporate feebleness. Our missions count that as a necessity which we are inclined to look on as a luxury. Already

the mission field is impatiently revolting from the divisions of the Western Church to make bold adventure for unity in its own right. We of the Churches represented in this Conference cannot allow our spiritual children to outpace us. We with them must gird ourselves to the task, the early beginnings of which God has so richly blessed, and labour side by side until our common goal is reached.

Some of us, pioneers in this undertaking, have grown old in our search for unity. It is to youth that we look to lift the torch on high. We men have carried it too much alone through many years. The women henceforth should be accorded their share of responsibility. And so the whole Church will be enabled to do that which no section can hope to perform.

It was God's clear call that gathered us. With faith stimulated by His guidance to us here, we move forward.

REPORT OF SECTION II
Received By the Full Conference, *nem. con.,* August 19, 1927
THE CHURCH'S MESSAGE TO THE WORLD—THE GOSPEL

The message of the Church to the world is and must always remain the Gospel of Jesus Christ.

The Gospel is the joyful message of redemption, both here and hereafter, the gift of God to sinful man in Jesus Christ.

The world was prepared for the coming of Christ through the activities of God's Spirit in all humanity, but especially in His revelation as given in the Old Testament; and in the fulness of time the eternal Word of God became incarnate, and was made man, Jesus Christ, the Son of God and the son of Man, full of grace and truth.

Through His life and teaching, His call to repentance, His proclamation of the coming of the Kingdom of God and of judgment, His suffering and death, His resurrection and exaltation to the right hand of the Father, and by the mission of the Holy Spirit, He has brought to us forgiveness of sins, and has revealed the fulness of the living God, and His boundless love toward us. By the appeal of that love, shown in its completeness on the Cross, He summons us to the new life of faith, self sacrifice, and devotion to His service and the service of men.

Jesus Christ, as the crucified and the living One, as Saviour and Lord, is also the centre of the world-wide Gospel of the Apostles and the Church. Because He Himself is the Gospel, the Gospel is the message of the Church to the world. It is more than a philosophical theory; more than a theological system; more than a programme for material betterment. The Gopsel is rather the gift of the new world from God to this old world of sin and death; still more, it is the victory over sin and death, the revelation of eternal life in Him who has knit together the whole family in heaven and on earth in the communion of saints, united in the fellowship of service, of prayer, and of praise.

The Gospel is the prophetic call to sinful man to turn to God, the joyful tidings of justification and of sanctification to those who believe in Christ. It is the comfort of those who suffer; to those who are bound, it is the assurance of the glorious liberty of the sons of God. The Gospel brings peace and joy to the heart, and produces in men self-denial, readiness for brotherly service, and compassionate love. It offers the supreme goal for the aspirations of youth, strength to the toilers, rest to the weary, and the crown of life to the martyr.

The Gospel is the sure source of power for social regeneration. It proclaims the only way by which humanity can escape from those class and race hatreds which devastate society at present into the enjoyment of national well-being and international friendship and peace. It is also a gracious invitation to the non-christian world, East and West, to enter into the joy of the living Lord.

Sympathising with the anguish of our generation, with its longing for intellectual sincerity, social justice and spiritual inspiration, the Church in the eternal Gospel meets the needs and fulfils the God-given aspirations of the modern world. Consequently, as in the past, so also in the present, the Gospel is the only way of salvation. Thus, through His Church, the living Christ still says to men "Come unto me! . . . He that followeth me shall not walk in darkness, but shall have the light of life."

REPORT OF SECTION III
Received By the Full Conference,
nem. con., **August 19, 1927**

THE NATURE OF THE CHURCH

God who has given us the Gospel for the salvation of the world has appointed His Church to witness by life and word to its redeeming power. The Church of the Living God is constituted by His own will, not by the will or consent or beliefs of men whether as individuals or as societies, though He uses the will of men as His instrument. Of this Church Jesus Christ is the Head, the Holy Spirit its continuing life.

The Church as the communion of believers in Christ Jesus is, according to the New Testament, the people of the New Covenant; the Body of Christ; and the Temple of God, built upon the foundation of the Apostles and Prophets, Jesus Christ Himself being the chief corner stone.

The Church is God's chosen instrument by which Christ, through the Holy Spirit, reconciles men to God through faith, bringing their wills into subjection to His sovereignty, sanctifying them through the means of grace, and uniting them in love and service to be His witnesses and fellow-workers in the extension of His rule on earth until His Kingdom come in glory.

As there is but one Christ, and one life in Him, and one Holy Spirit who guides into all truth, so there is and can be but one Church, holy, catholic, and apostolic.

The Church on earth possesses certain characteristics whereby it can be known of men. These have been, since the days of the Apostles, at least the following:

1. The possession and acknowledgment of the Word of God as given in Holy Scripture and interpreted by the Holy Spirit to the Church and to the individual. (a)

2. The profession of faith in God as He is incarnate and revealed in Christ.

3. The acceptance of Christ's commission to preach the Gospel to every creature.

4. The observance of the Sacraments.

5. A ministry for the pastoral office, the preaching of the Word, and the administration of the Sacraments.

6. A fellowship in prayer, in worship, in all the means of grace, in the pursuit of holiness, and in the service of man.

As to the extent and manner in which the Church thus described finds expression in the existing Churches, we differ. Our differences chiefly concern:

1. The nature of the Church visible and the Church invisible, their relation to each other, and the number of those who are included in each. (b)

2. The significance of our divisions past and present. (c)

Whatever our views on these points, we are convinced that it is the will of Christ that the one life of the one body should be manifest to the world. To commend the Gospel to doubting, sinful and bewildered men, a united witness is necessary. We therefore urge most earnestly that all Christians in fulfilment of our Saviour's prayer that His diciples may be one reconsecrate themselves to God, that by the help of His Spirit the body of Christ may be built up, its members united in faith and love, and existing obstacles to the manifestation of their unity in Christ may be removed; that the world may believe that the Father has sent Him.

We join in the prayer that the time may be hastened when in the name of Jesus every knee shall bow and every tongue confess that Jesus Christ is Lord to the glory of God the Father.

NOTES

(a) Some hold that this interpretation is given through the tradition of the Church; others through the immediate witness of the Spirit to the heart and conscience of believers; others through both combined.

(b) For instance

1. Some hold that the invisible Church is wholly in heaven; others include in it all true believers on earth, whether contained in any organization or not.

2. Some hold that the visible expression of the Church was determined by Christ Himself and is therefore unchangeable; others that the one Church under the guidance of the Holy Spirit may express itself in varying forms.

3. Some hold that one or other of the existing Churches is the only true Church; others that the Church as we have described it is to be found in some or all of the existing communions taken together.

4. Some, while recognizing other Christian bodies as Churches, are persuaded that in the providence of God and by the teaching of history a particular form of ministry has been shown to be necessary to the best welfare of the Church; others hold that no one form of organization is inherently preferable; still others that no organization is necessary.

(c) One view is that no division of Christendom has ever come to pass without sin. Another view is that the divisions were the inevitable outcome of different gifts of the Spirit and different understandings of the truth. Between these, there is the view of those who look back on the divisions of the past with penitence and sorrow coupled with a lively sense of God's mercy, which in spite of and even through these divisions has advanced His cause in the world.

REPORT OF SECTION IV
Received By the Full Conference,
nem. con., August 19, 1927
THE CHURCH'S COMMON CONFESSION OF FAITH

We members of the Conference on Faith and Order, coming from all parts of the world in the interest of Christian unity, have with deep gratitude to God found ourselves united in common prayer, in God our heavenly Father and His Son Jesus Christ, our Saviour, in the fellowship of the Holy Spirit.

Notwithstanding the differences in doctrine among us, we are united in a common Christian Faith which is proclaimed in the Holy Scriptures and is witnessed to and safeguarded in the Ecumenical Creed, commonly called the Nicene, and in the Apostles' Creed, which Faith is continuously confirmed in the spiritual experience of the Church of Christ.

We believe that the Holy Spirit in leading the Church into all truth may enable it, while firmly adhering to the witness of these Creeds (our common heritage from the ancient Church) to express the truths of revelation in such other forms as new problems may from time to time demand.

Finally, we desire to leave on record our solemn and unanimous testimony that no external and written standards can suffice without an inward and personal experience of union with God in Christ.

NOTES

1. It must be noted that the Orthodox Eastern Church can accept the Nicene Creed only in its uninterpolated form without the *filioque* clause; and that although the Apostles' Creed has no place in the formularies of this Church, it is in accordance with its teaching.

2. It must be noted also that some of the Churches represented in this Conference conjoin tradition with the Scriptures, some are explicit in subordinating Creeds to the Scriptures, some attach a primary importance to their particular Confessions, and some make no use of Creeds.

3. It is understood that the use of these Creeds will be determined by the competent authority in each Church, and that the several Churches will continue to make use of such special Confessions as they possess.

REPORT OF SECTION V
Received By the Full Conference,
nem. con., **August 20, 1927**
THE MINISTRY OF THE CHURCH

We members of the Conference on Faith and Order are happy to report that we find ourselves in substantial accord in the following five propositions:

1. The ministry is a gift of God through Christ to His Church and is essential to the being and well-being of the Church.

2. The ministry is perpetually authorized and made effective through Christ and His Spirit.

3. The purpose of the ministry is to impart to men the saving and sanctifying benefits of Christ through pastoral service, the preaching of the Gospel, and the administration of the sacraments, to be made effective by faith.

4. The ministry is entrusted with the government and discipline of the Church, in whole or in part.

5. Men gifted for the work of the ministry, called by the Spirit and accepted by the Church are commissioned through an act of ordination by prayer and the laying on of hands to exercise the function of this ministry.

Within the many Christian communions into which in the course of history Christendom has been divided, various forms of ministry have grown up according to the circumstances of the several communions and their beliefs as to the mind of Christ and the guidance of the New Testament. These communions have been, in God's providence, manifestly and abundantly used by the

Holy Spirit in His work of enlightening the world, converting sinners, and perfecting saints. But the differences which have arisen in regard to the authority and functions of these various forms of ministry have been and are the occasion of manifold doubts, questions and misunderstandings.

These differences concern the nature of the ministry (whether consisting of one or several orders), the nature of ordination and of the grace conferred thereby, the function and authority of Bishops, and the nature of Apostolic succession. We believe that the first step toward the overcoming of these difficulties is the frank recognition that they exist, and the clear definition of their nature. We therefore add as an appendix to our Report such a statement, commending it to the thoughtful c o n s i d e r a t i o n of the Churches we represent.

By these differences the difficulties of inter-communion have been accentuated to the d i s t r e s s and wounding of faithful souls, while in the mission field, where the Church is fulfilling its primary object to preach the Gospel to every creature, the young Churches find the lack of unity a very serious obstacle to the furtherance of the Gospel. Consequently the provision of a ministry acknowledged in every part of the Church as possessing the sanction of the whole Church is an urgent need.

There has not been time in this Conference to consider all the points of difference between us in the matter of the ministry with that care and patience which could alone lead to complete agreement. The same observation applies equally to proposals for the constitution of the United Church. Certain suggestions as to possible church organization have been made, which we transmit to the Churches with the earnest hope that common study of these questions will be continued by the members of the various Churches represented in this Conference.

In view of (1) the place which the Episcopate, the Councils of Presbyters, and the Congregation of the faithful, respectively, had in the constitution of the early Church, and (2) the fact that episcopal, presbyteral and congregational systems of government are each today, and have been for centuries, accepted by great communions in Christendom, and (3) the fact that episcopal, presbyteral and congregational systems are each believed by many to be essential to the good order of the Church, we therefore recognize that these several elements must all, under conditions which require further study, have an appropriate place in the order of life of a reunited Church, and that each separate communion, recalling the abundant blessing of God vouchsafed to its ministry in the past, should gladly bring to the common life of the united Church its own spiritual treasures.

If the foregoing suggestion be accepted and acted upon, it is essential that the acceptance of any special form of ordination as the regular and orderly method of introduction into the ministry of the Church for the future should not be interpreted to imply the acceptance of any one particular theory of the origin, character or function of any office in the Church, or to involve the acceptance of any adverse judgment on the validity of ordination in those branches of the Church universal that believe themselves to have retained valid and apostolic Orders under other forms of ordination; or as disowning or discrediting a past or present ministry of the Word and Sacrament which has been used and blessed by the Spirit of God.

It is further recognized that inasmuch as the Holy Spirit is bestowed upon every believer, and each believer has an immediate access to God through Jesus Christ, and since special gifts of the Holy Spirit, such as teaching, preaching, and spiritual counsel, are the treasures of the Church as well as of the individual, it is necessary and proper that the Church should make fuller use of such gifts for the development of its corporate spiritual life and for the extension of the Kingdom of Jesus Christ, our Lord.

In particular, we share in the conviction, repeatedly expressed in this Conference, that pending the solution of the questions of faith and order in which agreements have not yet been reached, it is possible for us, not simply as individuals but as Churches, to unite in the activities of brotherly service which Christ has committed to His diciples. We therefore commend to our Churches the consideration of the steps which may be immediately practical to bring our unity in service to more effective expression.

In conclusion, we express our thankfulness to Almighty God for the great progress which has been made in recent years in the mutual approach of the Churches to one another, and our conviction that we must go forward with faith and courage, confident that with the blessing of God we shall be able to solve the problems that lie before us.

NOTES

1. The following is the view of the Orthodox Church, as formulated for us by its representatives.

"The Orthodox Church, regarding the ministry as instituted in the Church by Christ Himself, and as the body which by a special charisma is the organ through which the Church spreads its means of grace such as the sacraments, and believing that the ministry in its threefold form of Bishops, Presbyters and Deacons can only be based on the unbroken apostolic succession, regrets that it is unable to come in regard to the ministry into some measure of agreement with many of the Churches represented at this Conference; but prays God that He, through His Holy Spirit, will guide to union even in regard to this difficult point of disagreement."

2. In Western Christendom also there are conspicuous differences.

One representative view includes the following points:

(a) that there have always been various grades of the ministry, each with its own function; (b) that ordination is a sacramental act of divine institution, and therefore indispensable, c o n v e y i n g the special charisma for the particular ministry; (c) that Bishops who have received their office by succession from the Apostles are the necessary ministers of ordination; (d) that the apostolic succession so understood is necessary for the authority of the ministry, the visible unity of the Church, and the validity of the sacraments.

On the other hand it is held by many Churches represented in the Conference (a) that essentially there is only one ministry, that of the Word and Sacraments; (b) that the existing ministries in these Churches are agreeable to the New Testament, are proved by their fruits and have due authority in the Church, and the sacraments ministered by them are valid; (c) that no particular form of ministry is necessary to be received as a matter of faith; (d) that the grace which fits men for the ministry is immediately given by God, and is recognized, not conferred, in ordination.

Further we record that there are views concerning the ministry which are intermediate between the types just mentioned. For instance, some who adhere to an episcopal system of church government do not consider that the apostolic succession as described above is a vital element of episcopacy, or they reject it altogether. Others do not regard as essential the historic Episcopate. Those who adhere to presbyteral systems of Church government believe that the apostolic ministry is transmissible and has been transmitted through Presbyters orderly associated for the purpose. Those who adhere to the congregational system of government define their ministry as having been and being transmitted according to the precedent and example of the New Testament.

REPORT OF SECTION VI
Received By the Full Conference,
nem. con., **August 20, 1927**
THE SACRAMENTS

We are convinced that for the purpose in view in this Conference we should not go into detail in considering Sacraments—by some called "Mysteries." The purpose therefore of this statement is to show that there may be a common approach to and appreciation of Sacraments on the part of those who may otherwise differ in conception and interpretation.

We testify to the fact that the Christian world gives evidence of an increasing sense of the significance and value of Sacraments, and would express our belief that this movement should be fostered and guided as a means of deepening the life and experience of the Churches. In this connection we recognize that the Sacraments have special reference to the corporate life and fellowship of the Church and that the grace is conveyed by the Holy Spirit, taking of the things of Christ and applying them to the soul through Faith.

We agree that Sacraments are of divine appointment and that the Church ought thankfully to observe them as divine gifts.

We hold that in the Sacraments

there is an outward sign and an inward grace, and that the Sacraments are means of grace through which God works invisibly in us. We recognize also that in the gifts of His grace God is not limited by His own Sacraments.

The Orthodox Church and others hold that there are seven Sacraments and that for their valid administration there must be a proper form, a proper matter and a proper ministry. Others can regard only Baptism and the Lord's Supper as Sacraments. Others again, while attaching high value to the sacramental principle, do not make use of the outward signs of Sacraments, but hold that all spiritual benefits are given through immediate contact with God through His Spirit. In this Conference we lay stress on the two Sacraments of Baptism and Lord's Supper, because they are the Sacraments which are generally acknowledged by the members of this Conference.

We believe that in Baptism administered with water in the name of the Father, the Son and the Holy Spirit, for the remission of sins, we are baptised by one Spirit into one body. By this statement it is not meant to ignore the difference in conception, interpretation and mode which exists among us.

We believe that in the Holy Communion our Lord is present, that we have fellowship with God our Father in Jesus Christ His Son, our Living Lord, who is our one Bread, given for the life of the world, sustaining the life of all His people, and that we are in fellowship with all others who are united to Him. We agree that the Sacrament of the Lord's Supper is the Church's most sacred act of worship in which the Lord's atoning death is commemorated and proclaimed, and that it is a sacrifice of praise and thanksgiving and an act of solemn self-oblation.

There are among us divergent views, especially as to (1) the mode and manner of the presence of our Lord; (2) the conception of the commemoration and the sacrifice; (3) the relation of the elements to the grace conveyed; and (4) the relation between the minister of this Sacrament and the validity and efficacy of the rite. We are aware that the reality of the divine presence and gift in this Sacrament cannot be adequately apprehended by human thought or expressed in human language.

We close this statement with the prayer that the differences which prevent full communion at the present time may be removed.

FOREWORD TO THE REPORT ON SUBJECT VII

The report of Section VII, on the Unity of Christendom and the relation thereto of existing Churches, was presented to the Conference on Thursday, August 18, by the Chairman of the section, the Archbishop of Upsala, and after discussion, in which various amendments were proposed, "was referred to the Drafting Committee for the consideration of the proposed amendments." The text of the first draft, together with an abstract of the discussion, is found in the official Proceedings of the Conference ("Faith and Order"), pages 396-403.

In the absence of the Archbishop of Upsala, a revision of the Report was presented to the full Conference on Saturday, August 20, by the Archbishop of Armagh, the Vice-Chairman of the Section. After debate, in which it appeared that the revision would not receive the unanimous approval of the Conference, the President suggested as a proposal likely to meet all difficulties "that the Report should be received by the Conference in the same way as the other reports, but on the understanding that it should be referred to the Continuation Committee for further consideration," it being further explained "that the Continuation Committee would take such action as it considered advisable in view of the knowledge it had of the situation." This proposal was adopted by the Conference. The text of the revised report, together with a brief abstract of the discussion which followed, is found in the Proceedings of the Conference, pages 435-439.

At a meeting of the Continuation Committee held on August 20, 1927, the following action was taken:

With reference to the report on Subject VII which had been received by the World Conference on Faith and Order for transmission to the Continuation Committee, it was agreed that a committee be appointed with the duty of considering the whole situation with regard to Subject VII and reporting back to the Business Committee. The following were named:

Rt. Rev. the Bishop of Gloucester, Convener.

Rev. William Adams Brown, D.D.

Rt. Rev. James DeWolf Perry, D.D.

Gen.-Sup. D.Dr. Otto Dibelius

Rev. Timothy Tingfang Lew, Ph.D.

At the suggestion of the President of the Conference, the Archbishop of Upsala was afterwards added to the Committee.

Acting under the instructions thus given, the Committee prepared a revised draft of Report VII in which, without introducing any new matter of their own, they endeavored to meet the criticisms which had been made of the Report in its earlier forms by rearrangement of material, by more exact reference to previous actions of the Conference itself, and by following more consistently the precedent set in earlier reports of stating alternative positions where there was difference of view.

In the course of its deliberations the Committee received valuable suggestions from many members of the Conference, especially from the Archbishop of Armagh, Professor Merle d'Aubignè, and Archbishop Germanos. The latter contributed valuable notes on the attitude of the Orthodox Church to certain points raised in the Report.

The Report, thus amended and revised, was presented to the Business Committee on December 21, 1927, and after full consideration and the adoption of certain minor amendments is by them submitted to the churches for such consideration as they may desire to give it.

REPORT ON SUBJECT VII
THE UNITY OF CHRISTENDOM AND THE RELATION THERETO OF EXISTING CHURCHES

Reports II to VI register the degree of unity in the conception of the Church to which the Conference has thus far attained. It remains in this closing report to consider the consequences which follow for the existing churches.

I

Report II declares that "the message of the Church to the world is and must always remain the Gospel of Jesus Christ . . . the joyful message of redemption, both here and hereafter, the gift of God to sinful man in Jesus Christ."

Report III declares that "God who has given us the Gospel for the salvation of the world has appointed His Church to witness by life and word to its redeeming power . . . As there is but one Christ, and one life in Him, and one Holy Spirit who guides into all truth, so there is and can be but one Church, holy, catholic, and apostolic."

Report IV declares that "notwithstanding the differences in doctrine among us, we are united in a common Christian Faith which is proclaimed in the Holy Scriptures and is witnessed to and safeguarded in the Ecumenical Creed, commonly called the Nicene, and in the Apostles' Creed, which Faith is continually confirmed in the spiritual experience of the Church of Christ."

Report V declares that "the ministry is a gift of God through Christ to His Church and is essential to the being and well-being of the Church . . . The purpose of the ministry is to impart to men the saving and sanctifying benefits of Christ through pastoral service, the preaching of the Gospel, and the administration of the sacraments, to be made effective by faith."

Report VI declares that "Sacraments are of divine appointment and that the Church ought thankfully to observe them as divine gifts;" that they "have special reference to the corporate life and fellowship of the Church and that the grace is conveyed by the Holy Spirit, taking of the things of Christ and applying them to the soul through faith."

II

The unity of the Church implies a unity in Faith and Order, but it does not mean uniformity. There must be space for divers types of expression, provided that those things which safeguard the unity in essentials are maintained. The various communions should bring into the common life of the Church those elements which express their characteristic gifts, so that nothing of the rich variety which marks Christian experience will be lost, and the liberty of interpretation within the limits of the accepted faith will be preserved.

Further there are differences as to the ultimate form which it is God's will His Church should take. Some hold that this form "was determined by Christ Himself and is therefore unchangeable; others that the one Church under the guidance of the Holy Spirit may express itself in varying forms" (Report III), and therefore make place in their view of the Church of the future for diversity of doctrine, worship and order. Still others admit diversity of worship and order, but not of doctrine.

This difference of ideal affects the view taken of the steps through which the ideal is to be reached, some interpreting the limit of legitimate variation in doctrinal statement and in the administration of church ordinances more strictly than others; but there is widespread agreement that there must be some unity of faith and practice and some liberty of interpretation as to the nature of sacramental grace and of ministerial order and authority. (See the appended "Note to Section II.")

III

As the individual disciple is known by his fruits, so the unity of the disciples is shown by their fellowship in the service of the Master. Report V declares that, "pending the solution of the questions of faith and order in which agreements have not yet been reached, it is possible for us, not simply as individuals but as Churches, to unite in the activities of brotherly service which Christ has committed to His disciples;" but there is difference as to the exact form this coöperation should take.

In his Encyclical Letter of 1920, the Ecumenical Patriarch proposed "that a league or council of the churches should be formed for practical purposes." It has been suggested that such a council might be evolved from already existing organizations, such as the Continuation Committee on Life and Work, consisting of representatives officially appointed by almost all the Christian communions, and other organizations of similar nature. Some of us believe that such a council if formed should include, as its two branches, questions of life and work and of faith and order. Others believe that, for the present, it would be wiser for the movements represented by Stockholm and Lausanne to develop in independence, each following its own way; but there is general agreement that ultimately life, work, faith and order are expressions of an existing spiritual unity, and that each requires the other for its complete fruition. "We therefore commend to our Churches the consideration of the steps which may be immediately practicable to bring our existing unity in service to more effective expression" (Report V).

IV

As material for such consideration, the following suggestions which it was impossible adequately to discuss at Lausanne are passed on to the churches:

1. In preparation for closer fellowship, each communion should seek more intimate knowledge of the faith and life, worship and order of the others. Differences which are the outgrowth of complicated historical developments, may preserve some aspect of truth or of life which is of value to the church as a whole, or they may sometimes prove to be less important than they are supposed to be. As the different communions come to know one another better,

they will grow in understanding and in appreciation of one another.

2. It has not been possible for the Conference to consider with the care which it deserves the relation of the existing churches to one another or the place which each or any of them may hold in the undivided church. We commend to the churches the suggestions which have been made on this subject in the addresses delivered at the Conference. In the meantime, we welcome the movement already under way for the union of bodies of similar doctrine, polity and worship, and trust that it may continue with ever greater success.

3. Pending the complete organic union of the different churches, we note with satisfaction a number of movements for practical coöperation along social, evangelistic and other lines. Experience shows that it has been possible for widely separate bodies to co-operate in such movements with mutual profit and without surrender of principle. (See the appended "Notes to Section IV," Note A.) There is abundant evidence that when communions undertake together the divine task of bringing the love of Christ to those who do not know Him, they become closer to one another. Especially we commend to the churches the consideration of what steps can be taken to eliminate needless overlapping and competition in the local community; that in ways consistent with the genius of the several communions, our existing unity in Christ may be manifest to the world. (See the appended "Notes to Section IV," Note B.)

V

We note with gratitude to God the recent increase of effective coöperation in the mission field. The purpose of all missionary work is to carry the eternal Gospel to the ends of the earth, so that it may meet the spiritual needs of every nation and bring all men to the Saviour. Here more than anywhere else unity is essential. We note with sympathy the degree of union which has already been attained in many countries and the plans which are proposed for further union. We commend these plans to the churches for their careful consideration.

The demand which comes from the churches of the Mission field is that the Churches at home should grant them geater freedom of action, and that their hopes of unity should not be frustrated by the long-continued acquiescence in disunion at home which makes it difficult to recognize how fatal disunion is to the new indigenous churches.

VI

Complete fellowship in the Church will be realized only when the way is opened for all God's children to join in communion at the Lord's table. Through prayer and thoughtful deliberation the steps must be found which will most effec ively lead to this goal. Ambiguous statements and hasty measures may hinder rather than hasten the work of unification. Yet it we are ever to become one, we must not shrink from the task. Some of us believe that full communion can be reached only at the end of the process of unification; others that it may be used by God as the means to that end. Whatever the way to the goal, complete unity will require that the Churches be so transformed that there may be full recognition of one another by members of all communions.

Nothing will do more to hasten the union for which we all long than that in our daily prayer, both as individuals and as churches, we should remember one another. It has been suggested that a common prayer be sent out in the name of the Conference to be used at a convenient time by all Christian Churches. Especially would we bear on our hearts before God our brethren who are passing through suffering, praying that grace may be given to them to stand firm under their afflictions, and that to them and to us alike, God will grant the spirit of sacrifice as we remember the word of the Lord Jesus: "If any man will come after Me, let him deny himself and take us his cross daily and follow Me." God give us, both as individuals and as churches, wisdom and courage to do His will.

Note to Section II

It must be noted that representatives of the Orthodox Church would guard their acceptance of any diversity in matters of Faith and Order (Section II) by the following limitations.

(a) The types of expression so far as these types have been established by Ecumenical Synods must be maintained.

(b) Liberty of interpretation comes within the sphere of the Church as a whole and not of different sections or individuals.

(c) They cannot agree that "there must be some liberty of interpretation as to the nature of sacramental grace, and of ministerial order and authority."

(d) They admit differences in worship so long as they do not diverge from the common doctrinal basis, on which is based the Holy Worship as handed down from the times of the Apostles.

Notes to Section IV, Par. 3

A. There are some who believe that cooperation should take the form of federation, either local, national, or international; others oppose federation, fearing that it may become a substitute for complete organic union. In the interest of clarity of thought it is important to remember that the word "federation" is used in at least three different senses. It may denote either

1. A substitute for organic union
2. A step on the road to organic union.
3. A form of organic union.

In discussing federation it is important to make clear in which of these different senses the word is used.

B. It is suggested that in the case of communions of similar doctrine and polity, the desired expression of unity may often be secured by the method of denominational comity. In the case of those communions which are separated by fundamental differences of view, the problem is more difficult and will require special consideration.

Your Commission is unable to recommend the adoption of these reports as statements of the faith of the Lutheran Church or as a basis for the union of the Churches for the following reasons:

(1.)   The Reports admittedly are not in proper form for adoption by the Churches as a basis of doctrinal agreement and of union.

(2.)   The Reports are inadequate as to definition.

(3.)   Certain subjects which we believe essential to a right conception of Christian truth are either not stated at all or stated in such terms as to leave the meaning of the statements quite unclear. As illustrations we may cite the doctrines of atonement, of justification by faith, and of the Word of God as the means of grace.

In view of the above, we recommend:

(4.)   That the Commission to be appointed be instructed to conduct a further study of the Reports and to present the results of that study in the form of a report through the Executive Board to the Convention of the United Lutheran Church in 1930.

The Commission should also be authorized to communicate to the Continuation Committee of the World Conference on Faith and Order such results of their study as may seem to be helpful to that Committee in its work.

With reference to the future

(a)   We endorse the proposal of the Lutheran delegates made at the Conference at Lausanne, to the following effect: "In order to secure a thorough and adequate consideration and to give the desired effect to the labors of this Conference, the whole material (contained in the Reports) should be referred to a small commission composed of trusted representatives of the various groups, namely the Orthodox, the Evangelical Lutherans, the Reformed and the Presbyterians (Calvinists), the Anglicans, the Methodists, the Baptists, the Congregationalists, etc. This commission should be charged with the duty carefully to examine these propositions in the light of the discussions during this Conference and to set forth the points of agreement and difference in doctrine and practice."

(b)   We believe that ecclesiastical order as well as a hopeful procedure will require that the Conference should be a Conference of the Churches, truly representative in character, but with limited powers.

(c)   It is our judgment that some authority must be agreed upon to which final appeal shall be made in regard to Church doctrines.

We would propose the following: That the Prophetic and Apostolic Scriptures of the Old and New Testaments be accepted as the only rule and standard for the determination of articles of faith.

XIV. MISCELLANEOUS

1. Visit of Bishop Kapi:

As a matter of record mention is here made of the visit of the Rt. Rev. Bela Kapi, Bishop of the Lutheran Church of Hungary and member of the Hungarian House of Lords, to the United States in the month of

March, 1928. Bishop Kapi came as a member of the delegation which visited this country to be present and participate in the unveiling of the statue to Louis Kossuth, Hungarian patriot and member of the Lutheran Church. The statue was unveiled at Riverside Drive and 113th Street, New York City, on March 15th. A luncheon was given to the Bishop and other members of the delegation on March 17th by the Lutheran Ministers' Association of New York, Dr. Samuel Trexler, President of the Association, presiding. Addresses of welcome were made by Dr. M. G. G. Scherer, Acting-President of the United Lutheran Church in America, Dr. John A. Morehead, Chairman of the Executive Committee of the Lutheran World Convention, Dr. Franklin F. Fry, Executive Secretary of the Board of American Missions.

On Sunday morning, March 18th, at ten o'clock, a service was held for the Hungarians of the city in Holy Trinity Church, 65th Street and Central Park West, New York, Dr. Paul E. Scherer, Pastor. Bishop Kapi preached. Words of welcome were spoken by the pastor, by Dr. M. G. G. Scherer, Dr. Samuel Trexler, Dr. F. F. Fry and Dr. J. A. Morehead. Under the auspices of the Board of American Missions and with the approval of the Acting-President of the United Lutheran Church, Bishop Kapi visited a number of Hungarian congregations throughout the country, at Pittsburgh, Cleveland, Akron and other places.

2. A letter was received requesting the financial support of The United Lutheran Church in America for the projected new building for the Church of the Atonement, Washington, D. C. The amount asked for was $50,000. This request had been presented to the Ministerium of Pennsylvania, with which the congregation is connected, as an uncompleted obligation of the General Council to establish through this congregation a national structure in the capital. The Ministerium answered that for such an undertaking any request should be made to the United Lutheran Church as a whole rather than to an individual Synod. The Executive Board declared that this matter was not within its jurisdiction and the President was instructed to correspond with the parties concerned.

3. Erie Convention:

In response to the request of delegates from the far west, that this convention begin a week earlier than usual in order to give them time to return to their fields of labor before Reformation Day, the Executive Board instructed the officers to arrange for the beginning of the Convention on Tuesday, October 9th, 1928.

It seemed unnecessary that there should be meetings of the three General Bodies in connection with the Erie Convention of The United Lutheran Church in America and therefore no such meetings have been called by the Executive Board.

4. As regards plans for a celebration of the quadri-centennials in 1929 and 1930, we would recommend the following:

(a) It is evident that the National Lutheran Council will aim to arrange for general celebrations of the quadri-centennials in 1929 and 1930. It is therefore recommended that the Executive Board be authorized to participate in such plans to the fullest extent possible.

(b) It seems desirable that during the year 1929 The United Lutheran Church in America lay added stress in all its Synods, Conferences and congregations upon catechization and confirmation of young people and adults. It is therefore recommended that the Committee on Evangelism be instructed to meet as soon as possible after the Erie Convention and to prepare plans for this effort. The plans are to be approved by the Executive Board.

(c)   Whatever else may be arranged for 1930, it would be well that the Convention of The United Lutheran Church in America in that year devote special attention to the Augsburg Confession. It is therefore recommended that the Executive Board be instructed to make arrangements for that purpose and to devise plans whereby all congregations can concur in the celebration.

5. **1930 and 1932 Conventions:**
Invitations were received from the Ministerium of Pennsylvania and the East Pennsylvania Synod requesting that the 1930 Convention of the United Lutheran Church be held in Philadelphia; also a communication from the Synod of the Northwest inviting the Church to hold its Convention in Milwaukee. The Executive Board considered these invitations and recommends that the 1930 Convention be held in Philadelphia and that the Convention in 1932 be held on the territory of the Synod of the Northwest, the exact place to be determined in conference with that Synod.

F. H. KNUBEL.

E. CLARENCE MILLER.

M. G. G. SCHERER.

The proposed amendment to Article V, Sec. 1 of the Constitution (II, 13) was taken up for consideration. On motion the Convention adopted the recommendation of the Executive Board to the effect that it deems the proposed change unwise.

At this point the Convention rose while the President read the following letter from Mr. Calvin Coolidge, President of the United States:

White House, Washington,
October 8, 1928.

My dear Dr. Knubel:
I am glad to have the opportunity of extending to The United Lutheran Church in America my hearty greetings and good wishes upon the occasion of your biennial convention in Erie. Your church has always joined with the forces of righteousness of every faith in standing for the ideals upon which our country was founded and upon which its hopes for the future are based.

I hope you will have a most successful convention, fruitful in works for the spiritual well-being of the nation.

Very truly yours,

CALVIN COOLIDGE.

The Rev. Dr. F. H. Knubel,
President, United Lutheran Church in America,
Luther Memorial Church, Erie, Pa.

The Committee of Tellers No. 1 reported that Dr. F. H. Knubel had received 411 votes out of a total of 456 cast. The Secretary declared that Dr. F. H. Knubel, having received more than a three-fourths majority of the votes cast, had been elected President of The United Lutheran Church in America.

The Committee of Tellers No. 2 in charge of the election of the Treasurer reported that Dr. E. Clarence Miller had received 439 votes out of 442 cast. The President declared Dr. E. Clarence Miller elected as Treasurer.

The Convention resumed consideration of the Report of the Executive Board, taking up the report concerning Irregularities of Retired Clergymen (III, A, 1 (a)). After some discussion the President requested the Rev. H. Offermann, Chairman of the Committee of Reference and Counsel, to prepare such verbal changes as might seem desirable and to offer such changes in the course of the afternoon session.

Tellers Committee No. 1, in charge of the election of Secretary, reported that out of 442 votes cast, the Rev. M. G. G. Scherer had received 425. The President thereupon declared the Rev. M. G. G. Scherer elected as Secretary.

The Convention adjourned with prayer by the Rev. C. A. Freed.

———————•———————

Afternoon Session

Wednesday, October 10, 2:00 o'clock.

Devotions were conducted by the Rev. Henry Manken, Jr., and the President called the Convention to order.

The Rev. G. A. Bierdemann, Chairman of the Nominating Committee, reported nominees.

For the Executive Board as follows:

Rev. A. C. R. Keiter; Rev. Charles D. Trexler; Rev. A. R. Wentz; Mr. Wm. E. Hirt; Mr. J. F. Kramer; Mr. George E. Neff; Rev. A. S. Hardy; Rev. P. E. Monroe; Rev. John Schmieder; Mr. J. W. King; Mr. E. J. Mosser; Mr. Chas. G. Smith.

For the Commission of Adjudication as follows:

Rev. Geo. Gebert; Rev. A. G. Voigt; Mr. E. K. Strong; Rev. C. H. Little; Rev. R. Neumann; Mr. G. A. W. Achenbach.

For the Committee on Church Papers as follows:

Rev. W. H. Greever; Rev. J. A. Leas; Rev. H. Offermann; Rev. J. L. Neve; Rev. W. E. Pugh; Rev. P. W. Roth.

The Rev. Arthur S. Hardy, Chairman of the Committee to Nominate the Executive Committee of the Laymen's Movement, reported the following nominees:

Mr. J. L. Clark; Mr. W. L. Glatfelter; Mr. Peter P. Hagan; Mr. Thomas P. Hickman; Mr. E. Clarence Miller; Mr. Harvey C. Miller; Mr. P. A. Myers; Mr. W. J. Showalter; Mr. Charles Steele; Mr. E. J. Young; Mr. Robt. F. Bowe; Mr. C. J. Driever; Mr. William Eck; Mr. Wm. H. Emhardt; Mr. Henry W. Harter; Mr. A. M. Hartzell; Mr. Jacob Pfeiffer; Mr. W. P. Seibert; Mr. Fred H. Wefer; Mr. Heiby W. Ungerer.

The Convention resumed consideration of the Executive Board's Report (III, A, 1, (a)) concerning Irregularities of Retired Clergymen.

In accordance with the request made at the morning session, the Rev. H. Offermann proposed the following changes:

1. That the second sentence of paragraph No. 1 be stricken. On motion the sentence was ordered stricken and the paragraph was adopted as amended.

2. That paragraph No. 2 be amended to read as follows: "Every such clergyman should likewise hold a definite relationship to a Synod." On motion the proposed change was approved and the paragraph was adopted as amended.

3. For paragraph No. 3, a reading, which as a result of discussion and amendment assumed the following form was adopted: "Whenever a pastor of a congregation is available, a retired clergyman or clergyman not serving under direct call of the Church should perform ministerial acts only with the approval and authorization of the pastor in charge where such acts are sought. Every ministerial act performed under such conditions should be promptly and correctly entered upon the records of the congregation within which the act is performed. This applies even to clergymen who may be serving the Church otherwise than as pastors of congregations."

4. That paragraph No. 4 be amended to read as follows: "Retired clergymen, or clergymen serving the Church otherwise than as pastors of congregations, should not be selected as lay representatives from any congregation, in order that the object of lay representation should be faithfully observed." Upon motion the paragraph was so amended, and as amended was adopted.

As amended the declaration was adopted as a whole, as here follows:

(1) Every retired clergyman or clergyman who is not serving under call from the Church, should be a member in good standing of some Lutheran congregation.

(2) Every such clergyman should likewise hold a definite relationship to a Synod.

(3) Whenever a pastor of a congregation is available, a retired clergyman or clergyman not serving under direct call of the Church should perform ministerial acts only with the approval and authorization of the pastor in charge where such acts are sought. Every ministerial act performed under such conditions should be promptly and correctly entered upon the records of the congregation within which the act is performed. This applies even to clergymen who may be serving the Church otherwise than as pastors of congregations.

(4) Retired clergymen or clergymen serving the Church otherwise than as pastors of congregations, should not be selected as lay representatives from any congregation, in order that the object of lay representation should be faithfully observed.

In the item concerning Uniformity in Dismissing and Receiving Ministers (III, A, 1, (b)), the Note to the Certificate of Transfer was changed so as to read as follows:

"When a pastor accepts a call to a parish in another Constituent Synod of The United Lutheran Church in America, the Certificate of Transfer should be placed in the hands of the President of that Synod as soon as the call is accepted."

The item (b) as thus amended was adopted.

Under the item on Apportionments (III, A, 2) the ruling of the President concerning the meaning of the words "communicant membership" on page 108 of the Minutes of the Richmond Convention was approved.

The item concerning Licensure and Ordination (III, A, 3) was next taken up.

A motion to adopt resolution No. 1 was lost.

Upon motion resolution No. 2 was amended by striking clause (b), leaving the paragraph to read as follows:

That The United Lutheran Church in America recommends to its constituent synods the practice of ordaining men to the ministry only after they have been regularly called to the work of the ministry.

The resolution was adopted as amended.

The Chairman of the Committee, the Rev. A. R. Wentz, was thereupon requested to recast the title and the preamble of the resolutions so as to harmonize them with the action taken. (See minutes second meeting, afternoon session.—Secretary.)

III, B, 4, (I), the item concerning the appointment by the Pacific Synod of electors for the proposed school of religion in the University of Oregon was adopted.

III, B, 4 (II). The action of the Executive Board on these resolutions was approved and a motion prevailed that the Executive Board confer with the delegates of the Pacific Synod during this Convention with reference to Item 1. According to a ruling of the President Item 2, being the resolution concerning the Pacific Theological· Seminary, was declared by the President to be outside of the authority of the Executive Board and that it should be dealt with by the Committee of Reference and Counsel.

The item concerning Special Days and Seasons (IV, A, 1) was adopted.

The item concerning presentation of causes to Synods (IV, A, 2) was adopted.

The item concerning regional representation on Boards (IV, A, 3) was adopted.

The item concerning cross appropriations (IV, A, 4) was adopted.

Item IV, B, 2 (b), recommendation concerning dissolution of home mission agencies adopted.

The ruling concerning construction of Section V, B, Item 4 of the By-Laws (IV, B, 3) was approved.

Action on the item concerning special provision for raising the deficit of the Foreign Mission Board (IV, B, 4 (a)) was postponed until the report of the Board of Foreign Missions comes before the Convention.

Items concerning Presidents of Synods as Missionary Superintendents (IV, B, 5, (d) and (e)) were adopted.

The item concerning appeal for the hurricane stricken area (IV, B, 5 (f)) was adopted.

The Agreement with the National Lutheran Home for the Aged at Washington, D. C., (IV, B, 15) was next taken up. Item 5 of the Agreement was amended to read "This entire action is to be reviewed within the period of ten years." The agreement as thus amended was adopted.

Moved and carried, That the heartiest congratulations of the Convention be conveyed to Mr. J. W. Kahler of the Synod of Ohio on this his eightieth birthday.

The Convention adjourned with prayer by the Rev. O. D. Baltzly.

———————•———————

Evening Service

Celebration of the Tenth Anniversary of The United Lutheran Church in America.

The Tenth Anniversary of The United Lutheran Church in America was celebrated by service in the Church, according to the program at eight o'clock P. M.

———————•———————

SECOND MEETING

Morning Session

SUNDAY SCHOOL CHAPEL, LUTHER MEMORIAL CHURCH,
Erie, Pennsylvania,
Thursday, October 11, 1928, 8 :45.

Matins were conducted by the Rev. J. A. Weyl.

The Convention was called to order by the President.

The minutes of Wednesday morning and afternoon sessions were read and approved.

Mr. Wm. H. Menges, Chairman of Committee of Tellers No. 1, reported on the elections held Wednesday afternoon.

For members of the *Executive Board* each of the following received a majority of the votes cast:

Rev. A. C. R. Keiter   Hon. Wm. E. Hirt
Rev. Charles D. Trexler   Hon. John F. Kramer
Rev. A. R. Wentz   Mr. George E. Neff

The President declared them elected.

For the *Commission of Adjudication* each of the following received a majority of votes cast:

Rev. George Gebert   Rev. A. G. Voigt
Hon. E. K. Strong

The President declared them elected.

For the *Committee on Church Papers* each of the following received a majority of the votes cast:

Rev. W. H. Greever   Rev. J. A. Leas
Hon. E. K. Strong

The President declared them elected.

For the *Executive Committee of the Laymen's Movement* each of the following received a majority of the votes cast:

Mr. J. L. Clark   Mr. E. Clarence Miller
Mr. C. J. Driever   Mr. Harvey C. Miller
Mr. W. L. Glatfelter   Mr. P. A. Myers
Mr. Peter P. Hagan   Mr. W. J. Showalter
Mr. E. J. Young

The President declared them elected. One member yet to be elected.

It was moved and carried, That in the election to fill this one vacancy in the Executive Committee of the Laymen's Movement, the names of the two who received the next highest number of votes to those elected be placed upon a special ballot to be cast at Friday's election.

The Secretary moved on behalf of the Executive Board that Section V, A, of the By-Laws be amended as follows:

"Strike out Item 5, which reads, 'A Home Mission and Church Extension Board;' also strike out Item 9, which reads, 'A Committee on Jewish Missions.'"

The motion having been duly seconded, was put and carried.

The Rev. S. W. Herman moved to amend the By-Laws, Section V, B, Item 4, by insertion of the words "unless he is an officer of the Board," so that the item shall read as follows:

"No member of any Board shall be eligible for election for more than two successive terms, unless he is an officer of the Board; and no person shall be a member of more than two Boards at one and the same time."

The motion was duly seconded, put and lost.

The item concerning presence of Chairmen of Committees at Conventions (IV, C, 1) was next considered and the recommendation was adopted.

The action of the Executive Board in reference to the Luther League was approved (IV, C, 6 (c)).

The recommendation of the Executive Board concerning Co-ordinations (V) was adopted.

The Budget recommended by the Executive Board (VII, 5) was adopted.

Moved and carried, That a Committee of Fifteen be appointed which, in connection with the Finance Committee, shall devise plans by which the desired result may be attained.

The provision of the Executive Board with reference to the disposition of the offerings taken at this Convention (VII, 11) was approved.

Under the item concerning the Lutheran Church House (VIII, 1) the following resolution was adopted:

"The United Lutheran Church, in its Sixth Biennial Convention assembled, has heard with gratitude and pleasure, that its Board of Publication has made possible the financing of the Lutheran Church House in New York City by advancing the sum of $151,573.37 up to this time, and agreeing to advance an additional sum of $50,000 to liquidate the existing mortgage when that becomes due;
"Therefore, be it resolved, that the appreciation of The United Lutheran Church be and is hereby tendered to this Board for its generous and timely help in this regard."

The regulations of the National Lutheran Council (X, 3, (1)) were approved.

The nominations for membership in the Larger Committee of the Lutheran World Convention (XI, 4) were approved.

Recommendations 1, 2 and 3 concerning continuance of participation in the World Conference on Faith and Order (XIII, (4)) were adopted; likewise statements concerning the inadequacy of the reports, recommendations concerning their further study by the Commission, and the judgments of the Commission with reference to the future, were adopted.

The recommendations concerning celebrations in 1929 and 1930 (XIV, 4) were adopted.

The recommendation of the Executive Board concerning the

places for the holding of the Conventions in 1930 and 1932 was read and a substitute was moved that the convention be held in Milwaukee in 1930. During the discussion of this substitute, invitations were extended from Jacksonville, Florida, and Denver, Colorado. The substitute motion was put and carried.

Upon motion of the Rev. C. P. Swank, the selection of Milwaukee as the place of the convention in 1930 was made unanimous.

The Convention adjourned with prayer by the Rev. P. D. Brown.

—————•—————

Afternoon Session

Thursday, October 11, 2:00 o'clock.

Devotions were conducted by the Rev. J. J. Scherer, Jr., and the President called the Convention to order.

The Rev. H. Offermann, Chairman of the Committee of Reference and Counsel, offered the following resolution:

Resolved, That this Convention expresses its heartiest congratulations to
Rev. H. E. Jacobs on the 60th anniversary of his ordination.
Rev. G. U. Wenner on his 60th anniversary as pastor of Christ Church, New York.
Rev. J. J. Heischmann on his 50th anniversary as pastor of St. Peter's Church, Brooklyn, N. Y.
Rev. W. H. Myers, Reading, Pa., on the 50th anniversary of his ordination.
Rev. J. W. Kapp, Cincinnati, Ohio, on the 50th anniversary of his ordination.
Rev. J. C. Kunzmann, Seattle, Wash., on the 50th anniversary of his ordination.
Rev. H. K. Fenner, Louisville, Ky., who served 56 years in the ministry, 51 of them in one church.

The resolution was unanimously adopted, and the Committee of Reference and Counsel was requested to convey these greetings.

The Rev. A. R. Wentz presented the following reformulation of the report of the Committee on Uniformity in Licensure and Ordination, in accordance with the previous action of the Convention:

"Whereas, the Lutheran doctrine of the ministry, based upon the Word of God and confirmed by the practice of the early Church, holds that the ministry is an office and not and order (Augsburg Confession, Article V), and requires that the minister be 'regularly called' (Augsburg Confession, Article XIV),

"Therefore, be it resolved, that The United Lutheran Church in America recommends to its constituent synods the practice of ordaining men to the ministry only after they have been regularly called to the work of the ministry."

The report of the Committee on Common Service Book, scheduled for Saturday, was by common consent presented at this point by the Rev. Luther D. Reed.

REPORT OF THE COMMON SERVICE BOOK COMMITTEE

Five meetings of the committee, continuing over eight days, were held during the biennium. At the first meeting Dr. Reed was elected chairman, and Dr. Getty, secretary.

The committee lost one of its oldest members in point of service, in the death of the Rev. Ezra Keller Bell, D.D., LL.D., September 13, 1927. Dr. Bell represented the General Synod on the Joint Committee from 1913 to 1918, and actively participated in the deliberations which resulted in the preparation and adoption of the Common Service Book. His membership on the Common Service Book Committee of the United Lutheran Church was continuous from 1918 until his death. His associates on the committee bear testimony to the high esteem in which his character and work were ever held. By appointment of President Knubel, the Rev. Prof. H. D. Hoover, Ph.D., D.D., S.T.D., succeeded Dr. Bell as a member of the committee.

The committee reports completion of the Family Service Book and of the Children's Service Book and Hymnal; completed arrangements with the Publication Board for the issuing of an Altar edition of the Common Service Book; preparation of a new music edition of the Common Service Book; continued work on a new joint translation of the Small Catechism; and the beginning of work on additional English Occasional Services and on a German edition of the Common Service Book.

Family Service Book

The committee believes that the Church will welcome the appearance of the Family Service Book, which, after years of careful labor, has just appeared from the press. The preparation of this book was originally entrusted to a Sub-Committee consisting of the Revs. Paul Z. Strodach ,D.D., Albert T. W. Steinhaeuser, D.D., and Ezra K. Bell, D.D., LL.D. Dr.

Steinhaeuser contributed a great deal to the general plan and some of the detail, but he and Dr. Bell were called to the Church Triumphant before the work could be completed. The general features of the Book and a large amount of typical material were considered and approved by the full committee several years ago and reported to the Buffalo Convention in 1922. Dr. Strodach, by earnest personal effort which the Church cannot fail to appreciate, and with the cordial cooperation of the Publication House, carried the work of the Sub-Committee to completion. After consultation with advisory members of the General Committee, the Book was given to the press. It is now offered to the Church in the assurance that it will meet a real need.

It contains an exceedingly rich body of devotional material, much of which is original. The arrangement of Services is interesting and provides a new approach to the subject. There is a brief but complete form of service for each morning and evening in the week. These brief services are responsive in character, so that the active participation of each member of the household may be secured, though this is not essential to the use of the book. The opening versicles are followed by a brief Lesson, and this in turn by a prayer. The lessons are grouped in a Lectionary which has been developed on the basis of the Church Year under topical heads for each week. The intercessions and prayers are also grouped under a weekly arrangement, with Sunday having as its general theme the Lord's Day, the Church, the Parish, etc.; Monday: Home and Inner Missions, those ministering to others, etc.; Tuesday: Foreign Missions, missionary interests, etc.; Wednesday: the children of the household, relatives, friends, neighbors, etc.; Thursday: the Nation, Christian education, those who teach, and all at school; Friday: the Ministry, Christian workers, and all who toil; Saturday: Pastors and Church Officers, preparation for the Lord's Day, etc. There is also a large collection of general prayers for all occasions and subjects. The Book, which the Committee believes to be of unusually comprehensive scope, and superior quality, will lead our families in their daily devotions through the full range of Christian experience in harmony with the life of the Church as it unfolds in the Christian Year. It is hoped that Synods and Conferences will urge all our pastors and people to study and use the Family Service Book in their homes.

THE CHILDREN'S HYMNAL AND SERVICE BOOK

A Sub-Committee, consisting of the Rev. Drs. Ohl, Stirewalt and W. E. Fischer, cooperated with a Sub-Committee of the Parish and Church School Board in the preparation of the Children's Service Book and Hymnal. The Rev. Dr. Strodach, representing the Publication House, also collaborated in the work. This book is now in press, and the Committee believes that its early appearance will supply the Church with a very satisfactory Service Book and Hymnal for the first three grades, that is, children from three to eleven years of age. The book contains a general service and eleven special services for Church Festivals and other occasions; a Children's Psalter; a specially prepared Children's Lectionary, with brief passages, chiefly from the Gospels; and a group of Prayers. The Hymnal contains about 260 hymns, many being entirely new to our collections. A great deal of original work is contained in the book, in new hymns, translations, and tunes specially written for it. The Committee believes that it will not only well meet the needs of this particular period in the educational program of the Church, but that it will prepare the way for the use in later years of the Parish School Hymnal and the Common Service Book.

ALTAR EDITION OF THE COMMON SERVICE BOOK

The Committee has arranged with the representatives of the Publication House for the early appearance of an Altar Edition of the Common Service Book. This will contain all the portions of the Common Service Book required for use by the minister at the Altar, viz., The Service; Matins and Vespers; Introits, Collects, Epistles and Gospels; Collects and Prayers; General Prayers, and the Psalter. The pages of the text edition of the Common Service Book will be reproduced exactly, page by page, in large type, the new type page being 8½ by 5¼ inches in size. The book will contain approximately 340 pages. It will be handsomely bound and will be a worthy addition to the altar appointments of the Church.

ADDITIONAL OCCASIONAL SERVICES

In response to numerous requests for the preparation of forms of Service for various occasions not now provided for in the Common Service Book, the Committee has appointed a Sub-Committee, consisting of the Rev. Drs. Strodach, Scherer and Hoover, to report on the preparation of forms for dedication of cemeteries, organs, bells, altars, etc., a form for the reception of members, and other minor offices.

It is recommended that the Common Service Book Committee be authorized to prepare forms for various dedications, commissionings, and such other minor services and occasions as the Committee shall deem proper and necessary. These forms when adopted by the Committee to be published by the Board of Publication.

GERMAN EDITION OF THE COMMON SERVICE BOOK

A Sub-Committee, consisting of the Rev. Drs. Steimle, E. E. Fischer, Strodach, and R. Morris Smith, is working with a Sub-Committee of the Committee on German Interests in the effort to prepare a German Edition of the Common Service Book. This work has grown out of a request of the Committee on German Interests, which is desirous of providing liturgical forms, and ultimately a hymnal also, which may be used by all the German congregations of the United Lutheran Church. In the work now in hand, viz., the Order for Baptism and similar orders, it has been agreed that "the Occasional Services as found in the Common Service Book, shall be regarded as the standard," necessary flexibility, of course, being recognized within this general rule. It is hoped that, if this work can be carried to completion, it will provide the German congregations of the United Lutheran Church with a liturgy and hymnal which will unify their practice, supplant the great variety of forms and hymnals now in use, and thus bring the devotional life of these congregations into harmony with the English-speaking part of the Church.

New Music Edition of the Common Service Book

The year 1928 marks the tenth anniversary of the completion of the Common Service Book and Hymnal and its adoption by the United Lutheran Church. The past decade has witnessed a gradual but general introduction of the book by most of our congregations in all parts of the Church. It is now in use from coast to coast, from the Lakes to the Gulf, in Canada, Porto Rico, and, in a more limited way, in our missions in India and Japan. Translations of at least portions of it already exist or are being prepared in German, Italian, Spanish, Telugu and Japanese. Altogether, more than 400,000 copies have been sold, and its influence in molding and unifying the devotional life of our congregations and institutions has been incalculable.

The Church has tested the Common Service Book thoroughly as to its effectiveness, in meeting the actual needs of the Church in general, and with respect to details of content, arrangement, and musical settings. It is gratifying to know that, while minor criticisms have naturally enough been made, scarcely any major criticisms have been offered. We cannot but conclude that the book as a whole is well fulfilling its important purpose.

Definite suggestions for improvement all center in the music edition, no dissatisfaction being expressed with the text of the liturgy, and little with the text of the Hymnal. With respect to the music edition, the facts seem to be that the Church has shown an overwhelming preference for the first setting of the liturgy, the second being but rarely used; that there is a very general desire for the insertion of at least the first stanza of hymns between the staves; that quite a few of the rich collection of hymn tunes provided in the Book are not generally sung; and that it would be a gain if the arrangement of the Burial Service could be simplified and if more of the Occasional Services could be included in the music edition.

In addition to these facts, drawn from the experience of congregations using the Book, it is also true that quite a large number of congregations have not yet introduced it, and by their continued use of one or the other of the books issued by the several General Bodies before the Merger, are delaying the development of a common Church life and consciousness among us. It is clear that the eventual adoption of the Common Service Book by many will be facilitated by a simplification of the musical material and by the insertion of the first stanza of hymns between the staves in conformity with the arrangement of books now used by these congregations.

In view of these facts a Sub-Committee, consisting of the Rev. Drs. Strodach, Reed, Getty, Ohl, and Scherer, with Dr. Henry Jacobs as consultant, gave earnest consideration to the details of a new music edition. The General Committee, after consultation with President Knubel and Mr. Hultberg, reviewed the project in detail and now presents the recommendations which follow, in the belief that the publication of a new musical edition will meet the desires expressed by many, and will facilitate the further introduction and use of the Book without the loss of essential features or material lowering of standards.

The Committee therefore recommends the adoption of the following resolution:

Resolved, that the United Lutheran Church authorize the preparation and publication of a new music edition of the Common Service Book, the same to contain no changes in the present text of the Liturgy or the Hymnal, but to contain certain changes in arrangement and musical settings.

Because of the importance of the matter as affecting the official Book of the Church, the details of proposed changes are reported fully for information.

With respect to contents and arrangement:

1. That the Second Setting be omitted and provision made to publish it in pamphlet form
2. That the following simplified arrangement of the Order for Burial be followed:
   Print the Order continuously
   Use Psalms 130 and 23.
   Use the first Responsory.
   Use the Nunc Dimittis, one setting only.
   Other Psalms, Responsories and Canticles with their settings, to be grouped in proper order immediately following the Order; reference to be made to those in rubrics at proper places.
3. That the Table for Morning and Evening Lessons, Page 304ff., be omitted.
4. That all Orders be included, excepting:
   Confirmation of Lay Baptism.
   Private Confession.
   Communion of the Sick.
   Lessons and Prayers for the Sick.
   Commendation of the Dying.
5. That the form of the page now used in the edition known as No. 590, be maintained in the regular edition of the Common Service Book (with changes provided in this report) and that another edition be published in which the first stanza of each hymn shall be printed between the staves. (See minutes, fourth meeting, afternoon session, and fifth meeting, morning session.—Secretary.)
6. That the Appendix be omitted.

With respect to hymn tunes:

1. Recommendations growing out of the omission of the Appendix.
   34. Substitute Antioch (34 Ap.) for Nativity.
   82. Spanish Hymn (82 Ap.) for Aberystwyth.
   135. Drop Azmon from the book.
   217. Dort (217 Ap.) for Italian hymn—latter used elsewhere.
   256. Armstrong (256 Ap.) for Falfield, used elsewhere.
   257. Drop Spohr.
   272. Add Laban (272 Ap.) as second tune.
   277. Drop Solitude.
   337. Add Woodworth (337 Ap.) as second tune.
   339. Drop Clymer.
   355. Substitute St. Catherine (355 Ap.) as second tune for Compline
   371. Add Martyn as third tune.
   376. Drop Boylston.
   380. Add Christmas (380 Ap.) as second tune.
   411. Drop Holborn.
   431. Use Sicilian Mariner's Hymn (431 Ap.) as second tune.
   465. Drop Holley.
   479. Use Miriam (479 Ap.) as second tune.
   578. To remain as 578, omit star and rubric at bottom.

Altogether nineteen numbers affected (one really remaining untouched, 578*). Of these tunes in the Appendix, eleven are used, four to displace tunes now in the body of the book; seven are used as second tunes. Seven appendix tunes are dropped from the book.

2. In connection with hymns having two or more tunes.
   39. Drop Star of the East.
   42. Drop Crüger.
   86. Drop Gloria.
   93. Drop Gethsemane.
   136. Drop Faith.
   179. Drop Newington.
   190. Drop Sursum Corda.
   192. Drop Bread of Heaven.
   275. Drop Downs.
   294. Drop Hanover.
   324. Drop Regnator orbis.
   334. Drop Wer Gott vertraut; add Bishopgarth (483) but print as first tune.
   381. Use "Faith" as first tune. Resolven as second tune.
   393. Substitute Quam Dilecta (573) for Ibstone.
   408. Substitute Hanford (259) for Leith.
   520. Drop Morington.
   564. Drop Edina.
   565. Drop St. Raphael.

Altogether seventeen numbers affected. Sixteen of these tunes are dropped (one being substituted for another tune elsewhere); one tune is added at 334; two are substituted for present tunes; in the one case, a second tune is added.

3. Further recommendations.
   55. Substitute Saxby (137) for Leigh.
   59. Substitute Grace Church (185) for Constance.
   63. Substitute Rivaulx (165) for Commandments.
   64. Substitute Breslau (97) for Ludborough.
   79. Substitute Angelus (233) for Cannons.

123. Substitute Diademata (Barnby, 134, 2d tune) for Olivet.
176. Substitute O du Liebe (92) for Everton.
206. Substitute Laus Regis (126) for Derwent.
306. Substitute Durham (243) for Peterborough.
316. Substitute Rivaulx (165) for Commandments.
364. Substitute St. Matthias (175) for Compline.
373. Substitute St. Chrysostom (351) for St. Justin.
388. Substitute Gorton (473) for Aberystwyth.
395. Add Weber (465) in Book of Worship.
405. Substitute Angelus (233) for Cannons.
462. Substitute Thanksgiving (366) for Ludborough.
487. Substitute Monkland (311) for St. Basil.
569. Substitute Litany (84) for Eighth Gregorian Tone.

Altogether eighteen numbers affected. In all but one case more useful and singable tunes are substituted for present tunes; in the one case, a second tune is added.

A total of fifty-four numbers will be affected by all the changes proposed.

TRANSLATION OF LUTHER'S CATECHISM

In February, 1926, President Knubel submitted, with his approval, an invitation from the Board of Elementary Education of the Norwegian Lutheran Church to unite with representatives of other Lutheran Bodies in North America in the preparation of a translation of Luther's Small Catechism. This project was in part due to a desire on the part of its sponsors to fittingly celebrate the Quadri-Centennial of the Catechism in 1929 by publishing a "Jubilee Edition" with the endorsement of a number, if not all, of the Lutheran Bodies in this country. Behind this desire there was a more weighty reason. The several synodical bodies all have their editions of the Catechism, but between these various English versions there are wide differences, both as to form and content. It has been felt by many that if a new translation could be made by representatives of several of the general bodies, preserving the exact meaning of Luther, but rendering his work into idiomatic English, it would do much to unify the spirit and practice of American Lutherans. The advantages of a Standard English text, thoroughly representative of our Church as to form and used in catechetical instruction by all the Lutheran groups in America, are obvious.

The Common Service Book Committee after full consideration accepted the invitation to co-operate in this undertaking, asking that the historic American translation, as given in Dr. Henry E. Jacob's Book of Concord, and many other places, be given a guiding influence in the development of any new translation.

The General Bodies taking part in this undertaking and their representatives on the Joint Committee were:

Norwegian Lutheran Church—Rev. J. N. Anderson, Rev. C. A. Melby, Ph.D.
Joint Synod of Ohio—Rev. Emmanuel Poppen, Rev. J. Sheatsley, D.D.
Augustana Synod—Rev. G. A. Fahlund, D.D., Rev. S. J. Sibelius, D.D.

Danish United Church—Rev. K. M. Mathiesen.
Synod of Iowa—Rev. M. Reu, D.D., Rev. J. Bodensiek.
Lutheran Free Church—Rev. George Sverdrop.
United Lutheran Church—Rev. John C. Mattes, D.D., Rev. G. A. Getty,
D.D.
Several other synods were invited to participate, and while they have
not been represented on the Joint Committee, they have followed the work
with interest, and it is hoped that they will adopt the text as it is finally
approved by the Joint Committee.

Eight meetings of the Joint Committee have been held, covering eleven
days of conference and discussion, besides which there has been considerable
work done by sub-committees. Doctor Reu was requested to submit to
the committee the original texts of the Catechism as they came from
Luther's hands in 1529 and 1531. His texts, with critical notes thereon,
have since been published and constitute a valuable contribution to the
literature on this subject. Upon the basis provided in this document, the
Joint Committee began its work of rendering the original German text
into English. All other available English versions, beginning with Cran-
mer's of 1548, were freely consulted and the so-called "Schaeffer text"
received special consideration. A provisional edition of the new translation was published in December, 1927. Criticisms were invited and at the
last meeting of the Joint Committee, May 22, 1928, these were considered
and acted upon, among them a considerable number submitted by the Common Service Book Committee.

The translation of the Joint Committee is complete, and includes the
Preface, Morning and Evening Prayer, Table of Duties, etc. We append
to this report the text of the Five Parts and recommend the adoption of
the following resolution:

(1) Resolved, That the United Lutheran Church rejoices with all other
Lutheran Bodies in the possession of Luther's Small Catechism, and in the
influence for good which this work has exerted throughout the world; that
we commend the effort of the Lutheran Synods of North America in undertaking jointly to signalize the 400th anniversary of the Catechism by preparing a new and uniform translation, true to the original text and expressed
in idiomatic English; and that we assure these co-operating Synods of our
own deep interest in this undertaking and of our gratification in having a
part in it.

(2) Resolved, That the Common Service Book Committee be instructed
to continue its study of the text of this new translation of Luther's Catechism and to co-operate with the other Lutheran Bodies to the fullest
extent in the effort to make it as nearly perfect and as generally satisfactory
as possible.

(3) Resolved, That when the final text is adopted by the Joint Committee
and approved by the Common Service Book Committee, it shall be published as the Jubilee edition of Luther's Small Catechism; but this resolution
shall not deprive the Common Service Book Committee of the right to

make such subsequent alterations in the text as that committee may deem imperatively necessary.

Respectfully submitted,

LUTHER D. REED, *Chairman.*

G. ALBERT GETTY, *Secretary.*

LUTHER'S SMALL CATECHISM

Uniform Text, Newly Revised and Edited by an Intersynodical Committee.
A Jubilee Offering for the Four Hundredth Anniversary of the Original Publication of the Small Catechism.
1529-1929.

PART I.
THE TEN COMMANDMENTS.

In the plain form in which the head of the family shall teach them to his household.

THE INTRODUCTION.

I am the Lord thy God.

THE FIRST COMMANDMENT.

Thou shalt have no other gods before Me.
What is meant by this Commandment?
Answer. We should fear, love, and trust in God above all things.

THE SECOND COMMANDMENT.

Thou shalt not take the Name of the Lord thy God in vain.
What is meant by this Commandment?
Answer. We should fear and love God so that we do not curse, swear, conjure, lie, or deceive, by His name, but call upon Him in every time of need, and worship Him with prayer, praise, and thanksgiving.

THE THIRD COMMANDMENT.

Remember the Sabbath day, to keep it holy.
What is meant by this Commandment?
Answer. We should fear and love God so that we do not despise His Word and the preaching of the Gospel, but deem it holy, and gladly hear and learn it.

THE FOURTH COMMANDMENT.

Honor thy father and thy mother.
What is meant by this Commandment?
Answer. We should fear and love God so that we do not despise our parents and superiors, nor provoke them to anger, but honor, serve, obey, love, and esteem them.

THE FIFTH COMMANDMENT.

Thou shalt not kill.

What is meant by this Commandment?

Answer. We should fear and love God so that we cause our neighbor no bodily harm or suffering, but help and befriend him in every bodily need.

THE SIXTH COMMANDMENT.

Thou shalt not commit adultery.

What is meant by this Commandment?

Answer. We should fear and love God so that we are chaste and pure in word and deed, and that husband and wife love and honor each other.

THE SEVENTH COMMANDMENT.

Thou shalt not steal.

What is meant by this Commandment?

Answer. We should fear and love God so that we do not take from our neighbor his money or property, nor get them by unfair dealing or fraud, but help him to improve and protect his property and living.

THE EIGHTH COMMANDMENT.

Thou shalt not bear false witness against thy neighbor.

What is meant by this Commandment?

Answer. We should fear and love God so that we do not deceitfully belie, betray, backbite, nor slander our neighbor, but excuse him, speak well of him, and put the most charitable construction on all his actions.

THE NINTH COMMANDMENT.

Thou shalt not covet thy neighbor's house.

What is meant by this Commandment?

Answer. We should fear and love God so that we do not seek deceitfully to gain possession of our neighbor's inheritance or home, nor obtain them under pretense of a legal right, but assist and serve him in keeping all that is his.

THE TENTH COMMANDMENT.

Thou shalt not covet thy neighbor's wife, nor his manservant, nor his maidservant, * nor his ox, nor his ass, nor anything that is thy neighbor's.

What is meant by this Commandment?

Answer. We should fear and love God so that we do not estrange or entice, away our neighbor's wife, servants, or cattle, but use our endeavors that they may remain and discharge their duty to him.

What does God declare concerning all these Commandments?

---

* Translation of Luther's text for these two phrases is "cattle."

Answer. He says: I the Lord thy God am a jealous God, visiting the iniquity of the fathers upon the children unto the third and fourth generation of them that hate Me; and showing mercy unto thousands of them that love Me, and keep My commandments.

What is meant by this declaration?
Answer. God threatens to punish all who transgress these commandments. We should, therefore, fear His wrath, and in no wise disobey His commandments. But He promises grace and every blessing to all who keep these commandments. We should, therefore, love Him, trust in Him, and gladly keep His commandments.

PART II.
THE CREED.
In the plain form in which the head of the family shall teach it to his household.

THE FIRST ARTICLE.
Of Creation.

I believe in God the Father Almighty, Maker of heaven and earth.

What is meant by this Article?
Answer. I believe that God has created me and all that exists; that He has given and still preserves to me my body and soul, my eyes and ears, and all my other members, my reason and all the powers of my soul, together with food and raiment, home and family, and all my property; that He daily provides abundantly for all the needs of my life, protects me from all danger, guards and keeps me from all evil; and that He does all this out of fatherly and divine goodness and mercy alone, without any merit or worthiness in me; for all which I am in duty bound to thank, praise, serve and obey Him. This is most certainly true.

THE SECOND ARTICLE.
Of Redemption.

And in Jesus Christ His only Son, our Lord; Who was conceived by the Holy Ghost, Born of the Virgin Mary; Suffered under Pontius Pilate, Was crucified, dead, and buried; He descended into hell; The third day He rose again from the dead; He ascended into heaven, And sitteth on the right hand of God the Father Almighty; From thence He shall come to judge the quick and the dead.

What is meant by this Article?
Answer. I believe that Jesus Christ, true God, begotten of the Father from eternity, and also true Man, born of the Virgin Mary, is my Lord; Who has redeemed me, a lost and condemned creature, bought me and

freed me from all sins, from death, and from the power of the devil; not with silver and gold, but with His holy and precious blood, and with His innocent sufferings and death; in order that I might be His own, live under Him in His kingdom, and serve Him in everlasting righteousness, innocence and blessedness; even as He is risen from the dead, and lives and reigns to all eternity. This is most certainly true.

THE THIRD ARTICLE.
Of Sanctification.

I believe in the Holy Ghost; The holy Christian Church, the Communion of Saints; The Forgiveness of sins; The Resurrection of the body; And the Life everlasting. Amen.

What is meant by this Article?

Answer. I believe that I cannot by my own reason or strength believe in Jesus Christ my Lord, or come to Him; but the Holy Ghost has called me through the Gospel, enlightened me with His gifts, and sanctified and preserved me in the true faith; in like manner as He calls, gathers, enlightens, and sanctifies the whole Christian Church on earth, and preserves it in union with Jesus Christ in the one true faith; in which Christian Church He daily forgives abundantly all my sins and the sins of all believers, and at the last day will raise up me and all the dead, and will grant everlasting life to me and to all who believe in Christ. This is most certainly true.

PART III.
THE LORD'S PRAYER.

In the plain form in which the head of the family shall teach it to his household.

THE INTRODUCTION.
Our Father, Who art in heaven.

What is meant by this Introduction?

Answer. God thereby tenderly encourages us to believe that He is truly our Father, and that we are His children indeed, so that we may pray to Him without fear and in perfect trust, just as dear children come to their loving father.

THE FIRST PETITION.
Hallowed be Thy Name.

What is meant by this Petition?

Answer. God's Name is indeed holy in itself; but we pray in this petition that it may be hallowed among us also.

How is this done?

Answer. When the Word of God is taught in its truth and purity, and we, as God's children, lead holy lives, in accordance with it. This grant us, dear Father in heaven! But whoever teaches and lives otherwise than as God's Word teaches, profanes the Name of God among us; from this preserve us, Heavenly Father!

THE SECOND PETITION.

Thy kingdom come.

What is meant by this Petition?

Answer. The kingdom of God comes indeed of itself, without our prayer; but we pray in this petition that it may come to us also.

How is this done?

Answer. When our heavenly Father gives us His Holy Spirit, so that by His grace we believe His holy Word, and live godly lives here on earth, and in heaven for ever.

THE THIRD PETITION.

Thy will be done on earth, as it is in heaven.

What is meant by this Petition?

Answer. The good and gracious will of God is done indeed without our prayer; but we pray in this petition that it may be done among us also.

How is this done?

Answer. When God destroys and brings to naught every evil counsel and purpose of the devil, the world, and our own flesh, which would hinder us from hallowing His Name, and prevent the coming of His kingdom; and when He strengthens us and keeps us steadfast in His Word and in faith, even unto our end. This is His good and gracious will.

THE FOURTH PETITION.

Give us this day our daily bread.

What is meant by this Petition?

Answer. God indeed gives daily bread to all men, even to the wicked, without our prayer; but we pray in this petition that He would lead us to acknowledge our daily bread as His gift, and to receive it with thanksgiving.

What is meant by daily bread?

Answer. All that is required to satisfy our bodily needs; such as food and raiment, house and home, fields and flocks, money and goods; pious parents, children and servants; godly and faithful rulers, good government;

seasonable weather, peace and health; order and honor; true friends, good neighbors, and the like.

THE FIFTH PETITION.

And forgive us our trespasses, as we forgive those who trespass against us.

What is meant by this Petition?

Answer. We pray in this petition that our heavenly Father would not regard our sins nor deny our prayers on their account; because we neither merit, nor deserve those things for which we ask; but that He would grant us all things through His grace, even though we sin daily, and surely deserve nothing but punishment. And we will certainly, on our part, heartily forgive and gladly do good to those who may sin against us.

THE SIXTH PETITION.

And lead us not into temptation.

What is meant by this Petition?

Answer. God indeed tempts no one to sin; but we pray in this petition that God would so guard and preserve us, that the devil, the world, and our own flesh, may not deceive us, nor lead us into error and unbelief, despair, and other great and shameful sins; but that, when so tempted, we may finally prevail and gain the victory.

THE SEVENTH PETITION.

But deliver us from evil.

What is meant by this Petition?

Answer. We pray in this petition, as in a summary, that our heavenly Father would deliver us from all manner of evil, whether it affect the body or soul, property or reputation, and at last, when the hour of death shall come, grant us a blessed end, and graciously take us from this world of sorrow to Himself in heaven.

THE CONCLUSION.

For Thine is the kingdom, and the power, and the glory, for ever and ever. Amen.

What is meant by the word "Amen"?

Answer. It means that I should be assured that such petitions are acceptable to our heavenly Father, and are heard by Him; for He Himself has commanded us to pray in this manner, and has promised to hear us. Amen, Amen, that is, Yea, yea, it shall be so.

PART IV.
THE SACRAMENT OF HOLY BAPTISM.

In the plain form in which the head of the family shall teach it to his household.

I. *What is Baptism?*

Answer. Baptism is not simply water, but it is the water used according to God's command and joined to God's Word.

What is this Word of God?

Answer. It is that which our Lord Jesus Christ spoke, as it is recorded in the last chapter of Matthew:* "Go ye therefore, and teach all nations, baptizing them in the Name of the Father, and of the Son, and of the Holy Ghost."

II. *What gifts or benefits does Baptism bestow?*

Answer. It works forgiveness of sins, delivers from death and the devil, and gives everlasting salvation to all who believe, as the Word and promise of God declare.

What is this word and promise of God?

Answer. It is that which our Lord Jesus Christ spoke, as it is recorded in the last chapter of Mark: "He that believeth and is baptized shall be saved; but he that believeth not shall be damned."

III. *How can water do such great things?*

Answer. It is not the water, indeed, that does such great things, but the Word of God, joined to the water, and our faith, which relies on that Word of God. For without the Word of God, it is simply water and no baptism. But when joined to the Word of God, it is a baptism, that is, a gracious water of life and a washing of regeneration in the Holy Ghost, as St. Paul says to Titus, in the third chapter: "According to His mercy He saved us, by the washing of regeneration, and renewing of the Holy Ghost; which He shed on us abundantly through Jesus Christ our Saviour; that being justified by His grace, we should be made heirs according to the hope of eternal life. This is a faithful saying."

IV. *What does such baptizing with water signify?*

Answer. It signifies that the old Adam in us together with all sins and evil lusts should be drowned by daily sorrow and repentance, and be put to death; and that the new man should daily come forth and rise, to live before God in righteousness and holiness for ever.

---

* *American Revised Version*: "Go ye therefore, and make disciples of all the nations, baptizing them into the Name of the Father, and of the Son, and of the Holy Spirit."

Where is it so written?

Answer. St. Paul, in the sixth chapter of the Epistle to the Romans, says: "We are buried with Christ by baptism into death, that like as He was raised up from the dead by the glory of the Father, even so we also should walk in newness of life."

OF CONFESSION.

What is Confession?

Answer. Confession consists of two parts: the one is, that we confess our sins; the other, that we receive absolution or forgiveness from the pastor as from God Himself, in no wise doubting, but firmly believing, that our sins are thereby forgiven before God in heaven.

What sins ought we to confess?

Answer. Before God we ought to acknowledge ourselves guilty of all manner of sins, even of those of which we are not aware, as we do in the Lord's Prayer. But before the pastor we should confess only those sins which we know and feel in our hearts.

What are such sins?

Answer. Here examine yourself in the light of the Ten Commandments, whether as father or mother, son or daughter, master or servant, you have been disobedient, unfaithful, slothful, ill-tempered, dissolute, or quarrelsome, or whether you have injured any one by word or deed, stolen, neglected or wasted aught, or done any other evil.

PART V.
THE SACRAMENT OF THE ALTAR.

In the plain form in which the head of the family shall teach it to his household.

I. *What is the Sacrament of the Altar?*

Answer. It is the true Body and Blood of our Lord Jesus Christ, under the bread and wine, given unto us Christians to eat and to drink, as it was instituted by Christ Himself.

Where is it so written?

Answer. The holy Evangelists, Matthew, Mark, and Luke, together with St. Paul, write thus:

"Our Lord Jesus Christ, in the night in which He was betrayed, took bread; and when He had given thanks, He brake it and gave it to His disciples, saying, Take, eat; this is My Body, which is given for you; this do in remembrance of Me."

"After the same manner also He took the cup, when He had supped, and when He had given thanks, He gave it to them, saying, Drink ye all of it; this cup is the New Testament in My Blood, which is shed for you, and for many, for the remission of sins; this do, as oft as ye drink it, in remembrance of Me."

II. *What is the benefit of such eating and drinking?*
Answer. It is pointed out in these words: "Given and shed for you for the remission of sins." Through these words the remission of sins, life and salvation are given unto us in the Sacrament; for where there is remission of sins, there is also life and salvation.

III. *How can the bodily eating and drinking produce such great benefits?*
Answer. The eating and drinking, indeed, do not produce them, but the words: "Given and shed for you for the remission of sins." For beside the bodily eating and drinking, these words are the chief thing in the Sacrament; and he who believes them, has what they say and declare, namely, the remission of sins.

IV. *Who, then, receives the Sacrament worthily?*
Answer. Fasting and bodily preparation are indeed a good outward discipline, but he is truly worthy and well prepared who believes these words: "Given and shed for you for the remission of sins." But he who does not believe these words or who doubts them, is unworthy and unprepared; for the words: "For you," require truly believing hearts.

The recommendation concerning additional Occasional Services was adopted.

During the general discussion of the section concerning the new music edition of the Common Service Book, a motion was made and seconded to amend item 5 relative to "contents and arrangement" by striking out the words "first stanza" and substituting "first three stanzas."

The President ruled that further discussion would have to be postponed until the regular order for the report of the Common Service Book Committee on Saturday.

The special order for the report of the Commission of Adjudication was taken up at 3:30 o'clock. The Rev. R. E. Tulloss read the report as follows:

REPORT OF THE COMMISSION OF ADJUDICATION

No business demanding the attention of the Commission of Adjudication was brought to its attention until within the last few weeks of the biennium. In consequence, no meeting was held prior to the sessions arranged in connection with this convention. Sessions were held on October 9th, 10th and 11th, 1928.

Organization was effected by the election of the following:

President: Dr. Henry E. Jacobs
Vice President: Dr. Luther Kuhlman
Secretary: Dr. R. E. Tulloss

An appeal, dated August 29th, 1928, was prepared and forwarded to the Commission by the Executive Committee of the Synod of California. After an examination of this appeal and of the circumstances under which it was presented, the following resolution was unanimously adopted:

"Whereas, under the Constitution of The United Lutheran Church in America, an appeal may properly come before the Commission 'by resolution' of a Convention of The United Lutheran Church in America, or 'by appeal from any of the Synods;' and

"Whereas, according to the officially adopted rules under which the Commission operates, questions which may be referred to the Commission 'shall be by resolution duly adopted by a Convention of The United Lutheran Church in America or by a Constituent Synod;' and

"Whereas, the appeal now presented for our consideration was prepared and forwarded by the Executive Committee of a Synod, and

"Whereas, there is no evidence that the Synod, in convention assembled, by specific resolution authorized or directed the Executive Committee to make such appeal; therefore, be it

"Resolved, That inasmuch as the appeal comes from the Executive Committee of the Synod of California and not from the Synod itself, under the Constitution and rules above noted, the appeal cannot be received for consideration by the Commission."

Respectfully submitted
HENRY E. JACOBS, *President.*
R. E. TULLOSS, *Secretary.*

The President called attention of the Convention to the fact that no action could be taken upon this report otherwise than as provided in the By-Laws.

Mr. Arthur P. Black presented the report of the Laymen's Movement.

REPORT OF THE LUTHERAN LAYMEN'S MOVEMENT FOR STEWARDSHIP

The biennium, 1926-1928, has been the most fruitful period in the history of our Laymen's Movement. Our threefold program has been greatly enlarged and extended. This happy result has come about quite as much because of the sympathetic attitude and helpful counsel of pastors, Church councils, and faculties of our colleges and seminaries, as because of the clear vision of the forward-looking and consecrated men on our executive and administrative committees. We are all coming to a clearer understanding of the imperative need of real rather than make-believe co-operation between the Pulpit and the Pew.

The Every Member Canvass

The chief objective of our Laymen's Movement during the twenty-two years of its history has been the promotion of the Every Member Canvass as an annual feature of our permanent church program. As a church we have not taken as kindly to the Every Member Canvass as some of our sister denominations, notably the Methodists, the Baptists, and the Presbyterians. We have suffered in more ways than one as the result. We are profiting by our experience. That is a cause for rejoicing.

The Banner Year

More congregations made use of the Every Member Canvass during the year 1927-8 than in any previous year. The requests for information literature established a precedent, both in number and size. For the first time it was necessary to use extra help for several months in our mailing and stenographic departments. The record would have been still more satisfactory had it not been for the break in our program caused by the Pension Endowment Fund Campaign. Our three secretaries gave full-time service to that worthy campaign from the middle of December to the middle of February, Secretary Hess in the Pittsburgh, Alleghany, West Virginia, and Canada Synods; Secretary Rinkliff in the Northwest Synod, and Secretary Black in the Maryland Synod. During this period the Every Member Canvass campaign was at a standstill. Undoubtedly, there were congregations which in other years made use of the Every Member Canvass during December, January and February, which did not make use of it the past year. The fact that in spite of this decisive break in our program there were more and larger requests for literature justifies the belief the year 1928-9 will be another banner year.

A Changed Attitude, and Why

The record made the past year clearly indicates a changed and changing attitude on the part of many pastors and church councils. Several reasons may be assigned, but the outstanding one is that they are becoming more and more convinced the Every Member Canvass is the very best medium for making a congregation what God intends it to be—a Christian enterprise for the building up and advancement of His Kingdom. Our Laymen's Movement has fostered this conviction by consistently and insistently putting it on a spiritual rather than a dollar and cents basis. Our efforts to get away from the purely mercenary idea in the promotion of the

Every Member Canvass have met with a gratifying response on the part of many church councils and more pastors. We believe the explanation may be given in a single word—*stewardship*. Insofar as possible we are making the Every Member Canvass program a stewardship program. Several of our Synods are helping out mightily in this respect, and we are hoping for the day when all of them will be in line.

EVERY MEMBER CANVASS LITERATURE

The following statement will give the reader a general idea of the wide use made of our Every Member Canvass literature during the campaign of 1927-8. Excepting samples mailed to pastors and other church officials, and the officials in our educational institutions, we mail out literature upon request only. Experience has proved it is largely a case of "love's labor lost" to broadcast literature, however important it may be:

(a) Making Church History (annual church folder), 400,000
    copies $1,452.39
(b) Making The Grade (story of Church progress), 300,000 copies   998.85
(c) Stewardship Pledge Cards, 500,000 copies.................................   328.89
(d) Budget Dollar Slips (the benevolent dollar), 310,000 copies....   330.50
(e) Stewards of Christ (study in stewardship), 106,500 copies....   451.60
(f) Stewardship Study Program (how to start it), 50,000 copies   246.50
(g) Every Member Canvass Folder, Duplex Envelope Folder,
    Church Budget Folder, 10,000 copies each to supplement
    existing supply, 30,000 copies...   113.65
(h) Statistical Circular (general data), 50,000 copies...................   69.12
                                                                                    _____
        Totals (1,746,500 copies) $3,991.50

THE ANNUAL CHURCH FOLDER

With the exception of the annual church folder this literature was issued, distributed, and paid for, by our Laymen's Movement. There is no charge for any of our literature. The annual church folder is authorized each year at the annual meeting of our Secretaries' Conference, the members of which are secretaries of the different boards and agencies of our U. L. C. A. The copy for each board or agency is prepared by its secretary. The cost of printing is pro-rated among the different boards and agencies on the basis of space used. The distribution is made by our Laymen's Movement which pays all costs incident thereto. We regard this folder an invaluable aid to every congregation as it gives a general survey, from the highest authoritative sources, of our United Lutheran Church in America at work.

STUDENT AID

The student aid phase of our program has been growing by leaps and bounds, as the following data will show: (a) during the biennium 1922-1924 aid was granted sixteen students; (b) during the biennium 1924-1926 aid was granted seventy-four; (c) during the biennium 1926-1928 aid was granted 135. During the present year we shall aid not fewer than 145.

Results Beginning to Tell

We have reached the point in our student aid program where results are beginning to tell. In 1926 there were six of our beneficiaries graduated from our seminaries. In 1927 there were 16. In 1928 there were 24. Of the total number, 46, there are 44 who have regular pastoral charges.

Applicants Not Solicited

During the past three years we have added approximately fifty new students to our rolls each year. During the past two years we have not solicited a single applicant. So far as our Laymen's Movement is concerned, it is no longer necessary to solicit men for the ministry. Our problem now is to choose from among those applicants who apply to us direct or through their pastors, synodical authorities, college faculties, or seminary faculties. Not a few on our student aid rolls are not only "out in front" in the classroom, but leaders in athletics and campus activities in general. Only one out of 105 failed in his studies in 1927, and only two out of 135 in 1928. It is doubtful if there is a more outstanding group in our whole student body today than the ministerial group. This augurs well for the future of the United Lutheran Church in America.

Growth of Student Aid Budget

Our Laymen's Movement has paid a total of $77,550 to date for student aid. The following table shows the growth of our student aid budget year by year:

1923-4	$ 3,600
1924-5	5,150
1925-6	17,150
1926-7	24,860
1927-8	26,790
Total	$77,550

During 1928-29 our student aid budget will approximate $28,000

Working Out a Difficult Problem

Many highly perplexing questions are involved in the student aid problem. Their proper solution calls for the highest degree of tact, forbearance, patience, and co-operation. Pastors, synodical authorities, college faculties and seminary faculties, almost without exception, co-operate wholeheartedly with our Laymen's Movement. If we at any time have failed to reciprocate it has been a mistake of the head and not of the heart. We have profited more than once by their wise counsel, and we have tried to show our appreciation by making our rules and regulations conform as nearly as possible to theirs. By and large, we feel we are working out our student aid problem mutually satisfactory to all concerned.

CHRISTIAN STEWARDSHIP

Our Laymen's Movement is doing its best to awaken the great body of our laymen to a clear understanding and a fuller appreciation of the principles of Christian Stewardship as taught both in the Old Testament and the New Testament. One of our greatest problems, probably the greatest is to convert the average layman to the truth that stewardship means something besides the giving of money. The average lay mind seems "set" on the wholly erroneous idea that stewardship and money are synonymous. It is a sorry fact that too many pastors entertain this unscriptural idea also. The advanced ground taken by many of our outstanding pastors and forward-looking synodical authorities on this all-important question during this biennium is bound to result in untold good to our Church. Stewardship is as broad as Christianity. It is the heart of missions. Christianity without missions is a hollow mockery.

WHAT WE ARE TRYING TO DO

We are trying to do several things: (a) to explain the fundamental principles of stewardship as outlined in the Bible; (b) to get our laymen away from the mercenary idea of what it is; (c) to show that stewardship has to do with (1) our time; (2) our personality; (3) our influence; (4) our talents; (5) our very life, as well as our money; (d) to bring to the attention of pastors and laymen alike the wealth of literature upon the subject; (e) to lead them to read their Bible with the thought of stewardship in mind; (f) to organize their church program on a stewardship basis—in a word, to give stewardship its rightful place in the life of our Church. We appreciate the opportunity given our secretaries to present the subject in so many synods, conferences, congregations, group meetings, and summer schools during this biennium. We hope others will continue the work we have begun. It is a work that challenges the best minds, lay as well as pastoral, everywhere. It is a work that must be done if our denomination is to keep its place among the other large Protestant denominations.

OTHER ACTIVITIES

Aside from majoring on (a) the Every Member Canvass, (b) Student Aid, and (c) Stewardship, our secretaries, under the direction of our two controlling committees, (1) make annual visits to the seniors in our seminaries to acquaint them with our program and contact them personally; (2) establish friendly relations with our new pastors from year to year, and (3) co-operate with the other agencies of our Church in working out their program. We feel that every working agency of our Church should have a good word to say for every other working agency as well as its own. All are working for a common goal. Co-operation rather than competition is our watchword.

ASSOCIATE SECRETARY C. W. HERMAN HESS

Mr. Hess' major activities during the biennium included work in (a) ten Synods, (b) eleven Conferences, (c) four Synodical Brotherhoods, (d) four Summer Schools, (e) six colleges, (f) forty congregations. Miscellaneous engagements included Sunday school conventions, orphans' homes, old people's homes, ministerial associations, memorial addresses, and church council meetings. Mr. Hess is a director of the Orphans' Home at Zelienople. He was president of the Pittsburgh Synodical Brotherhood several years. He was director of the Pension Endowment Fund Campaign in the Pittsburgh, West Virginia and Alleghany synods, with headquarters in Pittsburgh, and also did work in that campaign in the Canada Synod by special request. One of Mr. Hess' specialties is setting up meetings for recruiting members for our Laymen's Movement. He works out of New Castle, Penna., his address being 604½ Spruce Street, that city.

ASSOCIATE SECRETARY GEORGE L. RINKLIFF

Mr. Rinkliff came with our Laymen's Movement in April, 1927. He has put in a strenuous year and a half, his work covering territory from New Jersey to Montana, and from Minnesota to Mississippi. His major activities have been in the West and South. All told, he has worked in 167 meetings, 123 of which were church congregations. He has worked in fourteen Synods, several Conferences, Brotherhood conventions, summer schools, Women's Missionary Society conventions, and pastoral associations. Mr. Rinkliff formerly was a newspaper man. He has written several very timely and readable articles which have been published in *The Lutheran* at intervals during the past year. He was director of the Pension Endowment Fund Campaign in the Northwest Synod, with headquarters in Minneapolis. He works out of Springfield, Ohio, his address being 222 West Euclid Ave., that city.

HEADQUARTERS MOVED TO OUR NATIONAL CAPITAL

January 1, 1927, our Laymen's Movement headquarters were moved from Springfield, Ohio, to Washington, D. C. We are located in Our Home Life Building, corner of Vermont Avenue and L Street, close to the heart of the business district, therefore easy of access for all visitors. All official inquiries should be sent to this address.

RECOMMENDATIONS

1. That the annual, simultaneous, every-member canvass be reindorsed, and that pastors and councils be requested to make it a part of their permanent program.

2. That the month preceding the every-member canvass be set aside as Stewardship Month, during which special emphasis shall be placed on the stewardship of (a) time, (b) personality, (c) influence, (d) talents, (e) life, and money emphasized only incidentally.

3. That every congregation in the United Lutheran Church in America be asked to promote a definite program of stewardship, (a) in the Sunday school, (b) in the Missionary Society, (c) in the Brotherhood, (d) in the mid-week service, (e) in the Luther League, (f) in the Light Brigade, the official head of each to direct the work, under the leadership of the pastor.

4. That the student aid program of the Lutheran Laymen's Movement for Stewardship be approved.

J. L. CLARK, *Chairman.*
ARTHUR P. BLACK, *Executive Secretary.*

Mr. Black was followed by Mr. J. L. Clark, who called the attention of the Convention to the special work of the Laymen's Movement in educating young men for the ministry. At the close of his address the Convention rose and stood while the President led in prayer.

The recommendations of the Committee were adopted.

The Rev. J. A. Morehead presented the report of the Committee on Church Papers as follows:

REPORT OF THE COMMITTEE ON CHURCH PAPERS

Your Committee on Church Papers as now constituted consists of the Rev. John Aberly, D.D., Mr. L. Russell Alden, Reverends Henry Anstadt, D.D., C. E. Gardner, D.D., J. A. Leas, D.D., J. A. Morehead, D.D., LL.D., E. P. Pfatteicher, D.D., Ph.D., Mr. I. Searles Runyon, Dr. William J. Showalter.

At the first meeting of the biennium, 1926-28, the Rev. Dr. J. A. Morehead was elected chairman and the Rev. Dr. E. P. Pfatteicher, secretary.

Meetings of the Committee were held on December 9, 1926, April 21 and

December 15, 1927, and a meeting by correspondence on June 8, 1928. In addition, the Executive Committee met with representatives of the *Lutheran Quarterly* and the *Lutheran Church Review* on February 24, 1927, and the Executive Committee met again on December 20, 1927.

Your Committee had before it three matters of major importance and many questions of minor importance during the past biennium. The three matters listed as of major importance are: the resignation of the Rev. Dr. George W. Sandt as Editor-in-chief of *The Lutheran;* the calling of a conference of those interested in the publication of the *Lutheran Quarterly* and the *Lutheran Church Review* with the intention of seeking a merger of these publications; and the consideration of a carefully prepared "dummy" of an ideal religious weekly by experts in the publication world.

In a letter written to Dr. Morehead as Chairman of the Church Paper Committee on Luther's Birthday, November 10, 1927, Dr. George W. Sandt, who had served as editor of *The Lutheran* for 31 years, requested that he be relieved of a burden which was becoming very heavy. Dr. Sandt's letter is as follows:

Rev. J. A. Morehead, D.D., LL.D.,
Chairman of the Church Paper Committee,
39 East 35th Street, New York City.
My dear Mr. Morehead: As I intimated to you in the spring, I believe the time has come when I should be relieved of bearing the further responsibility as editor of *The Lutheran.* At my time of life it is impossible for me to keep in living touch with the movements and activities of the Church, both within the body of which I am a member and outside of it as well, and as I believe this to be necessary if the editorial department is to be rightly conducted, I herewith tender to the Church Paper Committee through you, its chairman, my resignation as editor of *The Lutheran,* to take effect January 1st, 1928.
I have seved as editor thirty-one years, and feel that the time has come when I should be relieved, though I still hope to be active in a literary way as circumstances permit and opportunity affords.
                    With high regards,
                              GEO. W. SANDT.

Your Committee felt deeply moved by this resignation, realizing how much of Dr. Sandt's whole life had gone into the making of *The Lutheran.*

The resignation was accepted with regret. The Publication Board was requested to confer with the Executive Committee of the Church Paper Committee concerning a retirement allowance. Dr. Nathan R. Melhorn was elected to fill the unexpired term with permission to employ temporary editorial assistance within the limits of a budget to be agreed upon. A subcommittee of the Committee on Church Papers was appointed to study the problem of additional editorial personnel.

Your Committee entered the following appreciation of Dr. Sandt on its records:

Doctor Sandt was a pioneer in the present period of religious journalism in North America when church papers are organs of an entire communion or a considerable section of a denomination. Until 1896, when the General Council of the Lutheran Church acquired control of two weeklies and one monthly, the religious press was largely in the control of individuals. Personal views were not only presented but many controversies were distributed and kept alive by printers' ink. Dr. Sandt was elected managing editor and soon after editor-in-chief of the "official organ" of the General Council, and undertook the arduous task of so conducting a weekly that all interests of the Church, individual and collective, should be served. He continued in that position until 1919, when the General Council was merged into the United Lutheran Church in America. He then was chosen as editor-in-chief of the official organ of the U. L. C. A. He was re-elected biennially thereafter, election for his present term of office occurring at Richmond, Va., in 1926.

As a writer, Dr. Sandt possesses the style which was developed when an editorial position carried with it an obligation to use and to promulgate the best type of language. His knowledge of religious issues, especially such as have been before the Church since 1865, is broad and accurate. He considers the individual rather than society the objective of Christian organization. Confessionally, he would, no doubt, rank himself with conservatives.

Besides the work he has accomplished for the Church in an editorial capacity he has served in other departments. He was a member of the Board of Home Missions in the General Council and is at present on the Home Mission Board of the Ministerium of Pennsylvania. He is a director of the Philadelphia Theological Seminary and of the Mary J. Drexel Home, the Lankenau Hospital and of the Artman Home. His interest in "inner mission" operations is very deep and of long standing.

Dr. Sandt was born at Belfast, Pa., in 1854. He is an alumnus of Lafayette College and of the Philadelphia Theological Seminary in the class of 1883. During 1884 to 1889 he was a member of the Faculty of Augustana College in the Department of English.

The second major item concerns the calling of a conference in the interests of merging the two theological quarterlies of Gettysburg and Mt. Airy, in the hope that this merger may be extended further and further until finally there may come into existence a Lutheran Theological Quarterly of America worthy of the name.

The conference of the committees delegated with this task was convened on February 24, 1927, by Dr. Morehead. The purpose of the conference was stated in these words:

"to consider the practicability of the consolidation of the existing theological journals with a view to the establishment of a scientific theological quarterly for the service of the entire Lutheran Church and the development of Christian thought for the welfare of the Christian Church at large."

Drs. Paulson, Hoh, Reed and Jacobs (C. M.) represented the *Lutheran*

Church Review; Drs. Delk, Stamm, Wentz and Fischer the *Lutheran Quarterly;* Drs. Morehead, Aberly and Pfatteicher the Committee on Church Papers. The session lasted throughout the day. It adopted a series of recommendations to be presented in turn to the owners of the two publications concerned. The two groups met independently and ratified the recommendations whereupon the merger was effected. Your Committee's task was considered completed when the two groups were brought into conference. As information, it is a pleasure to report that the owners of the *Lutheran Quarterly* and the *Lutheran Church Review,* having accomplished the consolidation of these two periodicals, began with the year 1928 the publication of the new theological journal under the title of *The Lutheran Church Quarterly.*

Your Committee desires to inject the statement at this point that it has carefully considered the advisability of launching a popular monthly as suggested at Richmond, which is to take its place beside the weeklies, *The Lutheran* and *Der Lutherischer Herold* and the new and rather technical Quarterly. It believes, however, that it is serving the Church best by holding this venture in abeyance for the immediate present.

The third major item concerns the deliberations of the Committee resulting from the submission to it of a "dummy" copy of *The Lutheran* submitted by several experts in the matter of publications. A most profitable meeting of the committee was held. Dr. Melhorn was present at the session. A subsequent meeting was held and after a second full discussion of the subject it was

> *Resolved,* that it is the judgment of the Committee and Editors that the journalistic principles embodied in the "dummy" copy of *The Lutheran* submitted through Dr. Showalter at the previous meeting are recognized as generally correct and that they should be adopted as far as they are serviceable in the accomplishment of the mission of *The Lutheran* as an official church paper.
>
> *Resolved,* that our Church Papers Committee puts itself on record as favoring the use of original stories by Lutheran writers for the appropriate pages of *The Lutheran.*
>
> *Resolved,* that we suggest to the Editors the advisability of reducing the space now used for "Helps for Devotions in the Home," giving one-half of this space for the weekly publication of a sermon.
>
> *Resolved,* that everything that is practicable should be done to develop the news section of *The Lutheran. Der Lutherischer Herold* is to be developed also.

Your Committee offers the following resolutions:

1. *Resolved,* that we place on record our unanimous and profound appreciation of the long and faithful service of Dr. George W. Sandt, distinguished as he has been in this work by a superior command of good English, by sound Christian thinking, and by devotion to the Word of God and the confessions of the Church. We are proud of the fact that through his service as Editor he has won recognition for *The Lutheran* not only in this country but also abroad.

2. *Resolved,* That the Convention authorize the Committee to send Dr. Sandt a telegram of appreciation and greetings.

3. *Resolved,* That we express our joy in the happy consummation of the merger effected between two of our Theological Quarterlies as the first step in the production of a representative Theological Quarterly as the mouthpiece of the best thought of American Lutheranism.

4. The Committee on Church Papers unanimously nominates and recommends to the Convention of The United Lutheran Church for election for the ensuing biennium, the Rev. Dr. N. R. Melhorn as Editor of *The Lutheran* and Dr. C. R. Tappert as Editor of the *Lutherischer Herold.*

Your Committee places in nomination the names of Dr. J. A. Leas, Dr. W. H. Greever and Dr. H. F. Offermann.

Respectfully submitted,

THE COMMITTEE.

On motion the resolutions were adopted.

The editors nominated in resolution No. 4 were declared elected.

The Rev. S. Billheimer presented the report of the Committee on Memorials from Constituent Synods as follows:

REPORT OF THE COMMITTEE ON MEMORIALS FROM CONSTITUENT SYNODS

The following memorials from district synods have been placed in the hands of your committee. They are herewith tabulated, with the action or reply suggested by this committee.

1. *Ohio Synod:*   Concerning the arrangement of words and music of the hymns in the Common Service Book.

"That the Synod of Ohio, United Lutheran Church in America, hereby petition The United Lutheran Church in America to request the Common Service Book Committee of The United Lutheran Church in America to print the words of hymns between the staves of music in the preparation of any further editions of the Common Service Book."

Reply: In view of the changes in this regard contemplated by the Common Service Book Committee and set forth in their report, we recommend that action on this memorial be postponed until the time of that report. The Committee on Memorials from Constituent Synods, however, wishes to put itself on record as favoring the inclusion of at least three stanzas between the staves of music wherever practical.

2. *Pittsburgh Synod:*   Concerning a fuller index of hymns.

"Resolved, That the Pittsburgh Synod memorialize The United Lutheran Church in America to request the Common Service Book Committee to prepare a fuller Index of Hymns according to subjects and days of the church years to be printed in future editions of the Common Service Book."

Reply: The Committee recommends this memorial from the Pittsburgh Snyod for adoption.

3. *Susquehanna Synod of Central Pennsylvania*: Concerning plans for personal evangelistic work.

"That the Susquehanna Synod of Central Pennsylvania memorialize The United Lutheran Church in America, in Convention at Erie, Pa., that the Church Years of 1930 and 1931 be dedicated to the spiritual and numerical upbuilding of the Home Church, and that the Executive Board of The United Lutheran Church prepare an outline of plans for personal evangelistic work, that we may be able to do our part in bringing the unchurched of our faith and the unsaved of our land into the Kingdom."

Reply: While realizing that the Committee on Evangelism has in part anticipated in its report the action proposed by this memorial, the Committee on Memorials from Constituent Synods nevertheless recommends the adoption in detail of the plan urged by the Susquehanna Synod.

4. *Kansas Synod*: Concerning work for deaf mutes.

"Motion prevailed to memorialize The United Lutheran Church to inaugurate through the Board of American Missions a department of work for Deaf Mutes in America and that the Board give consideration to Rev. E. C. Sibberson to head this work."

Reply: The Committee recommends that this matter be referred to the Inner Mission Board for earnest consideration.

5. *Pittsburgh Synod*: Concerning a new theological survey commission.

"Resolved, That the Pittsburgh Synod memorialize The United Lutheran Church to the effect that a new theological survey commission be appointed to consist of paid educational experts of the Lutheran Church from outside the United Lutheran Church, which commission shall make a church-wide survey of our theological seminary situation and prepare a program detailing the number and strategic locations of the seminaries necessary to the most effective prosecution of the work of theological education in the United Lutheran Church.

Reply: In view of the conferences now being held looking to the possible consolidation of Seminaries, we recommend that no action be taken on this memorial.

6. *Alleghany Synod*: Concerning an interpretation of Article XVI of the Augsburg Confession.

"Be it resolved by the Alleghany Synod in Annual Convention in the Moxham Lutheran Church of Johnstown, Pa., May 24, 1928: That we hereby respectfully memorialize the United Lutheran Church at its Sixth

Convention to give to the Church at large an interpretation of the XVI Article of the Augsburg Confession with respect to the phrases, 'To engage in just wars' and 'to serve as soldiers' in the light of present day thought and conditions."

Reply: The Committee recommends that this memorial be referred to the Committee on Moral and Social Welfare.

7. *Synod of New York*: Concerning the Inner Mission Board.

"That the New York Synod memorializes The United Lutheran Church in America at its Convention in 1928 to merge the Inner Mission Board with the Board of American Missions."

Reply: The Committee recommends that in view of the many and diverse interests at stake this matter be referred to the Executive Board for thorough investigation and careful study.

8. *Ministerium of Pennsylvania*:

(a) Concerning a change in the Formula for Ordination.

"Resolved, That the Ministerium of Pennsylvania petition the United Lutheran Church to amend the Formula for Ordination so as to read, 'I commit unto thee the office of the Word and Sacraments, according to the faith of the Evangelical Lutheran Church.'"

Reply: The Committee recommends that this petition be referred to the Common Service Book Committee.

(b) Concerning a change on the parochial report.

"Resolved, That the Ministerium of Pennsylvania petition the United Lutheran Church to change the rubric on the parochial report so as to make the items under the current expenses uniform to all congregations."

Reply: We recommend reference to the Statistical and Church Year Book Committee for conference and report.

(c) Concerning a periodical to give information on benevolent operations.

"Resolved, That the Ministerium of Pennsylvania memorialize the United Lutheran Church to publish for distribution a periodical in which all needed information concerning its benevolent operations is intelligibly presented."

Reply: The Committee recommends approval and suggests reference to the newly appointed special committee of fifteen.

9. Invitations for the next convention have been received from Detroit, San Francisco and Philadelphia.

In view of the action taken this morning, no recommendation is necessary.

Respectfully submitted,

STANLEY BILLHEIMER, *Chairman.*

Recommendation I was approved. (See minutes fifth meeting, morning session.—Secretary.)

Motion was made and carried to postpone action on recommendation No. 2 until the report of the Common Service Book Committee is before the Convention. (See minutes sixth meeting, morning session.—Secretary.)

Moved and carried to postpone action on recommendation No. 3 until the report of the Committee on Evangelism is before the Convention. (See minutes fourth meeting, morning session.—Secretary.)

Motion was made and carried to postpone action on recommendation No. 4 until the report of the Board of American Missions is before the Convention. (See minutes third meeting, afternoon session.—Secretary.)

Motion was made and carried to postpone action on recommendation No. 5 until the report of the Commission on Theological Education is before the Convention. (See minutes fifth meeting, afternoon session.—Secretary.)

Motion was made and carried to adopt recommendation No. 6 concerning interpretation of Article XVI of the Augsburg Confession.

Motion was made and carried to adopt recommendation No. 7 concerning the Inner Mission Board.

Item 8 (a), recommendation concerning formula of ordination adopted.

Item 8 (b), recommendation concerning Parochial Report adopted.

Recommendation 8 (c), concerning information on benevolent operations, was adopted.

The Convention adjourned with prayer by the Rev. N. Willison.

———————— •◦• ————————

Thursday Evening

The Laymen's Movement and the Board of American Missions held banquets, according to program, at six o'clock in the Hotel Lawrence.

THIRD MEETING
Morning Session

SUNDAY SCHOOL CHAPEL, LUTHER MEMORIAL CHURCH,
Erie, Pennsylvania,
Friday, October 12, 1928, 8:45.

Matins were conducted by the Rev. Ellis B. Burgess.

The Convention was called to order by the President.

The minutes of Thursday morning and afternoon sessions were read, corrected and approved.

The Rev. C. Theo. Benze presented the Report of the Board of Foreign Missions as follows:

REPORT OF THE BOARD OF FOREIGN MISSIONS
Directory of the Board

Headquarters: The Lutheran Foreign Missions House, 18 E. Mt. Vernon Place, Baltimore, Md.

OFFICERS

President: Rev. Prof. C. Theodore Benze, D.D., 7304 Boyer St., Mt. Airy, Philadelphia, Pa.

Vice-President: Rev. J. S. Simon, D.D., Hagerstown, Md.

Recording Secretary: Rev. George Drach, D.D., 18 E. Mt. Vernon Place, Baltimore, Md.

Treasurer: Rev. Luther B. Wolf, D.D., 18 E. Mt. Vernon Place, Baltimore, Md.

General Secretaries: Rev. George Drach, D.D., and Rev. Luther B. Wolf, D.D.

Field Secretary: Rev. M. Edwin Thomas, D.D., 2022 Market St., Harrisburg, Pa.

MEMBERS OF THE BOARD
TERMS EXPIRE IN 1928

Rev. J. S. Simon, D.D., Hagerstown, Md.

Rev. A. Steimle, D.D., 174 West 93rd St., New York

Rev. L. C. Manges, D.D., 1431 Walnut St., Harrisburg, Pa.

Rev. P W. Koller, D. D, 68 Sherman Ave., Mansfield, Ohio

Paul Van Reed Miller, Esq., 642 Widener Bldg., Philadelphia, Pa.

Mr. M. P. Moller, Hagerstown, Md.

Mr. H. L. Bonham, Chilhowie, Va.

TERMS EXPIRE IN 1930

Rev. C. Theodore Benze, D. D., 7304 Boyer St., Philadelphia, Pa.

Rev. R. C. G. Bielinski, Delanco, N. J.

Rev. H. W. Snyder, D.D., 114 Lelia St., Johnstown, Pa.

Rev. Jacob L. Morgan, D.D., 612 S. Main St., Salisbury, N. C.
Rev. G. Albert Getty, D.D., 40 S. Duke St., York, Pa.
Mr. James M. Snyder, 401 Chestnut St., Philadelphia, Pa.
Prof. C. W. Foss, PhD., 3808 Eighth Ave., Rock Island, Ill.

TERMS EXPIRE IN 1932

Rev. J. L. Sieber, D. D., 352 Church Ave., Roanoke, Va.
Rev. S. W. Herman, D.D., 121 State St., Harrisburg, Pa.
Rev. J. T. Huddle, D.D., 738 Eleventh St, N. W., Washington, D. C.
Mr. William Menges, Menges Mills, Pa.
Rev. Charles A. Dennig, 211 East St., Warren, Pa.
Mr. Martin H. Buehler, Glens Falls, N. Y.
Mr. Charles H. Dahmer, Scarsdale, N. Y.

COOPERATING MEMBERS
REPRESENTING THE AUGUSTANA SYNOD

Rev. Lars G. Abrahamson, D., 3449 Seventh Ave., Rock Island, Ill.
Rev. G. A. Brandelle, D.D., 627 44th St., Rock Island, Ill.

REPRESENTING THE UNITED DANISH CHURCH

Rev. V. W. Bondo, 3310 Washington Ave., Racine, Wis.
Rev. I. M. Andersen, Kenosha, Wisconsin.

ADVISORY MEMBERS
REPRESENTING THE WOMEN'S MISSIONARY SOCIETY

Mrs. W. F. Morehead, Salem, Va., and Mrs S. R. Kepner, Pottstown, Pa

STANDING COMMITTEES

Executive: The officers and Steimle, Sieber, Koller, James M. Snyder.
India Mission Committee: Simon, Koller, Abrahamson, James M. Snyder, M. H. Buehler.
Japan Mission Committee: Steimle, Morgan, Bielinski, Bonham, Bondo, Andersen.
Africa Mission Committee: Herman, Getty, Huddle, H. W. Snyder, Brandelle.
China Mission Committee: Sieber, Manges, Dennig, Foss, Dahmer, P. Miller.
South America Missions Committee: Manges, Foss, Moller, Dahmer, P. Miller, Wm. Menges.
Candidate Committee: Koller, Sieber, Dennig, H. W. Snyder, Mrs. Morehead, Mrs. Kepner.
Literature Committee: Bielinski, Simon, Steimle, James M. Snyder.

List of Foreign Missionaries
INDIA
MADRAS PRESIDENCY
Guntur District

Guntur: Dr. and Mrs. J. Roy Strock (College and Town Charge), Rev. and Mrs. C. H. Swavely (Mission Treasurer), Rev. and Mrs. F. J. Fiedler

(High School, St. Paul's Hostel, College Hostel), Mr. and Mrs. Wm. Bembower (Orphanage Compound and Vocational School), Anna Kugler, M.D., Arline Beal, M.D., Lottie L. Martin, R. N. (Hospital), Anna E. Sanford (Bible Training School for Women), Edna Engle (Mohammedan Women and Girls), Edith Eykamp, Emma Johnson (Girls' High School), Nellie S. Cassell, M.D., Grace L. Moyer, M.D., Hilda M. Kaercher, Mabel H. Meyer, R.N.

Chirala: Rev. and Mrs. L. A. Gotwald, Rose Brummer, R.N., Emma Baer.

Tenali: Dr. and Mrs. Victor McCauley.

Repali: Rev. and Mrs. Luther B. Slifer, Ellen B. Schuff, Louisa A. Miller.

Narsaravupet: Rev. and Mrs. C. P. Tranberg, Jessie S. Thomas, Alice J. Nickel, Frances M. Segner.

Sattenapalle: Rev. and Mrs. C. B. Caughman.

Rentichintala: Rev. and Mrs. H. Goedeke, Clara Leaman (Girls' School and Converts' Home), Metta K. Blair, R.N.

Nellore District

Tarlupad: Rev. and Mrs. G. A. Rupley.

East Godavery District

Rajahmundry: Rev. and Mrs. R. M. Dunkelberger, Rev. and Mrs. J. E. Graefe, Rev. and Mrs. O. V. Werner (Theological Seminary), Betty A. Nilsson, M.D., Verna Lofgren, R.N. (Hospital), Helen Brenneman (Girls' School), Charlotte B. Hollerbach (Lace Industry), Emilie Weiskotton, Christina Eriksson, R.N.

Dowlaishwaram: Rev. and Mrs. Thure A. Holmer.

Peddapuram: Mr. and Mrs. Ray L. Cunningham.

Samulkot: Mary S. Borthwick, Ruth Swanson.

Yelleswaram: Rev. and Mrs. W. T. Benze.

West Godavery District

Bhimawaram: Rev. and Mrs. F. L. Coleman, Agnes Christenson, Lilith N. Schwab.

Narsapur: Rev. S. C. Burger.

Tadepalligudom: Rev. and Mrs. A. Schmitthenner.

Tallapudi: Rev. and Mrs. L. E. Irschick.

Missionaries Emeritus: Rev. L. L. Uhl, D.D., Agnes I. Shade, Katherine Fahs.

Furlough: Rev. and Mrs. H. H. Sipes, Florence M. Welty, Selma Anderson, Rev. and Mrs. J. C. Finefrock, Hilma Levine, R.N., Maida Meissner, R.N., E. Pauline Whitteker, Rev. and Mrs. A. F. A. Neudoerffer, Agatha Tatge, R.N., Rev. Dr. and Mrs. Isaac Cannaday, Rev. and Mrs. J. R. Fink, Rev. and Mrs. G. R. Haaf, Rev. and Mrs. M. L. Dolbeer, Dr Mary Baer, Rev. and Mrs. H. H. Moyer.

LIBERIA

Monrovia, Liberia, Africa: Mrs. C. E. Buschman, Miss Mabel Dysinger,

Sister Laura Gilliland, Miss Bertha Koenig, Mr. and Mrs. James W. Miller, Rev. and Mrs. F. H. Bloch, Rev. and Mrs. E. A. Lape, Miss Elsie Otto, Rev. K. R. Jensen, Jacob R. Jensen, M.D., Rev. and Mrs. Harvey J. Currens, Rev. and Mrs. Harry Heilman, N. R. Sloan, M.D., Rev. A. H. Kaitschuk, Marie Jensen, R.N., Rev. and Mrs. David D. Dagle, Rev. and Mrs. Robert Oberly, Irene B. Bloch.

Furlough: Mrs. C. H. Nielsen, Rev. and Mrs. O. E. Bluehdorn, Rev. and Mrs. Paul M. Counts, Rev. and Mrs. J. D. Curran, Mr. and Mrs. J. I. Haltiwanger

JAPAN

Kumamoto: Rev. Dr. and Mrs. L. S. G. Miller, Rev. and Mrs. D. G. M. Bach, Anna Powlas, Maud Powlas, Martha B. Akard, Marion E. Potts, Martha M. Harder.

Tokyo: Rev. and Mrs. John K. Linn, Grace M. Beers, Helene Harder, Mary Heltibridle, Maya Winther.

Kurume: Rev. and Mrs. J. M. T. Winther.

Saga: Rev. and Mrs. W. F. Heins.

Ogi: Faith Lippard, Amy Thoren.

Moji: Rev. and Mrs. J. Arthur Linn.

Fukuoka: Rev. and Mrs. C. E. Norman.

Kobe: Rev. and Mrs. S. O. Thorlaksson.

Furlough: Rev. Dr. and Mrs. C. K. Lippard, Helen Shirk, Rev. and Mrs. George Schillinger, Rev. Dr. and Mrs. Edward T. Horn, Rev. and Mrs. Arthur C. Knudten, Rev. and Mrs. C. W. Hepner, Rev. and Mrs. A. J. Stirewalt.

SOUTH AMERICA

British Guiana, New Amsterdam: Rev. and Mrs. Robert H. Daube.

Buenos Aires, Argentina: Rev. and Mrs. J. M. Armbruster, Rev. Paul O. Machetzki, Corinne Menges, Myrtle Wilke.

Furlough: Rev. and Mrs. H. E. Haas.

CHINA
Shantung Province

Tsingtao: Rev. and Mrs. P. P. Anspach, Erva Moody, Rev. L. G. Cooper, Lydia Reich, R.N., Rev. and Mrs. C. H. Reinbrecht.

Kiaochow: Rev. and Mrs. Theo. Scholz.

Tsimo: Elvira Strunk.

Furlough: Rev. and Mrs. Wm. Matzat, Rev. Dr. and Mrs. C. J. Voskamp, Dr. and Mrs. P. E. Loudenslager, Kate Voget, Freda Strecker.

INTRODUCTION

Jesus said, "Verily, verily, I say unto you, he that believeth on Me, the works that I do shall he do also; and greater works than these shall he do, because I go unto My Father (John 14: 12)." We claim the fulfillment of this promise in our foreign mission fields. Through the faith and labor of our missionaries and native workers, supported by the devotion and sacrifices of the United Lutheran Church in America, by the administration of the means of grace, the Word and Sacraments, in the power of the Holy Spirit, "the blind receive their sight, and the lame walk, the lepers are cleansed, and the deaf hear, the dead are raised up and the poor have the gospel preached to them (Matthew 11: 5)."

Our foreign fields are so far away and so far apart that those who do not continually keep in touch with them are apt to underestimate the value of the work which is done in them. Not the only way but certainly the best way to find out what is being done is to visit our foreign fields. During the past few years an increasing number of persons visited one or more of our missions in an official or unofficial capacity. Their reports have increased the foreign mission interest of the home Church and have strengthened the ties which bind our missions to us.

Two years before his death Dr. F. G. Gotwald, with his wife and daughter, visited his son, our missionary in India. They saw as much of our mission work there as they could. Miss Eleanora M. Demmler of Evans City, Penna., with her sister and brother, visited our mission in Liberia, Africa.

Mrs. J. Nicum and later Mr. and Mrs. John A. Armbruster, parents of our missionary in Buenos Aires, stopped to see what our Church is doing in that great South American city. Dr. George Drach spent ten months on an official visit to our missions in India, China and Japan. Dr. L. B. Wolf paid official visits to our missions in Argentina and Liberia. Dr. F. H. Knubel and Dr. E. Clarence Miller, with their wives, spent several weeks in the India fields during the month of February, 1928. Mrs. H. B. Reller, of Pittsburgh, Penna., also was there at the same time, and also visited Japan. What they all saw and heard and described to us may well be summarized in the words of the first great foreign missionary, St. Paul, when he reported to the Church at Jerusalem and said that God had wrought "miracles and wonders," by which He "opened the door of faith unto the Gentiles."

If you who read this report had visited our foreign missions at any time during the past two years, you, also, we are certain, would have seen things you could never forget. You, too, would have seen miracles and wonders of grace in Jesus Christ, whereby His Church is being established on firm foundations and is being extended in ever increasing strength and influence among non-Christian peoples. You also would be led to say that the United Lutheran Church in America does not sufficiently appreciate and certainly does not adequately support its foreign missions in India, China, Japan, Africa and South America.

SOME ADVANCE AND BETTER ORGANIZATION

Momentous changes are taking place in our foreign fields. These changes relate in particular to the organizations of the missionaries in their respective fields and to the development of the indigenous churches. As we watch this development we must not become overanxious and move too fast nor, on the other hand, should we allow ourselves to hold back progress by too much assertion of foreign authority. We must seek to fulfill our function as the wise and loving parent Church which earnestly and joyfully desires the daughter churches abroad to reach their age of maturity and independence with mutual feelings of love and esteem.

In every one of our foreign fields problems of reorganization have called for solution. We have been obliged to revalue our missionary methods and management, and to readjust the relations of the missionaries to each other and to the growing churches in the mission fields. It is a difficult task which requires understanding and patient tact on all sides. We ask those who are watching the process with interest or taking part in it with ardor, to unite in prayer to God for His guidance and blessing. Churches are in the making and God must direct and help us or we will not succeed.

How serious and far-reaching these problems are, may be judged from the following record. During the visit of Dr. Wolf in Argentina in 1923 the mission there was reorganized. While Dr. Drach was in India in 1925 the constitution and by-laws of the Lutheran Church in the Andhra country were being formulated. His visit to China inaugurated new policies and regulations in every department of the work of that field. While in Japan he urged a revision of the relationship of the missionaries to the Japanese pastors and congregations, which led to the drafting of a new constitution. The chief purpose of the visit of Dr. Wolf to Liberia in July, 1927, related to the reorganization of that mission for more efficient coordination of work. The principal recommendations of Drs. Knubel and Miller deal with problems of mission administration and church organization.

MISSIONARIES COOPERATING

In all our foreign fields our missionaries are performing their part of the great task with deep and unselfish devotion to God and the spread of His kingdom. The Church nowhere has a body of more loyal and faithful servants than in its foreign fields. They deserve praise in all the churches both at home and abroad. It is to be regretted, however, that some of them have been tempted to become somewhat discouraged because the home Church has failed to support their efforts to the extent which would enable them not only to hold together the established work but also to take advantage of their opportunities to reach unevangelized parts of their respective fields and unreached classes of society in their respective communities.

The present indebtedness of the Board of Foreign Missions, which has accumulated since the merger in 1918, in all fairness must be interpreted as the result of its effort to meet at least to some degree the insistent financial needs of our growing missions. This the Board has done in the confident hope that the home Church sooner or later would accept its responsibility and provide larger income both through the fixed apportionments and by special gifts for designated purposes. The Board still believes that the United Lutheran Church in America wants to do bigger and better foreign mission work every year, and that this convention will find ways and means to cancel its indebtedness and give the Board financial ability to match the consecrated zeal of our foreign missionaries.

The following is a summary of statistics of all missions for the calendar year 1927.

SUMMARY OF STATISTICS OF ALL MISSIONS
January 1, 1928

Missions	Mission-aries	Native Workers	Bapt. Members	Congre-gations	Acces-sions 1927	Pupils in School	Value of Mission Property
India	97	3708	136,555	1405	6006	32,810	$1,116,600
Japan	42	47	2,500	25	300	700	600,000
China	16	144	2,390	35	170	1,669	185,000
Liberia	34	45	300	6	....	500	75,000
Argentina	5	10	664	8	169	1,560	208,000
B. Guiana	2	8	300	7	....	250	20,000
Totals	196	3962	142,709	1486	6645	37,489	$2,204,600

CHANGES IN MISSIONARY FORCE

The number of missionaries, including women missionaries, supported by the Women's Executive Board and wives of missionaries, has decreased during the biennium by five. The present total is 196. No new ordained missionaries were sent to India or Japan, where there have been a few losses by death, transfer and resignation. Their number increased in Liberia from twelve in 1926 to sixteen in 1928, including unordained men missionaries. One new ordained man was sent to British Guiana and two to China. The number of women missionaries in all fields increased from 56 in 1926 to 60 in 1928.

Two faithful and efficient men laid down their lives in the performance of their missionary duties, Rev. H. E. Dickey, who died at Repalle, India, on October 2, 1926, and C. H. Nilesen, M.D., who died at Muhlenberg, Liberia, Africa, on January 29, 1928. We mourn their loss and in spirit lay upon their graves in our foreign fields tributes of esteem and praise for the character of their work and the testimony of their lives in the service of the Saviour of the world.

The new missionaries appointed, commissioned and sent out during the past two years are as follows: To India—Frances M. Segner; to Liberia—Jacob R. Jensen, M.D., Dorothy R. Hueter (Mrs. Bluehdorn), Rev. and Mrs. Harvey J. Currens, Rev. and Mrs. Harry Heilman, N. R. Sloan, M.D., Rev. and Mrs. A. H. Kaitschuk, Miss Marie Jensen, Miss Irene B. Bloch; to Japan—Helen H. Harder, Mary E. Heltibridle; to Argentina—Myrtle

Wilke; to British Guiana—Rev. and Mrs. Robert H. Daube; to China—Rev. L. Grady Cooper, Lydia Reich, R.N., Rev. and Mrs. C. H. Reinbrecht.

The following missionaries have resigned: India—Rev. Ernest Neudoerffer, now professor at the theological seminary in Waterloo, Ontario, Canada, whose devoted wife, nee Anna Rohrer, died in the Kitchener-Waterloo Hospital on October 19, 1927; Rev. and Mrs. H. Toft and Rev. and Mrs. A. Anderson, who were transferred on July 1, 1928, together with their stations Gunipur and Bissemkattak to the East Jeypore Missionary Society of South Jutland, Denmark; Rev. and Mrs. Albert Schwerdtfeger, Rev. and Mrs. W. F. Adolphsen, Rev C. S. Hayner, who have accepted pastorates in America; Japan— Rev. and Mrs. Louis G. Gray, who have gone to serve as missionaries in the Virgin Islands under the Board of American Missions, and Reba Hendrickson; China—Rev. Dr. and Mrs. J. F. Krueger, who have moved to Springfield, Ohio, where Dr. Krueger has entered upon his duties as professor of practical theology in Hamma Divinity School; Liberia—Amelia Wiebking, R.N., Dorothy Hueter (Mrs. Bluehdorn), Mr. and Mrs. George Cope, Marie Martens, R.N., Mary Bauer, R.N.

COOPERATING SOCIETIES AND SYNODS

The Luther League of America, after having raised $31,000 for Andhra Christian College in India, has taken as its next objective one of the buildings in Villa del Parque, Buenos Aires, to be known as Luther League Hall, for which $12,000 will be contributed. In addition many state, district and congregational leagues are supporting assigned objectives, such as foreign missionaries, Parishes abroad and proteges.

The Women's Missionary Society has continued to give the cause of foreign missions unstinted devotion and enthusiastic cooperation by providing funds for the salaries and allowances of all women missionaries, supporting in full all their work, and providing all necessary buildings and equipment. The society has done so well that every visitor to our foreign fields is impressed with the character and equipment of the work supported by our women. For the year ended June 30th, 1927, the Women's Missionary Society furnished a total of $187,242.43.

The cooperation of the Augustana Synod, the United Danish Church and the Icelandic Synod is greatly appreciated. More recently their contributions have increased, stimulated in the United Danish Church by the return to Japan of Rev. and Mrs. J. M. T. Winther and the call of their daughter, Maya, to serve in our Japan mission. Mrs. Emmy Ewald's visit to our India field in 1927 cannot fail to increase the interest of the Augustana Women's Missionary Society, which has pledged the support of Ada Elizabeth Kron, R.N., as an additional representative of that society in our India mission. The appropriation of the Augustana Synod is $30,000 and of the United Danish Church $12,000.

WIDER CONTACTS AMONG LUTHERAN BOARDS

Cordial relations with other American Lutheran Foreign Mission Boards are cultivated through the Lutheran Foreign Missions Conference. In connection with its annual convention last January in Chicago this conference inaugurated a general public meeting, which it is hoped will become a permanent feature of its regular conventions.

INTERDENOMINATIONAL AND INTERNATIONAL RELATIONS

The Board continues to derive much benefit from participation in the annual meetings of the Foreign Missions Conference of North America, whose executive committee is called the Committee of Reference and Counsel. President Dr. Benze succeeded Secretary Dr. Drach as member of this committee and Dr. F. H. Knubel succeeded Dr. Wolf as a member of the International Missionary Council. Dr. Knubel on his return from India attended the enlarged meeting of this council at Jerusalem during Holy Week, 1928.

LOSSES

Two foreign missionary leaders in our church have gone to their eternal reward. Dr. M. J. Epting, of Savannah, Georgia, died there on July 14, 1927. He came into the merged Board as President of the Board of Foreign Missions of the United Synod in the South, and served since the merger as chairman of the Board's committee on the Japan mission. Rev. J. L. Morgan, D.D., President of the Synod of North Carolina, was elected as his successor.

Rev. Ezra K. Bell, D.D., of Baltimore, Maryland, departed this life on September 13, 1927. He was President of the Board of Foreign Missions of the United Lutheran Church since its organization. He served until his increasing physical disability forbade a reelection in 1926, when he was succeeded in his office by Rev. Prof. C. Theodore Benze, D.D., of Mt. Airy, Philadelphia, Pa. But Dr. Bell continued as a member and honorary president of the Board until his death. Rev. G. Albert Getty, D.D., was elected to fill his unexpired term.

REV. EZRA K. BELL, D.D., LL.D.

Born November 14, 1853.

Died September 13, 1927.

Member of the Board of Foreign Missions from 1899 to 1927.

President of the Board of Foreign Missions of the General Synod from 1916 to 1918.

President of the Board of Foreign Missions of the United Lutheran Church from 1918 to 1926.

Honorary President from November 1926 to the day of his death.

Eminent in the Councils of the Church.

Interested in the whole work of the Church.

A leader in Foreign Missions.

Highly honored by the Board.

Missed by all fellow-workers.

Nominations—The Board nominates the following for terms expiring in 1934:

Rev. J. Edward Byers, D.D., 2900 Guilford Ave., Baltimore, Md.

Rev. George A. Greiss, D.D., 38 S. 8th St., Allentown, Penna.

Rev. H. C. Brillhart, D.D., 19 Spruce St., Leetonia, Ohio.

Rev. E. R. Jaxheimer, 8068-87th Road, Woodhaven, L. I., N. Y.

Mr. A. Y. Leech, Jr., 926-15th St., N. W., Washington, D. C.

Mr. W. A. Rast, Cameron, S. C.

MISSIONARIES ON FURLOUGH

No part of the Home Base work should get more attention than the missionaries on furlough.

The Board must first attend to their physical condition. With this end in view, all Foreign Mission Boards have united in the preparation of a uniform blank, to be filled out by missionaries on their return to America and given consideration, with any medical operation deemed necessary, before the missionary is expected to do any deputation work among the churches. All missionaries are advised to take a few months rest at home, before they begin to visit largely among the churches. Rest and health are of prime importance and the furlough will not accomplish its best purpose for the missionary, unless we can send him back to his tasks renewed in body and mind and refreshed in soul.

Temporary change was made in financing furlough studies due in part to lack of funds. The general idea has been approved that some part of the furlough should be utilized in a course of study, and this should be general for all missionaries during their first and second furloughs, for at least part of the time. The Board had to set some limits to this policy, now, but it will only be temporary, until funds come in more adequately.

All missionaries should aim to do as much work in advocating missions in the Home Churches, as is consistent with their health, rest and studies. Especially those who are home on third or fourth furlough should spend much time to set forth in an attractive and concrete form their own endeavors and the effect of the great cause they represent, on the nations of the non-Christian world. All missionaries have free access to the secretary of the field and are invited to attend the meetings of the Board's committee on the field.

The Board is making such plans as will enable returned missionaries to be located in the Church, so as to reach the congregations in all parts in the most helpful manner, with up-to-date information.

FAREWELL SERVICES

It is customary to hold farewell services for outgoing missionaries. Usually they are held in churches which are particularly interested in the individual missionary. But whoever they are, and wherever they go, every missionary passing through the port of New York, is given a farewell meeting in that city under the auspices of a committee of which Rev. A. Steimle, D.D., is chairman. Steamer boxes with a memento for every day of the voyage, prepared by the missionary societies of the congregations connected with the New York Synods, are presented to the outgoing missionaries and their families. The missionaries have expressed their appreciation of these meetings with their unique features.

Whenever missionaries sail from San Francisco or Seattle the Board arranges farewell meetings there and invariably gets the hearty cooperation of the Presidents of the Pacific coast Synods and of local pastors.

CANDIDATES

Securing recruits for our various fields calls for the Board's most careful attention and thought. It is no easy matter to choose men and women to fill the positions created by the growing and changing needs of our foreign fields. Different men and women, with varied abilities and qualifications, are called for in this great work of the Church. It may not be enough that the individual candidate be certain of his inner call to foreign mission work. Nor again is it enough that intellectually he be fully qualified. It is no easy task to discover how a candidate will meet the situation in Japan, China, India, Africa or South America.

The Board can, at least, make fair provision against a break-down by careful physical examinations by good doctors and by submitting these examination papers to the Board's medical advisers. Uniform medical blanks for candidates have been prepared by the Foreign Missions Conference of North America and are in use among all our American and Canadian Boards. The Board regards approved physical fitness as a fundamental requisite for service in any of our fields, and as especially demanded in our tropical fields.

The personal equation is not so easily arrived at. Confidential letters written by friends of the Board, teachers and professors of candidates, may be regarded as a good way to estimate the qualifications of candidates. Personal interviews with candidates always are valuable. The whole matter of recruiting new missionaries is one that needs careful study. To reach a conclusion concerning qualifications, intellectual and spiritual, the Board cannot move too carefully. Of course for special positions definite training is necessary and it can only be had, in some cases, by a difficult and costly process. In case of special missionaries great care must be exercised in their preparation, because of the cost involved and the uncertainty as to their remaining true to their early promises and their missionary ideals.

FIELD SECRETARY

Rev. M. Edwin Thomas, D.D., the Board's Field Secretary, has endeavored to cultivate the Home Church for the foreign missions cause in the following ways:.

1. Sunday presentations of the cause. In the morning with an address. In the evening with an illustrated lecture.

2. Itineraries of a week or more covering all the week days except Saturday. It was difficult to secure representative audiences, hence this method was largely supplanted by

3. Personal interviews with pastors and leading laymen. For the last year the Parish Abroad plan has been presented to many pastors. Much interest was manifested, as pastors welcome cooperation in improving the spirit of missions among their people.

4. While visiting Synods and conferences efforts were made to meet the members and acquaint them with the problems and progress of our Board. discussions were held, with much interest.

5. Summer schools and assemblies. Group meetings or round-table disclussions were held, with much interest.

Considerable time has been given, in public addresses and private interviews, to the financial problems of our Board. Methods have been suggested whereby assistance could be rendered. A 100 per cent. apportionment has been stressed.

The outlook to-day is very hopeful for larger cooperation on the part of pastors and congregations.

DEPARTMENT OF SPECIAL GIFTS

Through the efforts of the Department of Special Gifts the Board receives an annual income of approximately one hundred thousand dollars. Many congregations, Sunday schools, classes, missionary societies, young people's societies and individuals desire to support special work in our foreign fields and the Department of Special Gifts furnishes the opportunity by making regular assignments. Smaller annual contributions, ranging from $25.00 upward are made for the support of native workers and boys' scholarships, which are assigned by number. The total number supported at present is 574. Larger annual contributions are given for the support of Parishes abroad, which are assigned by name. Patrons are kept in touch with their assigned Parishes Abroad by correspondence with the fields. This new plan, which enables contributors to have direct contacts with their Parishes Abroad, is rapidly growing in favor and our foreign missionaries have pledged their heartiest cooperation.

The most intimate and satisfactory relationships are established between assigned foreign mission pastors and their supporters. While the missionaries are at work in their respective fields they carry on correspondence with their supporters and when they come home on furlough they make personal reports of their work abroad. The annual contribution has been raised to $1200, and it is hoped that the supporters will increase this amount until in each case the entire financial expenditure for the missionary is provided by the supporter. Several congregations are supporting two or three foreign mission pastors and all of them have financially assisted their representatives in the foreign fields in various ways. Several have raised special funds for automobiles to be used in the work of the missionaries.

The California Synod is raising money for a special training class of evangelists among caste people in India. Dr. C. K. Lippard is raising $35,000 for Kobe, Japan.

FOREIGN MISSION PASTORS

$1200 or more Annually

Supporters	Pastor	Missionary	Field
1. Allentown, Pa., St. John's	W. C. Schaeffer, Jr.	O. V. Werner	India
2. Allentown, Pa., Christ's	G. H. Kinard	H. H. Moyer	India
3. Altoona, Pa., Second	George N. Lauffer	Harry Goedeke	India
4. Ashland, O., Trinity	A. H. Smith	J. M. Armbruster	Argentina
5. Baltimore, Md., Second	J. E. Grubb	L. W. Slifer	India
6. Baltimore, Md., St. Mark's	R. D. Clare	I. Cannaday	India
7. Baltimore, Md., St. Paul's	P. A. Heilman	J. D. Curran	Liberia
8. Boyertown, Pa., St. John's	D. F. Longacre	C. E. Swavely	India
9. Brooklyn, N. Y., Redeemer	H. T. Weiskotten	A. F. A. Neudoeffer	India
10. Canton, Ohio, Trinity	E. C. Herman	George Rupley	India
11. Canton, Ohio, Trinity	E. C. Herman	A. C. Knudten	Japan
12. Canton, Ohio, Trinity	E. C. Herman	Harlow E. Haas	B. Guiana
13. Chambersburg, Pa., First	Henry Anstadt	J. W. Miller	Liberia
14. Charleston, S. C., St. Andrews	C. B. Foelsch	C. K. Lippard	Japan
15. Dayton, Ohio, First	Charles L. Venable	G. N. Schillinger	Japan
16. Dayton, Ohio, First	Charles L. Venable	Victor McCauley	India
17. Dayton, Ohio, First	Charles L. Venable	To be assigned	
18. Dixon, Ill., St. Paul's	Lloyd W. Walter	C. G. Caughman	India
19. Fort Wayne, Ind., Trinity	P. H. Krauss	L. A. Gotwald	India
20. Fort Wayne, Ind., Trinity	P. H. Krauss	E. A. Lape	Liberia
21. Grand Rapids, Mich., Trinity	R. J. White	R. H. Daube	B. Guiana
22. Greensburg, Pa., Zion	A. W. Steinfurth	A. Schmitthenner	India
23. Hanover, Pa., St. Mark's	J. S. Tome	To be assigned	Liberia
24. Harrisburg, Pa., Memorial	L. C. Manges	G. R Haaf	India
25. Harrisburg, Pa., Zion's	S. W. Herman	R. M. Dunkelberger	India
26. Harrisburg, Pa., Zion's	S. W. Herman	L. Grady Cooper	China
27. Harrisburg, Pa., Zion's	S. W. Herman	J. K. Linn	Japan
28. Hummelstown, Pa., Zion	C. G. Leatherman	P. O. Machetzki	Argentina
29. Huntington, Pa., St. James	E. L. Manges	P.E.Loudenslager, M.D.	China
30. Icelandic Synod		S. O. Thorlaksson	Japan
31. Johnstown, Pa., First	Henry W. Snyder	A. J. Stirewalt	Japan
32. Mansfield, Ohio, First	Henry C. Roehner	J. C. Finefrock	India
33. Mansfield, Ohio, First	Henry C. Roehner	C. E. Norman	Japan
34. Luther League, N. Y. State		F. W. Heins	Japan
35. Norristown, Pa., Holy Trinity	D. L. Yount	Leon Irschick	India
36. Perkasie-Hilltown, Pa.	C. R. Brobst	George Cope	Liberia
37. Philadelphia, Pa., Messiah	J. Ross Stover	J. E. Graefe	India
38. Philadelphia, Pa., St. John's	Chas. J. Gable	W. Theo. Benze	India
39. Philadelphia, Pa., Tabernacle	W. J. Miller, Jr.	M. L. Dolbeer	India
40. Philadelphia, Pa. Nativity	J. C. Fisher	H. H. Sipes, Jr.	India
41. Philadelphia, Pa., Temple	A. Pohlman	N. R. Sloan, M.D.	Liberia
42. Philadelphia, Pa., St. Matthews	E. Heyl Delk	C. J. Voskamp	China
43. Pittsburgh, Pa., Mt. Zion	G. Elmer Swoyer	J. A. Linn	Japan
44. Pittsburgh, Pa., First	A. J. Holl	F. L. Coleman	India
45. Pottstown, Pa., Emmanuel	I. B. Kurtz	F. J. Fiedler	India
46. Reading, Pa., Trinity	Herman F. Miller	Edward T. Horn	Japan
47. Richmond, Va., First	J. J. Scherer	Robert S. Oberly	Liberia
48. Rockford, Ill., Trinity	H. M. Bannen	C. W. Hepner	Japan
49. Rockford, Ill., Trinity	H. M. Bannen	V. Ch. John	India
50. Rockford, Ill., Trinity	H. M. Bannen	F. H. Bloch	Liberia
51. Shelby, Ohio, First	D. Bruce Young	P. P. Anspach	China
52. Shippensburg, Pa., Memorial	W. W. Barkley	J. Roy Strock	India
53. Sterling, Ill., St. John's	E. C. Harris	S. C. Burger	India
54. Wilkinsburg, Pa., Calvary	L. A. Krouse	C. P. Tranberg	India
55. Wilkinsburg, Pa., Calvary	L. A. Krouse	D. D. Dagle	Liberia
56. Wilmington, Del.	Dr. C. M. Stine	Ray Cunningham	India
57. Winchester, Va., Grace	Chas. A. Freed	L. S. G. Miller	Japan
58. York, Pa., St. Matthew's	J. B. Baker	Harry Heilman	Liberia
59. York, Pa., Zion	G. Albert Getty	J. Russell Fink	India
60. Zanesville, Ohio, St. John's	W. M. Hackenburg	P. M. Counts	Africa

PARISHES ABROAD SUPPORTED

No.	Supporter	Parish Abroad	Field	Amount
1.	United Danish Ch............Kurume, Moji, Shimonseki	.....Hida, Amagi, Japan...$	8,200
2.	St. Luke's, Omaha, Neb........Gao Dschwang.....China		150
3.	First, Warren, Pa............Minamata ....Japan		1,000
4.	Men's Bible Cl., Harrisburg, Pa..Tsingtao, R.Rm....China		100
5.	St. Luke's S. S., Allentown, Pa..Yin Chia Tsun.....China		100
6.	S. S., Friedens, Pa............Mallavolu ....Palnad, India.........		250
7.	Bethlehem, Harrisburg, Pa.....Tunduru ....Narsapur, India.......		500
8.	Grace S. S., Mt. Carmen, Pa...Panidem ....Sattenapalli, India....		105
9.	St. James' S.S., Turbotville, Pa..Teh ....Liberia, Africa......		100
10.	Messiah, McEwensville, Pa....Dodler ....Sattenapalli, India.....		50
11.	Redeemer S.S., Harrisburg, Pa...Andukur ....Sattenapalli, India.....		75
12.	Redeemer, Harrisburg, Pa.....Purupadu ....Sattenapalli, India.....		50
13.	St. John's, Freedom, Pa........Kandlagunta ......Palnad, India.........		75
14.	Moxham S. S., Johnstown, Pa...Blind School .....Rentichintala, India...		500
15.	Mr. and Mrs. Kueter, Rochester, N. Y............Chintapalli ....Sattenapalli, India		50
16.	S. S., Trindle Springs, Mechanicsburg, Pa..........Fan Chia Tan.....China		100
17.	St. Paul's, Leetonia, Ohio.....Velduty H. E. Sch.Palnad, India.........		200
18.	S. S., Muhlenberg, Phila., Pa...Tangeda ....Palnad, India.........		200
19.	Pine St. Ch., Danville, Pa.....Gondapalli ....Yelleswaram, India....		100
20.	St. John's, Lewistown, Pa.....Tai Tung Chen.....China		565
21.	Trinity, Pottsville, Pa........Kumamoto, Suido..Japan		500
22.	Women's Miss. Society, Stephens, Pittsburgh, Pa.....Kommara ....Tadepalligudem, India.		55
23.	St. John's, Swissvale, Pittsburgh, Pa...............Ling Shan........China		100
24.	St. Paul's S. S., Spring Grove, Pa............Velduty ....Palnad, India.........		400
25.	Grace, Altoona, Pa............Narsaravupet ......India		500
26.	Holy Communion, Phila., Pa...Fukushima, Osaka..Japan		700
27.	First, Madam Cotta Society Greensburg, Pa............Domeru ....Tallapudi, India.......		500
28.	Bethlehem, Pa., Rosemont.....Jeddangi ....India		100
29.	Grace, L. L., Baltimore, Md...Adigopala ....Palnad, India		100
30.	St. Matthew's S. S. Class Toledo, Ohio...............Vissakoder ....Bhimawaram, India....		80
31.	W. M. S., H. Trinity, Jeanette, Pa...............Tsao An ....China		100
32.	Redeemer S. S., Buffalo, N. Y..Okubo, Tokyo ....Japan		825
33.	Holy Trinity L. L., Miss. Cl., Pittsburgh, Pa..............Inimetla ....Sattenapalli, India		75
34.	St. Paul's S. S., Altoona, Pa...Mutyalammapadu ..Palnad, India.........		100
35.	Trinity S. S., Germantown, Pa..Sattenapalli, Ch....India		205
36.	S. S. H. Trinity, Buffalo, N. Y..Sakhinatipalli ...Narsapur, India.......		330
37.	E. L. S. S., Tyrone, Pa.......Sanoyea Agriculture Dept......Liberia, Africa.......		200
38.	S. S., Incarnation, Phila., Pa...Gorlamudi ....Bhimawaram, India....		110
39.	Trinity S. S., Camp Hill, Pa....Sun Gia ....China		50
40.	St. Paul's Y. W. M. S., Altoona, Pa................Pillutla ....Palnad, India.........		50
41.	Augsburg S. S., Harrisburg, Pa.Gurzala ....Palnad, India.........		580
42.	Christ, Wm. Smith, Aspers, Pa..Panidem Rural Sch.Sattenapalli, India....		105
43.	Bethel, Phila., Pa............Higher E. School..Sattenapalli, India....		500
44.	St. John's P. M., Steelton, Pa..Muhlenberg, Cong..Liberia, Africa.......		100
45.	Bethany S. S., Braddock, Pa...Mulakaluru ......Narsaravupet, India...		100
46.	St. John's S. S., Erie, Pa......Kottapalli ....Bhimawaram, India....		100
47.	S. S. Assn., Greensburg, Conf., Pa................Tallapudi ....India		1,000
48.	S. S., H. Comm., Utica, N. Y...Manchili ....Bhimawaram, India....		55
49.	S. S., Bethany, Pittsburgh, Pa..Dachepalli ....Palnad, India.........		515

Total pledged...................$20,605

PUBLICITY AND LITERATURE

With the limited means at the disposal of the Board as much publicity as possible is given to our foreign mission work. After each meeting of the Board news items are released and published in our church papers. The publicity department has arranged with special committees in our foreign fields for monthly news letters and articles to be published in the magazines of the Board in "The Lutheran," "Lutheran Boys and Girls," "Lutheran Young Folks," "Luther League Review," and papers published by the Augustana Synod and United Danish Church.

"Der Missionsbote" has been ably edited by Rev. G. Julius Hoeppner, of Norristown, Pa., since the resignation of Rev. R. C. G. Bielinski, in 1925. Dr. Drach has continued to edit "The Foreign Missionary," the English monthly magazine of the Board, which has nearly 8000 subscribers. This number could easily be increased if all pastors would voluntarily serve as agents, or appoint agents to secure subscriptions in their congregations and Sunday schools.

In addition to the Annual Report of our Foreign Missions, sent free to every pastor, the Board has published and circulated a number of pamphlets and leaflets, such as "The Parish Abroad," "Needy Fields," and "Seeing Things in the Far East."

A part of the publicity work of the Board is done in the Department of Stereoptican Slides and Lectures. Twenty-four lectures with colored slides on our six mission fields are in constant use and have given very good satisfaction wherever the pictures have been shown.

FOREIGN MISSION DAY

Every encouragement has been given to reintroduce in all Sunday schools the observance of Foreign Mission Day at the close of the Epiphany Season. Free literature, programs and envelopes are offered to those who will use them. We trust that this convention will approve the recommendation of the Board that on Foreign Mission Day in 1929, and again in 1930, special offerings in all churches and schools be taken to help cancel the indebtedness of the Board. The plan which the Board suggests is that an average of fifty cents per communicant member be solicited for this special purpose.

REORGANIZATION OF THE ADMINISTRATIVE WORK OF THE BOARD

The Board began its operations after the merger with three General Secretaries, Drs. Wolf, Drach and Brown. After the death of Dr. Brown the attempt was made to conduct the business of the Board, owing to its increasing financial burdens, without filling the place thus vacated, although the operations of the Board were expanded by adding the mission in China. Later Dr. Thomas was added to the staff as Field Secretary for the cultivation of the Home Church for larger financial support.

During the past biennium the Board has given itself to a thorough study of its administrative and financial problems. A reorganization of its work has been planned by its division into four departments, a Home Base department, a Foreign Fields department, a Literature department, and a Finance department, with departmental secretaries in charge and one Executive Secretary who is charged with the general supervision of the entire work of the Board and to whom the Board will look as the responsible officer for the execution of its policies. The Standing Committees of the Board will correspond to these departments with such sub-committees as may be deemed necessary. The Executive Committee shall consist of the officers of the Board, chairman of the standing committees and three others.

The Board elected the Rev. Paul W. Koller, D.D., President of the Synod of Ohio, as its Executive Secretary. He has accepted the call and will assume office December 1, 1928.

The present staff of Secretaries has loyally accepted the decision of the Board to reorganize its work and has placed its knowledge and experience at the command of the newly elected Executive Secretary. The final allocation of the present staff to the departments will be made by the Board in cooperation with the Executive Secretary and will be put into effect with his assumption of office.

The Board has also directed the Missions to bring their fiscal years into harmony with the fiscal year of the Board and of the United Lutheran Church.

INDIA

"No work our Church is doing anywhere is more prosperous and promising than our missionary work in India," is the slogan proposed by Drs. Knubel and Miller after their recent visit to our mission field in India.

Perhaps the rank and file in our Lutheran Church in America does not sufficiently appreciate the value of our mission work in India. After eighty-five years of continuous and consecrated effort, beginning with the pioneer Rev. C. F. Heyer, M.D., familiarly called Father Heyer, we now have a Lutheran Church in the Andhra or Telugu country. Its organization is one of the outstanding achievements of our American Lutheran Church. How proud we ought to be of our daughter church in India! We greatly rejoice that she has reached the age of maturity and is ambitious for independence. As she starts out on her own career we regard her with loving solicitude and wish her happiness in her work and predict for her great power and influence in helping to accomplish the as yet unfinished task of Christianizing India. To be sure her independence is not yet complete. She will need our help and advice and will welcome our continued financial cooperation. The spheres in which complete independence must wait on self-support are especially those of higher education and inner mission work in the hospitals. Moreover, there are still many details of congregational life, evangelistic effort and village education, which will require a longer period of readjustment.

The departments which have been transferred to the Synods and the Andhra Lutheran Church are gospel, evangelistic and congregational work and primary schools in the villages. Elementary and higher elementary schools are to be under the general supervision of four missionaries, assisted by a staff of supervisors. Ministerial acts ordinarily are to be performed by Indian pastors. Church councils are to administer discipline. District missionaries thus relieved of a large part of their administrative duties are to do definite evangelistic work among unreached classes of society under the direction of the Council of missionaries. The educational and medical departments are to be in charge of boards of control, elected by the Council, which will recommend to the Board all financial appropriations and exercise veto power on all items requiring Board action. The constitution of these boards of control is to be subject to revision at any time and must be reviewed in any event at the end of five years of experimentation.

MISSIONARIES

The number of missionaries in India has decreased slightly during the past two years but not sufficiently to cripple permanently the force at work in the field. On the other hand the number of Indian pastors has increased to 50, and evangelists are being trained in a special class at Luthergiri for work among Sudras, middle class people, who are coming into the Church in increasing numbers. The work of the women missionaries has been carried on and developed in a most satisfactory manner. The total number of missionaries in India, counting those on furlough, is as follows: 31 ordained men, 2 unordained men, 32 wives and 35 single women missionaries.

We mourn the loss of one of the most zealous and successful district missionaries, Rev. H. E. Dickey, who died at his station, Repalle, on October 2, 1926, stricken down in the strength of his manhood in the midst of abounding activity; also of a number of faithful Indian pastors and other workers.

During the past two years Rev. and Mrs. Oscar V. Werner were transferred from Ranchi, Bihar, to Luthergiri, Rajahmundry, to teach in the theological seminary and Bible training school. Rev. Dr. and Mrs. Isaac Cannaday, after having finished their term of service in India, left Ranchi in March, 1928, to spend a well-earned furlough in America. Thus our last personal link with the Gossner Evangelical Lutheran Church in Chota Nagpur has been severed. The National Lutheran Council, however, still is giving this church much-needed financial assistance.

We cannot in this report mention the names and describe the work of all our missionaries in India, but we can say without fear of contradiction, that they all are doing their assigned tasks faithfully and well.

EAST JEYPORE FIELD

The return of West Jeypore to the Schleswig-Holstein Missionary Society of Germany has relieved us of a heavy burden which, however, we cheerfully bore in order to preserve an important mission field in India for the Lutheran Church. Our last appropriation to this society was paid during the first half of the year 1928. On July 1st we ceased all payments, our missionaries having withdrawn before that date.

The Schleswig-Holstein Society gave us as a mark of gratitude all of the East Jeypore field with stations and mission property at Salur, Parvatipur, Gunipur and Bissemkattak. The last two named stations were transferred with the consent of the Schleswig-Holstein Society on July 1, 1928, to the newly organized missionary society in South Jutland, Denmark, which at its organization in March, this year, established a cooperative relationship with the Church of Denmark Missionary Society. The services of Missionaries Toft and Andersen were transferred at the same time and subsequently they moved to Gunipur and Bissemkattak. The East Jeypore Missionary Society is to pay nothing for the mission property but has reimbursed our Board for the salaries and allowances of Missionaries Toft and Andersen from October 1, 1927 to the date of the transfer.

The disposal of the Salur and Parvatipur stations is still undecided. Some of our missionaries want us to keep them because they lie in the Telugu speaking area and the congregations there eventually could be incorporated into the Lutheran Church of the Andhra country, while others favor the total abandonment of all work at Salur and Parvatipur, if the Schleswig-Holstein Society will not take them back. Abandonment would mean that Roman Catholics would get this field, in which they have become very aggressive.

ANDHRA CHRISTIAN COLLEGE

Dr. J. Roy Strock, who on his return to India succeeded Rev. Hiram H. Sipes as principal of the college, has tried to find the right solution to the problem of locating Andhra Christian College, for which he and his wife raised nearly $250,000 in America. The solution waits on the decision of the Madras Presidency in regard to the site of the Andhra University. Some of our missionaries are in favor of staying in Guntur and developing our first-grade college there, despite the refusal of the Church Missionary Society of England to cooperate with us at Guntur. Others think that the Andhra Christian College should be located at Bezwada, thus insuring the cooperation of other Protestant missions in the Andhra country. The Board has asked our mission to invite all other Protestant missions to join us at Guntur. Still the final decision must wait the act of the Madras legislature. Meanwhile we rejoice in the pledged cooperation of the Joint Synod of Ohio, which has assigned Rev. Nicholson to serve next year as professor in the college at Guntur. Moreover, the expenditure of the Andhra Christian College Fund has begun by the appropriations for permanent scientific apparatus, amounting to about $5,000.

New Buildings

The new boys' high school building in Guntur was completed and occupied in 1927, thus giving adequate accommodations for this school, which is being conducted in connection with the college. The number of pupils has reached the gratifying total of 599 in the college and 381 in the high school. After the withdrawal of Mr. V. Ch. John, who had been elected to membership in the Madras Legislative Council, a political position of influence, Rev. F. J. Fiedler became the head-master of the high school.

New church buildings have been erected at Tenali, Sattenapalli and Narsapur. Those at Tenali and Sattenapalli each cost approximately $8000. Contributions for the first mentioned, which still awaits completion, have been given by St. Paul's Lutheran Church of Richmond, Indiana, Rev. J. P. Miller, D.D., pastor. The Seventh Street Lutheran of Lebanon, Pa., Rev. C. E. Leibegott, pastor, is providing for the Narsapur church, which will cost about $6000. The mission also has begun the erection of the Nicum Memorial Church on a new site at Dowlaishwaram, to be built according to plans approved for the Sattenapalli church and to cost about the same. The old church building is to be converted into a higher elementary school for boys.

Lest we duplicate information we leave the recital of the progress of the work of our women missionaries and of the erection of new buildings at Bhimawaram, Repalle, Guntur, Chirala, and Rajahmundry to the report of the Women's Missionary Society.

Medical Work

On her return to India in December, 1927, the mission again put Dr. Anna S. Kugler in charge of the hospital at Guntur. Dr. Betty Nilsson after the death of her mother in America, at Easter, 1927, remained at her post of duty at the head of the hospital in Rajahmundry. Dr. Mary Baer, after staying in India nine years beyond the time of her furlough, is now on her way to America. What the mission needs and urges is a group of men physicians and the education of Indian men in the science of medicine and surgery.

One of the outstanding Indian leaders is Dr. Samuel John, who has done excellent work as a physician and surgeon at Nidadavol and in the Tuberculosis Sanitorium at Rajahmundry. Indians, however, cannot get the degree of doctor of medicine unless they take a post-graduate course in England or the United States. To secure his degree Mr. Samuel John has been sent to England for a two years' course of study, after which it is hoped he may come to America on a visit.

The Board appeals to all physicians and surgeons in the United Lutheran Church for a fund of about $4000 to complete in England the medical education of Samuel John.

Mission Industries

Another department of mission work deserves special mention in this report, namely the mission industries. In addition to the flourishing lace industry, centering at Narsaravupet in the Guntur field and in the new buildings of the Lace Industry at Rajahmundry, there is more or less industrial work at every boarding school in the mission. The purpose of this work is to train the boarding boys and girls to be useful as well as educated members of society in the communities to which they will return after their school days.

It is to be regretted that lack of funds has delayed the development of the Mission Farm School on the Lam Reserve near Guntur, which should become an Agricultural Training School for the entire mission.

The mission printeries at Guntur and Rajahmundry are spreading the Good News through the printed page.

Reduced Appropriations

The Board has been obliged since 1925 to reduce its appropriations for the India mission as well as for the other missions; but it found itself able as a result of larger anticipated income from apportionments, to grant the India mission the same amount during the fiscal year, July 1, 1928 to June 30, 1929, as during the calendar year 1927, namely $187,000. This amount is for the running expenses of the work in charge of the men. The Women's Missionary Society provides an additional amount for the work of the women missionaries. Salaries and allowances of the men will call for an expenditure of $53,000 during the fiscal year. The total estimate for the India mission, including all items except the work of the women missionaries and their salaries, is $256,200. Whatever is needed for new buildings must be extra.

Federation of Lutheran Churches and Missions

The All-India Lutheran Conference, which functioned for many years as a common agency for cooperative programs and projects, has given way to the Federation of Lutheran Churches and Missions in India. A tentative constitution has been submitted to the Board, which in turn presents it to this convention of the United Lutheran Church. The proposed constitution is printed in full in appendix A of this report.

The following table will give a good idea of the relative strangth of the missions and churches in this Federation in India.

Statistics of Lutheran Missions and Churches in India, 1927

NAME OF MISSION OR CHURCH	Baptised Members	Communicant Members	Total No. of Baptisms		No. of Missionaries including Wives	No. of ordained Missionaries	No. of Indian Pastors	No. of the whole Indian Staff	Contribution on the field during the year
			Children of Christian Parents	Non-Christians					
1. Santal Mission	17,028	257	498	405	48	14	21	432	$ 3,935.00
2. E. L. Church in C. P.	2,270	1,050	81	48	31	9	5	266	1,369.00
3. Gossner E. L. Church	111,406	65,801	3,907	1,461	6	4	50	958	12,223.00
4. Jeypore E. L. Church	18,300	4,800	780	436	10	5	5	325	3,350.00
5. Andhra E. L. Church	129,865	54,178	5,031	195	99	31	50	3,339	135,009.00
6. O. E. L. Mission	4,658	......	130	829 5	17	8	2	216	927.00
7. Danish Mission	4,727	......	177	180	53	11	13	327	3,882.00
8. Tamil E. L. Church	25,155	10,779	783	495	60	15	36	774	58,898.00
Total	313,409	136,892	11,387	9,214	324	97	182	6,637	$219,593.00

Explanatory Notes:

1. The Santal Mission of the Northern Churches is a combined effort of Norwegians and Danes in Europe and America, among Santals in North East India and Assam.
2. The Evangelical Lutheran Church in the Central Provinces is in the field of the Evangelical National Society of Sweden, among the Gonds.
3. The Gossner Evangelical Lutheran Church is in Chota Nagpur, among the Kols, Mundas and Oraons.
4. The Jeypore Evangelical Lutheran Church is in the field of the Schleswig-Holstein Mission.
5. The Andhra Evangelical Lutheran Church is in the field of our mission in the Telugu country
6. The Ohio Evangelical Lutheran Missionary among Telugus is the successor of the Hermannsberg Mission.
7. The Danish Mission has headquarters in Madras.
8. The Tamil Evangelical Lutheran Church is in the fields of the Leipzig and Church of Sweden Missions, South of Madras.

AFRICA

LIBERIA REPUBLIC

The great continent of Africa commands much more attention since the World War. That part which, under the control of the African, should receive more sympathy and help than those parts which are under European influence. All mandated parts have become the general concern of the League of Nations, of which Liberia is a member.

Our medical work at the main station has been hindered by the sickness and death of Dr. C. H. Nielsen, on January 21, 1928. But the vacancy made by this sad loss was at once filled by the appointment of Dr. J. R. Jensen; and the medical work will be strengthened by the calling of Dr. Norman R. Sloan to join our staff in 1928.

The medical work in the interior was again taken in hand on the return of Dr. E. A. Lape in the summer of 1927. Miss Amelia Wiebking left the work as nurse of the Phoebe Hospital in 1928, and Miss K. M. Jensen has been appointed to take her place. Dr. John Ziegler, a native of Liberia, has finished his studies and internship in America, and expects to join the mission's medical staff in a year or two. His debts have made him delay entering the work.

The enforced withdrawal from the work of Mr. George Cope is a great set-back to agricultural work. He fully expects to return as soon as domestic conditions permit. Meanwhile efforts are being made to carry on with the help of local assistance.

The theological school is in the hands of Rev. K. R. Jensen, and the High School work is looked after by other members of the staff, awaiting the arrival of the new appointee for this position, the Rev. A. H. Kaitschuk, who will join the mission shortly.

The evangelistic work is maintained at all the interior stations. Nothing of special note has transpired, but the congregation at Harrisburg, (Girls' School Side of St. Paul River), is showing new life. The Day Memorial Church, for which the Women's Executive Board has $3,560 in hand, is in process of erection, and work is being pushed to completion. At all our interior stations Revs. P. M. Counts, D. D. Dagle, O. E. Bluehdorn, Miss Bertha Koenig and Sister Laura Gilliland have done faithful work.

The building operations and general industrial work shops are under the direction of our faithful and efficient builder, Mr. J. W. Miller. He is erecting the Neibel Memorial Bungalow, and will utilize that fund and draw on the R. D. J. A. Fund for any additional money needed.

Our Africa mission greatly needs a new Boys' School building. The mission was authorized to purchase the Massaquoi house, as a residence for the President of the Mission Conference, and every effort is being made to equip this mission with suitable missionary residences.

This biennium was signalized by the visit of General Secretary Dr. L. B. Wolf to Liberia in July of 1927. It was not intended as a visit of inspection, but rather as an effort to give effect to the new organization of our mission. To those interested, the reading of Appendix B is urged. It will give any one a very good idea of what a field must have in the way of organization, when missionaries are separated by miles of trackless or roadless distances, and can only rarely meet for consultation.

Liberia has cost in life and money a great deal to our Church. We claim for its work a continuance of effort and sacrifice. Soon sixty-nine years will have been rounded out. A better day is dawning and our missionaries are as much devoted to their work, and hopeful of its ultimate success, as those of any other field.

JAPAN

Our missionaries declare that both the direct and indirect influence of Christianity on Japan is constantly growing stronger. As a matter of fact our mission in the islands of Hondo and Kyushu is in a most flourishing condition. The more recent provision of equipment for the stations on the main island has greatly encouraged our missionaries. In Tokyo on the site purchased several years ago an attractive and substantial two-story church building has been erected, which is a credit to our Lutheran Church in the capital city of Japan. Another and less substantial church has been built in another part of the city, where success has crowned the work of Pastor Iwanaga.

The hub of the Lutheran Church in Japan is the theological seminary at Tokyo. After the resignation of Rev. J. P. Nielsen and the departure of Rev. Edward T. Horn, D.D., on furlough, Rev. John K. Linn carried on alone, which he was able to do because of the exceptional staff of Japanese professors: Rev. I. Miura, Rev. S. Sato and Prof. N. Asagi. On his return to Japan in the fall of this year Dr. Horn will go back to his work as theological professor.

It is fortunate that when Missionary Stirewalt left Japan on furlough, he could leave the Bethany Home for Widows and Children, and the Old People's Home in charge of Miss Grace Beers. These homes are institutions of mercy which grew out of our relief work after the great earthquake.

Nagoya and Toyohashi, where Rev. A. C. Knudten labored before he took his furlough, have been under the care of Rev. Mr. Hirai, who will be remembered as one of the Japanese students in America several years ago. A temporary church building on a rented site is used in part as a residence for the Japanese pastor in Nagoya.

Thanks to the J. E. Cooper legacy of $16,000, Osaka now has a permanent site, on which a parsonage has been built, which is used temporarily as a church by the congregation under the pastoral care of Rev. K. Takimoto. Rev. and Mrs. C. W. Hepner have gone to Germany on furlough and expect to come later to America. The congregation in Kyoto is served by Rev. T. Yonemura, whose daughter, Eiko, has finished her education in America and is returning to Japan to become a teacher in the girls' school at Kumamoto. Rev. S. O. Thorlaksson, representing the Icelandic Synod, is in charge at Kobe, where a new site for the church and parsonage has been purchased with funds collected by Dr. C. K. Lippard.

Work in North Kyushu is under the supervision of Missionaries J. Arthur Linn and E. Clarence Norman, cooperating with their Japanese pastors and evangelists. Rev. Mr. Norman also has charge of the Fukuoka Newspaper Evangelism office.

At Kumamoto, headquarters for work in the island of Kyushu, are located the large and flourishing schools for boys and girls. Additional equipment for the girls' school including the second unit of the dormitory is being gradually provided by the Women's Missionary Society, which also has pledged $2,500 a year for four years to endow the school in order to secure government recognition. Miss Martha Akard as American principal, Mr. Murakami as Japanese dean and Miss Marion Potts as a teacher in the school, are very much pleased with its record of progress.

At the commencement exercises of the boys' school, Kyushu Gakuin, on March 3, 1928, a class of one hundred and five young men was graduated. The efficient Japanese principal is Prof. S. Toyama, the American dean is Dr. L. S. G. Miller. Rev. H. Inadomi, who teaches in the school, is the pastor of the congregation which worships in the Brown Memorial Church. Another congregation in the city is served by Rev. M. Ishimatsu. Rev. G. W. Schillinger is returning to Japan this fall to resume his duties as teacher of English in Kyushu Gakuin. The Misses Anna and Maud Powlas supervise the work at the Colony of Mercy, for which the Women's Missionary Society has provided a much needed missionaries' home and has planned a Kindergarten building, which is to be a memorial to Mrs. E. C. Cronk.

Kurume is the city where Rev. and Mrs. J. M. T. Winther in 1900 began the work of the United Danish Church. Their return to this city this year, after an absence of several years in Denmark, was welcomed with rejoicing by the congregation and the out-stations of that field. Miss Maya, their daughter, will join them this fall, as the first woman missianary to represent and be supported by the United Danish Church.

Rev. and Mrs. W. F. Heins, New York State Luther League missionaries, and the Misses Faith Lippard and Amy Thoren, are working in Saga and Ogi, where there are congregations and kindergartens. Omuta and Minamata, the southermost station, are in charge of Japanese workers. All the Japanese pastors, evangelists and teachers are doing faithful and efficient work and are enthusiastically cooperating to build up a strong, vigorous, self-supporting, self-propagating Lutheran Church in the islands of the Empire of the Rising Sun.

SOUTH AMERICA
BRITISH GUIANA

This Mission has had a biennium of quiet growth. In New Amsterdam, on the Berbice River, among the Arawak Indians and among the immigrated East Indians, the work has gone on with encouraging signs of progress.

A new missionary, Rev. Robert H. Daube, was called, commissioned and entered the work in 1927. He was a much-needed addition to our staff. Rev. Harlow Edgar Haas came home on furlough that year. Since the taking over of the work by our Church in 1915, the Board had carried on with one missionary; but with the opening of our Industrial plant in New Amsterdam a second man is needed. Our Indian work, which is in a progressive condition, should get more attention, as well as the work among the immigrated Hindus. We have given some attention to the Hindu peoples, and Catechists are employed among them with good prospects of success. There is quite a large community of these people in the colony, especially in the large towns on the coast, Georgetown and New Amsterdam.

The Mission in this British Colony presents two very interesting branches of work. The old historic church in New Amsterdam dates back to the settlement of the country by Dutch Lutherans. They founded Ebenezer congregation almost two hundred years ago; and as in all their colonies they endowed this church. Services were conducted as long as a Lutheran pastor lived in New Amsterdam. When a pastor from Holland no longer was found, the Government of the British Colony became responsible for the endowment until one of the colonists came to the United States, united with the East Penn. Synod and for many years looked after the interests of the mother congregation in New Amsterdam and carried on an organized work along the Berbice River and among the Arawak Indians. These Indians live in the interior more than 100 miles from the mouth of the river in the wilds of dense forests.

Two Arawak congregations, with schools, are in good condition. This Mission is most encouraging and should be pushed more vigorously. It has shown signs of vigorous and healthy life, both in church and school. The colony's government encourages the mission schools by grants-in-aid and in other ways.

The ethnic group within the Church and Mission from New Amsterdam down to the Arawak Indian congregations and their schools, is a mixture of several racial strains and with the large influx of Hindus the race question will grow more complex. Dutch, English, Hindu, Indian and Negro, with other racial blendings are to be found in the Colony.

Mission work is carried on under the encouraging hand of the British Colonial Government, which makes life and mission work for our American missionaries very pleasant.

ARGENTINA

This part of the Evangelical Movement in South America has been the most rapid in its growth of any foreign work under the Board. It is now only eight years since the Board took over the struggling plant in Buenos Aires, the greatest metropolis of the South American continent. By wisely selecting the site for the Movement in Villa del Parque, the founder and first missionary of the United Lutheran Church in America deserves great credit. He certainly, both in site chosen and in the method of work he inaugurated, laid a sure foundation for this prosperous enterprise.

At the time of the last report Dr. L. B. Wolf had just completed the work of reorganization, and during this biennium every step made has shown that the field was ready for the organization which the missionaries recommended to the Board. The national workers in the school and church have merited all the responsibility which has been laid on them.

Our congregations have increased in number and membership, our schools have prospered and our Colegio Nacional has taken a strong hold on the whole community. We have in all our schools, including Sunday schools, 1,560 pupils. In our Colegio Nacional, in the lower and upper classes, in the Mehring Memorial, there are 474 boys and girls reading; and such work has great influence.

Our staff of workers has been increased by Miss Myrtle Wilke. Two of our sub-pastors, Messrs. Soler and Villaverde are coming at their own cost to America to study at Wittenberg College, to prepare for future work. Some of our North American friends who have visited South America may assist in some way these young men, but no Board grant has been asked for them in their preparation.

The Board is fully convinced that in the great city of Buenos Aires and out into the country we should push our movement and strengthen both our school and church work in all ways possible. Some congregation in North America should undertake to support Rev. Hugo Froese, whose willingness to join our staff and whose experience in work in Argentine and command of Spanish, would make him a most helpful asset to our working force. Only our shortage in funds prevents the Board from calling him at once to serve in our Mission. Who will respond to this loud call?

The growth in church membership and the congregational life has been healthy. Three young men are preparing for the Christian ministry. The Sunday schools connected with all the schools are well attended, with an enrollment in the confirmation classes of 40 and in the Sunday schools of 536. There is an increase in communicants of 72, and in baptized members of 169. A total communicant membership of 440 is reported, of whom 162 are men and 278 are women.

A Luther League of 190 members, a Girls' Society of 93, a Women's Society of 40, and a Children s Club of 31 show that the churches are well organized for all members and all classes of work.

CHINA

Our China Mission, as now conducted by the United Lutheran Church in America, has completed almost five years. We can never forget that much sacrifice was brought and faithful labor expended since its organization in 1898 by the Berlin Mission Society and their able missionaries. Two new missionaries have been added to our foreign staff during the two years of the period under report. Since January, 1928, however, the foreign staff has suffered severe loss in the withdrawal of Dr. J. F. Krueger, which in part is off-set by the commissioning and sending out of Rev. L. Grady Cooper and Lydia Reich, R.N., and the appointment of Rev. Charles H. Reinbrecht. Thus our missionary force, including the wives of missionaries, now numbers eighteen. Dr. and Mrs. C. J. Voskamp were on furlough during the biennium and will return this fall to their post in Hankow in connection with the Work assigned him by the Board.

In the report of the Mission to the Board the following appears: "The reappraisal and reorganization of the Mission work have led to a better understanding of the Mission." The financial outlook so far as the property purchase is concerned, is good. The Board, in taking over the property from the Berlin Society has up to date paid $70,867.00, and there remains only $114,133.00 yet due on the total ten-year payment of $185,000.

The Board continued negotiations for sometime on the question of paying interest on balances due the Berlin Society at the end of each year. As a result it was mutually agreed that no interest would be paid by the United Lutheran Church Board to the Berlin Society after December 31, 1926.

Every letter from our missionaries could not but fill us with anxiety. War and strife prevailed in China. Banditry went on unhindered. But no evil befell our missionaries, though it was a time of peril for our native Church and Christians in the Shantung province.

During the turmoil our Tsingtao station became a place of refuge for other missionaries and some of them gladly turned in and helped to carry on our work. The Mission did some special evangelistic work among the soldiers in Kiaochow, as they passed back and forth; and our Church became the center of famine relief for the distribution of funds to the poor and distressed in our field.

BIBLE WOMEN

Our Bible women had a specially blessed year among the women in our field. The training of Bible women for work in the district was carried on by Miss Freda Strecker with much success at Kiaochow, and both at the main stations and in the outlying villages encouraging results attended their efforts.

MISSION SCHOOLS

New schools were opened and Miss Brown and Miss Ruth Bracken of the Southern Presbyterian Church gave valuable help in conducting this branch of work. A Men's Bible Class was organized in Tsingtao and became a charter member of the International Sunday School Association in America. In Tsimo the Sunday school in the Girls' School building was attended by 60 men, quite a number of women and 20 children.

The Mission is trying to help to solve the educational problem of new China. It is doing all it can to meet the regulations and conform to them in the management of its educational work. Our Primary Schools have 1,123 scholars. In our Middle School in Tsimo we have 44 boys and 13 girls; in all schools we have a total attendance of 1,669. Five young men attended the Theological School at Shekow, and in our Bible Schools for Christian workers at Kiaochow there are 15 men and 15 women students. Teachers in mission schools number 76.

NATIVE CHURCH

The native church carries on its work in 35 preaching places in the field, and the number of preachers and evangelists is forty-two.

The baptized members number 2,390. Of these, twelve hundred and thirty-seven are communicants.

The accessions last year were 196 and inquirers, 245. Both in spiritual growth and in numbers the Mission has every reason to be encouraged to press on.

MEDICAL WORK

The medical department has not had much to show in the way of progress. The enforced temporary furlough of Dr. P. E. Loudenslager and the employment of Miss Reich in the study of Chinese at the language school in Pekin, have retarded the establishment of this department.

Our dispensary, however, at Tsimo, without an American doctor, under the direction of Mrs. W. Matzat, a trained nurse, assisted by a Chinese physician, gave physical relief to 1,450 patients during the last year. The Mission rejoices that it can look forward to enlarged medical work in Tsimo and Kiaochow and new developments in Tsingtao after the return of Dr. Loudenslager.

PROPOSED LUTHERAN COLLEGE IN CHINA

Rev. Prof. K. B. Westman, Missionary of the Church of Sweden, in China, and head of the Joint Lutheran College at Taochwalun, Yi Yang, Hunan Province, visited the Board Rooms and laid the full scheme for the reorganization of the Lutheran College before our Board Secretaries.

A new constitution was submitted to our Board together with all the facts of its previous existence since its founding in 1920. Buildings have been erected at a cost of $75,000. The running expenses have averaged $9,000 per year and the student body 30 with 13 professors.

The Missions cooperating are asked to make a grant of from $2,000 to $3,000 per year and the college is to be governed by a Board of Directors of six members to be chosen, as follows:

1. Two (2) members and substitutes shall be elected by the Church of Sweden Mission Board in addition to the superintendent of this mission, who shall be *ex-officio* chairman of the Board, and three (3) members and substitutes elected by the Council of the Lutheran Church of China. The elected members shall serve for a period of three (3) years. The Board shall be responsible to the Church of Sweden Mission Board and the Council of the Lutheran Church of China for the administration of the institution. It shall give an annual report to these two bodies.

The Board has taken action in favor of the reorganization of the college so as to provide one college for all Lutheran Missions and Churches in China, and has instructed our Mission in China to give careful consideration to its policy for college education in relation to this Joint Lutheran College at Taohwalun, Yi Yang, Hunan, China.

PROPOSED LUTHERAN COOPERATION WITH THE NATIONAL CHRISTIAN COUNCIL OF CHINA

The reorganization plan of the National Christian Council of China proposes to deal with the entire Lutheran Church in China as an integral unit of this new organization. The Lutheran Church in China now has a membership of 15,662. It is proposed to accord Lutherans four members of the Council in a total membership of 78. The whole question will be considered by our mission in consultation with the other Lutheran Missions in China. No definite agreement has been reached as yet.

CONCLUSION

What conclusion will the reader of this report reach? It is evident that our foreign mission program has assumed a wide comprehensiveness of effort both at the home base and in the foreign fields. This should appeal to the whole-hearted devotion of all our churches. With fields in three continents and work in six fields, with missionary contacts among people speaking eight different languages, with a mandate from God to preach His Word to nations whose religious and cultural backgrounds differ as widely as primitive animism and Confucianism or Hinduism, with changing industrial and social conditions, producing such significant events as the war in China, the unrest in India, the rise of Japan to a world-power, the awakening of Africa, with newly organized Lutheran churches in India and Japan, with a missionary responsibility for no less than 25,000,000 people, living within the bounds of our mission fields, we call upon all pastors and congregations in the United Lutheran Church to give more thought to the great work which our Church is doing in Foreign Missions.

The Board must have more financial support. The cause of foreign missions should receive more adequate recognition in the apportionment, from which the bulk of the Boards income is received. It must get more than 67 per cent. from the amount apportioned. Fortunately, the income from special gifts in support of foreign mission pastors, Parishes Abroad and Proteges is increasing, and the cooperating Augustana, United Danish and Icelandic Synods are more nearly meeting their pledged appropriations. Still the income from all sources is not sufficient to carry on the Church's work already established in our foreign fields. The character of foreign mission work demands increasing expansion, constant growth, uninterrupted progress.

The imperative needs of our foreign fields may be reduced to this appeal for increased financial income. We have a splendid corps of missionaries. Young men and women are eagerly offering themselves for service abroad. The spirit of missions in our Church is alive and growing. But this interest has not yet been capitalized sufficiently to meet the pressing needs of our foreign mission work. Opportunities to reach the middle and upper classes await the effort of our missionaries in India. Mission station equipment in Japan calls for immediate attention. The prospects in our China field are remarkable. Urgent new work among interior tribes in Liberia is meeting with splendid success. The way is opening in British Guiana to reach multitudes of aboriginal Indians and immigrant Hindus. Spanish speaking Argentinians are coming in larger numbers to see the need of the Evangelical Movement in South America. In the face of these clearly indicated and most urgent opportunities, the Board stands helpless unless the Church immediately rises to new heights of foreign mission consecration and effort. The Board appeals to this convention and the whole Church to make it possible to enter into a fuller realization of the Saviour's promise, that His Church is to do "greater works" for the Kingdom of God in all the earth.

RECOMMENDATIONS

1. The Board of Foreign Missions bows in gratitude before the Great Head of the Church; acknowledges His Divine favor in the past and prays that His blessings may further attend its work and that the Church may be inspired with increasing zeal for this cause.

2. *Foreign Mission Day Appeal.* Resolved, That the Board of Foreign Missions be permitted to appeal during the Epiphany season of 1929 and 1930 to all congregations and individuals, as well as Sunday schools, for offerings on Foreign Mission Day to cancel the entire indebtedness of the Board of Foreign Missions.

3. *Percentage of Apportionment.* Whereas, the income of the Board of Foreign Missions is not sufficient to carry on the Church's work as already established in our foreign fields,
   Resolved, That this Convention instruct the Executive Board to re-study the subject of the distribution of the apportionment among the various causes with a view of increasing the percentage allotted to the Board of Foreign Missions.

4. *Special Gifts.* Resolved, That all congregations, in addition to meeting the full apportionment, Sunday schools, societies and friends of the Cause, be encouraged to make special foreign mission contributions for assigned purposes such as Foreign Missionaries, parishes abroad and proteges.

5. *Legacies.* Resolved, That as an exception to the rule adopted at the last convention of the United Lutheran Church, the Board of Foreign Missions be allowed to use funds from undesignated legacies for payments due the Berlin Missionary Society for the property of our mission in the Shantung Province in China.

6. *Federation of Lutheran Churches and Missions in India.* Resolved, That the United Lutheran Church in America rejoices to see that Lutheran Missions and Churches. in India are forming a Federation in the interest of a common task in that land, and approves the tentative constitution of this Federation.

Respectfully submitted,

C. THEODORE BENZE, *President*
L. B. WOLF, *General Secretary.*
GEORGE DRACH, *General Secretary.*

Appendix A

CONSTITUTION OF THE FEDERATION OF EVANGELICAL LUTHERAN CHURCHES IN INDIA

PREAMBLE

In the name of the Father, and the Son, and of the Holy Spirit. Amen.

Having been called by the Gospel and made partakers of the Grace of God, and by faith, members of our Lord and Saviour Jesus Christ, and through Him, of one another,

We, members of Evangelical Lutheran Churches (Synods) in India, recognizing our duty as people of God to make the inner unity which we have with one another manifest in the common confession, defence, and maintenance of our faith, and in united efforts for the extension of the Kingdom of God, realizing the vastness of the field that God has assigned us for our labors in India, and the greatness of the undeveloped resources within our beloved Church, conscious of our need of mutual assistance and encouragement; and relying upon the promise of the divine Word that He who hath begun this work will perfect it until the day of Christ Jesus, we, while praying for the unity of all believers in Christ, hereby unite and now invite and until such end be attained, continue to invite all Evangelical Lutheran Churches (Synods) in India, one with us in the faith, to unite with us, upon the terms of this constitution in one general Federation.

ARTICLE I. NAME

The name and the title of the body, organized under this constitution, shall be The Federation of Evangelical Lutheran Churches in India.

ARTICLE II. MEMBERSHIP

Section 1. All Evangelical Lutheran Churches in India shall be entitled to membership in this Federation.

Sec. 2. The following shall be recognized as Evangelical Lutheran Churches.

Every Church which (1) receives and holds the canonical Scriptures of the Old and New Testaments as the inspired Word of God, and as the only infallible rule and standard of faith and practice, according to which all doctrines and teachers are to be judged;

(2) accepts as important testimonies drawn from the Holy Scriptures the three ecumenical Creeds; namely, the Apostles', the Nicene, and the Athanasian;

(3) receives and holds the Unaltered Augsburg Confession together with the Small Catechism of Luther as a correct exhibition of the faith and the

doctrine of the Evangelical Lutheran Church, founded upon the Word of God;

(4) recognizes the Apology of the Augsburg Confession, the Smalkald Articles, the Large Catechism of Luther and the Formula of Concord as of great importance in the historical development of the Evangelical Lutheran Church and as a valuable Lutheran heritage.

ARTICLE III. OBJECT

The Object of this Federation shall be to express outwardly the spiritual unity of Lutheran Churches (Synods), to cultivate cooperation among all Lutherans in the promotion of the general interest of this Federation, to seek the unification of Lutherans in India in one true faith, and thereby to develop and unfold their specific spiritual gifts.

ARTICLE IV. ORGANIZATION

The Federation of Evangelical Lutheran Churches in India shall function through two bodies, namely, a Conference, and an Executive Council, as defined in the following articles.

ARTICLE V. THE CONFERENCE

Section 1. The Conference shall consist of representatives of the constituent Churches in the following manner:

(a) Every constituent Church, two delegates.

(b) Further, for every ten ordained ministers or major portion thereof, up to a maximum of six, one delegate.

(c) Further, for every 5,000 communicant memberships or major portion thereof, up to a maximum of six, one delegate.

(d) Additional members, not to exceed ten, to be coopted by the Executive Council.

Sec. 2. The Conference shall meet at least once in three years.

Sec. 3. A quorum shall be a majority of the delegates to the meeting of the Conference, provided that at the time of counting the quorum, at least half of the constituent Churches are represented on the floor.

ARTICLE VI. THE EXECUTIVE COUNCIL

Section 1. The Executive Council shall be composed of one member from each constituent Church, to be selected by the body concerned, and additional members, not to exceed four, to be coopted by the Executive Council, and of the officers in case these are not already members of the Executive Council.

Sec. 2. All vacancies shall be filled up by the Executive Council itself until the churches concerned elect regular members.

Sec. 3. The tenure of office of members of the Executive Council shall ordinarily be from Conference to Conference.

ARTICLE VII. OFFICE BEARERS

Section 1. The Officers of the Conference shall be as follows: president, vice-president, secretary.

Sec. 2. The Officers shall be elected by the Conference but vacancies shall be filled up by the Executive Council.

Sec. 3. The Officers of the Conference shall also be the officers of the Executive Council.

Appendix B

CONSTITUTION OF THE AMERICAN LUTHERAN MISSION IN LIBERIA, AFRICA

ARTICLE I. NAME

The name of this body shall be the Conference of the American Lutheran Mission (formerly known as Muhlenberg Mission) in Liberia.

ARTICLE II. AMENABILITY

The Conference shall be amenable to the Board of Foreign Missions of the United Lutheran Church in America.

ARTICLE III. OBJECT

Its Object shall be to direct and control the Mission work and workers in harmonious cooperation for the extension of the Kingdom of Christ among the Kpele tribes, those of allied dialects and in the territory of approach to the Kpele people.

ARTICLE IV. MEMBERSHIP

Section 1. Its membership shall consist of all missionaries and wives of missionaries.

Sec. 2. Its voting membership shall consist of the missionaries after one year's residence on the field; likewise wives of missionaries, except those who are not in a position to enter into the mission activities.

Sec. 3. Non-voting members shall be entitled to all rights and privileges except voting.

ARTICLE V. OFFICERS

Section 1. The officers of the Conference shall be President, Vice-President, Recording Secretary, and Treasurer, whose terms of service and duties shall be defined in the By-Laws.

Article VI. Mission Council

Section 1. The Mission Council shall consist of the President of the Conference as chairman, one woman supported by the Woman's Board, and one other member, said Council empowered to call in as temporary members not more than two persons most interested in the question under consideration.

Sec. 2. The supreme authority of the conference shall be vested in this Mission Council with authority to make effective every activity of the Mission, subject to the Board of Foreign Missions of the United Lutheran Church in America.

Sec. 3 (1) The members of this Council shall be elected by the Conference for a term of three years each, and a temporary member shall be elected to act for any member going on furlough.

(2) Provisions for members going on furlough shall be made at the annual Conference meeting, and in case of emergency the Council shall nominate not more than two persons, one of whom shall be elected through correspondence.

Sec. 4. (1) The chairman of the Council shall have no other assignment of work than that of supervising, visiting, and counselling the missionaries and Christian workers and such other duties as grow out of his office as chief executive of the Mission.

(2) He shall make regular reports to the Mission Council for review and approval before transmitting them to the Conference and the Board.

Sec. 5. The Council shall be responsible for the coordinating and unifying of the work in the various sections of the field, and shall direct missionaries to this end, always seeking to promote a good moral and spiritual atmosphere throughout the field and a spirit of sympathetic fellowship among the missionaries and mission workers.

Sec. 6. The Council shall be the Board's advisor as to the general condition of the field and the needs of same, and shall be the official medium of communication between the Board and the Conference, receiving all remittances from the Board, and transferring them to the treasurer, and submitting quarterly financial statements to the Board.

Sec. 7. The Council shall be the official representative of the Board and Conference to the Government of the Republic of Liberia, and make all other official representations, either *per se* or by deputation.

Sec. 8. The Council shall be responsible for an annual audit of all station and official mission accounts, and for all other necessary audits; and shall sign all orders on the treasurer and all orders for mission supplies, controlling the supplies at each station.

Sec. 9. The Council shall prepare an annual report of the mission, based upon reports from the individual missionaries, including the statistical report.

Sec. 10. The Council shall properly man the various stations of the field, and shall have authority to extend or abbreviate terms of service and furlough periods, under the advice of the Medical Committee, provided that the missionaries shall always be heard on these matters before final action is taken. As far as possible, all missionaries shall be informed before they leave America of the work to which they are assigned.

Sec. 11. Members of Council on furlough shall be the representative of the Council to the Board and shall act in such capacity as the Board may deem advisable, presenting more clearly the needs of the field to the Board through the Africa Committee, it being understood that the member shall present nothing official to the Board which has not been approved by the Council.

Sec. 12. The Council shall prepare a complete agenda of the Conference business which shall be presented to that body for action.

Sec. 13. These rules governing the Mission Council shall not be changed by the Conference except on the recommendation of the Mission Council.

Article VII. Committees

Section 1. The following standing committees shall be elected at the annual Conference to act until their successors are elected: (1) Education, (2) Medical.

Sec. 2. The committees of the Conference shall function as provided in the By-Laws, and their reports shall be in the hands of the Council to be incorporated in the Agenda, two weeks before the annual Conference meeting.

Article VIII. Meetings

Section 1. Regular meetings shall be held annually at such time and place as the Conference may determine.

Sec. 2. Special meetings of the Conference may be called as determined by the By-Laws.

Article IX. Quorum

The Conference may adopt By-Laws in harmony with this Constitution, subject to the approval of the Board of Foreign Missions.

Article X. Amendments

This constitution may be amended subject to the approval of the Board by a three-fourths vote of the voting members on the field, provided such amendment has been presented at a previous meeting of the Conference.

THE TREASURER'S FINANCIAL STATEMENT

The audited account of the Board for the biennium is found at the conclusion of the report. Our Church's fiscal year begins on the first of July of each calendar year, and ends on June 30th the following year. This biennium begins July 1, 1926, and ends June 30, 1928.

The apportionment voted for this period was $1,230,000. The churches responded:

	Amount Apportioned	Received	Per cent of Apportionment
Year 1926-27	$600,000.00	$381,000.00	.635%
Year 1927-28	630,000.00	426,000.00	.676%

It is noted there was a fair increase in 1927-28 over 1926-27 apportionment, amounting to $45,000. From all sources the Board received the following for biennium:

Receipts	1926-27	1927-28
On Apportionment	$381,000.00	$426,000.00
Other synods	14,546.89	24,497.50
Donations other than apportionment from churches, Sunday schools and individuals ..	98,450.91	96,265.43
Donations on board's debt		8,630.05
Legacies	691.45	200.00
Interest on investments and bank	6,973.61	6,606.79
Publication subscriptions	2,847.95	4,594.29
Other income	1,309.17	2,517.23
Total	$505,819.98	$569,311.29
Received from Women's Missionary Society.	$187,300.00	$242,431.96
Other special funds	141,161.43	112,766.06
Total	$328,461.43	$355,198.02
Grand Total	$834,281.41	$924,509.31

Expenditures	1926-27	1927-28
Budget and specials to missions	$379,226.28	$351,667.81
Salaries to missionaries	132,317.31	136,472.76
Travel of missionaries to and from fields	38,373.53	40,933.64
Expenses of missionaries on furlough		10,731.12
Salaries of secretaries of board	10,200.00	10,200.00
Salaries of clerks, stenographers, etc.	6,490.45	6,224.98
Expenses of secretaries and board members	7,209.11	5,054.78
Expenses of candidates and students	6,052.67	5,330.99
Outfit of new missionaries	1,400.00	200.00
Special allowances and pensions	2,928.98	3,513.00
*Part payment Shantung Mission property ..	19,375.00	20,007.10
Contributions to intermissionary organizations	2,700.00	2,854.90
Purchase of property, Buenos Aires	5,765.36	1,068.75
Interest on Shantung property	2,883.00	1,769.90
Publications	6,005.71	6,345.30
Publicity	4,560.99	1,833.40

Interest on bank loans	7,183.52	9,674.46
Office supplies—telephone, telegraph and cables—postage and other expenses	5,599.87	5,235.50
Interest on annuities	2,645.06	3,332.92
Upkeep of property	1,031.29	1,279.83
Auditing	925.00	860.00
Total expenses general work	$642,873.13	$624,491.98
Women's Missionary Society	$204,451.66	$229,475.38
Disbursements special funds	9,087.21	41,355.15
Grand total all expenditures	$856,412.00	$895,322.51

* China property bought for $185,000 had payment on it of $10,000 in 1924. Since then it was agreed to pay annually $17,500 with three per cent interest on yearly balances. On January 1, 1927, it was agreed to remit this, and since then payments were continued. On June 30, 1928, $113,125.00 remained unpaid.

The Women's Contribution

As received and spent	1926-27	1927-28
From Women's Missionary Society — all purposes	$187,300.00	$242,431.96
From Women's Missionary Society—expenses all purposes	204,451.66	229,475.38
Deficit or excess	$17,151.66	$12,956.58

Other Funds
Andhra Christian College Fund

The chief of these was the Andhra Christian College, India, for higher education. It was underwritten in the amount of $270,000.00 and at the close of the biennium it stood as follows on the thirtieth day of June, 1928, as paid in, $234,669.02.

Reformation Diamond Jubilee Fund

This fund as reported at the Richmond Convention showed a balance of $74,803.83 at the end of June, 1926. It has been expended on special projects and at the close of June, 1928, showed a balance in the account of $33,559.16.

Annuities

By the last report our annuities as of June 30, 1926, amounted to $35,952.00. Our list of annuities for the biennium follow, and amounted to $32,500.00.

Since the last report the following sums were received for which bonds were issued bearing interest from 5.9% to 10%. No better way can be found to dispose of money whose interest one may need in his or her life time, than this plan affords. It is safe. It meets fully all legal difficulties. It is better than a will made in the Board's favor. Money is invested during the life time of the annuitant and the interest is paid semi-annually.

ANNUITIES

1926		
July	A Friend	$10,000.00
July	George W. Scherer	500.00
July	Laura Rehm	200.00
Sept.	Fredericka M. Heeb	100.00
Nov.	Carrie Sypher	1,000.00
1927		
Feb.	Carrie Sypher	2,000.00
March	Edwin H. Sharretts	5,000.00
Oct.	Dora M. Bishop	500.00
Oct.	Chas. A. Thress	100.00
Nov.	Laura A. Roth	250.00
1928		
Feb.	John P. Kellar, Jr.	1,000.00
Feb.	Carolina Dunn	5,000.00
April	John Jay and Annie W. Hill	2,000.00
May	C. M. Sandt and wife	5,000.00
	Total	$32,500.00

BEQUESTS

The bequests received during the period were as follows and amounted to $49,649.74. As pointed out legacies undesignated were held and expended for buildings in accordance with the Richmond resolution. The amount of the undesignated legacies was $11,189.17. The largest legacy received was from Mr. Cooper, a life-long friend of our Japan Mission.

Bequests

1926			
July	Elizabeth Kern	$481.45	Undesignated
Aug.	Florence T. Seagers	1,000.00	"
Oct.	Irene Danner Reinwald	900.00	Land and Buildings
"	Henry Forny	450.00	" " "
"	Henry Bowman	200.00	" " "
Nov.	Amelia Eichelberger	1,000.00	" " "
Dec.	Athalina Hicks	137.62	" " "
1927			Land and Buildings
Jan.	Pauline Glass	300.00	" " "
Feb.	Cooper Estate	12,375.00	" " "
March	Etta Harroway	5,000.00	" " "
"	Emma Viola Clark	3,511.48	Trust Fund
"	Katherine Thompsen	25.00	Land and Buildings
April	Malindo S. Stroh	270.00	" " "
"	Rosine Wiegers	1,000.00	" " "
May	Leddin Estate	50.00	" " "

May	Cooper Estate	2,000.00	Land and Buildings
"	Mary Ellen Smith	600.00	Trust Fund
"	Mary McLennan	465.00	Land and Buildings
"	Peter Woll, Jr.	1,272.72	" " "
July	Alice Elizabeth Seltzer	2,000.00	Trust Fund
"	Laura Stoever	2,000.00	Land and Buildings
"	Anna Elizabeth Snyder	225.00	" " "
Aug.	M. H. Adkins	930.00	" " "
"	Cooper Estate	2,000.00	" " "
"	Barbara Cone	1,000.00	" " "
Nov.	Annie M. Asper	402.78	" " "
"	Abraham Helsing	100.00	" " "
1928			
Jan.	Granville B. Repass	5.180.00	Trust Fund
Feb.	Caroline Tiglar	1,000.00	" "
"	Elizabeth Gayde	25.00	Land and Buildings
March	Granville B. Repass	1,298.69	Trust Fund
"	Henry Meyer	100.00	Land and Buildings
"	Etta Harroway	2,000.00	" " "
April	Emma Suber	50.00	" " "
"	Henry F. Meyers	100.00	" " "
June	Melissa J. Linhart	200.00	Trust Fund
	Total	$49,649.74	

Our Foreign Mission Board presented to the Executive Board for the apportionment for each year of the coming biennium the following as based on the needs of the fields and home base for the years 1930 and 1931. The plea put up to the Executive Board by the Foreign Mission Board was that in the division of the whole apportionment the Foreign Mission cause should get at least 31.72% of the whole amount apportioned. This would be restoring the rate per cent which was fixed at the Washington Convention in 1920. Elsewhere the Board presents its plea in the resolutions to the Convention.

BUDGET FOR 1930-1931

	Year 1929-30	Year 1930-31
India	$281,820.00	
Japan	130,075.00	
Liberia	56,210.00	
China	55,110.00	
Argentina	33,330.00	
British Guiana	6,930.00	
Home base and unforeseen	72,297.00	
Interest on loan	10,202.00	
Total	$645,974.00	$710,572.00
Commitments voted on various projects, cash to be raised above that for general work	$65,200.00	$65,200.00

An analysis of home base expenses for the year ending June 30, 1928, showing per cent of the cost of Promotion and Education, Administration, and Miscellaneous Disbursements, as compared with the total receipts of the board for the year 1928.

Promotion and Education:

Expenses of missionaries on furlough, including travel, house rent, etc.	$10,731.12
Expenses of candidates and students	5,330.99
Publications	6,345.30
Publicity	1,907.80
Travel and secretarial	4,054.78
	$28,369.99

Per cent of total receipts of ($924,509.31) $28,369.99 ·.......... .0266

Administrative:

Secretaries' salaries	$7,200.00
Salaries of clerks, stenographers and accountant	6,224.98
Expenses of secretaries' travel, and of board meetings	4,000.00
Office supplies and cables, telegrams, telephone, express, etc.	5,233.50
Auditing accounts	860.00
	$23,518.48

Per cent of total receipts of ($924,509.31) $22,655.95 .... .0245

General:

Special allowances and pensions	$5,513.85
Intermissionary organizations	2,814.90
Interest on bank loans	9,674.46
Annuities interest	3,332.92
Local property	1,279.82
	$22,655.95

Per cent of total receipts of ($924,509.31) $22,655.95 .... .0245

Per cent of total receipts ($924,509.31) $74,544.92 .... .0766

ALL RECEIPTS AND EXPENDITURES
Since Beginning of the Merger Board 1918-1928

	Receipts	Expenses	Deficit	Excess
Cash carried over from three merging boards	$84,475.66			
General Fund, 8 months	105,827.55	$156,818.85	$50,991.30	
Women's Mis. Society	38,670.64	22,293.19		$16,377.45
1918-19 Other Specials	30,425.83	18,201.00		12,224.83
Total cash received and expended	$174,924.02	$197,312.04		
General Fund	355,540.35	397,693.33	42,152.98	

	Receipts	Expenses	Deficit	Excess
Women's Mis. Society	134,258.41	103,484.38		30,774.03
1919-20 Other Specials	85,924.13	26,466.04		59,458.09
Total cash received and expended	$575,723.89	$527,643.75		
General Fund	382,012.55	429,220.40	47,207.85	
Women's Mis. Society	113,815.29	139,754.23	25,938.94	
1920-21 Other Specials	111,936.95	87,767.41		24,169.54
Total cash received and expended	$607,764.79	$656,742.04		
General Fund	475,335.08	441,695.87		33,639.19
Women's Mis. Society	186,201.00	194,689.00	8,488.00	
1921-22 Other Specials	100,732.54	11,286.19		89,446.35
Total cash received and expended	$762,268.62	$647,671.06		
General Fund	492,995.46	543,914.52	50,919.06	
Women's Mis. Society	206,233.50	160,284.06		45,949.44
1922-23 Other Epecial	62,405.17	50,553.47		11,851.70
Total cash received and expended .?....	$761,634.13	$754,752.05		
General Fund	555,048.54	522,533.05		32,515.49
Women's Mis. Society	209,192.22	248.918.84	39,726.62	
1923-24 Other Specials	121,154.60	114,693.23		6,461.37
Total cash received and expended	$885,395.36	$886,145.12		
1924-25 (11 mos.) General Funds	$516,107.33	$634,680.97	$118,573.64	
Women's Mis. Society	296,056.80	251,117.26		44,939.54
Other Funds	53,349.65	67,753.72	14,404.07	
Total cash received and expended	$865,513.78	$953,551.95		
1925-26 General Fund ..	623,280.22	652,810.42	29,530.20	
Women's Mis. Society	284,248.33	348,737.61	64,489.28	
Other Funds	76,663.16	57,548.34		19,114.82
Total cash received and expended	$984,191.71	1,059,096.37		
1926-27 General Fund ..	505,819.98	642,873.13	137,053.15	
Women's Mis. Society	187,300.43	204,451.66	17,151.23	
Other Funds	140,161.43	9,087.21		131,074.22
Total cash received and expended	$833,281.84	$856,412.00		
1927-28 General Fund ..	569,311.29	624,491.98	55,180.69	

Women's Mis. Society	242,431.38	229,495.38		12,956.58
Total cash received and expended	$924,509.31	$895,322.51		

Grand Total, Cash rec. and expended..	$7,059,682.11	7,221,111.02

Total deficit, all accounts	$701,807.01	
Total excess, all accounts		$642,362.35
Total deficit on General Fund	$531,608.87	
Total excess on General Fund		$66,154.68
Total deficit on Women's Missionary Society	$155,784.07	
Total excess on Women's Missionary Society		$150,997.04
Total deficit on other funds	$14,404.07	
Total excess on other funds		$353,800.89
	$701,807.01	$570,952.61

The above statement shows how all accounts are grouped under three heads: The General Fund, the Women's Missionary Society Fund, and Other Funds, which are called "Specials" and are only spent as donors direct. The Board assembles these funds separately to help, by a brief summary, to a better understanding of the Board's finances, and the cash received and expended.

A. *General Fund,* Year by Year	Received	Expended
Cash carried over from merging boards......	$84,475.66	
1919 ending July 31, 1919 (8 mos.)..........	105,827.55	$156,818.85
1920 ending July 31, 1920	355,540.35	397,693.33
1921 ending July 31, 1921	382,012.55	429,220.40
1922 ending July 31, 1922	475,335.08	441,695.89
1923 ending July 31, 1923	492,995.46	543,914.52
1924 ending July 31, 1924	555,048.54	522,533.05
1925 (11 mos.) June 30, 1925	516,107.33	634,680.97
1926 ending June 30, 1926	623,280.22	652,810.42
1927 ending June 30, 1927	505,819.98	642,873.13
1928 ending June 30 1928	569,311.29	624,491.98
Total	$4,665,654.01	$5,046,732.52

B. The following statement shows the receipts and expenses of the Women's Missionary Society. The Board receives monthly remittances which are credited on the Board's books, and as instructed, are forwarded to the mission fields for salaries, regular work and specific objects. Attention is called especially to the girls' school buildings in Japan, the high school building known as "Emma V. Day Memorial," and the Phoebe Hospital, in Africa, which account for a large part of receipts and expenses in this account.

Money received and expended since the merger, for ten years, was as follows:

	Received	Expended
1919 ending July 31, 1919	$38,670.64	$22,293.19
1920 ending July 31, 1920	134,288.41	103,484.38
1921 ending July 31, 1921	113,815.29	139,754.23
1922 ending July 31, 1922	186,201.00	194,689.00
1923 ending July 31, 1923	206,233.50	160,284.06
1924 ending July 31, 1924	209,192.22	248,918.84
1925 (11 mos.) ending June 30, 1925	296,056.80	251,117.26
1926 ending June 30, 1926	284,248.33	348,737.61
1927 ending June 30, 1927	187,309.43	204,451.66
1928 ending June 30, 1928	242,431.96	229,475.38
Total	$1,898,408.58	$1,902,205.61

C. Other Funds or Specials

The Board calls attention to such funds under this head as the Reformation Diamond Jubilee, the Foreign Mission Forward Fund, and the Andhra Christian College Fund, as to a large extent accounting for this fund. It instructs its treasurer to keep separate accounts of all such money and carry out the specific objects for which it was given. For the period since the merger, the receipts have been as follows, and the outgo on various objects are recited as follows:

	Received	Expended
1919 ending July 31, 1919	$30,425.83	$18,201.00
1920 ending July 31, 1920	85,924.13	26,466.04
1921 ending July 31, 1921	111,936.95	87,767.41
1922 ending July 31, 1922	100,732.54	11,286.19
1923 ending July 31, 1923	62,405.17	50,553.47
1924 ending July 31, 1924	121,154.60	114,693.23
1925 (11 mos.) ending June 30, 1925	53,349.65	67,753.72
1926 ending June 30, 1926	76,663.16	57,548.34
1927 ending June 30, 1927	140,161.43	9,087.21
1928 ending June 30, 1928	112,766.06	41,355.15
Total	$895,519.52	$484,721.76

D. Investments. The Board's investments cover three kinds of receipts: All legacies, which according to will, create funds, the interest of which alone is available in perpetuity annually for specific objects, that is, funds of which the Board is by will made trustee; other funds, which by the conditions named in their solicitation were to be invested, e. g., one-third of the Reformation Diamond Jubilee Fund, for Higher Education in India; funds, which were set aside as permanent funds by the Board's action; and a large part of the Andhra Christian College Fund, amounting to $91,000.00, for conservation "till building operations can be begun." All these, together with our annuity fund, now amount to $264,558.89.

E. A statement may be in place in regard to the Board's indebtedness. This divides itself into two parts,—that which is borrowed from the bank, and that which is due the Board's special funds, which must sooner or later be replaced and spent as promised. The total overdraft, according to the last audit, June 30, 1928, was $335,042.16, to which must be added $11,972.67 overspent on the Foreign Mission Forward Fund, making a total debt of $347,014.83. Of this amount the Board borrowed on collateral and its officers' credit $176,500.00 at 5½%, and the remainder, $170,514.83, from funds which must sooner or later be replaced and spent for the objects and projects for which they were raised.

An effort has been started, by private solicitation, to pay off the Board's loans. Cash and pledges have been secured in the amount of $21,830.00.

It should be remembered that pre-merger commitments involved the Board in large expenditures, which the Apportionment was not able to meet;— 65% raised was the limit for most part of the ten years. One commitment alone, the preservation of the Breklum Mission, involves the Board in an expenditure of $248,500. Our South American Mission in Buenos Aires cost for property and initial expenses not less than $250,000. China and its claims began in 1925 and cost to the end of 1928 $183,124.00 for property and running expenses—a total of $681,474.00 for Breklum, South America, and China. Besides, the natural growth of all the old fields demanded larger budgets for an increased force of missionaries, and the rapid development of their work. But, with great determination, the Board has set itself to work to make ends meet, and to balance its budget for each year of the coming biennium. As a glance at statement "A" will show, only twice in ten years, in 1922 and 1924, was there a balanced budget with excess receipts of $66,154.70. Eight months after the Board began to function it had to borrow money from special funds in the amount of $50,991.30. The Board made an effort to pay off this growing debt by the Foreign Mission Forward Fund, but it had only limited success; but it borrowed no money from banks to carry on 'till the end of 1924. Now its interest charges will be about $14,000.00 for bank and Andhra College Fund.

THE BOARD'S DEFICIT AND EXCESS FROM YEAR TO YEAR AS SHOWN IN STATEMENT "A"

	Deficit	Excess
1919 year ending July 31, 1919	$50,991.30	
1920 year ending July 31, 1920	42,152.98	
1921 year ending July 31, 1921	47,207.85	
1922 year ending July 31, 1922		$33,639.19
1923 year ending July 31, 1923	50,919.06	
1924 year ending July 31, 1924		32,515.49
1925 year ending July 31, 1925	118,573.64	
1926 year ending July 31, 1926	29,530.20	
1927 year ending July 31, 1927	137,053.15	
1928 year ending July 31, 1928	55,180.69	
Totals	$531,608.87	$66,154.70

The serious increase of indebtedness in 1927 and 1928 was in part due to the Richmond resolution which prevented the Board from crediting undesignated legacies, amounting to $37,037.12, to the General Fund.

The Board has set up its budget for the current year, after a most careful study of its reasonable expectations, based on the last three years' receipts and expenditures. By June 30, 1930, a balanced budget may be attained, if our income is maintained and our expenses are kept down, as in 1928.

The best indication that the Board's efforts are getting results is the reduction of its general expenses in the last year, in the amount of $18,381.44, and in the increase of its general income in the amount of $63,491.31, thus making an advance toward a balanced budget in one year of $81,872.75.

In the statement "A" General Fund, the amount of cash carried over from merging Boards is set down as $84,475.66. To understand the new Board's financial condition this cash carried forward must be explained. The General Work in the three Boards was always distinguished from the special, for which funds were separately raised and spent. However, while the three Boards kept separate accounts of their special and general funds, they, except one, held all their cash in one bank account. All the Boards, except one, invested annuities and recorded them as liabilities until the death of the annuitant. Hence, to understand the indebtedness of the Board, the condition of the account of the new Board must be faced, as the books of accounts show. The Church voted that all Boards are to receive all assets and assume all liabilities of the merging Boards. At time of the merger the various accounts show:

General Synod:
Amount in the Reformation Diamond Jubilee Fund $73,050.82
Cash carried over to Merger Board 56,250.23
Cash expended for General Work. as of Nov. 1, 1918 .... 16,800.59

Board of the United Synod of the Evangelical Lutheran Church in South:
Cash carried over as of January 23, 1919 .... 16,023.00
Special Funds carried over from Board:
  (1) Holland Memorial $9,625.77
  (2) Chapel Fund for Japan 5,716.83   27,205.20
  (3) Silver Jubilee, Japan Missions 2,362.60
  (4) Annuities, unprotected by securities 9,500.00
Accounts show as expended and as lacking securities to cover annuities $11,182.20

General Council:
1. Special Fund, as a claim, May 22, 1919, known as the Quadri-Centennial, as per Board Minute Book, of May, page 75 .... 13,672.52
2. Cash carried over as of January 23, 1919 .... 12,202.43
  Cash expended on General Work at time of merger, showing a deficit 1,470.07

SUMMARY OF OVERDRAFT OF SPECIAL FUNDS AND ANNUITIES AT TIME
OF MERGER

General Synod $16,800.59
United Lutheran Church of the South 11,182.20
General Council 1,470.07

Total indebtedness at time of merger $29,453.86

This statement shows that the Merger Board began to function with a heavy handicap of debt. As shown on preceding pages it never paid its way on General Account except twice in the ten years,—1922 and 1924. It began in debt to its special funds; it remains in debt to them in the amount of $170,514.83, and has bank loans to pay of $176,500.00. The churches must come to the help of the Foreign Board, and at once; or this great and promising work will be crippled,—nay injured in the house of its friends. Nothing is so urgent as this, in the Church.

REPORT OF THE TREASURER

For the two years ended June 30, 1928 and 1927
Balance Sheet, June 30, 1928

ASSETS

Cash in banks ....$ 56,290.07
Investments at book values, as annexed:
Bonds and stocks:
  Free ....$ 87,381.05
  Pledged as collateral to secure loans
    payable 114,156.26
                          $201,537.31
  Local real estate, mortgages, ground rents, etc.   50,021.58
  Property located at Kodikanal, India........   13,000.00
                                  264,558.89
                                $320,848.96

LIABILITIES

Loans payable to The National Bank of Baltimore:
Secured by bonds aggregating, at book values,
  $114,156.26 ....$100,000.00
Unsecured 76,500.00
                                176,500.00
                                $144,348.96

FUNDS

Trust funds $158,742.63
Annuity funds 67,752.81
Andhra Christian College fund 208,187.12
Reformation Diamond Jubilee Advance fund 33,569.16
Kobe Equipment fund 13,581.80

India Industrial fund 797.52
Pohlman fund 1,400.00
Land and Building fund 8,681.98
Luther League Educational Building fund.........   104.28
Susan K. Chester fund 351.51
                                                  _____
                                                  $493,168.81

Less, funds overdrawn (borrowed from other funds):
    Women's Missionary Society fund.$ 1,805.02
    Foreign Mission Forward fund....   11,972.67
    General fund 335,042.16
                                      _____
                                                  $348,819.85
                                                  _____
                                                              $144,348.96

Note: The above balance sheet does not include:
    Liabilities incurred in the purchase of properties in foreign mission fields not definitely ascertainable at June 30, 1928, but known to exceed $121,000, or
    Any investment in such properties (other than that located at Kodikanal, India) the value of which is also unknown at this date.

Balance Sheet, June 30, 1927
ASSETS

Cash in banks ....$ 27,676.21
Investments at book values:
    Bonds and stocks:
        Free ....$ 81,788.20
        Pledged as collateral to secure
            loans payable 114,594.36
                                       _____
                                                  $196,382.56
        Local real estate, mortgages, ground rents, etc.   41,103.39
        Property located at Edmonstone, India.......   5,000.00
                                                             _____
                                                             242,485.95
                                                             _____
                                                             $270,162.16

LIABILITIES

Loans payable to The National Bank of Baltimore:
    Secured by bonds aggregating, at book values,
        $114,594.36 ....$100,000.00
    Unsecured 55,000.00
                                                    _____
                                                    155,000.00
                                                    _____
                                                    $115,162.16

FUNDS

Trust funds $149,263.94
Annuity funds 54,652.81
Andhra Christian College fund 148,696.48
Reformation Diamond Jubilee Advance fund....... 37,610.05
Pohlman fund 1,400.00
India Industrial fund 395.44
Kobe Equipment fund 5,749.56
Land and Building fund 25,370.34
                                                  _____
                                                  $423,138.62

Less, funds overdrawn (borrowed from other funds) :
    Foreign Mission Forward fund......$ 12,603.39
    Women's Missionary Society fund... 14 761.60
    General fund 280,611.47
                                    307,976.46

                                                $115,162.16

Note: The above balance sheet does not include:
Liabilities incurred in the purchase of properties in foreign mission fields
not definitely ascertainable at June 30, 1927, but known to exceed $150,000, or
Any investment in such properties, (other than that located at Edmonstone, India) the value of which is also unknown at this date.

RECEIPTS AND DISBURSEMENTS

For the yeear ended June 30, 1928

RECEIPTS

	General Fund	Women's Missionary Society Fund	Other Funds
United Church on apportionment......$426,000.00			
Women's Missionary Society		$242,431.96	
Icelandic Synod	1,200.00		
Augustana Synod	13,472.00		$ 150.00
Danish Synod	9 825.50		
Donations received through Board treasurer and general fund	96,265.43		
Donations for Board's debt	8,630.05		
Bequests	200.00		20,085.47
Donations for specific funds			74,020.62
Annuities			13,850.00
Interest on investments	6,606.17		4,658.97
Interest on bank balances	.62		
"The Foreign Missionary"	2,819.45		
"Der Missionsbote"	1,774.84		
Rental of slides	157.62		
Rental of properties	714.43		
Profit on sales of bonds	708.99		
Payment received on account of R. B. Manikam's loan	936.19		
	$569,311.29	$242,431.96	$112,766.06
Total fund receipts		$924,509.31	
Investments sold		19,100.00	
Bank loans received		30,000.00	
Total receipts		$973,609.31	
Less, Investments received as bequests, included in above receipts, at face value......		5,180.00	
Total cash receipts		$968,429.31	

DISBURSEMENTS

	General Fund	Women's Missionary Society Fund	Other Funds
Budgets paid to missions	$345,305.68	$123,786.92	
Specials paid to missions	6,362.13	32,235.73	
Salaries of missionaries	136,472.76	57,827.29	
Traveling expenses of missionaries to and from fields	40,933.64	10,804.25	
Expenses of missionaries on furlough.	10,731.12	156.19	
Salaries of secretaries	10,200.00		
Salaries of clerks, stenographers, etc..	6,224.98		
Expenses of treasurer, secretaries and Board representatives	5,054.78		
Expenses of candidates and students ..	5,330.99		
Outfit allowances for missionaries	200.00	600.00	
Special allowances and pensions	3,513.85		
Disbursements from specific funds....			$ 41,355.15
Contributions to intermission organizations	2,854.90	565.00	
Partial payment on purchase of Shantung Mission	20,007.10	3,500.00	
Interest in full on Shantung Mission debt	1,769.90		
Purchase of real estate for Buenos Aires Mission	1,068.75		
"The Foreign Missionary"	3,849.30		
"Der Missionsbote"	2,496.00		
Expenses of slides	74.40		
Publicity	1,833.40		
Office supplies and expenses	2,603.98		
Telephone, telegraph and cables	479.46		
Postage and expressage	932.66		
General office expenses	545.00		
Auditing	860.00		
Expenses of local properties	1,279.82		
Interest on bank loans	9,674.46		
Annuities	3,332.92		
Transfer to Women's Missionary Society of legacy received in prior period	500.00		
	$624,491.98	$229,475.38	$ 41,355.15
Total fund disbursements		$895,322.51	
Investments purchased		35,992.94	
Bank loans repaid		8,500.00	
Total cash disbursements		$939,815.45	

SUMMARY

	General Fund	Women's Missionary Society Fund	Other Funds
Fund receipts	569,311.29	242,431.96	112,766.06
Fund disbursements	624,491.98	229,475.38	41,355.15
Excess or deficiency of fund receipts	$ 55,180.69	$ 12,956.58	$ 71,410.91
		$29,186.80	

For the year ended June 30, 1927

RECEIPTS

	General Fund	Women's Missionary Society Fund	Other Funds
United Church on apportionment	$381,000.00		
Women's Missionary Society		$187,242.43	
Icelandic Synod	1,200.00		
Augustana Synod	4,925.00		
Danish Synod	8,421.89	58.00	
Donations received through Board Treasurer and General Treasurer for General fund	98,450.91		
Bequests	691.45		$ 30,781.82
Donations for specific funds			89,414.86
Annuities			18,800.00
Interest on investments	6,876.14		1,164.75
Interest on bank balances	97.47		
"The Foreign Missionary"	1,336.87		
"Der Missionsbote"	1,511.08		
Rental of slides	285.88		
Rental of properties	570.00		
Refund of salary for previous period from R. J. White	453.29		
	$505,819.98	$187,300.43	$140,161.43
Total fund receipts		$833,281.84	
Instalment received on mortgage owned		200.00	
Final distribution received on bond owned		113.12	
Bank loans received		104,000.00	
Total cash receipts		$937,594.96	

DISBURSEMENTS

	General Fund	Women's Missionary Society Fund	Other Funds
Budgets paid to missions	$368,780.22	$119,623.20	
Specials paid to missions	10,446.06	20,499.02	
Salaries to missionaries	132,317.31	52,763.19	
Expenses of missionaries to and from fields	38,373.53	10,232.93	
Salaries of secretaries	10,200.00		
Salaries of clerks, stenographers, etc...	6,490.45		
Expenses of treasurer, secretaries and Board representatives	7,209.11		
Expenses of candidates and students ..	6,052.67	133.32	
Outfit allowances for missionaries	1,400.00	1,200.00	
Special allowances and pensions	2,928.98		
Disbursements from specific funds			$ 9,087.21

	General Fund	Women's Missionary Society Fund	Other Fund
Contributions to intermissionary organizations	2,700.00		
Partial payment on purchase of Shantung Mission	19,375.00		
Purchase of real estate for Buenos Aires Mission	5,765.36		
Interest on Shantung Mission debt to June 30, 1926	2.883.00		
"The Foreign Missionary"	3,192.58		
"Der Missionsbote"	2,813.13		
Expenses of slides	264.26		
Publicity	4,560.99		
Office supplies and expenses	2,307.81		
Telephone, telegraph and cables	597.27		
Postage and expressage	1,386.49		
General office expenses	1,044.04		
Auditing	925.00		
Expenses of local properties	1,031.29		
Interest on bank loans	7,183.52		
Annuities paid	2,645.06		
	$642,873.13	$204,451.66	$9,087.21

Total fund disbursements	$856,412.00
Final instalments on mortgage payable.	2,484.11
Bank loans repaid	20,000.00
Investments purchased	70,838.99
Total cash disbursements	$949,735.10

SUMMARY

	General Fund	Women's Missionary Society Fund	Other Fund
Fund receipts	505,819.98	187,300.43	140,161.43
Fund disbursements	642,873.13	204,451.66	9,087.21
Excess or deficiency of fund receipts	$137,053.15	$ 17,151.23	$131,074.22
		$23,130.16	

RECONCILEMENT OF CASH

For the two years ended June 30, 1928

Balance, July 1, 1926	$39,816.35
Cash receipts, as annexed:	
For the year ended June 30, 1927 ....$937,594.96	
For the year ended June 30, 1928 .... 968,429.31	
	$1,906,024.27
	$1,945,840.62

Cash disbursements, as annexed:
For the year ended June 30, 1927 .... 949,735.10
For the year ended June 30, 1928 .... 939,815.45
                                                              —————————— 1,889,550.55

Balance, June 30, 1928 ....$56,290.07

INVESTMENTS, June 30, 1928

		Book Values	Market Values
Bonds:			
1,500	Altoona & Logan Valley Elec. Ry 4½s, 1933 ....$	1,500.00 $	1,320.00
1,000	American Utilities Co. 6s, 1945, Series "A"	1,000.00	990.00
6,000	Associated Electric Co. 4½s, 1953........	5,655.00	6,240.00
5,000	Atlantic Coast Line 4s, 1952 (L. & N. Div.)	4,293.75	4,600.00
2,000	Baltimore Mortgage Co. 5½s, 1936, Series "A"	1,930.00	1,980.00
5,500	Baltimore Mortgage Co. 6s, 1937, Series "CC"	5,500.00	5,555.00
4,000	Baltimore & Ohio R.R. Co. ¼s, 1948......	3,050.00	3,765.00
3,000	Baltimore & Ohio R.R. Co. Equip. 4½s, 1940, "D"	2,969.40	2,905.32
2,000	Baltimore & Ohio R.R. Co., S. W. Div., 5s, 1950	1,985.00	2,070.00
4,000	Bonded Mortgage Co. 5½s, 1936, Series "E"	3,856.00	3,900.00
8,000	City of Baltimore, New Sewerage Impr. 4s, 1961	7,200.00	7,960.00
4,000	Central Illinois Public Service Co. 1-4½s, 1967	3,790.00	3,700.00
2,000	Central Indiana Gas Co. 1-5s, 1931........	2,000.00	2,000.00
1,000	Central Indiana Power Co. 1-6s, 1947.....	1,000.00	1,040.00
5,000	Central States Electric Corp. Conv. Deb. 5s, 1948	4,825.00	4,562.50
2,000	Chesapeake Mortgage Co. 6s, 1931, Series "C"	2,000.00	1,960.00
2,000	Consolidated Cities Lt., Pwr. & Trac. Co. 1-5s, 1962	1,659.90	1,870.00
3,000	Continental Mortgage Co. Coll. Tr. 1-6s, 1931, Series "A"	3,000.00	3,000.00
3,000	Kingdom of Denmark 5½s, 1955	2,985.00	3,015.00
1,000	Detroit Edison Co. 5s, 1933	1,000.00	1,031.25
2,500	Elec. & Peoples Trac. Stock Trust Ctfs. 4s, 1945	2,500.00	1,400.00
1,000	Elk Horn Coal Corp. Deb. 7s, 1931	1,000.00	820.00
5,000	Federated Utilities, Inc., 5½s, 1957.......	4,737.50	4,750.00
5,000	Florida East Coast Ry. 1-4½s, 1959..	3,950.00	4,875.00
2,000	Florida Power & Light Co. 1-5s, 1954.....	1,900.00	1,925.00
5,000	Illinois Central R.R. Co. 4¾s, 1966.......	4,825.00	5,012.50
2,000	Indiana Ice & Fuel Co. 6½s, 1947........	2,000.00	1,900.00
4,000	Interstate Power Co. 5s, 1957	3,900.00	3,860.00
1,000	Johnston Passenger Ry. Co. 4s, 1931......	1,000.00	780.00
19,000	Maryland Electric Ry. Co. 1-5s, 1931	19,000.00	18,715.00

5,000	National Union Mortgage Co. 6s, 1931....	5,000.00	4,950.00
5,000	Na ional Union Mortgage Co. 6s, 1936....	5,000.00	4,950.00
500	Nassau & Suffolk Lighting Co. 1-5s, 1945..	500.00	497.50
1,000	Oklahoma Ry. Co. 1st & Ref. 5s, 1941.....	1,000.00	690.00
2,000	Penn Central Light & Power 4½s, 1977...	1,920.00	1,840.00
4,000	Peoples Light & Power Corp. 5½s, 1941..	3,880.00	3,840.00
3,000	Phila. Co. secured 5s, 1967, Series "A"....	3,032.25	2,985.00
1,400	Phila. Elec. Co. 1st S. F. 5s, 1966........	1,400.00	1,473.50
1,000	Phila. Suburban Gas & Elec. Co. 1st & Ref. 5s, 1960	1,000.00	1,025.00
1,000	St. Louis County Gas Co. 1-5s, 1951......	1,000.00	1,010.00
1,000	Scranton Ry. Co. 1st Cons. Mtge. 5s, 1932.	1,000.00	785.00
4,000	Scranton & Wilkes-Barre Trac. 1-5s, 1951	3,320.00	4,040.00
4,000	Seaboard Air Line 1-4s, 1950	3 392.61	3,100.00
3,000	Seaboard Air Line R.R., Seaboard & Roanoke 1st Extended 5s, 1931.............	3,022.50	2,940.00
1 000	No. 79 Madison Avenue Corp. 6s, 1937....	1,000.00	960.00
3,000	Southern Pacific Co. 4½s, 1968, interim receipts	2,992.50	2,910.00
4,000	S. W. Missouri R.R. Co. Genl. & Ref. 5s, 1931	4,080.00	520.00
1,000	Standard Mortgage Co. 6s, 1929, Series "F"	1,000.00	980.00
2,000	Standard Mortgage Co. 6s, 1930, Series "C"	2,000.00	1,960.00
1,500	Standard Pwr. & Lt. Co. 6s, 1957	1,492.50	1,507.50
3,000	The Sun Mortgage Co. 1-5½s, 1932, Reg..	3,000.00	2,700.00
2,000	Texarkana & Fort Smith Ry. Co. 1-5½s, 1950	2,010.00	2,090.00
1,000	Tri City Ry. & Lt. Co. 1st & Ref. 5s, 1930	1,000.00	950.00
4,000	Union Electric & Gas Co. 1st & Ref. 6½s, 1941	4,000.00	3,800.00
8,000	United Rys. & Elec. Co. of Baltimore 4s, 1949	5,760.00	5,560.00
1,000	United Rys. & Elec. Co. of Baltimore Funding 5s, 1936	1,000.00	740.00
8,000	United Rys. & Elec. Co. of Baltimore 6s, 1930	7,940.00	7,720.00
1,000	U. S. First Liberty Loan Conv. 4¼s	1,000.00	1,010.00
1,000	U. S. Third Liberty Loan 4¼s	1,000.00	1,000.00
15,100	U. S. Fourth Liberty Loan 4¼s	13,663.40	15,402.00
2 000	West Penn Rys. Co. 1-5s, 1931............	2,000.00	1,950.00
		$195,417.31	$193,387.07

Stocks:

30 Shs.	Mutual Bldg. & Loan Assn. of Baltimore City, par $100 ....$	3,000.00
24 Shs.	West Baltimore Bldg. & Loan Assn. of Baltimore, par $130	3,120.00
		$ 6,120.00

Local real estate, mortgages, ground rents and notes:
Ground rents on properties at 920, 924, 1040 and 1042 W. Fayette St., Baltimore, Md..... $ 4,959.88

Mortgage on 2511 N. Calvert St., Baltimore, Md., at 5 per cent.	5,000.00
Mortgage on 5716 Hegerman St., Philadelphia, Pa., at 6 per cent.	3,200.00
Note of L. B. Wolf and Alice B. Wolf, due June 29, 1929, at 5 per cent.	5,000.00

Notes of Charles R. Fisher, guaranteed by G. B. Morehead, at 6 per cent:

Due September 10, 1928 ....$	2,250.00	
Due September 10, 1929	2,215.00	
Due September 10, 1930 ....\..	715.00	
		5,180.00

Note of Mrs. W. J. Harper (now Mrs. Hattie K. Hogg), due December 31, 1921, at 8 per cent.	2,000.00
Property at 18 E. Mt. Vernon Place, Baltimore, Md.	16,000.00
Equity in property at 132 E. Woodland Ave., Baltimore, Md.	8,681.70
	$ 50,021.58
Property located at Kodikanal, India	$ 13,000.00

SUMMARY

	Book Values
Bonds	$195,417.31
Stocks	6,120.00
	$201,537.31
Local real estate, mortgages, ground rents and notes	50,021.58
Property located at Kodikanal, India	13,000.00
Total book values	$264,558.89

Respectfully submitted,

L. B. WOLF, *Treasurer*

Baltimore, Md., July 30, 1928.

We have audited the accounts of the Board of Foreign Missions of the United Lutheran Church in America for the two years ended June 30, 1928, and we certify that, in our opinion, the foregoing statements submitted by its Treasurer are correct.

LYBRAND, ROSS BROS. & MONTGOMERY,
Accountants and Auditors.

Dr. Benze introduced the secretaries in the following order: Dr. George Drach, who spoke of the daughter churches in the foreign fields; Dr. L. B. Wolf, who spoke of the financial affairs of the Board; Dr. Paul W. Koller, the newly elected Executive Secretary, who outlined the reorganization of the administrative work of the Board; Field Secretary Dr. M. Edwin Thomas, who presented missionaries on furlough, each of whom made a brief address. These were Dr. A. J. Stirewalt of Tokio, Japan; Dr. C. K. Lippard, Kobi, Japan; the Rev. A. C. Knudten of Nagoya, Tyoyhashi; Dr. Edward T. Horn, Theological Seminary, Tokio, Japan; Dr. J. F. Krueger, Tsing Tao, China; Dr. Mary Baer, Chirala, India; Miss Catherine Fahs, former superintendent of nurses in Guntur; the Rev. and Mrs. Isaac Cannaday; the Rev. J. C. Finefrock, India; the Rev. H. H. Sipes, Jr., of Guntur; the Rev. and Mrs. M. L. Dolbeer, India; the Rev. J. Russell Fink, Sattenapalle, India; the Rev. H. H. Moyer, India; the Rev. A. F. A. Neudoerffer of Rajahmundry, India; Messrs. James Soler and James Villaverde of Buenos Aires and Mr. Eugene de Jerus of New Amsterdam, British Guiana.

Dr. Benze then acknowledged the assistance of the various co-operating bodies, both within the United Lutheran Church and in other bodies. He read a cablegram from Monrovia, Liberia, Africa, informing him of the safe arrival of the Rev. Kaitschuk and Dr. Sloan, and containing the following: "The Mission sends greetings to the General Convention. We continually remember you in our prayers."

Dr. Benze read the following resolution of the Gossner Lutheran Church by instruction of the Board of Foreign Missions, and requested that it be received as a supplement to the General Report:

"Resolution of the General Conference of the Gossner Lutheran Church in Chota Nagpur and Assam held March 22, 1928, at Ranchi, Bihar, British India.

"The General Conference of the Gossner E. L. Church in Chota Nagpur and Assam records with gratitude its sincere and deep appreciation of the most brotherly and cordial relationship between this church and the Foreign Mission Board of the United Lutheran Church in America and for its help in building up and strengthening the Church. Now that the Baltimore Board had to withdraw its missionaries, the Conference still hopes that the active interest of the United Lutheran Church and its Foreign Mission Board will continue in the future. The Conference may not expect help in the form of lending missionaries, but in order to conserve, consolidate and develop the Gossner work, the financial help of the United Lutheran Church is considered to be imperative."

Dr. E. Clarence Miller presented the Report of the President and Treasurer on their recent trip to the mission fields in India.

OUR INDIA MISSION
Report of President F. H. Knubel and Treasurer E. Clarence Miller

Can a man love India, especially if he has read some recent books like "Mother India"? He can, for her 350,000,000 inhabitants love her, and our scores of missionaries love her, and we who journeyed there have come to love her also. This report is written with the hope that the reader may know at least something of such an emotion, for our Church cannot do service in India unless Christian love be the motive.

We visited the land because flags of distress are flying over foreign mission fields today. This is true of our India field, which has suffered severe financial cuts because of our Board's indebtedness. It is, however, very generally true. The former age of missionary prosperity has passed away and an era of difficulty has come. Furthermore the principles, policies and methods of missionary endeavor need fundamental re-examination in the light of new conditions in the world. These new conditions are of a religious, political, racial, educational and industrial character. The facts were manifest at the meeting of the International Missionary Council which we attended on our return from India and which served to confirm us in our estimate of the problems.

It was impossible to journey at the same time to China and Japan or to other countries where our Church is in service. However, India is by far our largest operation at present, and at least some of our recommendations are of general application to all missionary work. A preliminary report to the Foreign Mission Board contained all of our recommendations, and as a consequence those which are of a detailed character may be omitted from this more general statement.

We crossed the Atlantic, realizing that Christ is the water and salt of life; we passed Gibraltar, knowing that He is the rock of ages; we sailed the Mediterranean, recognizing that He is the center of the nations; because of Him, for Him, with Him we went. Our eyes, ears, minds and hearts were open, for we desired to learn, to receive more than to give. No judgments were permitted to shape themselves in our minds while the first warm impressions of the mission work were upon us. Our conclusions have developed later under calm, prayerful deliberation and discussion. We continually asked ourselves and the workers: What needs to be made known to the Church in America? What have been the notable successes and failures? What parts of the work need change for improvement in India or at home? What advances must be planned?

The itinerary for our survey had been arranged with greatest wisdom by the missionaries. It was impossible to inspect every station, but all typical operations were visited and the remainder explained. Great congregations met us, reaching in one instance to probably 5,000 people. The humblest villages and homes were also visited. Colleges, schools and hospitals were thoroughly inspected. We addressed and conferred with the leading men of various religions at both Rajahmundry and Guntur, special meetings having been arranged for us. Every possible opportunity was seized for individual inquiries of our missionaries and our India Christian leaders. A dozen times conferences were held with groups of Indian leaders at different places, and all of them were gathered for conference during the last days at Guntur. On these occasions no missionaries were present. Our work ended with four full days of steady conference. During the first of these the All-India Lutheran Conference met, with representatives present from many of the other Lutheran missions (German, Swedish, Danish, etc.) The second day was for a special meeting of our own Andhra Evangelical Lutheran Church, with missionaries and Indian synodical representatives present. The third and fourth days were given to intimate, frank conference with the entire body of missionaries alone. A dozen or more papers had been studiously prepared by missionaries, dealing with all phases of the work. Several were accompanied by illuminating graphs, and complete copies of all were handed to us for later study. They are of permanent value and are open for consultation. All of these facts reveal that even in a comparatively short time we could complete a satisfactory survey. Our welcome was an enthusiastic one on the part of all concerned, and the missionaries threw their work and their homes and their hearts wide open for us.

American Ignorance

Men often speak and sing of the benighted condition of the heathen. Our first recommendation and appeal to the home Church is that it free itself of its own darkness. There is ignorance in America as well as in India, and the ignorance here is as to India and our work in that land. The responsibility of carrying out this recommendation is partly upon our people themselves and partly upon the Foreign Mission Board. As concerns our people, the thousands of pastors can be distinctly helpful. In general, however, our men and women must become ashamed of their ignorance. There remains among us a huge amount of indifference to foreign mission endeavor. Some of it arises simply from a lack of Christian consecration and consequent lack of love for humanity. Some of it is born of thoughtless acceptance of the idea that other religions possess beautiful thoughts and that their followers might better be left to these faiths. More of it grows out of the failure to recognize that the foreign mission service is simply a part of the Church's whole work. We fail to think of the wholeness of the Church's work and the necessity of all parts thereof. Strangely foreign missions have come to be regarded popularly as a work of supererogation, as something more than duty requires, and the foreign missionary is an unusual Christian hero. It was even regarded as an unusual thing that officers of the Church would visit the India work, whereas this was no more unusual than a similar journey to the work in Canada, or in Chicago. When opportunity offers our members should never neglect to visit the mission fields. They will see genuine world wonders. While we were in India a woman of our Church, in the course of a trip around the world, was thrilled by her inspection of the mission. Even without a journey much, indeed all that is necessary, can be learned by careful study of a few well-chosen books. Above all must we recognize that foreign mission work is not only a preaching of the Gospel to the heathen, but that it also involves intricate and interesting problems of far-reaching human importance which challenge the strongest minds and hearts that we have.

As was said, however, the responsibility that the home Church be informed rests also and heavily upon the Foreign Mission Board. There is need of a complete, clear and ceaseless plan of home cultivation. The following elements should be included therein and are approved by the missionaries themselves: a carefully directed use of all missionaries on furlough, with an eye to the entire home territory; an avoidance of that which is merely sentimental and thus calculated to stir only a temporary emotion; the exclusion of immediate financial objectives from this educa-. tional plan; a stimulation of the Church to serious study of the missionary problems, even the unsolved ones, for the Church is unconscious that great problems exist and therefore, not understanding, easily belittles the entire effort; in addition to the problems, a presentation of the stirring facts concerning the work; and finally the setting forth of a settled and sane program of development which will challenge enduring enthusiasm.

India's People

A genuine understanding of missionary endeavor must include some knowledge of the lands and the people where it is conducted. We do not presume to believe that we have come to know India thoroughly, although we have studied earnestly and continue to do so, but the further items of this report demand some statement of our impressions of the country. The study is a bewitching one. Inevitably one is impressed and even oppressed by the masses of the people, over three times the population of the United States living in an area half the size of the United States. It is quickly to be recognized that on the whole they are a kindly, industrious, religious, superstitious folk, with an unusually high percentage of comely individuals. Gradually a more consolidated conclusion concerning them develops, growing out of the following considerations. Over ninety per cent are illiterate. Men, women and children labor strenuously, at starvation wages, so that weariness and under-nourishment prevail. A spirit of healthy play seems to be lacking, even among the children, produced at least in part from the

physical condition just mentioned. It is inevitable that under such circumstances (illiteracy, physical weakness, lack of play) the lives of the
people will be pitifully empty. This idea of empty lives impressed us ever
more strongly, and to one who knows human nature but a little it is
evident that impurity will tend to run riot in such lives. This emptiness
of life is here stressed, however, to emphasize the reality that India is
fallow ground for the sowing of any conceivable influence. Another fundamental fact in the life of the people serves to increase this openness to
any controlling influence. We cannot undertake here to discuss Hinduism at
length, but must comment upon the fact that it is the pervading religion,
philosophy, of the people. Indian life is literally saturated with it. The
ideal of Hinduism is peace, emphasizing that the single goal of existence
is the attainment of inner peace It is clear that such a quest, entirely
controlling life, must glorify passivity in the end, must produce submissive-
ness, and will render the life an open opportunity for action from without.

If we have at all rightly estimated this attractive people, then a third fact
in their national existence reveals conclusively how readily they may become the prey of strong influences. The nation seems to be hopelessly
divided along various lines. India has a number of states, some of them
under true control of the central government, but others virtually independent. Worse than this is the division caused by a variety of languages (not merely dialects) so that those in one section cannot at all
understand those in another. Beyond these conditions are the barriers of
innumerable castes, always uncrossable, and the separation of castes from
outcastes. The strong antagonism between Hinduism and Mohammedanism
creates an added division, the latter including probably one-fifth of the
population. How can a people, whose unity is crisscrossed with cuts to the
depths, successfully resist forces from without?

In brief, India seemed to us to be emphatically an impressionable land.
Having recognized this condition, we noted the companion fact that powerful forces, influences, are at work there today and are aiming to control.
We can barely mention some of them. The British Government is there
with all that such a government involves. Mohammedanism is virile with
its aggressive efforts. Hinduism is ever ready to assume new strength
and would gladly, octopus-like, absorb even Christianity, adapting to itself
portions of Christian truth, even changing thereby its own essence but
also devitalizing Christianity. Education has come with its mighty force,
supported by the government and encouraged by the great numbers of
magnificently intellectual Indians; some of the states are introducing, as
well as they can, compulsory education. Industrialism presses in from all
sides, offering employment, irrigating and reclaiming the land, and promoting
purely secularistic, materialistic views. Racial consciousness has become
strong, and now a wave of nationalism is sweeping India aiming to overcome even the divisions of the people.

We have sought to picture thus what seemed to us a great mass of humanity, impressionable and susceptible to influence, and gripped today by mighty forces. India is plastic, almost fluid, waiting for whatever is able to impress itself. Indian life is being honeycombed and some things of age long standing will fall. It seems unlikely that anything in the way of revolution can occur, but tremendous changes will take place quickly. The burden of this entire portion of our report concerning the land and its people is that the India of twenty-five years hence will be a different land. It is the responsibility therefore of our Church and especially of our missionaries and our Foreign Mission Board to aim to understand the tendencies, to forecast the future, and to shape all plans in accordance. This must be a guiding principle throughout, and will affect such matters as the organization of the work, evangelization, and educational and merciful operations. It also emphasizes the need of Lutheran solidarity in India.

THE MIGHTIEST FORCE IN THE LAND

One more influence is at work in India, Christianity, back of which is the dynamic energy of our Lord. It is true that of the 350,000,000 inhabitants only 5,000,000 are Christians, but the missionaries have the distinct attention of the Indian, their message is being keenly studied, and they are not hated but loved. Their lives of unselfish service are recognized as the best indication of the spirit of Christianity, and are praised even by Hindu and Mohammedan leaders. Lutheran operations of an important character exist, with 300,000 followers. Of these our mission of the United Lutheran Church is the largest. We have come back to America to emphasize at home our calm judgment that *there is no work our Church is doing anywhere, of any kind, which is more prosperous and more promising than our mission work in India.* If only that sentence can be engraved in the hearts of all, we shall believe our journey to have been worth the effort and are willing that all other words of ours shall be forgotten. It is the center of our report.

We have 136,000 Christians in our mission. Do our people ever try to measure even the numerical size of that Indian Church? Only one American synod of ours is larger; namely, the great Pennsylvania Ministerium. To be more definite, we might take two of our larger synods, the New York Ministerium and the Illinois Synod, and have therein almost exactly the membership of the Guntur and Rajahmundry Synods which constitute the Andhra Evangelical Lutheran Church of India. The items of growth are even more startling and shame us by comparison. In seven years the India Church has made an advance of fifty per cent in membership, and at the same time, with all the poverty of the people, increased its own gifts for support of the work exactly one hundred per cent. No synod in all America matches Guntur and Rajahmundry in such items of growth. There are over fifty Indian pastors and 3,700 workers of all kinds. We have 1,400 congregations covering 1,800 towns and villages. The schools have 33,000 pupils, including high schools and college. Our hospitals and dispensaries treated 66,000 patients last year. Try to visualize those cold figures as meaning just that many eager faces and beating human hearts.

What kind of Christians are they? How often that question has been asked of us, since we have returned. Our answer is that as here in America they are good, bad and indifferent, only that over there one recognizes more easily the change that comes to a home or a life when Jesus Christ has entered it. Had we the space many a great congregation could be cited and many a thrilling example of individual consecration. Mention must be made, however, of our gratification over the fine type of the Indian leaders. Pastors, catechists, heads and teachers of high schools and grade schools, physicians, nurses, prominent laymen—they are men and women whom to hear and to know commands respect and love, giving confidence for that future when the India Church will need less of our American guidance.

Turning to our missionaries in India, words fail entirely to tell the esteem of our hearts for them since we have seen them where they labor. The Church in America should know that they are a sincere and consecrated body of men and women, who understand the problems of India, who are working with careful Christian thought, whose plans are never formed without most thorough consideration, who welcome every helpful suggestion, and who deserve our full confidence. We may well thank our Lord for them. They are conscious at all times that they represent our entire Church at home. Naturally there are outstanding personalities among them, but it is evident in general that length of service constitutes an important item in the entire influence of the mission. The aim should be to bring about lengthy total service for all missionaries. There have been too many brief terms; within the last twelve years eight missionaries have resigned before the end of a first term. On this account a more careful search and selection should be made, especially as to personality and physical condition. General qualifications need emphasis as well as specific qualifications. Furthermore all candidates should have more special missionary training before they leave the home country. Likewise the use of the furlough periods of missionaries should be more completely assisted by the Board of Foreign Missions. In a previous connection we have made reference thereto. Here, however, we recommend that any desire by a missionary for a proper further training shall have the support of the Board. The furlough of every missionary should also be used by the special committee of the Board for lengthy, intimate conference with him. The members of that committee will in this way secure something of the gains which were ours through our conferences while in India. We dare not leave this portion of our report concerning missionaries without indicating that facts were submitted to us, which our Board will receive from us, showing the need for six new missionaries at once and further an average of two additional missionaries each year.

SOME SERIOUS PROBLEMS

The shortage of missionaries leads us directly to a sad element in our survey, the limitations imposed by the overspent condition of the Foreign Mission Board's treasury. This has resulted during the last few years in successive cuts of the budget. Dozens of times our inquiries concerning unsatisfactory conditions were satisfactorily answered by the dull words, "the cuts in the budget." Finally it became so ridiculous a repetition that even the Indians smiled when it was given. There were sad and accusing manifestations of it. A rule exists that for the erection of a church building the congregation must contribute a certain portion, the remainder of the cost coming from America. We saw several instances where walls of a church have been erected entirely by the Indian congregation, and the structure remains unfinished and decaying—because of "the cuts in the budget." In this connection also we dare not omit mention of the contrast in physical equipment between the work of our Church as a whole and the work of the Women's Missionary Society. In general the latter is in definitely better condition. We are submitting to the Foreign Mission Board an analysis carefully prepared for us by a missionary which details the present necessities for physical equipment. Our chief recommendation in this respect is, however, that whatever arrangements become necessary in order to bring about a balanced budget for the Foreign Mission Board no further cuts be made in the India budget. Remembering the central sentence of our report, as emphasized above, it would manifestly be a ruinous policy to cut into the essential sustenance of one of our prosperous and promising works. If further curtailment becomes necessary it can be made in some other manner, without endangering a most flourishing operation.

The items of the budget and of physical equipment just mentioned lead us to speak briefly in this general report of the financial arrangements in India. Naturally the treasurer of the United Lutheran Church made thorough inquiry into and was shown the entire financial system. The detailed report to the Foreign Mission Board contains mention of some of his recommendations for changes, and he is ready to explain them completely to that Board.

We have also made reference to a contrast between the work conducted by our Church as a whole and the work which is under the special supervision of the Women's Missionary Society. The latter portion of the India operations merits a distinct mention of its truly wonderful character. Furthermore noteworthy adjustments have been made both in India and here at home so that harmonious development shall result. However, one hears in India and in America, and reads in publications from both sources the terms "Men's Work" and "Women's Work," the use of which should be resolutely abandoned. It is unjust because all married women (wives of missionaries) are now included as missionaries under "Men's Work." It creates a vicious distinction in the minds of those who use it and of those who hear it, and if followed to its legitimate conclusion would imply that we have here in America a men's church and a women's church, the latter being the Women's Missionary Society. Further adjustment of the entire situation is desirable and possible, while maintaining fully the definite organization and remarkable and indispensable accomplishments of the Women's Missionary Society. Meanwhile the present inequality in the India equipment as between the two classes of operation exists as a challenge to our Church until all equipment over there is on a parallel.

There are even more important changes in organization which we believe to be desirable and which would involve a fresh study by the Foreign Mission Board of organizations controlling the work. This is especially one of the situations where the probable facts twenty-five years hence should be considered and set as a goal of attainment. The movement must be in the direction of a transfer of authority to the ultimate and rightful possessor thereof. The hope of all concerned naturally is that in the end there shall be in India an Andhra Evangelical Lutheran Church which lives healthily and cares fully for itself. For many years we in America and our missionaries will be needed as guides and supporters, but we must never for an instant forget the desire to establish in India an autonomous Church.

In attacking this problem we must set out with a clean-cut distinction in principle as to the authority possessed by the congregations in India, by the two synods there, by the Andhra Church, by the Council of Missionaries, and by the Foreign Mission Board. The process of transferring authority to the native Church is one which is common to all missionary work and we may therefore study the experiences of others. However, there is no ready-made solution of the problem, and we may freely study and solve it in accordance with our own conditions. We may and must confidently seek and win the sympathetic co-operation of the missionaries and Indian leaders in this study, for their assistance will be invaluable. A number of detailed suggestions as to organization have been included in the special report to the Foreign Mission Board so that only the more outstanding ones need mention here. We believe that our Board at home can transfer much detail of decision to India, reposing it in the Council of Missionaries and in the Andhra Church. There are unused reserves of power in the missionaries and in the Indian leaders, which will be called forth only as responsibility is laid upon them. Gradually boards, similiar to those in our Church at home, should be created in the Andhra Church. We recognized what seemed to be too intense a spirit of democracy in our Indian work, in that for instance sufficient confidence and power is

not reposed in committees, officers are changed too frequently, and supervision is not of a sufficiently sustained character.

EVANGELISM

We have come now to a portion of our report which need not detain
us long, but which we include with intense joy. The Church has had one
chief aim in the establishment of the India mission; namely, to evangelize
those who do not know the Saviour or have not received Him, and we
believe there has never been a period in the entire history of that mission
when the idea of evangelization has been stronger than it is now. Here
we have no recommendation for changes, but only commendation of the
spirit and work of the missionaries and their Indian helpers and a longing
that the home Church might thrill with the same purpose. We saw the
missionaries chafing under the necessities upon them to do much administrative work and merely to guide the Indians who are pastors and teachers.
We heard several of our missionaries preaching with evident passion and
joy in the Telugu tongue, while others were restless in not having sufficiently mastered the language as yet. We noted that at least portions
of the Indian church have caught the missionary zeal and as new converts
are themselves supporting missionary operations. There are instances of
laymen working there as itinerant evangelists or building chapels entirely
at their own expense. The Council of Missionaries has seriously discussed
plans for work among caste people, which contemplates freedom for
themselves from many details of administration in order to engage very
fully in direct evangelization; these plans have been submitted by them to
the Board of Foreign Missions. All educational and merciful work is
manifestly conducted throughout with the motive of revealing Him Who
came "to save to the uttermost." One hears continually of plans for tours
by automobile or by houseboat in order to do street preaching in village
after village. Much else might be added in detail, but we refrain. Life
is just as monotonous a daily round for foreign missionaries and their
converts as it is for American pastors and laymen, but one clearly notes
there what seems a stronger daily realization that "the love of Christ
constraineth us."

EDUCATION

Slightly fuller attention must be given to educational operations as our
next consideration. This covers the theological institution (Luthergiri),
Andhra College, the high schools, the hundreds of village schools, the
training institutions for teachers, and the various industrial training centers.
Many problems arise instantly, the discussion of which would use too great
a space in a general report but as to the fact of which the Church needs
information. It is here again that the future must be considered, especially
as to what the India government may ere long undertake and may demand
of mission schools, for our schools must be shaped towards that future.

Here also a distinction must be made between elementary schools and those for higher education, so that our mission observe a due proportion for both in accordance with the need for both and in accordance with probable governmental arrangements in the future. With the development of first-class secular education in all schools we must preserve a proper inclusion and infusion of religious education, for recently we heard a caustic criticism of missionary schools in general and also of American church schools in general that nothing else is so poorly taught in them as is religion. One more educational problem is presented by industrial training (agriculture, trades, lace-making, etc.), since it is necessary that all who conduct it be guided throughout by firm principles as to the purposes for which a Christian mission conducts this work. In America also these fundamental educational problems must be fully understood and discussed by the Church, for such understanding will give our people keener interest in and stronger sympathy for the tasks of the missionaries.

We merely indicate a few of the suggestions which have been made in this connection to the Foreign Mission Board. Andhra College has been established with the full sanction of the Church in convention, and must as a consequence receive such development as will make it a worthy institution. Possibly an educational expert should be sent to India for an examination of our educational operations, or at least a missionary with special qualifications should be called; the examination must include the teaching of religion. Some careful consideration is needed for the musical development of the missionary work, since we believe this can be improved with valuable results.

MERCY

As we turn to the work of mercy in India, three great hospitals stand before our eyes, each of them coupled with the name of a great woman physician, whose skilled hand and mind is controlled by a great Christian heart beating in longing throbs over her patients. These are testimonies of Christian love which have spread throughout the land and before which hundreds of thousands have bowed in genuine acknowledgment. We see also, however, the humble dispensaries scattered elsewhere to which the troubled in body may come, often to have their deeper troubles healed also. Furthermore we are thinking of a sanitarium on a hill where tubercular patients are received, which is strongly helped by one of the Indian congregations and is managed by a fine Indian Christian physician. Other pictures are recalled, all of which we wish our American Christians might see so that they too might thank the Lord for the American and Indian physicians and nurses busily, quietly, lovingly working day by day in the name of Jesus. There are still other beautiful works of mercy, some of which we saw and others not. It seems necessary to recommend that definite effort be made, however, to spread the spirit of Christian mercy into the congregations, so that the idea of serving love be given free play by the individual Christians in all their daily relations with their neighbors. This we found to be just as absent as is the case with American congregations. We can prove our faith by our serving love.

We are confident that the Board of Foreign Missions will truly care for all that we brought back as a burden of testimony on our heart, even though it could not find mention in this general statement. We conclude therefore with a reference to our conviction that there is need of the cultivation of closest relationship with other Lutheran work in India. A common testimony for positive Lutheranism is genuinely needed. The project for a joint Lutheran theological seminary should be re-examined with the hope that at least some portions of that plan may become a reality. However, the entire program of work should also be reviewed with the aim of discovering as many points as possible for united endeavor, without sacrificing anything truly needed by the individual missions.

To every reader who has followed us to this conclusion we repeat our central sentence: There is no work which the United Lutheran Church in America is doing anywhere, of any kind, which is more prosperous and more promising than our India mission. Let us all give thanks for its existence and its inspiration.

The Convention proceeded to the consideration of the report of the Board of Foreign Missions.

The President gave an opportunity for inquiries and remarks concerning the work of the Board and its report.

At this point the Revs. Ralph White and John Aberly discussed certain items of the report.

Resolution No. 1 was adopted by a rising vote.

Resolution No. 2. In connection with this resolution, Item IV, B, 4 (a) (b) of the Executive Board's report, action on which had been postponed, was brought up. It was moved and carried, That both the item of the Executive Board's report and Resolution No. 2 of the report of the Foreign Mission Board be approved.

Resolution No. 3 adopted.

Resolution No. 4 was amended so as to read, "Resolved, That all congregations, in addition to meeting the full apportionment, Sunday schools, societies and friends of the Cause, be encouraged to make special foreign mission contributions for assigned purposes such as foreign missionaries, parishes abroad and proteges.

The resolution was adopted as amended.

Pending consideration of Resolution No. 5 the Convention adjourned with prayer by the Rev. M. J. Kline.

Afternoon Session

Friday, October 12, 2.00 o'clock.

Devotions were conducted by the Rev. Arthur S. Hardy and the President called the Convention to order.

The Secretary presented the Report on the Roll of Delegates as follows:

Number of delegates elected: Clergymen, 271; Laymen, 269; total, 540.
Number of delegates in attendance: Clergymen, 270; Laymen, 239; total, 509.
Eighteen Synods have 100 per cent attendance of their delegations. One clergymen is absent; thirty laymen are absent.
Two delegates from the Evangelical Lutheran Church in the Andhra Country, India, are present.

The report was ordered spread upon the Minutes.

The Rev. H. Offermann, Chairman of the Committee of Reference and Counsel, presented the following items:

1. He submitted the following response offered by the Rev. H. A. McCullough to the letter of President Coolidge:

October 12, 1928.
DEAR MR. PRESIDENT:
We thank you most cordially for the communication of your hearty greetings and good wishes to our United Lutheran Church in America.

Your expression of faith in our endeavors and approval of our ideals encourage us to undertake greater things for the spiritual welfare of our country and the extension of our Church.

Very truly yours,
President of the United Lutheran Church in America.

His Excellency, Calvin Coolidge,
President of the United States of America,
Washington, D. C.

This response was adopted by a rising vote and the Committee was instructed to telegraph it to President Coolidge.

2. The following, submitted by the Rev. N. R. Melhorn, was adopted:

"*Resolved,* That the United Lutheran Church in America in Convention assembled acknowledges with grateful appreciation the messages of good will received from church leaders in Europe and America not in connection with this body and authorizes its president to send to each of them a suitable reply."

3.   Your Committee recommends the following action concerning the Near East Relief:

"The Convention of the United Lutheran Church hereby renews its sincere approval of the rescue and constructive training of the orphans in Bible lands under the agency of the Near East Relief."

The recommendation was adopted.

4.   The following submitted by the Rev. John A. W. Haas was adopted:

"*Resolved,* That the Executive Board, through the Secretary or through a committee appointed by the President comprising persons not members of the Board, shall prepare, print and distribute for the use of delegates at future conventions, a convention calendar consisting of a pamphlet or leaflets, in such form as is deemed advisable, wherein shall be set forth verbatim all recommendations, resolutions, actions, findings and judgments of commissions, boards and committees or officers requiring the approval, adoption, concurrence or other action of the convention together with appropriate references to the pages of the BULLETIN where such recommendations appear and where information supporting them may be found and also such other briefly digested information as will aid in arriving at an understanding of the question or issue involved."

(For an amendment see Minutes of fourth meeting, morning session.—Secretary.)

The Rev. C. A. Freed, Chairman of the Nominating Committee, reported nominations as follows:

For the Board of Foreign Missions:

Rev. H. C. Brillhart; Rev. J. E. Byers; Rev. G. A. Greiss; Rev. E. R. Jaxheimer; Mr. A. Y. Leech, Jr.; Mr. Paul Van Reed Miller; Mr. W. A. Rast; Rev. H. M. Bannen; Rev. E. W. Harner; Rev. A. H. Keck; Rev. H. J. Pflum, Jr.; Mr. C. W. Howe; Mr. H. C. Pontius; Mr. W. T. Stauffer.

For the Board of American Missions:

Rev. A. E. Bell; Rev. C. A. Freed; Rev. G. K. Rubrecht; Rev. J. C. Seegers; Mr. A. H. Durboraw; Mr. Wm. Eck; Mr. S. F. Telleen; Rev. A. S. Hardy; Rev. B. R. Lantz; Rev. J. F. Marlette; Rev J. C. Peery; Mr. P. M. Bredt; Mr. Geo. Fisher; Mr. Charles Lehmann.

For the Board of Northwestern Missions:

Rev. A. E. Bell; Rev. C. A. Freed; Rev. G. K. Rubrecht; Rev. J. C. Seegers; Mr. A. H. Durboraw; Mr. Wm. Eck; Mr. S. F. Telleen; Rev. A. S. Hardy; Rev. B. R. Lantz; Rev. J. F. Marlette; Rev. J. C. Peery; Mr. P. M. Bredt; Mr. Geo. Fisher; Mr. Charles Lehmann.

For the Immigrants Mission Board:

Rev. A. E. Bell; Rev. C. A. Freed; Mr. Wm. Eck; Mr. S. F. Telleen; Rev. B. R. Lantz; Rev. J. F. Marlette; Mr. P. M. Bredt; Mr. Charles Lehmann.

For the West Indies Mission Board:

Rev. A. E. Bell; Rev. C. A. Freed; Rev. G. K. Rubrecht; Rev. J. C. Seegers; Mr. A. H. Durboraw; Mr. Wm. Eck; Mr. S. F. Telleen; Rev. A. S. Hardy; Rev. B. R. Lantz; Rev. J. F. Marlette; Rev. J. C. Peery; Mr. P. M. Bredt; Mr. Geo. Fisher; Mr. Charles Lehmann.

For the Board of Education:

Rev. E. C. Herman; Rev. A. J. Holl; Rev. Wm. M. Horn; Rev. A. A. Zinck; Mrs. Adelaide Burge; Mr. A. L. Bulwinkle; Mr. W. J. Showalter; Rev. R. H. Benting; Rev. H. W. Elson; Rev. H. A. McCullough; Rev. O. F. Nolde; Mr. Paul R. Heymann; Mr. G. L. Maron; Mr. Charles Steele.

For the Inner Mission Board:

Rev. F. B. Clausen; Rev. J. F. Fedders; Rev. J. S. Schantz; Mr. A. H. Durboraw; Mr. W. J. Showalter; Rev. J. B. Baker; Rev. G. H. Bechtold; Rev. D. A. Davy; Mr. J. A. A. Geidel; Mr. J. V. Sutton.

For the Board of Publication:

Rev. H. C. Alleman; Rev. A. H. Holthusen; Rev. G. W. Nicely; Mr. Croll Keller; Mr. J. C. Lynch; Mr. O. W. Osterlund; Mr. D. F. Yost; Rev. George W. Englar; Rev. J. E. Harms; Rev. Paul H. Heisey; Mr. C. H. Boyer; Mr. Clarence C. Dittmer; Mr. C. D. Rissell; Mr. F. B. Walters.

For the Board of Ministerial Pensions and Relief:

Rev. Otto Kleine; Mr. A. Raymond Bard; Mr. J. L. Fisher; Mr. Henry W. Harter; Mr. O. A. Sardeson; Rev. W. J. Miller, Jr.; Mr. W. H. Bosserman; Mr. Harry Fischer; Mr. S. M. Goodyear; Mr. M. P. Moller, Sr.

For the Parish and Church School Board:

Rev. P. D. Brown; Rev. A. J. Turkle; Rev. F. M. Urich; Mr. Grant Hultberg; Rev. Ralph D. Heim; Rev. W. C. Schaeffer; Rev. Paul E. Scherer; Mr. Wm. Lehmann.

For the Board of Deaconess Work:

Rev. Earl J. Bowman; Rev. U. S. G. Rupp; Rev. W. C. Schaeffer, Jr.; Mr. John A. Hoober; Mr. Frederick H. Wefer; Rev. H. C. Roehner; Rev. C. P. Swank; Rev. Norman S. Wolf; Mr. John A. Hill; Mr. J. C. Kinard.

For the National Lutheran Home for the Aged:

Rev. Henry Anstadt; Rev. O. F. Blackwelder; Rev. J. L. Frantz; Rev. J. E. Harms; Rev. J. T. Huddle; Rev. Richard Schmidt; Rev H. E. Snyder; Rev. F. R. Wagner; Rev. John Weidley; Mr. L. Russell Alden; Dr. W. K. Butler; Mr. F. E. Cunningham; Mr. Harry T. Domer; Mr. W. H. Finckel; Mr. John H. Jones; Mr. F. W. Kakel; Mr. Harry L. Snyder; Rev. Harry Beidlemann; Rev. E. M. Grove; Rev. E. Roy Houser; Rev. John B. Knisely; Rev. Henry Manken; Rev. S. T. Nicholas; Rev. H. B. Stock; Rev. W. H. Traub; Rev. J. H. Wagner; Mr. Carl M. Distler; Mr. M. Haller Frey; Mr. E. S. Gerberich; Mr. W. H. Hager; Mr. E. P. Miller; Mr. D. R. Perry; Mr. Dan Smith, Jr.; Mr. A. F. Ulrich.

For the Executive Committee of the Laymen's Movement:

Mr. Thomas P. Hickman; Mr. Charles Steele.

The Rev. J. Bradley Markward presented the report of the Board of American Missions.

REPORT OF THE BOARD OF AMERICAN MISSIONS

HISTORY

The Board of American Missions is the result of an evolutionary process. It started with a germ idea named merging. It began as far back as the day of the Joint Committee on Ways and Means. Since General Bodies were to be merged for greater effectiveness, it was thought that it might be wise to merge Home Mission agencies for the same purpose. But it seems that the fullness of time for the carrying into effect of that plan had not yet come. Wisdom said wait. But even so, the Merger Convention held in New York looked with favor upon the idea of merging Boards and so started the process of making possible the working out to its completion a unification program. The Executive Board was clothed with power to act in this direction. The Board moved cautiously, but effectively. It brought the merging idea to the Buffalo Convention for its consideration of the process and the proposed product. It secured this action: "Resolved, that the Executive Board be empowered to effect such mergers wherever satisfactory to the Boards concerned." Then things began to be done.

A conference between the Committee on Boards and Committees of the Executive Board of the United Lutheran Church and the Five Home Mission Agencies finally merged into the Board of American Missions, was held in October of 1923, in Holy Trinity Church, New York City. It was a spirited conference. It brought the pros and cons respecting the merger idea to the fore. While nothing definite was accomplished, it was a good outlet meeting. Expression ofttimes prepares the way for more serious and measured thinking. It did here. Men interested in this great merger idea began to think anew about it and its great possibilities. They saw values which they had not seen before. Unification knocked again at their hearts and going in found a glowing hospitality there.

Accordingly, at a second conference on April 24, 1924, in New York City, this fine result came, as the expression of the sense of the conference: "There shall be a General Board of the United Lutheran Church which shall function through synodical authorities and shall have the power of determining the general policy, and be given such general administration as may be necessary for the harmonious co-ordination of the various Home Mission interests and Church Extension work."

This was considered favorably by the several Boards concerned and the next stage of the evolution of the merger idea was the birth of the Committee of Ten—two representatives from each of the five Boards. This committee worked out a missionary policy and passed it on to the Executive Board of the United Lutheran Church and it in turn brought it, with some minor changes and with its approval, to the Chicago Convention. The convention also approved. The merger idea was now well on its way.

Following the convention at Chicago, the Executive Board elected a Joint Commission, composed of twenty-one persons nominated by the several Boards.

This Joint Commission undertook its challenging tasks in faith and hope. It worked with enthusiasm and devotion. It believed that the proposed consolidation of the five great Home Mission Agencies "should be a real re-organization, not a mere federation; an organic unification, not a mechanical re-arrangement." In the two years of its strenuous and exacting work, it met many difficulties, but they were finally resolved. Therefore, the Commission was able to go to the Richmond Convention in October, 1926, with a Constitution and a Plan of Operation for the Board of American Missions, and they were accepted and adopted without one protesting voice. Then and there, the Board of American Missions became an actuality needing only organization and a happy start toward the conquest of this Western Hemisphere for Jesus Christ.

The Joint Commission carried out the instructions of the Richmond Convention as directed in the Method of Functioning. At a meeting held during the Richmond Convention the Commission's quest for an Executive Secretary was ended in the election of the Rev. Franklin F. Fry, D.D., whose acceptance was announced at the organization meeting of the Board in Philadelphia on December 28, 1926.

On January 1, 1927, the financial resources and all records relating thereto were turned over to the Board of American Missions. At the regular meeting of the Board in January, 1927, the work of the Board of Home Missions and Church Extension and of the Board of Northwestern Missions was given into the hands of the new Board, and likewise at the April meeting, the work of the Board of Immigrants' Missions and of the Jewish Committee, and at the meeting in July the work of the Board of West Indies Missions. This gradual transfer gave the new Board opportunity to acquaint itself with all the varied details of its task.

The Board of Home Missions and Church Extension carried out the action of the Richmond Convention and applied to the York County Court for an amendment of the name and terminology of their charter which would make the Board of American Missions the legal successor of that Board. On December 13, 1926, the final decree was handed down by the Court, signed by Judge McClain Stock.

The charter is one for a corporation of the first class in Pennsylvania, and is dated May 5, 1919. The Board of Home Missions and Church Extension thereupon passed out of existence, but the incorporation of the Northwestern Board, of the Immigrants' Board, and the West Indies Board, is still maintained in order to protect all property rights. The membership of these Boards will be the same as that of the Board of American Missions, so that no expense will be entailed by their continuation.

In conformity with the action of the Richmond Convention, headquarters were established in New York City. Since the Executive Board had arranged for the purchase of Lutheran Church House, rooms were secured in this building, located at 39 East 35th Street, which were occupied on

October 1, 1927. Before that time temporary offices at 437 Fifth Avenue and at 74 West 126th Street were in use.

The Board also adopted suitable By-Laws which are to be found in Appendix G of this report.

The Board of American Missions has had two years of experience on its field and it now comes to this Convention with its report for your serious and sympathetic consideration.

DEPARTMENT OF MISSIONS

For real thrill and human interest, nothing can surpass the romance of home missions. It would stir the blood and quicken the pulsations of the heart to see our capable, energetic group of five hundred missionaries of the cross.

The Executive Secretary has stood on the mountain top of vision and surveyed our mission fields from Halifax, Nova Scotia, to Hollywood, California, and from British Columbia to the West Indies. He has had a comprehensive view of this Promised Land of the West within eighteen months which has broadened his knowledge and sympathy and given him a true appraisal of his task.

It is simply tremendous. Its possibilities are enough to bankrupt the English language. It is one thing to read and hear about home missions; it is another to see where they are and to engage in direct grapple with the problems on the field. Hundreds of our missionaries who are investing their lives have advanced in stature. They are dedicating themselves to the cause for which Christ died. They have expressed in their own personality partnership with God and the stewardship of life.

The old idea is fast disappearing that our ablest men are called to self-supporting congregations and those of inferior grade are assigned to the mission field. That fiction would be shivered to atoms if you could go and see for yourselves. If there is one city on the continent which might seem like barren soil for a mission congregation, it is the city of screen stars, movie artists and film productions. About the time the Board of American Missions came into being, a missionary went to that city, and behold the result. More than two hundred members were added during the year, the mission assumed full support January 1, 1928, a campaign was put on to cancel a $5,000 mortgage, and a goal was set of 1,000 members by November, 1931. This is no mushroom mission; it is growing steadily and strongly.

One of our missionary superintendents said: "Give me a million dollars and Long Island, and I will make New York Christian." A little later he confessed privately that it was just as well no one had accepted his offer. The possibilities of Long Island for Lutheran development can hardly be put into words. To cite only one illustration. With the right man as missionary leader, a hole was dug in the ground, the cornerstone was laid, a congregation was organized, and a church edifice was consecrated, *all within twelve months*. Can you point to any investment with larger and quicker returns?

If ever you feel a sinking of heart at the tardy growth of a mission and need a spiritual tonic, make a trip to Chicago and visit the North Austin Church and its remarkable pastor, the Rev. F. W. Otterbein. He has made Aladdin's Lamp look pale. Eight years ago they bought a combination of church, Sunday school and parsonage. Two years later it was so over-crowded that they were forced to build the first unit of the church—a basement seating 700. Two years after that the seating capacity was at such a premium that they were obliged to complete the structure, seating more than 1,100. Again two years later, with the sanctuary filled Sunday morning and evening, they were at their wits' end. By a happy inspiration, the pastor introduced a third service at 8 A. M. It was a success from the start. The congregation growing at the rate of 400 a year could be distributed over three services. Think of getting 800 to 1,000 people out to church on Sunday morning at 8 o'clock. Their latest move was to purchase additional land to build an L which will seat another thousand people. Some record! but they did it. The communicants at the Easter festival this year exceeded two thousand. Now they have started an over-flow Sunday school for our next mission in that neighborhood. Yes, truth is stranger than fiction. Who can lose heart or yield to discouragement with such an array of facts?

A careful comparison shows that our home mission congregations lead the self-supporting ones in the percentage of adult accessions. We point with gratitude to the fine record of young men our missions have sent into the ministry. Iowa Falls, Iowa, for example, a mission organized eleven years ago, has already two of its young men in the active ministry, serving mission congregations in the still farther West. Muscatine, Iowa, a mission that became self-supporting during the biennium, has recently had the joy of seeing two more of its young men ordained to the Gospel ministry, making four at present in the service of the Church; two of them as pastors of mission congregations, with the fifth son in one of our theological seminaries.

It makes one stand erect, expand his chest and take a new grip on life. No "zero churches" on this list. With the banner of the Lord lifted high, we have joined the loyal legions and follow in His train. Already we have planted our outposts in Alaska and claimed the American Continent for Christ and His Church. At the Richmond Convention, it was reported that a mission had been established in Juneau, Alaska. With faith un-faltering and the vision splendid, we have gone a thousand miles farther into that land as the Board of American Missions, and driven our stakes in Fairbanks. Our young missionary, the Rev. A. J. Buckingham, who does not see a Lutheran missionary in twelve months, wrote to the Pacific Synod in Victoria, British Columbia, that he was prevented from coming because it meant a journey of two thousand miles to Synod and the balance in the treasury of the mission would not warrant the expenditure.

The United Lutheran Church has six Synods within the limits of one State, the Keystone State. If, with the strength of Hercules, you could lift the territory of the Pacific Synod, turn it around a bit, and then lay it on the map of the United States, it would extend all the way from Atlantic City to Salt Lake City, and from Philadelphia to Montreal. Think of traveling 2,600 miles to go to Synod! The Synod of the Northwest covers the wide expanse of five imperial States, from Wisconsin to Montana. The Rocky Mountain Synod reaches out from Wyoming to Texas. We are dealing with magnificent distances and planting the United Lutheran Church throughout the land.

What is the actual record of the Board of American Missions? It has supervision over 578 missions and eighty-six additional preaching points, of which 390 are in the Division of English Missions. This is no holiday pastime. It is serious business. It is a task of continent-wide dimensions. This includes all five departments of the Board's work and in every one except the Jewish Department there has been steady advance. One hundred and two mission congregations have been organized or received on the budget during the biennium, sixty-six in the English division alone. The appropriation for these sixty-six missions for the first year was $65,436. This is an average of $1,000 a year for each of them. We are working on the scale of the King's business. Read Appendix A and get the names of these mission congregations and their Synodical affiliation.

Within these two years thirty-three English mission parishes have assumed self-support and three others, namely, Ascension, Baltimore, Church of the Reformation, St. Louis, and St. Luke's, Waterloo, have merged with self-supporting congregations. Eight additional missions, because of their unpromising character, owing to changed conditions, have been disbanded or been discontinued from the budget. The list of missions which became self-sustaining is given in Appendix B. Eleven bilingual mission congregations also became self-sustaining.

Our missionary staff is as devoted and enthusiastic a body of workers as is to be found in any denomination. The gratifying harvest of the biennium is largely the result of the intelligent missionary zeal and consecration of this staff of workers. We have had contacts with missionaries in many of our Synods. We know the problems they are called upon to solve and the difficulties under which they labor. We appreciate the burden of heart that often comes as the result of carrying almost unaided the load of the mission congregation. All honor to those who do not despise the day of small things and who are laying strong and secure the foundations of the great congregations of tomorrow. Their chief reward is the consciousness of doing the Master's work and winning His "well done."

Many of the Synods without complaint are doing their utmost to supplement the work of the Board of American Missions on their territory, limited because of lack of funds, especially in the way of helping their mission congregations to secure lots and raise funds to augment church extension loans. Other Synods are raising Church Extension Funds to be expended within their own bounds. The Synods, too, through their constituted authorities are making a systematic study of their fields and planning their Home Mission programs to cover a period of years. The spirit of co-operation on the part of Synodical Boards or Home Mission Committees with the thought of securing the maximum result for the money and effort expended is most commendable.

Our vacant missions have been reduced to twenty-eight, the smallest ever since the organization of the United Lutheran Church. Most of these are being served by field missionaries or student supplies. The challenge to advance was never more commanding. Each Synod that has cities of considerable size on its territory sees the compelling need to plant the Church in the growing suburbs. The young men in the Seminaries are willing to enlist in the Home Mission cause. We ask the Church to provide the means that we may occupy the land for our Lord and Saviour.

CHURCHES SUPPORTING MISSIONS

One of the best avenues of assistance in the great cause of American Missions is for congregations or individuals to assume the support or partial support of a Home Mission. The appended list includes only English missions. Equal opportunity is offered for a mission of the linguistic group. The amount is easily within reach, and correspondence on the subject is solicited. The Honor Roll to date follows:

First Church, Altoona, Pa., Rev. M. J. Kline, D.D., pastor, supports Emmanuel Mission, Rochester, N. Y., Rev. F. E. Reissig, pastor.

Zion Church, Harrisburg, Pa., Rev. S. W. Herman, D.D., pastor, supported Trinity Mission, Harrisburg, Pa., Rev. R. L. Meisenhelder, pastor, until January 1, 1928, when the mission assumed self-support.

Zion Church, Harrisburg, Pa., contributed Church Extension aid to St. Matthew's Church, Harrisburg, Pa., Rev. G. Z. Stup, pastor.

The Sunday School of the Church of the Resurrection, Buffalo, N. Y., supports Messiah Mission, Denver, Colo., Rev. Wilson P. Ard, pastor.

St. Paul's Church, Columbia, S. C., Rev. H. A. McCullough, D.D., pastor, supports St. Paul's Mission, Los Angeles, Calif., Rev. John E. Hoick, pastor.

Memorial Church, Harrisburg, Pa., Rev. L. C. Manges, D.D., pastor, supports First Church, Valley Junction, Iowa, Rev. George Ehrich, pastor.

Miss Julia S. Wattles, Pittsburgh, Pa., supports Grace Mission, Houston, Texas, Rev. William J. Hoebel, pastor.

Mt. Zion, Pittsburgh, Pa., Rev. G. E. Swoyer, pastor, supports Epiphany Mission, Pittsburgh, Pa., Rev. Arthur C. Waldkoenig, pastor.

WHAT'S NEW IN AMERICAN MISSIONS

The oldest stock in America is enlisting the newest work of the Board of American Missions. It recalls Lutheran pioneer mission work among the American Indians. Who does not remember the graphic story of the Swedes on the Delaware and Campanius' translation of Luther's Catechism for the American Indian? Before us rises also the familiar figure of Conrad Weiser, Jr., Henry Melchior Muhlenberg's father-in-law, as Indian interpreter, head of the Indian Bureau of the Colonial Government of Pennsylvania. "Absolutely trusted by both parties, this man of sterling worth, who was a convinced Lutheran most of his life, exerted a wide-reaching religious influence upon the Indian." To this we heartily subscribe.

Hitherto, no missionary efforts have been made by the United Lutheran Church to convert and educate the American Indian. At the last meeting of the Board, it was decided to take over Rocky Boy Mission on an Indian Reservation in Montana. Five hundred and fifty Indians live on the Reservation, representing 125 families. They have been there for eleven years. The number the year before was 465, proving that the race is not dying out.

There are 355,000 Indians in the United States, and a considerable percentage of them are located in Montana, "Land of Mountains." Rocky Boy Mission covers eighty acres and is under the protection of the United States Government. Its supervision has been entrusted to the National Indian Association, which has offered to transfer its rights to us. These wards of the nation will become the wards of the United Lutheran Church in America. True to its name, the Board of American Missions will begin work among American Indians.

Norwegian Lutherans, Swedish Lutherans, Missouri Lutherans, Joint Synod of Ohio Lutherans, United Danish Lutherans, Presbyterians, Methodists, Congregationalists, Baptists, and others, are doing successful work among the Indians. The Roman Catholic Church has supported Indian missions for many years and has given generously of its men and money. Uncle Sam visits them regularly through the mails.

After a careful study of all the facts and possibilities, the Board of American Missions resolved to take over Rocky Boy Mission in the name of the United Lutheran Church in America. It is our only mission among these native Americans. The Government official speaks of it as an unusual opportunity for great service. No other provision is made for the religious training of these people and their children. This is true missionary work and will have slow development. Its results do not depend upon numbers. It will require patience, courage and unfaltering faith.

Surprising is it not, almost providential, that a sterling young Indian, who has completed the graded course of the public schools with credit, has offered himself for the Gospel ministry. Paul Mitchell is ready to enter one of our Lutheran schools. His father, Malcolm Mitchell, is the Indian interpreter of the Mission, an excellent type of a Christian Indian. He is a truly converted man and has made an open confession of faith in Jesus Christ. Paul Mitchell has volunteered to be the first Indian missionary of the United Lutheran Church in America to his own people.

The Board has counted the cost and measured it with the challenging opportunity that knocks at our door. Other Protestant denominations and other branches of the Lutheran Church have heard the call and heeded it; shall not the United Lutheran Church in America show the same spirit toward these needy Americans?

Division of Linguistic Interests

The entire work of this department is to be viewed as one task,—chiefly that of gathering Lutherans of the various tongues and homelands, of serving their needs in their home tongues, and of holding them for the church of their faith in order to save the future generations for the Lutheran Church of tomorrow.

The mission task of the United Lutheran Church at its home base is two-fold: That which seeks the children of the American Lutheran Church in new communities and serves them in the language of the country,— and that which provides for the first generation and part of the second generation of immigrants according to their linguistic requirements until such time as they can join the first group. The linguistic policy of the United Lutheran Church was adopted at the Washington Convention in 1920.

This work is comprised under six groups:

    I. German Missions.
   II. Slovak—Hungarian Missions.
 III. Finnish Missions.
 IV. Esthonian Work.
  V. Italian Missions.
 VI. Jewish Missions.

The first four groups, including Letts, Lithuanians and Assyrians, represent work among people of Lutheran faith and traditions, the fifth group represents work among Christians of Catholic traditions, and the sixth, work among non-Christians.

I. German Missions

The largest mission group under the supervision of the Linguistic Committee of the Board is the German mission department. All missions using the German language exclusively or alongside of the English language are placed under this department. Such missions are to be found in the Manitoba, the German Nebraska, the Wartburg, the Canada and the Texas Synods, and in the New York Ministerium. Other German-English missions are on the fields of the Ministerium of Pennsylvania, the Pittsburgh Synod, the California and Pacific Synods. There were exactly one hundred such mission congregations at the close of the biennium, scattered over the whole North American continent from the province of Quebec to that of Alberta in Canada and from Massachusetts to the Lone Star State in the southwest, close to the Rio Grande.

Among our German and German-English missions, a strong trend towards the introduction of the English language has manifested itself during the decade of the United Lutheran Church in America. The transition from the German to the English language has progressed rapidly so that now three-fifths of our missions are bilingual. Purely German missions are found only in the Manitoba Synod, which covers the Canadian Northwest, where the people among whom we labor are immigrants of recent date. Even there signs of transition are noticeable and several new missions started out with equal rights for both languages in order to take care of non-German Lutherans in the neighborhood.

This process of transition confronts the Board with peculiar difficulties, as it is not always an easy matter to find the right kind of pastors for bilingual missions. Pastors who are able to use both languages equally well are rare indeed, and they are much sought after by the older and larger churches which offer higher salaries and better living conditions than our missions. Pastors who know one language well and the other poorly cannot give satisfaction to one part of their constituency, in consequence of which the work suffers. Our older church schools, colleges and seminaries do not teach the German language to such an extent that the students become really masters of this language unless they had gained this knowledge previously. This fact coupled with the other of greater inducements elsewhere results in a deplorable lack of missionaries for this particular work.

Some of our German Synods with a large mission territory felt constrained about fifteen years ago to open schools of their own for the preparation and education of ministers suited for their peculiar needs. These educational institutions, widely separated from each other, are Waterloo College and Seminary in Eastern Ontario, Saskatoon College and Seminary in Central Saskatchewan, and Martin Luther Seminary at Lincoln, Nebraska. The last two in particular are mission schools in the truest sense of the word. They prepare that native ministry which is invaluable, pastors born and raised among the people whom they are to serve and best fitted to lead the people through the period of transition. Without these schools the bilingual mission work on the respective territories and adjacent mission districts would be severely handicapped.

As the Synods in question are too weak financially to care properly for these institutions, and as the work carried on there doubtless benefits the whole Church, the Board of American Missions has continued the aid previously given to them by the Board of Northwestern Missions. Such support being authorized by the Board's Constitution, grants were made as follows: $4,000 a year to Saskatoon College and Seminary, and $200 per year for the support of needy students in Martin Luther Seminary at Lincoln. The Board also gives some financial assistance to Breklum-Kropp, whose graduates are obligated to spend a two years' course in an American seminary, to familiarize themselves with the conditions and the language of the country.

Six mission parishes with eleven congregations became self-supporting during the biennium. They are the Rankin parish and Gratan parish in Ontario, Canada Synod, with three congregations each; the mission at Rosenfeld, Manitoba, Manitoba Synod; St. Paul's, Doniphan, Nebraska, German Nebraska Synod; St. Paul's, Guttenberg, Iowa, and Friedens, Chicago, Wartburg Synod.

Nineteen new missions have been organized or received. In the Manitoba Synod: Strawberry Creek, Fishburn, Lunnford, Fawcett, Alcomdale and Sunnybrook in Alberta, served by Field Missionary A. Goos; Rich Valley, Fox Dale, Volbrand, Boro Green, Runciman and Sturgeon Lake in Saskatchewan, served by Field Missionary George Weidenhammer; Shellmouth and Jackfish Lake in Manitoba as additions to two former mission parishes. In the Wartburg Synod: West Allis and Cudahy, Wisconsin, and Stephen Ludwig Roth congregation in Chicago. In the German Nebraska Synod: St. Petri at Creston. And in the Texas Synod: Falfurrias.

Six new churches were built, at New Sarepta, Alberta, and Dresden, North Dakota, Manitoba Synod; West Allis, Wisconsin, and Martin Luther mission, Chicago, Wartburg Synod; Tivoli and Pawnee in the Texas Synod. Five new parsonages were built or acquired: Luseland, Saskatchewan, Manitoba Synod; Creston, German Nebraska Synod; Miles and Ray Point in the Texas Synod; and Tabor mission, Chicago, which enlarged and beautified its church at the same time, Wartburg Synod.

From this record it may be seen, that the Manitoba Synod is in possession of the most fertile mission field under this department, and how wonderfully the work there is progressing may be learned from the fact that on this territory alone thirty-six new churches and eighteen parsonages were erected since 1910. Pastor W. Wahl was appointed as additional Field Missionary in Alberta, and his support has been assumed by the

Women's Missionary Society. It is interesting to note the special type of his work, namely, that of settling immigrants in suitable communities and opening new settlements. This is really "building" the Church in that region from the foundation stones up.

It is the aim and purpose of this department to assist and urge the missions toward self-support, in which we have been measurably successful. Still there are a few that received support for many years and show little prospect of self-sustentation. What is to be done in such cases is one of the problems of home mission work.

The missionaries of this department deserve the thanks of the Church for the self-sacrificing work they perform under very trying conditions. This applies in particular to those laboring to gather the spiritual harvest in the Canadian Northwest, where in many places real pioneer conditions still exist and the pastor must share the poverty and hardships of his people. When parishioners are scattered over many square miles of prairie or bush country, and the roads are the poorest imaginable; when the little parsonages are almost bare of every comfort and convenience and often too small for the family; when the missionary is so isolated that he does not see a brother minister except at the annual meeting of Synod; when he must face climatic conditions of severe rigor, the long winter with its terrible cold and blinding blizzards that endanger health and limbs; and when for all this he receives a salary of $1,000 to $1,200 a year—it takes strong faith and courage and love to the uttermost to be a missionary.

Some missionaries in the service of the Board have lost their lives for Christ's sake. On October 2, 1926, one of our faithful missionaries sacrificed his life. Pastor John Kaehler had taken charge of the mission parish Massey-Chalk River, Ontario, in the early summer of 1925, right after his graduation from Waterloo Seminary. He was successful in his work and the mission flourished. On October 2, 1926, he took the train at Massey for a trip of two hundred miles to Chalk River, in order to conduct services there the next day. When he left the train he made a misstep, fell under the rolling wheels and was cut in half. Only two weeks earlier another of our missionaries was called suddenly from the service by a stroke, Pastor L. Grauenhorst of Lincoln, Nebraska, who had labored 35 years. In January of the present year a third one was called to his eternal home, Rev. H. Reumann, of Collinsville, Conn., whose time of faithful service in the New York Ministerium had extended through forty years.

The workers go, but the work remains and increases from year to year. At present there are fewer opportunities for purely German mission work than formerly in the United States. German immigration has been limited to 51,000 a year. Probably two-thirds of this number are Lutherans and most of them settle where they find churches of their faith. What new mission work our department can establish in the larger cities must be bilingual from the beginning. But things are different in Canada, for there the Government is trying by every possible means to attract immigrants and especially Germans, who belong to the preferred nations. It is among these newcomers that most of the new missions of the Manitoba Synod have been started. The Synod expects an ever increasing stream of these immigrants and with it ever multiplying opportunities for new mission work. Lead on, O King Eternal! Jesus, still lead on!

For statistical report of Department of German Missions see Appendix D.

II. SLOVAK-HUNGARIAN MISSIONS

The immigrants have come to stay. They fill our mines and factories, and may be found in the varied industries of the country. Due to the quota law their influx has been greatly diminished, especially from southern and eastern Europe. This fact has given rise to the inquiry whether the immigrant program is still of serious importance. It is a many-sided question. For our purpose we can consider only the religious side.

Our United Lutheran Church has given serious attention to the needs of the foreign-born in America. Constant effort has been made to assist in adjusting him to the American environment. The major effort has been to minister to his spiritual needs through the preaching of the Gospel rather than through the employment of social agencies. The Word and Sacraments have been offered to the immigrants in their mother tongue,— they do hear us speak in their own language the wonderful works of God. Due to the diversity of national groups, the task is a serious one. The problem of providing pastors for these strangers has always taxed the resources of the Church.

We have under our care six national groups: Slovak, Hungarian, Windish, Lettish, Lithuanian, Assyrian. The Slovak group is the strongest in congregations and has more pastors than the other five groups combined. This was the first nationality that attracted our attention because there are more Protestant adherents among the Slovak immigrants than among any other group. In extent of territory our operations extend over seventeen constituent Synods of the United Lutheran Church.

On this entire field there are 101 congregations, 55 of which are regularly organized and are served by 33 ordained pastors. Three parishes are vacant, and the Superintendent, Dr. A. L. Ramer, has 43 missions on his itinerant list. He has rounded out two decades of service since his return from Hungary, where he spent two years in studying the language. Recently he completed his fourteenth transcontinental missionary journey in the interests of these people.

Forty-six of the organized congregations have church buildings and twenty-six have parsonages. During the past biennium five church edifices were consecrated, one parsonage was bought, and one church made extensive additions and renovations. Two students were ordained and one ordained minister came from Hungary. Seven Slovak missions were added in Canada. Hungarian missions were begun in New York and Bethlehem, Pa. A Lithuanian mission was reorganized in Philadelphia, Pa. This makes a total of ten new missions.

An event of unusual interest during the biennium was the first Hungarian service ever held in New York under the direction of the United Lutheran Church in America. It took place in St. Peter's Church, March 11, 1928. Our Hungarian missionary, the Rev. Stephen Ruzsa, was in charge. An encouraging start was made. Bishop Bela Kapi, of the Evangelical Lutheran Church of Hungary, preached the sermon the following Sunday in the Church of the Holy Trinity. Drs. J. A. Morehead, M. G. G. Scherer, and Samuel Trexler, and the Executive Secretary, brought greetings.

During the succeeding weeks Bishop Kapi visited our Hungarian Missions in Pittsburgh, Cleveland, Akron, Buffalo, Philadelphia, and South Bethlehem. Everywhere he was received with the utmost cordiality and good will. Great influence for good was wrought by his visit, not only among the groups of his nationality which he met, but also among other persons and institutions which were brought into contact with this eminent representative of the Church in Hungary.

A Slovak Deaconess began her ministry of mercy in the Slovak congregation in New York. This congregation carries on a type of social work not only for its own membership but for the Slovak people living in the Bronx. It is the most effectual means of approach to the Slovak community in the Metropolis. People who had been estranged from the Church for a long time have returned to their faith through Christian service in their temporal distress. Spiritual ministrations in the many and diverse institutions within the metropolitan area of New York have reached multitudes of unfortunates who had been deprived of the comforts of the Gospel.

When one considers the tremendous difficulty which lies in the way of preparing a capable ministry for the different groups of foreigners, the task seems almost beyond reach. The ministry offers small inducement to a people who left the homeland to seek material gain. The language of their adopted country was strange and difficult to acquire. Educational facilities for this special training were inadequate and at times unsympathetic.

The men who have been prepared thus far to serve these people have given a good account of their stewardship. The congregations give evidence of their zeal and fidelity. The Board has enrolled a total of fifty-eight young men. Thirty of them have been ordained. Twenty-five congregations had student supplies for a term of years. Today twenty of these own houses of worship and ten have pastors.

For list of pastors, congregations and synodical affiliation see Appendix D.

III. Work Among Finns

The latest official statistics reveal the fact that 65,000 Finns have come into Canada. This is vastly in excess of any previous record. We appealed urgently to our Church in Finland to send men to supply this extraordinary need. The reply was prompt and to the point: All Lutheran missionaries in Finland and all candidates for the ministry are required in the homeland.

Suomi Theological Seminary at Hancock, Mich., has only a limited enrolment of students. Less than five were ordained in the last two years; only one in 1928. A conference with the officials of the Suomi Synod was held in the Lutheran Publication House, Chicago, in 1927, and again in 1928. Vital issues were given serious consideration.

The question of major consequence was the tragic lack of men and of missions. On the wide territory of the United States and Canada only eleven mission parishes are supported by the Suomi Synod, and two of these have been vacant during the biennium and served by the Missionary Superintendent, the Rev. V. Koivumaki, and seminary students. These parishes represent twenty-eight organized congregations and forty-two preaching points. They are scattered over thirteen States of the Union and two provinces of Canada. The Board of American Missions appropriates fifty per cent of the support. Such a dearth of parishes is simply appalling. Why, we are not even scratching the surface! The majority of Finns in this Western continent do not realize that we are concerned about their spiritual welfare.

It must be remembered that other Finnish church bodies besides the Suomi Synod are at work among the Finns. Thousands of those who have emigrated to America are Bolshevists and anti-Christian and they are proving a menace to Church and State. They censure the Church for its lack of interest and support and often try to create violent disturbances when religious services are held.

In Canada the problem is most acute. Can you wonder that the United Church of Canada spent a million and a quarter dollars last year for home mission work in that country alone? This is almost equal to the total income of the Board of American Missions for missionaries, mission congregations, and church extension in Canada, the United States, and the West Indies, during the biennium. A substantial proportion of the Canadian budget was appropriated for Finnish work. Since we cannot meet the emergency, they claim, the United Church of Canada will step in and do its share. This is not proselyting, they insist, it is helping to minister to Finns for whom we are unable to make provision.

The Suomi Synod at its last convention at Astoria, Oregon, June 7-10, decided to present the question of supporting Canadian Finns to the Board of American Missions of the United Lutheran Church in America, asking them to start the work independently among the Finnish people in Canada as soon as possible.   President A. Haapanen states that the Convention came to this conclusion for the following reasons:

Because of the urgent need of religious work among the increasing and scattered Finns in Canada;

Because our Synod is not able in any larger measure to meet the needs of religious care of our people in Canada at present;

Because the other denominations are just now planning a strong and copious program for proselyting our people in Canada. Of course, we do not need to doubt their unselfish and good purpose in the work for our people. However, they have a different conception of the essential doctrines of the Lutheran faith;

Because with full confidence we believe that the Board of American Missions of the United Lutheran Church is able to take care of the situation there and to start a progressive work immediately.

He adds that the Suomi Synod would be willing to co-operate in the work in every possible way in securing men, maintaining mutual understanding, etc.

Overtures have been made by the United Church of Canada to some of our missionaries of the Suomi Synod but with scant success. Is it nothing to us? Are we our brother's keepers? Do we pass it with a shrug of the shoulders and then dismiss it from our thoughts and prayers?

During the biennium the Board paid $7,009.86 toward the salaries and expenses of thirteen missionaries and the Missionary Superintendent, serving the nine mission parishes mentioned above.

For the scholastic year 1926-1927, $463 was paid toward the expenses of four students in the Theological Seminary at Hancock, Mich. For the scholastic year, 1927-1928, $863.50 was paid toward the expenses of five students at the same Seminary.

IV. ESTHONIAN WORK

At the request of the Board, Professor Edward F. Aksim, of Saskatoon College spent the summer of 1927 in surveying Esthonian work in Canada. Similar surveys had been made in the Eastern part of the United States in 1925, and on the Pacific Coast in 1926.

A service for the Esthonian people was conducted by him in the Church of the Holy Trinity, New York City, in which much interest was aroused. When the results of the survey were submitted to the Board, it expressed its conviction that there is real need for mission work among these people, and efforts have been made to secure a suitable Esthonian missionary to take up this work.

V. ITALIAN MISSIONS

The newest development of work among Italians is the organization of the Junior congregation in Holy Trinity Church, Erie, Pa., by its missionary pastor, the Rev. F. Scarpitti. Should delegates to this convention desire to visit this mission, it is located at 635 West 17th Street.

It comprises fifty young people between the ages of ten and twenty. Every member is required to make the following declaration when admitted into membership:

"I, ..., solemnly promise to follow Jesus Christ; to study the Holy Scriptures; to pray daily; to attend regularly the services of the Church; to support the financial program of the Church to the best of my ability; and to consecrate myself to the service of Jesus Christ for the spiritual enlargement of my own life, and for the salvation of other young people of this community and elsewhere."

While this promise may seem too advanced for a juvenile mind, it has brought these young people face to face with the reality of practical Christianity. They have grasped its significance and earnestly tried to live up to it.

The attendance at the Sunday morning service is never below forty. This service is held exclusively in the English language and the Common Service is used. The Church Council, composed of youthful energetic boys and girls, administers the affairs of the Junior Church. They are well disciplined. If any of the Councilmen should become lax in the performance of his duties or is absent for two consecutive meetings, he is automatically discontinued. Their motto is: "Serve unceasingly." The congregation's motto is: "Every member with a task to perform."

The devotional and social life of these young people has been quickened and deepened. Home life has been spiritually enlarged. Parents are gratified at the influence these children exercise over the household. Family altars have been instituted through them. They realize that power and happiness can be obtained only in constant communion with God. The most serious problem which faces Italian missions is the indifference of young people to church attendance. Since our Italian mission schools must recruit pupils from unchurched homes whose parents give no encouragement to these children because they have little sympathy for Protestantism, it seems an invariable rule that as soon as the pupils reach the age of fifteen or sixteen, believing that they have outgrown the Sunday school age, they sever all connection with the mission church. After many years of teaching and painstaking efforts, they are lost to our work.

The mission in Erie believes it has remedied these difficulties and the situation is markedly improved. No difficulties are experienced in keeping these people in Sunday school; in fact, they are more faithful in attendance and more interested in the study of the Word of God. Thus are the words of the prophet verified: A child shall lead them. Last Easter the confirmation class of twelve children was recruited from the Junior Church, four of them coming from non-Protestant families. Particular emphasis is laid upon stewardship. Under the present regime they are given duplex envelopes by which they contribute regularly for current expenses and benevolence. The real value of this new organization is educational. They are learning the various channels by which the Church functions. In ten months of its existence, the Junior Church has contributed $25 for synodical apportionment; $25 for current expenses; $10 to Ministerial Pensions fund; $15 toward the missionary's salary; $5 for missions; $5 for local evangelistic work. This is only the beginning of a religious experience in the lives of these young people. The Junior Church is the future congregation which will write history for Holy Trinity.

The Board has eight missions among Italians, an increase of two during the biennium. They are located at San Francisco, Fresno and Sacramento, California; Chicago, New York, Philadelphia, Erie, and Monessen, Pa. These missions are served by six pastors. It is gratifying to report the ordination of the Rev. Secundino Bertrando by the Synod of Illinois in 1927, and that he assumed charge of the Chicago Mission. St. Peter's Italian Mission in Philadelphia is under the pastoral care of the Rev. M. Renzetti. During the three years of his ministry there eighty new members have been received. Bible study is conducted every Wednesday evening. The Friday evening prayer meeting is said to be one of the best attended of any Italian Protestant Church of the city. Beginning with a group of four, it now has an average attendance of nearly forty. Other activities include sewing classes, library, Junior Luther League, daily vacation Bible school, and a boy scout troop. Last year the Sunday school had an average attendance of fifty-seven, and through them parents are reached by the workers.

The mission congregation was reorganized April 27, 1928, and the Constitution of the United Lutheran Church in America, translated into Italian by the pastor, was approved. The staff is reinforced by four women workers: Miss Anna P. Hess, Miss Emma L. Hess, Miss Mary E. Hunter, and Miss Nerina Rossi. The women workers reach the women and children of the community through the Martin Luther Neighborhood House.

VI. JEWISH MISSIONS

The Lutheran Church at all times has felt an obligation to minister to the Jews. As early as 1882 a Lutheran missionary, Pastor P. Werber, labored in Baltimore under the Zion Lutheran Society, whose headquarters are in Minneapolis. He left a strong impression on many Jews, some of whom still speak of him with admiration and love. He died in 1896, but it was not until 1920 that our own United Lutheran Church took up the work that Pastor Werber laid down.

Baltimore: Our Salem Hebrew Lutheran Mission was founded eight years ago. The Rev. Henry Einspruch has been its missionary ever since.

From the beginning a large number of friends rallied to its support. Today it has a beautiful mission property with class and club rooms, chapel, a fine library and reading room, costing $45,000, on which there is resting at present a mortgage of $7,500. An earnest effort will be made to cancel this obligation during the coming biennium.

How Salem Mission has been able to make such a fine showing in so brief a time is worthy of being told. Two and a half years after the mission was founded, an appeal was made through "The Hebrew Lutheran" for a building. Some three months afterward, Miss Margaret Mehring, a member of the Maryland Synod, made the mission a gift of twenty thousand dollars toward the purchase of a mission property. Encouraged by that gift, other friends came forward and lent their help, so that today our Baltimore Mission not only has the finest Jewish Mission building in the United Lutheran Church, but one of the best in the country.

At the meeting of the Maryland Synod in May, 1928, Mr. Dan B. Bravin, the associate missionary of Salem Mission, was ordained to the Gospel ministry. The Baltimore Mission has now two ordained men on its staff.

Our woman worker, Miss Grace Bredehoft, has had a most successful year in her department among the women and children. Considering that the field is not an easy one, she has performed a yeoman-like piece of work. This is the interesting program of the Mission: There are regular services in the Mission Chapel and on street corners, Bible classes for men and women, Sunday school, daily vacation Bible classes, educational meetings for boys and girls, including stereopticon and moving pictures, summer outings in the parks and on the bay, visits to homes, stores and hospitals, club work, manual training, and the circulation of thousands of copies of Christian literature, Bibles and New Testaments.

The Missionary Pastor, as also the Associate Missionary, extended the interest of the Jewish mission cause in many congregations of our co-operating Synods, and through the "Hebrew Lutheran," the mission monthly—now having a circulation of more than 3,000—the interest has been deepened by systematic information and education.

Two mission journeys were made during the year in the interest of extending the message of the mission to Jews living in the South. In Columbia, Charleston, and other cities, the Missionary Pastor visited many Jews. He was able to circulate among them many copies of the New Testament as well as other literature.

Salem Mission continues to lead in the role of a pioneer in the field of Christian literature for Jews. Beginning with the first of this year, the mission has published an all-English bi-monthly for Jews, called "The Mediator." Its circulation is at present over 7,000. Every Jewish leader, Rabbi, educator, the Jewish press and reading Jews generally are receiving it regularly. Requests have come for it from the Hebrew University in Jerusalem, from Rabbis, from News Clipping Service Bureaus and other Jewish agencies.

At the Jewish Mission Conferences held last year in Budapest and Warsaw under the auspices of the International Missionary Council, our Church was represented by the Baltimore missionary. As the result of these conferences it is hoped that at the meeting of the Home Missions Council (America) to be held in January of 1930, Jewish evangelization will receive a prominent place.

The Baltimore Mission enjoys the good fortune of having five Synods co-operating with it morally and financially. They are the Synods of Maryland, Virginia, North and South Carolina and Georgia. The financial returns have not been as large as expected, but we are hoping that their interest and sense of responsibility will increase with the years.

Philadelphia: Our mission in Philadelphia has two salaried workers, the Rev. Paul I. Morentz, and a woman missionary, Mrs. Agnes B. Herter, in charge of the work among children. The Philadelphia plan of conducting Jewish work by Lutheran congregations under the counsel and leadership of the Jewish missionary is in active operation. Its purpose is to enlist Lutheran congregations of that city for personal missionary work among the Jews of every age and station of life within their immediate neighborhood.

A corps of volunteer workers among church people distribute literature among the Jews in the communities in which their respective churches are located and they are learning gradually to witness personally and effectively to their Lord. This threefold method of evangelism, namely, Literature, Witnessing, and Personal Work, has by the grace of God produced the following results.

In Philadelphia alone we have eighteen centers from which Christian literature is being distributed among the Jews. A conservative estimate of the number of people engaged in such distribution is about one hundred.

Outside of Philadelphia we have thirty-two such contacts, some of which are represented only by one active and interested Christian. In this important seed-growing branch of the work, nine different states and one foreign country (four communities in Mexico) are represented. During the past year personal work brought 187 Jews in contact with the missionary, with whom he had frequent conferences. Of course, not all are equally interested, but earnest inquirers are among them, some of whom are attending Christian services regularly and a few are nearing the point of baptism. Two adults have been baptized, one of whom has spent a year at Wittenberg College as a special student, purposing to enter the seminary next year.

Toledo: In the Toledo Mission the Rev. Isadore Schwarz resigned during the biennium and the Rev. Harry Rubinstein is carrying on as summer supply. Already he is giving full proof of his loyalty and activity and has won a place in the hearts of Toledo Lutherans. Miss Alta Samelson has been highly successful in her training of children. She conducts a week-day religious school, a Sunday school and a daily vacation Bible school in addition to visiting the homes of the people. So runs the record of winning the Jews to the religion of the Cross. It is proving a blessing to the same people of whom Jesus came.

Pittsburgh: In Pittsburgh Christ's Mission to the Jews was organized by the Rev. John Legum, one of the noblest Hebrew missionaries of the Lutheran Church in America. During the first year of the biennium, the Rev. John A. Yount was in sole charge of the station until August 1, 1927, when his resignation became effective. During that time the mission was kept open every day, visits were made, inquirers met, regular Bible study classes were continued, and missionary services conducted. Earnest efforts have been made to discover a suitable missionary to the Jews, but to date they have been unavailing and the Pittsburgh Mission is vacant at this time.

DIVISION OF LATIN AMERICA

Porto Rico

San Juan is a city of eighty thousand people. It is fifty years older than St. Augustine, Florida. Its White House (Casa Blanca) was two and one-half centuries old when the cornerstone of the White House in Washington was laid. It is a busy centre of trade rapidly becoming Americanized. Its transportation facilities have improved amazingly. Autobuses with a five cent fare run on frequent schedule to all parts of the city. Within the past nine months tourist steamships anchor in the harbor often several times a week. Visitors by the thousands have stimulated business to a remarkable degree. Our Lutheran people from the States are coming in increasing numbers and getting firsthand acquaintance with what we are doing. The missionaries are glad to greet them and show them every mark of attention. The new Central High School would be a credit to any American city. The public school system has been developed to a high standard. Instruction in Spanish is given in the first four grades, but beginning with the fifth grade the instruction is in English.

So densely populated is the island with a million and a half people that one is seldom out of sight of a human dwelling or out of sound of a human voice. Its lavish display of flowers and palms is a constant delight, while its fertility in fruits and vegetation with vast stretches of pineapple, grapefruit, bananas and sugar cane lends charm to the natural panorama.

The old couplet holds true, "Where every prospect pleases and only man is vile." The curse and blight of the island is its low moral standard. No blame or censure is attached to it. Social standing is not affected. The tie between brothers and sisters is weakened. Children are denied a real home. The streets are filled with undernourished, under-privileged and neglected little ones. Fathers have no sense of responsibility for the training of their children. They satisfy the law's demands by providing a mere pittance every month for their material support. The boys and girls grow up only to follow the same shocking standards at an early age.

To combat this serious menace and inculcate Christian teaching and practice many Protestant denominations are actively at work in Porto Rico. They include Lutherans, Presbyterians, Anglicans, Methodists, Congregationalists, Baptists, Disciples, and United Brethren, not to mention the Y. M. C. A. and the Salvation Army. Naturally, the strongest church is the Roman Catholic, but all of them are striving heroically to elevate the morals of the people and to cultivate right living.

An interesting by-product of our mission work has been to stir the Church of Rome to greater activity. In Catano, e.g., where we are the only Protestant Church, Roman Catholic priests were indifferent and indolent until the Lutheran Church sent its missionaries; then a sudden transformation took place. The Spanish priest was removed. Two priests from the United States were appointed. That spelled another story. In a real sense, Roman Catholics in that growing town can thank the Lutherans for quickening their own church life.

Our work in the capital city is limited to San Pablo Church in Puerta de Tierra with two congregations and two mission stations. It is in the downtown business section. Within a stone's throw is Automobile Row and farther on the school for tropical medicines under the control of Columbia University. Nearby are a Roman Catholic and an Anglican Church and a large public school. The new capitol building costing already more than three millions of dollars, the Carnegie Free Library and the Y. M. C. A. are in the same section. Fortunately, the government is constructing a magnificent ocean boulevard which will front directly upon our church plant.

The second story of the school building is a six-room apartment. This was occupied by Dr. and Mrs. Ostrom for years and later by Pastor Pedersen. Within the past two months it has undergone needed repairs and renovations to accommodate the Rev. Eduardo Roig and his family who have taken up their residence there.

Across the bay is Catano with a church, a parsonage, and a school under the care of the Rev. Salustiano Hernandez. This congregation is blessed with a group of active laymen well known in the community who give the missionary loyal support. Connected with the parish are three mission stations.

One of our centers of mission activity is Bayamon. We have two churches there with two pastors, two kindergartens with trained teachers, a fine parsonage, a rented flat and a cottage, which was occupied by Sister Nanca Schoen and Miss Frieda M. Hoh, R.N. The Rev. Gustav K. Huf is pastor of Santisima Trinidad congregation and lives in the parsonage next door. The Sunday school has outgrown its quarters completely and is hampered in further expansion until more adequate space is provided. Plans have been approved for a concrete building on the present church lot for Sunday school and religious education purposes. It is expected that the building will be ready for occupancy during the year. It will supply a long-felt need.

Uptown in Bayamon is Sion congregation, whose Pastor is the Rev. Guillermo E. Marrero. In this section of Comerio Street the people literally swarm, particularly the children. The largest Lutheran Sunday school on the island meets here. The property is in serious need of attention. The present building has served its purpose for twenty years. Financially the people are unable to do much, but they need the ministrations of the Church and respond in loyal attendance.

Sister Nanca Schoen developed our educational work in a most commendable fashion. She was in charge of five kindergartens, instructing the teachers every week and visiting the schools regularly. At present she is on furlough in the Milwaukee Motherhouse. Our registered nurse, Miss Frieda Hoh, was her devoted associate and proved herself an unfailing sympathetic helper. Too much praise cannot be accorded her for her loyalty and faithfulness. She takes care of the sick and neglected children. It would touch your heart to see the suffering and afflicted ones to whom she ministers daily. It is a Christ-like thing. The familiar words of our Lord, "Inasmuch as ye have done it unto these my children, even the least of these, ye have done it unto Me," apply to her in an unusual degree. Her facile pen has assisted the work of publicity and brought additional funds from many interested friends throughout the Church.

The cottage for women missionaries has been a center of missionary work almost from its inception. It is a haven of refuge and a welcome retreat for our over-worked and over-weary missionaries on furlough in the islands. Like other frame buildings it shows the effects of the tropics and is in danger of falling down. It is located in a cool, quiet spot suitable for rest and meditation and at the same time is close to the scene of their activity. The project of replacing the cottage with a more substantial building is under favorable consideration. It would serve also as suitable headquarters for our industrial work.

The Rev. Albert Ell, a member of the Texas Synod, who had been ministering to Mexicans along the Rio Grande, was added to the ranks of our missionaries in Porto Rico. He is serving the Toa Baja-Dorado field. Mr. Frank Colon assists him in developing Maracayo, Santa Rosa, Campanilla and Higuillar stations.

The Board counts itself fortunate in enlisting the services of Mr. Balbino Gonzalez, who will enter Mount Airy Seminary in September for a course of one year. He took the four years' course in the Evangelical Seminary of Porto Rico, under Dr. McAllister, an alumnus of Gettysburg College. Since December 1st, 1927, he has been ministering to two of our organized congregations, Betania at Maracayo and Nuestro Salvador at Juan Domingo.

It was a laudable spirit which prompted our missionaries and laymen in Porto Rico to put on a canvass for the Ministerial Pension Fund. They had not been asked to contribute toward it because of their purely missionary territory. Our people were of one mind that they could not afford to miss the blessing and appealed for permission to have a share in the campaign. At the Missionaries' Conference in San Pablo Church, Puerta de Tierra, early in February, 1928, a unanimous resolution was passed that a goal of $1,000 be set and every effort made to reach it. The house to house canvass lasted only one week, April 8-15. The pledges exceeded the amount by 150 per cent and totaled $2,500. It was the first united effort on our Porto Rican field for the U. L. C. A. and its complete success put heart into all of our workers.

After a decade of active, faithful ministry as Field Superintendent, the Rev. Fred. W. Lindke, tendered his resignation, effective July 1, 1928. He arrived in the States July 9th and is enjoying a season of rest at Mulberry, Indiana, prior to taking on future work.

A large and flourishing Sunday school is conducted at Gandul within the corporate limits of San Juan. It is under the direction of Mr. Juan Zambrana, a native helper and zealous worker. Religious services are conducted every week by Pastor Roig. Extensive improvements, recently made, have added much to the attractiveness and equipment of the building.

VIRGIN ISLANDS

The oldest territory to fly the American flag is the Virgin Islands. Christopher Columbus landed in St. Croix on his second voyage November 14, 1493, and named it Santa Cruz. At the time of the transfer of the Virgin Islands to the United States much valuable property was acquired from the Danish National Church. This included five churches, three parsonages, three old people's homes, two homes for sick and neglected babies known as the Queen Louise Homes and the Ebenezer Orphanage. These works of mercy have been continued under the administration of the Board.

We have three fine church properties in St. Croix. The field covers an area of 15 miles with Frederiksted at one end, Christiansted at the other and Kings Hill midway. Since September, 1926, the entire field of St.

Croix was served by Dr. Alfred Ostrom, veteran missionary in the islands. All honor to him for his untiring devotion which was at the cost of constant physical strain. He won the hearts of all the people. They regarded him affectionately as their spiritual father. Under his able leadership the three congregations contribute regularly toward their support. For the first time these missions have pledged a total of $1,080 for 1928 and up to June 30th the proportionate amount was paid in full.

Shortly before the close of the biennium a call was extended to the Rev. Louis G. Gray as Pastor of the Frederiksted-Kings Hill Parish. He and his family sailed for the Virgin Islands and took charge of the work in July. A similar call has been sent to the Rev. Ivar O. Iverson, a graduate of the Northwestern Theological Seminary, as Pastor of the Christiansted Parish.

Miss Ethel M. Mosteller was commissioned in Christ Church, York, Pa., her home congregation, in January, 1927. For a time she was matron of Ebenezer Orphanage, an institution for orphan girls. Upon the arrival of Sister Emma Francis and Sister Edith Prince of the Philadelphia Motherhouse to take up that work, Miss Mosteller became Parish Worker in the Frederiksted congregation, where she is doing excellent service. Sister Maren Knudsen, of the Motherhouse at Copenhagen, is the beloved and successful matron of the Queen Louise Home in Frederiksted. With rare unselfishness she has given twenty years of unfailing activity. Sister Clara Symre of the Baltimore Motherhouse is the efficient matron of the Home in Christiansted.

The Rev. J. C. Pederson, a missionary in many lands, is in charge of the St. Thomas-St. John's Parish. He succeeded Pastor Nels T. Nesgaard, who had accepted a call to a Lutheran congregation in Detroit. Pastor Pedersen has given full proof of his ministry and on Pentecost of this year he confirmed a class of thirty-six. This congregation also assists the Board by financial contributions. The church in St. Thomas is a noble landmark, dating back to 1661. Services on the Island of St. John are conducted chiefly by the clerk, Mr. Carl E. Francis.

There are two Leper Colonies in the islands, one at Christiansted, St. Croix, with ninety lepers, the other in Porto Rico with sixty lepers. For years these latter unfortunates were forced to live on a lonely rocky island. Now the government has built a modern attractive sanatorium at San Piedras, where the lepers are given every comfort. In both colonies our missionaries take their part in conducting religious services along with the other denominations and minister to their material needs and the relief of their suffering.

Our missionaries desire to express their thanks through the Board to the congregations, Sunday schools, missionary societies and Luther Leagues for the Christmas boxes in which they find needed supplies for the poor and for gifts to the children in the kindergartens. Special acknowledgment is made of the generous gift of $500 annually from the Light Brigade for Sick and Neglected Babies.

WEST INDIES

The greatest asset in the West Indies today is the competent, conscientious, consecrated missionaries of Jesus Christ. Our missionary force during the biennium numbered 38; a field superintendent, 7 missionary pastors, 12 missionary helpers, 10 kindergarten teachers, 5 deaconesses and 3 women workers. These served 19 congregations and 11 mission stations, in addition to the educational work and the care of sick and neglected children. We have ten parsonages and three school buildings. The organizations include 29 Sunday schools, 7 daily kindergartens, 8 Luther Leagues, 9 Junior Luther Leagues, 8 Daily Vacation Bible Schools, 6 Light Brigades and an Altar Guild.

WORK AMONG NEGROES

The Board has given thoughtful consideration to work among negroes. The present status is indicated by the following resolution adopted February 23rd, 1927:

"Concerning the wider question of the United Lutheran Church in America beginning work among negroes, your Committee is not prepared to give a specific opinion. We have had the matter under advisement. We have not dismissed it. We have no intention to evade the responsibility or avoid the problem. We are simply not ready at this meeting to give an answer to the question.

"That the problem presents difficulties of a very definite and positive character no one will deny. That it calls for particular and prayerful thought, everyone will admit. That there is an answer, we confidently believe. In this, as in every difficult problem which confronts the Church, the Holy Spirit will offer the proper solution. His guidance we are seeking. His leadings we will endeavor to follow.

"At present we ask for the patient and prayerful co-operation of the Church."

NEW YORK

Directly connected with the missions in the West Indies is the work being done in New York City among West Indians who have sought a home in that unique section, Harlem, which is known the world over as the greatest negro city in all history, the Mecca of all the ambitious among those in whose veins flows the slightest trace of negro blood.

Our mission, the Church of the Transfiguration, affectionately known as the colored people's "little church around the corner," has had a marvelous growth, having received over a hundred members annually for the past six years. Since these people, because of their color, find it hard to secure work, they move frequently to other cities, where for the time being work is more plentiful, and as a result, there are only about six hundred active members. These people come literally from the ends of the earth, although the larger number are from the West Indies. Not all were Lutherans, for about one third of the present membership was recruited from other denominations and from the world.

The congregation is well organized, having all the various activities found in uptodate congregations. As many as five services have been held on Sunday and sometimes two services at the same time; this being possible because the church is four stories, furnishing room for three simultaneous meetings. At special services many people are turned away since the church is too small for the membership. Over $5,000 is raised by the congregation annually, an amazingly large sum for people who, because of their race, must take the poorest paid jobs and who, because they are negroes, must pay higher for inferior homes and food than white people pay for the best.

The congregation rejoices this year in having one of its own sons ordained to the ministry. The Rev. Paul West was born in St. Croix, Virgin Islands, but spent his youth in Santo Domingo and Porto Rico. He spent five years at Wagner Memorial College and three years at Mt. Airy Seminary. He was ordained by the New York and New England Synod, with which the congregation united. He is the second colored minister to be ordained by this Synod, which last year ordained Rev. N. L. M. Chisholm, an American Negro, who has been working under our Board. The opportunity for work among the 14,000,000 negroes of America is unlimited since more than half of them are untouched by any church. Shall the church withhold the support when men are saying, "here am I, send me?"

Spanish Work in New York. Our mission among Spanish people was organized primarily to conserve the labors of our missionaries on the Porto Rico field, whose members moving to New York City were lost to the Lutheran Church. Naturally, the growth in this mission is not rapid, not only because of the smaller number of Lutherans among the Spaniards, but also because the people are widely scattered. There is little or no prospect of establishing self-supporting churches among these people since they rapidly anglicise and are readily received by the established congregations because they are of the white race. The great need is a community center where the people can be cared for until they have learned the language and adjusted themselves to their new environment. Such a center with a pastor speaking Spanish, would be able to hold these people and win many others of the race who have lost all contact with the Roman Church. The present work is in charge of Student Leopoldo Caban, a native of Porto Rico. Mr. Caban studied at Wagner Memorial and is now in his senior year at Gettysburg. He has maintained a high standing in his classes and is a welcome reinforcement to our mission staff. If the church would furnish the means more men could be secured from Spain and an aggressive work undertaken in Latin America as well as on the Mexican border.

EDUCATION OF MISSIONARIES

The Plan of Operation as adopted at Richmond declares:

"Since the development of a permanent missionary staff requires not only the support of students in college and seminary but also additional special- ized training, the Board shall, in co-operation with the Board of Education, the educational institutions of the United Lutheran Church, the Women's Missionary Society, Laymen's Movement, and others, provide for the edu- cation and training of a succession of missionaries needed for the fields of the Board, giving special attention to the spiritual needs of racial or language groups. To this end the Board shall seek the benefit of estab- lished scholarships and where necessary, aid existing schools, and also establish additional schools, especially in fields outside of the United States. In this entire connection the Board has in mind the preparation of men for life service as home missionaries."

This article refers primarily to aid to be given after the conclusion of a candidate's seminary course. During the first biennium of the Board's existence it could not, for financial reasons, add this phase of activity to the work allotted to it. We have, however, co-operated with all the agen- cies noted in this article and wish to make special acknowledgement of the generous financial support furnished by the Women's Missionary Society for the education of students under our Division of Linguistic Interests. At the same time we wish also to express our gratitude for the aid fur- nished by the Laymen's Movement.

A short history is given at this point of the work transferred.

Kropp - Breklum. The need of men for work among German- speaking people was so great in both the General Synod and General Council that long before the formation of the United Lutheran Church these bodies established institutions in Germany to supply the American field. The General Synod institution was located at Breklum, Germany, while the General Council institution was at Kropp. At the time of the formation of the United Lutheran Church the World War prevented con- tact with these institutions and immediately afterwards Dr. E. F. Bach- mann was sent to Germany and later on Dr. Fred. Gotwald, both of whom endeavored to obtain a merger of these institutions, but it was not deemed practical and there was a readjustment whereby the institution at Breklum was the preparatory school while Kropp became the seminary.

In order to bring the matter clearly before the United Lutheran Church, Director Rohnert attended the Convention at Richmond, where the Execu-

tive Board brought in an exhaustive report on the subject. A budget of
$6,000 for the Breklum-Kropp institution was adopted and an additional
$1,000 by the Board of Northwestern Missions, to be paid through the
Board of Education. This amount was increased at the January meeting
in 1927 of the Board of American Missions, in accordance with the
conference held at Richmond between representatives of the Board of Education, Board of Northwestern Missions and the Director of Breklum-
Kropp, which was also approved by the Executive Board, the amount is
now $1,500 a year from the Board of American Missions. It would appear
that this appropriation must continue unless some new adjustment is made.
Neither the Board of Education nor the Board of American Missions could
in fairness reduce their appropriation without mutual agreement and the
approval of the convention.

Since the War the institution has been resumed on a reduced scale, so
that its future is practically dependent upon the money received from the
Board of Education and the Board of American Missions.

The number of students coming to this country since the War is necessarily limited,—first, because of the shortage of manpower in Germany and
secondly, because of our immigration law.

American training is absolutely necessary, for without knowledge
of the English language it is impossible for men to secure calls. A large
number cannot be expected annually for some time. Additional support of
candidates is required in this country, since our Board after consultation
with the Board of Education, requires that these candidates spend two
years in the seminaries of this country. Heretofore, this cost has been
borne by the seminaries to which the men were assigned by the Board
of Education. One seminary has refused to give any further support and
others are becoming more reluctant. It is necessary also for the Board
to furnish traveling expenses from Europe, because almost all of these
men are without financial resources.

Martin Luther Seminary, Lincoln, Nebraska. This seminary was founded
by the German Nebraska Synod in 1913 on the receipt of $20,000 in cash
and securities from Mr. Osterloh, a member of Dr. Wupper's congregation
in Hooper, Nebraska. Dr. Wupper became the first president of the
institution.

The institution was incorporated under the laws of Nebraska as an institution of the German Nebraska Synod, a part of the General Synod. A
concrete building in Lincoln, Nebraska, was purchased with room for
twenty-four students and quarters for the president and his family. The
property is valued at $25,000, although purchased at $11,000. It was
formerly a sanatorium and one purchaser gave it up, losing the initial payment, which made the offer of the Synod quite attractive.

After the Washington Convention the Northwestern Board commenced aiding students at the institution, which naturally relieved the Synod of this burden, so that the money previously raised by the Synod could be paid toward the upkeep. Later on, a congregation was organized for the seminary families and made a mission.

In 1927 our Board aided twelve students at the cost of $2,262, and this year we are aiding nine students at a cost of $1,525. The rule is that no student shall receive more than $200. Some receive much less.

Saskatoon. In view of the great need of missionaries for its vast territory, the Evangelical Lutheran Synod of Manitoba and other provinces at its convention at Winnipeg, Manitoba, in 1911, resolved to open an institution in which young men from the congregations might be prepared for the theological seminary. The Synod at this time was only fourteen years old with twenty-two parishes and 4,000 communicants.

The school was begun at Edmonton, Alberta, November 20th, 1913, in a rented house. The following year Saskatoon was selected as the permanent seat of the institution. The property at present is valued at $63,000. The number of men graduated has been small, but the institution is growing and since it has obtained recognition from the University of Saskatchewan will be able to build up a good school. The institution was chartered by Provincial Act in 1924. Since 1920 the Northwestern Board has been paying $4,000 a year toward the professors' salaries, which has been continued up to the present time under the Board of American Missions.

Student Aid in Various Institutions. Most of our Slovak and Hungarian students have been sent to Muhlenberg College and Mt. Airy Seminary, although some have studied at Chicago and other institutions. Last year we had five in the Seminary and nine in Muhlenberg. A tutor in Slovak was also paid by the Board for special instruction of the men both in college and seminary.

Under agreement with the Suomi Synod the Board assists in the support of students preparing for the ministry in their institution at Hancock.

The work in the West Indies not being connected with any constituent synod requires the Board to support men for the ministry. Last year one colored student was in the Seminary and a Spanish student supported at Gettysburg.

DEPARTMENT OF CHURCH EXTENSION AND FINANCE

The question of separate boards for the administration of home missions and of church extension has been a much debated subject. The experiences of the general bodies before the formation of the United Lutheran Church revealed that the largest development occurred when the church extension work was administered by a separate Board. However, the intimate relationship existing between church extension and home missions gave such advantage to a unified management that at the time of the merger of the three general bodies, their boards were all combined in the Board of Home Missions and Church Extension.

The Joint Commission gave the subject very careful study and endeavored by the establishment of a Department of Church Extension and Finance, with the treasurer of the Board as secretary *ex officio,* to secure all the advantages of a separate board, while at the same time maintaining the unity and co-ordination that can only be secured when the work is under one management.

The work in the Department of Church Extension and Finance during its first eighteen months has been largely concerned with the multitudinous details of reorganization as related to the financial and property interests of the five predecessor Boards, whose assets totaled two million dollars. This constituted a most difficult task that prevented the undertaking of certain other duties assigned to this department, but which will be cared for in the coming biennium.

The first task was that of securing an accounting system which would provide adequate records of such large resources. The firm of Lybrand, Ross Bros. & Montgomery, whose reputation is national, was engaged for this task, and as a result, the Board of American Missions has a system of accounting that is not excelled by any Board in the Protestant Church. Special mention should be made at this point of the service rendered in this work by Mr. Henry F. Heuer, a member of our Board.

The second task was the solution of the grave financial problems that confronted the Board at its inception on January 1, 1927. During the six months from July 1 to December 31, 1926, the predecessor Boards spent $118,609.99 more than they had received. In addition, Church Extension loans had been promised totaling more than $110,000. Also at this date the five Boards had short term loans at the banks which, together with their unpaid bills and the expenses of the Joint Commission (which had been advanced from the treasury of the United Lutheran Church), totaled $34,642. To meet this array of liabilities, the merging Boards, which on June 30, 1926, had cash balances of $170,196.12, turned over to the Board of American Missions cash balances of only $51,586.13, of which more than one-half was in trust funds which could not be used for current expenses. Furthermore, the apportionment for 1927 was that of the previous biennium which made no provision for the larger work to be accomplished after the unifying of the Church's various home mission agencies. In view of all these conditions, the Board takes a pardonable pride in the financial report presented to this convention.

Nevertheless, the lack of funds has seriously held back the development of the home field, especially in the work of Church Extension, where the Board's source of income is restricted chiefly to gifts from individuals,

legacies, and returned loans. The present apportionment is barely sufficient to meet the missionaries' salaries and the necessary expenses of
operation. It is the Board's confident hope that this convention will commend our cause to the membership of the United Lutheran Church, so
that by personal solicitation the necessary funds may be secured to
strengthen this important arm of the Church.

Overdue Loans. We rejoice that the collections on overdue church extension loans have been greater during the eighteen months of the administration of the Board of American Missions than during any like period
previously. The returns from this source, however, should be not less
than $150,000 a year, if the Church is to keep faith with those whose gifts
made the Permanent Loan Fund possible. These monies were given on
the promise that the loans would be returned at stated periods and be
loaned for the erection of churches over and over again throughout the
succeeding generations. It reflects a serious mental attitude, therefore,
when some of the churches that were exceedingly anxious to obtain a
loan on any terms in after years plead the statute of limitations, or request
a large discount as an incentive to repay, or even request the cancellation
of the entire loan. The new Plan of Operation has already created a
new interest on the part of Synodical authorities on this subject of overdue
loans, and we anticipate a large increase in repayments during the next
biennium.

The Board's greatest resource in building up a Permanent Loan Fund
is that derived from legacies, and it is therefore earnestly urged upon the
Church that increasing numbers of those who have been blessed with this
world's goods will remember the cause of Church Extension in their wills.
Since July 1, 1926, the following bequests have been received, some of
which, however, are only partial payments:

Elizabeth Kern	$ 481.45
C. L. Cline	500.00
Henry Bowman	200.00
Amelia H. Eickelberger	2,000.00
Theodore C. Birnbaum	3,759.99
Athalinda Hicks	137.62
Etta M. Harroway	14,000.00
Emma Viola Clarke	1,318.80
Peter Woll, Jr.	1,266.11
J. E. Cooper	14,000.00
Mary Ellen Smith	2,635.81
J. B. Kaercher	18,412.94
Margaret McGill	150.00
Rosa B. Repass	1,000.00
Annie M. Asper	402.79
Etta A. Wallis	1,500.00
N. C. Smith	1,000.00
Laura M. Stoever	2,000.00

Nellie S. Anderson	1,299.00
W. F. Lobach	2,250.00
Melissa J. Linhart	100.00

Loans to Churches. During the biennium loans have been made to churches in the amount of $297,800. While this sum is unusually large, especially in proportion to the receipts for this purpose, nevertheless, it is only a small part of the amount that was asked of the Board. To meet the pressing necessities of our growing church this Board should have funds which would enable them to grant four times this total.

Donations of Interest. In order to help churches where a sufficiently large church extension loan could not be granted or where it is not possible for them to furnish proper security for a loan according to the requirements of the Permanent Loan Fund, donations for the payment of interest on mortgages procured locally have been granted. The amount of money thus contributed in the past biennium totals $100,851.67. This form of aid, however, must necessarily be curtailed in the future, since funds for this purpose are no longer on hand.

Annuities. $18,000 were received on annuities since the last report which gives the Board a total of $70,350 in annuities.

Synodical Funds. One requirement placed upon the Department of Church Extension and Finance by the Plan of Operation adopted at Richmond has not been met as yet, due to the fact that it was impossible during the biennium to obtain from all Synods, local Church Extension Societies, and Mission Associations, the audited statements of expenditures required by this action. Believing that a partial report would be misleading rather than furnish the information sought by the Convention as required in this supplementary report, the statement is omitted at this time with the assurance that at the next Convention a full accurate report will be furnished and made a feature of all future reports of this Board.

PROMOTION AND PUBLICITY

Tell it to the Church. Give the facts to the people !

That is the policy of the Board in publishing its good news. The entire staff has been diligent in presenting the cause of Home Missions in all sections of the Church and to all groups of our constituents. Our advancing cause has been brought home to Synods, conferences, congregations, ministerial associations, student groups, women's synodical missionary societies, and summer assemblies, while the latest developments have been given to the Church through our Church periodicals.

Conference with Synodical Presidents:

A spirited discussion with the presidents of Synods was held in Edgewater Beach Hotel, Chicago, in November, 1927. The new financial policy was outlined, the budget appropriations to Synods considered and the Plan

of Operation reviewed. With few exceptions every synodical president
was in attendance.

Field Days for Church Extension:

Cleveland and Toledo put on successful field days in 1928. A two-day
program was set up. Drs. Markward and Larimer, General Superintendent
Ramer, Divisional Secretary Seibert, and the Executive Secretary, represented the Board and its staff; President Koller, Missionary Superintendent Herold, Field Missionary Strobel, Dr. Sittler, Chairman of the Home
Mission Committee, and others, presented the cause from the pulpits of our
Cleveland churches Sunday morning. A union service was held in the
evening in the interests of Church Extension. All missions were visited
by the entire group the following day and a complimentary dinner was
given by the Church Extension Society at which a definite objective was
reached. The mission in Parma, one of the newest suburbs of Cleveland,
was launched, property was purchased, and a church building was projected.

In Toledo twenty-three congregations in that strong Lutheran center
heard the missionary message on Sunday. A stimulating conference on
"Missions of Today and Tomorrow" was a feature at the meeting of the
Ministerial Association. A twenty-five year program for missions in
Toledo and vicinity was given definite shape by Dr. F. E. Strobel, Field
Missionary, which won unanimous approval, and an annual budget of $2,500
for local church extension was pledged.

A similar field day is planned for Chicago, October 21st.

Home Mission Conferences:

Dr. John J. Myers, Missionary Superintendent of the Pittsburgh Synod,
arranged a conference of Home Missionaries of the Synod each year of
the biennium. The attendance was highly gratifying and the enthusiasm
refreshing. President Burgess, General Superintendent Hoffman, and the
Executive Secretary, discussed missionary problems and opportunities and
answered many practical questions. Similar conferences were held by the
Ministerium of Pennsylvania. the Synod of the Northwest, and other
synodical bodies.

Evangelistic Services:

Out on the Pacific Coast, General Superintendent Hillerman has been
in great demand during the entire biennium, in holding one week's daily
services in scores of our missions. The result has been most commendable
and stirred our struggling enterprises to renewed faith and consecration.
His theme is Home Missions and Evangelism, which is given to the people
in such striking fashion as to arouse the indifferent and quicken missionary
fervor and zeal.

Publications:

Three booklets were issued for free distribution: A Twentieth Century
Adventure, Interpreting our Home Mission Work, and Open Doors. Tracts

containing the latest facts were prepared on English Missions, German Missions, Immigrants' Missions, Jewish Missions, and West Indies Missions. These were favorably received throughout the Church.

Summer Schools:

Most of the summer assemblies have included American Missions on their program. Representatives of the Board and the Staff accepted invitations from all parts of the United Lutheran Church to present a course of study and give popular addresses on the great cause which has appealed to the imagination and kindled the interest of the whole Church.

CO-OPERATION ALONG ALL LINES

The Board of Education:

A contribution of $2,500 for the biennium has been made by our Board to the Board of Education for the support of Kropp-Breklum, in Germany, in preparing students to serve in our mission fields

The Board of Education assists our Board in the support of the pastors at Durham, N. C., Rock Hill, S. C., Clemson College, S. C., Lafayette, Ind., Seattle, Wash., West Chester, Pa., Boulder, Colo.

The Inner Mission Board:

Our Board assists also in providing a house for the Rev. H. Becker, of Winnipeg. He has charge of the immigrant work in Northwestern Canada under the supervision of the Board of Inner Missions.

The presentation of the Gospel message to the Children of Silence received favorable consideration. Work among the deaf is needed in every section of the Church. It is a national problem rather than a synodical one. Religious services for the deaf can be provided in our mission churches all over the United Lutheran Church in America. By the use of the sign language, such services are conducted simultaneously with the regular worship of another congregation in the same building without disturbance or interference. In response to a request for support from the Inner Mission Board of one of our Synods, the Board has expressed its willingness to take over the work as a type of Lutheran evangelism.

The Women's Missionary Society:

Our thanks are due and given in generous measure to the Women's Missionary Society for its constant co-operation. As a mark of gratitude and appreciation, six members of the society were invited to attend the stated meetings of the Board. Mrs. William E. Black and Mrs. Virgil B. Sease served as Advisory Members. Mrs. T. W. Kretschmann represented the society in the interest of English Missions, Mrs. Frank E. Jensen in Linguistic Interests, Miss Amelia D. Kemp in Church Extension, and Miss Flora Prince in Latin-American interests. They were heartily welcomed and their presence proved helpful.

Thirty-six missions are supported by the society. Within the two years three assumed self-support and four were added to the list. This energetic organization has so loyally and willingly helped to underwrite our work that it must be an encouragement to note the victories won by some of the congregations which they have aided. Note, for example, the churches at Longview, Wash., and University, Seattle; Gary, Indiana; Kalamazoo, Mich., and the crowning work of that devoted servant of God, the late Rev. A. J. Sommer, who was called to his heavenly home while in the midst of erecting a fitting church building at Denver, Colorado, as a memorial to the sainted Dr. Samuel B. Barnitz, missionary hero and statesman.

Students preparing for the ministry of our linguistic groups receive aid from them. Women workers in the West Indies and the States who are making such a worthy contribution to the progress of our Italian, Hebrew, Slovak, Spanish, Negro and Southern mountain work, are made possible by their support.

Church Extension loans, interest donations and special gifts to the amount of $46,435 were granted by the Women's Missionary Society.

Committee on Church Architecture:

All plans of our mission churches are submitted to this Committee for approval before an appropriation is made. These plans are reviewed with commendable promptness and constructive criticisms are offered. An outstanding need is a supply of approved plans for churches of moderate size and cost. These could be used to advantage within the bounds of different Synods and prove a valuable aid in the promotion of our work.

The Board of Deaconess Work:

The relation of the Deaconess Board to the Board of American Missions has been thoroughly harmonious. The Milwaukee Motherhouse had assigned to our work Sister Nanca Schoen; the Baltimore Motherhouse, Sister Clara Smyre, Sister Mary Junas, Sister Rose Zemanek; the Philadelphia Motherhouse Sister Emma Francis and ,Sister Edith Prince. The assistance of these trained workers in the ministry of serving love has been invaluable. Without their wholehearted co-operation the record would tell another story. The Board is indebted to the Danish Motherhouse in Copenhagen for Sister Maren Knudsen, whose ministry of mercy challenges our admiration and awakens gratitude to God. Special recognition is given also for the training of Miss Nerina Rossi and Miss Nieves Villarini by the Philadelphia and Baltimore Motherhouses.

The Board is grateful to the *Laymen's Movement for Stewardship* for the financial aid to seven students for the ministry who are now in our service.

Augustana Synod:

The Board welcomes this opportunity of acknowledging its debt of gratitude to the Augustana Synod for giving it the valued services of Dr.

Alfred Ostrom, as well as its gifts to the Christmas boxes and its support of the industrial work in the West Indies.

In Memoriam

At the first stated meeting of the Board of American Missions, tidings of the passing of *Mr. J. B. Franke,* of Fort Wayne, were announced. Whereupon the following resolutions were adopted:

Resolved, That we express our gratitude to God for raising up such a loyal churchman and living exponent of the principles of our faith and we rededicate our lives to the great cause he honored and served so truly.

Resolved, That we record our high regard for his sterling qualities and his unwearied devotion to the cause of the Master. We shall cherish his memory as a living treasure.

Resolved, That we assure his widow and daughter of our heartfelt sympathy and commend them to the God of all comfort and consolation Whose grace is sufficient. May the Eternal God be their refuge and may they feel the pressure of the Everlasting Arms.

Resolved, That a copy of this Minute be sent to the family, be published in *The Lutheran* and be made a part of our report to the next Convention of the United Lutheran Church.

The Rev. A. Stewart Hartman, D.D., gave forty-five years of his life to Home Missions. He was a member of the Staff and served the Board as Educational Secretary. The summons came so peacefully on the day after Palm Sunday, 1928, that loved ones by his side scarcely knew he had gone. He has joined the company of immortals. The Board has placed on record an appreciation of his untiring service:

Dr. A. Stewart Hartman passed into the life immortal on April 2, 1928. He was one of the great and commanding figures of our Church. His most distinguished service was rendered to the cause of Home Missions. For many years he was the General Secretary of the Board of Home Missions of the General Synod. When the Board of Home Missions and the Board of Church Extension were merged he was made Associate Secretary of the new Board. The Board of Home Missions and Church Extension of the United Lutheran Church elected him to the office of Educational Secretary and when the Board of American Missions came into being he was continued in this office and was serving in this capacity at the time of his death.

Like poets, secretaries are born, not made, though the many years of contact with the mission enterprise and mission problems helped to call forth his native genius for such a great work as he did. He brought rapid mental processes to bear upon the task of solving the many problems that flocked like doves to the Home Mission windows. He had a great and hospitable heart, whose doors were always open to the cries of the discouraged and self-sacrificing missionaries. He was understandingly sympathetic with these modern apostles who were so often underpaid and undersung and overworked. While he expected results from their labors, he was no slave driver. He aimed to be an inspirational leader and an encouraging friend.

He was a powerful champion of his cause. The years that are gone still reverberate with his passionate eloquence in behalf of the extension of the Kingdom of God in our country. Some of us have stirring memories of the masterful speeches Dr. Hartman made in the great assemblies of Lutherans. They were like bugle calls to high duty. They were like burning revelations of vast possibilities. They were like martial music that urges soldiers to march on to great conflicts. He knew how to persuade and to move men. He made his church feel that it was fronted with an opportunity of challenging bigness in this country.

Dr. Hartman easily took a high place alongside of the great home secretaries of other denominations. He knew them intimately and he enjoyed a fine fellowship with them. Most loyal to his own church, yet he made a generous and effective contribution to the general Kingdom interests.

Six missionary pastors entered into life. Three of them served English mission congregations, and three German mission congregations. They are: The Rev. James A. Huffard, D.D., the Rev. H. J. Mathias, the Rev. Henry Reumann, the Rev. A. J. Sommer, the Rev. John Kaehler and the Rev. L. Grauenhorst.

Dr. Huffard, a former president of the Virginia Synod, after serving our mission in Luray for nineteen years, closed his ministry in Kingsport, Tennessee.

Rev. H. J. Mathias suffered a stroke of apoplexy and died in San Bernardino, California, where he had ministered since 1923.

The Rev. Henry Reumann had served our mission to Collinsville, Connecticut, for ten years, and was laid to rest in Pleasant Valley Cemetery, near Poughkeepsie, N. Y.

The Rev. A. J. Sommer was pastor of Trinity congregation, now Barnitz Memorial, Denver, Colorado, and was in the midst of a building project when he heard the final summons.

The Rev. John Kaehler had served the mission parish of Massey and Chalk River, Ontario, since 1925.

The Rev. L. Grauenhorst ministered in Lincoln, Nebraska, for thirty-five years.

ORGANIZATION

Officers:
President—Rev. J. B. Markward, D.D.
Vice-President—Rev. H. W. A. Hanson, D.D., LL.D.
Recording Secretary—Mr. Grant Hultberg.
Treasurer—Rev. Z. M. Corbe, D.D.
Executive Secretary—Rev. F. F. Fry, D.D.

Members:
Terms expiring 1928—Rev. A. E. Bell, D.D., Rev. C. A. Freed, D.D., Rev. G. K. Rubrecht, D.D., Rev. J. C. Seegers, D.D., Mr. Albert Niemoth, Mr. S. F. Telleen, Mr. H. E. Young.
Terms expiring 1930—Rev. G. A. Benze, D.D., Rev. H. W. A. Hanson, D.D., LL.D., Rev. J. B. Markward, D.D., Rev. J. Maurer, D.D., Mr. C. J. Driever, Mr. Grant Hultberg, Mr. Harry Snyder.
Terms expiring 1932—Rev. F. O. Evers, Rev. J. M. Francis, D.D., Rev. George Gebert, D.D., Rev. L. H. Larimer, D.D., Mr. W. L. Glatfelter, Mr. H. F. Heuer, Mr. W. E. Black.

At the January, 1927, meeting of the Board, Mr. William E. Black was nominated to fill the vacancy caused by the death of Mr. J. B. Franke, and this nomination was approved by the Executive Board.

Divisional Committee on English Missions: Rev. J. C. Seegers, D.D., Rev. J. M. Francis, D.D., Rev. Jacob Maurer, D.D., Mr. C. J. Driever.

Divisional Committee on Linguistic Interests: Rev. F. O. Evers, Rev. George Gebert, D.D., Rev. G. A. Benze, D.D., Mr. Albert Niemoth.

Divisional Committee on Latin America: Rev. C. A. Freed, D.D., Rev. L. H. Larimer, D.D., Rev. A. E. Bell, D.D., Mr. H. F. Heuer.

Divisional Committee on Church Extension: Mr. Grant Hultberg, Mr. W. E. Black, Mr. H. E. Young, Rev. G. K. Rubrecht, D.D.

Divisional Committee on Finance: Mr. W. L. Glatfelter, Mr. S. F. Telleen, Mr. H. L. Snyder, Rev. H. W. A. Hanson, D.D., LL.D.

Committee on Conference with Foreign Board: Rev. J. B. Markward, D.D., Chairman, Rev. J. C. Seegers, D.D., Mr. H. F. Heuer.

Committee on Conference with Board of Education: Rev. H. W. A. Hanson, D.D., Chairman, Rev. G. K. Rubrecht, D.D., Mr. Grant Hultberg.

Committee on Conference with Inner Mission Board: Rev. F. O. Evers, Chairman, Rev. C. A. Freed, D.D., Mr. S. F. Telleen.

Committee on Conference with Deaconess Board: Rev. J. M. Francis, D.D., Chairman, Rev. A. E. Bell, D.D., Mr. W. L. Glatfelter.

Committee on Conference with other Lutheran Bodies: Rev. J. B. Markward, D.D., Chairman, Rev. G. K. Rubrecht, D.D., Rev. J. C. Seegers, D.D., Mr. Grant Hultberg, Mr. C. J. Driever.

Committee on Beneficiary Education: Rev. H. W. A. Hanson, D.D., Chairman, Rev. J. C. Seegers, D.D., Rev. L. H. Larimer, D.D., Mr. S. F. Telleen, Mr. W. L. Glatfelter, Rev. F. O. Evers.

Committee to Study Relations of Field Missionaries to Board: Mr. H. F. Heuer, Chairman, Rev. J. B. Markward, D.D., Rev. J. C. Seegers, D.D., Mr. Grant Hultberg.

Nominations: The Board has placed in nomination the following names to fill vacancies occasioned by the expiration of term of office:

Rev. A. E. Bell, D.D. (Jewish); Rev. C. A. Freed, D.D. (West Indies); Rev. G. K. Rubrecht, D.D. (Home Missions); Rev. J. C. Seegers, D.D. (Home Missions); Mr. William Eck (Northwestern); Mr. S. F. Telleen (West Indies); Mr. A. H. Durboraw (Immigrants).

Staff:

Divisional Secretary of English Missions—Rev. J. F. Seibert, D.D.

General Superintendents of English Missions—Rev. I. C. Hoffman, D.D., Rev. A. D. R. Hancher, D.D., Rev. G. H. Hillerman, D.D.

General Superintendent of German Missions—Rev. Paul Ludwig.

General Superintendent of Slav-Hungarian Missions—Rev. A. L. Ramer, Ph.D.

General Superintendent of Finnish Missions—Rev. V. Koivumaki.

Attorney—George E. Neff, Esq.

English Missions

Thus far the wisdom of the Plan of Operation has been demonstrated and the need of Divisional Secretaries is evident. It is essential to have a Divisional Secretary for English Missions and the location of his headquarters has been satisfactory. The need of General Superintendents is evident, but there should be a better distribution of their energies. A more concentrated effort by our best trained men is needed on the territory of the weaker synods.

The Constituent Synods have assumed a larger part in the administration of Mission activities and are showing by their fine spirit of co-operation that they are ready to do their part, especially where they are well organized, many of them with salaried superintendents.

The weaker synods need our help. The Field Missionary System helps to answer the purpose, but should be reorganized for more effective work under the supervision of the Board. In the matter of the establishment of new Missions, in the problems of building operations by Missions, in Church Extension Aid, granted by the Board, the aid of an experienced superintendent is of invaluable service.

Duties of the *Divisional Secretary* of the Department of English Missions: Under the direction and supervision of the Executive Secretary, he shall have general oversight of the work. He shall be charged with the duty of stimulating and energizing the missionary spirit in the Constituent Synods of the United Lutheran Church in America. Under the direction and in co-operation with the Department of Church Extension and Finance, he shall, through the solicitation of funds from interested individuals, congregations and congregational organizations, endeavor to increase the income of the Board. He shall seek out new opportunities and new fields of service not covered by Constituent Synods.

The Rev. Dr. J. F. Seibert was elected Divisional Secretary of English Missions.

Duties of *General Superintendents* of English Missions: For the maintenance and development of the cause of English Missions as a general cause of the whole Church, General Superintendents shall be assigned work under the supervision of the Divisional Secretary with the approval of the Executive Secretary.

They shall keep in touch with the Mission Committee and Synodical Superintendent of such Synods as may be assigned to them. They shall advise Mission Congregations as to property and building plans and be ready to take temporary charge of Missions as directed.

They shall give attention to securing additional funds for Church Extension through gifts, bequests, and so forth, and shall seek out congregations and individuals to support a Home Missionary.

The following were elected as General Superintendents of English Missions: The Rev. Dr. I. C. Hoffman, the Rev. Dr. G. H. Hillerman and the Rev. Dr. A. D. R. Hancher.

LINGUISTIC INTERESTS

Until the growth of the work of the Linguistic Department justifies its complete organization under a Divisional Secretary, there is need of a general superintendent of German interests, who shall be under the direct supervision of the Committee on Linguistic Interests.

Considering that his chief work centers in the Middle West and the Northwest, it is desirable that his headquarters be in Chciago, where office room can be provided for him at 860 Cass Street, without additional expense to the Board.

The present needs of the Immigrants' Division includes a general superintendent of Slav-Hungarian Interests. And until a Divisional Secretary has been elected and the financial resources of the Board warrant an increase of salaried missionaries, and until we have strengthened and equipped the Missions already organized, it will be well to continue the present arrangement.

Inasmuch as the Italian Missions are under the supervision of the Mission Committee and Missionary Superintendent of the Synod to which each Mission belongs, there appears to be no adequate reason for the continuance of a General Superintendent for Italian work.

The Jewish Missions receive similar Synodical supervision and no change is needed.

Duties of the *General Superintendent* for *German Interests*: He shall be under the direct supervision of and report to the Executive Secretary. He shall co-operate with the Mission Committee and Synodical Superintendent of such Synods as may be assigned to him. He shall advise Mission Congregations as to property, building plans, and Church Extension Work. He shall solicit funds for the work of the Board and shall assist and encourage German Synods in their missionary operations and their educational work, in so far as it is supported by the Board.

The Rev. Paul Ludwig was elected as General Superintendent of German Interests.

Duties of the *General Superintendent* of *Slovak-Hungarian Work*: He shall be under the supervision and direction of the Executive Secretary. He shall visit Mission Congregations as directed and shall advise them as to property, building plans, and Church Extension Work. He shall assist and encourage work in his field and supervise Student Aid to such students as have been approved and are supported by the Board.

The Rev. Dr. A. L. Ramer was elected General Superintendent of Slovak-Hungarian Interests.

The arrangements made by the Board of Home Missions and Church Extension to continue the Rev. A. S. Hartman, D.D., as Educational Secretary were approved and carried out by the Board of American Missions until the death of this veteran missionary.

RECOMMENDATIONS

1. The Board of American Missions returns devout gratitude to Almighty God for His manifest guidance and blessing during its first biennium, and prays that the Head of the Church will give this Convention a clear vision of the boundless opportunities and unrealized possibilities in our cities and throughout its wide territory.

2. Recommended that the cause of Church Extension be commended to congregations and individuals of the United Lutheran Church in America so that by personal solicitation the necessary funds may be secured to strengthen this important arm of the Church.

3. Recommended that sympathetic consideration be given to the request of the Suomi Synod to start work among the Finnish people in Canada and that a conference on the entire question be authorized between representatives of the Board of American Missions and officials of the Suomi Synod, to be held under the auspices of the Executive Board of the United Lutheran Church in America.

4. Recommended that this Convention place upon the heart and conscience of the Church the obligation to think of and pray for the brother Lutheran who comes to us as a stranger and still as a brother in the faith; and that it bring home to our pastors and all our people the living fact that its linguistic work is not accidental but constitutes an integral part of the fulfillment of the Church's call to work on American soil.

J. BRADLEY MARKWARD, *President.*
GRANT HULTBERG. *Secretary.*
FRANKLIN F. FRY, *Executive Secretary.*

APPENDIX A

Congregations organized or Parishes placed on the Budget. Division of English Missions.

Ministerium of Pennsylvania

Lakewood, N. J. ....Emanuel
Haddonfield, N. J. ....Our Saviour
Philadelphia, Pa. ....Erloeser
Philadelphia, Pa. ....St. James'
Quakake Parish, Pa.
Hampden Heights, Reading Pa.......................Nativity
West Lawn, Pa. ....Advent

Ministerium of New York

Potter, N. Y. ....Zion
Valley Stream, N. Y. ....St. Paul's
Bay Shore, N. Y. ....St. Luke's
Babylon, N. Y. ....First
Great Kills, N. Y. ....Zion

North Carolina Synod
Andrews, N. C. ....St. Andrew's

Maryland Synod
West Forest Park, Baltimore, Md. ....Redeemer

South Carolina Synod
Batesburg, S. C. ....Faith
Blythewood, S. C. ....St. Mark's
                                                                        St. Andrew

Virginia Synod
Roanoke, Va. ....Emmanuel
                                                                        Glade Creek

Ohio Synod
Cleveland, O. ....Parma
Cleveland, O. ....Our Saviour's
Steubenville, O. ....

East Pennsylvania Synod
Runnemede, N. J. ....Trinity
Lansdowne, Pa. ....St. Paul
Woodbury, N. J. ....Trinity
Manoa, Pa. ....Trinity

Pittsburgh Synod
Beaver, Pa. ....Holy Trinity
Cleveland, O. ....Teutsch
Homestead Park, Pa. ....
New Castle, Pa. ....
Kearsage, Pa. ....
Canton, O. ....First
Wilkinsburg Manor, Pa. ....St. Paul's

Indiana Synod
Madison, Ind. ....St. Paul's
Indianapolis, Ind. ....Bethany

Illinois Synod
Villa Park, Ill ....Grace
Wheaton, Ill. ....St. Paul's
Olney, Ill. ....Trinity

Texas Synod
Harlingen, Tex. ....Grace
Houston, Tex. ....Redeemer

Michigan Synod
Detroit, Mich. ....Nativity
Detroit, Mich. ....Olivet
Fordson ....Emanuel

Georgia Synod
Miami, Fla. ....Trinity
Tampa, Fla. ....St. Paul

Kansas Synod

Cole Camp, Mo. ....Cole Camp

Synod of the Northwest

Minneapolis, Minn. ....Resurrection
Kenosha, Wis. ....Holy Trinity
West Allis ....Holy Trinity

Pacific Synod

Eugene, Ore. ....United
Fairbanks, Alaska ....St. John's
Salem, Ore. ....American

New York and New England Synod

Kenmore, N. Y. ....St. Mark's
Snyder, N. Y. ....Ascension
Bellrose, N. Y. ....Holy Trinity
Bellmore-North Bellmore Parish, N. Y........
Dumont, N. J. ....Redeemer
Forest Hills, Long Island, N. Y. ....Grace
Union, N. J. ....Christ
Bayside West, N. Y. ....Lutheran
Little Neck, L. I., N. Y. ....Christ

New York Synod

Richmond Hill Circle, N. Y. ....Holy Comforter
Richmond Hill South, N. Y. ....St. Matthew's
Schenectady, N. Y. ....Second
Maywood, N. J. ....Redeemer
Stewart Manor, N. Y. ....St. James'
Locust Manor, N. Y. ....St. Thomas'
Jamaica South, N. Y. ....St. Peter's
Rutherford, N. J. ....St. John's
    Total, 66.

APPENDIX B

Self-supporting or discontinued from the Budget. Division of English Missions.

Ministerium of Pennsylvania

Kingston, Pa. ....Holy Trinity
Scranton, Pa. ....St. Paul's

Maryland Synod

Ellicott City, Md. ....First
Baltimore, Md. ....Church of Ascension

West Pennsylvania Synod

Starview Charge, Pa.
York, Pa. ....Messiah

Virginia Synod

Bristol, Tenn. ....Redeemer
Salem, Va. ....College

Ohio Synod

Cleveland, O. ....St. James'
Columbus, O. ....Redeemer

East Pennsylvania Synod

Harrisburg, Pa. ....Trinity
Palmyra, N. J. ....First
Crum Lynne-Lester ....St. Matthew's
                                                              Lester

Pittsburgh Synod

Leetsdale, Pa. ....St. Matthew's
Moundsville, W. Va. ....First

Indiana Synod

Louisville, Ky. ....Memorial

Illinois Synod

Chicago, Ill. ....Norwood Park
St. Louis, Mo. ....Church of the Reformation

Iowa Synod

Davenport, Ia. ....St. Mark's
Muscatine, Ia. ....Grace
Waterloo, Ia. ....St. Luke's

Georgia Synod

St. Petersburg, Fla. ....Trinity
Weirsdale, Fla. ....St. John's

Nebraska Synod

Benson, Nebraska ....First

California Synod

Los Angeles, Calif. ....Hollywood

Synod of the Northwest

Helena, Mont.
Livingston, Mont. ....Redeemer
Aldens-Walters, Minn. ....Grace
                                        Faith
Lakeville, Minn. ....St. John's
Hiles, Wis.
New London, Wis. ....Trinity

Pacific Synod

Camas, Wash. ....Zion
Yakima, Wash. ....Holy Trinity

New York and New England Synod

Bellaire, N. Y. ....Good Shepherd
Dunton, L. I., N. Y. ....St. Paul's
Hartford, Conn. ....St. Paul's
Johnson City, N. Y. ....St. Paul's

Nova Scotia Synod

Conquerall Parish ....

New York Synod

Woodstock, N. Y. ....Christ
Hasbrouck Heights-River Edge, N. Y...........
New York, N. Y. ....Our Saviour
Bridgeport, Conn. ....First

West Virginia Synod

Clarksburg, W. Va. ....St. Mark's
Brandonville, W. Va. ....
    Total, 44.

APPENDIX C

STATISTICAL REPORT—DIVISION OF ENGLISH MISSIONS

Synod	Mission Parishes, June 30, 1926	Appropriation June 30, 1926	Mission Parishes, June 30, 1928	Appropriation June 30, 1928	Membership Conf.	S. S. Enroll.	Missions Rec'd Since June 30, 1926	Appropriations for New Missions for First Year	Self-Supporting Since June 30, 1926	Appropriation Released by Missions becoming self-supp.	Vacancies 1926	Vacancies 1928
Ministerium of Pennsylvania	18	10,400	21	14,250	3,510	3,515	7	5,366	2	900		2
Ministerium of New York	18	15,660	5	18,000	2,107	2,437	5	1,400			2	3
North Carolina	14	10,290	20	10,500	1,521	1,638	1	1,500	2	1,125	1	1
Maryland	8	6,830	11	7,675	771	799	2	3,000	2	575	3	1
South Carolina	7	3,000	9	2,800	597	814				650	1	1
West Pennsylvania	11	9,625	5	12,100	1,082	1,003	1	500	3	2,200	3	1
Virginia	19	20,000	10	18,450	2,291	2,393	3	3,600	2		2	
Ohio	22	15,625	23	15,450	3,368	3,477	4	3,250	3	940	1	1
East Pennsylvania	4	2,225	4	2,000	544	589						
Allegheny	28	22,640	33	22,360	4,482	3,274	7	3,800	2	980		1
Pittsburgh	15	12,600	16	13,050	1,160	1,368	2	1,600	1	600		2
Indiana	20	22,730	21	24,000	2,160	3,104	3	3,900	2	1,800	2	
Illinois	3	3,980	5	7,210	216	247	2	2,900				
Texas	1	850	1	400	217	290						
Sus. of Central Penna.	5	6,400	5	4,550	670	383			3			3
Mississippi	14	9,955	7	7,550	645	569			2	2,250		1
Iowa	12	19,985	17	18,500	1,659	1,658	3	4,820			1	
Michigan	6	14,575	12	19,340	622	626	2	4,700		1,100		3
Georgia	6	6,175	6	6,575	485	345					1	1
Canada	5	8,250	6	7,350	692	852	1		1	200		
Kansas	21	5,340	4	3,750	370	421			1	800		
Nebraska	13	21,590	20	21,205	1,563	1,830						4
California	31	11,180	12	11,205	853	760	1	3,700	1	3,870	4	2
Rocky Mountain	21	31,925	28	29,975	3,993	3,846	6	5,000	6	560	1	
Northwest	15	27,400	23	28,025	1,531	1,712	3	9,600	2	2,550		1
Pacific	3	11,880	18	16,145	1,705	1,589	9		4	200	4	
New York and New England	20	1,555	2	1,225	403	204			1	1,100		
Nova Scotia												
New York	20	13,200	22	16,475	2,984	2,766	7	5,900	4	1,100	3	1
West Virginia	6	6,180	4	4,500	656	678			2	850	2	1
Totals	**376**	**352,045**	**390**	**363,810**	**42,938**	**42,687**	**66**	**64,536**	**44**	**23,250**	**33**	**28**

APPENDIX D

STATISTICAL REPORT

German Missions

Synod	Missionaries June 30, 1928	Mission Parishes, June 30, 1928	Mission Congregations June 30, 1928	Membership Baptized	Membership Confirmed	Sunday School	Appropriation June 30, 1928
Canada	6	7	14	1,844	1,142	317	3,775
Manitoba	16	15	42	3,766	2,073	740	18,500
German Nebraska	13	14	18	1,882	1,228	627	10,450
Wartburg	9	9	10	1,577	1,120	890	10,280
Texas	5	5	10	982	628	461	3,540
New York Ministerium	4	6	6	571	442	146	3,325
	53	56	100	10,622	6,633	3,181	49,870

SLOVAK MISSIONS

Organized Missions:

Buffalo, N. Y.	John Ormai	N. Y. Ministerium
East Pittsburgh, Pa.	James Sopko	Slovak Zion
Garfield, N. J.	Ludwig Havel	Slovak Zion
New York, N. Y., St. Paul's	Louis Sanjek	N. Y. & New Eng.
	Sister Mary Junas	
Akron, O.	A. D. Dianiska	Slovak Zion
Port Clinton, O.	A. D. Dianiska	Slovak Zion
Trenton, N. J.	G. J. Chernansky	Slovak Zion
Camden, N. J.	Vacant	
Palmerton, Pa.	Vacant	
Jessup, Pa.	Vacant	
Pottstown, Pa.	Vacant	
Sheppton, Pa.	Vacant	
Bethlehem, Pa., So.	Vacant	
Philadelphia, Pa.	Vacant	
Grassflat, Pa.	Vacant	
Byesville, O.	Vacant	
Holdingford, Minn.	Vacant	
Tabor, Minn.	Vacant	
Calhan, Colo.	Supply	Rocky M't'n Synod

Vacant missions and preaching points are supplied by students and the General Superintendent.

Preaching Points:

Erie, Pa.
Saltsburg, Pa.
Hudson, N. Y.
Tarrytown, N. Y.
Proctor, Vt.
Philipsburg, Pa.
Dayton, O.
Middletown, O.
Dover, O.
Piney Fork, O.
Benwood, W. Va.
Gary, W. Va.
Gary, Ind.
Blue Island, Ill.
Muskegon Heights, Mich.
Copemish, Mich.
Phillips, Wis.
Fifield, Wis.
Cudahy, Wis.
Nashua, Mont.
Malta, Mont.

Belt, Mont.
Roy, Mont.
Geraldine, Mont.
Sand Coulee, Mont.
Everett, Wash.
Tacoma, Wash.
Ole Elum, Wash.
Elam, Wash.
Portland, Ore.
San Francisco, Calif.
Pueblo, Colo.
Birmingham, Ala.
Prince George, Va.
Bridgeburg, Ont.
Creighton Mine, Ont.
Timmins, Ont.
Fort William, Ont.
Montreal, Que.
Low, Que.
St. Clair, Pa.

HUNGARIAN

Allentown, Pa. ....Mission....Stephen Pottschacher ..Penna. Ministerium
Bethlehem, Pa. ....Mission....Stephen Pottschacher ..Penna. Ministerium
Palmerton, Pa. ....Mission....Vacant ....
New Brunswick, N. J...Mission....Alexander Szabo ....N. Y. Ministerium
Buffalo, N. Y. ....Mission....John Ormai ....N. Y. Ministerium
Pittsburgh, Pa. ....Mission....Alexander Poloskey ....Pittsburgh Synod
Perth Amboy, N. J.....Mission....Stephen Szmodis ....N. Y. & N. E. Synod
New York, N. Y........Mission....Stephen Ruzsa ....Pittsburgh Synod
Akron, O. ....Mission....Ralph Zimmerman ......Ohio

LETTISH

Philadelphia, Pa. ......Mission....Peter E. Steik...............Penna. Ministerium
New York, N. Y. ......Mission....Peter E. Steik...............Penna. Ministerium
Boston, Mass. ....Mission....Carl W. Selmer..........N. Y. & N. E. Synod
Sifton, Man. ....Mission....W. O. Zahlis.................Manitoba Synod
Lebau, Man. ....Mission....W. O. Zahlis.................Manitoba Synod
Selkirk, Man. ....Mission....W. O. Zahlis.................Manitoba Synod

WINDISH

Newark, N. J. ....Mission....Stephen Szmodis ....N. Y. & N. E. Synod

LITHUANIAN

Philadelphia, Pa. ....Mission....Peter E. Steik ....Penna. Ministerium

ASSYRIAN

Philadelphia, Pa. ....Mission....Yaure Abraham ....Penna. Ministerium

BOHEMIAN

Silverhill, Ala. ....Preaching Point ....

ITALIAN

New York City ....Cosimo Dell'Osso ....N. Y. & N. E. Synod
Philadelphia, Pa. ....Michele Renzetti ....Penna Ministerium
Phila. Neighborhood House....Miss Anna P. Hess ....
Phila. Neighborhood House....Miss Emma L. Hess ....
Phila. Neighborhood House....Miss Mary E. Hunter....
Phila. Neighborhood House....Miss Nerina Rossi ....
San Francisco, Calif. ....L. O. Pampana ....California Synod
Fresno, Calif. ....L. O. Pampana ....California Synod
Sacramento, Calif. ....L. O. Pampana ....California Synod
Monessen, Pa. ....   Fausto Pisani ....Pittsburgh Synod
Erie, Pa. ....Fortunato Scarpitti ....Pittsburgh Synod
Chicago, Ill. ....Secundino Bertrando ......Illinois Synod

Students for the Ministry in College and Seminary:

HUNGARIAN	SLOVAK	
Andrew Leffler ....John Janisak ....J. Albert Billy
	George Billy ....Joseph W. Billy
	Andrew Brndjar ....Stephen Medved
	Andrew Kanyuch ....John Balog
	Joseph Kavalek ....George Churlick
	John Mikletz

APPENDIX E

SUMMARY OF STATISTICS

All Departments

Number of Parishes 494
Number of Congregations 664
Number of Missionaries ordained and unordained..... 492
Baptized Membership 103,218
Confirmed Membership 55,664
Sunday School Scholars 49,178
Number of Parsonages 282
Value of Property $8,219,398
Indebtedness on Property $3,603,873

APPENDIX F

BY-LAWS

Article I. Meetings.

Regular meetings of the Board shall be held in the months of January, April, July and October each year.

Each meeting shall be held at the place and on the day and hour as determined by the Charter or action of the Board.

The annual meeting shall take place at the time of, and shall be the regular meeting for October.

Special meetings may be called by the President, or in case of his absence or inability to act, by the next ranking officer on notice to each member, mailed or otherwise given in time for its receipt at least ten days prior to the meeting.

All meetings shall be opened and closed with devotional services.

Article II. Organization.

As far as practicable and subject from time to time to such modification not inconsistent with the approved Plan of Operation governing the Board, and as the exigencies of its work may require, the organization of the Board shall embrace the following Departments and Divisions:

1. Department of Missions
    a. Division of English Missions
    b. Division of Linguistic Interests
    c. Division of Latin America
2. Department of Church Extension and Finance
    a. Division of Church Extension
    b. Division of Finance.

For the Board supervision of these Divisions, five committees shall be elected, to be composed as follows:

1. Divisional Committee on English Missions
    Three clergymen and one layman.
2. Divisional Committee on Linguistic Interests
    Three clergymen and one layman.
3. Divisional Committee on Latin America
    Three clergymen and one layman.
4. Divisional Committee on Church Extension
    Three laymen and one clergyman.
5. Divisional Committee on Finance
    Three laymen and one clergyman.

Article III. Election of Officers and Committees.

At the annual meeting of the Board, the following officers and committees shall be elected:

1. Officers
    1. President
    2. Vice-President
    3. Recording Secretary
    4. Treasurer
2. Committees
    1. An Executive Committee
    2. A Committee advisory to each Department or Division of a Department.

These officers and committees shall hold office until the next annual meeting of the Board and until their successors are elected and qualify. Vacancies occurring in any of said offices or committees may be filled at any succeeding meeting, each person elected to fill any such vacancy, to hold office or membership in committee for the unexpired term of his predecessor and until his successor is elected and qualifies.

Article IV.   The Executive Committee.

The Executive Committee shall consist of the President and Secretary of the Board (if the Secretary be not a paid employee), and the five Chairmen of the Divisional Committees, of whom four shall constitute a quorum. During the intervals between the meetings of the Board, this Committee shall possess and exercise all the powers and functions conferred on the Board by Charter and Constitution, the Board reserving the right to review all actions taken by the Executive Committee.

The Executive Committee shall meet regularly in each month in which the Board does not meet. Special meetings may be called at any time by the President.

Article V.   Committees Advisory to Departments and Divisions.

It shall be the duty of each Divisional Committee to study the work of the Division to which it is related; advise the secretaries of the same concerning methods and policies of carrying forward the work and bring to the attention of the Board any matters concerning the work which the judgment of the Committee may suggest. Each Committee shall meet as often as necessary, and always before each regular meeting of the Board in order to review all work done under the Division, to hear the Divisional Secretary's reports and such portions of the Executive Secretary's report as deal with their Division, for the purpose of simplifying in every possible way the work of the regular Board meeting.

These Committees shall have such powers as the Board may delegate to them or as the exigencies of the work may require.

Article VI.   Amendments.

These By-Laws may be amended or added to by a majority vote of the Board at any regular meeting, provided that notice in writing of the proposed amendment or addition has been given to the members not less than thirty days before it is to be acted upon, but no amendment or addition shall become effective until it is approved by the Executive Board of the United Lutheran Church in America.

TREASURER'S REPORT OF THE BOARD OF AMERICAN MISSIONS OF THE UNITED LUTHERAN CHURCH IN AMERICA

August 31, 1927.

CERTIFICATE OF AUDIT

We have audited the accounts of The Board of American Missions of the United Lutheran Church in America for the six months ended June 30, 1927, and of its predecessor Boards, the Board of Home Missions and Church Extension, the Board of Northwestern Missions, the Board of West Indies Missions, the Board of Immigrants' Missions and the Committee on Jewish Missions, all of the United Lutheran Church in America, for the six months ended December 31, 1926, and we certify that the annexed balance sheet at June 30, 1927, correctly sets forth the financial position of The Board of American Missions at that date and that the annexed Consolidated Statement of Receipts and Disbursements of The Board of American Missions and its predecessor Boards for the year ended June 30, 1927, contains all contributions and other income appearing in the records which were duly accounted for, and that all disbursements appearing therein were supported by proper vouchers.

LYBRAND, ROSS BROS. & MONTGOMERY.

BALANCE SHEET, June 30, 1927

ASSETS

*Cash	$ 99,299.29
Securities Owned, at ledger values	129,125.05
Advanced for the Women's Missionary Society	23,804.92
Loans to Churches	1,274,949.19
Furniture and Fixtures (United States and West Indies)	8,171.00
Real Estate	429,083.59
	$1,964,433.04

LIABILITIES

Loans Payable	$14,200.00	
Mortgage Payable	20,240.00	34,440.00
Net Assets		$1,929,993.04

FUNDS

General Fund		$461,822.61
Endowment Funds:		
Missions	$38,029.67	
Church Extension	19,872.21	
		57,901.88
Permanent Loan Fund	$972,559.29	
Permanent Surplus Fund	100,000.00	
		1,072,559.29
Church Building Fund		16,975.99
McMurray Trust Fund		32,938.38
Annuity Funds		69,350.00
Special Funds		50,199.36
Agency Accounts:		
Women's Missionary Society	$140,375.53	

Northwest Synod 2,200.00
Sundry Churches 25,670.00   168,245.53
Total Funds $1,929,993.04

THE BOARD OF AMERICAN MISSIONS and its predecessor Boards:
    THE BOARD OF HOME MISSIONS AND CHURCH EXTENSION,
    THE BOARD OF NORTHWESTERN MISSIONS,
    THE BOARD OF WEST INDIES MISSIONS,
    THE BOARD OF IMMIGRANT MISSIONS,
    THE COMMITTEE ON JEWISH MISSIONS.
of the UNITED LUTHERAN CHURCH IN AMERICA.

CONSOLIDATED STATEMENT OF RECEIPTS AND DISBURSEMENTS
For the year ended June 30th, 1927.

Balances, July 1st, 1926.. $170,196.12

RECEIPTS

United Lutheran Church, on apportionment...............$483,235.00
Women's Missionary Society 61,525.13
Individuals, Churches, Societies, Synods....................... 13,280.40
Returned Loans 38,750.00
Returned Donations 700.00
Interest and Dividends, including income from trusts 10,666.88
Annuities 17,000.00
Bequests 40,477.50
Donations, Specials and Designated Gifts.................... 7,795.11
Proceeds of Sale of Securities and on Sales Contracts 60,867.13
Loans 6,000.00
                                                                                                                740,297.15

Total Receipts $910,493.27

DISBURSEMENTS

Loans to Churches $169,400.00
Donations to Churches 51,205.18
Salaries:
    Missionaries 396,395.95
    Secretaries and Superintendents 31,749.92
Expenses of Missionaries 21,098.67
Expenses of Secretaries and Superintendents................ 17,543.76
Expenses of Officers and Board Members..................... 6,071.07
Seminary and Student Aid 14,693.82
Interest to Annuitants 3,963.00
Rentals 1,380.00
Repayments of Loans and Mortgages 14,140.00
Charitable Institutions, Virgin Islands 5,146.05
Transmission of Designated Gifts................................... 4,870.54
Investments:
    Real Estate $16,518.04
    Furniture and Fixtures, West Indies........ 993.45
                                                                                          17,511.49
Securities Purchased 36,943.75
Insurances, Taxes, Repairs, etc. 3,977.28
Office Supplies and Expenses 1,027.26
Printing and Stationery 803.51

Telephone and Telegraph	154.55
Auditing	1,775.00
Publicity	932.31
Expenses of Joint Commission	5,142.04
Interest on Loans and Mortgages	3,145.21
Prepaid Interest and Brokerage Fees on Bond Purchases	259.73
Office Equipment	872.76
Sundry Expenses	991.13
Total Disbursements	$811,193.98
*Balances, June 30, 1927	$ 99,299.29

* Invested in temporary loans through the Fifth Ave. Bank of New York, subject to call by the Treasurer.

ZENAN M. CORBE, *Treasurer.*

CERTIFICATE OF AUDIT

We have audited the accounts of The Board of American Missions of the United Lutheran Church in America for the twelve months ended June 30, 1928, and we certify that in our opinion the annexed balance sheet at June 30, 1928, correctly sets forth the financial position of The Board of American Missions at that date and that the annexed Consolidated Statement of Receipts and Disbursements of The Board of American Missions for the year ended June 30, 1928, contains all contributions and other income appearing in the records which were duly accounted for, and that all disbursements appearing therein were supported by proper vouchers.

LYBRAND, ROSS BROS. & MONTGOMERY.

BALANCE SHEET, JUNE 30, 1928
ASSETS

*Cash		$ 66,874.68
Securities Owned, at ledger values		185,422.55
Advanced Expense Accounts		975.00
Advanced for Women's Missionary Society		16,828.31
Loans to Churches		1,347,339.69
Equipment (United States and West Indies)		7,444.00
Real Estate		419,750.54
Accrued Interest Purchased		597.71
		$2,045,232.48

LIABILITIES

Loans Payable	$10,200.00	
Mortgage Payable	20,000.00	30,200.00
	Net Assets	$2,015,032.48

FUNDS
General Fund

Missions	$ 13,299.52	
Church Extension	391,187.58	
		404,487.10

Endowment Funds

Missions	$ 39,084.59	
Church Extension	20,252.21	
		59,336.80
Permanent Loan Fund		1,189,029.16
McMurray Trust Fund		39,373.50
Annuity Funds		71,812.63
Special Funds		80,512.76
Agency Accounts:		
Women's Missionary Society..	$142,610.53	
Northwest Synod	2,200.00	
Sundry Churches	25,670.00	
		170,480.53
Total Funds		$2,015,032.48

CONSOLIDATED STATEMENT
RECEIPTS AND DISBURSEMENTS
Year Ending June 30, 1928

*Balance, July 1, 1927 .... $ 99,299.29

RECEIPTS

United Lutheran Church on apportionment	$540,310.00	
Women's Missionary Society	86,440.21	
Individuals, Churches, Societies, Synods	15,079.07	
Returned Loans	53,948.91	
Returned Donations	4,116.11	
Interest and Dividends, including income from trusts	13,546.21	
Annuities	1,000.00	
Bequests	28,137.01	
Donations, Specials and Designated Gifts	3,096.67	
Proceeds of Sale of Securities and on Sales Contracts	29,792.36	
Easter Offering	5,872.77	
		781,339.32
Total Receipts		$880,638.61

DISBURSEMENTS

Loans to Churches	$128,400.00
Donations to Churches	49,646.48
Salaries:	
Missionaries	414,167.49
Secretaries and Superintendents	34,546.67
Expenses of Missionaries	15,331.30
Expenses of Secretaries and Superintendents	15,268.28
Expenses of Officers and Board Members	5,400.52
Seminary and Student Aid	14,851.56
Interest to Annuitants	6,213.40
Maintenance Contributions, Lutheran Church House	2,350.00
Repayment of Loans and Mortgages	4,240.00
Charitable Institutions: Virgin Islands	5,782.06
Transmission of Designated Gifts	7,449.86
Advanced for Women's Missionary Society for Boone, N. C.	13,000.00
Real Estate purchased	727.50

Furniture and Fixtures: West Indies	878.26
Securities Purchased	81,922.50
Insurance, Taxes, Repairs	3,882.43
Office Supplies and Expenses	810.31
Telephone and Telegraph	235.08
Auditing and installing system of accounting	1,797.09
Publicity	1,967.07
Interest on Loans and Mortgages	1,997.60
Prepaid Interest and Brokerage Commission on Bond purchases	877.47
Sundry Expenses	46.00
Home Missions Council	1,000.00
Advanced Expense Accounts	975.00

Total Expenditures	$813,763.93
*Balance, June 30, 1928	66,874.68
Total Receipts	$880,638.61

* Invested in temporary loans through the Fifth Ave. Bank of New York, subject to call by the Treasurer.

ZENAN M. CORBE, *Treasurer.*

MISSIONS ACCOUNTS
Balance Sheet, June 30, 1928.

ASSETS

Available Cash — General Fund	$13,579.46
Home Mission Endowment	1,572.09
Harroway Estate	6,042.39
Kaercher Endowment	468.86
Repass Estate	1,000.00
Asper Estate	402.79
Wallis Estate	1,000.00
Designated Gifts	336.15
*Total Cash	$24,401.74
Bonds	43,630.00
Stocks	3,500.00
Advanced Expense Accounts	975.00
Accrued Interest Purchased	77.72
	$72,584.46

LIABILITIES

General Fund	$13,299.52
Home Mission Endowment Fund	39,084.59
Harroway Fund	7,000.00
Kaercher Fund	9,206.47
Repass Fund	1,000.00
Asper Fund	402.79
Wallis Fund	1,000.00
Women's Missionary Society—for salaries, etc.	1,254.94
Designated Gifts	336.15
	$72,584.46

MISSION FUND BALANCES

General Fund	Assets	Liabilities	Principal
*Cash	$13,579.46		
Advanced Expense Accounts	975.00		
Women's Missionary Society		$1,254.94	
Principal			$13,299.52
	$14,554.46	$1,254.94	$13,299.52

Home Mission Endowment Fund
*Cash	$ 1,572.09	
Bonds	34,012.50	
Stocks	3,500.00	
Principal		$39,084.59
	$39,084.59	$39,084.59

E. M. Harroway Estate
*Cash	$ 6,042.39	
Bonds	942.50	
Accrued Interest	15.11	
Principal		$ 7,000.00
	$ 7,000.00	$ 7,000.00

J. B. Kaercher Endowment
*Cash	$ 468.86	
Bonds	8,675.00	
Accrued Interest	62.61	
Principal		$ 9,206.47
	$ 9,206.47	$ 9,206.47

Rosa B. Repass
*Cash	$ 1,000.00	$ 1,000.00

Annie M. Asper
*Cash	$ 402.79	$ 402.79

Etta A. Wallis
*Cash	$ 1,000.00	$ 1,000.00

Designated Gifts .... $ 336.15 $ 336.15

CHURCH EXTENSION ACCOUNTS

Balance Sheet, June 30, 1928.

ASSETS		LIABILITIES	
Cash—General Fund	$21,236.79	General Fund	$ 391,187.58
Church Extension Endowment	727.21	Permanent Loan Fund	1,189,029.16
McMurray	157.67	Church Extension Endowment Fund	20,252.21
Annuity	8,943.47	McMurray Fund	39,373.50
Designated Gifts	108.00	Annuity Fund Principal	70,350.00
Special Funds	9,177.03	Annuity Reserve Interest	1,462.63
Omnibus Investment	622.77	Omnibus Investment Principal	50,733.37
Agency—Northwest Synod	1,500.00	Omnibus Investment Reserve Interest	1,601.95
*Total Cash	$42,472.94	Special Funds	9,177.03
		Designated Gifts	55.00

Bonds ....$	116,533.75	
Investment Mortgages...	5,000.00	
Investment Notes	10,000.00	
Stocks	6,758.80	
Loans to Churches...........	1,204,029.16	
Real Estate	394,080.54	
Equipment	7,444.00	
Agency Loans to Churches	143,310.53	
Agency Real Estate......	25,670.00	
Balance due from Women's Missionary Society, Interest	15,568.25	
Balance due from Women's Missionary Society, Loans	2,515.00	
Accrued Interest Purchased (McMurray Estate)	228.33	
Accrued Interest Purchased, Annuity Fund	291.66	

AGENCY FUNDS

Women's Missionary Society ....$	142,610.53
Synod of Northwest......	2,200.00
St. Luke's, York, Pa....	25,000.00
Harmony Grove, Pa....	500.00
Cly, Pa.	170.00

GENERAL LIABILITIES

Loans Payable, Ostrom..$	10,200.00
Mortgages Payable, Harlem, N. Y.	20,000.00

$1,973,902.96 $1,973,902.96

FUND BALANCES

June 30, 1928

	Assets	Liabilities	Principal
General Fund			
*Cash ....$	21,236.79		
Advances Women's Missionary Society	18,136.25		
Bonds	17,140.00		
Investment Mortgages	5,000.00		
Real Estate	352,430.54		
Equipment	7,444.00		
Loans Payable		$ 10,200.00	
Mortgages Payable		20,000.00	
Principal			$391,187.58
	$421,387.58	$ 30,200.00	$391,187.58
Permanent Loan Fund			
Loans to Churches $1,189,029.16		•	$1,189,029.16
Church Extension Endowment Fund			
*Cash ....$	727.21		
Bonds	6,875.00		
Real Estate	12,650.00		
Principal			$ 20,252.21
	$ 20,252.21		$ 20,252.21
McMurray Fund			
*Cash ....$	157.67		
Accrued Interest Purchased....................	228.33		
Bonds	9,987.50		

Real Estate	29,000.00		
Principal			$ 39,373.50
	$ 39,373.50		$ 39,373.50
Annuity Funds			
*Cash	$ 8,943.47		
Bonds	47,577.50		
Loans to Churches	15,000.00		
Accrued Interest Purchased	291.66		
Income		$ 1,462.63	
Principal			$ 70,350.00
	$ 71,812.63	$ 1,462.63	$ 70,350.00
Designated Gifts			
*Cash	$ 108.00	$ 108.00 (a)	
Special Funds			
*Cash	$ 9,177.03		$ 9,177.03
Omnibus Investment Fund			
*Cash	$ 622.77		
Bonds	34,953.75		
Stocks	6,758.80		
Investment Notes	10,000.00		
Income		$ 1,601.95	
Principal			$ 50,733.37
	$ 52,335.32	$ 1,601.95	$ 50,733.37

Agency Account

Women's Missionary Society, Loans to Churches	$142,610.53	$142,610.53
Synod of Northwest, Loans to Churches	700.00	
Synod of Northwest, *Cash	1,500.00	2,200.00
St. Luke's, York, Pa.	25,000.00	25,000.00
Harmony Grove	500.00	500.00
Cly, Pa.	170.00	170.00
	$170,480.53	$170,480.53

* Cash invested in temporary loans through the Fifth Ave. Bank of New York, subject to call of the Treasurer.

(a) $53.00 of this amount has been credited to the Women's Missionary Society Account, $15,568.25, appearing in the Church Extension Balance Sheet.

RECORD OF BONDS
{ In Mission's Trust ... $ 43,630.00
In Church Extension ... 116,533.75
Book Value ... $160,163.75

5,000 Pac. Gas & El., 4½ per cent	$ 4,900.00
4,000 D. & H. Co., 4 per cent	3,775.00
1,000 C. B. & Q., 4 per cent	942.50
2,000 St. Louis Co. Gas, 5 per cent	2,000.00
5,000 Union El. Lt. & Pr., 5 per cent	5,137.50
1,500 B. & O., 4 per cent	1,500.00
5,000 B. & O., 5 per cent	5,285.00

4,000	Memphis P. & L. Co., 5 per cent	4,000.00
1,000	Consumers' Pr. Co., 5 per cent	1,000.00
6,000	Detroit Ed. Co., 5 per cent	6,175.00
4,000	L. V. Ry. Co., 4 per cent	4,000.00
5,000	N. Y. Tel. Co., 6 per cent	5,450.00
1,000	Jeff. & Placq. Dr. Dis., 5 per cent	1,000.00
1,000	Riverside Tract. Co., 5 per cent	770.00
7,000	Publ. Serv. El. & G. Co., 4½ per cent	6,947.50
5,000	C. & N. W. Ry., 5 per cent	5,303.75
5,000	L. & N. R. R. Co., 4 per cent	4,855.00
5,000	L. & N. R. R. Co., 4½ per cent	5,100.00
6,000	So. Pac. Ry., 4 per cent	5,692.50
1,000	Howard G. & C. Co., 6 per cent	1,000.00
2,000	St. Louis, Spr. & Peoria, 5 per cent	2,000.00
2,000	West Penn Rys., 5 per cent	2,000.00
3,000	El. & People's Tract., 4 per cent	1,875.00
5,000	West Penn Power, 5 per cent	5,243.75
5000	Ill. Central R. R., 4 per cent	4,743.75
1,000	Gallitzin School Dist., 5 per cent	1,000.00
1,000	Publ. Serv. Newark Ter., 5 per cent	952.50
5,000	No. Tex. & Mex. Ry., 5 per cent	5,012.50
5,000	Penna. Ry. Co., 4½ per cent	5,043.75
5,000	Ala. Pr. Co., 5 per cent	5,131.25
1,250	1st Liberty Bonds—4¼ per cent	1,250.00
300	3rd Liberty Bonds—4¼ per cent	300.00
30,650	4th Liberty Bonds—4¼ per cent	30,650.00
20,000	Boston, Cape Co. & N. Y. Canal, 5 per cent	20,127.50

$160,163.75

RECORD OF STOCKS {In Missions ....$ 3,500.00
{In Church Extension........................... 6,758.80

4	Shares Riverside Traction Co.	$ 96.00
70	Shares Citizens' Sav. & Tr. Co., York, Pa.	3,500.00
12	Shares Col. Ave. Trust Co., Phila., Pa.	3,412.80
10	Shares Fidelity T. & T. Co.	3,250.00

$10,258.80

LOANS TO CHURCHES
June 30, 1928

Location and Name of Debtor	Date of Loan	Maturity	Amount
ALLEGHANY SYNOD			
Bushman, Pa.:			
Mt. Olivet		1908	$ 166.77
CALIFORNIA SYNOD			
Alhambra, Calif.:			
Grace	1925	1930	4,000.00*
Berkley, Calif.:			
St. Michael's	1920	1929	2,500.00
Gardena, Calif.:			
St. John's	1926	1931	3,000.00
Glendale, Calif.:			
First	1917	1928	500.00

Huntington Park, Calif.:
St. Luke's ....1925 Demand 1,000.00
Los Angeles, Calif.:
Hollywood 1924 1929 5,000.00
Los Angeles, Calif.:
St. Paul's 1925 1930 3,000.00
Oakland, Calif.:
St. Johannis 1922 1930 2,500.00
Richmond, Calif.:
Grace 1926 1931 5,000.00
San Jose, Calif.:
Grace 1895 1900 2,000.00
Sanger, Calif.:
St. Paul's 1908 1913 360.00*
Santa Monica, Calif.:
St. Paul's 1926 1931 10,000.00

CANADA SYNOD
Brantford, Ont.:
St. Matthew's 1919 1930 5,000.00
Galt, Ont.:
St. Paul's 1913 1930 1,000.00
Guelph, Ont.:
St. Paul's 1915 1930 2,000.00
Hamilton, Ont.:
Trinity 1915-23 1928-30 7,080.00
Kitchener, Ont.:
First English 1913 1930 4,114.59
Montreal, Que.:
Redeemer 1910 1930 4,000.00*
Ottawa, Ont.:
St. Peter's 1913 1930 4,000.00

NORTH CAROLINA SYNOD
Durham, N. C.:
St. Paul's 1925 1930 5,000.00
Henderson, N. C.:
Grace 1922 1925 2,000.00
Highland, N. C.:
Good Hope 1927 1932 2,000.00
Raleigh, N. C.:
Holy Trinity 1922 1930 5,000.00
Rocky Mount, N. C.:
Trinity 1925 1928 5,000.00

SOUTH CAROLINA SYNOD
Batesburg, S. C.:
Faith 1927 1932 1,500.00
Clinton, S. C.:
St. John's 1925 1930 2,500.00
Columbia, S. C.:
Reformation 1926 1931 3,000.00

GEORGIA SYNOD
Birmingham, Ala.:
Christ 1921 1929 25,800.00

Location and Name of Debtor	Date of Loan	Maturity	Amount
Daytona, Fla.:			
Resurrection	1925-27	1930-32	10,000.00
Hollywood, Fla.:			
St. John	1927	1932	7,500.00
Macon, Ga.:			
Redeemer	1924	1929	5,000.00
St. Augustine, Fla.:			
Memorial	1926-27	1931-32	5,000.00
St. Petersburg, Fla.:			
Trinity	1921	1929	15,000.00
West Palm Beach, Fla.:			
First	1927	1930	2,400.00
ILLINOIS SYNOD			
Aurora, Ill.:			
Our Redeemer	1907-8	1910-13	2,500.00
Centralia, Ill.:			
Redeemer	1920	1927	5,000.00
Champaign, II.:			
Grace	1916	1929	2,000.00*
Chicago, Ill.:			
Belmont Park	1922	1930	3,500.00*
Epiphany	1916	1928	5,000.00
No. Austin	1926	1928	8,000.00
Norwood Park	1924	1929	5,000.00
Reformation	1918	1923	1,500.00
St. Andrew's	1924	1929	2,500.00
Mt. Zion	1916	1929	2,625.00*
St. Luke's	1907	1931	2,500.00
Our Saviour (Riverdale)	1913	1918	1,000.00
Woodlawn, Memorial	1923	1928	9,000.00*
Elmhurst, Ill.:			
Elmhurst	1923	1928	3,000.00
Epiphany	1926	1931	3,500.00
Maywood, Ill.:			
Broadview	1926	1931	6,000.00
Murphysboro, Ill.:			
First	1926	1931	5,000.00
Oak Park, Ill.:			
Oak Park	1926	1929	2,750.00
St. Louis, Mo.:			
Advent	1924	1929	5,000.00*
Reen Memorial	1915	1918	3,500.00
Reformation	1926	1931	6,500.00
St. Mark's		1884	961.17
Wheaton, Ill.:			
St. Paul's	1928	1933	4,000.00
Wilmette, Ill.:			
English		1929	5,000.00
Evanston, Ill.:			
St. Paul's		1926-31	28,500.00
INDIANA SYNOD			
Batesville, Ind.:			
Bethany	1912	1914	1,400.00

Location and Name of Debtor	Date of Loan	Maturity	Amount
Evansville, Ind.:			
Christ	1923	1928	2,000.00*
Indianapolis, Ind.:			
Bethany	1926	1931	4,000.00
Bethlehem	1924	1928	5,000.00
Gethsemane	1921	1926	3,000.00
Lafayette, Ind.:			
Holy Trinity	1900	1931	9,500.00
Memphis, Tenn.:			
First	1926	1931 32	7,500.00
Terre Haute, Ind.:			
Unity	1924	1929	4,000.00
IOWA SYNOD			
Council Bluffs, Ia.:			
St. John's	1919	1924	2,000.00
Des Moines, Ia.:			
Unity	1924	1929	3,000.00
Iowa Falls, Ia.:			
English	1918	1931	1,000.00
Mason City, Ia.:			
Central	1928	1933	5,000.00
Missouri Valley:			
St. Paul's	1926	1931	2,000.00
Muscatine, Ia.:			
Grace	1900-1 and 23	1905-28	4,000.00
Ottumwa, Ia.:			
St. Mark's	1917-20-21-23	1922-28	5,000.00
Princeton, Ia.:			
Zion	1898	1903	300.00
Valley Junction, Ia.:			
First	1920	1921	700.00
Waterloo, Ia.:			
St. Luke's	1917-20	1922-25	1,300.00
Waterloo, Ia.:			
Trinity	1928	1933	15,000.00
KANSAS SYNOD			
Fairmount, Mo.:			
Fairmount	1926	1931	5,000.00
Hutchinson, Ks.:			
Zion	1921	1929	1,500.00
Kansas City, Ks.:			
Trinity	1926	1931	10,000.00*
Kansas City, Mo.:			
St. John's	1926	Demand	10,000.00
Sedalia, Mo.:			
Trinity		1930	1,800.00
Tulsa, Okla.:			
First		1919	1,500.00
Valley Falls, Ks.:			
St. Paul's		1891-96	1,200.00
MANITOBA SYNOD			
Edmonton, Alta.:			
St. John's	1923	1926	1,500.00

Location and Name of Debtor	Date of Loan	Maturity	Amount
South Edmonton, Alta.:			
Trinity	1921		1,500.00
Brightholme, Sask.	1921	1921-29	450.00
Golden Bay, Man.	1922		500.00
Golden Spike, Alta.:			
St. John's	1927	1932	5,000.00
Esk, Sask.:			
Gartenland	1923		146.00
Harts Hill:			
St. John's	1914		30.00
Kinderley:			
Friedens	1914		75.00
Friedens Feld:			
St. Paul's	1922		100.00
Leduc, Alta.:			
Rosenthal	1922		75.00
Saskatoon:			
Trinity	1922		2,100.00
Saskatoon College	1915-20		6,475.00
Steinbach, Man.:			
St. John's	1925		1,000.00
MARYLAND SYNOD			
Baltimore, Md.:			
All Saints	1922-24	1927-29	7,000.00
Ascension	1923	1928	5,000.00
Luther Memorial	1920	1925	3,000.00
Redeemer	1928	1933	5,000.00
Dundalk, Md.:			
St. Timothy			10,000.00
East Riverdale:			
St. John's	1923	1928	1,000.00
Washington, D. C.:			
St. Stephen's	1927	1931	5,000.00
MICHIGAN SYNOD			
Annarbor, Mich.:			
Trinity	1893	1898	2,000.00
Butler, Ind.:			
Evangelical	1866	1869-73	500.00
Detroit, Mich.:			
Augsburg	1926	1931	3,800.00
Ea. Jefferson Ave.	1913	1918	2,000.00
Hope	1925	1930	7,000.00
Luther Memorial	1926	1931	7,000.00
Nativity	1927	Demand	3,500.00
Reformation	1926	1931	10,000.00
St. Paul's	1920	1926	5,000.00
Unity	1924	1929	11,567.05
Flint, Mich.:			
Trinity	1922	1927	5,000.00
Fort Wayne, Ind.:			
Christ	1917-26	1918-27	2,000.00
Gary, Ind.:			
Grace	1924	1929	10,000.00*

Location and Name of Debtor	Date of Loan	Maturity	Amount
Jackson, Mich.:			
Reformation	1926	1931	4,000.00
Kalamazoo, Mich.:			
Trinity	1928	1933	5,000.00*
Lansing, Mich.:			
Redeemer	1923	1928	4,000.00
Monroeville, Ind.:			
Evangelical	1867	1870-74	500.00
Pontiac, Mich.:			
Ascension	1926	1931	6,000.00
Saginaw, Mich.:			
Resurrection	1925	1930	2,500.00
Windsor, Ont.:			
Trinity	1924	1929	6,000.00
MISSISSIPPI SYNOD			
Goodman, Miss.:			
St. Mark's	1924	1927-29	300.00
Laurel, Miss.:			
Grace	1923	1928	2,500.00
NEBRASKA SYNOD			
Benson, Neb.:			
First	1908	1913	1,200.00
Ericson, Neb.:			
First	1899	1904	150.00
Fremont, Neb.:			
Salem	1924	1929	15,000.00
Hooper, Neb.:			
Grace	1916	1927	600.00
Lincoln, Neb.:			
Grace	1893	1898	4,000.00
St. James'		1930	3,500.00
Omaha, Neb.:			
Grace	1896	1901	3,000.00
South Omaha:			
First	1909-10	1914-15	2,625.00*
So. Sioux City:			
First English	1925	1928	5,000.00
York:			
First	1908-22	1913-27	800.00
GERMAN NEBRASKA SYNOD			
Burlington, Colo.:			
St. Paul's	1928	1933	500.00
Havelock, Neb.:			
Zoar	1916	1921	600.00
Lincoln, Neb.:			
Martin Luther	1926	1929-37	900.00
St. John's	1916	1919	750.00
Lodge Pole, Neb.:			
Immanuel	1922	1927-34	900.00
Norfolk, Neb.:			
St. Johannis	1920	1925	750.00

Location and Name of Debtor	Date of Loan	Maturity	Amount
NEW YORK MINISTERIUM			
Valley Stream, L. I., N. Y.:			
St. Paul's 1925		1930	3,000.00
NEW YORK & NEW ENGLAND SYNOD			
Baldwin, N. Y.:			
St. Peter's 1924		Demand	5,000.00
Bellaire, N. Y.:			
Good Shepherd 1925		1930	2,000.00
Blasdell, N. Y.:			
First 1926		1931	2,000.00
Brooklyn, N. Y.:			
St. Andrew's 1916		1921	8,000.00
Endicott, N. Y.:			
Nativity 1926		1931	2,000.00
Forest Hills, N. Y.:			
Grace 1927		1932	4,000.00
Flushing, L. I.:			
Messiah 1922		Demand	5,000.00
Franklin Square, N. Y.:			
Ascension 1925		1930	3,000.00
Hartford, Conn.:			
St. Paul's 1924		Demand	3,700.00
Little Neck, L. I.:			
Christ 1926		1931	3,000.00
Newark, N. J.:			
Grace 1906		1909	6,000.00
East Orange, N. J.:			
Advent 1924		Demand	800.00
New Britain, Conn.:			
Reformation 1926		Demand	4,900.00
Nutley, N. J.:			
Trinity 1927		1932	4,000.00
Queens (Dunton), N. Y.:			
St. Paul's 1925		1930	5,000.00
Rochester, N. Y.:			
Emmanuel		1927	5,000.00
Snyder, N. Y.:			
Ascension 1927		1932	5,000.00
Union Township, N. J.:			
Christ 1927		1932	3,000.00
Woodhaven, N. Y.:			
St. James 1924		1929	5,000.00
NEW YORK SYNOD			
Albany, N. Y.:			
St. Peter's 1914		1919	2,000.00
Brooklyn, N. Y.:			
Calvary 1905		1910	2,500.00
St. Philips' 1921-26		1929-30	5,000.00
Buffalo, N. Y.:			
Zion 1896		1901	2,000.00
Gerritsen Beach, N. Y.:			
St. James' 1926		1931	5,000.00

Location and Name of Debtor	Date of Loan	Maturity	Amount
Glen Morris, N. Y.:			
St. Andrew's	1915	1920-32	1,600.00
Gloversville, N. Y.:			
St. James'	1893	1895	200.00
Hasbrouck Hgts.:			
Holy Trinity	1923	1928	2,000.00
Hillside, N. J.:			
Calvary	1925	1930	5,000.00
Hoboken, N. J.:			
Holy Trinity	1911	1916	2,000.00
Howard Beach, L. I., N. Y.:			
St. Barnabas	1924	1929	3,000.00
Jamaica, N. Y.:			
Our Saviour	1924	1929	5,000.00
Incarnation (Baisley Park)	1925	Demand	3,000.00
Jersey City, N. J.:			
Calvary	1919	1924	2,500.00
New Haven, Conn.:			
First English	1904	1909	2,000.00*
Newark, N. J.:			
St. James'	1901	1906	400.00
Oswego, N. Y.:			
St. Matthew's	1888	1893-1900	2,150.00
Paterson, N. J.:			
First		1912-32	5,960.90
Pelham Park, N. Y.:			
Calvary	1925	Demand	5,000.00
Richmond Hill Circle, N. Y.:			
Holy Comforter	1926	1931	1,000.00
River Edge, N. J.:			
Grace	1923	1928	3,000.00
Schenectady, N. Y.:			
First	1922	Demand	3,500.00
Second	1928	1933	5,000.00
Springfield Gardens, N. Y.:			
Bethany	1925	Demand	5,000.00
Syracuse, N. Y.:			
Atonement	1918	1923-33	5,000.00
Teaneck, N. J.:			
St. Paul's	1928	1933	5,000.00
NORTHWEST SYNOD			
Appleton, Wis.:			
Trinity	1924	1929	5,000.00
Beloit, Wis.:			
Atonement	1908-18	1913-23	8,000.00
Billings, Montana:			
First English	1920	1925-28	6,200.00
Fond Du Lac, Wis.:			
Our Saviour	1926	1931	5,000.00
Grand Forks, N. D.:			
St. Mark's	1915	1929	900.00
Great Falls, Mont.:			
St. John's	1927	1932	10,000.00*

Location and Name of Debtor	Date of Loan	Maturity	Amount
Jefferson, Wis.:			
St. Mark's	1926	1931	1,000.00
Killdeer, N. D.:			
St. John's	1920	1925	2,093.00
Lansford, N. D.:			
Trinity	1920	1925	1,000.00
Lincolnton, Minn.:			
St. Andrew's	1925	1930	3,000.00
Livingston, Mont.:			
Redeemer	1912	1932	5,000.00
Madison, Wis.:			
Luther Memorial	1921-22-24-27	1926-32	39,300.00
Marinette, Wis.:			
St. James'	1922	1927	5,000.00
Marshfield, Wis.:			
Trinity	1924	1929	3,000.00
Milwaukee, Wis.:			
Pentecost	1924		1,500.00
Washington Park	1921	1929	15,000.00
Minneapolis, Minn.:			
Epiphany	1926-27	1931-32	5,000.00
Holy Communion	1910-13	1915-18	2,000.00
Mt. Carmel	1926	1931	4,000.00
Resurrection	1923	1928	2,000.00
St. James'	1916	1921	2,000.00
New London, Wis.:			
Holy Trinity		1925	2,500.00
Oshkosh, Wis.:			
St. John's	1924	1927	3,000.00
Oxboro (Bloomington), Minn.:			
St. Luke's	1927	1932	2,000.00
St. Paul, Minn.:			
Ascension	1925	1930	5,500.00
Superior, Wis.:			
Holy Trinity	1926	1929	5,000.00
Walters, Minn.:			
Faith	1923	1926	1,500.00
Waukesha, Wis.:			
St. Luke's	1926	1928-31	8,000.00*
Wauwatosa, Wis.:			
St. Matthew's	1921	1928	15,000.00
West Bend, Wis.:			
Trinity	1926	1931	3,000.00
Williston, N. D.:			
Trinity	1925	1928	8,200.00
Winnipeg, Man., Can.:			
First English	1912-21	1915-26	26,288.38
Winona, Minn.:			
Faith	1918	1923	350.00
Milwaukee, Wis.:			
Resurrection	1915	1920	700.00
Nova Scotia Synod			
Halifax, N. S.:			
Resurrection	1915	1930	5,000.00

Location and Name of Debtor	Date of Loan	Maturity	Amount
OHIO SYNOD			
Akron, O.:			
First Hungarian	1927	1932	5,000.00
Bowling Green, O.:			
First	1923	1928	3,000.00
Cambridge, O.:			
Christ	1913	1918	1,000.00
Cleveland, O.:			
Emmaus	1912	1916	1,150.00
Cleveland Hgts.:			
Messiah	1924	1929	5,000.00
East Cleveland:			
St. James'	1919	1924	2,000.00*
Columbus, O.:			
Hilltop	1919	1924	2,000.00
Indianola	•	Demand	3,333.33*
Immanuel	1891-96	1893-06	4,250.00
Redeemer	1923	1928	3,000.00
Continental, O.:			
Christ	1897	1897	300.00
Covington, Ky.:			
First	1920	1931	5,000.00
Dayton, Ohio:			
Grace	1912	1917	1,700.00
No. Riverdale	1914	1919	1,500.00
Westwood	1916	1921	1,500.00
Fremont, O.:			
St. Mark's	1921	1926	3,000.00
Kent, O.:			
First	1908	1913	1,000.00
Lakewood, O.:			
Trinity	1921	1926	10,000.00
Marion, O.:			
St. Paul's	1917	1922	1,000.00
Niles, O.:			
Trinity	1924	1931	5,000.00
Sebring, O.:			
Trinity	1915	1918	1,000.00
Springfield, O.:			
Fifth	1902	1904	2,000.00
Toledo, O.:			
Augsburg	1925	1929	5,000.00
Bethany	1927	1932	5,000.00
Home Acres	1922	1927	1,000.00
Messiah	1925	1930	2,000.00
Redeemer	1925	1930	5,000.00
PACIFIC SYNOD			
Bellingham, Wash.:			
St. Mark's	1924	1929	1,000.00*
Everett, Wash.:			
Trinity	1920	1929	5,000.00
Longview, Wash.:			
Trinity	1926	1931	10,000.00*

Location and Name of Debtor	Date of Loan	Maturity	Amount
Medford, Ore.:			
Zion	1928	1933	3,000.00
Portland, Ore.:			
Redeemer		Demand	1,200.00
Seattle, Wash.:			
Holy Trinity	1901-03	1902-06	3,500.00
St. James'	1923	1928	2,500.00
University	1926-27	1931	17,000.00*
Spokane, Wash.:			
St. Paul's	1924	1929	3,000.00
Vancouver, B. C.:			
Redeemer	1913	1918	5,000.00
Victoria, B. C.:			
Grace	1910	1913-25	5,967.50*
Yakima, Wash.:			
Trinity	1925	1930	3,500.00
EAST PENNSYLVANIA SYNOD			
Bristol, Pa.:			
Zion	1920	1925	3,000.00
Collingdale, Pa.:			
First	1926	1931	5,000.00
Drexel Hill:			
Grace	1925	1930	5,000.00
Essington, Pa.:			
Tinicum Memorial	1922	1930	3,000.00
Harrisburg, Pa.:			
St. Paul's	1924	1929	3,000.00
Merchantville, N. J.:			
Messiah	1927	1932	2,500.00
Narberth, Pa.:			
Trinity		1926-29	7,500.00
Palmyra, N. J.:			
First	1925	1930	5,000.00
Philadelphia, Pa.:			
Bethany (Memorial)	1891		500.00
Luther Memorial			5,000.00
St. Andrew's	1904		2,000.00
Runnemede, N. J.:			
Trinity	1928		2,500.00
Sea Isle City, N. J.:			
Messiah	1918	1919	500.00
Stone Harbor, Pa.:			
Our Saviour	1916	1921	1,000.00
Trenton, N. J.:			
Bethel	1924	1929	10,000.00
West Chester, Pa.:			
Calvary	1925	1926	1,500.00
PENNSYLVANIA MINISTERIUM			
Allentown, Pa.:			
Redeemer	1926	1931	3,000.00
Attleboro, Pa.:			
Redeemer	1906	1930	800.00

Location and Name of Debtor	Date of Loan	Maturity	Amount
Chester, Pa.:			
Nativity	1920	1929	2,500.00
Haddon Heights, N. J.:			
St. Paul's	1916	1930	2,000.00
Mountainville, Pa.:			
Trinity	1924	1927	5,000.00
Philadelphia, Pa.:			
Mediator	1923	1930	7,000.00
Gloria Dei	1924	1929	15,000.00
Grace (Roxboro)	1926	1929	3,000.00
St. Stephen's	1913	1918	5,000.00
Shaverton, Pa.:			
St. Paul's	1927	1932	2,500.00
Somers Point, N. J.:			
Grace	1927	1932	2,500.00
West Collingswood, N. J.:			
St. Luke's	1917	1930	3,000.00
Wilkes-Barre, Pa.:			
Trinity		1929	800.00
Wyomissing, Pa.:			
Atonement	1921	1929	5,000.00*
Reading, Pa.:			
Nativity	1928	1933	5,000.00
Oaklyn, N. J.:			
St. Mark's	1928	1933	2,500.00
Haddonfield, N. J.:			
Our Saviour	1928	1933	2,500.00
SUSQUEHANNA OF CENTRAL PENNA.			
Jersey Shore, Pa.:			
Grace	1908	1911	500.00
Scranton, Pa.:			
Grace	1902	1907	1,300.00
PITTSBURGH SYNOD			
Arnold, Pa.:			
Calvary	1923	1928	3,000.00
Ashtabula, O.:			
First	1912	1917	1,000.00
Butler, Pa.:			
Trinity	1923	1928	8,000.00*
Cleveland, O.:			
St. Johannis	1924	1929	5,000.00
East McKeesport, Pa.:			
St. John's	1911	1916	500.00
Garfield, Pa.:			
English		1907	500.00
Gary, Ind.:			
Honterus	1927	1932	5,000.00
Monessen, Pa.:			
St. Paul's	1910	1915	1,000.00
Pittsburgh, Pa.:			
First Hungarian	1926	1931	5,000.00
Messiah	1915	1930	2,000.00*
St. James'	1907	1930	2,000.00

Location and Name of Debtor	Date of Loan	Maturity	Amount
St. Paul's	1906	1909	700.00
Sharon, Pa.:			
Trinity	1926	1929	3,000.00
Swissvale, Pa.:			
St. John's	1908	1913	2,000.00
Wilkinsburg Manor	1927	Demand	5,000.00
Wesleyville, Pa.:			
Messiah	1920	1923	3,000.00
Farrell, Pa.:			
St. John's	1928	1933	4,000.00
ROCKY MOUNTAIN SYNOD			
Casper, Wyo.:			
Grace	1924	1924	5,000.00*
Colorado Springs, Colo.:			
First	1894	1929	2,895.00
Denver, Colo.:			
Messiah	1924	1927	2,000.00
Trinity	1908	1929	2,300.00*
Laramie, Wyo.:			
First Scandinavian	1925	1930	4,000.00*
Pueblo, Colo.:			
St. Mark's	1906	1929	1,500.00
SLOVAK ZION SYNOD			
Camden, N. J.:			
St. John the Baptist	1927	1932	2,000.00
East Pittsburgh, Pa.:			
Trinity Slovak	1924	1929	3,000.00
TEXAS SYNOD			
Dallas, Texas:			
First	1923	1928	3,000.00
Pawnee, Texas:			
Holy Cross	1927	1932	1,000.00
San Antonio, Texas:			
St. Luke's	1926	1931	5,000.00
VIRGINIA SYNOD			
Lynchburg, Va.:			
Trinity	1923	1926	5,300.00*
Roanoke, Va.:			
Emmanuel	1922	1929	1,650.00
WEST VIRGINIA SYNOD			
Charleston, W. Va.:			
Trinity	1925	1930	5,000.00
Clarksburg, W. Va.:			
St. Mark's	1926	1929	1,400.00*
Davis, W. Va.:			
St. John's	1893-98	1898-1901	601.00
Elkins, W. Va.:			
Holy Trinity	1908	1911	500.00
Wheeling, W. Va.:			
Edgewood	1926	Demand	500.00

WARTBURG SYNOD
Breitung, Mich.:
  Good Shepherd 1925   1930   1,500.00
Burr Oak, Ia.:
  St. Paul's   1924   1,200.00
Chicago, Ill.:
  Friedens 1923   1928   3,000.00
  Martin Luther 1926   1931   2,000.00
  St. Johannis 1916   1921   800.00
  Tabor 1927   1932   3,000.00
  Mont Clare 1921   1924-34   2,200.00
Guttenberg, Ia.:
  St. Paul's 1923   1928   4,900.00

---

* Agency Loans.

LOANS TO CHURCHES

Synod	Amount
Alleghany Synod	$ 166.77
California Synod	38,860.00
Canada Synod	27,194.59
North Carolina Synod	19,000.00
South Carolina Synod	7,000.00
Georgia Synod	70,700.00
Illinois Synod	123,836.17
Indiana Synod	36,400.00
Iowa Synod..	39,300.00
Kansas Synod	31,000.00
Manitoba Synod	18,951.00
Maryland Synod	36,000.00
Michigan Synod	97,367.05
Mississippi Synod	2,800.00
Nebraska Synod	35,875.00
German Nebraska Synod	4,400.00
New York Ministerium	3,000.00
New York & New England Synod	76,400.00
New York Synod	83,810.90
Northwest Synod	207,031.38
Nova Scotia Synod	5,000.00
Ohio Synod	80,733.33
Pacific Synod	60,667.50
East Pennsylvania Synod	57,000.00
Pennsylvania Ministerium	67,100.00
Susquehanna of Central Penna.	1,800.00
Pittsburgh Synod	50,700.00
Rocky Mountain Synod	17,695.00
Slovak Zion Synod	5,000.00
Texas Synod	9,000.00
Virginia Synod	6,950.00
West Virginia Synod	8,001.00
Wartburg Synod	18,600.00

$1,347,339.69

The Rev. J. Bradley Markward, President of the Board, addressed the Convention and introduced the speakers in the following order: The Rev. F. F. Fry, Executive Secretary of the Board; the Rev. Z. M. Corbe, Treasurer; the Rev. A. D. R. Hancher, Superintendent for the Southern District.

Resolution 1 was adopted by a rising vote.

Resolution 2 adopted.

Resolution 3 adopted. In connection with the consideration of this resolution the Rev. H. Offermann presented President Haapanen of the Suomi Synod, who extended the greetings of that Body to the Convention, expressed thanks for the help extended in home mission work and the desire of the Suomi Synod for further co-operation on the part of the United Lutheran Church.

The Rev. John C. Seegers, by appointment of the President, expressed the gratification of the United Lutheran Church at the presence of President Haapanen, and its sympathy in the problems of the Suomi Synod.

Resolution 4 adopted.

Item 4 of the Report of the Committee on Memorials from Constituent Synods, on which action had been postponed, was taken up. The Secretary read the memorial from the Kansas Synod concerning work for deaf mutes and the reply of the Committee on Memorials recommending that the matter be referred to the Inner Mission Board. The President stated that this recommendation of the Committee on Memorials was now before the Convention. Moved and carried, That the matter be referred to the Executive Board for consideration with power of decision.

The report of the auditors on the accounts of the Board of American Missions was accepted.

The Convention resumed consideration of resolution 5 of the Report of the Board of Foreign Missions.

The following substitute for the original resolution was offered by the President of the Board and adopted:

"*Resolved,* That as an exception to the rule adopted at the last Convention of the United Lutheran Church, the Board of Foreign Missions be allowed to use funds from undesignated legacies for payments due the Berlin Missionary Society for the property of our mission in the Shantung Province in China."

Resolution 6 of the Board of Foreign Missions was adopted.

The Rev. E. P. Pfatteicher offered the following resolution which was adopted by a rising vote:

"*Whereas* the United Lutheran Church in Convention assembled has heard with great profit the instructive report concerning the visit of President Knubel and Treasurer Miller to our mission stations in India, and

"*Whereas* we believe that said visit has been of great direct value to the Church at large, be it

"*Resolved,* That we extend to Doctors Knubel and Miller the heartfelt and sincere appreciation of the United Lutheran Church for their readiness to undertake and their ability to fulfill this important mission."

The Rev. Paul E. Scherer moved that the Convention commend the Report of Drs. Knubel and Miller to the Board of Foreign Missions for that Board's guidance in the prosecution of the work in India. The motion was adopted.

The auditor's report on the accounts of the Board of Foreign Missions was accepted.

The Convention adjourned with prayer by the Rev. J. F. Crigler.

Evening Service

The Evening Service was held according to program. The speakers were the Rev. F. H. Knubel and Mr. E. Clarence Miller, both of whom addressed the audience upon the subject of their recent visit to India.

The Opening Vesper Service was conducted by the Rev. C. T. Benze; the Rev. J. L. Morgan closed the service.

FOURTH MEETING

Morning Session

SUNDAY SCHOOL CHAPEL,
LUTHER MEMORIAL CHURCH,
ERIE, PENNSYLVANIA.
Saturday, October 13, 1928, 8.45.

Matins were conducted by the Rev. John C. Seegers.

The Convention was called to order by the President.

The Minutes of Friday morning and afternoon sessions were read and approved.

Moved and carried, That the Convention reconsider its action upon resolution 4 of the Committee of Reference and Counsel of Friday afternoon.

Moved and carried, To amend resolution 4 by striking out "shall prepare, print and distribute" and substituting "shall consider the preparation of, printing and distributing." The resolution was adopted as amended.

Mr. Harry Hodges, Chairman of Tellers Committee No. 2, reported elections as follows:

For the *Executive Committee of the Laymen's Movement*: Mr. Thos. P. Hickman received a majority of the votes cast. Mr. Hickman was declared elected.

For the *Board of Foreign Missions* each of the following received a majority of the votes cast:

Rev. H. C. Brillhart	Rev. E. R. Jaxheimer
Rev. J. E. Byers	Mr. A. Y. Leech, Jr.
Rev. G. A. Greiss	Mr. Paul Van Reed Miller

Mr. W. A. Rast

The President declared them elected.

For the *Board of American Missions* each of the following received a majority of the votes cast:

Rev. A. E. Bell   Rev. J. C. Seegers
Rev. C. A. Freed   Mr. A. H. Durboraw
Rev. G. K. Rubrecht   Mr. Wm. Eck
Mr. S. F. Telleen

The President declared them elected.

For the *Board of Northwestern Missions* each of the following received a majority of the votes cast:

Rev. A. E. Bell   Rev. J. C. Seegers
Rev. C. A. Freed   Mr. A. H. Durboraw
Rev. G. K. Rubrecht   Mr. Wm. Eck
Mr. S. F. Telleen

The President declared them elected.

For the *Immigrants Mission Board* each of the following received a majority of the votes cast:

Rev. A. E. Bell   Mr. Wm. Eck
Rev. C. A. Freed   Mr. S. F. Telleen

The President declared them elected.

For the *West Indies Mission Board* each of the following received a majority of the votes cast:

Rev. A. E. Bell   Rev. J. C. Seegers
Rev. C. A. Freed   Mr. A. H. Durboraw
Rev. G. K. Rubrecht   Mr. Wm. Eck
Mr. S. F. Telleen

The President declared them elected.

For the *Board of Publication* each of the following received a majority of the votes cast:

Rev. H. C. Alleman   Mr. Croll Keller
Rev. A. H. Holthusen   Mr. O. W. Osterlund
Rev. G. W. Nicely   Mr. J. C. Lynch
Mr. D. F. Yost

The President declared them elected.

For the *Board of Ministerial Pensions and Relief* each of the following received a majority of the votes cast:

Rev. Otto Kleine   Mr. J. L. Fisher
Mr. A. Raymond Bard   Hon. Henry W. Harter
                   Mr. M. P. Moller, Sr.

The President declared them elected.

For the *Parish and Church School Board* each of the following received a majority of the votes cast:

Rev. P. D. Brown   Rev. F. M. Urich
Rev. A. J. Turkle   Mr. Grant Hultberg

The President declared them elected.

For the *Board of Deaconess Work* each of the following received a majority of the votes cast:

Rev. Earl J. Bowman   Rev. W. C. Schaeffer, Jr.
Rev. U. S. G. Rupp   Mr. Frederick H. Wefer

The President declared them elected and stated that there was one layman yet to be elected.

For the *Inner Mission Board* each of the following received a majority of the votes cast:

Rev. F. B. Clausen   Mr. A. H. Durboraw
Rev. J. F. Fedders   Mr. W. J. Showalter

The President declared them elected and stated that there was one clergyman yet to be elected.

For the *Board of Education* each of the following received a majority of the votes cast:

Rev. E. C. Herman   Rev. Wm. M. Horn
Rev. A. J. Holl   Rev. A. A. Zinck
                   Mr. W. J. Showalter

The President declared them elected and stated that there were two laymen yet to be elected.

It was moved and carried, That in each case where the election was not complete, twice the number yet to be elected be regarded as the nominees of the Convention and that these be the persons having received the highest number of votes short of the number necessary for election, and that the balloting be limited to these nominees.

The Tellers were instructed to pass ballots for these elections.

The Rev. John C. Seegers presented the report of the Committee on Evangelism.

REPORT OF THE COMMITTEE ON EVANGELISM

The fact that the latest statistics reveal a decided gain in the numerical strength of the forces of Protestantism, and the additional fact that the largest net gain among these forces is credited to the United Lutheran Church, fill our hearts with gratitude to God that He has blessed the labors of our people. These facts, however, heartening and encouraging as they are, are not a cause for self complacency nor do they warrant any let up in our effort to add and anchor souls to Christ and His Church.

Stimulating as these facts may be, an honest analysis of the situation by the Church will demand a continuous effort on her part. She will still find it necessary to place the emphasis upon evangelism as the great work challenging her best thought and calling for her most earnest endeavor.

This is said not with the thought of pitting one cause against another, much less with the idea of making causes in the church competitive. All the phases of the Church's work are interdependent. When one suffers all suffer. But without hesitation we say the perpetuation of the church is definitely linked with and inseparably associated with evangelism. It is central and basic. It represents her mission in a supreme sense.

That there is need, a real necessity, for this work will not be seriously questioned by any one acquainted with the real situation confronting the Church. "Its necessity is very obvious whether we take a world-view and see three-fourths of the globe's population not even professedly Christian; or a more localized view and note over half of our nation claiming no church affiliation; or a survey of our own losses recorded or unrecorded." A careful study of the real situation will reveal, not only the necessity upon the church to do this work vigorously and hopefully, but also the opportunity opening up to her to fulfill her high mission on earth.

Be it said the church has not been idle in this respect. In spite of many criticisms and caustic strictures the fact remains that the church has been making progress. Her impress is being felt. She has not been standing still. Her accessions certify her activity. Her gains confirm her progress. Institutes have been held in the interest of evangelism in several district synods in the Middle West. One of our committee, Dr. C. J. Rockey, was privileged to assist in this work. In other synods the question received definite consideration and members of our committee took part in the deliberations.

The work of the committee has been carried on largely through the medium of correspondence, but this is not sufficient. We are of the opinion that the time has come to concrete the principles we have advanced into action. We believe the hour for an aggressive campaign for souls has struck. We believe the signs of the times indicate the wisdom of such a campaign. We believe it can be launched not only in faith, but with every hope of success. We need but cite the fact that others are doing so. We need but remind you that the emotional appeal is no longer being made. Men and women are going out as witness bearers. Individuals are making their testimonies to individuals. We believe, therefore that the time has come for the United Lutheran Church to conduct its work of evangelism in a more effective way. We would not shift the emphasis. We are definitely convinced that the emphasis must be placed upon the congregation. Evangelism to be successful must be the out-going of the congregation's life. It must be the constant and the uninterrupted program of every congregation. It is not a question of emphasis. It is a question of method.

The Richmond Convention in resolution authorized the committee to "employ a full-time secretary as soon as they deem it feasible, who shall work under the direction of the aforesaid committee." The committee has not seen its way clear to exercise the privilege authorized by the resolution. The committee does not think it wise or necessary to establish another board nor to create another secretarial office. And yet we are convinced that there must be some personal contact with the congregations or at least with the district synod if the work is to gather that momentum and power which it should have to become really effective. Contact by mail is not sufficiently vital. It seems to us, therefore, that provision for this personal contact must be made.

1. For the year 1929 the Committee recommends the holding of evangelism institutes within the bounds of every district synod affiliated with this body. We suggest that these institutes be held for one day.

2. We recommend that the Committee be authorized to send a personal representative to the district synods with a view of enabling and assisting every synod to formulate and project a program, which will make effective the work of evangelism within its bounds, and that expenses incident to this shall be met by the United Lutheran Church.

To give direction to the character of nature of these meetings the committee offers as a suggestion the following program. We believe it covers the entire question.

General Theme: "The Evangelistic Task."
Special subjects under the theme to be discussed.
    (a) The equipment of the Church for the task.

(b) Methods of accomplishing the task.

Hymn, Scripture, Prayer, Hymn, or any devotional service best adapted
to the environment in which the institute is being held.

First (1) Address: The Sufficiency of the Church Equipment.

    (a) Guaranteed by the commission given the Church.

    (b) By the person giving the commission.

    (c) By the means associated with the commission.

(2) Certified by Christ's Relation to the Church.

    (a) Present with the Church. Matt. 28:20 last clause, Mark 16:20.

    (b) Effective, in the Church. Matt. 16:18; Mark 16:20; Acts 2:47.

(3) Certified by the experience of the Church. (Refer to the Acts of
the Apostles and other records of epochal movements in the life of the
Church.)

Second Address—Methods of accomplishing the task.

(1) In general.

Quicken the Church to an appreciation of

    (a) Christ's Person and Work.

    (b) The value of the soul.

    (c) The efficiency of the means of grace.

Arouse the congregation to a sense of its responsibility.

    (a) As the primary body of the church.

    (b) As the potent spiritual factor in the community.

Stress the necessity of individual witnessing.

    (a) In the matter of church allegiance.

    (b) In the matter of Christian living.

Particular methods.

    (1) By the congregation.

    (2) By the individual.

Under 1. Emphasize the evangelistic note in the services.

    Set aside seasons for special endeavor—reclaiming and
    recruiting.

    Advertise and use appropriate literature.

Under 2. Recognize the source of power. Not by might nor by power,
    etc. See also I Cor. 6:9; Isaiah 6:5-8 and related
    scripture.

    Approach the prospect intelligently, hopefully and expectantly.

Under 3. Concentrate definitely on specific persons.

    Do not dissipate energy. Study them carefully and prayer-
    fully. Learn their peculiarities. Consider their environ-
    ment, their temperament.

Under 4. Invite and direct them to the church, and arrange for them to
    attend the services, etc.

This program contemplates an institute of two sessions. If an evening session is deemed feasible and desirable, it could take the form of an open forum, or a round table talk, at which the chief points suggested in the previous discussions could be emphasized and enlarged upon.

Problems and possibilities could be made the basis of an additional address. As these vary so much in different localities, the development would have to be colored by conditions existing in a given place or community.

The committee expresses its appreciation of the co-operation by the presidents of district synods and the chairmen of synodical committees.

Respectfully submitted,
JOHN C. SEEGERS,
For the Committee.

In connection with the presentation, the Revs. A. Pohlman, J. F. Crigler, L. W. Steckel and Mr. Chr. Hummel, addressed the Convention.

Recommendation 1 adopted.

Recommendation 2 adopted with the understanding that it be subject to arrangements with the Executive Board.

In connection with this report Mr. Oliver C. C. Fetta moved the following recommendations:

1. The United Lutheran Church in America adopts as a goal for every constituent member, congregation and synod, a net increase in the communicant membership of ten per cent each year.
2. That the Committee on Evangelism, in conjunction with the synodical presidents, proceed with this campaign promptly, assigning each synod a quota of not less than ten per cent of its communicant membership reported in 1928.
3. That the Church papers be requested to give full publicity to this movement by publishing from time to time the quota assigned each synod and the results achieved in comparative order, together with the names of all congregations meeting the quota.

After discussion by Messrs. Fetta, H. F. Heuer, J. Frank Dougherty, W. H. Hager and the Revs. J. C. Kunzmann and P. W. Roth, the recommendations submitted by Mr. Fetta were adopted.

At the request of the President, the Secretary read item three of the Report of the Committee on Memorials from Constituent Synods, being a memorial from the Susquehanna Synod concerning plans for personal evangelistic work. In view of the action just taken it was the sense of the Convention that this item had been covered.

Mr. Harry Hodges, Chairman of Tellers Committee No. 2, read the nominations for the pending elections as follows:

For the Board of Education: Mrs. Adelaide Burge, Mr. A. L. Bulwinkle, Mr. Paul R. Heymann and Mr. Charles Steele.

For the Inner Mission Board: The Revs. J. S. Schantz and D. A. Davy.

For the Board of Deaconess Work: Mr. John A. Hoober and Mr. J. C. Kinard.

Mr. Hodges reported that each of the following had received a majority of votes cast for the Board of the *National Lutheran Home for the Aged*:

Rev. Henry Anstadt	Rev. John Weidley
Rev. O. F. Blackwelder	Mr. L. Russell Alden
Rev. J. L. Frantz	Dr. W. K. Butler
Rev. J. E. Harms	Mr. F. E. Cunningham
Rev. J. T. Huddle	Mr. Harry T. Domer
Rev. Richard Schmidt	Mr. W. H. Finckel
Rev. H. E. Snyder	Mr. John H. Jones
Rev. F. R. Wagner	Mr. F. W. Kakel

Mr. Harry L. Snyder

The President declared them elected.

The Rev. David A. Davy presented the report of the Committee on Lutheran Brotherhoods.

REPORT OF THE COMMITTEE ON LUTHERAN BROTHERHOODS

"The Brotherhood, as an auxiliary of the Church, is completely back of every project of the Church." So it commendably declared at the Richmond Convention of 1926. In demonstration of the sincerity of its declaration, your committee is happy to incorporate the splendid report of Brotherhood activities and progress, during the past biennium, as submitted by its executive secretary and president.

THE BROTHERHOOD'S REPORT

One of the encouraging signs of our time is the increasing interest men are taking in the work of the Church. We seem to be awakening to the fact, that while we have carefully organized the women, and led them into positive, effective service, we have hitherto given too little thought to the organization of the men, for a like service. We are beginning to realize the incalculable loss the Church has suffered from this neglect.

PROGRESS

In the past two years the Brotherhood has devoted much time to bringing this fact home to the consciousness of the men. Many addresses have been made, and an extensive correspondence has been carried on to this end. The result has shown itself in a marked growth in the organization and enrollment of brotherhoods in the Brotherhood of the United Lutheran Church. The Brotherhood has won its way. Its vital importance to the Church is shown in the rapidly increasing host of laymen, who are taking a deep interest in the affairs of the Kingdom. If nothing more had been done, this result alone would show the vital importance of the Brotherhood to the Church. The awakening and organization and combination of the men is, without question, the key to the solution of our problems, and the prophecy of great achievement in the near future.

THE PENSION FUND

At the Chicago Convention in 1924, the Brotherhood agreed to co-operate with the Pension Board in securing the endowment of four million dollars for pensions for pastors. From that date, the Brotherhood has taken every opportunity to promote this cause. Many addresses have been made by the secretary, and by Brotherhood men throughout the whole country. Every month articles have appeared in *Lutheran Men,* giving information on the subject. The May number was almost wholly devoted to it. A large edition of this number was printed and distributed. Every brotherhood has co-operated heartily in the campaign, and conducted the canvass. The organization for this task, in every church that had a brotherhood, was ready for service, and as a result these churches exceeded their quota in practically every case. The churches that failed were churches without a brotherhood.

"LUTHERAN MEN"

Soon after the Richmond Convention, *Lutheran Men* was changed from a quarterly to a monthly, and increased from an eight-page to a twelve-page paper. This change has been received most favorably, and has done much to promote the work. The circulation of the paper is steadily growing, and has now passed the ten thousand mark. We have thus doubled our circulation in the past two years. Plans are now under way to rapidly increase this list, and from our knowledge of conditions, we feel safe in saying that in the next year, we fully expect to double the present number. *Lutheran Men* not only seeks to develop men in church work, but it also furnishes a complete program for the monthly meetings, on topics that give information concerning the Church and its work. The aim is to get our men informed concerning the work of the Church, and thus interested. Soon after the paper was changed to a monthly, a page was offered to the Laymen's Movement, for such material as it desired to publish. This offer was accepted, and Secretary Black has furnished, month by month, most excellent articles on "Stewardship." We are glad to note that this arrangement will be continued. The Brotherhood organization and the Laymen's Movement are in complete accord concerning all parts of the work, and are co-operating to the one great end, that our Lutheran Church may ere long, use its great latent power.

FEDERATION OF LUTHERAN BROTHERHOODS

At the Richmond Convention, both the Brotherhood Convention and the convention of the United Lutheran Church, adopted a constitution for a proposed Federation of Lutheran Brotherhoods in America. A convention to launch this organization was held in Milwaukee in October, 1927. Representatives were present from the Augustana Synod, the Danish Synod, the Iowa Synod, the Norwegian Synod, the Joint Synod of Ohio and the United Lutheran Church. This meeting was preceded by a meeting of the Lutheran Brotherhood Association, called for the purpose of closing the books of that organization and dissolving the same. Following this meeting, the question of the organization of the Federation of Lutheran Brotherhoods was taken up. After some discussion, the organization was launched. Dr. W. A. Granville of Chicago was elected president. The assets of the Lutheran Brotherhood Association were turned over to the Federation. A full corp of officers was elected, the Executive Committee formed, and the organization fully equipped for service. The men of the different Lutheran bodies present, took a deep interest in the proceedings and were enthusiastic as to the future service this organization will render our Lutheran Church. There was manifested a deep conviction that this will prove to be an historic event and will ultimately lead to a closer affiliation among our Lutheran bodies and possibly finally to a merger of our Lutheran forces and interests. The Brotherhood of the United Lutheran Church had an important part in this meeting. For many reasons it was of the highest importance that we should take an active part in forming this Federation, and we are pursuaded that the service rendered has shown anew the value and importance of our Brotherhood to the whole Lutheran cause in America.

FOUR VITAL OBJECTIVES

The Brotherhood is now presenting four definite objectives, to be taken up by each brotherhood. We are laying emphasis upon the need of every brotherhood definitely committing itself to this program. These objectives are:

A. The larger attendance of men at the services of the church.

B. Securing the return of the lapsed membership.

C. The winning of the outside man.

D. The holding of the boys in the church.

It is in these particulars that the church is weak. It will be conceded that to remedy this condition is vital to the progress of the church. It will also be granted that the pastor alone cannot do this. The difficulty has been that congregations have largely shifted this responsibility on the pastor. This has been unfair, both to the pastor and to the laymen. Both have responsibilities here, and it is only as the pastor and the laymen co-operate, that the church can enter upon a career of great progress. A committee on each of these objectives is now functioning in a number of our brotherhoods and most excellent results are being secured. It is only as the laymen are organized and given these duties, that it is at all possible to do them. Since all of these objectives are vital to the progress of the church, and since they can be done only by the Brotherhood, it reveals to us the fact that the Brotherhood is today of supreme importance to the welfare of the church.

HINDERANCES

Our principal hinderance in the work has been the spirit of separatism and individualism, resulting in a refusal or neglect of organizations of men, in our church, to affiliate with the Brotherhood of the United Lutheran Church. This attitude is difficult to understand, first, for the reason that the Brotherhood is the agency of the United Lutheran Church, and as such, is an integral part of its work. Loyalty to the church would, therefore, mean that we will co-operate with the whole work of the church. The United Lutheran Church was either right or wrong in establishing the Brotherhood; if it was right, then loyalty to the church will lead us to organize the men and to enroll them in the Brotherhood of the Church; if it was wrong, then it must be shown that it is wrong to organize men for Christian service. Secondly, many of the men belong to clubs and social organizations. In not a single instance do these non-church organizations stand out separately and apart. Every one of them is affiliated with the state and national organization, and the dues are paid by every member for the local, state and national organization, nor do we hear any objection raised on the part of the men to this order. Why not treat the church equally as well? The spirit of separatism is nothing but evil. It has always hindered the growth of our church and brought disaster to our possibilities. We can never win with this spirit. Our progress, the fulfillment of the mission Christ has given us, the achievement of that of which we are capable, the assuming and discharge of our responsibilities before God, lies along the line of co-operation, united action, acceptance of the whole plan of our United Lutheran Church. Separatism in the men's work, spells hinderance, halting, defeat and disaster.

A New Day

Without question, we are facing a new day in the attitude of men toward the church. Men are wanting a definite task. A growing number are no longer willing to sit in the pew and listen and let it go at that, or of "just belonging to the church." They want work, they are eager to render service. This spirit has found expression, both in our correspondence and in many personal interviews, and in active participation in the work, in many churches. The Brotherhood has now developed many outstanding leaders in many parts of the country. These men are showing many others the way, and by their enthusiasm and devotion, are rapidly adding to the list of those definitely committed to whole hearted Christian service.

The Brotherhood now stands in the most favorable position in its history. More and more men are seeing that the Brotherhood offers the greatest possibilities in the church. That the men, organized and combined, are the guarantee of our progress, and of the mightiest Christian, forward movement yet seen in America.

Rev. Jacob W. Kapp, D.D., *Executive Secretary.*
Approved by Mr. Charles J. Driever, *President.*

It especially is noteworthy that the Executive Committee of the Brotherhood now has arranged with the executive secretary, the Rev. Jacob W. Kapp, D.D., to devote his entire time to brotherhood promotion. Having accomplished so much, in conjunction with pastoral responsibility, large advances confidently may be expected, as Dr. Kapp consecrates his full energy and splendid abilities to the Brotherhood work.

In many localities, as indicated in the above report, there are unmistakable evidences of increasing Brotherhood interest and progress. From some districts, reports would indicate that "Brotherhood reconstruction" is in order. "It is tragic," as a member of your committee puts it, referring to the man power of the church, "that the strongest power, humanly speaking, in our Church, is so largely unharnassed." In the material realm we have the hydro-electric super power development; and the "rocket power" engine. In the realm of the spiritual does not God expect us to co-ordinate and most efficiently utilize the man power of the church, for the advancement of His cause and Kingdom?

At the very least, through subscription to and the reading of *Lutheran Men,* supplemental to *The Lutheran,* every man of our United Lutheran Church might and should come into vital relation with our United Lutheran Brotherhood. Is not the Brotherhood the God-appointed agency of the Church, for the effective concentration and potential release of the vital energy of United Lutheran men, empowered of the Holy Spirit?

Accordingly will not every pastor, every church council, every corps of conference and synodical officers, every leader of United Lutheran men co-operate for the strategic organization and inspiration of United Lutheran men within the Church; that Christ, in all things may have the pre-eminence and be glorified.

Respectfully submitted,

JOHN L. ZIMMERMAN,
W. C. SCHAEFFER,
J. E. HEINDEL,
H. A. KINGSBURY,
G. DALTON MYERS
RODNEY T. MARTINSEN,
G. M. JONES,
WILLIAM J. BAUERLE,
H. E. ISENHOUR,
A. E. ALBRIGHT,
W. A. HILTABIDLE,
WILLIAM B. AHLGREN,
C. OBENHACK,
H. G. WALTER,
DAVID A. DAVY, *Chairman.*

Besides Dr. Davy, Chairman of the Committee, Mr. C. W. Howe, Treasurer of the Brotherhood, addressed the Convention. The report of the Committee on Women's Work was next taken up.

REPORT OF THE COMMITTEE ON WOMEN'S WORK

The report of the Committee on Women's Work will be necessarily brief, so far as its own activities are concerned. A meeting of the committee was held at the time of the U. L. C. A. Convention in Richmond, and functions and possible spheres of usefulness of the committee were thoroughly discussed. It had been proposed that a general survey of all kinds of women's work in our Church should be made, but it has been discovered that this is a far larger task than at first imagined, and consequently, we could not carry it through as desired.

However, the original purpose and chief function of this committee are to keep in touch with the work and problems of the Women's Missionary Societies, to render such assistance as might be needed and to represent the United Lutheran Church in case of special problems or difficulties requiring adjustment. However, the Women's Missionary Society is functioning so smoothly and effectively and its relationships have been so clearly determined and settled by this time, that there have not arisen recently, any serious problems of policy or questions of relationships, which might have required our attention. We have reason to rejoice that all the major problems incident to the merger have been quickly and satisfactorily settled.

The biennium just closing has been marked by successful planning and continued achievement in the broad field of women's work for missions. The women have had such an unwavering faith, they have prayed so earnestly and they have toiled and given with such wise diligence and self-sacrifice, that the blessing of God upon their work is evident. The outstanding achievements of the biennium are presented in the interesting and valuable report of Miss Amelia D. Kemp, Executive Secretary of the W. M. S., a digest of which report is appended.

The financial reports of the society are not yet available at this writing, July 26, 1928, but it is expected that after the Johnstown Convention, a supplementary report may be prepared embodying the salient features of such reports. We bespeak the continued interest and support of the entire Church for the deeply spiritual work which these faithful women are doing in the field of Christian missions.

Respectfully submitted,

The Committee on Women's Work,

A. H. SMITH, *Chairman.*

WOMEN'S MISSIONARY SOCIETY

REPORT OF THE EXECUTIVE BOARD

A compelling urge drives us so irresistibly forward that we can have but a single glance backward as we review ten years of accomplishments and failures. In 1918 the combination of the Women's Missionary Society of the United Synod South, the Women's Missionary Society of the General Council, and the Women's Home and Foreign Missionary Society of the General Synod brought into being the Women's Missionary Society of the United Lutheran Church in America. These two years ending June 30, 1928, then, complete the first decade of our united society.

SYNODICAL SOCIETIES

We are thoroughly united as evidenced in our co-operation from ocean to ocean and from Canada to the Gulf in the thirty-two Synodical societies: Alleghany, California, Canada, East Pennsylvania, Georgia and Adjacent States, Illinois, Indiana, Iowa, Kansas, Maryland, Michigan, Ministerium of Pennsylvania, Mississippi, Nebraska (English), Nebraska (German), New York Ministerium, New York and New England, New York, Nova Scotia, North Carolina, Northwest, Ohio, Pacific, Pittsburgh, Rocky Mountain, South Carolina, Susquehanna of Central Pennsylvania, Texas, Virginia, Wartburg, West Pennsylvania and West Virginia.

EXECUTIVE BOARD AND OFFICERS

The officers and Executive Board as constituted are:

President, Mrs. Wythe F. Morehead, elected 1926; Vice-President, Miss Flora Prince, elected 1926; Recording Secretary, Mrs. Philip M. Rossman, elected 1926. Statistical Secretary, Mrs. Frank E. Jensen, elected 1918; re-elected 1920, 1922, 1924, 1926; Treasurer, Mrs. Walter C. Weier, elected 1918; re-elected 1920, 1922, 1924, 1926.

The Executive Board members are:

Mrs. William E. Black, Mrs. G. W. McClanahan, Mrs. Frank W. Seegers, Mrs. John G. Traver, Mrs. N. Willison (terms expire 1928).

Mrs. W. S. Dysinger, Mrs. James P. Reese, Miss Eleanora E. Demmler, Mrs. Milton J. Bieber, Mrs. Thomas W. Kretschmann (terms expire 1930).

Mrs. Oliver D. Baltzly, Mrs. Sidney R. Kepner, Mrs. A. B. Leamer, Mrs. Albert O. Mullen, Mrs. August V. Pohlman (terms expire 1932).

The Executive Board held six meetings in the biennium; four of these were held in the Executive Office, 1228 Fulton Building, Pittsburgh, Pa., one in Trinity Church, Rockford, Illinois, following the biennial convention; one in the Muhlenberg Building, Philadelphia, at the time of the Secretaries for the Departments came for special conference in May, 1927.

BOARD OF TRUSTEES

Members of the Board of Trustees are the same as for the Executive Board. Officers are: President, Vice-President, Recording Secretary the same as for the Executive Board. Treasurer, Miss Flora Prince. The meetings of the Board of Trustees are simultaneous with the Executive Board.

ADMINISTRATIVE COMMITTEE

The Administrative Committee consists of the five officers of the Executive Board. The committee met eight times in the biennium; six meetings were held at the Executive Office, 1228 Fulton Building, Pittsburgh, Penna.; one in the Muhlenberg Building, Philadelphia, May, 1927; one in New York, in July, 1927, at the time of the meeting of the Board of American Missions.

STAFF

Staff secretaries appointed for the biennium were: Secretary of Literature, Mrs. Charles L. Fry; Field Secretary, Mrs. Herbert C. Bell; Secretary for Women Students, Doctor Mary E. Markley and Miss Mathilde Peper; Light Brigade Superintendent, Mrs. E. Calvin Cronk; Executive Secretary, Amelia D. Kemp.

On March 12, 1927, after three months' illness in the Lankenau Hospital, in Philadelphia, Mrs. Cronk was called from earth to heaven. The children of the Church, all our missionary interests, and the missionaries personally, together with hosts in other churches, have lost a thoughtful friend. Tribute was paid to Mrs. Cronk from every quarter of the globe and our hearts were touched as we read these tributes which appeared in *The Lutheran,* in *Lutheran Women's Work,* in the *Missionary Review of the World,* and as we learned of the many memorial meetings in her honor. We record here the words of our president, Mrs. Wythe F. Morehead:

"How hard to think of her as forever still; she who was so alive! How hard to realize that between her winged words and our dull ears has fallen the curtain of eternal silence!

"We have been asked to speak of Mrs. Cronk in the relationships in which we knew her best. To me she was first of all my friends and fellow-workers. It was in 1906 at the organization of the Women's Missionary Conference of the United Synod of the South in Dallas, N. C., that our friendship began, and through twenty-one years it has continued with never the shadow of a misunderstanding to cloud it.

"At the same time our relationship to each other as workers in the missionary society began, and it is pleasant to recall that it was during our association in the work of the Women's Missionary Conference that she began to develop the talents which later made her an outstanding figure in the religious world; her ability to present vividly the missionary message through tongue and pen; her genius for organization; her delight in training the children of the Church; her success in achieving the wholly impossible. In those early days when we were always handicapped by a plentiful lack of funds, I was often tempted to curb her adventurous spirit, but I soon learned that when I gave her free rein she would succeed where a more timorous soul would have failed. Her spirits rose joyously to meet the wider opportunities which came to her with the merger and with her interdenominational contacts.

"Her loyalty to organization was unfailing and her interest in and knowledge of every detail not only of the Light Brigade and the Literature Committee, but in that of every department of the Women's Missionary Society, was amazing. She was quick to recognize talent in others and the development of younger workers was her special delight. Many a Joshua has she called to follow in her footsteps.

"Dear, brave, Adventurer, and truest of comrades, may flights of angels sing thee to thy rest!"

CRONK MEMORIALS

Two memorials are planned, honoring Mrs. Cronk's memory: A kindergarten to be known as the Katharine Scherer Cronk Kindergarten at the Colony of Mercy, Kumamoto, Japan, and a fund sufficiently large to endow the Chair of Religious Education in the proposed Woman's Colony.

In March, 1928, Miss Peper resigned to accept a position on the Faculty of Carthage College, Carthage, Illinois. Miss Peper has been most helpful in the work with students since 1921. "Her greatest service lay in her personal work. At least three students, one now in Japan, one under appointment to India, and another finishing preparation for foreign service, were wholly or largely helped in their decisions by Miss Peper."

In June, 1928, the Board of Education appointed Miss Mildred E. Winston as one of its staff secretaries. Miss Winston is a graduate of Susquehanna University in the Class of 1921 and holds the degrees of Bachelor of Oratory and Bachelor of Science from that institution. Following her Susquehanna graduation she taught in the English department of her home high school, Sunbury, Pennsylvania. For the past three years she has been a student at the Biblical Seminary in New York and in June, 1928, received their degree of Bachelor of Religious Education and from New York University the degree of Master of Arts. Miss Winston's record of accomplishments leads us to have great confidence for her work as a student secretary. At the Biblical Seminary she was president of the Student Government Association and for two summers she has held administrative positions at the Biblical Seminary. Miss Winston was one of the organizers of the first Federation of Young Women's Missionary Societies in what is now Susquehanna Central Young Women's Missionary Institute. She has been active in student work, not only in the metropolitan district but in the North Atlantic Region of the Lutheran Student Association. Her professors recommend Miss Winston most highly both at Susquehanna University and at Biblical Seminary. Miss Winston is a member of Zion Church, Sunbury, Pennsylvania.

In July, 1927, Mrs. C. K. Lippard, missionary from Japan, who has been in this country for nearly three years, accepted the appointment as superintendent of Light Brigades. Mrs. Lippard comes fresh from the mission field with a view of the work from both sides of the world.

In September, 1927, Miss Nona M. Diehl, of York, Pennsylvania, accepted the appointment as Secretary for Young Women, filling a vacancy which we had carried since May, 1926, when Miss Tilda E. Nelson resigned. Miss Diehl brings resources as a graduate of Goucher College (1917) and a fund of valuable experiences gained through ten years of high school teaching, Young Women's Christian Association contacts, Sunday school, Missionary Society and Church activities. Miss Diehl is president of the West Pennsylvania Synodical Young Women's Conference.

We cordially welcome these three new members to our staff and pledge unfailing support. Their reports speak well for the promise they give of fulfilling our high hopes for what each has undertaken.

DEPARTMENTS

Department secretaries for the biennium were appointed: Annuity, Mrs. David A. Davy; Box Work (Home), Mrs. Frances C. Reeves; Box Work (Foreign), Mrs. F. B. Clausen; Deaconess, Mrs. W. P. M. Braun; Extension, Mrs. D. Burt Smith; German, Mrs. Anna R. Fogel; Immigrant

Student, Miss Laura R. Swope; India Lace, Mrs. A. S. Woll; Life Membership and In Memoriam, Mrs. L. K. Sandford; Magazine, Mrs. L. K. Krechting; Patron and Protege, Miss Eleanor M. Robinson; Thank-Offering, Mrs. C. E. Gardner; West Indies, Mrs. F. F. Fry.

Mrs. F. B. Clausen was not able to accept appointment and Miss Anna R. Bunke was appointed and served one year in her stead. Mrs. D. Burt Smith could not serve and Mrs. A. C. Schenck has served in her place throughout the biennium.

LITERATURE COMMITTEE

According to constitutional provision seven members of the Literature Committee were appointed by the Executive Board as follows: Mrs. B. S. Copenhaver, Mrs. D. Burt Smith, Mrs. C. E. Hay, Mrs. Virgil B. Sease, Mrs. M. R. Gilbert, Mrs. E. S. Lewars, Miss Ruth Arnold Nickel. The other members of the Literature Committee by virtue of their department offices are: Mrs. L. K. Krechting, Mrs. J. F. Seebach, Mrs. C. P. Wiles, Miss Mary E. Markley, Mrs. W. P. M. Braun, Mrs. A. C. Schenck, Miss Nona M. Diehl, Mrs. C. K. Lippard.

CANDIDATE COMMITTEE

The president appointed the Candidate Committee: Mary E. Markley, Litt.D., chairman; Miss Flora Prince, Amelia D. Kemp.

INTERDENOMINATIONAL COMMITTEE

Instead of one representative on Interdenominational relationships, a committee was appointed as follows: Mrs. Phillip M. Rossman, chairman; Mrs. F. F. Fry, Mrs. A. V. Pohlman, Amelia D. Kemp.

ADVISORS TO CHURCH BOARDS

Board of Foreign Missions: Mrs. W. F. Morehead, Mrs. S. Y. Kepner.

Board of Home Missions and Church Extension: Mrs. Frank E. Jensen and Mrs. William E. Black to serve until January, 1927, when the Board of American Missions was established. At that date the following appointments were made: To the Board of American Missions, at large: Mrs. William E. Black, Mrs. Virgil B. Sease; Linguistic Division, Mrs. Frank E. Jensen; Latin America, Miss Flora Prince; English Missions, Mrs. T. W. Kretschmann; Church Extension, Amelia D. Kemp.

Board of Inner Missions: Mrs. P. M. Rossman, Mrs. E. L. Snyder.

Board of Education: Mrs. A. V. Pohlman, Miss Dorothea Hess.

Deaconess Board: Mrs. J. P. Reese, Mrs. W. P. M. Braun.

Ministerial Pensions and Relief: Mrs. J. G. Traver, Mrs. Oscar C. Schmidt.

West Indies Board: Mrs. F. F. Fry, and Immigrants' Board: Miss Laura R. Swope, and Mrs. T. W. Kretschmann were appointed to serve until the Board of American Missions was established in January, 1927.

INTERDENOMINATIONAL MEETINGS

We were represented in 1927 and in 1928 with our full quota of representatives at the Federation of Women's Boards of Foreign Missions and at the Council of Women for Home Missions.

At the Foreign Missions' Conference we had five representatives.

On the Central Committee for United Study of Missions our appointee is the Mission Study Secretary.

We have two members on the American Board of Governors of Madras Christian College in India: Doctor Mary E. Markley and Mrs. P. M. Rossman.

Within the past year the Executive Secretary has been made a member of the American Advisory Board for the Kodaikanal School in India for missionaries' children.

The Secretary of Literature is the official representative in the Missionary Education Movement.

SUMMER SCHOOLS

We have a lively participation in summer schools from coast to coast in membership in their committees and places on their faculties, as well as attendance on their sessions. This is an increasingly valuable factor in the training and maintaining of workers.

MISSIONARIES

Under the *Board of American Missions* we have the following missions in the United States and Canada:

California
  Alhambra, Grace
  Redlands, First
  Sanger, St. Paul's
  San Bernardino, First
  Santa Barbara, Grace
Colorado
  Boulder, Trinity
  Denver, Trinity-Barnitz Memorial
  Pueblo, St. Mark's
Connecticut
  New Haven, First
Illinois
  Chicago, Belmont Park
  Chicago, St. Paul's
Indiana
  Evansville, Christ
  Gary, Grace
Michigan
  Kalamazoo, Trinity
Missouri
  St. Louis, Advent
Montana
  Great Falls, St. John's
New Jersey
  Vineland, Redeemer

New York
  Endicott, Holy Nativity
North Carolina
  Watauga Parish
Ohio
  East Cleveland, St. James'
Pennsylvania
  Butler, Trinity
  Pittsburgh, Messiah
  Sewickley, St. Paul's
South Carolina
  Rock Hill, Grace
Virginia
  Lynchburg, Holy Trinity
Washington
  Bellingham, St. Mark's
  Longview, Trinity
  Seattle, University
Wisconsin
  Waukesha, St. Luke's
Wyoming
  Casper, Grace
  Laramie, Trinity
Quebec
  Montreal, Redeemer
British Columbia
  Victoria, Grace

In the Watauga Parish in North Carolina in addition to the pastor, we have Missionary Cora Pearl Jeffcoat. In New York City we have Sister Mary Junas at the Slav Lutheran Mission. Miss Alta Samelson is our missionary at the Jewish Mission, Toledo, Ohio, and Mrs. Agnes Herter at the Jewish Mission, Philadelphia, Pa. Sister Clara Smyre, Sister Maren Knudsen, Sister Emma Frances, Sister Edith Prince, and Miss Ethel Mosteller in the Virgin Islands, and Miss Frieda Hoh, R. N., in Porto Rico, comprise our West Indies staff. Sister Nanca Schoen, who had been in Porto Rico with Miss Hoh, returned to the United States in February, 1928, in ill-health and will remain here for an indefinite time.

SUPPORT OF MISSIONS

Synodical Societies are supporting wholly or in part these missions as follows:

Alleghany: St. John's, Great Falls, Montana.
California: Grace, Alhambra, California.
Illinois: Advent, St. Louis, Mo.
Indiana: Christ, Evansville, Indiana.
Michigan: Trinity, Kalamazoo, Michigan.
Ministerium of Pennsylvania: Redeemer, Vineland, New Jersey.
Ohio: St. James, Cleveland, and Miss Alta Samelson, Jewish Mission, Toledo, Ohio.
Pittsburgh: Trinity, Butler, Pa.
South Carolina: Grace, Rock Hill, S. C.
Under the *Inner Missions Board* at the Konnarock Training School, Konnarock, Virginia, their faculty is composed of our missionaries: Mrs. Catherine Cox Umbarger, A.B., Principal; Miss Marion Waldron, A.B., Miss Helen Wilkin, A.B., Miss Katherine Umbarger, Miss Elizabeth Umbarger, Miss Amy L. Fisher, R.N.
Under the *Board of Foreign Missions* we have missionaries in India, China, Japan, Africa, and South America. The roster is:

AFRICA

Mrs. Gertrude R. Buschmann
Miss Mabel Dysinger
Sister Laura Gilliland
Miss Elsie R. Otto

Miss Bertha Koenig
Miss Irene B. Bloch, A.B.
Miss K. Marie Jensen, R.N.

CHINA

Miss Erva Moody, A.B., A.M.
Miss Lydia F. Reich, R.N.

Miss Frieda Strecker
Miss Elvira May Strunk, A.B., A.M.
Miss Kathe Voget

INDIA

Miss Selma S. Anderson, A.B.
Miss Emma K. Baer, A. B.
Doctor Arline M. Beal
Doctor Mary Baer
Miss Mette K. Blair, R.N.
Miss Mary S. Borthwick
Miss Helen Brenneman, A.B.
Miss Rose Brummer, R.N.
Miss Agnes Christensen, A.B.
Miss M. Edna Engle, A.M.
Miss Christine Ericksson, R.N.
Miss Edith Eykamp, A.B.
Miss Charlotte Hollerbach
Miss Emma Johnson, A.B.
Doctor Anna S. Kugler
Miss Clara V. Leaman, A.B.
Miss Hilma Levine, R.N.

Miss Verna Lofgren, R.N.
Miss Maida Meissner, R. N.
Miss Louisa A. Miller, A.M.
Miss Lottie Martin, R.N.
Miss Alice J. Nickel
Doctor Betty A. Nilsson
Miss Annie E. Sanford, A.B., D. of Ped.
Miss Ellen Schuff, A.B.
Miss Lilith Schwab
Miss Frances Segner, A.B.
Miss Hildegarde R. Swanson
Miss Agatha Tatge, R.N.
Miss Jessie S. Thomas, A.B.
Miss Emilie Weiskotten
Miss Florence M. Welty, A.M.
Miss E. Pauline Whiteker, R.N.

Retired: Miss Agnes I. Schade, Miss Katherine Fahs, R.N.

JAPAN

Miss Martha B. Akard, A.M.
Miss Grace M. Beers, R.N.
Miss Helene H. Harder, A.B.
Miss Martha M. Harder, B.F.A.
Miss Mary E. Heltibridle, B.S.
Miss Faith G. Lippard, A.B.

Miss Marion Potts, A.B.
Miss Manie Powlas, A.B., B.S.
Miss Maude Powlas, A.B.
Miss Helen Shirk
Miss Amy J. Thoren, A. B.

SOUTH AMERICA

Miss Corinne Menges, A.B.   Miss Myrtle S. Wilke, A.B.

STATISTICS AND OTHER DATA ON MISSIONARIES

The following tabulations will be of interest:

Missionaries sent out by years:

Year	
1918	2
1919	1
1920	11
1921	9
1922	3
1923	5
1924	7
1925	6
1926	4
1927	6
1928	6*
Total	60

In ten years, 1918 to and including to sail October, 1928:

	Sent out	Resigned	Now in Service
To India	30	9	21
Africa	14	11	3
Japan	11	1	10
China	3	....	3
South America	2	....	2
Totals	60	21	39

* Including those to sail to India, October 3, 1928.

Year	Name	Field	Congregation and City	Synodical Connection
1918	Sister Jennie Larmouth	Africa	Carey, Ohio	Ohio
1919	Maude Powlas	Japan	St. Paul's, Hickory, N. C.	North Carolina
	Annie Powlas	Japan	St. Paul's, Hickory, N. C.	North Carolina
1920	Selma S. Anderson	India	St. Mark's, Omaha, Neb.	Nebraska (English)
	Emma K. Baer	India	Dover, Ohio	Ohio
	Barbara E. DeRemer	India	St. John's, Williamsport, Pa.	Susquehanna Central
	Eleanor E. Lange	India	Cedarburg, Wisconsin	Lutheran Synod of Buffalo
	Marie Martens	Africa	St. James', Concord, N. C.	North Carolina
	Alice J. Nickel	India	Second, Baltimore, Md.	Maryland
	Elsie R. Otto	Africa	Trinity, Wheeling, W. Va.	West Virginia
	Elizabeth Reese-Wiliens	India	Episcopal, Reisterstown, Md.	Diocese of Maryland
	Sister Ruth Robeson	Africa	Camden, Indiana	Michigan
	Lilith M. Schwab	India	First, St. Joseph, Mo.	Kansas
*1921	Elizabeth Szember	India	Wellesley, Ontario, Can.	Canada
	Mette K. Blair	India	Kountze Memorial, Omaha, Neb.	Nebraska (English)
	M. Edna Engle	India	India Mission	United Brethren Church
	Mary R. Fleming	India	Hillsdale, Baltimore, Md.	Presbyterian Church
	Reba McC. Hendrickson	Japan	St. Peter's, Middletown, Pa.	East Pennsylvania
	Maida M. Meissner	India	Advent, New York City	New York and New England
	Marian Eyster	India	First, Chambersburg, Pa.	West Pennsylvania
	Marion Potts	Japan	St. Luke's, Philadelphia, Pa.	Ministerium of Pennsylvania
	Viola Steigerwalt	India	Ben Salem, Philadelphia, Pa.	Ministerium of Pennsylvania
	E. Pauline Whitteker	India	Trinity, Lancaster, Pa.	Ministerium of Pennsylvania
1922	Mary Bauer	Africa	Chicora, Pa.	Pittsburgh
	Helen M. Shirk	Japan	St. James', Lebanon, Pa.	Ministerium of Pennsylvania
	Isie Weygandt	India	Marchsllville, Ohio	Ohio
1923	Bertha Dierolf	Africa	St. Paul's, Wilkes-Barre, Pa.	Ministerium of Pennsylvania
	Bertha Klein	Africa	Messiah, Philadelphia, Pa.	East Pennsylvania
	Clara V. Leaman	India	Fairmount, West Va.	West Virginia
	Verna Lofgren	India	Galesburg, Illinois	Illinois
	Lottie Martin	India	Messiah, Philadelphia, Pa.	East Pennsylvania
1924	Rose E. Brummer	India	Amsterdam, New York	New York
	Edith Eykamp	India	Polo, Illinois	Illinois
	Dorothea Hahn	Africa	Gossner Mission, India	New York Ministerium
	Emma Johnson	India	Trinity, Rockford, Ill.	Illinois
	Hildegarde R. Swanson	India	St. Paul, Minnesota	Augustana
	Miriam Treon	Africa	Zion, Sunbury, Pa.	Susquehanna Central
	Ethel Viele	India	Amsterdam, New York	New York

* In December, 1921, Doctor Irene Smedley, of Des Moines, Iowa, was appointed but not commissioned and went as Medical Assistant to India. Doctor Smedley remained in the mission less than half a year.

Year	Name	Field	Congregation and City	Synodical Connection
1925	Arline M. Beal	India	St. Paul's, Davenport, Iowa	Iowa
	Faith G. Lippard	Japan	Salem, Minneapolis, Minn.	Northwest
	Corinne Menges	South America	Menges Mills, Pa.	West Pennsylvania
	Erva Moody	China	Fillmore, Illinois	Illinois
	Elvira M. Strunk	China	St. Paul's, Allentown, Pa.	East Pennsylvania
	Amy J. Thoren	Japan	St. John's, Minneapolis, Minn.	Northwest
1926	Grace M. Beers	Japan	Zion, Indiana, Pa.	Pittsburgh
	Ruth F. Gilliland	Africa	First, Colorado Springs, Colo.	Rocky Mountain
	Martha M. Harder	Japan	St. Matthew's, Johnson City, Neb.	Nebraska (German)
	Amelia M. Wiebking	Africa	St. Stephen's, Baltimore, Md.	Maryland
1927	Helene H. Harder	Japan	St. Matthew's, Johnson City, Neb.	Nebraska (German)
	Dorothy R. Heuter	Africa	Christ, York, Pa.	West Pennsylvania
	Mary E. Heltibridle	Japan	St. Mary's, Silver Run, Md.	Maryland
	Lydia F. Reich	China	Epiphany, Milwaukee, Wis.	Northwest
	Frances Segner	India	Shippensburg, Pa.	West Pennsylvania
	Myrtle S. Wilke	South America	St. John's, Bendena, Kansas	Kansas
1928	Irene B. Bloch	Africa	Salem, Fremont, Neb.	Nebraska (English)
	Nellie S. Cassel	India	Virginia Heights, Roanoke, Va.	Virginia
	K. Marie Jensen	Africa	Ames, Iowa	Norwegian Lutheran
	Hilda M. Kaercher	India	Transfiguration, Philadelphia, Pa.	Ministerium of Pennsylvania
	Mabel H. Meyer	India	Gilead, Centre Brunswick, N. Y.	New York
	Grace L. Moyer	India	St. Paul's, Palmerton, Pa.	Ministerium of Pennsylvania

SUMMARY

Total sent out from 1918 to and including sailing October, 1928, 60.
Of this number there are now in service, 39.
Of this number resigned to marry within our missions, 8.
Marian Eyster became Mrs. August Schmotthenner in India.
Isie Weygandt became Mrs. Clarence Swavely in India.
Viola Steigerwalt became Mrs. Leon Irshick in India.
Bertha Dieroff became Mrs. Paul M. Counts in Africa.
Miriam Treon became Mrs. James Miller in Africa.
Sister Jennie Larmouth became Mrs. Robert Oberly in Africa.
Ruth Gilliland became Mrs. Ira Haltiwanger in Africa.
Dorothy Heuter became Mrs. O. E. Bluehdorn in Africa.

Of this number resigned to marry outside the missions, 2.
Elizabeth Szember from India.
Ethel Ville from India.

Of this number resigned for other reasons, 11.
Mary Bauer from Africa.
Barbara DeRemer from India.
Mary Fleming from India.
Dorothea Hahn from Africa.
Reba Hendrickson from Japan.
Bertha Klein from Africa.
Eleanor Lange from India.
Marie Martens from Africa.
Elizabeth Reese-Wilkens from India.
Sister Ruth Robeson from Africa.
Amelia Wiebking from Africa.

From and including sailing October, 1928:
From Synods of the United Lutheran Church, 53.

Canada (1) .... Elizabeth Szember
East Pennsylvania (4)....Reba Hendrickson, Bertha Klein, Lottie Martin, Elvira Strunk
English Nebraska (3)...Sela Anderson, Mette Blair, Irene Bloch
German Nebraska (2) ....Helene Harder, Martha Harder
Illinois (3)...Edith Eykamp, Emma Johnson, Erva Moody
Iowa (1) .... Arline Beal
Kansas (2) .... Lilith Schwab, Myrtle Wilke
Maryland (3) .... Mary Heltioridle, Alice Nickel, Amelia Wiebking
Michigan (1) ....Sister Ruth Robeson
Ministerium of New York (1) .... Dorothea Hahn
Ministerium of Pennsylvania (6)...........Bertha Dierolf, Hilda Kaercher, Grace Moyer,
                                Marian Potts, Helen Shirk, Pauline Whitteker
New York (3)...Rose Brummer, Mabel Meyer, Ethel Viele
N. Y. and N. E. (1)..Maida Meissner
North Carolina (3)..................................Marie Martens Annie Powlas, Maude Powlas
Northwest (3)................................. Faith Lippard, Lydia Reich, Amy Thoren
Ohio (3)...Emma Baer, Sister Jennie Larmouth, Isie Weygandt
Pittsburgh (2)..Mary Bauer, Grace Beers
Rocky Mountain (1)..Ruth Gilliland
Susquehanna Central (2).....................................Barbara DeRemer, Miriam Treon
Virginia (1)...Nellie Cassel
West Penna. (4) .....Marian Eyster, Dorothy Heuter, Corinne Menges, Frances Segner
West Virginia (2)...Clara Leaman, Elsie Otto

From other Lutheran bodies, 4.
Augustana Lutheran Church (2)............................Hildegard Swanson, Verna Lofgren
Buffalo Synod Lutheran Church (1)...Eleanor Lange
Norwegian Lutheran Church (1)........ ....K. Marie Jensen

From other churches, 4.

Presbyterian Church (1)..Mary Fleming
Protestant Episcopal (1)...Elizabeth Reese-Wilkens
United Brethren (1)..Edna Engle
Ben Salem (1)..Viola Steigerwalt

OUR PIONEER DOCTOR

It is with especial gratitude that we tell of the remarkable recuperation of Doctor Anna S. Kugler, senior missionary at the Guntur Hospital, who first went to India in 1883 and has given distinguished service through these years. She was ill in America from 1925 to 1927, but as vigor gradually returned, and before she set sail again in December, 1927, for her beloved India, she gave us the history of the Guntur hospital. This little book of 135 pages and attractive pictures, although an accurate account, does not include all the beautiful record of deeds of devotion which have characterized Doctor Kugler's skill as a physician and loyalty as a missionary.

OUR PIONEER NURSE

Miss Katherine Fahs, R.N., for thirty-one years the nurse in the Guntur Hospital on whom Doctor Kugler depended, and who gave untiring and unfailing service, retires October 1, 1928, and will live in this country. Eighty nurses are working throughout South India, having had no other training than that given by Miss Fahs. In so small a compass we cannot measure what Miss Fahs has done, nor what the influence of her life means to our Guntur Hospital.

OUR PIONEER TEACHER

Miss Agnes I. Schade went to India in 1890 and for thirty-five years was in Rajahmundry. From small beginnings the Central Girls' School grew to a place of commanding respect, due largely to Miss Schade's wise guidance as a gifted teacher and as an educational administrator. The India government recognized her normal school diploma, so that for twenty years her position as chief executive of the school was unchallenged. Hundreds of girls who attended the school have gone into the elementary schools to teach, and scores have gone into higher training from the Central Girls' School gratefully remembering Miss Schade, their honored Principal.

SUPPORT OF MISSIONARIES

At this writing Synodical Societies wholly or in part are supporting missionaries in the fields as follows:

East Pennsylvania: Doctor Anna S. Kugler in India and Miss Martha M. Harder in Japan.

German Nebraska: Miss Helene H. Harder in Japan.

Illinois: Miss Erva Moody in China.

Indiana: Miss Florence M. Welty in India.

Kansas: Miss Lilith Schwab in India.

Maryland: Doctor Mary Baer in India, Miss Mary Heltibridle in Japan, Mrs. Catherine Cox Umbarger, Principal, Konnarock Training School, Konnarock, Va.

Ministerium of Pennsylvania: Miss Emelie Weiskotten in India.

New York: Miss Rose Brummer in India.

Northwest: Miss Faith G. Lippard and Miss Amy J. Thoren in Japan.

Ohio: Miss Jessie S. Thomas in India; Miss Alta Samelson, Jewish Mission, Toledo, Ohio.

Pittsburgh: Sister Laura E. Gilliland in Africa; Doctor Arline Beal in India, and the Spring Garden Settlement in the city of Pittsburgh.

West Pennsylvania: Miss Annie E. Sanford in India.

West Virginia: Miss Elsie R. Otto in Africa.

Congregations wholly or in part are supporting missionaries as follows:

Baltimore, Md., Christ, has pledged salary of Doctor Nellie S. Cassel in India.

Brooklyn, N. Y., Good Shepherd, Miss Alice J. Nickel, in India.

Carlisle, Pa., St. Paul's, Miss Clara Leaman, in India.

Chicago, Illinois, Unity, Miss Edith Eykamp, in India.

Indiana, Pennsylvania, Zion, Miss Grace Beers, in Japan.

Lancaster, Pennsylvania, Trinity, Miss E. Pauline Whitteker, in India.

Milwaukee, Wisconsin, Epiphany, Miss Lydie F. Reich, in China.

New York, New York, Advent, Miss Agatha Tatge, in India.

Omaha, Nebraska, Kountze Memorial, Miss Mette K. Blair, in India.

Philadelphia, Pa., Holy Communion, Miss Mary S. Borthwick, in India.

Philadelphia, Pa., Temple, Mrs. Gertrude R. Buschmann in Africa and Miss Lottie Martin, in India.

Rockford, Illinois, Trinity, Miss Emma Johnson, in India.

Souderton, Pa., Emmanuel, Miss Selma Anderson, in India.

South Williamsport, Pa., Messiah, Miss Amelia Wiebking, in Africa, and have pledged the salary of Miss Marie Jensen, in Africa.

Washington, D. C., Missionary Union, Miss Marion Waldron, in the Konnarock Training School, Va.

York, Pa., Christ, Miss Ethel Mosteller, in the Virgin Islands.

The Women's Missionary Society and Luther Leagues of the Augustana Synod support wholly or in part in India: Doctor Betty A. Nilsson, Miss Agnes Christensen, Miss Christine Ericksson and Miss Levine.

The Norristown Conference of the Ministerium of Pennsylvania and the New York Conference of the New York Ministerium support Sister Mary Junas at the Slav Mission in New York City.

BUILDING PROGRESS IN THIS BIENNIUM

We have not carried a building program quite as extensive as in other years. However, we have done some building of a substantial character both at home and in the foreign field.

At Home. In Kalamazoo, Michigan, where for twenty-five years there has been a small struggling mission, there was dedicated on June 17, 1928, the new Church which stands on a corner of promising location for that town in which there are students in attendance at the State Teachers' College. Pastor Alvah K. Jones deserves a word of confidence.

In Blowing Rock, North Carolina, in our Watauga Parish, on June 5, 1927, the chapel was dedicated which will long serve the mountain people who have worshiped for years without a building. Miss Cora Pearl Jeffcoat, Rev. J. A. Yount the pastor, together with summer pastor, Student J. A. Seeboch, are doing a very real bit of service.

In Denver, Colorado, the cornerstone has been laid for the new building of Trinity Mission, the Barnitz Memorial. Our hearts are sad over the death of the pastor, Rev. J. A. Sommer, whose untiring efforts are largely responsible for the new life of the mission.

At Seattle, Washington, the University Church was able to dedicate its new building during the biennium. This is the mission which warms our hearts in its work among students. All honor to Pastor and Mrs. Otta A. Bremer! Another service this church renders is its hospitality to outgoing missionaries. Most of our Japan and China missionaries go out from Seattle and Pastor Bremer places himself and all the Church at the disposal of the missionaries.

At Boone, North Carolina, ground has been broken for the new church. This is good news and we shall watch the progress of the building with prayer and interest.

Foreign: Our one notable enterprise in new building in the foreign field was the school in Bhimavaram, India. This has been a claim for which it has taken patience to endure the delay. But at last the necessary $8,000 was sent and the building completed. The entire plant, however, remains incomplete until the bungalow, girls' hostel and walls are built. At Chirala, India, a girls' school is in progress.

In China, at Tsimo, a European building was remodeled and is now a girls' school.

In Japan, at the Colony of Mercy (Ji-Ai-En) a special gift from donors in America made possible the building of a missionaries' residence. This was an example of the really greatheartedness of our women. In April, 1927, the Executive Board sent out the call for $6,800 for this residence. On August 1, 1927, there was in hand in cash and in pledges $8,075.36, and of this amount all but $200 has been received and has been sent to Japan, the house is built and the missionaries have been living in it since Christmas eve, 1927. We wish to record that every cent raised for the house has been devoted to its building bills. In addition to the house an adequate and sanitary and safe water system was installed, the grounds put in perfect condition and cyclone protection provided.

AMONG OURSELVES

Your Executive Board and Administrative Committee have given unusual service in bringing the best they have to the careful deliberations of the many difficult problems which have been presented. Each action taken has been the culmination of discussions into which have come all sides of the questions involved.

Your Staff has a thoroughly workable working basis on which the society has rested. Each of the six in her own report has given an accounting for the biennium.

Your Literature Committee has done better work than ever before. It has been able to serve more of the department secretaries, it has served the executive office, it has served the Board and missionaries, with marked efficiency and really helpful work for them all. The very recent development of translations into the Japanese of some of our leaflets and material is a fine bit of far-visioned co-operation which is being fostered between the home base and the Japanese literature committee.

Your Candidate Committee has made earnest effort to secure every available and possible candidate. We are especially fortunate in those young women who have received appointment for this year.

Your Department Secretaries have made their reports to which we ask careful attention. Their work is increasing steadily and they have given unstinted service.

In our societies we have worked toward the bringing in of the Tenth Anniversary Fund, our Love Gift for the gratitude in our hearts in response to the many blessings we have received in these ten years. The work has progressed beyond any expectations or hopes we ever had. Much good has been accomplished everywhere. We have not, however, kept pace in income, so that now we must face the next ten years in the critical situation of finding it necessary to curtail in some places. Some of this necessity has come about through the advance costs in every area of life—travel, building costs, clothing, office supplies, and so on. Some of it has come in our losses in not having had sufficient forces and overworking some of the already tired missionaries who have had to come home, thus necessitating extra travel. Some of it has come by way of circumstances over which no possible control could be exercised. But we hope for great things from the Love Offering.

EXECUTIVE SECRETARY'S WORK

Your Executive Secretary's work for the biennium has consisted in office routine in handling the regular correspondence; in issuing annuity bonds; in general supervision of the many details which come to the Executive headquarters; in preparing agendas for the Administration Committee and Executive Board meetings; in the regular contributions of notes from headquarters which appear in *Lutheran Women's Work*; in preparing the

Monthly Prayer Calendar; in candidate corespondence and interviews; in answering the calls for representation of the Board wherever possible and in the promotion of better correlation.

In the 104 weeks of the biennium 82 public addresses have been made as follows:

Synodical Conventions	11
Conference Conventions	6
Local Societies	6
Sunday Schools	3
Luther Leagues	2
Thank-Offering Meetings	18
Tenth Anniversary	5
Young Women's	17
Mothers and Daughters	5
Summer Schools (series)	3
Ministers' Meeting	1
Christian Workers' Conference	1
Interdenominational City Federation	1
World Day of Prayer (City wide)	1
Church Dedications (woman's night)'	2
	82

(Seventeen of these were in Pittsburgh.)

In addition it has been necessary to make the following trips:

To New York especially for Candidate Committee and interviews	7
To Philadelphia especially for interviews concerning young women's work, candidates, gifts, literature, missionaries	6
To Baltimore especially for interviews with Secretaries of Board of Foreign Missions, gifts, missionaries	3
To Philadelphia for Literature Committee	1
To Baltimore for meeting of Board of Foreign Missions	3
To New York for meeting of Board of American Missions	4
To Rochester, N. Y., for meeting of Board of American Missions	1
To Detroit, Mich., Quadrennial Student Volunteer Convention	1
To Atlantic City, Federation of Women's Boards Foreign Missions and Foreign Missions Conference	1
To Philadelphia, Council of Women for Home Missions	1
To Richmond, Va., for convention United Lutheran Church	1
To Chicago, Ministerial Pensions and Relief Campaign	1
	30

BUDGET

For the biennium beginning July 1, 1928, and ending June 30, 1930, the budget for our Home Field, Foreign Field, and General Appropriations, which is proposed for adoption at the biennial convention, is herewith respectfully submitted. It is with great earnestness of purpose that we have made this budget. Many of its items require its most careful investigation. We present it seeking guidance and support for all that is contained or implied in its limits. A careful survey of the income of the society was the basis for making the final draft.

Proposed budget for July 1, 1928, to June 30, 1930:

HOME FIELDS

Support of Home Missions—salaries, loans, new work...............$120,715.00
Linguistic interests—including salaries of women workers............ 14,400.00
Northwest Missions 1,500.00
Jewish work—three women workers.. 7,200.00
West Indies work—children's homes, missionaries and travel.... 21,860.00

Total for Board of American Missions...$165,675.00
Board of Education—women secretaries 6,000.00
Board of Ministerial Pensions and Relief 10,000.00
Inner Mission Board—Konnarock School... 20,000.00

Total for home fields $201,675.00

FOREIGN FIELDS

Africa:
Salaries ....$ 14,200.00
Maintenance 10,800.00
Medical Work 4,000.00
Travel 4,000.00

Total for Africa...$ 33,000.00

China:
Salaries ....$ 9,500.00
Maintenance 15,000.00
Travel 1,500.00
Purchase Price 7,000.00

Total for China..$ 33,000.00

India:
Salaries ....$ 60,300.00
Maintenance 137,048.00
Travel 20,000.00
Colleges 5,000.00

Total for India...$222,348.00

Japan:
Salaries ....$ 24,750.00
Maintenance 50,000.00
Travel 4,000.00
Endowment—Janice James School 5,000.00

Total for Japan ....$ 83,750.00

South America:
Salaries ....$ 6,600.00
Maintenance 18,000.00
Travel 500.00

Total for South America 25,100.00

Total for Foreign Field $397,198.00

GENERAL APPROPRIATIONS

Scholarships for Students ....$ 5,400.00
Interdenominational—Missionary Education Movement, Council
 of Women for Home Missions, Federation Women's Boards,
 Committee Reference and Counsel, Missionary Review of
 the World 2,304.00
Literature Committee, salary secretary, office force, free liter-
 ature for all departments, rent of offices, supplies, postage
 and express, filing, etc. 42,564.00
Biennial Convention 14,000.00
Annuity—Semi-annual interest installments..................................... 20,000.00
Administration—Salaries, Pittsburgh office appropriation, Board
 meetings, travel of officers, account of Konnarock School
 and other meetings, maintenance of departments and com-
 mittees 51,560.00
Expenses of Parish Worker, N. C. 1,000.00
Miscellaneous special appropriation 400.00
Repayment of loan (part payment).. 20,000.00
Interest for two years 6,000.00
New Work and Emergencies.. 19,000.00
  Beegle Memorial (Repalle)............................$ 6,000.00
  Dormitory, Janice James' School................... 13,000.00
Cronk Memorial Professorship—Woman's College........................ 50,000.00

                                                                                 $232,228.00

SUMMARY

  Total for Home Fields.. $201,675.00
  Total for Foreign Fields... 397,198.00
  General Appropriations 232,228.00
                                                                         _____
    Total Budget $831,101.00

ELECTIONS

By reference to the first of this report it will be seen that only three of
the general officers—the President, the Vice-President, the Recording
Secretary, are eligible for re-election and the terms expire of five members of the Executive Board. Therefore, this convention is charged with
the responsibility of making elections as provided for in the constitution.

RECOMMENDATIONS

1. In view of the fact that the work of our organization has grown
far beyond the anticipation of the members of the Women's Missionary
Society at the time of the merger, and that notwithstanding the liberality
of our women in the matter of special gifts, there still exists a wide difference between the estimated income and our obligations; we therefore
recommend that an increase in the regular dues of the society be considered.

2. We recommend that consideration be given to assuming more scholarships for the Janice James' School in Japan.

3. We recommend that societies contributing $400 for immigrant student
scholarships be commended and that these amounts hereafter be applied

to the item in the Board of American Missions' budget for linguistic interests.

4. We recommend that a committee be appointed for the observance in 1933 of Doctor Anna S. Kugler's fifty years in India and the medical work extending over that same period.

5. We recommend that the budget adopted become effective January first following the biennial convention.

6. We recommend a centralization of Board offices in Philadelphia, and in such headquarters there be located the Executive Office of the Board, the Field Secretary, the Young Women's Secretary, the Light Brigade Superintendent, the Treasurer, the Literature Committee, and the financial work of the following departments: Annuity, Life and In Memoriam, and Patron and **Protege.**

7. We recommend that the Christmas offering of 1929 be devoted to the completion of the Beegle Memorial at Repalli, India, and that the 1930 Christmas offering be for some home mission interest to be determined later.

DEDICATION

It is in humility that we close another biennium, knowing how far short we have come of fulfilling satisfactorily all the demands which have been made upon us. The load of responsibility has been heavy, but we have trusted that, even though we have gone falteringly through this first ten years, we will be permitted to go on and take the next step. This is our confidence and our prayer. Our pledge is to renew efforts and to strengthen weak spots. The renewed efforts will mean more force at the home base. The weak spots will be strengthened only in so far as we have more women of the Church catching the vision glorious—sending to the treasury of spiritual power a great outpouring; sending to the treasury of money more of a share in our abundance; sending to the treasury of precious workers, more of our daughters. This is our dedication for the second ten years of our united society. May we be able to do it all for the Master.

Respectfully submitted,
Executive Board of the Women's Missionary Society,
AMELIA D. KEMP,
By Amelia D. Kemp, *Executive Secretary.*

Pittsburgh, Penna., July, 1928.

In the absence of the Rev. A. H. Smith, Chairman of the Committee on Women's Work, the report was presented by the Rev. M. J. Bieber and in connection with it the report of the Women's Missionary Society, whose President, Mrs. Wythe F. Morehead, was introduced and addressed the Convention bearing the greetings of the Society and laying stress on the financial achievements of the Society. She then presented Miss Amelia D. Kemp, Executive Secretary, who spoke of the Society's work and workers.

By appointment of the President, the Rev. H. Brezing, President of the Ministerium of New York, responded to the greetings of the Women's Missionary Society.

The Convention adjourned with prayer by the Rev. W. E. Pugh.

Afternoon Session

Saturday, October 13, 2.00 o'clock.

Devotions were conducted by the Rev. Alvin E. Bell.

The President called the Convention to order.

By unanimous consent the report of the Committee on Associations of Young People and that of the Luther League were taken over from the morning program and considered at this point.

The Rev. H. C. Roehner presented the Report of the Committee on Associations of Young People.

REPORT OF THE COMMITTEE ON ASSOCIATIONS OF YOUNG PEOPLE

Your committee is glad to report that the work of the young people's organization of the United Lutheran Church, the Luther League of America has continued its aggressive work among the young people of the Church. The last two years have been marked by excellent progress, more efficient work, and a widening of the influence and usefulness of the Luther League. It is not necessary for your committee to go into the detail of the work. The Luther League will make its report through the General Secretary, the Rev. Amos J. Traver.

Your committee deemed it would be wise and helpful if some uniform practices for the relations existing between Synods and the respective Luther League organizations on their territory could be formulated as a suggested plan of relationship. With that in view a questionnaire was sent to the presidents of the district synods of the United Lutheran Church inquiring as to the present relationship existing, and asking for suggestions for a uniform plan for all Synods and Luther Leagues.

There was a commendable response to the inquiry, indicating the growing interest and recognition of the importance of the work of the Luther League.

With the information from the presidents of synods, as a basis, the committee in meeting gave consideration to the whole question, and reached the following conclusion as a suggested plan for uniform relations between the synods and their Luther Leagues.

Suggested Relation Between Synods and Luther Leagues

1. That the synods appoint Committees on Luther League.

2. That the Synods appoint a representative on the Executive Committee of the Synodical Luther League.

(*Temporary arrangement*—Inasmuch as in a few cases the territory of synods overlap within some states, it is deemed advisable that the chairmen of the synodical committees on Luther Leagues in the Synods in such states, shall constitute a joint committee, representing the different synods in the state, in order to unify and harmonize the general Luther League relationships. This joint committee shall select one of its members to represent them in the executive committee of the State Luther League.)

3. The Synodical Committee on Luther League shall report to the synodical convention.

4. The Synodical Luther League shall loyally co-operate with the Luther League of America in its general program which is in harmony with the program of the United Lutheran Church.

5. The program of the Synodical Luther League shall be in harmony with the general program of the Synod.

6. The Synodical Luther League shall heartily co-operate in the work of the Synod.

7. It is suggested that the Synod shall grant an annual apportionment for state or synodical Luther League work. (This is now done by the Synod of Ohio, the Maryland Synod, the New York Ministerium, the New York Synod and by the New York and New England Synod.)

Your committee further recommends in view of the needs of the enlarging work and the work which should be done and cannot because of financial inability, that the Luther League of America be granted an allowance of $10,000 a year by the United Lutheran Church in America to assist it in its work.

It is doubtless known by the delegates present that our Church does not begin to compare in what she does in this way with what the denominations are doing. The work among the young people needs an enlarging program and more effective prosecution of the same.

No other matters were referred to your committee for action.

Respectfully submitted,

HENRY C. ROEHNER, *Chairman.*

The Committee on Associations of Young People.

On motion the recommendation of the Committee was referred to the Executive Board.

The Rev. A. J. Traver, after introducing two associate workers in the offices of the Luther League, namely, Miss Brenda Mehlhouse and the Rev. Robert J. Wolf, presented the Report of the Luther League.

REPORT OF GENERAL SECRETARY OF THE LUTHER LEAGUE OF AMERICA

Confidence is the key-word for interpreting The Luther League of America. There are increasing evidences of confidence in the League by leaders of the Church everywhere and the constant demand for organization literature tells a story of awakened interest by pastors and leaders in the life of the congregations. There is also a new confidence growing within the League. The Luther League leader of today is sure of his organization's place in the Church, is sure of the program he promotes, and is sure of the increasing importance of the League in shaping the future of the Church. The Church is finding the League and the League is finding itself. These two facts are tremendously significant for the understanding of the Luther League movement today.

ORGANIZATION

There is little territory in the United Lutheran Church still unoccupied. During the biennium we have added the Luther Leagues of the State and Synod of West Virginia, the Florida Synod, the Georgia Synod, the Rocky Mountain Synod, Northern California, German Nebraska Synod. We also welcome the Luther League of Canada into reaffiliation. Intensively there is emphasis on good organization methods. The whole youth movement is being more and more closely interwoven. League leadership is being consciously trained for its place in the United Lutheran Church leadership of tomorrow.

REGIONS.

The Midwestern Region, taking in a wide reach of territory from Colorado to Illinois, under the leadership of Secretary Herbert Fischer of Omaha, has been a great asset in developing the League in the mid-west. There is a sense of unity that could be produced in no other way. The Eastern Region, consisting of Connecticut, New York and New Jersey, has called a full-time secretary, Miss Ethel Tussing of Virginia, and the advantages of this type of service are already being felt. All these New York Synods are participating in her support. No investment in personnel could be more productive. Several Synods are also considering the possibility of full-time league secretaries.

PERSONNEL

The officers of the Luther League of America for 1927-29 are as follows:
Executive Committee: Honorary Members — Rev. L. M. Kuhns, D.D.,
Litt.D., Hon. E. F. Eilert, C.S.D., Secretary Harry Hodges. Active—
Mr. C. C. Dittmer, President; Miss Rosa Sox, First Vice-President; Mr.
Kenneth Shook, Second Vice-President; Mr. Herbert Fischer, Recording
Secretary; Mr. Charles W. Fuhr, Treasurer; Rev. Amos John Traver, Gen-
eral Secretary; Miss May Scherer, Missionary Secretary; Rev. Clarence A.
Portz, Life Service Secretary; Rev. Robert J. Wolf, Intermediate Secre-
tary; Miss Brenda L. Mehlhouse, Junior Secretary; Mrs. S. T. Peterson;
Mr. Paul Brindle; Miss Winnie Butt; Rev. M. J. Bieber, D.D.; Mr.
John Greiner, Jr.; Rev. C. M. Teufel; Mr. Walter Banker; Mr. Harry
Hodges; Rev. F. W. Otterbein; Rev. H. C. Roehner, D.D.

WORK LITERATURE

All literature for departments is now printed on a uniform size to fit into
a loose-leaf notebook cover. A Luther League handbook is thus made available for every worker. The aim has been to produce helps in the simple
form that the average local League worker will be able to use. In addition a number of plays and pageants of merit, written by members of the
League have been published. Pamphlets produced by several of the Boards
are also distributed.

THE LUTHER LEAGUE REVIEW

Nearly forty years ago this monthly was founded and edited by Hon.
E. F. Eilert, one of the pioneers in the Luther League movement. During
these years Dr. Eilert has continued to publish *The Review* in his large
New York plant, at considerable sacrifice. Beginning with January, 1928,
The Review has been published at a smaller plant, where printing costs are
lower. The Luther League of America will always owe a debt of gratitude
to Dr. Eilert for his years of patient interest in *The Review*.

The Review is now published in an enlarged form. During March, 1928,
a campaign for subscriptions was made through the Educational Department.
This resulted in 2,700 new and renewed subscriptions. The monthly subscription list is now about 7,000. *The Topics Quarterly,* edited by Rev.
C. P. Harry, D.D., has also been enlarged and is a popular addition tc the
devotional leader's source material.

THE LUTHERAN

The Luther League should be interested in the circulation of the weekly
official magazine of the Church. With this in mind the organization of the
League was put at the service of the Publication House during the fall of
1927, with the result that 5,000 new and renewed subscriptions were secured.

This plan of campaign is now established as a regular feature of the fall program of the League.

AGE DEPARTMENTS

The Luther League is divided into Junior, 9-12 years; Intermediate, 13-16, and Senior, 17 plus.. The General Secretary is in charge of the Senior Department. Mr. Wolf and Miss Mehlhouse head the Intermediate and Junior Departments.

The Intermediate Department is making steady growth, serving an age that is most critical in the life of youth. A literature has been produced that will aid any local Church leader in organizing. In addition to the promotion of the standard Intermediate League, this department has been actively engaged in Boys' Work. Many summer camps have been visited, Secretary Wolf has been in consultation with the management of many other camps and anyone interested in camping will find a great deal of helpful information available at headquarters. A study of the Boy Scout Movement shows over 800 troops in our churches. The Department is helping to co-ordinate their programs with that of the Church. A series of pamphlets is now published that deals specifically with the boy problem in the Church.

The Junior Department is foundational to League work. For the year 1929 the goal of the League will be the establishing of 1,000 new Junior Societies. All the departments that later function in the Intermediate and Senior Departments are to be found in the Junior League. Training in Bible, Church History and Missions are central to its program. Through the courtesy of the Light Brigade Department of the Women's Missionary Society the missionary programs are prepared by their editors for the Junior League. Institutes for Junior Workers have been held in many sections of the Luther League of America and have proved their worth.

The Luther League through its age departments seeks to give organization training to the youth of the Church that progressively leads them from childhood, by promotions from Junior to Intermediate and Intermediate to Senior, to consecrated intelligent membership in the Women's Missionary Society and Brotherhood.

PROGRAM DEPARTMENTS

Education, Missions and Life Service are the three program departments. Under Education are the following activities: Weekly Devotionals, excepting the Missionary Meeting, Daily Bible Reading, The Reading Course, The Study Group, and the Circulation of Lutheran Literature.

Under Missions are included, The Monthly Missionary Devotional, The Mission Study Class and the Missionary Objective. The last Biennial Objective, the Administration Building at Andhra Christian College, India, was gloriously over met. The goal set was $25,000 and over $32,000 was paid in. The present objective is the appropriation of $12,000 for the Religious Education Building at our Buenos Aires Mission, to be called Luther League Hall.

Under Life Service are included, Study Groups in Vocational Guidance, an Annual Life Service Day on Reformation Sunday, Pageants and Plays that bring home the appeal for consecrated lives, Rallies at which missionaries and deaconesses and other workers speak. The Service Shield, endorsed by the Board of Education is promoted and a Life Service Card used in recruiting.

FINANCES

The Sustaining Membership at $5.00 minimum has been a necessary part of the financial program of the League. Dues pay less than one-quarter of the budget. 25 cents per member per year for General League seems to be all that it is wise to expect. The League must depend upon the generosity of the Church to meet its budget. A full-time secretary is needed for the Missionary and Life Service Departments, but the League itself cannot finance this advance without raising dues. The Luther League desires to remain a young folks' organization. It must therefore be dependent.

1929 GENERAL CONVENTION

The Luther League of America will meet in the Eighteenth Biennial Convention at Omaha, Nebraska, July 6-10, 1929, as guest of the Nebraska State League. The young people of the Church are learning the technique of convention arrangement and the plans for this League gathering, the first in the middle west, are complete to the last detail. Pastors and leaders in the Church will find the enthusiasms of youth contagious.. There is splendid opportunity offered for the study of our Church youth at their best. Extensive and attractive schedules for sightseeing, before and after the convention have been provided. The program will definitely challenge youth with the call of Christ to life service. The prayers of the Church are sought for an outpouring of the Holy Spirit upon the youth convention of the Church.

DOUBLE VALUES

The Luther League is a power in the Church, today. Take out the work done by Luther Leaguers in any congregation and the vitality of the Church would be seriously lowered. Any investment made by the Church in Luther League work will return interest manyfold. But the Luther League movement must also be evaluated for its future. The leadership in the Luther League of America today will be the leadership of the Church of tomorrow. League fellowship promises a more closely united Church, a Church where sectionalism fades before vision and understanding. League training promises a new generation of leaders who understand the principles of organization life and who will commit themselves to a more efficient United Lutheran Church. League acceptance of quotas and sense of responsibility for meeting them promises a day when apportionments will be met as a Christian privilege. League calls to the consecrated life promise crowded seminaries and deaconess homes, and an army of lay workers for every project of the Church. The Luther League of today will be the leadership of the Church of tomorrow.

AMOS JOHN TRAVER,
General Secretary, Luther League of America.

The Rev. H. Offermann, Chairman of the Committee of Reference and Counsel, presented the following letter and resolutions of the Committee:

October 10, 1928.

Dr. F. H. Knubel, President,
Erie, Pennsylvania.
Dear Dr. Knubel:

Your kind invitation to attend the convention of the United Lutheran Church received some time ago. I hereby extend to you my sincere thanks. It goes without saying that I would have been more than pleased to attend. However, I regret to state that various circumstances make it impossible for me to accept the invitation.

Please extend hearty greetings to your convention from the United Danish Evangelical Lutheran Church in America. We rejoice to see the progress of your church body. "Your labor is not in vain in the Lord." God bless your convention and the great work of the United Lutheran Church.

With hearty greetings, I am

Fraternally yours,
N. C. CARLSEN, President of the United Danish Evangelical
Lutheran Church in America.

1. *Resolved,* That the President be authorized to send a suitable reply to the Rev. N. C. Carlsen, President of the United Danish Evangelical Lutheran Church in America, expressing our appreciation of his message of congratulations and good wishes.

This resolution was adopted.

2. The United Lutheran Church in America sends cordial greetings and good wishes to the General Convention of the Protestant Episcopal Church of the United States and prays God's blessing upon them in their deliberations and upon the churches which they represent.

This resolution was adopted.

He submitted also the following resolution offered by Mr. W. H. Stackel:

Resolved, That a special commission of seven men be appointed by the Executive Board to consider the advisability and method of having all trust

and endowment funds belonging to the Church and its various Boards managed and invested by a common agency of the Church, report of said
commission to be made at the next Convention.

This resolution was adopted.

He submitted also the following resolution offered by Prof.
E. S. Dreher:

Whereas, we are commanded to worship God in the beauty of holiness,
and

Whereas, directions for beautifying places of worship are found in Isaiah
60: 13, as follows:

> The glory of Lebanon shall come unto thee,
> The fir tree, the pine tree, and the box tree together
> To beautify the place of my sanctuary;
> And I will make the place of my feet glorious.

And whereas, there is a great indifference among all denominations,
including our own, to the spiritual value of beautiful things, especially with
reference to the exterior decoration of church buildings with flowers and
shrubbery;

Therefore, be it Resolved, That it is the sense of this body that the
decoration of churches, as indicated above, be enthusiastically encouraged.

On motion of the Committee, this resolution was referred to
the Committee on Church Architecture.

Dr. Offermann introduced the Rev. Dr. G. A. Brandelle, President of the Augustana Synod, who bore the greetings of that
body. He spoke of the progress of the United Lutheran Church
since its organization, of its support of the work of the National
Lutheran Council and of the cordial relations existing between
it and the Augustana Synod. By appointment of the President,
the Rev. R. E. Tulloss made the response to Dr. Brandelle.

Dr. Offermann introduced the Rev. V. Koivumaki, Superintendent of the Home Mission Work of the Finnish Evangelical
Lutheran Church of the Suomi Synod, who spoke in appreciation
of the assistance given them in their work by the United Lutheran
Church.

Mr. Hodges, Chairman of the Committee of Tellers No. 2,
reported the result of elections as follows:

For the *Inner Mission Board*: The Rev. J. S. Schantz received
a majority of the votes cast. He was declared elected.

For the *Board of Deaconess Work*: Mr. J. C. Kinard received a majority of the votes cast. He was declared elected.

For the *Board of Education*: Mrs. Adelaide Burge and Mr. Charles Steele received a majority of the votes cast. These were declared elected.

Mr. E. F. Eilert, President of the Board of Publication, presented the following report:

REPORT OF THE BOARD OF PUBLICATION

To the members of the United Lutheran Church in America: '

Your Board of Publication reports a biennium of continued progress in its work both as to the books and periodicals it has published and distributed as well as the substantial assistance it has been able to give to the Church.

Our work has indeed been a pleasure and we are indebted to the splendid services rendered by those assigned the duties of management, editorial, manufacture and sales.

It would be encouraging if you would give them some indication of your appreciation. The spirit of loyalty and devotion to the work permeates all our establishments at Philadelphia, Chicago, Pittsburgh and Columbia and is such as would make any Church corporation feel very proud.

ORGANIZATION

Our Board has continued to meet regularly with splendid, almost perfect attendance and conducted your business with unamity and not the least indication of dissension or disagreement. We have had our problems which were your problems but they have all been settled by a unanimity of action.

At the first meeting of the Board during the biennium, which was held on November 9, 1926, officers were elected as follows:

Hon. E. F. Eilert, C.S.D., President; Mr. John M. Snyder, Vice-President; the Rev. N. R. Melhorn, D.D., Litt.D., Secretary; and Mr. E. G. Hoover, Treasurer.

During the biennium the Board has suffered the loss of two of its members by death. George E. Schlegelmilch, Esq., Chairman of the Board's Committee on Real Estate and Accounting ever since the organization of the Board. died on June 9, 1927, after a lingering illness. Mr. D. F. Efird, also a member of the Board from its organization, died at his home near Lexington, South Carolina, on August 19, 1927. Both of these men had given devoted and conscientious service to the Board and both had for years served on the Publication Boards of their respective bodies prior to the formation of this Board. Suitable minutes were inscribed on the records of the Board and thanks are rendered to God for the lives of these devoted and conscientious Christian men who so abundantly gave of their time and energy to the service of the Church and the work of the Lord.

The vacancy caused by the death of Mr. Efird has been filled by the Executive Board by the election of F. William Cappelman, Esq., of Columbia, South Carolina. As successor to Mr. Schlegelmilch, Dr. George Schlegel of Reading, Pa., was elected, but found it impossible to serve. Mr. Kenneth Baker, Greenwood, South Carolina has now been nominated to fill this vacancy.

MEETING, AND STANDING COMMITTEES

The Board as a whole has met four times each year during the biennium. The Executive Committee have met each month.

The various Standing Committees have been made up as follows:

Executive Committee: E. F. Eilert, John M. Snyder, N. R. Melhorn, E. G. Hoover, C. M. Jacobs, S. W. Herman, D. F. Yost, G. E. Schlegelmilch, and O. W. Osterlund.
Religious Literature: C. M. Jacobs, F. P. Manhart, A. H Holthusen.
Secular Literature: S. W. Herman, Charles F. Steck, H. C. Alleman.
Manufacture and Sales: D. F. Yost, G. D. Boschen, A. H. Kohn.
Real Estate and Accounting: G. E. Schlegelmilch, O. W. Osterlund (succeeding Mr. Schlegelmilch), D. F. Efird, Charles Baum.

NEW BOOKS

During the biennium, the Board has issued a number of new publications, among which we desire to call particular attention to the following: "Social Problems," A Christian Solution, by the Rev. E. E. Fischer, D.D.; "Life Service," by the Rev. A. J. Traver; "Our Church Abroad," edited by the Rev. George Drach, D.D.; "Names of Jesus," by the Rev. Walter Krumwiede, S.T.M.; "Christian Doctrine in Outline," by Werner Elert, translated by the Rev. C. M. Jacobs, D.D.; "The Truth of Faith," by the Rev. J. A. W. Haas, D.D; "The Jesuits," by H. Boehmer, translated by the Rev Paul Zeller Strodach, D.D.; "Little Children Come Unto Me," by the Rev. Paul J. Hoh; "Handbook of Christian Theology," by the Rev. J. A. Singmaster, D.D.; "A Catechism in Christian Worship," by the Rev. C. P. Swank, S.T.D.

In the Religious Education Text Series, there have been published for the weekday schools "God's Great Plan for Mankind" and "God's Care of Mankind" by Eva M. Stilz, and "God and His Helpers" and "Jesus and His Friends" by Mrs. Mabel B. Fenner, each in separate editions for the teachers and pupils. For the vacation schools, there have been issued "The Heavenly Father and His Children," "Serving the Heavenly Father," "Stories of the Early Hebrew Heroes" and "Stories of Jesus" by Maud Junkin Baldwin. These texts, designed for the teacher, have been accompanied by Memory Work material and illustrations for the pupil.

The new *Parish School Hymnal* was published just in time for the Richmond Convention. The *Lesson Commentary* on the International Uniform Sunday School Lessons has been issued each year, and the volume for 1929 is ready now. The Year Book of the United Lutheran Church and *Der Lutherischer Kalender* have appeared each year and will soon be ready for 1929.

"The Church, the State and the School" by Judge C. E. Reno and the Rev. E. E. Fischer, D.D., was issued in time for the Richmond Convention.

"The Story Ever New," a Christmas Pageant by the Rev. Arthur H. Getz, and "The Banner of the Cross," a Pageant for Reformation, by the Rev. S. N. Carpenter, D.D., have been published.

The Church Year Calendar has been continued and received with increasing favor.

The total of new books published during the biennium amounts to 216,450 copies.

BOOKS REPRINTED

Among books reprinted during the biennium may be mentioned "Martin of Mansfeld," "The Story of the Church," "The Story of Jesus," "How to Teach in Sunday School," "The Lutheran Commentary," "Golden Treasury," "An Exposition of the Gospels," "Favorite Hymns," "Luther, the Reformer," "Lectures on the Epistles" by Seiss, "Christian Theology" by Valentine.

The Common Service Book has been reprinted in several editions and reprints have been issued of the Book of Worship, the Church Book, and Kirchenbuch.

Several of the Catechisms have been reprinted and a number of the books of the Graded Series and the Teacher's Training Course have required reissuance. This has also been true of the Confirmation Booklets, "Upon This Rock," "At the Altar and After" and "Helpful Words for the Newly Confirmed."

The total number of volumes reprinted during the biennium amounts to 472,350.

PAMPHLETS AND TRACTS

New pamphlets and tracts, including Christmas, Easter, Chlidren's Day and Rally Day Services, have been issued to the number of 649,000, and previously issued tracts and pamphlets have been reprinted in a quantity of 218,000.

HYMNALS

The new Parish School Hymnal has been favorably received and a total of 120,000 copies produced during the first twenty months after its publication.

Of the various Church Hymnals, there have been published since the previous report the following number of copies:

Common Service Book	71,100
Book of Worship	13,250
Church Book	8,800
Kirchenbuch	10,000

A total of 497,876 copies have been published to date of the various editions of the Common Service Book.

To meet the requirements of Sunday schools having orchestras, the music of the hymns in the Parish School Hymnal has been arranged for twenty-eight orchestra instruments by Mrs. Catherine Fitting Zendt. This orchestration will be published in seven books and will be available early this fall.

PERIODICALS

The various periodicals which have been issued by the Board are being printed in quantities as follows:

Weekly

The Lutheran	33,000	
Lutherischer Herold	5,000	
Lutheran Young Folks	106,000	
Lutheran Boys and Girls	51,000	
		195,000

Monthly

Augsburg Teacher	39,000	
Sunbeams	43,000	
Sunshine	27,500	
Little Ones	24,000	
Pictureland Weekly	18,000	
Jugend Freund	4,000	
Senior Lesson Leaves	16,500	
Intermediate Lesson Leaves	6,500	
Junior Lesson Leaves	5,500	
		184,000

Quarterly

Home Department Lesson Book	31,000	
Adult Lesson Book	100,000	
Senior Lesson Book	165,000	
Intermediate Lesson Book	**65,000**	
Junior Lesson Book	55,000	
Bible Teachings	3,100	
Bible Story	7,800	
Bible Outlines	1,800	
Bible History	5,100	
Bible Biography	3,400	
Bible Facts and Scenes	3,500	
Bible Readings	5,700	
Wonderland	3,200	
Workland	2,400	
Pictureland	3,400	
Parish School	2,000	
Bible Picture Cards	18,000	
Bible Charts	350	
		475,750

Grand Total		854,750

GRADED SERIES

The syndicate hitherto issuing the International Closely Graded Series has discontinued the publication of this material in its present form. A sufficient supply has, however, been provided of these lessons so that we anticipate being able to continue furnishing it to our Sunday schools using the lessons until the fall of 1930 when, it is anticipated, the new Graded Lessons now being prepared by the Parish and Church School Board will be ready for the use of our schools.

CHURCH PAPERS

The two Church papers, *The Lutheran* and *Lutherischer Herold,* have been published regularly each week during the biennium. *The Lutheran* has enjoyed a steady, if small, increase in circulation. With reference to *Lutherischer Herold,* we are compelled to state that it has not received the anticipated support and therefore shows a slight falling off in the number of subscribers.

The Board would respectfully suggest that the Convention stress the value of both these Church papers to the members of the Church.

PUBLICATION PROGRAM

To complete the Publication Program outlined to the Buffalo Convention has been more difficult than anticipated. Progress is being made and manuscripts for several books called for by this program are under preparation. Work has been pushed on the completion of Luther's Works and it is to be hoped that the remaining volumes in this work will come from the press before the next Convention. The Family Service Book, prepared by the Common Service Book Committee is in press and should be ready soon.

The Fourth Book in the Key Book Series was delayed but is now in press and will be issued under the title, "The Ministry of Love." This book has been prepared by the Rev. Foster U. Gift, D.D.

An Altar Edition of the Common Service in large type has been authorized by the Board. Publication of such a book will be started as soon as the Common Service Book Committee has determined the material to be included.

GENERAL BUSINESS

The figures on the total business done during the biennium are $1,440,518.20. The corresponding figures for the previous biennium were $1,373,597.36. The increase for the biennium is accordingly, $66,920.84,

In the fall of 1927 a considerable reduction was made in the price of Sunday school papers and lesson books. It was estimated that this reduction would, in the course of a year, amount to about $26,000. Unfortunately the volume of business did not increase during the year sufficiently to make up for this reduction. The volume remained practically constant. Accordingly, the second year of the biennium shows a decrease in Net Business as compared with the first year. The accompanying reports of the Business Manager, Mr. Grant Hultberg, and the Treasurer, Mr. E. G. Hoover, give the financial figures in detail.

New York Property

Title to the Lutheran Church House in New York City, mentioned in the report to the Richmond Convention, was taken by the United Lutheran Church in America. After most careful consideration of all matters relating to the purchase of this House, the conclusion was reached that the most advantageous way in which it could be accomplished would be for the United Lutheran Church, as a New York corporation, to make the purchase. Accordingly, the Board of Publication offered the Executive Board to advance to the United Lutheran Church the money needed for the purchase of the property and to furnish when required, the funds with which to pay the mortgage resting thereon. In carrying out this policy, the Board has thus far advanced to the Treasurer of the United Lutheran Church for the New York Church House, the sum of $151,573.37, and has agreed to advance an additional sum of $50,000 with which to pay the existing mortgage when that becomes due.

Ministerial Pension Endowment Fund

A subscription of $50,000, payable in five semi-annually installments, was made to the Board of Ministerial Pensions and Relief toward their $4,000,000 fund raised throughout the Church last spring. The first installment of $10,000 has already been paid.

Terms Expiring With This Convention

Those whose terms expire at this time are the Rev. H. C. Alleman, D.D., the Rev. S. W. Herman, D.D., the Rev. A. H. Holthusen, Ph.D., Mr. E. G. Hoover, Mr. A. H. Kohn, Mr. D. F. Yost, Mr. Otto W. Osterlund.

The Board has placed in nomination the following: Rev. H. C. Alleman, D.D., Rev. George W. Nicely, D.D., Rev. A. H. Holthusen, Ph.D., Mr. E. G. Hoover, Mr. D. F. Yost, Mr. O. W. Osterlund, Mr. Croll Keller.

We are indeed grateful to all in our Church who have made possible the success of our Publication House. It is with great pride and satisfaction that through your splendid co-operation we have been able to build up for our United Lutheran Church not only a beautiful edifice (a monument to Lutheranism) in Philadelphia, but a publishing business of growing volume, expanding contact and increased capacity for service.

Respectfuly submitted,

E. F. Eilert, *President.*
Nathan R. Melhorn, *Secretary.*

BOARD OF PUBLICATION BUSINESS MANAGER'S REPORT

CONSOLIDATED PROFIT AND LOSS ACCOUNT
FOR THE YEAR ENDED JUNE 30, 1927

Gross Sales of Books, Advertising, etc.............$747,187.74
Less Returns, Allowances and Discounts......... 12,590.40
Net Sales................................. ————— $734,597.34
Cost of Sales:
Purchases of Materials, Printing and Binding....$315,786.10
Printing Department Wages and Editorial Salaries 107,905.95
Authors and Contributors....................... 11,811.43
Royalties 1,543.52
Shipping and Mailing, including Postage......... 37,844.15
Freight, Expressage and Hauling................ 5,830.40
Rent 27,000.00
General Manufacturing Expenses............... 3,783.08
Insurance 1,793.29
Depreciation of Machinery, etc................. 11,855.03

$525,152.95
Deduct:
Sales of Waste, etc..............$ 1,689.18
Discounts on Purchases.......... 1,854.19
Increase in Inventories.......... 10,377.52   13,920.89   511,232.06

Gross Profit on Sales............................ $223,365.28
Selling, Administrative and General Expenses:
Executive and Office Salaries....................$ 70 872.78
Office Supplies and Expenses................... 3,462.68
Expenses of Board Meetings, etc................ 777.18
Telephone, Telegraph and Messenger............ 1,061.20
Advertising 2,242.49
Legal and Auditing............................ 2,097.03
Memberships 1,106.16
Traveling Expenses............................ 2,404.65
Commissions to Agents........................ 1,963.10
General Expenses............................. 5,898.43
Branch Offices:
Rentals $6,866.00
Postage 3,004.18
Freight, Hauling, Shipping, etc....... 2,478.56
Insurance 503.68
Taxes and Water Rent............. 215.49
Light 98.55
—————   13,166.46
Uncollectible Notes and Accounts Receivable
Written Off............................ 1,886.10
Depreciation of Furniture and Fxtures.......... 3,180.06
Appropriation to the United Lutheran Church.... 50,000.00
Pensions 900.00

$161,018.32
Profit on Machinery and Equipment Abandoned.. 1,318.92   159,699.40

		$ 63,665.88
Profit from Operation of Real Estate.......................		2,261.19
		$ 65,927.07

Other Income:
Interest on Investments	$2,519.00	
Interest on Bank Balances......................	2,369.19	
Interest on Notes and Accounts Receivable.......	99.75	4,987.94

Net Profit ....$ 70,915.01

CONSOLIDATED PROFIT AND LOSS ACCOUNT
FOR THE YEAR ENDED JUNE 30, 1928

Gross Sales of Books, Advertising, etc.............	$717,683.98	
Less Returns, Allowances and Discounts.........	11,763.12	
Net Sales		$705,920.86

Cost of Sales:
Purchases of Materials, Printing and Binding....	$290,238.86
Printing Department Wages and Editorial Salaries	114,411.06
Authors and Contributors........................	11,509.65
Royalties	1,183.51
Shipping, Freight and Mailing, including Postage.	45,405.80
Rent	27,000.00
General Manufacturing Expenses...............	3,163.02
Insurance	2,000.92
Depreciation of Machinery, etc..................	11,980.60

	$506,923.42

Deduct:
Sales of Waste, etc...............	$2,721.22	
Discounts on Purchases.............	1,113.31	3,834.53

	$503.088.89	
Add, Decrease in Inventories	4,972.70	508,061.59

Gross Profit on Sales............................... $197,859.27

Selling, Administrative and General Expenses:
Executive and Office Salaries....................	$ 73,044.83
Office Supplies and Expenses....................	3,675.26
Expenses of Board Meetings, etc................	829.48
Telephone, Telegraph and Messenger...........	1,217.99
Advertising	1,544.51
Legal and Auditing.............................	1,771.00
Memberships	789.00
Traveling Expenses.............................	1,988.64
Commissions to Agents.........................	889.25
General Expenses	6,044.87

Branch Offices:
Rentals	$5,550.00	
Postage	2,580.83	
Freight, Hauling, Shipping, etc......	2,617.88	
Insurance	500.77	
Taxes	257.05	
Light	113.92	11,620.45

Uncollectable   Notes   and   Accounts   Receivable
   Written Off 4,181.17
Depreciation of Furniture and Fixtures..........   3,436.28
Appropriations:
 United Lutheran Church...........$50,000.00
  Board of Ministerial Pensions
   and Relief................. 10,000.00
            ————————   60,000.00
Pensions 825.00
Loss on Machinery and Equipment Sold.........   186.20
                ————————   172,043.93

                    $ 25,815.34
Loss from Operation of Real Estate.........................   1,215.40

                    $ 24,599.94
Other Income:
 Interest on Investments...........................$3,046.95
 Interest on Bank Balances......................... 3,184.38
 Interest on Notes and Accounts Receivable........   2.20
                 ————————   6,233.53

  Net Profit ....$ 30,833.47
      Respectfully submitted,
        GRANT HULTBERG, *Business Manager.*

TREASURER'S REPORT OF JOHN RUNG LEGACY
Cash Balance, July 1, 1926......................................$1,131.92
Cash Receipts:

	Year ended June 30, 1927	Year ended June 30, 1928	Totals for the Biennium
Interest on Investments........	$275.00	$275.00	$550.00
Interest on Bank Balances.......	45.67	58.63	104.30
	$320.67	$333.63	$654.30

Cash Balance, June 30, 1928..............................$1,786.22

Statement at June 30, 1928
ASSETS:
Cash in Bank...$1,786.22
Bonds at Market Value, June 30, 1928................. 5,580.00
                ———————— $7,366.22
LIABILITIES:
Trust Fund $3,000.00

 Surplus on Hand...$4,366.22
      Respectfully submitted,
        E. G. HOOVER, *Treasurer.*

BUSINESS MANAGER'S REPORT OF ASSETS AND LIABILITIES
as of June 30, 1928
ASSETS:
Cash in Banks and on Hand..............................$166,545.78
Notes Receivable..............................$ 127.49

Accounts Receivable
Merchandise $148,551.05
Advertising 2,396.34
                           ————— 150,947.39

                           $151,074.88
Less, Allowance for Doubtful Accounts............ 10,000.00
                           ————— 141,074.88
Accrued Interest on Investments............................ 1,339.94
Merchandise and Stock on Hand in Philadelphia and Branch
    Houses 255,502.31
Securities, at Market Values, June 30, 1928.................... 93,130.00

                           $657,592.91
John Rung Legacy (E. G. Hoover, Treasurer)................ 7,366.22
Prepaid Insurance and Taxes................................ 4,833.83
Advance to the United Lutheran Church...................... 51,573.37
Land and Buildings, net of depreciation............$729,421.51
Machinery and Equipment, net of depreciation..... 48,035.53
Furniture and Fixtures, net of depreciation......... 17,085.93
Electrotype Plates, at estimated values............. 6,012.05
                           ————— 800,555.02

                           $1,521,921.35
                 LIABILITIES:
Accounts Payable...$ 18,316.27
Accrued Royalties 1,406.92
Amount due Subscribers on Subscriptions for
    Periodicals $65,517.29
Prepaid Advertising............................ 90.29
                           ————— 65,607.58
                          $ 85,330.77
John Rung Legacy Fund..................................... 7,366.22
Net Assets 1,429,224.36

                           $1,521,921.35

Respectfully submitted,
GRANT HULTBERG, *Business Manager.*
August 4, 1928.

We certify that we have examined the accounts of the Board of Publication of the United Lutheran Church in America for the two years
ended June 30, 1928, and that the foregoing statements, in our opinion,
correctly set forth its financial condition at June 30, 1928, and the results
of its operation for the two years ended June 30, 1928.

LYBRAND, ROSS BROS. & MONTGOMERY,
Accountants and Auditors.

In connection with the consideration of this report Mr. Eilert
introduced the Rev. C. R. Tappert, Editor of the *Lutherischer
Herold,* who spoke of the desirability of a wider circulation of that
paper, and Mr. Grant Hultberg, Business Manager of the Board

of Publication, who addressed the Convention concerning the financial affairs of the Board of Publication.

The report of the Auditors on accounts of the Board of Publication was accepted.

In due order the Convention resumed consideration of the Report of the Committee on Common Service Book, the particular item being the resolution concerning the proposed new music edition of the Common Service Book, and an amendment to specification 5 under the resolution, the amendment being a motion to print three stanzas instead of one between the staves. The motion on the amendment was carried by a vote of 186 to 173.

This amendment requires that the last clause of item 5 under the resolution shall read: "and that another edition be published in which the first three stanzas of each hymn shall be printed between the staves." (For further action see Minutes Fifth Meeting, Morning Session—Secretary.)

The motion on the adoption of the original resolution was put and carried.

The resolutions concerning the translation of Luther's Catechism were then taken up.

On motion the third resolution was recommitted. (See Minutes Fifth Meeting, Morning Session—Secretary.)

The Convention adjourned with prayer by the Rev. F. E. Strobel.

Evening Service

The program prepared by the Glee Club and the Dramatic Club of Thiel College was given at eight o'clock.

FIFTH MEETING

SUNDAY SCHOOL CHAPEL,
LUTHER MEMORIAL CHURCH,
ERIE, PENNSYLVANIA.
Monday, October 15, 1928, 8.45.

Matins were conducted by the Rev. E. A. Trabert.

The Convention was called to order by the President.

The Minutes of Saturday morning and afternoon sessions were read and approved.

The Rev. A. Steimle, President of the Board of Education, presented the report of that Board.

REPORT OF THE BOARD OF EDUCATION

The Board of Education of the United Lutheran Church in America submits its Sixth Biennial Report herewith:

This report is presented with gratitude to the great Head of the Church for His unfailing help. The Board records its conviction that the Church has placed upon it the responsibility of dealing with an enterprise of most far-reaching consequence for the Kingdom of God. We are pleased to report measurable progress. We rejoice in the continued and increasingly large number of friends and advocates of Christian higher education. We thank God and take courage as we record the history of the biennium, for the spiritual support which has been given the educational program of the Church by the prayers of God's people and for the renewed evidence of the spirit of Christian liberality.

MATTERS OF RECORD

Conference of Presidents With Board of Education

In December, 1927, a conference of all presidents of institutions convened in Washington upon the invitation of the Board. In all probability this will be made a permanent policy of the Board. Two conferences of college presidents have been held with staff members of the Board of Education in preliminary plans for Educational Year 1930, authorized and directed by the Richmond Convention.

Educational Year 1930

The proposal of the United Lutheran Church in Richmond Convention to observe the year 1930 as Educational Year, has apparently met with approval among several other general bodies of Lutherans. The National Lutheran Educational Conference meeting in January, 1927, adopted the following resolution:

"*Resolved*, That we have learned with satisfaction of the progress which has been made during the year toward the realization of the project of simultaneous campaigns on the part of all Lutheran Educational Institutions throughout the country during the year 1930, the four hundredth anniversary of the Augsburg Confession.

"We commend the action of the United Lutheran Church in setting aside

the year 1930 as 'educational year' in that body. We note with pleasure
the messages of approval of the general project from various persons in
the different branches of the Church. In view of these evidences of a
favorable reaction toward the proposal, be it

"*Resolved,* That we express ourselves as being in hearty approval of
holding a series of simultaneous campaigns during the year 1930, on the
part of all Lutheran educational institutions, each to appeal in its own way,
in its own field, to its own constituency. In cases where for some reason
a financial campaign during 1930 is not practicable, special emphasis should
be given to the cause of Christian education.

"We urge consideration of this proposal by the general church bodies
and synods related to our various schools, in the hope that by simultaneous
campaigns and combined emphasis upon educational needs during 1930,
the cause of education and the welfare of our schools may be largely
furthered."

This Conference again in session January, 1928, adopted the following:

"*Resolved,* (1)   That we have noted with deep satisfaction the progress
which has been made in the development of plans for the observance of
1930 as Educational Year throughout all branches of the Lutheran Church
in America.

"(2)   That we appoint a special committee consisting of Presidents
R. E. Tulloss, G. A. Andreen, O. Mees and Lars W. Boe to arrange for
an early meeting of college presidents and representatives of Lutheran
Church bodies, for the discussion of this project, to the end that by campaigns or other emphasis the cause of education may be stressed in the
year named throughout American Lutheranism."

The meeting suggested was convened in Chicago in March, 1928, with
a splendid representation and enthusiastic approach to more definite plans
for the observance of Educational Year. Foremost among the actions of
the Conference was a recommendation addressed to the National Lutheran
Council requesting the Council to provide for an All-American Lutheran
Convention to be held the twenty-fifth of June, 1930. Committees of the
group were named to "stimulate further interest and activity with reference
to the general project of educational emphasis and campaigns during 1930,
to convene representatives of educational institutions and church bodies for
further conference and to co-operate with the National Lutheran Council."

The Board of Education of the United Lutheran Church pursuant to
the action of the United Lutheran Church in Convention 1926, has communicated the Convention action affecting Educational Year to all synodical
units and by special action of the Board has requested all synodical bodies
to take action "with formal and definite resolution in harmony with the
action of the United Lutheran Church at the Richmond Convention, to
set aside the year 1930 as Educational Year and to provide for such campaign or campaigns as may be deemed justifiable upon its local territory,

on behalf of educational institutions or agencies customarily supported by the synods concerned."

In a group meeting of the representatives of the United Lutheran institutions, the total financial objective for education in the year 1930 will approximate $10,000,000 for the United Lutheran Church.

Reformation Day Appeal

Although the new schedule of special days, authorized by the Richmond Conventions for the Boards of the Church was really not effective as it pertained to the Board of Education until the year 1928, by special courtesy of the Board of American Missions, our Board was privileged to use the 1927 Reformation Season for educational and inspirational purposes and for the solicitation of an offering. The Board prepared a special program for the Reformation Anniversary for use in the Sunday schools and resolved that for 1927 an offering should be solicited for Pacific Seminary and Saskatoon College and Seminary. Every possible opportunity was used to get before the Church a plan of the observance of this day and to create a church consciousness upon the matter of its observance. Every means was employed to focus the attention of the entire Church upon Reformation Day. This schedule was without precedent in the history of the United Lutheran Church. The Board was exceedingly anxious in this initial venture that the Church should make a creditable response. We record our disappointment in the returns. We recognize the fact that it was but a beginning and we are assured that a considerable amount of education will be necessary before there can be realized anything approaching a general recognition of this day. We call fervently upon the Church to set apart Reformation Day in the interests of the cause of Christian Education. We are sure that this method is not the most effective way of helping our cause to attain financial recognition, but we are thoroughly convinced that it should prove the part of worth and wisdom to train our youth in the Sunday schools of the Church to a plan of giving of their substance to our specific cause. By resolution of the Board, the offering of Reformation Day, 1928, is to be devoted to the Lutheran College for Women.

Co-operation With the Board of Ministerial Pension and Relief

Two members of the secretarial staff co-operated with the Board of Ministerial Pensions and Relief in the campaign for promotional and intensive work. Secretary Bauslin acted as director in the Synods of Michigan and Indiana, and Secretary Harry assisted in the Ministerium of Pennsylvania.

Co-operation With the Icelandic Lutheran Church in North America

The co-operation with the Icelandic Synod as it affects the support of the Jon Bjarnason Academy in Winnipeg, Manitoba, Canada, continues. During the biennium the amount of $3,666.33 has been paid.

Co-operation in the Pacific Northwest

The plan of co-operation in education between the Pacific District of the Norwegian Lutheran Church, the Columbia Conference of the Augustana Synod, and the Pacific Synod of the United Lutheran Church in America, was reported to the Richmond Convention. We are advised by the representatives of the Pacific Synod that there have been no favorable developments in the biennium that has elapsed.

Co-operation in California

Negotiations have been pending for an intersynodical Lutheran Institution in California. Late in the biennium 100 acres were offered for a Lutheran University. An independent Board of Trustees, members of which must be Lutheran, has been incorporated. Some Lutheran groups in California have officially endorsed the project. The Committee on Institutions of the Board of Education, upon request of the Educational Commission of the California Synod of the United Lutheran Church, received and reviewed (1) the articles of incorporation of .... College, (2) covenant in re of a Lutheran College in California, (3) the by-laws of .... College and referred them back to the California Synod with comments. The matter has been altogether in the hands of the California Synod as it affects the United Lutheran Church in America.

Annuity Bonds

Annuity Bonds have been issued by this Board, during the biennium, in a total amount of $14,000.

Monroe Bequest

At the close of a long life of eighty-three years, Mrs. Harriet Earhart Monroe, an ardent advocate of Christian Education, for many years the devoted friend and benefactress of the Board of Education, bequeathed practically her entire estate to the Board of Education, including real estate in the City of Washington, District of Columbia. Under the terms of the will the residence, 204 "A" Street, S. E., is being transferred to the Board of Trustees of the Lutheran College for Women. The proceeds

of insurance policies have been assigned by the Board to the Scholarship
and Loan Fund for Women. "This Board reveres the memory of Mrs.
Monroe for the noble deeds of a noble life and commends to all who would
leave their tasks in adequate hands after they are gone her splendid
solution of the problem."

The Lutheran College for Women

The Board of Directors is drawn from the co-operating synods in the
proportion of one director for every twenty thousand communicant members
or major fraction thereof, providing that every participating synod shall
be represented by at least one director. In April, 1927, the Lutheran
College for Women was incorporated under the laws of the State of
Maryland. The officers of the Corporation and Board are: President,
the Rev. J. Henry Harms, D.D., Philadelphia; vice-president, the Rev.
W. E, Fischer, D.D., Shamokin, Pa.; treasurer, E. Clarence Miller, LL.D.,
Philadelphia; administrative secretary, the Rev. William A. Kump, Cham-
bersburg, Pa. The Board has taken title to a tract of land in Montgomery
County, Maryland, a short distance from the northern boundary of the
District of Columbia. By recent action the Maryland Legislature has
made this section a part of the metropolitan area.

In order that the interests of the college might be administered most
advantageously the Board elected the Rev. William A. Kump administrative
secretary. He became full-time representative of the college in December,
1926.,

The Board is able to report that since the appointment of the administrative secretary it has received gifts or pledges to the approximate amount
of $150,000. The estimated value of the college site, the original cost of
which was assumed by the Maryland Synod, is $150,000. The Women's
Missionary Society of the United Lutheran Church will endow the chair
of Religious Education in honor of their distinguished and lamented co-
worker, Katherine Scherer Cronk. A bequest to the college of $20,000,
made by Miss Margaret Mehring, of Key Mar, Md., will become in-
operative through the failure to meet a provision of the will that the college
"shall be established, incorporated and in actual operation during my life
time or within five years after the time of my death." Mrs. Harriet E.
Monroe before she died gave to the Board of Education in trust for the
Lutheran College for Women, properties in Washington, D. C., together
with her library and art objects. It is believed the college will realize
at least $25,000 from the sale of these properties. By resolution of the
Board of Trustees of Elizabeth College a fund of $4,000 is set aside from
the assets of that institution as an endowment fund for scholarships in

the Lutheran College for Women. The college is made the beneficiary in certain wills.

For many reasons no special financial effort has been made. However, the co-operating synods have approved of a plan to secure special gifts and memorials. This intensive effort will begin on Reformation Day, 1928. By action of the Board of Education on this day the Lutheran College for Women will receive offerings throughout the United Lutheran Church.

Breklum-Kropp

During the biennium six Kropp students have completed their course and have been assigned for further study to seminaries in the United Lutheran Church. In the fall of 1927, Bruno Paulson, Hans Peters and Kurt Sobbe entered the Seminary at Waterloo, Canada. Arrangements have been completed for Berthold Korte and Ernst Schmidt to enter the Chicago Seminary this fall and for Ernst Ringstroem to enter the Waterloo Seminary. In addition to these, the director of Kropp reports that two former graduates of Kropp, Hans Moertelmeyer and Eugen Buehler in 1927 entered the Manitoba Synod and assumed pastorates there. The director emphasizes that due to the growth of the Seminary it will be in a position, beginning in 1929, to send a larger number of men annually than heretofore.

The Board of Directors of the joint institution has elected Pastor Adelbert Paulsen, the son of Kropp's founder, as its president in place of Pastor Ketels, who resigned on account of advancing age. Pastor Thun, pastor for seamen in Altona, has been added to the Board.

Director Petersen of Breklum celebrated his silver jubilee in connection with that work January, 1928. In view of the considerable number of men in the ministry of the United Lutheran Church who have been instructed and influenced by him, it is recommended that this convention take appropriate action.

A gift of five thousand marks from a layman in America has greatly heartened the director of Kropp who declares that another such gift will enable the institution to retire its old debt and restore its credit, which is strained to the uttermost.

The reports of the Kropp and Breklum institutions will be found in the proper place in this report. They set forth very clearly the points of view under which the institutions are operated.

Conference of Board of Education and Board of American Missions Representatives, Affecting Memorial From Manitoba Synod

A Memorial from the Manitoba Synod, presented to the Richmond Convention, was referred by the convention to the Board of Education and the Board of American Missions. The representatives of these two Boards, Secretaries Fry and Bauslin, met in Philadelphia, December 12, 1927. They recommended to their respective Boards that serious consideration shall be given to an appreciable increase of appropriations by each Board to the work,—*first*, of the Manitoba Synod; *second*, to the work of Saskatoon College and Seminary, the strategic basis of a native ministry for the Canadian Northwest.

BOARD MEMBERSHIP AND ORGANIZATION

Professor R. S. Saby, Ph.D., of Gettysburg College was elected to fill the unexpired term (to 1930) of Mr. W. H. Stackel of Rochester, New York, resigned.

The advisory members for the past biennium

From the Women's Missionary Society,
　　Mrs. A. V. Pohlman, 5143 Race Street, Philadelphia, Pa.
　　Prof. Dorothea C. Hess, M.A., Hunter College, New York City.
From the Evangelical Lutheran Augustana Synod of North America:
　　Prof. George M. Stephenson, Ph.D.
　　G. A. Brandell, D.D., President of the Augustana Synod,
　　　　　　　　　　　　　　　　　　　　　　Rock Island, Illinois.

The following officers were elected by the Board for the biennium:

　　　　　　　President, Augustus Steimle, D.D.
　　　　　　　Vice-President, Hugo C. M. Wendell, Ph.D.
　　　　　　　Secretary, W. M. Horn, D.D.
　　　　　　　Treasurer, Mr. John M. Snyder.

In addition to the officers the following were elected members of the Executive Committee:

　　　　　　　J. H. Harms, D.D.
　　　　　　　E. P. Pfatteicher, D.D.
　　　　　　　W. J Showalter, Sc.D.

The Executive Staff for the work of the Board is as follows:
Secretaries

Charles S. Bauslin, D.D., 212 Evangelical Building, Harrisburg, Pa.
C. P. Harry, D.D., 210 W. Fornance Street, Norristown, Pa
Mary E. Markley, Litt.D., 39 East 35th Street, New York City.
Mathilde Peper (resigned April, 1928).
Mildred E. Winston, A.M. (from September, 1928).

The nominations of the Board for the terms which expire at this Convention are the following:

Clergy	Synod
*The Rev. W. M. Horn, D.D., Ithaca, New York	N. Y. & N. E.
The Rev. E. C. Herman, D.D., Canton, Ohio	Ohio
The Rev. A. J. Holl, D.D., Pittsburgh, Pa.	Pittsburgh
The Rev. A. A. Zinck, D.D., Milwaukee, Wis.	Northwest

Lay	
*Dr. W. J. Showalter, Washington, D. C.	Maryland
Dean Adelaid L. Burge, State University of Iowa, Iowa City, Iowa	Iowa
The Hon. A. L. Bulwinkle, Gastonia, N. C.	North Carolina

* Nominated to succeed themselves.

DISBURSEMENTS TO INSTITUTIONS

The following amounts were paid to educational institutions during the biennium ending June 30, 1928:

Theological Seminaries

Breklum-Kropp Budget	$12,000.00	
Breklum-Kropp Special	190.00	
Breklum-Kropp Transportion of Students	500.00	
		$12,690.00
Chicago Seminary Budget		1,833.33
Hartwick Seminary Budget		2,200.00
Martin Luther Seminary Budget		917.33
Pacific Seminary Budget	4,583.33	
Pacific Seminary Special	2,000.00	6,583.33
Southern Seminary Budget		6,516.66
		$30,740.65

Colleges

Carthage College Budget	$6,600.00	
Carthage College Special	428.25	
		$7,028.25
Gettysburg College Budget		2,750.00
Lenoir-Rhyne College Budget		2,750.00
Collegiate Institute Budget		2,083.33
Lutheran College for Women Budget		9,166.66
Marion Junior College Budget		2,083.33
Roanoke College Budget		5,500.00
Midland College Budget		18,333.33
(Western Seminary included)		
Newberry College Budget		6,600.00
Summerland College Budget		3,300.00
Muhlenberg College Budget	2,750.00	

Muhlenberg College Special	25.00	
		2,775.00
Saskatoon College and Seminary Budget	3,583.33	
Saskatoon College and Seminary Special	3,500.00	
		7,083.33
Susquehanna University Budget		2,750.00
Thiel College Budget		2,750.00
Wagner College Budget	3,666.66	
Waterloo College and Seminary Budget	4,583.33	
Waterloo. College Special, support of three Breklum-Kropp Students	190.00	
		4,773.33
Wittenberg College Budget		2,750.00
Icelandic Synod Budget (For Academy at Winnipeg		3,666.33
		$89,809.55
Total for Biennium		$120,550.20

DEPARTMENT OF INSTITUTIONS

The magnitude of the educational enterprise of the United Lutheran Church cannot be estimated by the amount of apportionment budgeted to the Board of Education by the United Lutheran Church. The Theological Seminaries and Colleges of the United Lutheran Church represent a property investment of $15,000,000. The operating cost of these institutions is approximately $2,000,000. The financial problems of these various institutions are not solved solely by increased enrollments. No college student ever pays more than two-thirds of the cost of his education. Increasing standards of effectiveness demand that our seminaries and colleges continue to have more money. Naturally, therefore, they turn to the Church that founded them and that looks to them to train a consecrated and intelligent ministry and laity.

Weidner Institute and Mont Amoena Seminary

By official action June 14, 1927, the Synod of Indiana voted to close at once Weidner Institute at Mulberry, Ind. The Synod assumed all obligations of the institution, approximately $20,000 in current and other indebtedness. The Board of Education at its meeting in June, 1928, took suitable action on the closing of Weidner, which has served the Church as a preparatory school and junior college since 1902.

Mont Amoena Seminary, Mount Pleasant, N. C., has been discontinued after sixty-eight years of service in the education of the daughters of the Church. Since 1859, distinguished educators—men and women—have been training to fine womanhood hundreds of girls from the southern states. Many of the graduates of Mont Amoena are the leaders in the Church today. In taking suitable action at its meeting in June, 1928, the Board of

Education was not unmindful of the wide influence of Mont Amoena in the upbuilding of the Kingdom.

Reports by Institutions

Reports are submitted from the administrative offices of the institutions of higher learning in the United Lutheran Church in America. They are arranged as Theological Seminaries and Colleges in order of their founding.

I. Theological Seminaries

HARTWICK SEMINARY, NEW YORK

Founded 1797. Chartered 1816

The Rev. Charles R. Myers, D.D., *President*

Notable progress was made during the past biennium. In October, 1926, the Synod of New York, under whose ownership and control the school functions, authorized a campaign of $500,000 for building and endowment. The citizens of Oneonta offered as their contribution $200,000 and 140 acres of land provided the college work would be transferred to that city, eighteen miles south of Hartwick Seminary. The offer was accepted, $637,000 was subscribed and the decision was reached to establish a standard College of Liberal Arts in Oneonta authorized and approved by the Board of Regents of the University of the State of New York. Since the close of the campaign additional contributions in pledges, land and special gifts have brought the resources to the total of $750,000.

General plans for the complete and ultimate campus development of seven college buildings have been approved. Detailed plans for first building, to cost $300,000 with equipment, have been accepted and the ground broken for its erection. The building will be ready for use in September, 1929. The architect is Dwight James Baum of New York of the associated officers of Dwight James Baum and John Russell Pope.

Changes in organization have been made. Hartwick Academy, Rev. Prof. J. C. McLain, Headmaster, remains at the present Seminary location as does the Theological Department with Dr. Frank Wolford as Dean. Hartwick College in Oneonta has Dr. Charles R. Myers, President, and Dr. O. M. Norlie, called from Luther College, as Dean.

Extensive repairs in Main Academy Building have been made. The residence occupied by President Myers, now known as Hiller Hall, will be used as a dormitory and recitation hall for theological students. The faculty of Academy and Theological Seminary has been strengthened by additional members. The college faculty organization is now being effected.

During the school year 1927-28 the Seminary was crowded to capacity. The scholastic work was of the highest. The President, being occupied with the college program, administrative responsibility at the Seminary was committed to Dr. O. L. Schreiber as acting Principal.

Thus "The Greater Hartwick" under the blessing and by the guidance of God has come into existence. All friends of Hartwick look to the future with confident hope as they rejoice in the development of the work of the oldest Lutheran School in America.

LUTHERAN THEOLOGICAL SEMINARY, GETTYSBURG, PENNSYLVANIA

Founded 1826

The Rev. John Aberly, D.D., *President*

This report covers briefly the one hundred and first and one hundred and second years of the Seminary's uninterrupted work. During the first year of the biennium the number of students enrolled was fifty-seven; during the second year sixty-eight. The first year six graduates and two special students were sent to the work of the Church, the special students entering mission work in Liberia. The second year twenty graduates were sent to various fields of service in the Church. The enrollment for the coming year promises a still further increase in the number of students.

The Synods supporting the Seminary have contributed to the Endowment Funds of the Seminary during the past two years the sum of $57,137. Besides this there have been special contributions, the chief of these being the gift of $5,000 from Dr. and Mrs. Jeremiah Zimmerman of Syracuse, N. Y., for the Lectureship on Effective Preaching. The Lectureship was inaugurated April 17-20, 1928, by Dr. James I. Vance of Nashville, Tenn. Dr. and Mrs. Zimmerman have also been adding generously to the Library so that the Zimmerman Collection now numbers over 11,000 volumes, many of them rare and valuable. The Alumni Lectureship has also become operative during this biennium. An endowment of $1,350 has been received on this Fund. Six thousand dollars have been received as annuities from friends. The total assets now in the various endowment funds are $548,460. The Synods supporting the Seminary have also increased their annual contributions to the running expenses of the Seminary so that an income of $8,000 is realized annually from this source.

The Board of Directors has adopted a program of expansion. This provides for two new professorships, a chapel, a gymnasium and assembly hall, new dormitories, increased endowments for the maintenance of the library, and additional scholarships, including graduate fellowships. The program calls for a minimum of $586,000 and a maximum of $761,000.

The curriculum of the Seminary has been revised. Arrangements have been made whereby graduates having the B.D. degree can do advanced work leading to the degree of Master of Sacred Theology. In 1927 one and in 1928 three were given this degree. In the undergraduate work the chief addition to the course has been that of clinical work. Through the co-operation of pastors each student is given practical work under the direction of the Department of Practical Theology.

THE SOUTHERN SEMINARY, COLUMBIA, S. C.

Founded 1830

The Rev. A. G. Voigt, D.D., LL.D., *Dean*

The chief purpose of the Southern Seminary from its founding in early days has been to provide an educated and competent ministry for the Lutheran Church in the South. Along with this main purpose runs the desire to make a contribution of capable men to the foreign mission work of the Church. During the past two years the Seminary has been able to fulfill its objects with a great degree of adequacy.

In the past biennium the institution has given to the Church for service twenty-five graduates. An enrollment of forty-one last year and of forty-two the preceding year is an evidence that the 65,000 confirmed members of the five Southern Synods have been awakened to the necessity of having enough educated ministers for their developing territory. These students almost all come from Southern homes and receive their preliminary education in the Lutheran Colleges in the South,—Newberry, Lenoir-Rhyne, Roanoke, and Collegiate Institute. Very few of the students in the Southern Seminary are not college graduates. The past biennium has confirmed again what has long been felt, that the development, efficiency and progress of the Lutheran Church in the South are bound up with the life, progress and prosperity of the Seminary.

The interest in the foreign mission work of the Church is strong among the students. They cultivate knowledge of the cause and imbibe inspiration in their Mission League in addition to the instruction given on the subject. In the fall of 1927 one, who since his graduation in 1925 had been waiting to be sent out by the Board of Foreign Missions and who in the meanwhile continued his preparation by post-graduate study in this country and Europe, was commissioned for China. Another student, a native of Japan, who graduated in 1926, returned to his own country after some post-graduate study. In the class which graduated recently there is one who will welcome the opportunity to enter the foreign field; and in the student body there are others with the same aspiration.

There has been material progress during the last two years. When the report was prepared for the last convention of the United Lutheran Church it was stated that ground was broken for a new building. That building for classroom purposes has been completed, a worthy adjunct to the magnificent main building, which with the exception of the chapel has been converted to dormitory uses. The endowment of the institution is steadily growing. The financial condition is improving in every respect. The intelligent interest of the churches in all the Southern Synods has been increased. The Seminary has at last emerged from the state of struggling to live to the state of vigorously wrestling for adequate equipment for the great service which providential indications appear to have imposed upon it.

HAMMA DIVINITY SCHOOL, SPRINGFIELD, OHIO

Founded 1845

The Rev. Rees Edgar Tulloss, D.D., Ph.D., LL.D., *President*

The Rev. Loyal Herbert Larimer, D.D., *Dean*

The Faculty. The faculty is composed of six full-time professors. Four others are listed as lecturers and professors, dividing their time between the College and the Seminary.

Professor Henry Carl Offerman, M.A., acting professor in the New Testament Department for the past two years, resigned May 1, 1928, to complete his work for the doctor's degree at Union Theological Seminary. Professor Offerman is an accomplished New Testament scholar. He has served Hamma Divinity School faithfully and efficiently. In his going from us we record our deep appreciation of his excellent contribution of scholarship and inspiration to our school.

Professor Allen Oliver Becker, D.D., for the past five years Professor of Christian Missions, giving courses in both the Seminary and College, has resigned to accept a call to a pastorate. Professor Becker's knowledge of Christian Missions, his zealous interest in the missionary work of the Church, to which he had given twelve years of service in India, together with his inspiring Christian character, made him one of the most influential members of the faculty. We record our deep loss as a school in his resignation.

Professor Carl Herman Oscar Schneider, Ph.D., special lecturer on philosophy of Religion and Exegesis for the past two years is engaged as special lecturer in institutions of Australia during the summer of 1928. Dr. Schneider has received a call to the Professorship of New Testament Exegesis in the University of Riga. He has also been offered a position in Wittenberg College and Hamma Divinity School. He is holding his decision in abeyance for some months. In event of his acceptance he will return to our Seminary for the second semester of 1928-29. Dr. Schneider is a distinguished scholar, with clear and hearty grasp of Evangelical doctrine. We are hoping for his decision to return to our school.

Professor John Frederick Krueger, D.D., Ph.D., LL.D., has accepted a call to a professorship in Practical Theology, comprising Homiletics, Liturgics, and Church Polity, and will assume his work at the beginning of the school year 1928-29. Dr. Krueger's attainments as scholar, his experience as educator, school administrator, and missionary to China, are known to the Church at large. We are happy in his coming. The courses in Christian Missions will be given by Dr. Krueger.

A professor for the New Testament Department will be chosen as soon as possible; in the meantime the work has been temporarily provided for. Preliminary steps have been taken also toward the securing of a professor specially trained in English and American literature in its relation to religious life and thought.

The Students. The enrollment for the past year was sixty-four resident students and fifteen correspondence students, making a total of seventy-nine. Twenty-seven graduated in the last class. All of this class were college graduates with the exception of one. These men had calls prior to their graduation. An average annual enrollment of fifty to sixty students at Hamma Divinity School can be maintained, and is probably what can be expected from the churches of her territory. Ninety-five per cent of our Seminary students have taken their college work at Wittenberg.

Aims and Methods. Hamma Divinity School holds clearly that its chief function is to prepare men as pastors for the churches. All departments of instruction co-operate towards this end. Students with special ability and desire for teaching in the schools of the Church are encouraged to pursue graduate work.

Requirements for admission are being advanced. Care is given to encourage only those who have the qualities of personal and spiritual fitness. The college faculty, together with the Religious Work Department of the College, gives excellent help to the Seminary in encouraging young men to consider the ministry. The co-operation of the Seminary and College faculties in stimulating a proper interest among students for the work of the ministry is helpful to the Seminary.

With the increased endowment and added equipment which we feel sure the 1930 campaign will furnish us, Hamma Divinity School will be able to serve the Church with increasing numbers of well-trained young men imbued with devotion to the progressive work of the Lutheran Church. Courses offered, methods of instruction employed, the calling of new men to the faculty, are all determined upon for the advancement of the Church.

THE LUTHERAN THEOLOGICAL SEMINARY AT PHILADELPHIA

Founded 1864

The Rev. Charles M. Jacobs. D.D., *President*

The Philadelphia Seminary was founded in 1864 by the Ministerium of Pennsylvania. The Charter of the Seminary provides that its professors must be elected by that Synod and not less than two-thirds of its Board of Directors must be elected by the same Synod. The remaining one-third of the Board of Directors may be elected by such other Synods as receive that right from the Ministerium of Pennsylvania. At the present time the New York Ministerium, the New York and New England Synod and the Pittsburgh Synod participate in the management of the Seminary through the election of four directors each. The total number of directors is thirty-six.

During the academic year 1927-28 the number of students in the Seminary reached the highest point in its history. The enrollment of undergraduates was eighty-eight and of graduate students twenty-five, making a total enrollment of 113. In the preceding year the number of undergraduate students was seventy-six and of graduate students fifteen, making a total of ninety-one. The advance enrollment for 1928-29 indicates that the number of undergraduate students will be larger than in the year just closed.

The faculty of the Seminary consists of seven professors, four instructors and two teaching fellows. It was augmented in 1927-28 by three special lecturers,—Prof. A. R. Wentz of the Gettysburg Seminary, giving a course in American Church History, and Dr. E. T. Horn and Rev. H. H. Sipes, Jr., giving a course in Foreign Missions.

In November, 1927, the Rev. Charles M. Jacobs, D.D., was elected President of the Seminary to succeed his father, the Rev. Henry Eyster Jacobs, D.D., LL.D., who had resigned the Presidency in the preceding year. Dr. C. M. Jacobs was inaugurated April 22, 1927.

At about the same time the Rev. F. W. Friday was elected by the Board to be Secretary and Registrar in charge of the executive office.

In May, 1928, the Board of Directors approved the report of the Committee on Seminary Expansion and resolved to ask the Church in 1930 for funds with which to remove deficits, complete endowments and erect new buildings. The total amount asked will be $1,200,000.00.

BREKLUM-KROPP SEMINARY

A. Theological Department—Kropp

W. Ernst Rohnert, D.D., Director

The American trip of the director at the beginning of the biennium just closed furnished inspiration, new zeal and new points of view for the work of our Seminary.

Some changes occurred in the faculty. Pastor Paul Puls, who taught in the Seminary twenty-five years ago, replaced Pastor Hansen in the fall of 1926. Pastor Dr. Hardeland, overburdened with duties, relinquished his chair of the Old Testament in February, 1927. Pastor Johannes Groening of Schleswig took his place. Dr. Hardeland at Easter, 1928, rejoined the faculty and took over New Testament lectures. In addition to these the director, Dr. Rohnert, and Miss Elizabeth Sager, teacher of English, constitute the faculty.

The number of students in 1926 was eighteen; 1927, twenty-three; 1928, twenty-seven. Three of these go to seminaries of the United Lutheran Church this fall. For a few months John W. Kirsch of Jersey City, son of a Kropp graduate, was enrolled as a student.

Since August, 1926, six students were graduated. To this number should be added two Kropp graduates of former years, Hans Moertelmeyer and Eugen Buehler who in 1927 entered the Manitoba Synod. Although neither was lawfully bound to enter the service of the United Lutheran Church, they gave us pleasure by doing so entirely of their own accord and are enjoying their ministry in this Church. All our present students have obligated themselves to enter the service of the United Lutheran Church. The number of candidates which we shall be able to furnish the United Lutheran Church from 1929 on will be measurably larger than that of late years, as all our classes have had a gratifying increase in numbers.

The deportment and spirit of our students were on the whole satisfactory. We are zealous to keep out undesirable elements and when they creep in, to weed them out speedily. The latter was done in two cases; in two other cases manifestly unfit men left of their own accord.

Co-operation with Breklum continued in closest harmony. The Kropp students, under the leadership of the director, were enthusiastic participants in the celebration of the silver anniversary of Director Petersen of Breklum, in January, 1928.

The American trip of the Director and his participation in the Convention of the United Lutheran Church at Richmond, above all his personal discussions with the responsible authorities of the Church, brought valuable results. They served to bring clarity into the questions hitherto not sufficiently clear concerning the relation of the Breklum-Kropp Seminary to the United Lutheran Church, and thus essentially improved the conditions necessary for the successful work of our Seminary for the Church. The Director conceived a deep love for the United Lutheran Church on this trip. He was impressed with the greatness of its work and the quality of its leaders. His desire to serve this Church was strengthened. The privilege accorded him of visiting the Seminaries of the Church and of grasping the hands and seeing the work of the pastors sent out from Kropp and Breklum will have valuable results in the future.

Our financial condition remains a difficult one. But we need to emphasize here, however, that the Board of Education as well as the Board of American Missions kept their promise of support most loyally, for which we herewith desire to express our warmest gratitude. However, we must labor unceasingly to induce the pastors who have come from Breklum-Kropp to make it their business annually to gather sufficient additional contributions. Along with this our express endeavor is, to secure larger gifts from Germany. The Board of the Breklum-Kropp Seminary will employ every effort to reach this goal. We are convinced that the further development of our Seminary and therefore its increased efficiency will come as soon as its financial basis is more secure.

Our ardent aspiration is honestly to serve the United Lutheran Church with all our powers. We are grateful if the Church will recognize this. For it is evident to every one familiar with the conditions, that in view of the great increase of German emigration to America and especially to Canada, the United Lutheran Church cannot dispense with the assistance given by our Seminary. Our specific and great task is to provide pastors of German blood for the Lutheran immigrants from the Old World and for the mission congregations to be organized among them, who are willing for Christ's sake to become loyal Americans and loyal Canadians. May God help us joyfully to give ourselves without stint to the fulfilling of this task. May He also cause the brothers and sisters of the United Lutheran Church to be willing to continue their assistance in this endeavor. May He bless the beloved United Lutheran Church and our service for it.

B. The Proseminary in Breklum
Pastor Fr. Petersen, Director

In presenting our biennial report to the United Lutheran Church we cannot do so without the expression of genuine and hearty thanks for the constant and regular assistance which has been given us by the Board of Education. To this expression of gratitude we would humbly add a request for the continuance of this assistance for our institutions and thus assure the possibility of giving the pre-theological training to young men destined for the ministry within the United Lutheran Church.

In correspondence with our specific task, we stress the study of the foreign languages, Latin, Greek, English, and Hebrew. We also emphasize a thorough course on the Bible and the History of Literature, including American literature. We have likewise sought to widen and deepen the knowledge of our students in the other prescribed courses.

The instruction was largely in the hands of the director. Inspector Pohl of the Breklum Mission gave instruction in English and the Catechism. Pastor Pacholke gave the courses in Bible, History of Literature, German Composition, Elocution and Latin. Pro-Rector Nielsen of the Mission Seminary taught Geography and Mathematics.

During the biennium eleven students were graduated and entered Kropp. The present enrollment is twenty-four.

The assistance given by the Board of Education and the Board of American Missions must be regarded as the financial basis of our work. With the aid of contributions from our friends in Germany and former Breklum students, from tuition and board paid by our students, and from the general collection in all the churches of the Schleswig-Holstein "Landeskirche," we have been able to carry on our work. We regret that we had to strain our credit at times, yet the debts which we were compelled to contract and which remain unpaid were not so pressing as to compel a retrenchment of our operations.

Our work receives more recognition than formerly in the Schleswig-Holstein "Landeskirche." The General Synod of that Church at Rendsburg authorized an annual collection, obligatory for all the congregations, for the years 1927-1930. The Synod of the Provostship Husum last year made an appropriation for the Breklum institution for the first time. At the twenty-fifth anniversary of the director many friends gathered from far and near and the bishop of Schleswig sent a lengthy telegram of congratulation.

With grateful hearts we look unto the Lord who has blessed us and has signally confessed Himself to our work, and we acknowledge with gratefulness the aid of our friends and especially the United Lutheran Church, which has made it possible to carry on our work during the past biennium. We are ready to continue to serve with gladness Him, who is our supreme Lord, and the United Lutheran Church, and we pray God that He may graciously bless our labors.

WESTERN THEOLOGICAL SEMINARY, FREMONT, NEBR.

Founded 1887

The Rev. Horace F. Martin, D.D., Ph.D., *President*
The Rev. Holmes Dysinger, D.D., LL.D., *Dean*

Two new courses were added to the Seminary curriculum during the last biennium, the one in Religious Education and the other for the training of Christian Workers. The former has special relation to the educational program of the congregation for the training of the young in the Christian life and activities of the Church, and aims at qualifying the young pastor for organizing and putting into successful operation a worth while and efficient educational program in his parish. The latter has as its objective the training of those who do not contemplate entering the active ministry, but who wish to equip themselves for efficient service as missionaries, parish workers, and Sunday school teachers and officers of the Church.

The enrollment for the first year of the biennium was seventeen, including two non-resident undergraduates. That of the second year of the biennium was sixteen, including four non-resident graduate students. Two of the latter are pursuing courses for advanced degrees.

Several changes have been made in the personnel of the faculty and the distribution of the work during the last two years. Owing to the illness of Dr. R. L. Patterson, Dr. W. F. Rangeler, who entered upon his duties as professor of Church History and Pastoral Theology at the beginning of the Seminary year 1926-27, was transferred to the Department of Practical Theology and English Bible the last year of the biennium. Professor James J. Raun of Midland College taught Church History during the last year. Since Dr. Patterson's continued illness has necessitated the severing of his connection with the institution, this arrangement is to be continued for the year 1928-29.

Dr. C. H. B. Lewis of the Parish Board of the United Lutheran Church has rendered excellent service as head of the department of Religious Education in the Seminary. The institution is to have the benefit of his continued assistance in this department the coming year.

CHICAGO SEMINARY, MAYWOOD, ILLINOIS

Founded 1891

The Rev. L. Franklin Gruber, D.D., LL.D., *President*

This institution was founded by the former General Council. It was first located in Chicago, on Addison Street on the north side. Its corporate title therefore is—"The Theological Seminary of the Evangelical Lutheran Church at Chicago, Illinois." In 1910 it was removed to its present beautiful location in Maywood, a western suburb eleven miles from Lake Michigan. Its physical equipment consists of eleven modern brick buildings, fifteen acres of ground, conservatively valued at a half million dollars.

The Seminary has seven full professorships for the departments of Systematic Theology, New Testament Theology, Old Testament Theology, Historical Theology, Practical Theology, Missions, and English Bible. It has also a widely known special instructor in Oratory and the Art of Expression. During the year a number of lectures and addresses are delivered by various Church officials and specialists and by other eminent churchmen.

Two courses of instruction are offered: A Standard Course, leading under certain requirements to the degree of B.D.; and an English Course, leading to the diploma of graduation. A Post-Graduate Course in residence is offered to graduates of Theological Seminaries, leading under special requirements to advanced degrees. During the year 1927-28 the following courses were given: Church History, History of Religions, Religious Education, English Bible, Apologetics, Archaeology and the Bible, and Greek New Testament. A number of special courses are given also for extra-mural students, to guide pastors and teachers in the continuation of their studies.

The Seminary Library consists of nearly twenty thousand volumes, temporarily housed on the second floor of the Administration Building until a modern Library Building can be erected. There is also a large reference library and reading room, containing the leading theological and other periodicals.

An interest-bearing fund of $37,000 has been provided to aid needy students, not more than $100 going to one student at a time. During the past year twenty-two students were assisted from this fund.

During the year 1927-28 the total enrollment numbered 119 students. Of these two were special students, nine were Juniors, seventeen were Middlers, sixteen were Seniors, ten were graduate students in residence, and sixty-five were extra-mural students. The resident students came from eleven States and Canada and represented forty-two different institutions of learning, eight of them American and foreign universities. Of the sixteen Seniors, ten received the B.D. degree.

The Seminary has had four presidents: The Rev. Prof. Revere F. Weidner, D.D., LL.D.; the Rev. Prof. Elmer F. Krauss, D.D.; the Rev. Prof. John E. Whittaker, D.D., LL.D.; and the president incumbent, who assumed charge in 1927.

The movement to put Chicago Seminary under more direct synodical control is now well under way, several of the contiguous Synods having already taken action to assume their part of this program, and having their official representatives on the Board of Directors.

Several additional buildings are still needed, among them a modern Library Building. A greatly increased endowment is also needed, the present $225,000 working endowment being wholly inadequate. This necessary endowment it is hoped will be acquired during the Educational Year of 1930.

A revision of the curriculum is being arranged and the aim is to attain such a standard, both for entrance and for graduation, as will be the equal of the best of the Theological Seminaries in the country.

THE PACIFIC THEOLOGICAL SEMINARY, SEATTLE, WASHINGTON

Founded 1911

The Rev. J. C. Kunzmann, D.D., *President*

For 1,900 miles from Minneapolis to the Pacific Coast and for 5,200 by the route of travel from the southern border of California to the northern border of Alaska, the Pacific Theological Seminary is the only Lutheran institution to prepare a native ministry. In this important section, the institution is handicapped by the fact that the Pacific Synod is the smallest Synod in our Lutheran Church with sufficient heroism to undertake such a great task and is the least able financially to carry it to success. It is surrounded by a divided Lutheranism whose only hope of union is the raising of a native ministry.

For this important task, the finely located fourteen-acre tract near the Washington State University, with two frame buildings and three portables (a nine-room house made to answer as administration building, refectory, chapel, library and classrooms), and two professors, the one the traveling and travailing president for finances, the other the encumbered president of the Synod, are surely an inadequate equipment. That the institution has been able to hold the field and make progress in spite of handicaps is due to God's special providence and indicates the great possibilities of the institution with adequate facilities. We are compelled to mark time and grow slowly under present conditions, and yet that growth has been remarkable under our circumstances.

The Pacific Seminary should be equipped for the work of our Church in this immense and rapidly populating section and nothing will enable that to be done except largely increased funds. A program of buildings has been adopted with the collaboration of the United Lutheran Church Committee on Church Architecture. Its first unit, the dormitory building, is to be used as a general building until our assured growth shall demand the erection of the others. In addition to furnishing better facilities for chapel, library, classrooms, administration quarters, it will enable the institution to house the young men who take their college course in the nearby State University, as well as to provide for our seminarians. As the beautiful suburb, Laurelhurst, round about our Seminary, is changing from farm lands and vacant lots to comfortable dwellings, our grounds must be graded and landscaped, and walks and drives laid in harmony with its surroundings. According to the estimates of the architect, this will require the sum of $130,000. As neither our small constituency nor the income of the Board of Education can furnish us the means to salary an adequate teaching and working force, endowments must be secured.

Many suggestions have been made to us by interested pastors and laymen, and we hope and pray that a conference of the authorities of our Church will be held and that plans will be adopted in view of the approaching year 1930, which is to provide the means for adequate equipment for all our institutions, to finally furnish the Lone Seminary in the West with such an equipment as the importance, the present and growing possibilities of the mighty West require. Our prospects for larger attendance in the coming year and in the years to come are excellent. With a reasonable equipment the results will bring joy to the saints on earth and in heaven.

MARTIN LUTHER SEMINARY, LINCOLN, NEBRASKA

Founded 1913

Rev. G. H. Michelmann, D.D., *President*

This seminary was founded and is supported by the German Evangelical Lutheran Synod of Nebraska with the primary purpose to supply a well-trained bi-lingual ministry for the territory of synod. But at the same time it aims to serve the Church as a whole, and several of its graduates are serving parishes in eastern synods and as far south as Texas.

The faculty of last year consisted of four teachers, Rev. G. H. Michelmann, D.D., Rev. O. W. Heick, A.M., Prof. A. Alexis, Ph.D., and Rev. A. Th. Mikkelsen, who as pastor of Martin Luther congregation, aided the professors of the Seminary by teaching English Bible, Catechetics and

Apologetics. At the end of the school year Dr. Michelmann was taken ill and will not be able to resume his work in the coming scholastic year. Dr. Michelmann is a man of outstanding character and great abilities who was always active in the interest of the institution and the Church as a whole. Prof. O. W. Heick, A.M., was appointed Acting Dean for the summer months. Rev. J. Huebner, S.T.M., San Bernadino, California, has been elected to succeed Rev. Mikkelsen as pastor and professor for the English subjects in the theological department.

The student body for 1927-28 numbered fourteen, two of whom graduated. All students with the exception of three were natives of Nebraska and Texas.

The entrance requirements for the theological department is full college education. A pre-theological course in the pro-seminary lasting from two to five years must be pursued by those who do not meet the above requirement.

The Seminary offers only the standard course which leads to the B.D., provided the student holds the A.B. from a college or its equivalent, and his scholastic standard is at least eighty-five. All other students have to take the full academic course for which a working knowledge of Greek, Hebrew and Latin is required.

We take this opportunity to express our appreciation for the financial aid which the Seminary has received from the Board of Education. And we also gratefully acknowledge that several of our students are beneficiaries of the Board of American Missions to which Board after graduation they are pledged.

As the only bi-lingual seminary within the United Lutheran Church south of the Canadian line supplying with ministers the churches in the transition period from German to English, Martin Luther Seminary has a missionary task which no other institution can fill.

NORTHWESTERN THEOLOGICAL SEMINARY, MINNEAPOLIS, MINN.

Founded 1921

The Rev. Joseph Stump, D.D., LL.D., L.H.D., *President*

The Seminary, founded, supported and controlled by the Synod of the Northwest, has greatly prospered during the biennium. The average attendance has been thirty-two. A class of eight was graduated in 1927 and a class of fourteen in 1928. The institution has four professors, one full-time instructor and two part-time instructors. It offers a Greek and Hebrew course and an all-English course for college graduates. It also conducts correspondence courses for pastors. It is free of debt, has a satisfactory plant and equipment, an endowment fund of $18,000, a library of four thousand volumes, and endowment pledges of over $100,000. It serves the Northwest territory between Lake Michigan and the Rocky Mountains, a distance of 1,700 miles.

II. COLLEGES

GETTYSBURG COLLEGE, PENNSYLVANIA

Founded 1832.

The Rev. Henry W. A. Hanson, D.D., LL.D., President.

During the past two years Gettysburg College has made encouraging progress in the development of an adequate physical equipment. Extensive changes have been made on the campus; improved roads have been installed; approximately three hundred trees have been planted; a new gymnasium and a new science hall have been dedicated.

The College has been most fortunate in receiving a gift which will cover the cost of a new library building. Extensive changes will be made in Gladfelter Hall, which, for fifty years, has served as the main recitation hall of the college. This building will now be remodeled into a modern recitation building. The funds for the project have already been provided. The old gymnasium, which has stood for three-quarters of a century, will be remodeled into an administration building.

All of the plans of the college are converging into a worthy celebration of the one hundredth anniversary of the college in 1932. The present building program, as adopted three years ago, will be completed in time for the celebration.

Gettysburg College is glad to report very substantial additions to its library. Through liberal gifts from loyal friends four thousand volumes have been added to the library during the last two years. In addition to this a fund of $6,000 has been set aside for the purchase of books during the coming two years.

In order to promote the highest possible standard of work on the part of the faculty, Gettysburg College has, during the past year, adopted a number of important features:

(1) The Sabbatic year has been adopted. Each professor is given a leave of absence covering one semester on full salary for foreign travel or advanced study.

(2) Each professor, during the course of the year, is sent as a visitor to one or more institutions in order to obtain first hand information on methods and objectives in his own department. The cost of this visitation is borne by Gettysburg College.

(3) A pension system has been adopted covering all members of the faculty whose period of service with the institution covers twenty years or more.

In an effort to promote a closer relationship between the students and the homes from which they come, Gettysburg College inaugurated a Father's Day and a Mother's Day. Each year witnesses a broadening of the influence of these two occasions on the life of the student body.

The college has been most fortunate in bringing to its campus outstanding religious leaders of our country.

A prominent feature in the work of Gettysburg College is the freshman program. The first two months on the college campus are probably the most important in the entire college course. The freshmen are brought to the campus a week before the formal opening of college. This week is devoted entirely to the building up of correct ideals and attitudes to college life and opportunities. The week is made all the more effective because of the fact that twelve seniors are selected to co-operate with the faculty in this week of intensive freshman instruction. During the entire freshman year the Orientation course aims to help the freshmen develop correct habits of life and thought. There is, perhaps, no single feature in the life of the college which has exerted more helpful influence than this carefully developed program covering the freshman year.

The enrollment for the year 1927-28 was 587 men and 76 women.

The students for the ministry number 105.

The faculty consists of fifty members.

The physical equipment of the college is valued at $1,500,000.

The interest bearing endowment is $800,000.

WITTENBERG COLLEGE, SPRINGFIELD, OHIO

Founded 1845.

The Rev. Rees Edgar Tulloss, D.D., Ph.D., LL.D., President.

New Buildings: The Chemistry Psychology Building, a four-story fire-proof building, was completed and equipped at a cost of $250,000. The building was dedicated on October 21, 1927, in the presence of a distinguished gathering comprising over five hundred of the leading psychologists and chemists of America. Blair Hall, designed to house the Department of Education and the model training school, was erected at a cost of $156,000 and was dedicated November 7, 1927, in connection with the holding of an educational conference.

The addition of these two buildings has greatly enlarged the class room and laboratory space available for the use of students.

In May and June, 1928, a successful campaign was carried on in Springfield, Ohio, for $300,000, for the erection of a Physical Education and Health Building. The work of erection will be begun this fall. It is hoped to have at least a portion of the building ready for use at the beginning of school in September, 1929.

Enrollment. The increase in enrollment has continued. In the College of Liberal Arts, the total registration reached 1,003 for the year 1927-28, as against a total of 398 eight years ago. The enrollment in the various special schools has continued to increase. The grand total of all students at the institution during the last year was 2,487.

In view of the continuing increase in enrollment in the College of Liberal Arts, extended study has been given to the question of limitation of the enrollment. After a complete discussion of all phases of the problem formal action was taken by the Board limiting the new entrants to the freshman class to 350. This will result in a limitation of the student body in the College of Liberal Arts to about 1,000 students. The enrollment now to be permitted will take ample care of the young people of the Church on Wittenberg territory and will permit the acceptance of a limited number of other high grade students.

During the biennium degrees have been awarded as follows:

	1927	1928
Bachelor of Arts	141	144
Bachelor of Music	4	3
Bachelor of Divinity	10	22
Master of Arts	7	5
Honorary degrees were granted as follows:		
Doctor of Divinity	6	5
Litt.D.	1	......
Doctor of Laws	1	2
Master of Arts	......	1

Faculty. The teaching staff has now reached a total of eighty-four, of whom about 43 per cent have the degree of Ph.D. or its equivalent as specified by the accrediting associations. This percentage is equalled by only a few colleges of the country. A recently published study of the training and teaching experience of the faculty members gives a list of forty outstanding universities at which the members of the staff have been trained, and twenty-nine internationally known universities and colleges at which the members of the Wittenberg staff have previously taught. This list includes Berlin, Goettingen, Grenoble, Leipzig and Oslo Universities abroad, and such American institutions as Chicago, Harvard, Illinois, Iowa, Johns Hopkins, Michigan, Minnesota, Ohio, Pennsylvania.

Accrediting. Wittenberg continues to hold the "Class A" rating on the University of Illinois list, and has full accrediting by the Association of American Universities and the Association of American University Women.

Tuition and Student Aid. The tuition has been set at $225 for the current year and $250 beginning September, 1929. Student aid has been increased in proportion to increase in tuition. The expenditures on this account for 1926-27 were $31,000 and for 1927-28 $38,000.

New Projects. Beginning with September, 1928, a comprehensive teacher training project has been in operation. In co-operation with the Springfield Public School System, a model training school has been established upon the Wittenberg Campus, and arrangements have been made for practice-teaching in the Junior High Schools of Springfield. This enables Wittenberg to give a teacher-training service equal to that found anywhere.

The Degree of Bachelor of Science in Education for those specializing in this field has been authorized by the Board. Wittenberg is the only Liberal Arts College in Ohio operating its own training school.

In Dayton, Ohio, the extension courses have largely increased in enrollment. In co-operation with the Dayton Y. M. C. A. a special Extension School offering Junior College Courses has been inaugurated.

The Radio Station, 256.3 meters, 1,170 kilocycles, is operating with increased power (500 watts). Announcements of the monthly programs are mailed to all pastors in Wittenberg territory. A regular feature is the comment upon the Sunday School Lesson which is given on each Friday evening.

Academy. After a service extending over a period of 82 years, the Wittenberg Academy has been discontinued. Adequate High School opportunities provided by local communities seem to obviate the necessity for continuing a school of this kind. Annual deficits in current operation could no longer be justified on the basis of a special service to a very limited group. Friends of the Academy will note with regret the cessation of its work, but will concede the adequacy of the reasons for its discontinuance.

CARTHAGE COLLEGE, CARTHAGE, ILLINOIS

Founded at Hillsboro 1846, Carthage 1870

The Rev. N. J. Gould Wickey, Ph.D., *President*

The biennium has witnessed four significant accomplishments:

1. There has been the maintenance of a high spiritual atmosphere. We believe there must be a direct relation between the teaching of religion and the practice of religion on the campus. No college is Christian merely because it offers courses in Bible and Religious Education. According to those who have been at Carthage many years, the spiritual life of the college has never been higher. Educators are speaking today of "the child fit for college." Carthage believes the time has come when we must speak of the college fit for the child.

2. We have rendered a distinct service to the Church. Outstanding missionaries of recent years are graduates of Carthage. At present 40 per cent of our boys and 20 per cent of the whole student body are preparing for definite church service. Fifty-five per cent of our students are Lutherans. A college must be true to its birthright.

3. The Board of Trustees have had the first reading of a new constitution. Constitutions of a former generation are inadequate today. Carthage is keeping pace with recent developments in college administration.

4. We met the conditions of the offer of the General Education Board in one of the most unique college campaigns ever conducted. We had the obstacles of criticisms, synods not allowing a total church campaign—only

selected list of givers, rain and floods, crop failures, the approaching Ministerial Pension Fund Campaign, the fact that we had to obtain the cash. Notwithstanding these difficulties we went over the top on February 3, 1928. So-called expert campaign directors declare that a successful campaign needs 20 to 35 per cent large gifts. Our campaign was successful with more than 90 per cent of the gifts in sums of $50 and less. The General Education Board gave us $175,000. Our Endowment Funds, not including personal notes and annuities, now total $850,000.

Besides the above major accomplishments, the Church will be interested to learn of the following:

1. The formation of a Social Committee to plan all-college functions each month. We believe the social life of the student must be supervised and constructive.

2. The establishment of a Carthage College News Bureau, which secures nationwide publicity for the college.

3. The organization of a Placement Bureau to serve students and alumni, especially those interested in the teaching profession. Students are also assisted to secure positions while attending college.

4. The formation of a college band.

5. The organization of an "a capella" choir,—the only one in the United Lutheran Church in America.

6. The establishment of a Department of Agriculture, the only one in the colleges of the United Lutheran Church.

7. The establishment of two new professorships:
   The Chicago Lutheran Professorship of Religious Education.
   The William Keller Frick Memorial Professorship of Bible.

With profound regret we record the death of Dean Anna Letta Simmons, one of the outstanding Lutheran women of the middle west. She served the college for fourteen years efficiently and sacrificingly. Her influence was wide and deep, her contacts many, her work goes on.

"No work begun shall ever pause for death."

ROANOKE COLLEGE, SALEM, VIRGINIA

Founded 1853

The Rev. Charles J. Smith, D.D., *President*

The enrollment for the Session of 1927-28 was 480. Of this number 261 were registered for the regular session and 219 for the summer courses. These students came from fifteen different states and one foreign country.

The work of the session was satisfactory from the standpoint of both faculty and students. (Forty-one young men received their degrees.) The number of failures was smaller than usual, due to the careful personnel work done in the offices of the deans.

During the past biennium, the college has completed the collection of $500,000 for additional endowment and has celebrated most happily the 75th anniversary of its founding.

The immediate projects now pending are those of erecting four new buildings and adding another half million dollars to the endowment funds. Mr. Dennis B. Welsh has been elected Treasurer of the Board of Trustees and assigned the duties of financial oversight including the gathering of funds to complete the above-mentioned projects.

With faith and courage Roanoke College looks forward to the best years of its history.

THE COLLEGIATE INSTITUTE, MOUNT PLEASANT, NORTH CAROLINA

Founded 1854

Prof. G. F. McAllister, A. M., *Principal*

The Collegiate Institute has made steady progress during the past biennium. The standards have been raised and graduates are accorded favorable rating by higher institutions. Thanks to the generosity of the late J. S. Efird, valuable additions have been made to the scientific apparatus and the laboratories have been brought up to date.

Institute men continue to heed the call to the Gospel Ministry. A number of new commitments were made by students the past session. Twenty-one young people graduated during the biennium and eight of these have the Gospel Ministry in view.

Notwithstanding marked improvements in our plant within very recent years, there is need for still further additions to the physical equipment and to the endowment. Persons of means are known to be considering substantial gifts to the Collegiate Institute, and it is hoped that their early commitments will lend impetus to the financial campaign planned by the Board of Trustees for the year 1930.

NEWBERRY COLLEGE, NEWBERRY, SOUTH CAROLINA
(Including Summerland)

Founded 1856

S. J. Derrick, LL.D., *President*

At the annual meeting of the board of trustees of Newberry College held recently, three matters of especial importance were adopted.

The standing committee was authorized to call to its assistance a committee of citizens of Newberry to assist in raising a fund for the renovating and remodeling of Smeltzer Hall in accordance with plans submitted by J. B. Urquhart, architect. The board believes that the local people have obligations above others, because of the many advantages they enjoy by having Newberry College in their community.

A special committee was appointed to work out a plan whereby the Synod of Georgia may become joint owner with the Synod of South Carolina of Newberry College. This plan is to be submitted for approval to the two Synods.

The year 1930 has been set apart by the United Lutheran Church in America for a campaign to increase the resources of the colleges and seminaries of the Church, each local synod to work for its own college.

The board therefore petitions the Synods of South Carolina and Georgia at their meetings next winter to set up a campaign for Newberry College.

SUSQUEHANNA UNIVERSITY, SELINSGROVE, PENNSYLVANIA

Liberal Arts and Theological Seminary

Founded 1858

The Rev. G. Morris Smith, A.M., D.D., *President*

During the academic year 1927-28 there was a total enrollment of 896. In the College of Liberal Arts there were 417. The rest are to be classified as students of Divinity, students in the Conservatory of Music, students in Expression, and Summer Session students.

The most conspicuous addition to Susquehanna's equipment during the past year has been the erection of the first unit of a new library, which was dedicated in June, 1928.

Death came to Dr. Charles T. Aikens on June 21, 1927. Dr. Aikens was president for almost 22 years. He guided the college during very difficult days and the remarkable growth of the institution in recent years is a monument to his business sagacity and genial spirit.

His successor is Dr. G. Morris Smith and the college looks forward under his administration to a new era of attainment.

During the last session the college was efficiently guided by Dr. Jacob Diehl, Executive Representative of the Board of Trustees.

MUHLENBERG COLLEGE, ALLENTOWN, PENNSYLVANIA

Founded 1867

The Rev. J. A. W. Haas, D.D., LL.D., *President*

During the biennium 1926-28 Muhlenberg College has completed its Science Building at a cost of $475,000, and it expects this fall to complete its library at a cost of $400,000. Of the million dollars subscribed in 1924, there has been collected up to the time of this report $815,000. The college has been compelled to assume a temporary debt of $300,000.

To meet the interest on the debt the Ministerium of Pennsylvania has made an annual appropriation of $15,000. Besides the Ministerium pays $3,000 for a professorship in religion.

Within the next few years the college expects to build a church for which through the will of Annie S. Hartzell there will be available $125,000. It will be necessary also to erect a gymnasium.

The number of students in 1927-28 was 476 and it appears that the limit of 500 set for the Fall of 1928 will be reached.

In the Preparatory School the college took care of 200 students.

The graduating class of this year, including the Fall College Day, will number 112. The teachers' courses had an enrollment of 850 in the winter and 383 in the summer. This makes a total enrollment of 1909.

The college has in its student body over eighty students preparing for the ministry.

Thiel College, Greenville, Pennsylvania

Founded 1870

The Rev. E. Clyde Xander, D.D., *President*

The progress of Thiel College has gone on apace. This has been general, but especially noticeable in the new confidence and perspective that is in evidence on the Campus, in the borough of Greenville, and throughout the territory of the Pittsburgh Synod.

Noteworthy work was accomplished by Rev. B. H. Pershing, who was acting president until September, 1927. Professor Pershing was interested in high scholastic standards and with the help of his co-workers was able to have Thiel accredited with the large universities throughout the East. This aim has not been omitted from the present administration. Entrance requirements have been made a little more rigid and a closer check-up has been made on the work of the student.

One of the outstanding events of the college year of 1927-28 was a special service held to honor the students who had attained a quotient of 3.25 in their work for the previous semester. President Vestling of Olivet College gave the address for the occasion.

The enrollment for the last biennium shows an increase over former years. The attendance for 1927-28 was greatly influenced by the financial depression, as it affected the coal industry in Western Pennsylvania. The Lutheran students constitute 40 per cent of the entire student body. The increasing interest manifest in the Pittsburgh Synod argues that this percentage will be on the increase.

Eight additional members were added to the faculty in the Fall of 1927. This places Thiel in a position to offer a fine type of service to her students on the basis of the number of faculty members in relation to the number of students. The Department of Religious Education, recently established and directed by Prof. Ralph D. Heim, has rendered splendid service, especially to our pre-theological students. On the strength of our increased faculty, Thiel has recently been recognized by the American Association of University Women. This should help attract many young women to Thiel who formerly sought other institutions of such rating.

The financial support of the college by the Pittsburgh Synod has been ever increasing. This last year (1927) the Pittsburgh Synod contributed $20,000 for the maintenance of her college. At the recent meeting of the Synod it was voted, "that the objective for the Educational Campaign for the year 1930 shall be $750,000 for Thiel College." In addition, the Board of Trustees has purposed to secure a new dormitory for women, costing approximately $125,000.

The graduating class of 1928 numbered 45 students, of whom six were pre-theological students. Thiel has made a fine contribution to the Church in regularly graduating a large number of men who have entered the Ministry. A local pastor of another denomination has just written to one of the young women of his faith, making inquiry about Thiel: "Thiel is ranked among Pennsylvania colleges as A No. 1. The atmosphere of the college is religious, which cannot be said of all colleges. I sent my children to Thiel—and I do not regret my action. Thiel is safe and sane and a good place to get an education." We aim to keep Thiel closely in accord with the spirit of the Church.

We anticipate the report of the recent Educational Survey made by the Board of Education. We are grateful to the Board for this outstanding piece of work, and hope that the unbiased presentation of the conditions and possibilities of our institution will make a tremendous appeal to the constituency of the college.

MARION JUNIOR COLLEGE, MARION, VIRGINIA

Founded 1873

The Rev. C. Brown Cox, A.M., D.D., *President*

The report of Marion Junior College for the biennium is one of normal operation, excepting the financial campaign which was conducted during 1927. The internal affairs of the college have moved pleasantly along established lines.

In 1927 the college made appeal to the constituency of the Lutheran Synod of Virginia for $100,000 for payment of building debts and beginning of endowment. The gross results of the campaign aggregated approximately $50,000 in cash and pledges. This amount is wholly inadequate to the needs. It develops, furthermore, that the pledges are very difficult to collect. Unless much more money can be secured from some source, the future of the college is endangered.

The problem of the college is wholly financial. The Lutheran Synod of Virginia has not given, and probably cannot give, sufficient funds to meet the needs. Unlike a college for men, an institution of the type of Marion cannot hope to draw considerable financial support from its alumnae. The fate of its many predecessors in the southern territory confronts the college, unless strong financial support can be secured outside of the Lutheran Synod of Virginia.

The Church cannot afford to let Marion die for lack of funds. Its long record of service and devotion to the Church merits sufficient support from Lutherans of wealth to perpetuate its usefulness.

Having given twelve years of service to the college, much of which was devoted to re-establishing it in the confidence of the Church and in preparing the way for an appeal to the Church, and this appeal having failed to receive adequate response. President Cox tendered his resignation in June, 1928.

WAGNER MEMORIAL LUTHERAN COLLEGE, STATEN ISLAND, NEW YORK

Founded 1883

The Rev. Charles F. Dapp, Ph.D., DD., *President*

Since the last meeting of the United Lutheran Church, Wagner College has made tremendous progress financially and educationally.

The Endowment Campaign of 1926 has already netted the college the sum of $475,000, and efforts are being continued to call in the last outstanding pledges.

A new combined administrative and recitation hall has just been authorized by the Ministerium of New York. This building will cost in the neighborhood of $275,000, and building operations will be well under way by the time the United Lutheran Church will be in session. This new building will occupy the key position in the comprehensive scheme of grouping and ground improvement prepared by the architects.

During the year two new men were added to the teaching staff of the college, thus bringing the number of full professors up to the number required by the Board of Regents of the State of New York.

By far the most outstanding proof of the progress of Wagner College was the recent action of the Board of Regents of New York in recognizing Wagner College as an institution of collegiate rank. This recognition puts the college on the list of approved colleges of New York State and permits the Board of Trustees of Wagner College to confer degrees. The class graduating in June was the first class to be awarded degrees, four men of the class who had completed the prescribed work being awarded the degree of Bachelor of Arts.

The first degree conferred by President Dapp in the name of the Board of Trustees was the honorary degree of Doctor of Divinity. The recipient of this degree was the Rev. Frederic Sutter, pastor of Trinity Lutheran Church, Stapleton, Staten Island, New York, and President of the Board of Trustees of Wagner College. This degree came to Dr. Sutter without his previous knowledge.

Following the practice in most colleges two distinct courses have now been inaugurated at Wagner College; namely, the Academic Course leading to the degree of Bachelor of Arts, and the Science Course leading to the degree of Bachelor of Science. All ministerial students must take the former course with its emphasis on the languages. It is expected that many pre-professional students will avail themselves of the opportunity of taking the Science Course. This course will enable future doctors and dentists to finish their education in seven years instead of eight years.

Last spring work on a fine new athletic field with a quarter mile cinder running track was begun and will be dedicated this fall. This field will be one of the finest in this section of New York and will give the students of Wagner College the opportunity of competing athletically with other schools of their class. A fine football team is now being developed.

Prospects are bright this fall for the largest enrollment in the history of the college. During the past year there were sixty-seven students enrolled in the college and forty-seven in the high school. Of these students eighty per cent have the Gospel Ministry as their objective.

Wagner College also elected a new president to take the place of the Rev. Dr. A. H. Holthusen, who resigned in 1927, in the person of the Rev. Charles F. Dapp, Ph.D., D.D., whose teaching and administrative experience was obtained in the West Philadelphia High School, the Philadelphia College of Pharmacy and Science, and the University of Pennsylvania.

MIDLAND COLLEGE, FREMONT, NEBRASKA

Founded 1887

The Rev. Horace F. Martin, D.D., Ph.D., *President*

The administration during the past two years has been confronted with many difficulties and problems. A decrease in the student body has reduced the expected income from tuition and fees. This decrease has been common to nearly all the church schools of the middle west. The University of Kansas reports a decrease in the student body the past year and the University of Nebraska reports a net increase of twenty students in all departments, although in previous years their net increase has been reported in hundreds. The increase in installment buying; the agricultural depression; the let-up of the after-war rush into colleges and universities, may account for the decrease in enrollment the past two years. Every effort is being made to increase the enrollment this fall.

Financial difficulties have been caused also by slow collections. The auditors reported that we should confidently expect about $42,000 to be paid in on the last installment of the Appeal Fund. Instead, only $17,000 was received. The auditors wrote off $90,000 as uncollectable from Appeal Fund pledges of 1924, although every effort is being made to collect all the pledges. Since Midland moved to Fremont in 1919, three campaigns for funds resulted in pledges approximating $625,000. Of this total more than $240,000 is delinquent.

Until income can be realized from the 1930 campaign, Midland must have help from the Church toward current expenses.

There are many things to cause encouragement. Midland is well located and has a fine Lutheran constituency that can be increased through mergers or federations with two other general bodies of Lutherans. The Nebraska Synod shows a net increase the past biennium of 5 per cent a year. The gifts from membership on the territory are increasing year by year.

The city of Fremont sends a large number of students to Midland. The business men of the city are supporting the school in a fine way.

A dormitory for women, known as Beegle Hall, has been completed at a cost of seventy thousand dollars. Five thousand was taken from the current expense fund to satisfy pressing bills and a note of $5,000 at the Fremont State Bank was signed by members of the Executive Committee to complete payment on the building. The latter obligation is the only debt against the dormitory.

Midland has been host to the Nebraska Church College Association, on which occasion more than two hundred delegates and visitors were in attendance. We also entertained the Nebraska Academy of Science, at which time one hundred and fifty delegates were present.

The debate teams took high rank in the state contests; our orators gave a good account of themselves in the three state contests in which they participated, securing two second places. The athletic teams made excellent records.

The largest class to be graduated from Midland, thirty-five, received B. A. and B. S. degrees. This class subscribed funds to pay the premium on a $5,000 life insurance policy taken out on the life of the president. The policy is a ten-year endowment to be applied to the endowment funds of the college.

We are heartily grateful for the financial help extended to us by the Board of Education and earnestly request that the amount previously contributed be doubled for the coming biennium.

LENIOR RHYNE COLLEGE

North Carolina

Founded 1891

The Rev. H. Brent Schaeffer, D.D., *President*

There are nine buildings on the campus, three erected during 1927-28, three old ones remodeled during 1928. $310,000 was expended on buildings, equipment and campus improvements, all of which with insurance was provided by friends of the college, with the exception of about $50,000.

The Endowment Fund of $450,000 should be increased to at least one-half million dollars. A portion of the above amount is involved in bank and mill failures and is not at this time yielding income.

Present property and resources total more than a million dollars.

Total enrollment for the biennium in regular college sessions was 598. Total enrollment in four summer terms was 1524.

North Carolina ranks Lenior Rhyne College as standard.

The prospects for the future are fairer than ever in the history of the college.

EVANGELICAL LUTHERAN SEMINARY OF CANADA

Waterloo College   Waterloo College School

Founded 1911

W. C. Froats, M.A., D. Paed., Dean

Efforts to secure a fourth seminary professor and a president for the institution proved unsuccessful throughout the year and the internal management of the institution continued to rest, as during the second semester of the previous year, in the hands of the executive heads of the three departments acting in consultation with an executive committee of the Board.

The Registrar, Dr. Willison, and the Dean, Dr. A. Potter, both resigned from our college. Their resignations became effective June 1, 1928. Dr. Willison served our institution as teacher for 17 years and Dr. Potter for five years. We regret very much to lose the services of these men. However, the Board is fortunate in securing Prof. W. C. Froats, M.A., D.Paed., Principal of the Morrisburg Collegiate Institute, as Dean and Professor of our college. Mr. Froats is a Lutheran and well qualified by experience and by his academic and pedagogical attainments for this position to which he is called by the Board.

Seventeen men were engaged during the past year in the work of instructing the students in the three departments of our institution. Of these seventeen, ten gave full time service; three were part-time men; and four were student assistants. Quite a number of these men taught in more than one department, so that while the total number employed in the institution was seventeen, the number on the various faculties were: Seminary 3, College 13, School 11.

At the close of this year eighty-nine students were in attendance at our institution. Here again it is to be noted that certain students, nine in number, are registered in more than one department. The Seminary enrollment was 14, College 41, School 43. Of the students enrolled in the college and school fifty-three are Lutherans.

The high educational standard of the institution is confirmed by the results of the last final examinations. All ten of our juniors in the college passed their examinations, and of the nine students who received the degree of B. A., Grade A, at the University of Western Ontario, six were students of Waterloo College.

Our financial position is quite weak. On this account your Board has appointed Prof. E. Neudoerffer to act as financial agent for the period of one year and to devote his entire time to the collection of funds for our own institution, provided that he is able to secure a supply professor in his place in the Seminary. Prof. Neudoerffer reports having received pledges and cash for the new Seminary Building to the amount of $20,245, and pledges and cash for the purchase of the Weber property amounting to $2,445. As financial agent under the proposed arrangement he expects to collect funds for all purposes of the institution.

All of which is submitted in humble gratitude to God and with sincere thanks to all our pastors and people who have supported in any way the • Evangelical Lutheran Seminary of Canada.

THE LUTHERAN COLLEGE AND SEMINARY, SASKATOON, SASKATCHEWAN, CANADA

Founded 1913

The Rev. H. W. Harms, *President*

The largest number of students in the history of the institution was reached, fifty-nine in all. Of these, ten attended lectures in the Theological Seminary, seven were registered as students of the University of Saskatchewan, three attended a collegiate institute in the city, three were special students, and thirty-six were enrolled in our High School Department. The student body was also of higher quality than in former times.

The new dormitory for girls was fully furnished and equipped through the endeavors of the Dean of Women, Miss Tappert, who raised the funds among her friends and from the women's auxiliaries of the Synod.

Synod again raised its apportionment to the institution in full. A beginning was made for an endowment fund by a friend in Pennsylvania who donated $50 in memory of his mother.

An Alumni Association was formed with the immediate objective of raising funds for the equipment of a chapel.

Through the efforts of Dr. C. P. Harry of the Board of Education, a branch of the Lutheran Student Association of America was organized among the students.

The importance of the institution for our Church in Western Canada is more apparent day by day as large numbers of Lutherans settle on the plains of Western Canada. The harvest thereby grows larger and with it the need for laborers, which Saskatoon alone can supply for this part of our Church. It is our prayer that the Lord of the Harvest may give us the means to carry on our educational work in a manner required by the opportunities granted by Him.

DEPARTMENT OF RELIGIOUS WORK IN STATE UNIVERSITIES AND OTHER SCHOOLS

Increased Activity of the Synods. One of the most encouraging features of the progress of the work has been the evidence of an increasing sense of responsibility for university students on the part of the Synods. It is axiomatic that a congregation is responsible for the care of souls in the community where it is located; and that the Synod should assist weak congregations or missions in discharging their responsibilities. The presence of an educational institution with a considerable number of Lutheran students from out of town in attendance adds to a congregation's responsibilities without adding much to its resources. Synods are facing this need and helping to meet it. The *New York and New England* Synod has voted increased interest and support for the work at Boston. The *six Synods* of the State of *Pennsylvania* have formed a committee to raise funds throughout the state to assist the congregation at the State College to erect suitable buildings. The *North Carolina* Synod will furnish half the support for a secretary-fellowship at the University of North Carolina, where there are nearly a hundred Lutheran students, but where there is no Lutheran congregation. (A secretary-fellowship is a plan by which a graduate student uses approximately one-half his time in work with students and in directing religious work among them. He receives a stipend equivalent to a graduate fellowship in the university where he serves.) The Synod of *Illinois* is paying the rental for Lutheran student headquarters and social rooms at the University of Illinois. The *Iowa* Synod gives substantial support to the work at the State University. The *Ministerium of Pennsylvania* and the *East Pennsylvania* Synod continue to furnish a large portion of the funds needed for the expenses of the work among students in Philadelphia. The Board of Education as the agent of the whole United Lutheran Church continues to aid these points and is developing the work according to the needs throughout the entire territory of the Church.

More Adequate Equipment. In the Minutes of 1926, page 388, is a list of places where more adequate equipment was needed. Nearly one-half of these points have taken definite steps to secure it. At some of them building operations are now in progress or have been completed during the biennium. At the University of *Washington,* Seattle, Washington, the first unit of the University Church was dedicated in April, 1927. It is a commodious and well appointed parish, educational and social building in which churchly provision for worship has been made pending the building of the church itself. The Rev. O. A. Bremer is pastor. A new church on a new site will be dedicated at Lawrence, Kansas, in September, 1928. The University of *Kansas* is located at Lawrence. The Rev. C. A. Puls is pastor. Plans have been adopted and the financial campaign is on for the new church of the Augustana Synod at Manhattan, Kansas, where the State Agricultural College is located. The Rev. Armour Edberg is pastor. Plans are being made for a new church on a new site at the University of *West Virginia*, Morgantown, W. Va., the Rev. D. M. Funk, pastor. At the University of *Colorado,* Boulder, the Rev. Walter A. Voss, pastor, and at *Purdue* University Lafayette, Indiana, the Rev. Henry Stolldorf, pastor, both of them taking charge of the fields in 1928, plans are being made for early church building. The same is true at the Pennsylvania State College for Teachers at *West Chester,* Pa., the Rev. Luther W. Evans, pastor. Better facilities usually mean better work. It is highly gratifying to note these improvements in the churches in which our university and college students worship and work.

Western Canada and the Pacific Coast. During the biennium your secretary visited the universities of the western provinces of Canada. At the University of *Manitoba* the work is in charge of the Rev. Bjorn Jonsson of the Icelandic Synod. A majority of the fifty Lutherans attending come from that Synod. At the University of Saskatchewan our capable and versatile President of Saskatoon College and Seminary, the Rev. H. A. Harms, is in charge. The seventy-five Lutheran students in Saskatoon are in three groups,—attending the Seminary, the University, and the Provincial Normal School. They have formed a Lutheran Student Association which meets frequently. Only about ten Lutherans attend the University of *Alberta* at Edmonton. They are cared for by Pastor A. Goos and other Lutheran ministers in the city.

The secretary visited the universities on the Pacific Coast during the Fall of 1927, stopping at the Universities of Washington, Oregon, and California; and on his return stopping at the Universities of Arizona, New Mexico, Colorado, Kansas and Nebraska.

The pastor of the new mission in Eugene, Oregon, the Rev. F. S. Beistel, is doing work among the seventy-five Lutherans attending the University of *Oregon.* At the other state institutions—the State College at Corvallis and the State Teachers' College at Monmouth — the work is cared for through the Oregon Lutheran Student Service Association. This association is composed of Lutherans of all synods. Its work is directed by a secretary, the Rev. William Schoeller, of the Joint Synod of Ohio, who visits the Lutheran students in these institutions and assists them in carrying on their Christian activities. Our Board makes an annual contribution to the association. The secretary is in constant touch with Pastor Schoeller. The Rev. Luther B. Deck of the Pacific Synod is a director of the association.

Lutheran students numbering about forty attending the University of *Arizona* are cared for by the Rev. Arnold Sitz, pastor of the local congregation which is connected with the Wisconsin Synod.

Cooperation with Other Synods. The *Augustana Synod* has increased its support of the work of this department to $3,000 a year. The Synod continues to entrust all its university work to our Board. The President of the Synod, the Rev. G. A. Brandelle, D.D., is an Advisory member of our Board. The secretary has maintained personal contact with many of the pastors of the *Norwegian Lutheran Church in America* who care for Lutheran students in state institutions in the Northwest, especially those at the universities of South Dakota, Montana, Minnesota, and Iowa State College.

The *Lutheran Student Association of America* has continued its activities among Lutheran students. Your secretaries have counseled with the students and taken part in many conferences which have been held under the direction of the L. S. A. A. and its regional organizations. The most notable of these was the conference held at Madison, Wisconsin, during the Christmas holidays, 1926-27. One hundred and seventy-five Lutheran students came as delegates from all parts of North America and from all Lutheran synods. They represented fourteen Lutheran colleges (seven of the U. L. C. A.); six theological seminaries (four of them U. L. C. A.); twenty-eight state universities and colleges, ranging from Massachusetts to Idaho and from the Dakotas to South Carolina, and from eleven other schools and colleges. There were present students from European countries, from Japan, China and India. The theme of the conference was the Student and the Church. Its outstanding values were that Lutheran students received a clear impression of the place and responsibility of our Church in present-day life; they sensed the imperative need of developing understanding and ultimate cooperation in all branches of the Lutheran Church in all parts of the world; they formed personal acquaintances across synodical lines which will bear fruit in better understanding and more cordial fellowship.

The Secretary. A brief report of this kind can give no adequate idea of the work done by the University Secretary. He has visited more than a hundred college and university campuses. He has attended as many sessions of conventions and large meetings. He has counseled with over two hundred committees and smaller groups. His interviews with individuals run well up over one thousand. He has made over two hundred addresses. He has travelled over 50,000 miles. The personal contact maintained by the department with over 175 pastors and many more students in educational institutions in all parts of the country has values which cannot be accurately measured but which assuredly are very great. Since the Spring of 1928 a Service Bulletin appearing monthly has helped further to maintain these contacts and coordinate the work of the department. It is sent to nearly two hundred and fifty pastors, and others interested directly in the work of the department.

In all the work the closest cooperation with the Department for Women Students is maintained. Indeed, the two departments function in all co-educational institutions as one.

The department would record its gratitude to our Lord Jesus Christ without whose constant grace and supporting power the task would be more than could be borne. May the Church continue in prayer for her students and for those to whom she has entrusted the difficult and delicate task of guiding them while at school.

DEPARTMENT FOR WOMEN STUDENTS

Correlation and Cooperation. This department, so far as possible, functions wherever women students of our Church are found. It cooperates, therefore, on United Lutheran campuses with the Department of Institutions, and on non-Lutheran campuses with the University Department. Only in colleges or schools for women alone situated in towns or cities where there is no local Lutheran Church, has this department no direct contact with other phases of the work of the Board of Education. And even in such institutions the Lutheran Student Association of America seeks the cooperation of the secretaries who are privileged to make occasional visits.

With the Women's Missionary Society of the United Lutheran Church, the Board of Education, through this department, maintains close cooperation. The committee on women students includes two members appointed by the Executive Board of the Women's Missionary Society. Since the creation of this department the Executive Board of the W. M. S. has annually budgeted a liberal amount of money for its support. The valuable services of a part-time associate in the person of Miss Mathilde Peper were made possible from January, 1921, to April, 1928, in part at least, by the budgeted gifts of the missionary societies of the New York and New England Synod, of the New York Synod, and of the Ministerium of Pennsylvania. Miss Peper resigned to become a member of the faculty of Carthage College. At the last meeting of the Board the following motion was unanimously adopted: "That the Board of Education in formally accepting the resignation of Miss Mathilde Peper express its deep appreciation of the fine personal and constructive work she has done in the Department for Women Students since 1921; and that it voice its satisfaction that she has gone into educational work at one of our United Lutheran colleges."

Addition to the Staff of Secretaries. At its meeting in June, 1928, the Board elected as assistant secretary for women students, Miss Mildred E. Winston, of Sunbury, Pa. Miss Winston received her bachelor's degree from Susquehanna in 1921. After teaching in the High School of Sunbury, she entered the Biblical Seminary in New York, from which she received the degree of Bachelor of Religious Education in 1928. She also has the Master of Arts degree from New York University.

Student Census. The increasingly successful annual census of the young men and women students of our parishes is the result of the continued and cumulative work of the student secretaries of synodical and conference Women's Missionary Societies. The first census for 1919-20 brought in the names of 1,259 women students. In 1922-23, 2,200 names of women students, and 2,300 names of men students were received. In the census taken September, 1927, 970 parishes reported 3,315 men students; 1,095 parishes reported 3,160 women students. The women students reported classified as follows: attending state institutions of higher learning, 1,035; attending Lutheran colleges, 460; attending all other universities or colleges, 1,100; attending training schools for nurses, 555. The classified names have been valuable to the secretaries in their campus visits and to the student pastors. The synodical and conference student secretaries have stimulated a wholesome interest in connection with questions relating to the students of the Church and with the especially pertinent question of higher education for Lutheran young women.

Candidate Committee. Through appointment by the Executive Board of the Women's Missionary Society, the secretary for women students since April, 1922, has been on the candidate committee and since 1924 has been chairman of that committee. The candidate committee is charged with finding the young women who are qualified to fill specific positions open to women under the various boards of the United Lutheran Church. To the Board of Foreign Missions and to the Board of American Missions, young women are recommended for appointment by the Executive Board of the Women's Missionary Society. The educational requirements for successful Christian work have been advancing steadily. Candidates must be sought among our college students or recent alumnae. Examination of the list of recently appointed and recommended candidates will show that they have received their undergraduate training in Lutheran colleges, in denominational colleges and in state colleges and universities.

Visits Made to Campuses. A comparison of different years will give some idea of the growth of the work. During the first year of the work of the department one secretary visited 49 campus groups. By June, 1922, 147 groups of students had been reached, sixty-one of these for the second time. By June, 1924, the different student groups visited reached 256, and by June, 1926, 285. By June, 1928, Miss Peper had visited groups of 151 different institutions. Miss Markley has visited 190 additional groups and 45 groups which at one time or another Miss Peper has also visited. These groups fall in 23 States, the largest number being in New York and Pennsylvania.

Student Conferences. The Lutheran Student Association of America held its first national conference at Augustana College in April, 1923. The second conference, international in character because of students from Canada and from European as well as from Oriental countries, was held December, 1926, in Madison, Wisconsin. Annually, usually in February, the various regional week-end conferences are held. During the biennium Miss Markley and Miss Peper have attended such regional conferences at Upsala, Susquehanna, Thiel, Augsburg, and Bethany Colleges.

The Lutheran Student Association interests itself in the problems facing the Church both at home and abroad. It is planning to accept the invitation from the Lutheran World Committee, Dr. J. A. Morehead, chairman, to have representatives at the convention in Copenhagen, in 1929. This past year its financial objective has been to assist the Lutheran Theological Seminary in Leningrad, Russia. About $3,000 has so far been forwarded to the National Lutheran Council for that purpose from student groups in Lutheran and non-Lutheran institutions in twelve (12) States and Canada.

The quadrennial Student Volunteer Convention was held December, 1927, in Detroit. Like the preceding conventions at Des Moines and Indianapolis, it was attended by many students of all bodies of Lutheranism.

Approximately 150 Lutheran students were met either at headquarters, at the church group meeting, or at the student dinner.

Lutheran student registration was as follows: from Lutheran Theological Seminaries, 7; Lutheran Colleges, 19; non-Lutheran Institutions, 21; Foreign Universities, 4.

Scholarship and Loan Fund for Women. By action of the Board at its meeting in December, 1927, $3,737.11 of the bequest of Mrs. Harriet Earhart Monroe was allocated to this important fund. With two earlier gifts of $1,000 each, this forms the principal of a fund which has helped seven young women prepare for distinctive Christian vocations.

Women Students and the Church. The past few years have shown conclusively the wisdom of knowing the women students of our Church if for no other reason than of finding the young women best equipped for doing the special pieces of work which the various Boards of the Church expect women to do. The point is best exemplified in the dependence of the Board of Foreign Missions upon students and alumnae for candidates for foreign fields. Questions of no little concern to the Church at large are: Where are our young women getting the undergraduate training that fits them for full-time Christian service? What United Lutheran educational institutions are giving to women the professional graduate training necessary for specific forms of mission service at home and abroad? What answer does the Church give to properly educated and qualified young women who offer themselves for full-time Christian service in the Homeland?

THE SURVEY OF THE EDUCATIONAL SITUATION IN THE UNITED LUTHERAN CHURCH IN AMERICA

The Constitution of the Board of Education of the United Lutheran

Church in America in Article VIII, Section 1, reads as follows:

Article VIII. Duties, Powers and Functions of the Board.

Section 1. Subject to the Constitution of the United Lutheran Church or its resolutions, the Board shall have full power to prosecute the work entrusted to it. It shall have authority to prepare general surveys of educational standards; to investigate any phase of educational work and make recommendations to institutions and synods; to appoint pastors and other agencies for the prosecution of religious work among students; to publish literature covering the various phases of its work under the direction of the Executive Board; to cooperate with synods in the establishment of new institutions where approved by the United Lutheran Church; to receive and disburse contributions for educational purposes and to hold and administer bequests and trusts for such purposes, and to perform such other duties as the United Lutheran Church may assign it.

The United Lutheran Church in Convention in Chicago, October, 1924, charged the Board of Education with the making of an educational survey in the following resolution:

"*Resolved,* That the Board of Education be asked to make a scientific survey of the educational situation in the United Lutheran Church, in those spheres not covered by the Commission on Theological Education, and that it consider the relation of our educational work to the whole status of religious education in our country and Canada.

"That the Board of Education, with the approval of the Executive Board of the United Lutheran Church, be empowered to employ impartial experts outside of the Lutheran Church.

"That the Board of Education be asked to report, if possible, at the next convention."

At the meeting of the Board of Education in December, 1924, the following were nominated and elected by the Board as members of the Survey Commission: E. P. Pfatteicher, D.D.; M. J. Kline, D.D.; C. F. W. Hoppe, D.D.; Howard R. Gold; Glenn M. Cummings, Esq.; Hugo C. M. Wendel, Ph.D.; Mrs. Wythe F. Morehead.

This Commission was at the December, 1925, meeting of the Board increased by the appointment by President Turkle of A. Steimle, D.D., and J. Henry Harms, D.D.

At the meeting of the Board on May 5, 1925, the Survey Committee reported correspondence and interviews regarding the plans, scope, and cost of Educational Surveys with such experts as Dr. Robert Lincoln Kelly, Executive Secretary of the Association of American Colleges and of the Council of Church Boards of Education, New York City; Dr. F. J. Kelly, Dean of Administration, University of Minnesota; Dr. George F. Zook, Federal Bureau of Education, Washington, D. C. These preliminary investigations in connection with finding the most competent educational leaders to conduct the Survey included a conference at the Hotel Astor, attended by John W. Withers, Ph.D., Dean of the School of Education, New York University; Robert J. Leonard, Ph.D., Director of School of Education, Teachers College, Columbia University; Galen Fisher, Ph.D., of the Institute for Social and Religious Research; Jesse Jones, Ph.D., of the Phelps-Stokes Foundation; Luther A. Weigle, Ph.D., Dean of Yale Divinity School; Mary E. Markley, A. Steimle, D.D., and Howard R. Gold, chairman of the Survey Commission. There were also conferences with a number of Lutheran educators.

The Survey Commission after most thorough and painstaking investigation in May, 1925, presented to the Board of Education as Joint Directors of the Survey:

Robert J. Leonard, Ph.D., Director of the School of Education, Teachers College, Columbia University.

Edward S. Evenden, Ph.D., Professor of Education, Teachers College, Columbia University.

With the names of the joint directors were presented full outlines of the Aims and Scope of the Survey; the Agreement between the Survey Commission and Teachers College, Columbia University; the budget of Cost of Survey. The Report of the Survey Commission was adopted by a unanimous rising vote by the Board of Education. (See minutes of Fifth Biennial Convention of the United Lutheran Church in America, Richmond, Virginia, October 19-27, 1926: Report of Board of Education, pp. 340-343.)

May 13, 1926, the President of the United Lutheran Church submitted to the Executive Board the entire action of the Board of Education relative to the Survey. On motion the Executive Board approved "the action of the Board of Education in employing experts outside of the Lutheran Church" (to conduct the Survey of the colleges and academies of the United Lutheran Church in America).

The Directors of the Survey associated with themselves F. B. O'Rear, Ph.D., associate in College Administration, Teachers College. Offices with adequate staff were furnished in Teachers College.

One of the first developments of the Survey was the formulation of a set of blanks of unusual thoroughness and significance which were sent out to the staff members of all United Lutheran Colleges and Junior Colleges. These questionaires were addressed specifically to the President, Deans of Instruction, Deans of Men, Deans of Women, Heads of Departments, Professors and Assistants, Librarians, Registrars, and Business Managers. There were blanks for students covering questions of geographical distribution, home background, courses chosen, extra-curricular activities, persistence in college, occupation after graduation, church affiliation, religious life. For students at non-Lutheran institutions and for pastors dealing with these students there were blanks carrying questions relative to the scope of the work being done by the United Lutheran Church among students in non-Lutheran institutions. In the formulation of these blanks, the directors had the assistance and advice not only of experts in the various lines of activity on the staff of Teachers College, but also of mature graduate students who had experience in the varied forms of college administration and instruction. From the returns on these several blanks, there were available impressive and comparable data.

According to the agreement, one of the directors was to visit every institution surveyed. There was one unavoidable exception to this. In every other case, two directors and three or four of their graduate students in college administration visited a campus, investigating in their stay of several days the various phases of work, interviewing students, consulting with professors, visiting classes, viewing buildings, examining records and treasurers' books, counselling with the administrative officers. The mechanical work involved collating data and notes may be judged from the statement in the typing office at Teachers College, that the amount of work handled in the course of the Lutheran Survey up to June 28, 1928, required 5,262 stencils, 7,404 hours of labor and 263,100 sheets of paper. On the basis of evidence available in such visits and of the data submitted in the blanks, the directors formulated for the various institutions their Reports and their Recommendations.

The Survey contains unique special studies, as for example in connection with College Curricula and the Church Boards of Education. These have been made possible through the direct financial aid, assistance and equipment of the Carnegie Foundation for the Advancement of Learning, Dr. Clyde Furst, Secretary; or through the prolonged study and investigation of graduate students in college administration and staff members of Teachers College.

In order that the facts obtained through the Survey might be available before the completion of the Survey, the Board of Education in May, 1927, passed the following resolution:

"That the Survey Commission be authorized to submit a preliminary report to Synods and Boards of Trustees of educational institutions if these bodies request it, or if in the opinion of the Survey Commission such information may be useful."

One synod requested and received such a preliminary report. To the proper officials of three other synods such a preliminary report was submitted.

During the progress of the Survey there has been, on the whole, commendable cooperation on the part of Church and college officials. At the December, 1927, meeting of the Board of Education the Conference of United Lutheran College and Seminary Presidents passed the following: "It is the sense of this Body that we express our deeply felt appreciation of the value of the Survey now being conducted and that we profoundly appreciate the ability, the fairness, and the evident desire to be genuinely helpful in their work, shown by those in charge of the Survey."

After two years of work, in May, 1925, the Directors of the Survey submitted their report, according to the original agreement, to an Advisory Committee chosen by the Survey Commission and by the Directors. The committee was Luther A. Weigle, Ph.D., Dean of Yale Divinity School; Charles P. Wiles, D.D., President of the Parish and Church School Board; Clyde Furst, Ph.D., Secretary of the Carnegie Foundation for the Advancement of Teaching; George J. Gongaware, D.D., Pastor of St. John's Church, Charleston, S. C.; George F. Zook, Ph.D., President of Akron University, Akron, Ohio. The written statement to the Survey Commission of this Advisory Committee follows:

"Pursuant to the request of the Commission chosen by the United Lutheran Church for a survey of the colleges, the Advisory Committee met with the Survey Staff and several officials of the Church, on May 3, 4, 5, 1928, in New York City, to examine the tentative draft of the report which had been prepared for the Survey Staff. The Advisory Committee spent three days and two evenings in a general review of the report and examined in detail the major recommendations of policy and the information on which they were based. In the course of this examination, the official representatives of the Church also made certain minor corrections in the supporting data and offered their impressions as to the feasibility of the various recommendations contained in the report. The Advisory Committee, however, accepts full responsibility for the present statement.

"The Advisory Committee understands that the Survey Staff necessarily restricted its examination to the material and the personnel phases of the institutions, without any attempt to define, interpret or evaluate the faith, the genius, or the spirit of the Lutheran Church. Nevertheless, the Survey Staff has done an outstanding piece of educational work. There is every evidence that the Survey Staff has taken extraordinary care to obtain extended information on which to base its report and that this information has been verified in sumerous ways, including extensive correspondence and personal visitation to the colleges.

"Attention is called also to the fact that for the first time in the conduct of an educational survey a large number of important features in connection with college life, which have hitherto not received adequate attention, were carefully investigated. New types of data also were secured and better scientific methods were employed in evaluating the large amount of information obtained than have been employed in any similar study. The result is an exceptionally comprehensive study of nine manuscript volumes.

"While the Survey Staff must accept responsibility for the accuracy of the information adduced in the report, it seems clear to the Advisory Committee that the methods employed in gathering the data upon which to base its report insure its accuracy, with possible minor exceptions. On the basis of this information, the Advisory Committee examined with considerable care the major recommendations relative to general educational policy and also those relating to the future policy to be pursued by each institution. As a result of the discussion relative to these recommendations, the Survey Staff in certain instances cordially consented to modify the tentative draft of the report. In all important respects, however, the report and the recommendations remain substantially the same as in the original draft.

"In its modified form the Advisory Committee wishes to record its hearty approval of the report including its recommendations and to express the hope that all those who are concerned with the recommendations will give them the most careful and serious consideration. The committee is clearly of the opinion that if the Church and the institutions will cooperate to carry them out, a very distinct forward step will be taken toward the solution of present difficulties in the colleges attached to the United Lutheran Church and toward a new and sounder policy relative to the educational policy which may well be followed by other church denominations.

"Without the assistance of numerous graduate students at Teachers College, the large contribution of service rendered by the Carnegie Foundation, and the tremendous efforts of the Survey Staff, it would have been quite impossible to produce so remarkable a report. The report is certainly worth several times what it cost, and the United Lutheran Church may well take pride that it has set a superior standard for surveys of denominational colleges which will indeed be difficult for others to follow."

Signed,

LUTHER A. WEIGLE.
CHARLES P. WILES.
CLYDE FURST.
GEORGE J. GONGAWARE.
GEORGE F. ZOOK, <i>Chairman.</i>

The Survey Report was later in May reviewed in great detail by the three secretaries of the Board of Education in the presence of Assistant Director, Dr. F. B. O'Rear. The entire document was checked for omissions or errors.

The Survey Report was presented in person by Directors Leonard and Evenden and by Assistant Director O'Rear June 25-27, at Teachers College, to the entire Survey Commission. The report of approximately 2,000 mimeographed pages was temporarily bound in nine volumes. The data submitted for the individual colleges and junior colleges was presented in chapters or studies under the following topics: Supporting Organizations and Clientele; Government of the College; Location; Accreditation; Faculty; Instruction and Instructional Officers; Curricula; Administrative Organization; Advisement of Men; Advisement of Women; Library; Physical Education and Athletics; Student Records and Registrar's Office; Physical Plant; Financial Support; Student Body; Provision for Religious Life of Students; Educational Theory of Extra Curricular Activities; Specific Organizations; Organization and Unification of the Social Program. There was also a chapter on the work of the United Lutheran Church among students attending non-Lutheran institutions. The study of the history, scope, work, and influence of the Board of Education of the United Lutheran Church in America is projected against a background of the comparable topics in connection with the Boards of Education of the Northern Baptist Convention, Congregational Churches of the United States, Disciples of Christ, Norwegian Lutheran Church of America, Methodist Episcopal Church, Presbyterian Church in the United States of America, United Presbyterian Church of North America.

The Survey Commission on June 28, 1928, through its chairman, the Rev. Howard R. Gold, introduced the presentation of the Report and Recommendations to the Board of Education as follows: "The Church, in authorizing the Board of Education to make this study, asked for a "scientific survey." This request the Commission has faithfully carried out and the study, the interpretations and the recommendations have all been made in a purely objective manner. We are transmitting to the Board a remarkably large body of data gathered with unusual care and thoroughness and sympathetically evaluated. The recommendations growing out of this data we believe are warranted by the facts and when made effective, will set high standards for the educational work of the Church."

The Board of Education considered the Report and Recommendations during three sessions. On the basis of data submitted, the Board of Education approved the Report as a whole and adopted the Recommendations.

Two types of Recommendations were submitted by the Survey Commission. The first type pertains to the individual colleges and junior colleges. These Recommendations having been approved by the Board of Education will be presented to the respective Boards of Trustees.

The second type of Recommendations pertains directly to the Board of Education. These are respectfully submitted to the United Lutheran Church in America for information and approval.

A. With respect to religious policy of the Board of Education:

(1) In the case of institutions which are not organically connected with a Synod of the United Lutheran Church, nor required by charter provision to have two-thirds of their boards of trustees members of the United Lutheran Church, the Board of Education should formulate criteria by which it may determine whether or not an institution is to be considered as affiliated with the United Lutheran Church and entitled to receive appropriations from the Board of Education.

(2) As an agency of the United Lutheran Church, the Board of Education is obligated to give special attention to those features of its institutions which differentiate them from privately endowed and state institutions, to define more specifically the distinctive marks of a *Christian* college, and to determine by investigation the extent to which these characteristics are present in its institutions.

B. With respect to educational policies of the Board of Education:

(1) To foster the development of cooperation among the Lutheran institutions and between the Lutheran institutions and others in order that these institutions may exercise a greater degree of leadership in the whole enterprise of higher education in the United States and develop special features of the program in the several colleges and thus provide for maximum use of available resources.

(2) To be guided in all decisions regarding educational policy on the

basis of carefully ascertained facts. This implies that the Board be equipped to engage continuously in survey and research.

(3) To foster existing institutions or establish new ones only when there is assurance that they can be maintained on a high educational level.

(4) To guide in the determination of educational policies within the individual institutions, their several constituences, and the United Lutheran Church as a whole, by

(a) proposing and promoting educational programs and principles;
(b) promoting continuous investigation and research making available expert advice on important educational and administrative problems, such as curricula, physical plant, budgeting and accounting, records, equipment, etc.;
(c) conducting frequent conferences on educational problems among the representatives of the various Lutheran institutions.

C. *With respect to the organization and operation of the Board of Education:*

It is assumed that the Board of Education will continue to make administrative and financial provisions for the four activities which may be regarded as its major functions:

(1) Rendering expert service to the educational interests of the Church and its institutions through the maintenance of a central professional staff.

(2) Aiding seminaries through subsidies and expert service.

(3) Aiding colleges through subsidies and expert service.

(4) Aiding student pastor work through subsidies and expert service.

It is impossible to recommend the precise percentage of the total income of the Board which should be spent for each of the four activities because, (1) their absolute or relative importance cannot be determined; (2) no data has been gathered concerning the needs of the seminaries, since this was not a part of the survey, and (3) the amounts needed for the support of the student pastor work are largely a matter of judgment and estimate, rather than of accumulated experience or consensus of opinion.

The total amounts available for distribution are so small, that the chief value lies in official recognition of the institution and the activity rather than in the weight of the subsidy itself.

It is to be regretted that the percent of the total Church budget apportioned to the Board of Education has decreased throughout the years. Again, while the Survey Staff cannot suggest what the percentage should be, since only a portion of the activities of the Church has been studied, the hope is entertained that the Church might increase the percent to education.

With respect to staff and Board, it is implicit within the very meaning and purpose underlying the creation of the Board of Education by the Church, that the Board be provided with expert staff members in order that it may be a functioning body, capable of reaching decisions on the basis of data gathered by its staff, and in turn serving the colleges and educational enterprises as a constructive sphere of influence. The first duty of the Board is to appoint a staff of properly qualified individuals. The salaries for these staff members, and the overhead charges, constitute the first claim upon the income of the Board.

As outlined in the Constitution of the Board (1920 Convention Minutes, pp. 258-259) there are to be the following secretaries:

(1) General or Executive Secretary
(2) Secretary for institutions
(3) Secretary for recruiting for the ministry
(4) Secretary for Lutheran students in non-Lutheran institutions
(5) Secretary for women students.

Four secretaries are now in the employ of the Board: one secretary for the first three functions outlined above; one for the fourth, and two for the fifth. The office of one secretary is at Harrisburg, of another at Norristown, and of two others at New York.

It is recommended that as soon as possible the position of General Secretary should be filled by an educator of outstanding qualifications. The position should be regarded as of equal or even greater importance than a college presidency. There should be corresponding recognition in salary.

It is recommended that provision be made for advancing the whole educational program of the Church by rendering expert advice and services with reference to (a) finance and publicity, (b) research and statistics, (c) theological seminaries, (d) colleges, and (e) student work in non-Lutheran institutions. As soon as possible staff members should be assigned to each of these special fields.

It is recommended that the staff should be concentrated at a central headquarters.

D. With respect to aid to colleges from the Board of Education:
The principle of aid or subsidy for definite projects *is recommended* instead of aid for general support.

It is the judgment of the Survey Staff that the projects in which the Church should aid the colleges are those which give the colleges their essential character and which differentiate them from either state or private institutions. Such differentiating activities fall within the field of religion, —as activities, worship, advice and instruction. *It is definitely recommended* that the department of religion be the first project aided in each institution.

To be eligible for aid each institution should be required to submit a plan stating the purpose, organization and scope of the department. Upon approval of this plan, the institution should be granted a sum sufficient for *one* appropriately educated full-time faculty member of this department. His work could include one or all of these fields: Bible teaching, religious education, or direction of religious work and activities.

It is recommended that the Board of Education spend whatever remaining funds are available for aid to colleges for the further promotion of religious instruction and activities in ways which may be from time to time determined, such as the conduct of experiments, maintenance of demonstration centers, preparation of teaching materials, and awards of scholarships or establishment of loan funds for the advanced education of workers in this field.

The total amount of money set aside for colleges in the years to come should not be less than the amount so spent at present. Every effort, consistent with the other obligations of the Board, should be made to increase it.

E. *With respect to aid to work among Lutheran students at non-Lutheran institutions*:

Since the promotion of the student work in the non-Lutheran institutions is one of the most important responsibilities of the Board of Education, in cooperation with the Synods, every effort should be made to obtain more adequate financial support. It is not likely that the Church can provide in its budget adequate amounts for this purpose. The best solution appears to be for the Board of Education to attempt to obtain an endowment for the enterprise. The goal for this endowment fund should be at least $1,000,000.

The Board should aid with advice and service of staff members all attempts to care for the religious life of Lutherans attending the non-Lutheran institutions, regardless of the number of such students at any institution.

The factors to be considered in determining the institutions at which financial aid is to be given and the amount of aid, should be:

(a) the importance and location of the institutions
(b) the number of Lutheran students
(c) the type and wealth of the congregation
(d) the resources of the Synod or Synods
(e) the personal and professional qualifications of the pastor
(f) an approved organization.

Where the aid extended by the Board of Education is $500 or more the proper organization is regarded as follows: establishment and maintenance of cooperative relations between the Synod or Synods in which the non-Lutheran institutions are located and the Board of Education of the United Lutheran Church, and the creation of a Board of Trustees for each unit to control the enterprise, such control to include: receipt and disbursement of funds, approval of the program and the employment of necessary staff. This Board should be composed of not fewer than five members, representing as may be determined by the Board of Education, the Congregation, the Synod or Synods, and the Board of Education itself. This Board should draft a plan showing how the work is to be organized and conducted, and when this plan is approved by the Board of Education, it will be eligible to receive funds.

On recommendation of the Survey Commission and by action of the Board of Education, neither the Survey nor any part thereof is to be released until the entire Survey is published. The present policy concerning preliminary reports is continued. Executive and administrative officers of the respective colleges will receive the first copies of the Survey. Later, delegates to the Erie Convention of the United Lutheran Church and the officials of the Church and Synods will receive copies of the completed report of the Board of Education. A limited number of copies moderately priced will be available to all who are interested in the great educational work of the United Lutheran Church.

On recommendation of the Survey Commission and by action of the Board of Education, the Secretary of the Board was instructed:

(1) To express appreciation to the Carnegie Foundation for the Advancement of Teaching for the contribution of $900 for a study of the curricula of the colleges of the United Lutheran Church in connection with the Survey.

(2) To acknowledge especially the valuable personal advice of Dr. Clyde Furst of the Carnegie Foundation for the Advancement of Teaching.

(3) To thank the Board of Trustees of Teachers College which has assisted both the Survey Directors and the Survey Commission by extending to them services and facilities equivalent to the sum appropriated by the Board of Education for the Survey.

(4) To send the following resolution to the persons concerned: "That we record our unqualified satisfaction with the expert service rendered the Survey Commission by the Directors of the Survey, Dr. Robert J. Leonard and Dr. Edward S. Evenden, and of the Assistant Director, Dr. F. B. O'Rear. Their work has been done with a thoroughness that must command not only our respect but the attention of the entire educational world as well. The performance of their duty was objective in method and sympathetic in spirit. By their genial personalities they have won our highest esteem. We believe that we could not have been more fortunate in our choice of Survey Directors."

Respectfully submitted for the Board of Education
A. STEIMLE, *President.*
WM. M. HORN, *Secretary.*

REPORT OF THE TREASURER OF THE BOARD OF EDUCATION

For the fiscal year ended June 30, 1927

GENERAL ACCOUNT

Balance, Cash on hand July 1, 1926... $ 2,477.44

RECEIPTS

Treasurer United Lutheran Church on Apportionment..	$111,125.00	
Treasurer United Lutheran Church, Women's Missionary Society	3,000.00	
Treasurer United Lutheran Church, Breklum-Kropp Seminary	68.50	
Synod of New York and New England, for Boston Work	2,559.92	
Augustana Synod—Religious Work Among Students in the Universities	2,000.00	
Swedish Lutheran Student Work—Harvard	200.00	
Breklum-Kropp Special	165.00	
Breklum-Kropp, Board American Missions	1,000.00	
Miscellaneous	60.00	
Income from Annuity Fund	2,463.27	
Interest on Deposits	211.11	
Loan	500.00	
		123,352.80
		$125,830.24

DISBURSEMENTS

Secretaries' Salaries	$ 10,999.92	
Secretaries' Traveling Expenses	3,569.28	
Stenographers	2,047.97	
Telephone and Telegraph	135.57	
Office Rent	480.00	
Postage	568.10	
Office Supplies	733.56	
Student Pastor's Salaries	9,785.16	
Student Pastor's Expenses	9,867.98	
General Expenses	14,173.51	
Printing and Publications	3,076.86	
Annuity Payments	3,237.37	
Women's Student Worker's Salary and Expenses....	2,210.15	
	$60,885.43	
		$125,830.24
Board and Executive Meetings—Expenses	1,168.41	
Special Account—Mrs. H. E. Monroe. For services rendered	300.00	
Pacific Seminary Budget	1,874.97	
Breklum-Kropp Budget	5,500.00	
Breklum-Kropp Special	1,233.50	
Waterloo Seminary and College Budget	1,874.98	
Chicago Seminary Budget	749.98	
Saskatoon Seminary Budget	2,916.62	
Hartwick Seminary Budget	900.00	

Southern Seminary Budget 2,624.96
Midland College Budget 7,499.97
Mt. Amoena Seminary Budget 833.31
Martin Luther Seminary Budget 374.97
Mt. Pleasant Collegiate Institute Budget 1,874.97
Newberry College Budget 2,700.00
Muhlenberg College Budget 1,125.00
Marion College Budget 1,874.98
Marion College Loan 2,500.00
Lenoir-Rhyne College Budget 1,125.00
Carthage College Budget 2,700.00
Wurtenberg College Budget 1,125.00
Gettysburg College Budget 1,125.00
Roanoke College Budget 2,250.00
Summerland College Budget 1,350.00
Susquehanna University Budget 1,125.00
Wagner College Budget 1,499.97
Wiedner Institute Budget 666.65
Thiel College Budget 1,125.00
Winnipeg Academy Budget 1,499.97
Woman's College Budget 4,583.27
Loan Budget 3,000.00
                                                            $121,986.91

Balance June 30, 1927 .... 3,843.33

ANNUITY PRINCIPAL CASH ACCOUNT
Balance on hand July 1, 1926..................... $ 323.13

RECEIPTS
December 16. Cash .... $ 1,000.00
1927
February 28. Cash 10,000.00
February 28. Cash 2,500.00
                                        13,500.00

                                        $13,823.13
DISBURSEMENTS
Investment Purchased .... $ 13,631.25
Balance June 30, 1927 .... $ 191.88

CALIFORNIA COLLEGE
Balance, July 1, 1926, and June 30, 1927.............. $ 60.00

SCHOLARSHIP AND LOAN FUND FOR WOMEN
Balance on hand July 1, 1926 .... $ 60.24

RECEIPTS
Miscellaneous receipts .... $ 215.00
Income from investments 50.00
                                        265.00

                                        325.24
DISBURSEMENTS
Cash Scholarships .... $ 300.00
Balance, June 30, 1927 .... .25.24

PERMANENT MINISTERIAL EDUCATION FUND
Principal Cash Account

Balance on hand, July 1, 1926 .... $ 143.84

RECEIPTS

Treasurer United Lutheran Church............. $ 405.00
Legacy Estate Henry Bowman 200.00

$ 748.84
Income on hand above account..................   551.39

Balance, June 30, 1927 ....   1,300.23

INVESTMENTS JUNE 30, 1927

Par Values   Book Values

ANNUITY FUND

$8000 Altoona and Logan Valley Elec. Ry. 4½'s, 1933	$6,400.00
5000 Baltimore & Ohio 6's, 1929	5,112.50
2000 Baltimore & Ohio 5's, 1948.....................	1,975.00
6000 Bell Telephone Co. of Pa. 5's, 1948....................	5,888.75
1000 Chesapeake & Ohio Eq. 5's, 1935	969.67
1000 Penna. R. R. Eq. 5's, 1934.....................	992.26
2000 Penna. R. R. Eq. 5's, 1935.....................	1,965.60
3000 Penna. R. R. Eq. 5's, 1938	2,974.80
1000 Phila. Electric 5½'s, 1947.....................	1,030.00
4600 Phila. Electric 5's, 1966.....................	4,574.37
2000 Phila. Sub. Water Co. 5's, 1955.....................	1,955.00
500 Bell Telephone Co. of Pa. 5's, 1948....................	506.25
2000 Scranton & Wilkes-Barre Trac. 5's, 1959........	1,680.00
4000 Baltimore & Ohio S. W. Div. 1st....................	4,055.00
13 Shares Western Union Tel. Co. Stock........	1,560.00
Marion College Note, 6 per cent balance due on or before August 1, 1927...............................	2,500.00
1000 Chelsea Hotel Co.	1,000.00
3500 Phila. Electric Power 1st 5½'s, 1972....................	3,631.25
5000 Quaker City Tank Line Eq. 5½'s, 1934................	5,000.00
4000 U. S. Post Offices Corp. 1st 5½'s, 1935............	4,000.00

$57,770.45

Real Estate—204 A St., S. E. Washington, D.C.   15,000.00

SCHOLARSHIP AND LOAN FUND FOR WOMEN

1000 Chesapeake & Ohio Eq. 5's, 1935.......................	969.68
1000 City of Mandon North Dakota 6's (Gift)........	1,000.00

1,969.68

PERMANENT MINISTERIAL EDUCATION FUND

1000 Baltimore & Ohio 6's, 1929.......................	1,022.50
1000 Northern States Power Co. 6's, 1948....................	1,000.00
500 Fort Spring Mag. Dist. Greenbrier Co. W. Va. 5's	500.00
1000 Phila. Sub. Water Co. 1955 5's	977.50
1000 Phila. Electric Power 1st 5½'s, 1972................	1,022.50
2000 Scranton & Wilkes-Barre Trac. 1st and ref. 5's, 1951	1,690.00

6.212.50

$80,952.63

Respectfully submitted,
JOHN M. SNYDER, *Treasurer.*

Philadelphia, September 26, 1927.

We have audited the accounts of the Treasurer of the Board of Education of the United Lutheran Church in America for the year ended June 30, 1927, and have verified the foregoing Treasurer's Report, pages 1 to 4, both inclusive, and we certify that all recorded receipts have been accounted for, that the disbursements were found to be supported by authenticated vouchers and that, in our opinion, the foregoing report is correct.

LYBRAND, ROSS BROS. & MONTGOMERY,
Accountants and Auditors.

GENERAL ACCOUNT

For the Fiscal Year Ended June 30, 1928.

Balance on hand, July 1, 1927 .... $ 3,843.33

RECEIPTS

Treasurer, United Lutheran Church, on Apportionment	$124,250.00	
Treasurer, United Lutheran Church, Woman's Missionary Society	3,750.00	
Treasurer, United Lutheran Church, Spec. Saskatoon College and Seminary	25.00	
Treasurer, United Lutheran Church, N. Y. Breklum-Kropp German Conference	25.00	
Treasurer, United Lutheran Church, E. Penna. Synod—Mt. Airy Seminary	25.00	
Treasurer, United Lutheran Church, E. Penna. Synod—Muhlenberg College	25.00	
Synod of New York and New England, for Boston Work	2,633.22	
Breklum-Kropp Relief—German Conference, New York	100.00	
Breklum-Kropp Relief—German Conference, New York	25.00	
Breklum-Kropp Relief—Laymen's Movement—three students	190.00	
Breklum-Kropp Relief—Board American Missions....	1,500.00	
Trinity, Reading, Pa.—Ruth S. Walker, for student work	10.00	
Woman's League—New York and Vicinity	50.00	
Income Estate—E. D. McLallen, 1927-28	10.50	
Augustana Synod—For Religious Work in Universities	2,000.00	
Synod Northwest Special for Carthage College	428.25	
Transferred from Reformation Day Offerings, S. S., U. L. C.	3,131.92	
Swedish New England Conf. (Augustana) — For Boston Work	216.66	
Income from Annuity Fund	3,110.12	
Interest on Deposit	224.94	141,730.61
		$145,573.94

DISBURSEMENTS

Secretaries' Salaries	$ 10,999.92
Secretaries' Traveling Expenses	3,361.53
Stenographers	2,243.42
Telephone and Telegraph	208.11
Office Rent	630.00
Postage	512.65
Office Supplies	395.56
Student Pastors' Salary	10,887.53
Student Pastors' Expenses	9,675.35
General Expenses	10,441.46
Printing and Publications	2,090.97
Annuity Payments	3,710.00
Woman Student Workers' Salary and Expenses	1,290.62
Accrued Interest on Securities Purchased	55.29
Board and Executive Meetings	1,019.30
Pacific Seminary Budget	2,499.96
Breklum-Kropp Budget	6,000.00
Breklum-Kropp Special	650.00
Waterloo Seminary and College Budget	2,499.96
Waterloo Seminary and College Special	190.00
Chicago Seminary Budget	999.96
Saskatoon College and Seminary Budget	1,999.93
Saskatoon College and Seminary Special	2,525.00
Hartwick Seminary Budget	1,200.00
Southern Seminary Budget	3,499.92
Martin Luther Seminary Budget	499.93
Lutheran Theological Seminary, Phila., Special	25.00
Midland College Budget	9,999.96
Mt. Pleasant Collegiate Institute Budget	2,499.96
Newberry College Budget	3,600.00
Muhlenberg College	1,500.00
Muhlenberg College Special	25.00
Marion College Budget	833.32
Lenoir-Rhyne College Budget	1,500.00
Carthage College Budget	1,800.00
Carthage College Special	10,428.25
Wittenburg College Budget	1,500.00
Gettysburg College Budget	1,500.00
Roanoke College Budget	3,000.00
Summerland College Budget	1,800.00
Susquehanna University Budget	1,500.00
Wagner College Budget	1,999.93
Thiel College Budget	1,500.00
Winnipeg Academy Budget	1,832.27
Woman's College Appropriation Budget	4,999.92

$131,893.98

Balance, June 30, 1928 .... $ 13,679.96

ANNUITY PRINCIPAL ACCOUNT

Balance, July 1, 1927 .... $ 191.88

RECEIPTS

Cash Annuity Bonds issued	250.00
Proceeds—5000 B. & O. 6's, 1929, called at 102½	5,125.00

Proceeds—2000 Scranton and Wilkes-Barre 5's,
called at 105 .... 2,100.00
  ——————— $ 7,666.88

DISBURSEMENTS

Purchased—5000 Appalachian Elec. Power 1st 5's,
1956 .... $ 4,950.00
Purchased—2000 Lack. and Wyo. Valley R. R. 1st 5's   1,935.00
  ——————— 6,885.00

Balance, June 30, 1928 .... $ 781.88

SCHOLARSHIP AND LOAN FUND FOR WOMEN
Principal Account

RECEIPTS

Harriet E. Monroe Fund—Transferred per resolu-
tion of Board dated Dec. 3, 1927............................... $ 3,737.11
Proceeds—Scranton and Wilkes-Barre Trac. 5's
called at 105 .... 1,050.00
  ——————— $ 4,787.11

DISBURSEMENTS

Purchased—1000 Scranton and Wilkes-Barre Trac... $ 760.00
Purchased—3000 Westmoreland Water Co. 2,970.00
Purchased—1000 Lack. and Wyo. Valley R. R. 1st
5's, 1951 .... 967.50
  ——————— 4,697.50

Balance, June 30, 1928 .... $ 89.61

Income Account
Balance on hand, July 1, 1927.. $ 25.24

RECEIPTS

Interest on Investments net 276.79
Income Annuity Bond 40.00
Church Atonement, N. Y., Memory Miss Hilda
Strass 50.00
Miss Matilde Peper 50.00
  ——————— 442.03

DISBURSEMENTS
Accrued Interest on Securities Purchased.................... 49.56
  ———————
Balance, June 30, 1928 .... $ 392.47

CALIFORNIA COLLEGE
Balances, July 1, 1927-June 30, 1928............................. $ 60.00

PERMANENT MINISTERIAL EDUCATION FUND
Principal Account
Balance, July 1, 1927 .... $ 748.84

RECEIPTS
Proceeds—1000 B. & O. 6's, called at 102½................ 1,025.00

Proceeds—2000 Scranton and Wilkes-Barre Traction, called 105 .... 2,100.00
Cash, Treasurer, U. L. C. 60.00
$ 3,933.84

DISBURSEMENTS

Bought 1000 Appalachian Elec. Power 1st, 5's, 1956   990.00
Bought 2000 Lack. and Wyo. Valley 1st, 5's............ 1,935.00
2,925.00

Balance, June 30, 1928 .... $ 1,008.84

Income

Balance, July 1, 1927 .... $ 551.39

RECEIPTS

Interest on Investments 388.62
$ 940.01

DISBURSEMENTS

To student for Ministry, Gettysburg Academy........ 200.00
Interest accrued on Investments................................... 21.95
221.95

Balance, June 30, 1928 .... $ 718.06

PACIFIC SEMINARY AND SASKATOON COLLEGE AND SEMINARY SPECIAL REFORMATION DAY OFFERINGS S. S., U. L. C.

RECEIPTS

Through Treasurer, Board of Education .... $ 4,024.63
Through Treasurer, U. L. C. 1,473.72
$ 5,498.35

DISBURSEMENTS

Transfer—Pacific Seminary, per Resolution, Jan. 27 $ 2,000.00
Transfer—General Fund of Board, per Resolution, Jan. 27 .... 2,000.00
Transfer—Expenses of Campaign, per Resolution, June 27 .... 1,131.92
5,131.92

Balance, June 30, 1928 .... $ 366.43

HARRIET E. MONROE ACCOUNT

Proceeds Equitable Life Insurance Co. of U. S......... $ 3,737.11
Transferred to Principal Account of Scholarship and Loan Fund for Women as per resolution of Board, Dec., 1927 .... 3,737.11
Note.—Executed by the Lutheran Orphan's Home of the South and payable to Elizabeth College, endorsed by Robert W. Kime, Esq., as Liquidating Treasurer of Elizabeth College .... $ 4,000.00
By resolution of Board, the above Note was delivered to E. Clarence Miller, Treasurer of Woman's College 4,000.00

INVESTMENTS
Annuity Fund

Par Value		Book Value
$8,000 Altoona Logan Valley Elec. Ry. 4½, 1933....	$	6,400.00
2,000 Baltimore & Ohio 5's, 1948		1,975.00
6,500 Bell Telephone Co. of Pa., 5's, 1948		6,395.00
1,000 Chesapeake & Ohio Eq., 5's, 1935		969.67
1,000 Penna. R. R. Eq., 5's, 1934		992.26
2,000 Penna. R. R. Eq., 5's, 1935		1,965.60
3,000 Penna. R. R. Eq., 5's, 1938		2,974.80
1,000 Phila. Elec., 5½'s, 1947		1,030.00
4,600 Phila. Elec., 5's, 1966		4,574.37
2,000 Phila. Suburban Water Co., 5's, 1955		1,955.00
4,000 Baltimore & Ohio S. W. Div., 1st 5's, 1950..		4,055.00
13 Shares Western Union Tel. Co. Stock		1,560.00
Note—Marion College, 6 per cent bal.		2,500.00
1,000 Chelsea Hotel Co., 6's, 1945		1,000.00
3,500 Phila. Elec. Power, 1st 5½'s, 1972		3,631.25
5,000 Quaker City Tank Line Eq., 5½'s, 1934		5,000.00
4,000 United Post Offices Corp., 1st 5½'s, 1935		4,000.00
5,000 Appalachian Elec. Power, 1st 5's, 1956		4,950.00
2,000 Lackawanna and Wyoming Valley, 1st 5's, 1951		1,935.00
		$ 57,862.95
Real Estate, 204 A. Street S. E., Washington, D. C.		15,000.00

SCHOLARSHIP AND LOAN FUND FOR WOMEN

1,000 Chesapeake & Ohio Eq., 5's, 1935	$	969.68
1,000 City of Mandon, North Dakota, 6's, 1926 (Gift)		1,000.00
3,000 West Moreland Water Co., 5's, 1952		2,970.00
1,000 Lackawanna & Wyoming Valley R. R., 1st 5's, 1951		967.50
		5,907.18

PERMANENT MINISTERIAL EDUCATION FUND

1,000 Northern States' Power Co., 6's, 1948	$	1,000.00
500 Fort Spring Mag. Dist. Green Briar Co., W. Va., 5's		500.00
1,000 Phila. Suburban Water Co., 5's, 1955		977.50
1,000 Phila. Elec. Power Co., 1st, 5½'s, 1972		1,022.50
1,000 Appalachian Elec. Power, 1st 5's, 1956		990.00
2,000 Lackawanna & Wyoming Valley, 1st 5's, 1951		1,935.00
		6,425.00
		$ 85,195.13

Respectfully submitted,
JOHN M. SNYDER, *Treasurer.*

Philadelphia, August 11, 1928.

We have audited the accounts of the Treasurer of the Board of Education of the United Lutheran Church in America for the year ended June 30, 1928, and have verified the foregoing Treasurer's Report, pages 1 to 5, both inclusive, and we certify that all recorded receipts have been accounted for, that all disbursements were authenticated and that, in our opinion, the foregoing report is correct.

LYBRAND, ROSS BROS. & MONTGOMERY,
Accountants and Auditors.

Dr. Steimle introduced the heads of the various colleges and other institutions who were present and then presented the Rev. R. E. Tulloss, President of Wittenberg College, who addressed the Convention in the interest of the educational work of the Church.

The Rev. J. Henry Harms, Chairman of the Committee on Institutions, then presented the following resolutions which were adopted:

"*Whereas,* the action of the Richmond Convention in 1926, setting apart the year 1930, the four hundredth anniversary of the Augsburg Confession, as Educational Year throughout the Church, has been reecived with such general favor and approval, and

"*Whereas,* it is increasingly vital to the Church in her mission to mankind that her colleges and seminaries shall be adequately equipped and financed without delay,

"*Be it resolved,*

"First, That the Board of Education give all possible aid in making Educational Year a complete success, and that as means to this end, the Board shall call one or more conferences of the representatives of the National Lutheran Educational Conference, Presidents of Synods, and the representatives of any other Church Bodies or agencies which may be interested, with a view especially to the formulation of the strongest possible program of publicity for this appeal to the whole Church which is of such vital consequence to all our institutions;

"Second, That Synods interested in the financing of the institutions on their territory during the year, be advised to organize this educational appeal, as to details, each in its own way to its own constituency with such help as may be available and desirable in the results of the consultations referred to above;

"Third, That all pastors of the Church be requested to take occasion frequently during the year 1930 to stress the cause of Christian Education and in every possible way to lay this burden of the adequate support of our colleges and seminaries upon the hearts of all our people, and to co-operate heartily with the representatives of their institutions in making this appeal successful."

Dr. Harms then spoke of the progress made by the Lutheran College for Women and presented the following resolutions:

"*Whereas,* we have heard with interest of the continued co-operation of nine of our Constituent Synods in the establishment of the Woman's College at Washington, D. C., and

"*Whereas,* there appears to be a demand for a college such as is being planned—a standard Christian college under the auspices of the Church for the education of our young women,

"*Be it resolved*

"1. That we commend the synods which are co-operating in this enterprise and wish them complete success in their undertaking.

"2. That we call attention of all our pastors to the service which has been prepared for use in all our Sunday schools on Sunday, November 10th, in the coming Reformation Season, by which it is intended to arouse interest throughout the Church in the proposed College for Women and to gather funds in aid of its establishment.

"3. That we commend the Woman's College to the favor and financial support of persons interested in the founding of such a College for the young women of the Church as speedily as possible."

Dr. Wm. A. Kump, Administrative Secretary of the College, further addressed the Convention concerning this institution and on motion the resolutions were adopted.

The Rev. J. Huebner, president of Martin Luther Seminary, Lincoln, Nebr., offered the following resolution pertaining to the Silver Jubilee of Director Petersen of Breklum-Kropp:

"*Whereas,* it has been brought to the attention of the United Lutheran Church in America, assembled in Convention at Erie, Pa., that Director Petersen of Breklum Seminary has recently celebrated his silver jubilee as professor in that institution,

"*Whereas,* as nearly one hundred of his former students are now actively engaged in the United Lutheran Church as pastors, college and seminary professors, and

"*Whereas,* all of these hold Director Petersen in very high esteem and grateful affection, praising his sound scholarship and his consecrated Christian character,

"*Be it Resolved,* That we express to Director Petersen our deep appreciation of his faithful services by which the United Lutheran Church has been benefited and extend to him our heartiest congratulations, wishing him many more years of fruitful labors in the Kingdom of our Lord,

"*And be it further resolved,* That the Secretary of the United Lutheran Church forward a copy of these resolutions to Director Petersen."

The resolution was adopted.

The Rev. C. P. Harry, Chairman of the Committee on Religious Work in State Universities, and Dr. Mary E. Markley, Secretary of the Department for Women Students, addressed the Convention.

The Rev. Wm. M. Horn, Secretary of the Board of Education, offered the following resolutions which were adopted:

Inasmuch as the Board of Education has received a request from representatives of the Board of Trustees of Midland College and Western Theological Seminary for its opinion concerning the advisability and feasibility of continuing the Western Theological Seminary or merging it with some other seminary,

Therefore, we recommend, That this Convention authorize and instruct the Board of Education to make a survey as to the advisability and feasibility of continuing the Western Theological Seminary or of merging the same with some other seminary of the United Lutheran Church in America.

The Rev. Howard R. Gold was given a seat and voice in the Convention. He presented the report of the Survey of the Educational Situation in the United Lutheran Church, included in the Report of the Board of Education.

Dr. Steimle then introduced Dr. Robert J. Leonard, one of the Joint Directors of the survey, who addressed the Convention. It was ordered that his address be made a part of the Minutes. The address follows:

ADDRESS OF DR. ROBERT J. LEONARD

When the Church in 1924 authorized the Board of Education to make a comprehensive study of the educational program, it must have been realized that a unique and important step had been taken. Unique because no other great church organization had undertaken a similar study, although since that time two other bodies have copied your action, the Disciples of Christ and the Presbyterians. Important because of the possible consequences of such a study upon the development of education.

Mingled with your hopes were doubtless fears and apprehension lest those selected to carry on the project be short-sighted regarding policy, out of close sympathy with Christian education, or so scientifically minded as to fail to grasp the meaning of the aspirations of the church leaders, which were implied but not stated.

As you know, your Board of Education pursued the very wise course of proceeding with great care and caution, and took almost two years to plan the study and select the personnel.

Those chosen to serve you were familiar with colleges and universities in this country, and were accustomed to the technical procedures adapted to the ends in view.   Although each was actively affiliated with some Protestant Church no one of us was adequately informed as to the distinctive educational or religious problems of the United Lutheran Church in America.

Accordingly, the first few months were given over to a study of the history of the Church in the United States, its educational aspirations, the development of its institutions and the organization and operation of the Board of Education.

For two years most of the waking hours of Dr. Evenden, Dr. O'Rear and myself have been given to the survey.   We have become acquainted with the officers of the Church, the members of the Board of Education and the Survey Commission, the Presidents of the institutions, and many faculty members.

We have come to know and appreciate something of the reasons for your devotion to the Church, the integrity of your leaders, and the seriousness of your purposes.

Although it was understood that it was your desire to have the study made by those outside your own church organization, we have proceeded as though we were part of the organization itself, and the conclusions to which we have come, and the recommendations which have been made, have been far more carefully conceived and formulated than if we ourselves were to be later concerned with their execution.

The problems confronting your institutions are approximately the same as those of all other Christian colleges.   Regardless of the approach you may make, you are soon driven to the central issue.

Why does the church in this day attempt to maintain its own institutions, and how should those institutions differ from others?

There are in this country approximately 975 institutions for higher education.

One-third are supported by public taxation and may be regarded as in the realm of the state;

One-third are supported by tuition and private gifts and may be thought of as in the realm of philanthrophy, and

One-third are supported by church organizations and may be considered as in the realm of religion.

The oldest, and for a century, the most influential groups were those in the realm of religion. Of the ten colonial colleges, including Harvard, Yale, Princeton, William and Mary, eight were founded by God-fearing men for the Christianization of the Indians, and for preparing young men for the ministry. You know the success of these colleges—graduates filling pulpits, teaching, rearing large families, were in the front rank in promoting education and Christianity. To each new settlement came not only churches but church colleges; the founding of these colleges directly parallels the western movement, and the flow of immigration. By the middle of the nineteenth century there were Christian colleges dotting the whole country and enjoying intellectual as well as spiritual leadership.

And then came the rising tide of state-supported institutions—starting in the South, North Carolina and Virginia, spreading to the middle west, and re-enforced by the Land-Grant Act of 1862—institutions new in type and purpose, at first boasting an open mind toward all truth, scoffing at, or only weakly supporting the position that spiritual truth is the most important truth of all!

Backed by great public resources, the promise of a freer type of life for students and numerous attractions for faculty members, they soon assumed the position of leadership by sheer force of the size of the student bodies, the breadth of the program, and the superior physical facilities.

And the church college, originally responsible for higher education and for the setting and maintenance of standards, by degrees, either voluntarily left the custody of the church, to receive large grants from private sources and from foundations, or was relegated to a position of secondary importance.

For twenty years or more the church colleges have occupied a competitive position, somewhat of a defensive character. By the process of upgrading they have tried to hold their own and become as well regarded academically as the state universities or the endowed colleges. Perforce, the standards of the state institutions have been copied, and each year the church college has become more like them in educational program, athletics and sports, social life and general objectives. To retain their place in the educational world, they have tended to sacrifice the very thing for which they were established, and the only reason for their claim upon church support.

Such is the general situation among Christian colleges in the United States, and such is true of the Lutheran situation in broad, general outline. The problem is not only to make and keep the colleges of high grade as to scholarship, but to bring to the front conspicuously the one purpose which differentiates them from state and private institutions—religion.

It would be far from the truth, and most unfair to convey the impression that your institutions are irreligious, or failing by conscious effort to promote the highest Christian standards, but it is fair to say, and it should be said plainly, that your institutions have been so pressed to obtain the necessary funds for bare existence that all the finer things have suffered.

The Church has been all too willing to establish an institution, call a distinguished minister as President and then throw the burden of raising funds and erecting buildings upon the President. His talents which should be directed toward inspiring students and faculties, and promoting Christian character, are spent in running financial campaigns and in the work of an educational promoter.

No Lutheran college now maintains a religious program adequate for the great ends of the Church, in terms of leadership, or facilities for worship, activities or instruction! It is not because of the lack of desire, but for the lack of funds, and the added reason that such is not considered as basic need for religious work, just as great in the church colleges as by the controlling educational agencies.

There is latent within every Lutheran institution the consuming desire to build Christian character, to release to the leadership of the Church qualified individuals, and to enthrone within the institution the key activity.

That the organized Church, through its Board of Education, should spend its funds for the direct promotion of religious instruction and activities, seems from every point of view the most constructive course to be taken.

By so doing notice is served to the world of the preferred value placed upon religion in the college, and assurance is given that each institution will maintain at least a minimum religious program.

There are two occupations whose insignia is a lighted lamp, the miner and the teacher. The miner with a candle at his forehead, and the teacher with a lamp upon the table. About the time of Martin Luther a German writer defined a miner as one who goes into the grave to find coal that we may be warm, jewels that we may be adorned, and gold that we may trade!

I wonder how he would have defined the teacher. Perhaps—the teacher is one who goes into the mind and heart of youth, and there by sympathetic understanding finds talents that may be developed, motives that may be heightened and a whole life that may be dedicated to useful service.

There are scores of such individuals in your institutions. They may be discouraged because of meager support, or disheartened because they do not see the results of their work, but I am sure they will be reassured if religion can become a more conspicuous objective, and can be more adequately supported.

Prof. Edward S. Evenden, Ph.D., further explained to the Convention the work of the survey and F. B. O'Rear, Ph.D., Associate Director of the survey, outlined the contents of the nine volumes of the report which were exhibited to the Convention.

On motion the recommendation under "D" was adopted.

Moved and carried, That the extent of the spread of this publication be referred to the Survey Commission here present, members of the Board of Education and the college presidents, to report to this Convention. (See Minutes Sixth Meeting, Morning Session—Secretary.)

By a rising vote the Convention expressed to Drs. Leonard, Evenden and O'Rear its appreciation of the spirit in which their work has been done as well as of its value.

The report of the auditors on accounts of the Board of Education was accepted.

Under the heading of unfinished business the report of the Common Service Book Committee was taken up, and a motion was passed to reconsider the action taken on the resolution concerning the proposed music edition of the Common Service Book.

The Rev. O. D. Baltzly proposed the following amendment which was adopted:

That the first stanza of a hymn of three stanzas, the first and second stanzas of a hymn of four stanzas, the first, second and third stanzas of a hymn of five or more stanzas, shall be printed between the staves.

The original resolution as amended was adopted.

Dr. Reed presented again the resolutions concerning the translation of Luther's Catechism, with the third revised in the following form:

Resolved, That when the final text is adopted by the Joint Committee and approved by the Common Service Book Committee, it shall be published as the Jubilee edition of Luther's Small Catechism; but this resolution shall not deprive the Common Service Book Committee of the right to make such subsequent alterations in the text as that Committee may deem imerpatively necessary.

The resolution as revised was adopted.

The resolutions adopted as a whole.

It was moved and carried, That the right of voting in this Convention be given to an alternate from the East Pennsylvania Synod in the absence of one of the principal delegates.

The Convention adjourned with prayer by the Rev. John Aberly.

Afternoon Session

Monday, October 15, 2.00 o'clock.

Devotions were conducted by the Rev. A. H. Keck.

The President called the Convention to order.

The Rev. H. Offermann, Chairman of the Committee of Reference and Counsel, read the following telegram:

"Greetings from our Church. God's richest blessing upon The United Lutheran Church in America.
"H. J. URDAHL, President of the Norwegian
Lutheran Free Church."

It was moved and carried, That the Committe be authorized to send a suitable reply.

The Chairman of the Committee read the following cablegram:

"Rajahmundry, October 13, 1928.
"The Andhra Church in Convention sends greetings to Mother Church.
"PRESIDENT BURGER."

Moved and carried, That a cablegram conveying the greetings of the United Lutheran Church be sent by the President to the Evangelical Lutheran Church in the Andhra Country, India.

The Committee presented the following resolution:

Resolved, That the United Lutheran Church in Convention assembled expresses its high appreciation of the splendid services rendered by our Publication House and all those who are connected with its business in the various departments. It most heartily commends the spirit of loyalty and devotion to the work which permeates all establishments of the business at Philadelphia, Chicago, Pittsburgh and Columbia. It also recognizes the inestimable value of the two Church papers, *The Lutheran* and *Lutherischer Herold,* published regularly each week, and it again recommends these papers most earnestly to all the members of the Church.

The resolution was adopted.

Also the following resolution of the Committee was adopted:

Resolved, That we express our grateful appreciation to the pastor, Church

Council, choir, and members of Luther Memorial Church, as well as to all the Lutheran pastors and churches at Erie, the Chamber of Commerce, and all others who have offered us their hospitality.

The following resolution offered by the Rev. A. S. Hardy and amended by the Committee was referred to the Executive Board:

Resolved, That at elections in future conventions, no stars or other distinguishing marks, except such abbreviations as denote synodical affiliations, be placed opposite names upon the ballots, and that the resolution of the Chicago Convention providing such distinguishing marks be herewith rescinded.

The following resolution was proposed and adopted:

Resolved, That the Secretary be authorized to urge upon all Boards, Committees and Commissions the desirability of presenting their final reports for the printed Bulletin in the briefest possible form and in the clearest possible language.

The Chairman of the Committee then presented Dr. L. W. Boe, of the Norwegian Lutheran Church in America and President of St. Olaf's College. Dr. Boe addressed the Convention and conveyed the greetings of Dr. Aasgaard, President of the Norwegian Lutheran Church, to Dr. Knubel, President of The United Lutheran Church in America.

By appointment of the President, the Rev. J. A. W. Haas made the response on behalf of the Convention.

The Rev. Alonzo J. Turkle presented the report of the Commission on Theological Education as follows:

REPORT OF COMMISSION ON THEOLOGICAL EDUCATION

The Commission on Theological Education in the United Lutheran Church, authorized by the Chicago Convention of the United Lutheran Church in America, and continued by the Richmond Convention (see Minutes for 1926, pages 542 and 662) met in Philadelphia, Pa., October 12, 1927.

An organization was effected electing Rev. Dr. Alonzo J. Turkle, Chairman, Mr. W. H. Stackel, Secretary. Other members of the Commission are: Rev. L. F. Gruber, D.D., LL.D., Maywood, Ill.; Rev. C. E. Walter, D.D., York, Pa.; Rev. C. M. Jacobs, D.D., Philadelphia, Pa.; Rev. John A. W. Haas, D.D., LL.D., Allentown, Pa.; Rev. A. G. Voigt, D,D., LL.D., Columbia, S. C.; Rev. Paul W. Koller, D.D., Mansfield, Ohio; Rev. C. H. Little, D.D., Waterloo, Canada; and Judge H. W. Harter, Canton, Ohio.

The second meeting was held in Philadelphia, Pa., on February 22, 1928. The Commission was favored with the presence of President Knubel in the first meeting of the biennium, whose counsel was greatly appreciated.

CONFERENCE OF SEMINARY FACULTIES

It has been a matter of great satisfaction to the Commission that two conferences of Seminary faculties have been held since the last Convention of the Church.

The first of these conferences was held in June, 1927, at Gettysburg, Pa. It was attended by representatives of the Gettysburg, Susquehanna, Philadelphia, Chicago and Northwestern Seminaries and of the Hamma Divinity School. The Conference organized by the election of President C. M. Jacobs as Chairman, and Professor A. R. Wentz as Secretary. There were four sessions held at which matters of common interest were discussed and it was resolved to continue the conferences in future years.

The second conference was held at Philadelphia, June 19th and 20th, 1928. Nine Seminaries were represented at this conference, as follows:

Hartwick, Gettysburg, Philadelphia, Susquehanna, Southern, Chicago, Western, Northwestern and Hamma Divinity School.

Four sessions were held under the chairmanship of Dean Manhart of Susquehanna University. It was resolved to hold the Conference in 1929 at Susquehanna University.

The Commission believes that these conferences have been productive of much good. While no definite actions have been taken, the conferences have served to give the professors in our various institutions an opportunity to become more intimately acquainted and the discussions of matters of common interest have led to a large number of informal understandings between the institutions that will not only reduce friction, but must lead eventually to closer co-operation than has been possible in the past. We believe that this part of the Commission's program has been decidedly worth while.

CONSOLIDATION OF SEMINARIES

In harmony with Recommendation No. 2, Page 541, Minutes of 1926 Convention, the Commission issued an invitation to the Presidents and the Presidents of the Boards of Directors of Gettysburg Seminary, Philadelphia Seminary, Susquehanna University and Hartwick Seminary to enter into a conference for the purpose of considering whether the needs of the Church may not be served by consolidation or by such affiliation as may unify or correlate their work. These representatives met in Harrisburg on November 15, 1927. The following were present: Rev. C. W. Leitzell, D.D., Board President, and Rev. C. R. Meyers, D.D., Seminary President representing Hartwick; Rev. John Weidley, D.D., Board President, and Rev. John A. Aberly, D.D., Seminary President representing Gettysburg Seminary; Rev. L. P. Young, D.D., Board President, and Rev. F. P. Manhart, D.D., LL.D., Dean of Seminary representing Susquehanna; E. Clarence Miller, LL.D., Board President, and Rev. C. M. Jacobs, D.D., Seminary President representing Philadelphia Seminary.

In the general discussion of the consolidation of seminaries recognition was given to the fact that the representatives had not authority to speak officially, but a full and frank consideration was participated in by all present.

The following action was taken:

"*Whereas,* the question of the closer affiliation of seminaries has been referred to the various theological institutions on contiguous territories."

"*Whereas,* it is exceedingly important that this question be decided soon, as programs of seminaries are waiting for its decision.

Resolved, Item I—that the representatives of Hartwick, Gettysburg, Susquehanna and Philadelphia Seminaries assembled at the call of the Commission on Theological Education of the U. L. C. at Harrisburg, Pa., November 15, 1927, request the controlling authorities of these institutions to consider this question, and in case of favorable consideration appoint conference committees.

Item II—that along with this request to the controlling authorities we take the liberty of giving it as our opinion that, provided plans can be worked out so that nothing essential for which the various institutions have stood need be sacrificed, we would favor consolidation.

Accordingly the matter was presented to the Boards of the four Seminaries, and Committees were appointed by Gettysburg, Philadelphia, and Susquehanna for authoritative conference, Hartwick took the following action: "Whereas: We, the Board of Trusteees of Hartwick Seminary are convinced of the absolute need of a Theological Seminary on the territory of our Synod of New York, and in view of the fact that we have on this territory the center of the greatest population in the United States and also the potential center of Lutheran strength, THEREFORE: We cannot favor any merging of Seminaries which would deprive this territory of a Lutheran Theological Seminary." The Hartwick Board requested the president to attend the conference but he was prevented by sickness.

Pursuant to their appointment by their respective Boards and to the call of the Commission on Theological Education, the Conference was held in Harrisburg, Pa., June 22, 1928. Those present from Gettysburg were: Rev. John Aberly, D.D., Rev. Edwin Heyl Delk, D.D., Rev. John Weidley,

D.D., Robbin B. Wolf, Esq., and Mr. William H. Menges; from Philadelphia: Rev. Charles M. Jacobs, D.D., Rev. George Gebert, D.D., Rev. F. H. Uhrich, D.D., Rev. J. A. W. Haas, D.D., LL.D., E. Clarence Miller, LL.D., and from Susquehanna: Rev. R. Morris Smith, D.D., Rev. F. P. Manhart, D.D., LL.D., Rev. T. Reisch, D.D., Messrs. M. P. Moller, Charles Steel, and Sterling Decker.

This meeting reaffirmed the action taken at the meeting of representatives of the same institutions on November 15th, 1927, as follows: "Provided plans can be worked out so that nothing essential for which the various institutions have stood need be sacrificed we would favor consolidation." This action was unanimously adopted as well as the following: "We are agreed that the doctrinal basis of such a consolidated Seminary should be the doctrinal basis of the United Lutheran Church in America." Committees were authorized and appointed to give consideration to the questions involved in the legal aspects, organization and control, and location of the consolidated Seminary. The chairman of the Commission has been invited to call another conference when these committees are ready to report.

The Theological Curriculum

The Commission has been making a further study of the findings reported to the Richmond Convention through two committees. The principles underlying theological education, the requirements for faculty positions, and for student admission to undergraduate courses of the Seminary, have been given special consideration. The Commission has had some discussion of the theological curriculum recommended in the report of the Commission in 1926 (Minutes, pages 524-541). The Commission has made no modification in that report and recommends that it be referred to the Conference of Theological Faculties with the request that it be discussed by that Conference and the findings reported to the Commission. To facilitate this action, the Commission asks permission to reprint this portion of its report as a separate leaflet for general distribution to those interested.

Practical Experience for Theological Students

The section of the report of the 1926 convention concerning the desirability of practical contacts and practical experience for theological students has been under discussion also. In this connection, the Commission desired to present the report of the sub-committee as follows:

The desirability of practical contacts and practical experience has been stated in the report of the Commission to the U. L. C. (Minutes of 1926, Page 529g). The question which the Commission has to consider is how these contacts can be formed and how large a place for forming of such contacts may have during the period that men are actively preparing for the ministry.

This is one of the really difficult problems with which Theological Seminaries are confronted and it may well be questioned whether any solution of the problem can be found that can be applied equally by all seminaries. Like most of the other problems with which the Commission has to deal, it is primarily one of emphasis. Shall the emphasis in theological education be placed on the practical work of the ministry or shall it be placed upon the acquisition of theoretical knowledge? The answer, no doubt, should be that both sides of theological education should receive their proper emphasis and the question then becomes "How can the seminaries give an adequate amount of practical experience to their students without letting down their theoretical and intellectual standards?" The higher the intellectual demands which a seminary makes upon its students, the more limited is the time which can be spared for the work of forming practical contacts.

The problem is complicated by the differences between the theological seminaries themselves. One important factor is that of location. Where a seminary is located in a rural community, the possibilities of general contact with the practical work of the Church and with many different kinds of men are necessarily limited. On the other hand, where the seminary is located in a metropolitan center the number of such activities that open to students is so large that the temptation becomes very strong to neglect the theoretical side of theological education and engage chiefly in one or another form of practical work. This simply illustrates one of the difficulties in the solution of the problem. The following general rules are suggested:

First. Theological seminaries should encourage their students to engage in practical activity and should, if possible, provide opportunities for such activity. They should, however, be closely in touch with these activities of their students, and student work should always be under the regulation and control of the seminary itself.

Second. During the first two years of the seminary course, every student should be definitely engaged in some specific work, either in a congregation or under some general agency of the Church. In this work he should have some well-defined responsibility under the supervision of the pastor or other person in charge of the work. Where possible, he should serve as an assistant pastor and thus be brought into touch with a variety of Church activity.

Third. Vacation times should be used by theological students for the further development of contacts with men. It is not necessary and it is not in all cases desirable, that this work should be definitely the work of the Church. There are other occupations of a secular character in which men may secure that insight into human nature which must, after all, lie at the basis of a successful administration of the work of the Church.

SPECIALIZED TRAINING

With reference to specialized training in theological seminaries the following was adopted by the Commission:

This subject is closely connected with that which has been discussed above. The practical contacts of theological students with the work of the Church are not only a means to their own development, but may also serve a useful purpose in revealing the special talents which the student has for one or another of the many lines along which the Church's work is done.

SCHOOLS FOR LAY-WORKERS

With regard to the training of men for the fields of Religious Education, Inner Missions and Foreign Missions, theological seminaries should be warned of the danger to the Church which may arise from early specialization. It is highly important that the specialists in all our lines of work should have a thorough knowledge and a sympathetic understanding of the work of the Church outside of their own special fields. The foreign missionary should know the home Church before he goes into the foreign field, and the inner missionary should have a thorough understanding of the problems of the congregation. There is, perhaps, no single field in which specialization begun too early contains more danger for the Church than in the field of religious education. If religious education is to become anything more than a fad, our religious educators must possess the full training that is required of men who enter into the other ordinary activities of the Church.

While all this is true, it nevertheless remains a fact that for the work of Foreign Missions, Inner Missions and Religious Education, a special training is necessary over and above that which men get from the general theological course.

The Commission therefore believes: That the proper time of special education for Foreign Missions, Inner Missions, and Religious Education, is at the end of the seminary course. Such instruction as is given in these subjects during the first three years should be given with a view to acquainting future pastors with these lines of work and specialized courses such as are required for actual foreign mission work and the like should be built up on the general courses previously given.

The Commission also considered the subject of training schools for lay-workers and reports the following conclusions:

The training of lay-workers is a field that differs very widely from the general field of theology. In connection with this work two dangers need to be avoided.

The first is that schools, which start as schools for lay-workers will eventually become theological seminaries of low grade and serve as short-cuts by which men of insufficient preliminary education will endeavor to enter the ministry of the Church. The other danger is that laymen who have had a certain amount of training in such schools will become troublesome members of their congregation and be possessed of the idea that they are as well qualified to conduct the affairs of the congregation as the pastor.

These two dangers offer the strongest argument for connecting schools for lay-workers with the theological seminaries which would then be in control of the standards and the content of the education given to laymen.

It may be doubted whether any seminary of our Church is so equipped at the present time that it can add courses for lay-workers to the regular courses of instruction now being given. The matter is one that requires prolonged and serious study, before a definite program should be adopted. There can be no doubt at all that such a study ought to be made if only to prevent the development within our Church of mushroom schools whose courses are defective both in content and method.

Two other subjects have been under discussion. These are Advanced Theological Education, and the provision which the Church should make for it (Minutes of 1926, page 539, VII, 6) and the possibility of establishing Extension Schools for Pastors. Concerning these two subjects the Commission is not yet prepared to make a definite report.

GENERAL PROPOSITIONS

The Commission presents the definite conclusions embodied in the following statements:

1. We believe that for the best interest of the Church the theological seminaries should be more definitely bound to the United Lutheran Church.
2. We believe from our survey and data in hand, that only one seminary should serve a definite territory, and where there is more than one seminary on that territory that they should take steps to consolidate.
3. We believe that the number and boundaries of such territory should be fixed by the United Lutheran Church in such manner as it shall determine.
4. We believe that the standard requirement for admission into the undergraduate courses of our seminaries should be that of graduation from a standard college or its equivalent.
5. We believe that the whole subject of beneficiary education should be studied by the Church.
6. We believe that the Church should call the attention of seminary boards to the importance of satisfying themselves thoroughly as to the teaching ability of men proposed to them for faculty positions.
7. We believe that all graduate work leading to degrees should be done in residence and be made of the same value as that of other graduate schools.
8. We believe that all seminaries should foster to the fullest degree the spiritual life of their students and that they should make very definite provision for this very necessary part in the development of the theological student.

Respectfully submitted,

ALONZO J. TURKLE, *Chairman.*

W. H. STACKEL, *Secretary.*

The following resolution was adopted:

Resolved, That the Commission on Theological Education be enlarged to a membership of fifteen, to be appointed by the Executive Board, and that it be directed to prepare for submission to the United Lutheran Church at its next convention a Theological Seminary policy along the lines suggested in Items 1, 2 and 3 of the General Propositions included in the present report.

Item 5 of the Report of the Committee on Memorials from Constituent Synods, action on which had been postponed to this time, was brought up for consideration. The Rev. E. B. Burgess, President of the Pittsburgh Synod, withdrew the memorial.

The Rev. Wm. L. Hunton presented the report of the Parish and Church School Board and introduced the Revs. Charles H. B. Lewis, S. White Rhyne and D. Burt Smith, Secretaries, each of whom addressed the Convention.

THE REPORT OF THE PARISH AND CHURCH SCHOOL BOARD

THE SPHERE AND OBJECT OF THIS BOARD

The sphere of this Board in its general program of education seems not to be as clearly understood by all as it should be. The Board according to the charter and constitution given to it by the Church and approved by the Convention at Washington, announces specifically a very broad and comprehensive program of objectives toward which it should strive.

"The object of this Board shall be to develop and execute a system of literature for use in the home, the parish and the Church schools; to organize schools for weekday Christian training; to plan methods of school administration; to recommend books for the library; to outline programs for Summer Assemblies, Sunday School Conventions and Normals and all festival occasions of the Church; to prepare hymnals; to have oversight over and control of whatever pertains to the best interests of the parish and the Church school. It shall carry on its work in the name of The United Lutheran Church in America, and in accordance with the Doctrinal Basis, Constitution, Acts and Rulings of said United Lutheran Church in America."

Thus it will be seen that this Board is the natural and logical directive agency for all educational work in our parishes. Keeping in mind its aims the Board has at various times sought the co-operation of other agencies and has always shown its desire to advise and help and is at this time specially striving to co-ordinate all the parish educational activities and thus increase the efficiency and the harmony with which these various agencies can work in our congregations.

We express approval of the plan for co-ordination and recommend that every effort be put forth to unify and make a co-ordinated educational program for our congregations.

INTERSYNODICAL CONFERENCE ON ELEMENTARY CHRISTIAN EDUCATION

Your Board has been co-operating with other Lutheran bodies in holding special conferences on Elementary Christian education. These conferences have been held in Chicago. The following synods have been represented: Augustana, Danish United, Iowa Synod, the Lutheran Free Church (Norwegian), the Norwegian Church in America, the Joint Synod of Ohio and the United Lutheran Church. The accredited representatives of our Board have been the Rev. Charles P. Wiles, D.D., and the Rev. W. L. Hunton, D.D.

The conferences have discussed the fundamental principles of our church program of Christian education, various types of curriculum and the possibilities of a closer co-operation, even to the extent of considering a possible uniform program for the entire Lutheran Church.

Differences in principles and practices which showed themselves in the discussions were plainly pointed out and frankly considered. A better understanding on the part of the editors representing the various sections of our Church has resulted. While some seemed to feel discouraged and to expect more rapid results we feel that these conferences have been quite helpful.

We recommend that the Board continue to participate in such conferences and encourage further co-operation in the hope of ultimately attaining greater uniformity in our Christian educational curricula.

TEXT BOOKS AND LESSON MATERIAL

The chief effort of the Board during the past biennium has been given to the development of new text books for our various types of church schools. The Board recognizes the need of text books which in content and method are on a par with the best educational text books. It has for this reason given special thought to the selection of writers and unusual diligence in supervising the preparation of the various texts.

RELIGIOUS EDUCATION TEXTS

The series of religious education texts designed especially for use in Weekday Church Schools was chiefly in outline two years ago. We now with pleasure announce the completion of the Primary and Junior texts, a total of twelve volumes as follows:

PRIMARY

First Year	"God and His Helpers"	Pupil
	"God and His Helpers"	Teacher
Second Year	"Jesus and His Friends"	Pupil
	"Jesus and His Friends"	Teacher
Third Year	"God's Good Gifts"	Pupil
	"God's Good Gifts"	Teacher

JUNIOR

First Year	"God's Great Plan for Mankind"	Pupil
	"God's Great Plan for Mankind"	Teacher
Second Year	"God's Care for Mankind"	Pupil
	"God's Care for Mankind"	Teacher
Third Year	"God Working Through Mankind"	Pupil
	"God Working Through Mankind"	Teacher

The Primary texts were prepared by Mrs. Mabel B. Fenner, a former supervising principal in a Cleveland, Ohio, Kindergarten, and the Junior texts by Miss Eva M. Stilz, a teacher in the Philadelphia Public Schools.

The aim of the Board has been to have a complete primary and junior department. The demand for higher grades is somewhat limited and general material is more available. As the need develops and their use in the churches seems to warrant, upper grades will be added to this course.

DAILY VACATION CHURCH SCHOOLS

During the biennium a complete series of Daily Vacation Church Schools has been planned and the books have been prepared by our Children's Division editor, Mrs. Maud Junkin Baldwin.

The books which have been completed and are ready for use, with titles, are as follows:

PRIMARY

1. "The Heavenly Father and His Children."
2. "Serving the Heavenly Father."

JUNIOR

4. "Stories of the Early Hebrew Heroes."
5. "Stories of Jesus."

Book 3 for Primary Grade and Book 6 for Junior Grade are in manuscript and will be ready for Vacation Church Schools next summer.

THE CHRISTIAN LIFE COURSE

Having thus carried out the requests of the Church and prepared a Graded Course of text-books for Weekday Church Schools and another for Vacation Church Schools, the present plan is to give special attention to the preparation of the text-books of the new Christian Life Course, which is our official Lutheran Graded Series. This course has been outlined and is already approved by the Church as follows:

1. *Beginners or Christian Kindergarten*
   WONDERLAND

2. *Primary*
   (a) WORKLAND }
   (b) PICTURELAND } 3 years

3. *Junior—Intermediate*
   (a) Bible Story ⎱
   (b) Bible Readings ⎬ 3 years
   (c) Bible Truths ⎰

4. *Intermediate* (Junior High)
   (a) Bible Characters
   (b) Bible History ⎱ (New Testament) ⎱ 3 years
   (c) Bible History ⎰ (Old Testament) ⎰

5. *Senior*
   (a) The Faith of the Church
   (b) The Work of the Church
   (c) The History of the Church
       (To include the History of the Bible in the Church)

Several preliminary conferences have been held, the purpose being to determine the underlying pedagogical and biblical principle which should govern the writers of the text-books. These conferences have included in addition to our editors and authors of the prospective books several professors of Religious Education and pastors who have given unusual attention to the development of the curricula and program of Christian education in our parishes. With this preliminary work done the Board now feels it is free to push the development of this series and aims as rapidly as the writers can produce the texts, to edit the same and arrange for their publication. We confidently believe that a number of these texts will be ready for the use of our schools during the coming biennium.

We express appreciation of the results attained and approve the method of procedure and urge upon the schools of our congregations to use the official literature which the Church is providing through its Parish and Church School Board.

THE LESSON COMMENTARY

The eighth volume of this annual supplementary help for our teachers in the use of the Uniform lessons has been published. This Commentary, it should be remembered, is supplementary to all other literature which furnishes teaching material on the Uniform lessons. It treats the subject in a comprehensive and clear manner. The Commentary has had the highest commendation from authorities outside of our Lutheran Church. Its increasing circulation within the Church is evidence of its approval by those who are its beneficiaries. The current year, dealing as it does with great doctrines, teachings, and social problems in the light of God's Word, is a particularly valuable issue of the Commentary.

HYMNALS

Immediately following the completion of The Parish School Hymnal, the Board authorized its Committee on Hymnals to prepare a children's hymnal. The Committee of this Board for this task included Dr. Wm. Hoppe, Dr.

W. L. Hunton, Dr. J. D. M. Brown, together with Dr. D. Burt Smith. A sub-committee of the Common Service Book Committee co-operated. The members were Dr. J. F. Ohl, Dr. W. E. Fischer and Dr. M. L. Stirewalt, together with Dr. Strodach.

The new hymnal which will appear in the near future is the result of a study of more than fifty hymnals of Primary and Junior grade, the selection of hymns being made largely on the basis of use. Special emphasis has also been laid upon the securing of new and original hymns and tunes, a very large contribution to this collection having been made by the Rev. J. F. Ohl, Mus.D., D.D., to whom the special thanks of the Board and the Church are due for his contributions. The title of the new hymnal is to be "The Children's Service Book and Hymnal."

Your Board was encouraged through its Hymnal Committee to proceed in the preparation of this book by the remarkable favor with which The Parish School Hymnal was received by the Church. Probably no other book thus far issued by our Publication Board has met with more universal favor and with less criticism.

Favorable reception of The Parish School Hymnal and the frequent request for orchestration moved the Publication Board to undertake the preparation of a complete orchestration which will be furnished for churches in eight volumes, through which music for twenty-two instruments will be provided. This was the work of Mrs. Catherine S. Zendt, the daughter of one of our Lutheran pastors, Rev. H. K. Fitting, of Quakertown, Pa.

Your Board has provided regularly the music services for Christmas, Easter, Children's Day and Rally Day. In the preparation of these services special attention has been given to the occasion and the type of service. the music texts have been determined with great care.

Through these services and hymnals the worship of our Church schools can be brought to a much higher standard and be made far more devotional than in the past.

LEADERSHIP TRAINING

During the past year the Board, believing that Leadership Training was one of the greatest needs of our educational work in our congregations, inaugurated an intensive campaign to further the work. A special issue of The Parish School, announcements in The Augsburg Teacher and our other periodicals and special correspondence with all pastors and schools resulted in a quickened interest and secured a wide response. Probably more have been engaged in Leadership Training work during the past year than at any other time in the history of our Church. The Board is at the present time providing the Lutheran Advanced Standard Training Course and planning for its revision and enlargment. It is also giving credits for the New Standard Training Course and co-operating in the development of many specialization units.

Special training schools have sprung up in various communities. For such Leadership Training Schools the Board recommends courses in outline and gives such supervision as is possible. It also under definitely prescribed regulations provides diplomas for graduates of these training schools who have secured the proper number of units of credit.

It is recommended that all training schools, whether community, conference or synodical, co-operate with the Parish and Church School Board for the completion of their work. In this manner unification of our Lutheran training work as well as its standardization will result.

The Board recognizing the necessity of some intensive Leadership Training work appointed a special committee on Leadership Training Camps, composed of M. Hadwin Fischer, Ph.D., Th.D., Rev. F. R. Knubel and Prof. Gilbert P. Voigt, Ph.D. The Chairman has made a thorough study of the problem and after investigating various sites suitable for camps and the methods prevailing ·in other camps, inter-denominational and denominational, recommended to the Board the establishment of a Lutheran Leadership Training Camp. A site was selected near Brysonia, Adams County, Pa. An Adams County Committee raised the funds for the purchase of the site and offered the same to our Parish and Church School Board.

The Board authorized the acceptance of the site and the appointment of a holding corporation which under the direction of the Board shall be responsible for its management and maintenance. A number of synods have pledged contributions toward the erection of proper buildings and tentative dates for the opening of the camp have been agreed upon. It is proposed that the first season of the camp shall be from June 10th to September 2, 1929.

The General Director is the Rev. M. Hadwin Fischer, Ph.D., Th.D., Gettysburg, Pa., and the Assistant Director, Miss La Vene Grove, Harrisburg, Pa.

A constitution has been approved and the following men have been named as the members of the holding corporation:

The Rev. M. Hadwin Fischer, Ph.D., Th.D.

Mr. Alvin Nissly, Hanover, Pa.
Mr. M. E. Knouse, Biglerville, Pa.
Mr. H. S. Smeltzer, Harrisburg, Pa.
Carl M. Distler, Esq., Baltimore, Md.

Dr. D. Burt Smith, Philadelphia, Pa.
Mr. Geo. M. Jones, Reading, Pa.
Mr. A. Monroe Hall, Williamsport, Pa.
Prof. J. Ernest Wagner, Johnstown, Pa.

Recognizing the need of better trained teachers and leaders in the educational work of our congregations we commend the work to the attention of our pastors and people and recommend that every facility for Leadership Training in our parishes be used to the limit of the ability of our churches.

The Parish School

The Parish School, the official magazine of the Board, has continued during the past biennium as a quarterly magazine of Christian education. While the support of the Church has not been such as to encourage either the publishers or the editors, the editors have felt that a more frequent issue and a greater variety of subjects and more practical treatment of themes would make the magazine more helpful to the Church. Therefore, with the usual liberal support of the Publication Board, in approving the plan, it is now proposed that beginning with the October issue, this magazine will be issued as a monthly, ten months in the year. In this manner it will be possible to give attention to all departments and all phases of our educational program. The magazine will be departmentalized and a number of specialists in the various phases of our Christian education will contribute to the columns of the magazine. It will be of such high character and practical value as to warrant the appeal to place The Parish School into the hands of every teacher and supervisor of a Church school.

Church School Architecture

Frequent requests for information and advice in the erection of buildings for use as Church schools has led the Board to create a standing Committee on Church School Architecture of the United Lutheran Church to develop model plans for buildings for use in Christian education and to create a Bureau of Advice and Help in the proper organization and equipment of Church schools, and also to assist in planning the remodeling of existing buildings, and in the securing of proper equipment for the educational work in our parishes.

Personnel

The editorial and field forces of the Board have not changed during the biennium. The following is the staff:

Editors:
 Charles P. Wiles, D.D.
 William L. Hunton, D.D.
 D. Burt Smith, D.D.
 Mrs. Maud Junkin Baldwin, B.R.E.

Field Secretaries:
 Charles H. B. Lewis, D.D.
 The Rev. S. White Rhyne.

These editors and secretaries are at the service of the Church and gladly do all in their power to aid synods, conferences and congregations to develop their educational program to a high standard of efficiency.

FIELD WORKERS, LEADERSHIP TRAINING, ETC.

Your Board has thus far been able to place only two field secretaries. Their work has been eminently satisfactory, the results showing the wisdom of having such workers in the field. The fruits of their work also have created a desire for additional district secretaries. These the Board plans to secure as rapidly as its funds will permit.

Our Field Secretaries or District Directors of Religious Education have had assigned to them during the past biennium the supervision of the work of Leadership Training in their districts. This is only a temporary expedient. The Board is convinced that Leadership Training in our churches is so urgently needed as to require the selection of a general director of Leadership Training at the earliest possible moment.

EDITORIAL CHANGE

By a special arrangement the Women's Missionary Society has co-operated with the Parish and Church Schoool Board in providing the paper, *Lutheran Boys and Girls,* for use in Sunday Church Schools and Children's Missionary organizations. Mrs. E. C. Cronk was the first editor for the Missionary Department of this paper. Due to her lamented death a vacancy occurred and on recommendation of the Missionary Society Miss Jane Gilbert was nominated to the Board of Publication as the editor of the missionary material in *Lutheran Boys and Girls.* Miss Gilbert is the daughter of the late Dr. Gilbert, for many years pastor of Zion's Church, Harrisburg, Pa., is fulfilling her duties in this respect with satisfaction to the editors.

The terms of the following four members of the Board expire at this meeting: Charles P. Wiles, D.D.; Wm. Hoppe, D.D.; Frank M. Urich, D.D.; Mr. Grant Hultberg.

Doctors Wiles and Hoppe, President and Vice-President respectively, having served two full terms, the Board has nominated the Rev. A. J. Turkle, D.D., of Pittsburgh, Pa., and the Rev. P. D. Brown, D.D., of Columbia, South Carolina, as their successors. Frank M. Urich, D.D., and Mr. Grant Hultberg, present members of the Board, are renominated.

The Board desires to place on record its regret at losing from its membership both its President and Vice-President, who have been among its most useful and influential and active members.

SUMMARY OF THE 1928 SURVEY OF UNITED LUTHERAN CHURCH SCHOOLS

There are, in all parts of the United Lutheran Church, altogether 3,830 Church schools from which reports should have been received, distributed through the districts as follows: Eastern District (Pennsylvania and New York Synods and Ohio, Maryland and West Virginia), 2,366 schools, of which 46 per cent reported; Central District (Synods of Indiana, Michigan, Illinois, Northwest, Iowa, Kansas, Nebraska, German Nebraska and Wart-

burg), 667 schools, of which 56.4 per cent reported; Southern District
(Synods of North Carolina, South Carolina, Virginia, Georgia, Mississippi,
and Texas), 525 schools, of which 67.6 per cent reported; Western District
(California, Pacific, and Rocky Mountain Synods), 88 schools, of which 66
per cent reported; Canada (Synods of Manitoba, Canada, and Nova Scotia),
184 schools, of which 32.3 per cent reported; there being a total of 50.6 per
cent of all schools reported.

In the matter of Grading some improvement is noted over the report of
two years ago. Of the schools reporting 70 per cent have Cradle Rolls;
in the Kindergarten 91.2 per cent observe the grading standard of 4 and 5
years, while the remainder are scattered through eight variations from
the norm; in the Primary Department, 79.5 per cent follow the standard (6,
7 and 8 years) while the others are spread over 29 variations from the
standard; in the Junior Department, 82 per cent follow the correct standard
(9, 10 and 11 years), while the other 18 per cent cover 32 variations from
it; in the Intermediate Department 81 per cent use the standard (12, 13
and 14 years), the remainder scattering over 39 variations; the Senior Department standard (15, 16 and 17 years) is observed by 78 per cent of the
schools, 40 variations being reported; the Young People's Department standard (18 to 23 years inclusive) is used by 83 per cent of those reporting
such departments with 42 variations; while 88.6 per cent of the schools
having Adult Departments have the correct standard of 24 years and over,
there being 17 variations reported; 30 per cent of the schools reporting have
Home Departments. The improvement over two years ago varies from
8 per cent to 17 per cent increases in the correctness of the standards in
various departments, there being fewer variations from the norms, also.

Compared with the reports of two years ago, an improvement is noted
in the matter of Average Attendance in the schools reporting. This year,
in the Eastern District the average attendance is 64.2 per cent compared
with 61.4 per cent two years ago; in the Central District this year the
average attendance is 65.7 per cent, compared with 61.4 per cent two years
ago; in the Southern District, the average attendance is 63 per cent, compared with 63.6 per cent of two years ago; the Western District is the same
as two years ago, 63.7 per cent, and Canada shows an increase of 64.4 per
cent, being the record this year against 62.5 two years ago; for the whole
church, the average attendance is 64.4 per cent, compared with 62.5 per
cent two years ago.

There is a slight improvement noticeable in the number of schools having
regular meetings for their officers and teachers, there being 57.2 per cent
of the schools having such conferences, 78 per cent of this number having
such conferences monthly; two years ago 53.3 per cent of the schools held
such meetings.

In the matter of the Curriculum, 72 per cent use Lutheran Graded Lessons
in the Kindergarten, 17.4 per cent using International Graded, and 7.6 per

cent using Uniform Lessons, the other 3 per cent using about eight varieties of lessons other than those mentioned. In the Primary Department, 56 per cent use Lutheran Graded, 13.2 per cent use International Graded and 28 per cent use Uniform Lessons, the other nearly 3 per cent using seven other kinds of lessons. In the Junior Department, 42 per cent use the Lutheran Graded, 8.5 per cent use International Graded, and 48 per cent use Uniform Lessons. In the Intermediate Department 30.9 per cent use Lutheran Graded, 5.8 per cent use International Graded, and 59 per cent use Uniform Lessons, 1 per cent using Wartburg Lessons, and the remainder five varieties of lessons, some of which are strictly language lessons. In the Senior Department, 24.4 per cent use Lutheran Graded, 1 per cent use International Graded, and 69.2 per cent Uniform Lessons, the others using about three varieties of other lessons. In the Young People's Department, 3 per cent use Lutheran Graded, 93 per cent use Uniform Lessons, while 1 per cent use Teacher Training Lessons and the others introduce other features. In the Adult Department the Lutheran Graded find favor with 1 per cent, the Uniform being used by 96.6 per cent and the others use the Bible or some local course.

45.6 per cent of the schools distribute *Lutheran Young Folks,* 36 per cent distribute *Lutheran Boys and Girls,* 0.5 per cent report using *Jugendfreund,* and 3 per cent use papers published by David C. Cook Co.

Weekday and Vacation Church Schools are reported as follows: 8 per cent report Weekday Schools only, 19.4 per cent report Vacation Schools only, and 3 per cent more report having both weekday and vacation schools, therefore a total of 30.7 per cent of the schools have either or both weekday and vacation schools. If that proportion held through the Church (supposing that every report came in) then there would be about 310 having weekday schools only; 743 having vacation schools only, and about 120 having both.

Although the Parish School Hymnal has been on the market but two years, 24.6 of the schools report using it, with others promising to introduce it this year, 11.2 per cent more use the Sunday School Book, 10 per cent use Dr. Cronk's, about 2 per cent use the Lewar's book, about 48 per cent use books issued by Lutheran authors, and the other 52 per cent using a wide variety of hymnals issued by independent publishers.

Leadership Training shows some improvement this year. Two years ago only 29 per cent of the schools reported having such classes, but this year about 33 per cent of the schools report Leadership Training classes of various kinds, 30 per cent of these classes being held during the Sunday school hour, and the Dr. Oliver text-book ranking highest with 41.4 per cent of the classes, 8 per cent of the classes are affiliated with Lutheran Community classes, and 9 per cent more with Interdenominational schools.

Missionary Instruction meets with favor with but 32.9 per cent of the schools, the overwhelming majority of which have this instruction monthly,

55 per cent of these schools spreading this instruction over all departments, others having it in but one or two departments. However, 40 per cent of the schools have Missionary Offerings, the three methods which seem most popular being monthly offerings, special offerings and the use of the Duplex envelope, there being about 30 per cent for each of these plans, with the other 10 per cent of the schools using about five or six other methods.

PLANS FOR PROGRESS

The Board has been hampered in its work through conditions which it is now making special efforts to overcome. A lack of revenue has prevented the building up of an ample force of field workers. A limited editorial staff has been in a measure responsible for the Board's inability to produce literature as rapidly as it has desired. With the increased number of texts available for use in the various types of church schools and with the responsibility fixed for the general supervision of the entire parish educational program, it is confidently hoped with increased revenue and increased workers to show great progress both in the development of new literature and in the education of the Church in the use of the literature which we already have.

With the co-operation of the churches and the support of our pastors and people, your Board, through its editors and field workers, is looking toward the future development of Christian Education in our congregations under its direction with the greatest optimism.

RECOMMENDATIONS

1. We express approval of the plan for co-ordination of all the educational interests in our parishes and recommend that every effort be put forth to unify and make a co-ordinated educational program for our congregations.

2. We recommend that the Board continue to participate in the Intersynodical Conference on Elementary Christian Education and that its representatives encourage further co-operation in the hope of ultimately attaining greater uniformity in our Christian educational curricula.

3. We express appreciation of the results attained in the development of texts for Weekday and Vacation Church Schools and approve the method of procedure. We urge upon the schools of our congregations the use of the official literature which the Church is providing through its Parish and Church School Board.

4. In order that a greater unification of our training work and more uniform standardization may result, it is recommended that all Leadership Training Schools, whether community, conference or synodical, co-operate with the Parish and Church School Board in planning and completing their work.

5. Recognizing the need of better trained teachers and leaders in the educational work of our congregations we commend the new Leadership Training Camp to the attention of our pastors and people. We also recommend that every facility for leadership training in our parishes be used to the limit of the ability of our churches.

Approved by the Board.

CHARLES P. WILES, *President.*

WILLIAM L. HUNTON, *Secretary.*

THE TREASURER'S REPORT OF THE PARISH AND CHURCH SCHOOL BOARD

Receipts and Disbursements

For the period from July 1, 1926, to December 8, 1926.

Cash in bank, July 1, 1926	$ 6,631.27	
Receipts, United Lutheran Church on apportionment	3,400.00	
		$10,031.27

DISBURSEMENTS

Salary of Field Secretaries	$ 2,550.00	
Expenses of Field Secretaries	819.13	
Expenses of Members of Board and Committees	214.89	
Expenses of Board Meetings	196.92	
Stationery	8.78	
Auditing	25.00	
		3,814.72
Cash in bank, December 8, 1926		$ 6,216.55

H. M. M. RICHARDS, *Treasurer.*

Philadelphia, February 4, 1927.

We have audited the accounts of the Parish and Church School Board of the United Lutheran Church in America for the period from July 1, 1926, to December 8, 1926, and we certify that, in our opinion, the foregoing statement of Receipts and Disbursements for the period from July 1, 1926, to December 8, 1926, is correct.

LYBRAND, ROSS BROS. & MONTGOMERY,

Accountants and Auditors.

TREASURER'S REPORT

Receipts and Disbursements

For the year ended June 30, 1927

Cash in bank, July 1, 1926		$ 6,631.27
Receipts:		
United Lutheran Church, on apportionment	$10,795.00	
Interest on bank balances	14.38	
		10,809.38
		$17,440.65

Disbursements:
Salaries of Field Secretaries..$ 5,850.00
Expenses of Field Secretaries.............................. 1,594.77
Expenses of Members of Board and Committees........ 968.65
Expenses of Board Meetings.................................... 432.78
Stationery and Supplies 60.74
Auditing 50.00
Premium on Surety Bond.................................... 17.60
                                                                          ———— 8,974.54
                                                                                    ————————

Cash in bank, June 30, 1927.. $8,466.11

GEO. M. JONES, Treasurer.

Philadelphia, August 29, 1927.

We have audited the accounts of the Parish and Church School Board of the United Lutheran Church in America for the year ended June 30, 1927, and we certify that, in our opinion, the foregoing statement of Receipts and Disbursements for the year ended June 30, 1927, is correct.

LYBRAND, ROSS BROS. & MONTGOMERY,
Accountants and Auditors.

CASH ACCOUNT
For the year ended June 30, 1927.

Cash in bank, July 1, 1926 .... $ 6,631.27

RECEIPTS

United Lutheran Church, on apportionment....................$10,795.00
Interest on bank balances... 14.38
                                                                          ———— 10,809.38
                                                                                    ————————
                                                                                    $17,440.65

DISBURSEMENTS

Salaries of Field Secretaries ....$ 5,850.00
Expenses of Field Secretaries 1,594.77
Expenses of Members of Board and Committees............ 968.65
Expenses of Board Meetings.................................... 432.78
Stationery and Supplies 60.74
Auditing 50.00
Premium on Surety Bond 17.60
                                                                          ———— 8,974.54
                                                                                    ————————

Cash in bank, June 30, 1927.. $8,466.11

CASH ACCOUNT
For the year ended June 30, 1928

Cash in bank, July 1, 1927 .... $ 8,466.11

RECEIPTS

United Lutheran Church, on apportionment..................$12,485.00
Interest on bank balances 148.07
                                                                                 12,633.07

                                                                                 21,099.18

DISBURSEMENTS

Salaries of Field Secretaries..$ 6,625.00
Expenses of Field Secretaries...   792.57
Expenses of Members of Board and Committees............ 1,177.73
Expenses of Board Meetings..   570.35
Literature and Survey Expense...   538.51
Auditing 25.00
Premium on Surety Bond...   25.00
                                                             9,754.16

Cash in bank, June 30, 1928.. $11,345.02

Respectfully submitted,
GEO. M. JONES, <i>Treasurer.</i></center>

Philadelphia, August 9, 1928.

We have audited the accounts of the Parish and Church School Board of the United Lutheran Church in America for the years ended June 30, 1927 and 1928, and we certify that, in our opinion, the foregoing Cash Accounts for the years ended June 30, 1927 and 1928, are correct.

LYBRAND, ROSS BROS. & MONTGOMERY,
Accountants and Auditors.

Pending consideration of this report the Convention adjourned with prayer by the Rev. Roy G. Catlin.

————•————

Evening Service

A special service was conducted by the Board of American Missions in Luther Memorial Church on Monday evening, October 15th. During this service addresses were made on work among the American Indians, among the Jews and in Latin America. Musical selections were given in Hebrew, Italian, German and Slovak; and a pageant was enacted by the children of the Italian Lutheran Church of Erie. The service gave an impressive vision of the varied lines of activity in which the Board of American Missions must engage in order to reach the people of this western world.

SIXTH MEETING

Morning Session

SUNDAY SCHOOL CHAPEL,
LUTHER MEMORIAL CHURCH,
ERIE, PENNSYLVANIA.
Tuesday, October 16, 1928, 8.45.

Matins were conducted by the Rev. J. F. Fedders.

The Convention was called to order by the President.

The Minutes of Monday morning and afternoon sessions were read and approved.

Mr. Carl M. Distler, President of the Inner Mission Board, presented the report of that Board.

REPORT OF THE INNER MISSION BOARD

Inner Mission work, broadly speaking, has always been done by the Lutheran Church in America. Even in a specific technical sense we may claim the founding of the church in this country as a fruit of the Inner Mission, which brings the Gospel to the scattered, endangered and lost members of the household of faith who are not reached by the regular ministrations of the church. It is true, however, that as an organized agency of the church the Inner Mission is of recent origin, and the Inner Mission Board of the United Lutheran Church in America is much younger and less known than the Board of Foreign Missions and that of Home Missions.

The great work of Dr. Passavant marks the real beginning of Inner Mission work in America. He established a remarkable record, so far unexcelled, by the founding of the first Protestant Hospital, that in Pittsburgh, in 1848. He also established a number of other hospitals and orphans' homes.

It took more than another half century of individual initiative and constant efforts before the church included the Inner Mission officially in her great missionary program. At first the General Bodies appointed standing committees on Inner Mission work out of which finally developed the Inner Mission Board of the United Lutheran Church in America, organized formally with the merger of the General Synod, the General Council and the United Synod of the South in 1918. The latter two bodies had standing committees, whereas the General Synod had had an incorporated Board for three years previous to the merger. Under the inspiring leadership of its President, the Rev. F. H. Knubel, D.D., LL.D., now the president of the United Lutheran Church in America, that Board

did much pioneer work and its constitution and official declarations are
so sound and forceful that they still may serve for the guidance of the
Inner Mission work of the church. In the former General Council, the
Rev. J. F. Ohl, Mus.D., D.D., did pioneer work both by his personal
endeavor in Philadelphia institutions as the Ministerum of Pennsylvania's
Superintendent of the City Mission, and as president of the Inner Mission
Society of Philadelphia, of which he was one of the founders in 1902.
He continually urged the Inner Mission ideals in the body with which he
was connected. His book "The Inner Mission," the first of its kind in this
country, remains a source of valuable information and high inspiration.

It will be good to get a general view of Inner Mission work. A clear
conception of its biblical basis and character is essential. The Inner Mission
is as necessary to complete the great missionary task of the church as the
better known phases of her efforts at home and abroad "to make disciples
of all nations."

Carrying the Gospel to the ends of the earth we call "Foreign Missions."
Taking the Gospel to the scattered fellow-believers and others in our own
land and of organizing them into congregations is "Home Missions." But
what of the indifferent, the spiritually dead, the wicked, the lost, within
the church herself? What of the great masses, though perhaps baptized
and confirmed, who never go to church services, and who are real Christians
no more than the unenlightened people of Africa? Has the church no
mission to these? To bring the Gospel to those within the scope of the
church, and yet not reached by the regular ministrations of the church,
is a real mission. Though widely diversified in its forms of work, yet it
is after all but one great mission, and, functioning within the church herself, is properly called the "INNER MISSION."

The Lord Jesus, in His earthly ministry, was above all engaged in Inner
Mission work, as He distinctly said, "I am not sent but unto the lost sheep
of the house of Israel." In principle the Inner Mission would limit
itself to the members of our church, but in practice gladly extends her
ministry of serving love beyond the "inner circle" and stretches out her
helping hand to any person estranged from God, to any Christian in
spiritual danger, and to any one in bodily distress.

In point of time the Inner Mission phase of the church's work could
not begin to operate until after the church had become established for
some time and some of her members had begun to grow cold and turn
back. Then the call to this work came to all directly from the Lord
Himself, not merely to the church at Sardis, "Be watchful, and strengthen
the things that remain, that are ready to die; for I have not found
thy works perfect before God." (Rev. 3:2). Resounding thoroughout the
ages this call still comes to the entire church.

To accomplish this purpose the church must follow the example of
Jesus, and of the Apostolic church, who combined the Word and the works

in bringing the kingdom of God to men. Christ and the Apostles did not limit themselves to preaching and teaching, but also healed the sick and helped many other forms of bodily distress. The great purpose of Jesus in performing His many miracles and feeding multitudes was not, however, primarily to relieve distress, but above all to make manifest the coming of the kingdom of God to men. Not *sickness,* but *SIN,* is the cause of suffering of the body and of agony of the soul. To take away sin, the wages of which is death, physical and spiritual, temporal and eternal, is the beginning and the end, the basis and the climax of Christ's great work. To redeem the entire man, body and soul, and to lead him back to God reconciled; to make of a sinner a saint; of a rebel a child of God, therefore is and must remain the great purpose of the church in all her work. All else, however important in its sphere, and legitimate within certain spheres and functions, must take a secondary place.

Why, then, is Inner Mission work so largely works of mercy? Because genuine Christian love cannot pass by on the other side, but, like the Good Samaritan, would help all who are in distress. Nor will she approach the distressed with the question, "Who are you?"; "How did you come into this trouble?"; "Why should I help when others are under more direct obligations?" These questions are asked when the emergency is passed, and should the individual be found unworthy of help, then the real Inner Mission task begins—the reaching out after the soul. Nothing dare be spared in the effort to restore in body and soul such a prodigal son, such a degraded woman, mere wrecks of humanity, caricatures of man created in the image of God.

This then is our "Mission"; in every sense of the word a "mission"; on a par with the Foreign and Home Mission work of the church, and, like these, not limited to certain classes. The Inner Mission must include all, from the ungodly of the highest social and intellectual standing to the outcasts of society.

It is evident therefore that Inner Mission work includes far more than "Christian Social Service," because many come within her particular scope who are in no bodily distress whatever except such due to over-indulgence. Because sickness and destitution are external evidences of distress, and because those suffering therefrom are most easily reached, and make the strongest appeal, the bulk of the Inner Mission work in our country is still done among those who need physical assistance. As the members of the church become better informed and also financially more willing to aid in Inner Mission work, the church will be enabled to reach out to the cultured in a larger degree than is possible at present.

The characteristic feature of Inner Mission work as distinct from humanitarian efforts, is the bringing of the Gospel, the Word of God; and as distinguished from the usual teaching and preaching by the church in regular congregational work and in Home Missions, it is the "work." We find little humanitarian welfare work apart from that of the church up to about one hundred years ago, and little of any organized effort by the church to express her faith by unselfish loving service to those in distress. Throughout the Middle Ages such emphasis is placed upon charity and good work that the Gospel is pushed into the background. Soon after the Reformation the Word of God was so exclusively emphasized that the ministry of love was neglected and gladly left to the State, the church co-operating to some degree.

The combining of both, the ministry of the Word with the ministry of mercy, produced the Inner Mission. The teaching and preaching of the Word together with works of Christian love and mercy give us the full Gospel and produce genuine Christianity.

THE INNER MISSION BOARD AT WORK

It pleases God to work through consecrated individuals rather than through official actions by the church. Practically all of its institutional work the church owes to private initiative and local interest and support. Consecrated men and women have acted simply because they could not do otherwise. The Lord placed a burden upon their hearts, gave them a vision, and compelled them to act in the spirit of the great Apostles, who write, "The love of Christ constraineth us."

It is likewise true, however, that not every vision and call is from God. A number of sad failures are evidences of misguided zeal. For that reason it is advisable that the church exercise some general supervision over the institutions asking her members for support, that before new institutions are founded she be advised and heard, that unnecessary work be not undertaken, and that overlapping and unpleasant rivalry be avoided, all of which is as important as arousing the church to a keener sense of responsibility and inspiring her to greater efforts. All these functions the United Lutheran Church in America exercises through her Inner Mission Board, organized at the time of the merger along with the other Boards.

There are three great tasks at which the Inner Mission Board is working. In addition, there are some special activities assigned by the church, or undertaken with her approval.

I. Congregational Work

The church has recognized that the primary aim of its Inner Mission Board is to develop the Inner Mission spirit and service of the congregation. This means to effect more truly in all congregations in the United Lutheran Church in America and in all of its individual members the reality of the Inner Mission. This is a return to the spirit and practice of the early church. When one member suffered all members suffered with him, and came eagerly to his relief. The congregation which realizes this ideal makes itself responsible for the needy, the distressed and the wandering in its own community. It aims to bring into the fold all who have strayed or have never found the joy which is the holy possession of the Christian.

In the effort to realize this ideal the Board has approved the following CONGREGATION PROGRAM:

1. The development of the life of all its members, leading to a natural and ready service to those within and without.
2. The congregational ideal of every member in some form of Christian service.
3. Realizing in each member the universal priesthood of believers.
4. The congregation as a force rather than as a field.
5. The use of "A Message for the Day" for "Shut-ins" and "Shut-outs" in the congregation.
6. A worth while task for every member.
7. A survey of the congregation.
8. A survey of the community.
9. The possibility of community co-operation in deeds of serving love.

To help make effective this program a CONGREGATIONAL SURVEY form has been prepared for free distribution. It is suggested for use every two years. Its purpose is to discover the spiritual resources of the congregation. It reveals often the material resources unknown before. The needs in the congregation itself, but dimly sensed, are revealed.

As a corrollary to the congregation survey there has also been prepared for free distribution a COMMUNITY SURVEY form. This aims to discover the conditions and needs of the people in the community. When the resources of the congregation are known or their development indicated as a possibility, and the needs around the church discovered, it is obvious that the congregation must be organized for service to meet these needs, and bring its Christian love into service.

There was a day when the church did all the merciful work which was done in a community. This is no longer true. Most of this work is now done by State, County, City, and purely secular organizations, with no regard to the great Christian impulse of love. New opportunities await our zeal in supplying a Christian ministry of love to such institutions. This may be accomplished by more of our Lutheran people entering this service, or by local congregations carrying on a regular program of Christian service in local institutions.

It is surprising to know how many Lutheran people, some of them of course only nominally Lutheran, are being provided for in such secular institutions. While some faithful pastors and people have for years visited such institutions, yet many of these folks have been long neglected by the church. Little provision, in some cases none, has been made for their spiritual care. A survey of the country, still incomplete, has clearly revealed this fact. As a result of this survey such need has been pointed out to local congregations, who have in most instances organized at once a loving and effective ministry of love to these scattered and neglected people. In addition to a purely spiritual ministry, entertainment and recreation has been provided by our congregations, chiefly by young peoples' organizations.

In our larger cities, congregations have found themselves unable to cope with these problems before them. They have, therefore, found a means of meeting them through the organization of INNER MISSION SOCIETIES. By these a truly blessed work is being done. Most of such Societies publish monthly journals telling of their work, their plans, and their hopes. It will be helpful to subscribe for them. The superintendents would welcome invitations to speak of their work or to have someone do so for congregations.

In many places, however, this work must of necessity be congregational if it is to be done at all. Many of our church activities call for the initiative of the whole church. Inner Mission work must be done at the initiative of the congregation. This work specifically begins right at home. Heal that which is sick. Bring back that which is lost. This is the task of every living member of the church. We emphasize the Every Member Canvass as an administrative feature of the church. Here is the spiritual every member canvass. Following up the delinquent, straying and destitute may eventually lead to the founding of an institution. This will in turn lead to a better understanding of Inner Mission work. It will give us a new realization that the purpose of all our work is to lead men back to Christ. But the right attitude must always be maintained, that institutions are a tool, a means of Inner Mission work not its aim and objective.

So the Inner Mission interest of the congregation should be threefold:

1. Congregational activity radiating from the membership, led beyond its limits to range all through the community by the demands such activity will create.

2. Reveal the need of local institutions which are essential to carry on the work as it should be done. Here congregations often begin to band together for the greater effort over a wider field. Participation in such work gives great inspiration because it affords the object lesson showing what combined effort can accomplish when it sets its hand to a task for Christ.

3. The local work leads to an understanding of a larger necessity for work which must first be fostered by the church as a whole. Work for immigrants and seamen, and such activities as work for mountain people must often be first fostered by the whole church before local synods or organizations can take them over.

To make this work effective there must be some simple form of congretional organization. A CONGREGATIONAL INNER MISSION

COMMITTEE has been suggested. This committee might be made up of representatives of the various organizations of the congregation with the pastor. Very often a well qualified person can soon be found to take something of this further burden from the pastor. Such a committee if active, will be constantly finding new opportunities for the congregation to show its Christian love in practical form. There are many little things which may be done. There are, however, some large tasks which require all our resources of faith and love. They challenge the best thought and consecrated energy of our people. The very poor do not come to our churches. We must go out and find them. The down and outs never come near us. We must go where they are. This has led to street preaching. Such preaching is now being done in three centers where our church is strong. It has been found by pastor and people to be a really great privilege. Much blessing has come to those who have rendered such service, and souls have been brought back to Christ.

The Congregational committee might well form a study group. In addition other such groups could be formed. There will be available, possibly before this Convention, pamphlets and books which will be just the thing needed. The new Key-Book will be useful for such a purpose.

The Board is now engaged in a GENERAL SURVEY of the whole church, Synod by Synod. Its aim is to discover the possible resources of each Synod for Inner Mission work. It also is revealing the needs for work of certain kinds upon synodical territory. With a broad vision of the situation for the whole church, wise planning can be done for proper expansion. Out of this survey will come the possibility of bringing to the church a full, well-rounded Inner Mission program. It will surely enable the Board to suggest to district Synods a more complete development of Inner Mission work upon their territory.

A second great task of the Inner Mission Board is:

II. INSTITUTIONAL WORK

An institution of mercy is an expression of the Christian love of the church. The church has seen the need, and has made provision to meet it. It is quite natural that such institutions should be synodical or local in character. Local ownership, control and support have been demonstrated as the more successful method. A greater and more personal interest is aroused than with a general institution. Here the members of our churches can show their love. They can help the poor and needy personally. As the church supports these institutions it reveals its love.

But at the same time, some institutions may reveal a failure of Christian love by the members of the church. It is a failure not of the church, but of the individual. Did love control as it should, we would, for instance, often take an orphan into our own home rather than send him to an orphanage. No doubt children would be much better off in one of our

institutions than in certain homes. But a true Christian family is the ideal
if it can be attained. That it can be attained is now being demonstrated
by certain of our own Synods. Notably the Inner Mission Board of the
Ministerium of Pennsylvania is doing a fully successful piece of child
placement work. Of this more is said elsewhere in this report. This
same principle applies to other institutions than orphanages, but at present
to a lesser degree.

We must be careful, however, to understand that our institutions will
always be needed. In the very nature of the case some may be better
cared for in an institution than in a private home. Some need rather
constant and others expert care. Our institutions will always have their
claim upon our support. Others will no doubt be established as need
arises. But we must guard against the temptation to lose the vital, personal touch in helping the unfortunate. To do something ourselves out
of love for Christ is better than giving of our means to support merciful
activities.

The Board has no control over our institutions. It does gather information and advises. It learns of successful methods both from church institutions and from those of a purely secular character. It can be and has
been particularly helpful in conferring with those who contemplate the
founding of an institution or society. Some pitfalls have been avoided
through the help of the Board.

In many of such institutions we are co-operating with Lutherans of
other General Bodies. About half of them are on this basis. The list
of institutions appended to this report classifies the institutions under two
headings: those owned, controlled, and supported by the United Lutheran
Church in America, or any of her constituent parts; and those in which
we share ownership, control and support with Lutherans of other General
Bodies. While this classification is not perfect, it is the best found to this
time. It is recognized that it is in this field of the church's work that
co-operation with other Lutherans can first be accomplished. This has
been done and is working for the most part quite happily and effectively.

At present the United Lutheran Church in America is interested in
78 institutions of mercy and Inner Mission Societies. Of these institutions and societies 33 are entirely supported and controlled by our church
or groups within it. We have 10 institutions giving loving care to orphans
and half-orphans, and some other children. In them are housed 1,281 children at an annual expense of $328,655. For their care in old age the
church provides for our old folks 12 homes, caring for 308 people, at a
cost of $215,382 (part for buildings). In two instances Orphanages and
Old Folks' Homes are combined. In these, 317 are cared for, with an
expenditure of $43,242. Our work for defectives has just begun. We
now have three such institutions with 116 souls, the cost being $124,591
(part for buildings).

Safeguards are thrown around young men and young women in 10 Hospices. 489 have thus a Christian home at an expenditure of $114,511. The church provides five Hospitals for the Christian care of its people while they are under medical attention. In a year 21,589 people were treated in these hospitals with an annual expense of $1,230,336. Seamen's and Immigrants' Homes take care of 7,611 at an outlay of $42,340. Many thousands also use the reading rooms provided, in addition to the dormitory.

A very important development is shown in the Inner Mission Board of the Ministerium of Pennsylvania which is at work directing and co-ordinating the Inner Mission activities of the territory covered by the Ministerium. Thousands of people receive the loving ministry of this Board, their annual budget being about $50,000.

Fifteen Inner Mission Societies are doing a work almost beyond belief. Their workers go into all kinds of institutions and homes. They bring relief, gather in again and restore those who have strayed. The total of their annual expenditure is $250,000. One Society alone forms contact each year with 33,000 persons. It is easily possible that as many as 300,000 people know the ministry of these societies.

The work of our two Motherhouses will be set forth in another place. It is fitting to mention, however, that in connection with our Motherhouses there are 173 Deaconesses, many giving full time to some form of Inner Mission work. The expenses of these two Motherhouses are $183,003.

Of institutions difficult to classify we have fifteen, caring for 3,798 needy and pathetic persons. In doing this blessed work there is an annual outlay of $145,852.

The Board of American Missions has two institutions in the Virgin Islands. Here we find 464 sheltered by the church at an expense of $5,463.

The Foreign Mission Board also carries on an Inner Mission work in far distant lands. In connection with our Mission Stations there are four institutions with 16,953 people, for which is expended $47,149.

In America, the Lutheran Church has 381 institutions, which care for 447,946. Many thousands of others are touched by this activity. For this work the church spent $7,551,443 in a year, a small part of it being for the erection of buildings. In addition many congregations do a relief and welfare work, which it is impossible to tabulate. No doubt the Lutheran Churches in America as a whole give as much as ten millions of dollars a year to its work of Christian love.

About one-third of this work is done by the United Lutheran Church in America. The money contributed to this amounted to $2,650,828 in a year. The work is so quietly done that we are hardly conscious of its large dimensions.

Since the organization of the United Lutheran Church in America eight NEW INSTITUTIONS have been developed. During that period many offers of property have come to Synods or to the Board. On account of the restrictions or the location of the property it has been found necessary to advise against their acceptance. It is becoming very clear that the wise thing to do in founding new institutions is to make haste slowly. Enthusiasm has more than once carried the church into difficulty. Such property has become a burden instead of a service to the church. It is now clearly recognized that no institution will succeed unless there is at least one individual who is on fire with zeal for that particular cause. Even under such circumstances failure may result through the failure to arouse others to its support.

Among the most important problems at this time is that of CHILD WELFARE WORK. Rapidly growing organization in this work by secular organizations has left the church far to the rear. Several Synods however, are busy at this matter. The Inner Mission Board of the Ministerium of Pennsylvania is now recognized by the courts and child welfare agencies as the organization that will care for all Lutheran children in Eastern Pennsylvania. A most efficient service is given by this Board. In the main, however, we are failing as a church to thus care for the children of our church. The Board hopes soon to suggest to Synodical Inner Mission Committees what can be done and how it should be done.
New Institutions.

Three new institutions have begun work in this biennium.

1. *Williams-Henson Home for Boys, Knoxville, Tenn.*

After some years of negotiations and prayerful planning, first steps have now been taken by this home to fulfill its large task. Without question this will develop into one of the most far-reaching activities for the church, one which will be fruitful in the saving of our boys.

2. *The Lutheran Hospital, Reuss Memorial, Cuero, Texas.*

Texas has been added to the list of the states which now have Lutheran Hospitals. The Texas Synod has purchased and owns this new hospital. The cost was $30,000. The purchase was consummated on January 1, 1928, with all but $4,825 of the price raised in cash and pledges. It is the only institution of its kind in the whole Southwest. The hospital was built by Dr. Reuss in 1916 for $65,000, and with equipment cost $75,000. The founder died soon after its completion. The building is of brick and reinforced concrete and is fireproof. It has fifty-two rooms, thirty-five beds, ten physicians and surgeons. A charity ward and free clinic has been operating for some months. Spiritual care is given by the pastor of St. Mark's, who is also president of the Board. Besides his efforts a sick and devotional committee of the local congregation is busy. An auxiliary has been organized which provides for the linens and other necessary equipment of this nature. Nine rooms have been equipped with entirely new metal furniture as memorials. Extensive improvement and renovations at a cost of $6,000 have been made since title to the hospital has been taken over.

An X-ray and clinical laboratory of the latest improved type has been installed, the only one for many, many miles around.

3. *Home for the Aged, Jeffersonville, Ky.*

This home for old folks is now in operation. It has been made possible through the interest of the people of our Louisville, Ky., and vicinity churches. It was recently dedicated and is already busy with the loving care for our old people. A fine property has been secured and put into good shape. It was a happy day when this institution began its work.

Dedications of Institutions.

1. *Salem Orphanage* has been dedicated with its fine new building on the former site of Elizabeth College at Salem, Va. The buildings were designed by the late George Baum, of Philadelphia, and are up-to-date in every way. The Virginia people made of the dedication day a holy-day. The institution serves and is supported by our Southern Synods.

2. *Lowman Home, White Rock, S. C.* After many years of devoted work the new buildings at Lowman have been completed and were dedicated within the last few months. Dr. E. F. Bachman, Vice-president of the Inner Mission Board preached the dedicatory sermon. These buildings are a model of efficient arrangements and above all of a most moderate cost for the finest material. Those contemplating institutions might well visit this institution before their plans are made. The institution for helpless people is a fact largely through the persistent efforts of Dr. W. H. Greever.

3. *Home for the Aged, Jeffersonville, Ky.* This institution has also been dedicated within the last few months. Mention has been made of it above. It serves to help in meeting a real need now before the church.

4. While not a dedication, yet it is but proper to mention in this connection that the Ohio Synod has now taken title to Feghtly Home for Old People, Tippecanoe City, Ohio. This institution was for years the property of the General Synod, and supported by an endowment left to the Board of the Home. The courts have now approved the passing of the title to the Ohio Synod. Developments of this institution may be expected under the ownership of this Synod.

Need of Old Folks' Homes.

A preliminary study of the work of the church in maintaining homes for old folks leads to the following tabulation:

We now have 12 Homes for Old People entirely under the control and management of the church or groups within it. There are in addition three such homes in which we co-operate with other Lutherans. The total number cared for in these homes is about 400. There are twenty Synods interested to a greater or less degree in the support of these homes. The synodical location of the homes is:

Ministerium of Pennsylvania—two homes, caring for 98.

The three New York Synods—six homes with 108 people.

Maryland Synod—one home with 56 persons.

Pittsburgh Synod—two homes with 63 old folks.

Ohio Synod—one home with 16.

South Carolina Synod—one home with 11 people (residents here are restricted to those who live in Charleston, S. C.)

Nebraska Synod—one home with 44 old people.

California Synod—one home, number unknown.

Pennsylvania, with almost half the membership of the United Lutheran Church in America, has four such Homes. The territory west of the Mississippi River has two such Homes with about 50,000 members of our church supporting one, and about 5,000 supporting the second.

III. EDUCATIONAL WORK

One of the most effective means of informing our people about the Inner Mission work of the church is the preparation of proper literature. For the last two bienniums but little has been possible in this line. We now, however, are glad to report a resumption of this service to the church.

The Board has co-operated in the preparation of the "Key-Book," on "Christian Love," which will, no doubt, be ready for distribution shortly. This book will prove to be of real value to the church in a proper understanding of this important work.

As this report is being written, the copy for a booklet entitled "SAVED TO SERVE" is in the hands of the printer. This is one of the outstanding contributions of the Board to the Church. This booklet started out to be the suggestion of a thousand things to do in developing the Inner Mission of the church. While the number of suggestions does not begin to reach this total, yet it includes many practical hints for congregational activity in Inner Mission work. Each suggestion is one that has worked successfully in some congregation or congregations. The machinery required for this work is indicated, as well as a brief statement concerning the Inner Mission. This latter forms the basis and motive for the work.

A new series of "A MESSAGE FOR THE DAY" will be off the press and ready for distribution beginning with Advent Sunday. This is a little folder with a brief form of worship with sermon for the use of "Shut-ins" and "Shut-outs." It may be used in the home or wherever Sunday employment takes a person, possibly at the same hour for Public Worship. This little folder has proven a blessing to many of the people of our church who are prevented from attending the regular services of the church. Over 6,200 copies are now distributed each week.

An "INNER MISSION MANUAL" is now in preparation. It is often difficult to secure information about Inner Mission work. This book aims to supply just such information as is now needed. It gathers up the principles and methods of Inner Mission work as well as indicating what and where work is now being done. It will give detailed yet concise information. It will form a good study book for interested groups. It should be ready early in the new year.

A limited amount of GERMAN LITERATURE has been secured and is available at a small charge for those who may wish it.

The WOMAN'S MISSIONARY SOCIETY has supplied the Board with some copies of the Inner Mission leaflet in their FACT SERIES. The Board is grateful to the Society for these leaflets and trusts that they will have a wide distribution throughout the church.

One of the most important contributions of the Board to the church has been the plan for the Office of LAY READER. After years of conference this matter was presented in the form of resolutions to all the Synods. In brief these resolutions suggest that there is an opportunity to use some of our well qualified laymen to perform some of the functions of the pastor, in vacant congregations and as supply under the proper restrictions and direction of the Synod. The president of Synod or Conference, the Inner Mission Committee of Synod or some other duly authorized person or committee have oversight over their work, and to them report is made by the Lay Reader of his activity. Some of these laymen are doing valiant service for the Church in mission or vacant congregations.

A perplexing problem, that still remains unsolved, is the proper use by our church of our TRAINED YOUNG PEOPLE. This problem is shared with the Board of Education. But few of our well trained young folks, most of them college graduates, find full time, paid work for them in the church. Each year a few are placed, but in increasing numbers they offer themselves for work in our congregations. We use but few of them. Many, as a result, are going into the employment of other churches and purely secular work. Some find their way into Social Service Work, and do not often feel entirely comfortable in this atmosphere.

A further problem is the TRAINING OF WORKERS. Our institutions particularly feel the lack of proper trained workers. But the problem is much broader than this. It also includes the training of our young people in our own schools in the purely technical phases of work as well as maintaining their faith. Some effort to meet this problem is found in the local training schools meeting one evening a week in some of our cities. Some of our colleges look forward to possible courses. At least one of our Theological Schools has just this ideal in mind, but has not been able to find the way open.

Some NEW TENDENCIES are manifesting themselves today. There is a disposition to belittle the serving love of the church at work. Some are telling us that Social Service is the big and American way to do the work. Many of our young people have been deceived by this plausible propaganda. The church has, however, laid herself open to criticism in failing to appreciate the value of the scientific findings of recent years. With a fine Christian spirit and motive and the most expert knowledge the work we have to do would move on apace. Yet it is encouraging to know that some of the most thoughtful Social Service leaders are reaching the conclusion that there is a missing link somewhere in their work. There is the latest scientific knowledge, but much Social Service work is showing weakness or even failure. This offers a new opportunity to the church to supply what is missing. If we can become the loving link between scientific knowledge in social matters and the people who need the ministry of love at its best, then we will give to the needy world a real service, and win many souls to Christ.

An important activity has been the visitation of our Theological Seminaries by a representative of the Board every two years. A new angle has, however, now presented itself. The Seminary students are visiting us. For each of the two years of this biennium the SENIORS OF THE GETTYSBURG THEOLOGICAL SEMINARY have come to New York and Philadelphia, and spent a number of days visiting Inner Mission and Social institutions and agencies. The leaders in all these activities, of the church or purely secular, have given freely of their time to explain their work and answer many questions. This has been time well spent and has proven immensely profitable to the young men.

IV. IMMIGRANT WORK

This new Department of the Board's work has assumed a growing importance. Recently there has been added to it the supervision of the development of Seamen's Work.

The work for Immigrants is done in co-operation with the Lutheran Emigrant House Association of New York, which provides a home and office for our Secretary for Immigrant work. This Association has had a continuous existence since 1868. It was organized as a free Association when the church found herself unable to meet the needs of the incoming immigrants. It has been supported by gifts from individuals who became members of the Association, and some contributions from congregations. An Immigrant House was maintained for many years, which was sold at the time of the World War. Since that time an office only has been maintained, located at 281 Seventh Ave., New York City. It is of ready access from steamship piers and railroad stations, and the transit facilities of New York.

Advice and information, which often save from disaster, are freely given to the immigrants. The Immigrant Work is largely a personal service. It meets personally incoming immigrants at the piers, or ministers to those detained at Ellis Island, to which the Secretary has an annual pass. It assists immigrants on their way to their destinations. Employment is often secured. Lodging is found. Tickets on steamship lines are secured for returning immigrants. It helps both the incoming and outgoing Lutheran people of Europe. It gives its ministry to people of all nationalities gladly.   The proper housing of immigrants while possibly delayed in New York is one of really serious problems of this work.

It is in the PORT WORK for immigrants that a large service is given. Such work is now done at New York City, Montreal, and Winnipeg, Canada.   In addition a large work is done in Philadelphia by a full time missionary.   The Board is directly responsible for the three points indicated above.   This is but a temporary arrangement, to continue only until the local Lutheran Synods can assume the full charge of the work. A growing deficit in the Fund which carries this work has prevented many enlargements of it.   The deficit has been caused by the necessity of undertaking work in Canada for which no budget provision was possible until some years later.   Now that budget provision has been made, the deficit continues to grow through the lack of a full apportionment.   The other work of the Board has suffered therefore.

In the PORT OF NEW YORK effective work continues.   The work has grown despite the curtailment of immigration.   As we become better known abroad more information concerning incoming Lutherans reaches our hands.   The Secretary made a visit abroad last year to establish new and valuable contacts and to bring about a better understanding of our purpose.

To such an extent has the work grown that a new worker is required in addition to the Secretary and the workers connected with Lutheran Emigrant House Association.   These workers have visited 186 incoming ships in the biennium, meeting them at the piers, where the greatest number of the immigrants are now discharged, without the necessity of being transferred to Ellis Island.   During this same period, in addition to those served in leaving the ship, 925 persons have been met at railroad stations, 1,328 people in search for work have had employment found for them, and 57 of those sent to Ellis Island have had the ministry of our church.

The work has grown rapidly in CANADA.   The restrictions on immigration in the United States has caused the opening of the doors in Canada. Here the work is carried on under the direction of the Inner Mission Committees of the Canada and the Manitoba Synods.   These Committees in turn direct the activities of full time Immigrant Pastors.   To these Committees the Board contributes a portion of the salary of the Immigrant Pastors.   The funds which we supply are supplemented by the contributions of the Synods concerned and the Board of American Missions. The amount of our contributions is being slowly reduced, looking forward to the time when the Synods concerned shall be able to assume the full support of the work themselves.   These Synods deserve much credit for their deep interest in the work and their willingness to do all possible towards its support.

The Immigrant pastor at MONTREAL reported to the Inner Mission Committee of the *Canada Synod* that 36,937 immigrants entering the

Eastern Ports of Canada had been served in some way. The large majority of these immigrants did not remain in Eastern Canada but went at once to the Western Provinces. Some remain in the eastern section and have been helped to self-support and independence through the Christian service of the church.

At WINNIPEG, the Immigrant pastor reported to the Inner Mission Committee of the MANITOBA SYNOD that of the large number met by him 4,266 had been inducted into Lutheran Congregations and communities of Western Canada. To many others personal service was given to help over some of the rough spots. Busy early and late, making valuable and complete records of each individual and spreading a vast amount of information about the church, these men have been of inestimable service, and are presenting something of the challenge of the incoming immigrant of our faith into Canada.

The most important work of this Department of the Board's work is the FOLLOW-UP WORK. This involves the receipt of names of expected newcomers to America, meeting them upon their arrival, informing the local pastor or other agency which has made itself responsible, of their coming, and seeking thus to bring them into vital, living relation with a congregation in their new home. For the United States this work is done through our Immigrant Office, and for Canada, through the Inner Mission Committee of the Canada Synod.

During this biennium 11,585 names and addresses of such immigrants were sent to pastors and organizations. Some improvement in the report of pastors of local congregations has occurred. It still is true that a few of our pastors, possibly through unsuccessful former efforts, fail to report at all, and the immigrant is often lost so far as the church is concerned. This is a distinct loss to the church. It is gratifying to know what ready response comes from the brethren of other Lutheran General Bodies when immigrants are reported to them. They readily assume care of them and bring them into their congregations.

Surveys are now being made by the Secretary of the Gulf Ports with the hope that work may be organized for sailors coming into these Ports as well as for the Immigrant.

Co-operations with other Lutherans on the West Coast is being investigated. Conferences have already been held and the possibility exists that the Board may soon be able to come to the Executive Board for its approval of such co-operation.

The Port Work for Immigrants opens a new avenue of service for volunteers at our Ports of Entry. They can often serve to great purpose in personally conducting newly arrived immigrants about our cities or towns upon necessary errands, taking them to railroad stations to continue their journey on to their new homes, and assisting in the office work which is required in connection with this work.

V. Southern Mountain Work

Since 1924 the Women's Missionary Society has fostered the enterprise of the Inner Mission Board in the extreme southwest of the State of Virginia. The work is now fully established at Konnarock in Smythe County, under the title "Konnarock Training School," with the opening date December, 1925, and the formal dedication May 14, 1926.

The building is not located on a railroad nor in a city, but is in the very heart of the mountains, easy of access to the people living on the hillsides. As witness to the readiness of the community to make use of the school it is interesting to note that in 1926 Smythe County authorities made an arrangement with the Konnarock Training School to enroll 56 children as day pupils for whom the County pays regularly. Heretofore these children have had no school where they might go. Thirty-three girls are boarding pupils. The basis of admittance for a boarding pupil is determined by the circumstances of the homes.

The Faculty of the Konnarock Training School is a well qualified group of consecrated Christian teachers. First grade through the eighth grade are taught and in addition to the curriculum of the class room a modest introduction to music and the arts is provided.

During the past year, one of the rooms in the building was fitted up as a temporary dispensary and some interesting clinics were held in the school. A dentist gave his services and a surgeon came once for a tonsil clinic. Still another clinic provided examination of eyes and fitting of glasses for the children who needed such care, and it may be noted that they would not have had this attention in their homes.

At the school and at three other points in the mountains Daily Vacation Bible Schools have been proven helpful to the community. Volunteer teachers have come each summer. In 1927 a total of 60 children were reached.

The investment consists of the school building, equipped to house about forty children and the Faculty in dormitory rooms, dining room, class rooms, and chapel. There are 335.7 acres of land, with timber, apple orchard and meadow.

The children of the mountains at Konnarock Training School get a glimpse of the possibilities life holds for them. Our dividends will come if we can make that glimpse become a wide vision. The children should be fitted to go back into their mountains ready for meeting the home difficulties with new, better and Christian principles for everyday living. This is the aim of the work in the mountains under the direction of the Konnarock Training School fostered by the Women's Missionary Society under the auspices of the Inner Mission Board of the United Lutheran Church in America.

VI. Special Matters

1. *The Death of Dr. Gerberding.*

During the biennium the Board suffered a severe loss in the death of

Dr. Gerberding. He had been a member of the Board from its organization and his wisdom and experience as one of the pioneer Inner Mission students had been invaluable to the Board. It was with a real sorrow that the Board was under the necessity of adopting the following resolution:

In the sudden and tragic death of the Rev. G. H. Gerberding, D.D., LL.D., the Inner Mission Board of the United Lutheran Church in America has lost a member, who as pastor, professor and author, for a period of fifty years, served the church with distinguished ability. A man of strong convictions, implicitly obedient to the Word, knowing only Christ crucified for our sins and risen again for our justification, uniting in his own life a child-like faith and genuine piety, stressing these in all his teachings, and deeply interested in the church's activity at home and abroad. He stood as a tower of strength amid the vagaries of the present, beloved of all whom he served. In his preaching, teaching and writing, Dr. Gerberding constantly emphasized the Inner Mission principle that a living faith must express itself in a life of serving love, and hence his interest in the work committed to this Board. We mourn his loss; thank God for his eminently useful life; and express to his family our sincerest sympathy.

RESOLVED, That this appreciation be spread on our minutes, and that a copy thereof be sent to the family, and another to *The Lutheran*.

THE INNER MISSION BOARD,

E. F. BACHMANN, *President*   WM. FREAS, *Executive Secretary*.

2. To fill the vacancy caused by the death of Dr. Gerberding, Rev. John F. Fedders, Milwaukee, Wis., was chosen. His election was approved by the Executive Board.

3. On account of his physician's advice Dr. Bachmann insisted upon the acceptance of his resignation as the President of the Board. Dr. Bachmann had served in this capacity since the organization of the Board in 1918. His deep interest and zeal have had much to do with the progress of the work of the Board. He was always deeply concerned about accomplishing our task in and for the church. After much hesitation and deep regret the Board agreed to relieve Dr. Bachmann of his duties as president, electing him as Vice-President. In his place, Mr. Carl M. Distler, Esq., Baltimore, Md., was elected as President of the Board. Mr. Distler has been a member of an Inner Mission Board since 1915, and brings to his soon finished task a thorough knowledge of the Inner Mission and a burning zeal for it.

4. The Board is again glad to commend the retiring members of the Board. Among them is the Inner Mission pioneer, Rev. J. F. Ohl, Mus.D., D.D., who has also been a member of the Board since its organization. Dr. Ohl has seen and had a large part in the development of Inner Mission work from very small things to activities of large proportions. For about thirty years he has been in the midst of the actual work as the Inner Missionary in Philadelphia. Under his constant urging and exhortation the Ministerium of Pennsylvania was led to organize its Inner

Mission work years ago. The far-reaching plans then begun have developed greatly and become the norm for such work for the whole church. The Board officially expresses its gratitude for the service which he has rendered to our work and to express the hope that he may still continue to advise with us in the further growth of this activity of the church.

The President of the Board also retires from active service with this Convention. His loss will be keenly felt, as, in addition to his wide knowledge of the work, he has also served as the legal adviser of the Board.

5. The General Inner Mission Conference has become an organization which is making a real contribution to our Inner Mission thinking and activity. In it are represented all the Lutheran General Bodies in America. The discussions and suggestions of this Conference have great value. While lacking entirely official character, it has become the meeting place of Inner Mission workers for the exchange of ideas and experiences. It is looking forward, and rendering now a real service to the church and the work.

6. There are now in process of preparation Inner Mission Survey maps. They will serve to show at a glance the present Inner Mission work of the church. They will indicate where possible overlapping occurs. They will suggest where new activity should be begun. They should prove to be of real value in planning the future of the work.

7. Both the Secretaries of the Board gave full-time service to the Ministerial Pensions Campaign. The Board was glad to render this service to the cause. We rejoice in the success of this great effort by the church.

8. The Board now is happy in its new headquarters at the Lutheran Church House, with ample space to carry on the work. We find congenial working conditions in the truly Christian spirit which pervades all the work at the Church House.

Respectfully submitted,

CARL M. DISTLER, *President*   WM. FREAS, *Secretary.*

VII. TREASURER'S REPORT

STATEMENT OF RECEIPTS AND DISBURSEMENTS

For the year ended June 30, 1927

RECEIPTS

	General Fund	Immigrant Work Fund	Mountain Work Fund
United Lutheran Church	$12,700.00	$3,175.00	
Woman's Missionary Society		2,000.00	$15,497.88
Konnarock School Scholarship, received through the New York Synod			200.00
Board of Home Missions and Church Extension for Immigrant work		750.00	

Donations from individuals	136.00	126.49
Sales of literature	752.21	
Loans	8,300.00	
	$21,888.21	$6,051.49 $15,697.88

DISBURSEMENTS

	General Fund	Immigrant Work Fund	Mountain Work Fund
Salary of Secretaries ....$	3,999.96	$3,000.00	
Salary of clerks, stenographers, etc........	1,552.50		
Salary of School Superintendent			$ 1,100.00
Other School expenses			7,897.88
Salaries of Pastors		3,299.88	
Expenses of Secretaries	3,918.52	117.84	
Expenses of Board Members, etc.	670.56		
Literature purchased	2,016.82		
Office rental, net	626.60		
Printing and stationery	72.00		
Postage and express	294.69		
Auditing	150.00		
Office supplies and expenses	328.78	221.00	
Loans repaid	7,650.00		
Interest on bank loans	58.67		
Lutheran Emigrant House Association of New York		800.00	
Lutheran Settlement House	25.00		
School Buildings and Equipment			6,500.00
Office furniture and fixtures	16.50		
	$21,380.60	$7,438.72	$15,497.88
Excess or Deficiency of Receipts.......	$507.61	$1,387.23	$200.00

STATEMENT OF RECEIPTS AND DISBURSEMENTS

For the year ended June 30, 1928

RECEIPTS

	General Fund	Immigrant Work Fund	Mountain Work Fund
United Lutheran Church ....$	13,040.00	$4,535.00	
Women's Missionary Society			$ 9,166.63
Donations from individuals	67.00	35.00	5.00
Sales of literature	742.49		
Loans	12,400.00		
	$26,249.49	$4,570.00	$ 9,171.63

DISBURSEMENTS

	General Fund	Immigrant Work Fund	Mountain Work Fund
Salaries of Secretaries	$ 3,999.96	$2,875.00	
Salaries of clerks, stenographers, etc......	1,249.50		
Salary of School Superintendent			$ 1,100.00
Other School expenses			8,066.63
Salaries of Pastors		3,999.84	
Expenses of Secretaries	2,510.76	470.18	
Expenses of Board Members, etc.........	676.51		
Literature purchased	80.65		
Maintenance Contribution, Lutheran Church House	813.96		
Printing and stationery	391.00		
Postage and express	298.01		
Auditing	150.00		
Office supplies and expenses	425.33	138.14	
Loans repaid	11,950.00		
Interest on Bank Loans	57.52		
Lutheran Emigrant House Association of New York		600.00	
Lutheran Settlement House	28.00		
Moving expenses	315.00		
Office furniture and fixtures	46.25		
Tabor Home	25.00		
Germantown Orphanage	10.00		
Mountain Work, Traveling expenses	57.87		
Mountain Work, equipment			5.00
Konnarock School Scholarship			200.00
	$23,085.32	$8,083.16	$ 9,371.63
Excess or Deficiency of Receipts	$3,164.17	$3,513.16	$200.00

BALANCE SHEET
June 30, 1928
ASSETS

Cash in bank and on hand ....$	103.49
Due from Executive Board for June, 1928 apportionment and Specials	4,133.43
Due from Secretary for Traveling Expenses	16.89
Inventory of Salable Literature, at estimated value..............	497.71
Stamps	4.24
Advance to Secretary for Immigrant work, for Traveling Expenses	100.00
	$ 4,855.76
Office Furniture and Fixtures, at estimated value...............	397.75
Land, 335.7 acres, Konnarock, Va.	7,140.00
School Buildings and Equipment, Konnarock, Va.	43,751.08
	$56,144.59

LIABILITIES

Vouchers payable		$ 3,817.88
Loans payable:		
The Fifth Avenue Bank of N. Y.....$	400.00	
C. M. Distler	300.00	
E. C. Miller	400.00	1,100.00
		4,917.88

FUNDS

General Fund ......,.................	8,802.14	
Special Fund for Immigrant Work	8,666.51	
Special Fund for Mountain Work	51,091.08	
		51,226.71
		$56,144.59

Respectfully submitted,

WM. FREAS, *Treasurer.*

Philadelphia, July 28, 1928.

We have audited the accounts of the Treasurer of The Inner Mission Board of the United Lutheran Church in America for the two years ended June 30, 1928, and we certify that, in our opinion, the foregoing balance sheet as of June 30, 1928, and the statement of receipts and disbursements for the two years ended June 30, 1927 and 1928, are in accordance with the books of account and are correct.

LYBRAND, ROSS BROS & MONTGOMERY,
Accountants and Auditors.

INNER MISSION INSTITUTIONS AND SOCIETIES

A.—United Lutheran Church in America
(Owned, controlled and supported entirely by the United Lutheran Church in America, one or more of its constituent Synods, one or more of its congregations, or by associations within constituent Synods).

I. *Orphans' Homes*

1. St. John's Orphans' Home, Buffalo, N. Y.
2. Tressler Orphans' Home, Loysville, Pa.
3. Lutheran Orphans' Home, Salem, Va.
4. Lutheran Orphans' Home, Topton, Pa.
5. Nachusa Lutheran Orphanage, Nachusa, Ill.
6. Oesterlen Orphans' Home, Route 10, Springfield, Ohio.

II. *Old Peoples' Homes*

1. Mary J. Drexel Home, Philadelphia, Pa.
2. National Lutheran Home for the Aged, Washington, D. C.
3. Lutheran Church Home for the Aged and Infirm, Buffalo, N. Y.
4. Lutheran Home for the Aged, Erie, Pa.
5. Old Peoples' Home of the Pittsburgh Synod, Zelienople, Pa.
6. Feghtly Home, Tippecanoe City, Ohio.
7. Franke Home, Charleston, S. C.
8. Lutheran Home for the Aged, Southbury, Conn.
9. The Lutheran Church Home for the Aged and Infirm of Central New York, Clinton, N. Y.
10. Home for Old People, Jeffersonville, Ky.

III. *Orphans' and Old Peoples' Homes*

1. Orphans' Home and Asylum for the Aged, Philadelphia, Pa.
2. Tabitha Home, Lincoln, Nebr.

IV. *Institutions for Defectives*

1. Lowman Home for the Aged and Helpless, White Rock, S. C.

V. *Hospices*

1. The Luther Hospice for Young Men, Philadelphia, Pa.
2. The Lutheran Hospice for Young Women, Akron, Ohio.
3. Unity Lutheran Church Home for Girls, Chicago, Ill.
4. State Luther League Hospice, Omaha, Nebr.

VI. *Hospitals*

1. Childrens' Hospital, Philadelphia, Pa.
2. Lutheran Hospital, Reuss Memorial, Cuero, Texas.

VII. *Miscellaneous Institutions*

1. The Lutheran Settlement, Philadelphia, Pa.
2. Kensington Dispensary for the Treatment of Tuberculosis, Philadelphia, Pa.
3. River Crest Preventorium, Mont Clare, Pa.
4. Spring Garden Neighborhood House, Pittsburgh, Pa.
5. Bethesda Home, Meadville, Pa.
6. Lutheran Children's Bureau, Philadelphia, Pa.
7. Lutheran Bureau, Philadelphia, Pa.
8. St. John's Lutheran Settlement House, Knoxville, Tenn.
9. The Inner Mission Center, Brooklyn, N. Y.
10. The Williams-Henson Home for Boys, Knoxville, Tenn.

VIII. *Seamen's and Immigrant Missions*

1. Seamen's and Immigrant Mission of the Ministerium of Pennsylvania, Port of Philadelphia, Pa.

IX. *Inner Mission Societies and City Missions*

1. The Inner Mission Society of the Ev. Lutheran Church, Phila., Pa.
2. The Inner Mission Society of the Ev. Lutheran Church in Brooklyn and vicinity.
3. The Inner Mission Society of the State of Connecticut.
4. Inner Mission Society, Charleston, S. C.
5. The Inner Mission Society of Washington, D. C.
6. The Inner Mission Society of Trenton, N. J.
7. The Philadelphia City Mission.
8. The Inner Mission Society of the Chicago Area, Chicago, Ill.

X. *Deaconess Motherhouses*

1. Lutheran Deaconess Motherhouse, Baltimore, Md.
2. Mary J. Drexel Home and Philadelphia Motherhouse, Philadelphia, Pa.

XI. *Synodical Inner Mission Board*

1. Board of Inner Missions of the Ministerium of Pennsylvania, Philadelphia, Pa.

B.—Allied to the United Lutheran Church in America.
(Not owned, controlled and supported by the United Lutheran Church in America, but in whose ownership, control and support United Lutheran Church congregations have a part.)

I. *Orphans' Homes*

1. Emaus Orphans' Home, Middletown, Pa.
2. Orphans' Home and Farm School, Zelienople, Pa.
3. Wartburg Orphans' Home and Farm School, Mt. Vernon, N. Y.
4. Orphan Home of the Children's Friend, Jersey City, N. J.

II. *Old Peoples' Homes*

1. Mary Louise Home for the Aged and Infirm, Mt. Vernon, N. Y.
2. Old Folks' Home—Lutheran Womans League of Albany, N. Y.

III. *Institutions for Defectives*

1. Passavant Memorial Home for the Care of Epileptics, Rochester, N. Y.
2. Good Shepherd Home, Allentown, Pa.

IV. *Hospices*

1. Trabert Hall (for young women), Minneapolis, Minn.
2. Lutheran Hospice for Young Women, Pittsburgh, Pa.
3. Lutheran Hospice for Girls, Baltimore, Md.
4. Tryon Homestead (for young women), Philadelphia, Pa.
5. The Student House, Pittsburgh, Pa.
6. Girls' Hospice, Milwaukee, Wis.
7. Hospice for Girls, Reading, Pa.

V. *Miscellaneous Institutions*

1. Layton Home for Incurables, Milwaukee, Wis.
2. Tabor Home for Children, Doylestown, Pa.
3. Children's Receiving Home, Maywood, Ill.
4. Artman Home for Lutherans, Sellersville, Pa.
5. Wilbur A. Herlich Memorial Home, Towners, N. Y.

VI. *Hospitals*

1. Passavant Hospital, Pittsburgh, Pa.
2. Lutheran Hospital, of Manhattan, New York City.
3. Milwaukee Hospital, Milwaukee, Wis.
4. California Lutheran Hospital, Los Angeles, Calif.
5. Robinwood Hospital, Toledo, Ohio.

VII. *Seamen and Immigrant Missions*

1. Seamen's Mission, Hoboken, N. J.
2. Lutheran Emigrant House Association, of New York.

VIII. *Inner Mission Societies*

1. Lutheran Welfare Society in the Twin Cities.
2. Lutheran Inner Mission Society of Pittsburgh, Pa.
3. Inner Mission Society of the Ev. Lutheran Church in New York.
4. Inner Mission Society of the Ev. Lutheran Church of Buffalo, N. Y.
5. Inner Mission Society of the Ev. Lutheran Church of Baltimore and vicinity.
6. Inner Mission Society of the Ev. Lutheran Church in Reading, Pa.
7. Inner Mission Society of Milwaukee, Wis.

Nachusa Lutheran Orphanage

A long felt need at the Nachusa Lutheran Orphanage was supplied when two cottages and a modern school building were provided. These buildings were dedicated early in the biennium. The cottage type of building has proven to be the most practical, and has many advantages over the dormitory type. An average of forty-seven children have been cared for under conditions that are as near private home-life as possible in a children's home.

The Orphanage sustained a great loss on April 25th, 1928, when the Main Building was totally destroyed by fire. There was no loss nor injury of life, but the property loss was very conservatively placed at $25,000. The Board immediately took steps to rebuild, and when completed the new building will be of fire-proof construction, and fully modern in all its appointments. The most up-to-date plans for child welfare work will be followed. It is hoped the building will be ready for occupancy by December 1st, 1928.

This marks the twenty-fifth year of service for the Nachusa Orphanage, and a special program commemorating the event will be given.

The Mary J. Drexel Home for the Aged

This Home is so named by its founder, Mr. John D. Lankenau, in memory of his wife, Mary Joanna Drexel. Though by charter limited to Protestant men and women of German birth or descent, residents of Philadelphia at least five years before admission, the Home is always filled to capacity and has a long waiting list. This is largely due to some peculiar advantages enjoyed by the members of the Home family, e.g., regular chapel services with the deaconesses and the girls of the Lankenau School, personal freedom limited only by the interests of the family or the welfare of the individual, every day a visiting day, and an opportunity to attend concerts, lectures, pageants and other public entertainments of the Lankenau School; also a resident physician in the house and in case of serious illness admission to the Lankenau Hospital located on the same grounds.

The Home cares regularly for 51 men and women—married couples occupy the same large room, most of the others have single rooms. During 1927 six members of the Home family were laid to rest, having reached an average of 85 years and having been in the Home an average of 9 years. Among the aged men and women are some who have been prominent as active members of their congregations, and others who had drifted away from the Church and from their Lord for years. The former we rejoice to provide with a Christian haven of rest after faithful labors, the latter we are glad to have brought into contact with the gospel before they are called out of this life. Here is real Inner Mission opportunity.

The National Lutheran Home for the Aged, Washington, D. C.

The work of the Home has been maintained without interruption. The two years now closing, since sending in our last report, have been years of blessing. Removals by death have not been many. Life seems to be renewed when applicants are admitted to the shelter of the Home. There is always a long waiting list.

The surroundings are pleasant. The help is efficient. The service is adequate.

We are constantly in need of more funds. Larger buildings must be erected if we are to care for the many aged who are appealing for admission.

By the circulation of "Home News," a quarterly pamphlet, information is going out to a larger circle of friends. Gifts in money, clothing, provisions, are increasing. The one great need is a fund sufficiently large to endow the Home, and thus make it a perpetual haven for the worthy aged who are dependent upon the Church for creature comforts in their declining days.

The capacity of the present building is 58. The rooms are all filled. There are many applicants on the waiting list.

Lutheran Church Home for Aged and Infirm, Buffalo, N. Y.

REV. WM. FREAS, D.D.

Dear Reverend:

In reply to your letter concerning our Home, 217 E. Delavan Ave., would state that the object of our Home for the past two years has been faithfully carried out. It is a home for the aged and infirm members of the Lutheran Church. Members of other denominations have also been received. There are at present 27 women and 14 men as inmates of the Home. Our Board consists of 15 members, five pastors and ten laymen, who are connected with churches belonging to the United Lutheran Church. Our pastors have services at the Home every Sunday afternoon. The Ladies' Aids of the various churches have appointed days on which they visit the Home. Also Sunday Schools, Bible Classes and Luther Leagues visit the Home and entertain the old people.

The Women's Auxiliary meets monthly, also quarterly with the Board.

The President is Mr. L. H. Eppers; Vice-President, Dr. F. A. Kahler; Treasurer, Wm. L. Henrich, and Secretary, Rev. T. H. Becker.

Respectfully,

217 E. Delavan Ave.   MRS. J. SCHRAGEN, *Matron.*

Feghtly Home, Tippecanoe City

This Home as you know, cares for old ladies. The capacity is limited, only fifteen can be cared for with the present equipment. During the year this Home became an institution of the Synod of Ohio. Its property and assets have been turned over to us by the General Synod and the United Lutheran Church. One cannot help but admire the splendid way in which the Board of Directors and the Matron have conducted the affairs of the Home. It will be a question to decide in the near future as to whether it shall serve the whole church of the state or remain a small institution with a limited field of usefulness.

Franke Home, Charleston, S. C.

The Franke Home at Charleston, South Carolina, is a child of the Lutheran Church of that city, born of the faith and nutured by the love and generosity of Jacob Washington Franke, and sustained today largely by the income from his munificent bequest and also by the prayers and gifts of the people.

It has been in active service for twenty years, and during the past two years has ministered lovingly to its guests who are under the daily ministries of beneficence of Sister Dorothy Hesse.

Plans are now under way to install an elevator, this comfort feature being fostered enthusiastically by the Ladies' Auxiliary Society.

This institution is located in a prominent setion of the city, and its grounds comprise more than half a city block. The buildings are in excellent repair and the administration of this charity of the Church is proving most effective for those who are entertained there and is a tangible witness in the community to the sterling faith and Christian spirit of our people.

The Lutheran Church Home for the Aged and Infirm of Central New York, Inc.

This Home has entered into its eighth year of service for the homeless, aged, Lutheran people. The property is free of debt and a $3,000 building fund has been gathered with additional pledges of $4,000 outstanding. An endowment fund of $4,000 is on hand. It was advisable to postpone the construction of a new building until more building capital is available. Lutheran congregations of Central New York are being visited with a view to enlist wider interest and additional support.

The Home consists of one building with accommodations for ten residents, a matron and a cook, and ten acres of land. It is located near Clinton, N. Y., eight miles south of Utica, near a trolley, in pleasant and healthy surroundings. It serves the district of Central New York. From a radius of 75 miles peeople have been cared for. God's blessings have been evident in this enterprise undertaken in Christ's Name. The need is beyond doubt. The service rendered is a credit to the Church and to the loyal members and friends of the Association. May the divine Author of love and charity strengthen our hands and hearts.

Orphans' Home and Home for the Aged, Germantown, Philadelphia, Pa.

The Germantown Orphans' Home was opened in 1859, and admits children between the ages of two weeks and ten years; and the Aged Home for Men and Women, over sixty years of age. During the biennium considerable progress, both in the care of our wards and of the property, is to be noted. The population June, 1928, includes eighty-six boys and sixty-five girls of all ages, and forty-six men and women.

The Home is located in one of the city's finest residential sections, becoming increasingly valuable; well marked by the handsome Schmidt entrance it impresses the public as a credit to the Church.

The children enjoy the advantage of our Public Educational system. The school record shows considerable enrollment in Junior High, High and students at Business College, and such as Drexel Institute and Muhlenberg College. A Kindergarten only is conducted at the Home. The Summer Bible School, in session daily during July, with a faculty of Lutheran Public School Teachers, in view of the felt need for comprehensive religious instruction, is given especial consideration.

The record of improvements and development show attention to every building and a consistent effort to better the surroundings of young and old. The building formerly used as Baby Cottage, was entirely rebuilt at a cost of approximately $11,000 and is virtually a new building. An old stable, was razed according to our comprehensive plan and a fine modern stone garage and vegetable storage building erected at another location.

The expenses of the Institution for the year ended April 1, 1928, were $63,975.36.

Dependent upon the churches of the Ministerium for the major portion of its support, the Home is alert to every opportunity for service among the Orphans and Aged.

Tabitha Home, Lincoln, Nebr.

Tabitha Home, Lincoln, Nebr., was opened 1886 for children, aged, and helpless. It came into possession of the General Synod, Western District Synod in 1906. During the 22 years the home has been tenderly going forward in its work in quite a large indebtedness. Many improvements were made and a building for the children was erected. The average number of guests in the home for the past two years was one hundred twenty-six, sixty-eight children and fifty-eight aged and helpless. Fifteen aged and helpless died during the biennium. The orphanage department of Tabitha has never had a death in all these years. City water, sewerage and a modern poultry house were the improvements made last year. There is perhaps no other home of the church which gives shelter with so small equipment as Tabitha does. Tabitha Home is happy to report that the last two years were the best, more work, more funds and more divine blessing than ever before. We give heartfelt thanks to God and to the Church.

The financial statements for the biennium:

June 30, 1927

Income from apportionment, Synods and other sources...........$40,787.08
Expenditures for salaries and running expenses 50,710.29

June 30, 1928

Receipts from apportionment and other sources, including $6,400.00
  endowment 51,125.26
Expenditures for salaries and running expenses 42,492.70

The Luther Hospice for Young Men, Philadelphia, Pa.

With gratitude to God we record that the work progressed satisfactorily during 1927. The house kept well filled and an average of 70 men carried. Seven denominations were represented. About 50 per cent. of the men were Lutheran. Among the foreign countries represented were Germany, Sweden, Scotland. From the home land we had men from Pennsylvania, New Jersey, New York, Massachusetts, Virginia. The majority, of course, came from the home state of Pennsylvania. Sixty per cent of the men were business men and the remainder students. Every effort was made to keep the work as near to its ideals as possible, both spiritually and physically. Conducting it as an extension of the Christian family, Mrs. Schantz and I endeavored, with the family prayers and with the personal contact, to maintain that helpful atmosphere which should be found in every home. The men co-operated in the work splendidly in every way. Positions were secured for new-comers and in several cases financial assistance was given to men starting out in their work. Several younger boys whose families were broken up and who had to start with low wages were entertained for considerably less than the regular rate. The rate per week ranges from $10.50 to $12. Among other things the men were urged to do was to remain faithful to their churches, to spend their leisure evenings and especially their Sunday afternoons right.

United Lutheran Church Girls' Club, Chicago, Ill.

During the past biennium the Club has been operating at maximum capacity. The greatest need is for enlargement. Many are turned away because of "no room." The debt has been reduced to $12,500.

We appreciate the many distinguished visitors who have called.

The "Golden Rule" is the rule of the Club. Lutheran girls coming to Chicago are invited to write to the Superintendent, Mrs. D. A. Davy, 5402 Magnolia Ave., Chicago, Ill.

Hospice of Luther League of Nebraska

Since the Richmond Convention we have been strengthening our work by interesting more and more young people from Leagues and congregations out in the smaller communities of our state who come to the metropolis of Omaha to work or to pursue a course of study in our schools in the city, to come to the Hospice either permanently or until they have made other contacts and friends and leave us to stay with them. The work is entirely self-supporting in that we ask for no contributions from the Leaguers of the state, other than one offering a yeear for our new equipment fund. The rátes charged the residents are below or equal to the same standard of board and room elsewhere in the city. The Hospice is a real home for the Lutheran young folks and welcomes alike transients or permanent guests. Since the Richmond Convention the Hospice has entertained over a hundred and fifty guests, among whom are many prominent Lutheran clergymen and laymen of the United States. The Hospice is centraly located, facing one of Omaha's numerous parks—an ideal location. "When in Omaha stay at the Hospice."

The Children's Hospital of the Philadelphia Motherhouse

This hospital occupies the first floor of the west wing of the beautiful and spacious building known as the Mary J. Drexel Home and Philadelphia Motherhouse of Deaconesses. Since it was opened on May 15, 1890, more than 29,000 patients have been admitted, 1,142 during 1926, and 1,065 in 1927. The excellent Laboratory and X-ray facilities of the Lankenau Hospital located on the same grounds and for adults only, are at the service of the Children's Hospital. At the dispensary more than 2,500 children annually are treated in about 20,000 visits. Daily devotions are conducted with the patients and Sunday school is held regularly with the convalescents. Christmas and Easter are celebrated with special programs rendered by the children themselves with genuine joy, though some may not be able to sit up. Appropriate decorations and gifts contribute much to the festive spirit. Not a few of the little patients have never before come into contact with Christian worship and most of them enter heartily into the spirit of the services. Frequently children who have been confined to the hospital for several weeks, after returning to their homes send their mothers to inquire about the hymn book used, from which one or more of the songs and prayers have become precious to them. As an Inner Mission Agency, therefore, this hospital takes an important place.

May the good seed sown bear much fruit!

Spring Garden Neighborhood House, 1286 Spring Garden Ave., N. S., Pittsburgh, Pa.

The Women's Missionary Society of the Pittsburgh Synod has, since 1913, maintained a worker in the Spring Garden field. She is under the supervision of the pastor of Grace Church.

This work is primarily with the children. It includes weekday Bible classes, daily Summer school, Scouts, Campfire Girls, Story Hour, movies and handcraft. In the Summer the adjacent playground is the center of activities.

Enrollments in Summer school and weekday Winter classes is 75.

This work feeds into and supplements the regular church activities. Many scores of former Grace Church members now are in other congregations. The present communicant strength is 170.

Bethesda Home

Bethesda Home has moved forward during the biennium. The bequest of $50,000 from the estate of the late John B. Kaercher, and that of Lulu D. Bair, of $7,000, together with a number of smaller bequests have given us a nucleus for an Endowment. This will be increased with additional funds from several other sources. A new cottage costing $32,000, erected during the year, by the Women's Missionary Society of the Erie Conference will accommodate 36 problem girls. We have at this time 132 in the Home with 11 additional in private homes. Permanent homes have been found for six children. J. C. Yeany, brother of the Superintendent, who has been Farm Manager since the beginning of the Home, has been called by the Board as assistant Superintendent and Farm Manager, to enable the Superintendent to devote more time to the presentation of the cause to congregations.

Much attention is being given to health, dental work, etc. Improvements have been made to the water system, lawns enlarged and beautified and the whole plant of the Home has a prosperous appearance. The staff of workers has been enlarged and all are giving service that will be of inestimable value to the children, now and in the years to come.

Lutheran Settlement, Philadelphia, Pa.

The Settlement Congregation has shown great interest in the unchurched population of this community, many of its members have engaged in personal work, and some have been successful in bringing souls into the Church. Interest, however, has not been limited to this community, but has gone beyond into various activities of the Church at large. Time and again gifts have been sent by the various organizations within the Settlement to home and foreign mission fields. Forty-three members united with the Congregation during 1926 and 1927; 79, of whom most were infants, were baptized during the same period. Holy Communion was administered regularly. Ill families were represented by one or several members in the Church, and 210 families were likewise represented in the Sunday school.

The Sunday school, besides defraying its own expenses, contributed regularly to Mission causes. Speakers from the various fields have acquainted the school with the missions.

The three Luther Leagues, Senior, Intermediate, and Junior, have all functioned successfully.

The Week-Day classes and clubs, numbering close to fifty, ministered to a large number of boys and girls, men and women. The families represented in Sunday school were also in the weekday classes, but in addition there were 315 more families represented in the latter. The total aggregate attendance in all activities for 1926 and 1927 was 112,115.

The Settlement House has thus made many contacts in the community, and much preventive work has been accomplished through its classes, clubs, clinic, and home visitations. Good has been promoted and evil curbed.

Family case work loomed large in our work, help was rendered in numerous ways—rent, food and clothing were among the most frequent aids; 7,733 visits were made and 2,280 interviews conducted.

The regular staff of five women workers was assisted by the associate pastor, two seminary students, and 55 volunteers. The running expenses for the two years were approximately $28,000, which sum was raised through contributions, and dues given by the members of the Inner Mission Society of Philadelphia.

Kensington Dispensary for the Treatment of Tuberculosis, Philadelphia, Pa.

The Kensington Dispensary for the Treatment of Tuberculosis has treated, without regard to creed, color or condition, hundreds of patients this biennium. It has given home treatments to those who need it. Milk and personal needs are always supplied and every form of Tubelculosis treated by a competent medical staff.

Home visiting and follow-up work by our visiting nurses constitute a large welfare program also, and as a receiving station for all children needing Preventorium care at "River Crest" it is doing the largest work.

"River Crest" Preventorium, Mont Clare, Pa.

"River Crest" Preventorium has during the past biennium erected a modern group building at an approximate cost of $200,000. Hundreds of children, predisposed and exposed to tuberculosis, here receive the care they need.

Convalescent care is also given and this ideal spot is doing a work which simply cannot be measured in words.

Children ranging in age from 4 to 14 years are eligible. During the summer months our groups are larger, and are supervised by trained counsellors.

Beautiful woods and spacious playgrounds afford ample recreation. Fresh milk, eggs, and vegetables produced on our own farm, are the great bodybuilders, and the Christian treasured teachings with our morning and evening worship, will, we pray, be soul-builders.

Endorsements by Philadelphia Health Council and the State of Pennsylvania prove the merit of any institution, and "River Crest" is proud to be among that list.

Seaman's and Immigrant Mission, Philadelphia, Pa.

The work was begun in 1898; a seamen's home, at 1402 East Moyamensing Ave., was bought in 1908; value of property, $30,000; owned by Philadelphia Association for the Care of German seamen; President, Carl Berger; Seamen's pastor, Rev. Erich Saul; 26 beds, reading room, writing room, library, dining room.

Statistics—Lodgers at the Home, 1,906; sleeping nights, 15,268; vessels visited, 288; seamen met on vessels, about 2,000; periodicals distributed, about 4,000; testaments, 500; services held at the Home, 94; sailors present 1,186; sailors visited at hospitals, 450; sailors assisted with money amounting to $2,792.42; sailors assisted with free lodgings, 2,415; sailors assisted with free meals, 845; sailors assisted with employment, 751; money from sailors for safekeeping and forwarding, $220,026.75.

Lutheran Inner Mission Society, Inc., Washington, D. C.

This organization of the Lutheran Churches of the District of Columbia was formerly under the direction of the Lutheran Alliance of the City of Washington. During the past year it was incorporated into a distinct and separate Society to carry on the work of mercy and Christian service in the name of the Lutherans of the National Capital.

The Board of Directors now have the co-operation of the Joint Synod of Ohio, and of the two Missouri Churches in the city. However, the by-laws give the control and direction to the United Lutheran representatives. The Board consists of fifteen members. During 1927 we had an ordained minister, Rev. J. M. Stick, who resigned December 27. January 1, 1928 we called Frances Dysinger, A.B., of Fremont Nebraska, as Administrative Secretary. Our work covers Juvenile court, alms house, jail, hospital and other institutional visitations. Much work is done in Walter Reed Military Hospital, Mt. Alto Military Tuberculosis Hospital, and St. Elizabeth's Insane, where many shell-shocked boys are treated.

The National Capital furnishes exceptional opportunities along this line for service. Our Churches are beginning to realize their privilege and are measuring up to it by an intense interest and devotion. We have, since January 1, gathered over 500 members, and with the Churches backing us on their budget, we have the support of over 2,500 persons. Our budget is not very large, about $3,000 per annum, but the service we are able to render is unlimited.

Trenton Lutheran Inner Mission Society

Services at Mercer Hospital, January and July.

Lesson for the Day, Five Hospitals.

Occasional services held at—Florence Mission, N. J. Children's Home, Mercer County Jail, Mercer County Work House.

Weekly Catechetical Class, State Home for Girls.

Child taken care of at Orthopaedic Hospital.

Lutheran Young People supplied to—Mercer County Jail, 10; State Home for Girls, 5; Odd Fellows' Home, 25.

The Lutheran placed in—The Trenton Free Public Library, The Y. M. C. A., The Y. W. C. A.

One public meeting held, Dr. Freas, speaker.

Relief furnished for five families, food and clothing.

Books purchased and distributed—Catechisms, 6; Bibles, 6.

Ten layettes for infants made and distributed as needed.

Three baskets of fruit to Lutherans at Odd Fellows' Home.

Musical entertainments furnished—Odd Fellows' Home, State Home for Girls, Florence Mission, Children's Home.

The Philadelphia City Mission

This is a department of the Inner Mission Board of the Ministerium of Pennsylvania, office, 803 Muhlenberg Building. The work of the City Mission is chiefly in hospitals, homes and prisons. In these its staff of missionaries annually holds upwards of 500 services, and makes from 15,000 to 17,000 individual visits. One member of the staff continues to go to the sessions of the Juvenile Court several mornings of the week to take charge of children committed to the care of the Lutheran Children's Bureau. In finding positions for the unemployed, placing homeless, aged, sick and others needing care in institutions, and in frequent office interviews much helpful service is also rendered; and unconnected Lutherans found by the Missionaries are directed to a Lutheran Church and brought into communication with the pastor. To all this work there is a background which statistics do not reveal. Figures tell nothing of the lives influenced by the preached Word, of the cheer and comfort brought to the sick, of the hope awakened in the hearts of the shut-in, of the support and guidance given the tempted, and of the efforts made to lift up the fallen.

Inner Mission Society of the Chicago Area, Chicago, Ill.

U. L. C. A. Pastors and Congregations have co-operated splendidly during the biennium in the development of the Society and its program. More than 3,000 members are enrolled. Present activities comprise family and individual welfare, regular institutional visitation at the University of Illinois Research Hospital, occasional visitation at various city and county institutions, and denominational nurture of Lutheran children at the Mooseheart Home.

A suitable field is being sought for a settlement work. *The Message for the Day,* published by the Inner Mission Board, portions of Scripture, and scriptural picture cards and tracts have been distributed. *Inner Mission Message,* which was started as a quarterly, is now published monthly. A budget of $8,000 was provided for in 1927, and an additional $4,000 was added for the current year.

A U. L. C. A. Home for the Aged and Infirm, which is urgently needed in the Chicago zone, has been selected as an institutional objective, and as the first unit of a Colony of Mercy. A Life Annuity System, which offers a life income to investing donors, has been put into operation. For information, address Brother Davy, Supt., 860 Cass St., Chicago, Ill.

The Board of Trustees, which is elected by the U. L. C. A. ministers and Congregational Chairmen of the Chicago Area at present includes—Mr. Emil Bach, Mr. C. J. Driever, Rev. Otto Doering, Mr. O. L. Ewert, Rev. J. R. E. Hunt, D.D., Rev. Albert Kaitschuk, Mrs. H. C. Krueger, Mrs. J. Allen Leas, Rev. Geo. P. Lottich, Mr. F. H. Mobley, Mr. Adolf Monsen, Mrs. A. M. Neumann, Mrs. E. Luther Spaid, Rev. E. F. Valbracht, and Mr. O. J. Volkman. The Rev. E. F. Valbracht is president.

The Philadelphia Motherhouse of Deaconesses

This is one of the outstanding Inner Mission agencies of the United Lutheran Church. As reported elsewhere more fully, the Philadelphia Motherhouse conducts a *Home for the Aged* and a *Children's Hospital;* also a *Kindergarten,* most of whose children are not members of a Lutheran congregation and many without any other definite Christian influence. The children usually attend two years and during this time learn many of the stories of the Bible, especially of the life of Jesus, memorize prayers, songs and brief passages and at Christmas and Easter are impressed with the great facts of the life of Christ. Of still greater importance to the Church is the *Lankenua School for Girls,* founded by the Motherhouse in 1890 and gradually devloped into a school with standard courses for resident and day students. Because of the confidence the school enjoys on the part of parents and educators, fully one-half of the pupils come from non-Lutheran and some from non-Christian families, but all are instructed in the fundamentals of the Christian religion to which are devoted three class periods a week, beginning with the simplest facts in the I Grade, and leading up to Christian Doctrine, Ethics and Church History in the Senior High School. It is gratifying to know that with few exceptions the graduates have gratefully accepted the truths of the Christian religion and the ideals of a Christian life. As many of these girls are from families of means, the influence of this school reaches groups usually beyond the direct Inner Mission efforts.

Above all, however, the Philadelphia Motherhouse serves the Inner Mission cause through its deaconesses, trained for educational, institutional and social work. Sisters of this Motherhouse are in charge of the Lankenau Hospital with over 4,000 patients a year; the Kensington Dispensary for the Treatment of Tuberculosis, the Preventorium of which "River Crest" is doing typical Inner Mission work; the Tabor Home, where 75 children from unfortunate families are raised under Christian leadership; the Lutheran Home for the Aged in Erie; the Hospice for Girls in Reading, Pa., opened on June 30, 1928 by the Berks County Inner Mission Society, the Executive Secretary of which is likewise a deasoness of this Motherhouse. All this besides the incidental, but by no means unimportant, Inner Mission work done by the deaconesses in parishes.

The training of other Christian workers has been discontinued since the Sisterhood has gone over the hundred mark and needs all the available space at the Motherhouse so that special students cannot be properly accommodated. The two-year introductory course for the diaconate is, therefore, adjusted exclusively to the needs of candidates. In special cases, however, day students can be admitted.

Many requests for deaconesses had to be refused during the past biennium, preventing the Church from a still larger expansion of its Inner Mission activities. It is evident that the demand for deaconesses far exceeds the supply, but when met more fully by thoroughly qualified and consecrated young women of the Church, the Inner Mission cause will share in the advance.

The Emaus Orphan House

The Eamus Orphan House, Middletown, Pa., is supported by the income from the George Frey estate and is not under the control of the Lutheran Church, for which reason no financial report is made. The interest of the Church arises from the fact that, by the terms of the Frey will, the institution is Lutheran in spirit, the Board of Control is comprised entirely of members of St. Peter's Lutheran Church, Middletown, and the children are given instruction in the Lutheran Catechism and become members of St. Peter's Lutheran Sunday school and church.

Thirty-two children, aged from six to sixteen, equally divided as boys and girls, are in the home and receive excellent care. Many of these children are from non-Lutheran parentage. The principal, Dr. Colin S. Few, and the tutor and matron, Mr. and Mrs. Fred S. Bauchmoyer, exert a splendid moral influence over the children. The children are well disciplined and happy and the spirit of the institution is that of a Christian family. No expense is spared in providing for the physical well-being of the children, and they are given the spiritual, moral and mental preparation which should fit them for life.

All the children attend the services in St. Peter's Church, Middletown. During the past year fifteen were enrolled in the Pastor's catechetical classes and eight were received into church membership by baptism or confirmation. Children leaving the home are followed up through the Lutheran pastor in the community in which they locate. The home is open at all times to visitors from the Lutheran church. The gifts and interest of many congregations and individuals of the Lutheran Church, particularly from this immediate vicinity, are deeply appreciated.

Orphans' Home and Farm School, Zelienople, Pa.

The Orphans' Home at Zelienople, Pa., has been engaged in this phase of Inner Mission activity since 1852. For the first two years the work was conducted in connection with the Passavant Hospital in the city of Pittsburgh. In 1854 the farm at Zelienople, Pa., was purchased, buildings were erected, and the work has been going on ever since.

This institution is regarded the first or one of the two first orphanages (Protestant) in America.

We care for, on an average, 150 children each year; orphans, half-orphans, and otherwise dependent children.

Our work is operated on the cottage plan, twenty-five to thirty children to a cottage. A lady helper in charge of each cottage.

The age limit is 17 years of age. However, if a boy or girl has not finished high school by that time they have the privilege of finishing their school work.

Two young men from our Home were ordained to the Gospel ministry at the recent meeting of the Pittsburgh Synod. One of our girls graduated from Thiel College and will in two years go to Africa as a missionary.

The work is now under a Board of Directors elected by the Pittsburgh Synod.

A Superintendent's residence is under process of construction. The house now occupied by the Superintendent will be used as a nursery. Heretofore, we received children from three years on up. We will soon be in a position to take care of the babies.

The Wartburg Orphans' Farm School, Mount Vernon, N. Y.

Founded in 1866 and possessing a charter, which permits every known Inner Mission activity, the Warburg Home has been a haven of refuge to thousands of homeless children of every sort and to a large number of aged Lutherans. During the past year more than 400 children have been cared for. The annual budget has passed the $100,000 mark. Practically all of this money is raised by voluntary contributions. On the physical side the Home has increased its assets continuously. Today the property value approaches $2,000,000. Two plants are now being operated, one in Mount Vernon, the other at Kensico Lake, where the Home purchased 236 acres of most desirable land a few years ago. In Mount Vernon there are still 93 acres with 19 buildings; on the new location three buildings have been reared during the past year at a total expenditure of $85,000. A 2,000-foot road has been constructed and two pumphouses have been built and equipped. The first Children's Cottage, dedicated on July first, a memorial gift of Mrs. Margaret Achenbach, of New York City, for her parents, Mr. and Mrs. D. Bultmann, marks a new departure in Lutheran Child Welfare work. Twelve children will be cared for in this cottage, brothers and sisters remaining together under the same roof. Plans have been drawn for a "Rest Home," and another Old Folks' Home. The present new buildings are but units in a comprehensive plan of development, which has been prepared against all future needs.

Marie Louise Heins Memorial, Mount Vernon, N. Y.

This Old Folks' Home, begun in 1897, is among the smaller Homes of the Lutheran Church. Its capacity is limited to 36 persons. None but Lutherans in good standing are accepted. The admission fee is $1,000. **During** the years of its existence the Home has cared for almost 200 aged Lutherans. The expenses are met almost entirely by the inmates themselves. A legacy of $15,000 from the estate of Mrs. Marie Geyer was received during the past year and created an endowment fund. The Home is valued at $150,000. Under the direct supervision of the Wartburg Orphans' Farm School the Old Folks' Home is governed by the same officers.

The Passavant Memorial Homes for the Care of Epileptics, Rochester, Pa.

These Homes have continued their work of mercy. A kind Providence has kept away many evils and provides food, clothing and comfortable shelter for one hundred twenty patients. Our new year starts with forty-nine male and sixty female patients. The same corps of faithful deaconesses and helpers continues to serve. They have all been with the institution for more than ten years and seem to understand well how to treat the afflicted ones of the family.

During the year a new cottage has been erected on the grounds to the east of Elizabeth Hall. It is a very fine looking building and the rooms are light and airy. It is a very fine building. It was occupied the 18th of June. It will shelter at least seventy-five people and the cost will be $80,000, all of which is provided for. The expense for the year was $27,776.92. The Homes have no debts. Just now there is no room for men folks but plenty for females.

In the annual Report of the institution we read:

"The mystery of epilepsy has not yet been discovered. We gaze upon convulsive bodies but fail to see the mighty force which fills and shakes the mortal tenements. Physically strong, with mind clear and active, in a moment consciousness gone, and body apparently suffering great agony. If the Creator of these wonderful human bodies would only reveal the secret cause and remedy of this dread malady—how grateful thousands of people would be!

Trabert Hall, Minneapolis, Minn.

It is better and less difficult to keep a girl from falling than to lift her up after she has fallen.

For nine years the Lutheran Welfare Society of the Twin Cities have maintained a home at 625 East 14th Street, Minneapolis, Minnesota, for girls working in the city. This place, formerly known as the Hospice for Young Women, but now called Trabert Hall, is not just a boarding house but as real a home as it can be made, and those in charge feel that they have succeeded fairly well when they hear the many words of appreciation that have come to them not only from the girls in residence but also from the mothers and relatives who come to visit from time to time.

The standards of living at Trabert Hall are high. Nearly all who come want a Christian home and that is the kind those in charge endeavor to give them.

Trabert Hall is not a money-making institution. It charges a girl from $5.75 to $7.25 a week for room and three meals a day, and, when all food and fuel and repairs and equipment and salaries and interest and a thousand dollars on the mortgage every year, and many other expenses have been paid, there is very little left in the treasury, but the good that has been done to hundreds of girls, more than 90 per cent. of whom are Lutherans, those in charge forget about the money and are glad that through the serving of so many young folks they, too, have served the Lord.

Lutheran Hospice for Young Women, Pittsburgh, Pa.

Founded, 1918.
Value of property, $150,000.
Number of guests, including transients, 295.
Annual expense, about $10,250.
These figures are for the year 1927, and vary little from year to year.

Lutheran Hospice for Girls, Baltimore, Md.

Located at 509 Park Ave., and conducted by the Inner Mission Society. The Hospice can accommodate 32 girls and has been filled during the past two years.

Two years ago a mortgage of $1,000 rested on the Hospice which has been paid off and the property has a value of $40,000 today. The property is in good condition, the only improvement being the installing of an incinerator.

Our Hospice is a Christian Home where family life and the spirit of helpfulness is emphasized. We have been the means of helping many a girl to a larger and fuller vision of life.

The Hospice Mission Circle contributes to Home, Foreign and Inner Mission work through their gifts and personal service.

The Tryon Homestead, Philadelphia, Pa.

The Tryon Homestead has taken care of a large family of girls, students and business girls. We have co-operated with the various Boards and helped, by employment, persons referred to us through Rev. Saul.

The house has been decidedly improved, grounds also, and our young friends appear to be very happy and contented. If we could only find more of them anxious to enjoy the privileges which this beautiful home-like place, with its splendid director offers.

Children's Receiving Home, Maywood, Ill.

The Children's Receiving Home, Maywood, Ill., is fostered by the Lutheran Woman's League of Chicago and vicinity.

The Home was opened in 1919 in a substantial residence, on grounds occupying one square, which soon became inadequate.

In October, 1926, a large, commodious building of brick, costing approximately $100,000 was dedicated. It contains single bed rooms, boys' and girls' dormitories, study rooms, kindergarten, in charge of a trained kindergartener, office, parents' reception room, living room, nursery, in charge of a trained nurse, kitchen, store rooms, dining room, and fully equipped laundry. It will accommodate about 60 children. It is substantially and attractively furnished, the gifts chiefly of interested friends.

From January, 1926 to January, 1928, there were 90 children received and 39 dismissed. In June, 1928, there were 47 enrolled.

The total disbursements for the maintenance of the Home in 1926 was $8,407.58, while in 1927 is was $18,385.23.

The former home, thoroughly renovated, provides a hospital, quarters for some of the workers, and a large play room.

A real home atmosphere prevails. Thoughtful physical care, training in a love and reverence for holy things, and attention to the little courtesies of life are a part of the daily regime. All of the children of school age attend the church services of St. John's Church of Maywood.

Artman Home, Ambler, Pa.

The Artman Home for Lutherans, located on Bethlehem Pike, Ambler, Pa., is a home for Lutherans, designed primarily for pastors' widows and other persons definitely connected with the work of the Church. It has, however, enlarged its scope and now receives others as well. During the past year the home had 14 permanent and 7 transient guests, coming from at least 12 congregations of the Ministerium of Pennsylvania, and the East Pennsylvania Synod. A large mansion with 20 rooms, surrounded by seven acres of ground, houses the guests while a parsonage, just completed at a cost of over $7,000, provides a home for the director and his wife. The endowment of $50,000 supplies about one-third of the annual cost of maintenance. Another third is received from interested friends. The remainder is a deficit that can be met only by the generous support of our churches. The Board, composed of clerical and lay members selected from the membership of the Synods on whose territory the home is located, is doing all in its power to provide for the needs of these one-time workers of the Church.

Lutheran Hospital of Manhattan

Lutheran Hospital of Manhattan was founded in 1911, chartered in 1913, and is recognized by the College of Surgeons as a Grade A, 100-bed Hospital. The total bed capacity is 121: 90 adult beds, 10 children's beds, 20 bassinettes, and 1 incubator. 74 beds are in wards, 23 in semi-private rooms, and 24 in private rooms.

The work of the Hospital is general. A dispensary is maintained, and clinics held every day except Sunday. Members of the Medical Service Association, an organization of staff and courtesy doctors, make free calls to the homes of the poor.

During the past two years 5,145 patients were admitted, 3,176 being in the wards, 1,015 in semi-private rooms, and 954 in private rooms. The total number of Hospital Days was 64,266. During the same period, the Dispensary Service treated 2,828 patients with a total number of 8,521 visits. Clinic and Ward prescriptions are compounded at cost in the Drug Room and in many cases without charge.

The cost of maintaining the Hospital and Dispensary was $370,698.44. The Hospital depends for its support upon receipts from patients, membership dues, and donations; and receives no financial support from State, county or city funds, nor from the United Hospital Fund of New York City.

Seamen's Mission and Seamen's House, Hoboken, N. J.

Unchurched not by choice but by necessity are the seamen. A floating existence calls for props to substitute for the stability family life and home give to the resident worker. The message of God brought to the seaman in his language, the home kept in the spirit of his country are the stabilizers used by the mission. The port of New York is the most important link in the chain of Seamen's Missions. There is hardly a seaman who does not touch this harbor. For thousands it becomes the home port. The call for the Lutheran Mission is greater than the means to answer it. 160 lodgers a night, 300 visitors in the reading room, a thousand letters a week; five hospitals where sick calls are to be made; visits aboard ships; help to the destitute and convalescent; good books aboard ships; taking care of seamen's savings. In all work one aim: to bring Christ to the hearts of men.

Two buildings were added to the institution during the last two years. The staff was increased by one trained worker. Value of property, $150,000.

Lutheran Welfare Society in the Twin Cities

The Lutheran Welfare Society originally organized in 1905 is governed by an elected board of 18 members, 5 of whom are women. The following synods are represented in the board: Augustana, Buffalo, United Danish, Free, Iowa, Norwegian, Ohio and United.

July 1st, 1928, the membership of the society was 2,419, and *Lutheran-*

Welfare, the monthly journal, had 4,483 subscribers. The 1928 budget requires $74,224.25. Receipts: annual earnings, $31,850; Minneapolis Community Fund allotment, $13,500, and the balance is provided by voluntary offerings. The second annual membership "roll Call" observed as "Lutheran Welfare Week," resulted in $9,670.94 in cash and pledges. The property valuation is about $115,000.

The society employs a regular staff of 16 trained mission workers. A large number of volunteer workers, mostly Lutheran students, supplement the work of the regular staff. The Women's League in Minneapolis and the St. Paul Auxiliary appropriated $5,019 to the society during 1927. Additional women's auxiliaries are being organized in different sections of the state, the first being the Northfield Unit, organized November 8, 1927.

The Norwegian Lutheran Church at its regular biannual convention in June, 1928, decided to transfer the Twin City welfare work of its Board of Charities to the society and appropriated $7,500 toward the expense, the same to take effect January 1, 1929. The activities involved are—city mission work and institutional ministrations, home finding and child placement, juvenile court work and work with unmarried mothers. Three ordained city missionaries and three case workers are involved in the transfer.

By invitation of the Minneapolis Council of Social Agencies the general office of the society occupies a suite of rooms in the Citizens' Aid Building, 404 South 8th Street; the new office building used exclusively by the religious and social agencies of the city. The findings of a comprehensive survey of the Lutheran Welfare situation in St. Paul is to be published by the end of the year and a St. Paul office is under consideration.

Departments: (1) *City Mission,* five workers served 728 (figures are for 1927) families in distress through 2,885 visits and 3,364 interviews. (2) *The Luther House,* 828 South 6th Street, a Christian settlement, with day nursery, kindergarten, mother's club, employment bureau, children's classes, missionary services, Sunday school, resident department, playground and community service served 1,143 different individuals. (3) *Missionary Training School* enrolled 11 day students and 38 evening students. (4) *Trabert Hall and Annex,* 625 East 14th Street, sheltered 440 young women. Service is on a cost basis. (5) *Children's Receiving Home,* 875 Aldine Ave., St. Paul, and the Children's Department served 115 cases, 64 boys and 51 girls. Placement investigations, 92, approved, 31, placed, 31. (6) *Children's Summer Camp,* Lake Pepin, Wis., cared for 106 children. (7) *Street Services* were conducted weekly during July and August, reaching over 2,000 hearers.

The officers of the society are: Rev. H. B. Kildahl, President; Rev. A. W. Walck, 1st Vice-President; Dr. Silas Anderson, 2nd Vice-President; Mrs. F. E. Moody, Secretary; Prof. V. L. Erickson, Treasurer, and Ambrose Hering, D.D., Executive Secretary.

The Inner Mission Society of the Evengelical Lutheran Church in New York City, Incorporated

The Society maintains headquarters at 412 W. 145th St., New York City, from which its workers go out to institutions, prisons, courts and private homes with a ministry of Christian mercy. There are four paid workers giving full time, two giving part time and a large number of volunteers. The Society helps to maintain the work of the Lutheran Chapel on Welfare Island, conducts a German and an English service each Sunday, as well as provides comforts, reading matter and many treats for the old people in the city institutions on the island. We have now a full time City Missionary who gives his time to institutional ministrations.

The Society conducts, also the social service department of the Lutheran Hospital, providing a worker as Registrar for the Out Patient Department and caring for the needs of ward patients and their families.

A Family and Child Welfare Department ministers to the needs both physical and spiritual of many families, neglected children, homeless men and women. Clothing is collected and distributed, and more than $1,200 expended yearly for emergency relief.

A monthly publication is sent to members of the Society who subscribe and the organization is supported entirely by voluntary contributions from churches and individuals. There are at present over 1,300 members.

The Wilbur A. Herrlich Memorial Farm, at Towners, N. Y., is owned and operated by the society, as a vacation home for children.

The total budget of the society for 1928 is $22,980, an increase over 1927 of about $2,000.

The Wilbur A. Herrlich Memorial Farm

This institution is owned and operated by the Inner Mission Society of New York, at an annual cost of $5,500. 400 city children, chosen from the poorest homes, are given two weeks each of country air, healthful recreation and spiritual nurture. A staff of nine persons, assisted by 15 volunteers, include group counsellors, a trained nurse, recreational supervisor, housekeeper and director.

The program for the Home is carefully balanced so as to provide health, recreation and spiritual and habit-forming instruction. It is definitely a Christian Home. Both boys and girls between five and twelve years of age are eligible. The parents of these children are unable to pay for their children, the work being supported by voluntary contributions. The Institution is in its seventh year, on its own property of 40 acres, but the society has a record of 15 continuous years of service in Vacation Home work.

Lutheran Inner Mission Society of Reading and Vicinity

During 1927-1928 we put on a campaign for a hospice. Result—Paid in cash, $14,794.57; Pledges, $3,250; Annuity Bond, $5,000: Total, $23,044.57.

A piece of property was bought costing $11,250, and the balance of money used for repairing and furnishing up the hospice so that no funds remain.

Over 16,000 calls made to sick, shut-ins and families.

Over 60,000 pieces of Christian literature distributed.

One hundred and twenty addresses delivered.

Over 400 unchurched Lutherans referred to pastors for church connection.

Three hundred seventy-five babies referred to cradle roll teachers to be registered for Sunday school.

One hundred family welfare problems called to attention of the society.

Sixty-five child welfare problems called to attention of the society.

Regular visitation every week at four city hospitals and monthly visitation to six other institutions, as County Home, Widows' Home, etc.

Membership of 1,274.

The Passavant Hospital of Pittsburgh, Pa.

A brief summary of the work of the Passavant Hospital for the past two years discloses the following:

There were 3,223 patients admitted in the previous year and only 3,160 last year. Nursing days in the former year were 40,337, last year only 38,071. We cannot explain the reason for this decrease unless it is due to the various hospitals having increased their bed capacity.

Of the 3,223 patients in 1927, 2,420 were pay; 39 were part pay, and 714 were free. Of the nursing days in 1927, 26,768 were pay days, 4,055 were part pay, and 9,514 were free. Of the 3,160 patients in 1928, 2,219 were pay; 156 were part pay, and 785 were free. The nursing days were 25,314 pay, 3,135 part pay, and 9,622 free.

The Dispensary and Emergency visits were for 1927 and 1928 respectively, 10,512 and 11,130.

The receipts in 1927 amounted to $167,473.11 and the expenditures to $167,077.53. In 1928 the receipts were $184,375.18 and the expenditures, $189,514.17.

From the State of Pennsylvania during the last year we have received $15,000 besides legacies from Mr. Chas. Wattles amounting to $16,136; from Mr. Pollock, $450, and from Mr. McMurray, $900.

According to the State's method of computing the cost per patient per day, a private room patient cost $4.72 and a ward patient, $3.60.

The Lutheran Inner Mission Society has been faithful in the attendance of the sick, conducting chapel services once a week and Bible lesson during the school term.

Board of Inner Missions of the Ministerium of Pennsylvania

Five years have elapsed since this Board was established. It is the first Synodical Board of Inner Missions to be organized in the United Lutheran

Church. Its management is vested in a Board consisting of the President of the Ministerium, three pastors and three laymen. For its support the Ministerium makes an appropriation of $24,000. In addition, the Board receives contributions from organizations and private individuals; partial support of the children is also given by the various counties. The total expense for the biennium was $86,000. The Board has in its service four pastors, three women missionaries and two office workers. Two pastors are at work in the City Mission, one in the Seamen's Mission; the Executive Secretary is also in charge of the Children's Bureau and the Lutheran Bureau. In this work he is assisted by the women missionaries. Offices are located in the Muhlenberg Building, Philadelphia.

For effective administration the Board carries on its work through four departments.

Philadelphia City Mission

This is the oldest agency of the Ministerium. Two full time pastors and a number of volunteers carry on the work. During the biennium more than 900 services were conducted in penal institutions, hospitals and homes. In the course of the work of visitation almost 30,000 individual visits were made. Four infant and one adult baptisms were administered and 161 persons received the Holy Communion. The missionaries officiated at thirty-one funerals. Pastor Weaver represents the Lutheran Children's Bureau in the Philadelphia Juvenile Court.

Seamen's and Immigrant Mission

In co-operation with the Philadelphia Association for the Care of German Seamen, the Board carries on an extensive work among seamen in the port of Philadelphia. A large, well appointed home is the center in which the many activities are carried on. In addition to the rooms for lodgers, there are reading and writing rooms and a large recreation room. The missionary visits incoming ships, the local hospitals and looks after the welfare of sailors in general. No record of the number of visitors is kept but in the biennium the Home provided 2,200 men with over 15,000 sleeping nights.

Restriction of immigration has cut down this part of the work considerably. Both Pastor Saul and the office of the Board carry on a large correspondence in behalf of the newly arrived immigrants. Pastor Saul also ministers to those who are detained at the station in Gloucester awaiting deportation to their native land.

The Lutheran Children's Bureau

This work has passed the experimental stage and at the end of the year 1927, the Bureau had 252 children in its care, an increase of 73 in the biennium; during the same period 53 children were discharged.

An increasing number of Lutheran families are opening their homes and hearts for these dependent children, many of whom could not otherwise be provided for. In addition to the secretary and office staff, three women missionaries give full time service. Branch offices are maintained in Allentown, Reading, Pottsville, Wilkes-Barre, and Scranton.

Assistance is given to pastors and in co-operation with the Courts and public agencies in this ever widening field. The total disbursements were $62,000.

The Lutheran Bureau

Services are regularly conducted and visitations made in the State Sanitorium for Tuberculosis at Hamburg. Ours is the only Protestant Church doing such work. Patients from all over the State are sent here and the ministrations of Pastor R. E. Kern and the Board's missionary, Miss Gassner, are greatly appreciated. A similar work is carried on at White Haven by Pastor Geiger.

At Sleighton Farm for Girls the Lutheran girls receive religious instruction weekly from Miss Sachs and the Secretary conducts a monthly Communion Service.

The outstanding work of the biennium was the revival of the Mission for the Deaf. Services had been conducted intermittently during the previous sixteen years. The Board from the time of its organization made a number of attempts to organize this phase of Inner Mission work. A number of circumstances brought about the present development. Parents of Lutheran deaf children at the Pennsylvania Institution for the Deaf and men and women who had been confirmed by the late Rev. Dr. Jacob Fry, made earnest requests for spiritual help. With the entrance of Mr. Edward F. Kaercher to the Philadelphia Seminary in 1926, the plans took shape. Mr. Kaercher is deaf and is a graduate of Gallaudet College for the Deaf. Working with the Secretary of the Board he assisted in the establishment of three congregations, St. Philips, Philadelphia; St. Thomas', Allentown, and St. Andrew's, Reading. Services are also conducted at Norristown, Trenton and Lancaster. Contacts are being established with Lutheran and unchurched deaf throughout the territory.

The Pottsville Conference through its Inner Mission committee conducts services in the County Prison, County Home and Asylum and has regular chaplains for each hospital. A splendid co-ordinated work is carried on.

Through this department an Information Bureau and Library for Inner Missions is maintained.

Mr. Distler introduced the Executive Secretary, the Rev. Wm. Freas; the Rev. E. A. Sievert, Secretary in charge of Immigrant's and Seamen's Work; Mrs. W. F. Morehead, President of the

Women's Missionary Society, which is doing work among the Southern mountain children; the Rev. Ernst Walter, Superintendent of Tabitha Home; the Rev. F. F. Eberhardt, of the Texas Hospital; and the Rev. J. F. Ohl, Superintendent of the City Mission in Philadelphia.

The Rev. O. C. D. Klaehn was introduced and spoke of the Immigrant Work in Canada and appealed to the United Lutheran Church for help. Before he took his seat a voice from the floor said that the appeal had been heard and that provision had been made by two members of the Convention to take care of at least one missionary. The two members were Mr. Peter P. Hagan and Dr. E. Clarence Miller.

The auditor's report on accounts of the Inner Mission Board was accepted.

The Rev. John Weidley presented the report of the Board of Trustees of the National Lutheran Home for the Aged, Washington, D. C.

REPORT OF THE NATIONAL LUTHERAN HOME FOR THE AGED

"Withhold not good from them to whom it is due, when it is in the power of thine hand to do it."

The fear of poverty is a moral disease from which all civilization suffers.

Age brings infirmity. While it lessens the enjoyment of life it increases desire for living. Fear becomes a prevailing passion. Caution grows as the years pass. Nature increases the wish to live, while it reaps the sins of pleasure. So very much is dependent upon how the earlier years have been spent.

Though the age be prosperous, the food abundant, clothing fine, there always seem to be those coming to the evening time of life having nothing with which to maintain themselves. Meanwhile there are many suggestions for thrift, by individuals, by communities, by states and by nations. Lay aside a little from the month's wages. Have your life insured. Purchase bonds. In spite of this, misfortune may come to those who least expect it, and at a time when they are no longer able to recover.

There are children who lose interest in their parents, and permit them in old age to shift for themselves.

There is also a class which gives itself to the care of others, which eventually finds itself without money, or home, or friends.

Some there are who, having accumulated enough for old age, permit themselves to be deceived by relatives or so-called friends, entrust their money to them, and it never comes back. Thus they become dependent upon the Church, or the State, or some form of charity. These must not be neglected. The obligation of love is upon us to make provision for the unfortunate and the helpless. This is one of the first enterprises of the Christian Church. Seven deacons were appointed to care for the widow and orphan.

While this is one of the first it is by no means the least of the benevolent works of the Church. No apology need be made for its mission. We cannot think ourselves to be Christian if we neglect the care of those within our reach who need brotherly assistance.

The National Lutheran Home for the Aged, Washington, D. C., is a standing testimonial of love for the aged and the needy. Thirty-five years it has been doing this blessed work of mercy.

The building is thoroughly equipped. The family is cared for by a consecrated Deaconess. She has the aid of trained assistants.

A Board of Lady Managers, composed of members of the Washington Lutheran congregations, gives careful attention to the management of the Home family.

There is connected with the building a beautiful chapel in which service is conducted every Sunday. The Lutheran ministers of Washington have charge of the devotions.

Not only do we provide food, and clothing, and shelter. There are missionary meetings, social entertainments, automobile excursions to interesting places in and about the District of Columbia.

The building is beautifully located, with ample space about, and removed from the noise of the streets.

The rooms are always filled. There is a long list of applicants awaiting their turn to be admitted. Sometimes requests for admission are as frequent as two a week. If we are to care for these, new and larger buildings must be erected. Funds are being gathered for an addition, but the query is, whence shall we get the money to maintain it after it is erected?

A plan has been agreed upon by the Executive Board of the United Lutheran Church, to be presented for consideration at this Convention, by which the present relationship of the Home shall be maintained for a period of ten years. At that time the question is to be considered anew.

The membership of the family is 47 women; 9 men.

During the biennium 13 members have died.

In the same period 13 new members were admitted.

The Board of Directors is very grateful to the Church for its aid in the maintenance of the Home. For the evidences of growing interest, for bequests, for annuities, for special gifts in food, clothing, good-will, and prayer, we are truely thankful.

An invitation is extended to all Lutherans who visit in our beautiful Capital city to visit the Home. Inspection is solicited. Those who come from time to time are favorably impressed. There are some who come with a preconceived notion of seeing a poverty-house. They go away with changed mind, for they have seen a Christian Home.

The report of the treasurer is herewith submitted. We are greatly indebted to Mr. H. T. Domer for his careful and systematic service.

Respectfully, for the Board

JOHN WEIDLEY, *President.*

TREASURER'S REPORT OF THE NATIONAL LUTHERAN HOME FOR THE AGED

BALANCE SHEET
For the two years ended June 30, 1928 *and* 1927
June 30, 1928
ASSETS

Cash:

American Security & Trust Co.	$ 5,470.31	
Columbia National Bank	5,968.17	
The National Savings & Trust Co.	27,885.59	
Washington Loan & Trust Co.	318.23	
In transit from General Treasurer	1,200.00	
		$ 40,842.30
Securities, at book values, as annexed		51,835.00
Share of Fetterly Bequest to be received at death of life tenant		1,606.83
Real estate, etc., at book values:		
National Lutheran Home property, Washington, D. C.	39,469.48	
New building	91,555.64	
Farmer's cottage	3,000.00	
New barn	2,000.00	
Grundy County tract, Tennessee	200.00	
		136,225.12
		$230,509.25

FUNDS

Trust funds	$32,691.14
Annuity funds	17,333.34
New Building Fund	91,955.64
Maryland Synod Building Fund	31,890.26
General Fund	56,638.87
	$230,509.25

June 30, 1927
ASSETS

Cash:
American Security & Trust Co.	$11,507.90	
Columbia National Bank	392.46	
The National Savings & Trust Co.	21,889.62	
Washington Loan & Trust Co.	318.23	
		$ 34,108.21
Securities, at book values		52,385.00
Share of Fetterly Bequest to be received at death of life tenant		1,606.83
Real estate, etc., at book values:		
National Lutheran Home property, Washington, D. C.	27,598.00	
New Building	91,555.64	
Farmer's cottage	3,000.00	
New barn	2,000.00	
Grundy County Tract, Tennessee.................	200.00	
Deposit with Thomas J. Fisher for option on additional land adjacent to Home	100.00	
		124,453.64
		$212,553.68

FUNDS

Legacy and trust funds	76,186.20	
New Building Fund	91,955.64	
Annuity Fund	12,000.00	
Maryland Synod Building Fund	25,761.43	
General Fund	6,650.41	
		$212,553.68

CASH RECEIPTS AND DISBURSEMENTS

For the year ended June 30, 1928

	General Fund	Trust Funds	Maryland Synod Building Fund	Annuity Funds
RECEIPTS				
* United Lutheran Church, apportionment	$12,540.00			
Inmates of Home		$4,864.67		
Donations, general	388.57			
Donations for specific purposes.			$ 6,128.83	$ 5,333.34
Admission fees	2,005.00			
Sale of farm products.......	403.53			
Income from securities, etc.....	3,564.87			
Interest on bank balances	859.17			
"The Home News"	67.15			
Miscellaneous receipts	621.11			
Proceeds of sales of investments.	2,100.00	700.00		
	$22,549.40	$5,564.67	$ 6,128.83	$ 5,333.34

	General Fund	Trust Funds	Maryland Synod Building Fund	Annuity Funds
DISBURSEMENTS				
Board of Lady Managers for for domestic expenses ....$	6,500.00			
Farm labor and expenses......	2,213.83			
Gas, electricity and fuel.......	1,783.51			
Engineers' wages	960.00			
Medical and nursing expense ..	2,573.03			
Religious services	235.00			
Funeral expenses	1,108.28			
Repairs to building, plumbing, etc.	2,053.63			
Salary of president	310.00			
Salary of treasurer	500.00			
Expenses of board meetings....	52.25			
Auditing expenses	132.58			
Printing, stationery and postage	56.99			
Telephone	205.70			
Taxes and water rent	188.24			
Insurance	74.80			
"The Home News"	227.36			
General expenses	153.45			
Interest and annuities paid.....	1,642.02			
Land purchased	11,871.48			
	$32,842.15			

	General Fund	Trust Funds	Maryland Synod Building Fund	Annuity Funds
Excess or deficiency of cash receipts ....$	10,292.75	$5,564.67	$ 6,128.83	$ 5,333.34
			$ 6,734.09	
Cash balance, July 1, 1927...............			34,108.21	
Cash balance, June 30, 1928..............$	40,842.30			

* Includes $1,200 for June, 1928, apportionment, not entered on books nor deposited in bank until July 2, 1928.

For year ended June 30, 1927

	General Fund	Trust Funds	Maryland Synod Building Fund	Annuity Funds
RECEIPTS				
United Lutheran Church apportionment ....$	12,700.00			
Inmates of Home		$ 955.00		
Donations, general	947.15			
Legacies	11,736.00			
Donations for specific purposes.			$19,766.18	$10,000.00

Admission fees	1,295.00		
Sale of farm products	101.01		
Income from securities, etc.	1,918.96		
Interest on bank balances	324.27		
"The Home News"	53.45		
Miscellaneous receipts	322.68		
	$29,398.52	$ 955.00	$19,766.18 $10,000.00

DISBURSEMENTS	General Fund	Trust Funds	Maryland Synod Building Fund	Annuity Funds
Board of Lady Managers for domestic expenses	7,610.00			
Farm labor and expenses	2,908.79			
Gas, electricity and fuel	1,623.20			
Engineers' wages	965.00			
Medical and nursing expense	2,544.32			
Religious services	205.00			
Funeral expenses	571.01			
Repairs to building, plumbing, etc.	392.98			
Salary of president	310.00			
Salary of treasurer	500.00			
Expenses of Board meetings	47.35			
Auditing expenses	141.38			
Printing, stationery and postage	91.07			
Telephone	168.94			
Taxes and water rent	129.86			
Insurance	31.20			
"The Home News"	220.99			
General expenses	238.95			
Interest and annuities paid	2,394.24			
Securities purchased	200.00	5,327.81	2,970.00	10,000.00
Admission fees refunded	400.00			
Architect's fee			1,320.00	
Trust funds refunded		439.71		
	$21,694.28	$5,767.52	$ 4,290.00	$10,000.00
Excess of cash receipts	$ 7,704.24	$4,812.52	$15,476.18	

$18,376.90

Cash balance, July 1, 1926 .... 15,740.31

Cash balance, June 30, 1927 ....$34,108.21

SECURITIES OWNED
June 30, 1928

Par Values	BONDS — Descriptions	Book Values
$ 300	Boro of North York, Pa., School District 4½s, 1944 ....$	300.00
500	Fort Spring Magisterial District, County of Greenbrier, W. Va., Road 5s, 1934.........	500.00
500	Island Oil & Transport Co. 8 Pct. Participating Gold Note Certificate of Deposit...........	500.00
500	Milford Improvement Co., N. J., 5s, 1930.....	500.00
1,000	United Rys. & Electric Co. of Baltimore Income 4s, 1949	1,000.00
50	U. S. First Liberty Loan 3½s	50.00
750	U. S. Second Liberty Loan 4¼s	750.00
300	U. S. Third Liberty Loan 4¼s	300.00
50	U. S. Fourth Liberty Loan 4¼s	50.00
5,000	Washington Gas Light Co. 10 year 6s, 1933, Series "A," Registered	5,000.00
5,000	Washington Ry. & Electric Co. 6s, 1933	5,000.00
500	York & Peach Bottom Ry. Co. 5s, 1932.......	500.00
		——— $14,450.00

STOCKS

Shares	Descriptions	Book Values
18	American Telephone & Telegraph Co. ....$	1,800.00
4	Baltimore & Ohio R. R. com.	400.00
1	Codorus Canning Co. (In name of Susanna Rebert)	100.00
4	Codorus National Bank of Jefferson, Codorus, Pa.	400.00
4	Drovers and Mechanics National Bank, York, Pa.	400.00
5	Garford Motor Truck Co. Common A, no par value (Company liquidated, stock of no value)	10.00
30	Potomac Electric Power Co. 5½ Pct. Preferred.	3,000.00
11	Union National Bank, Westminster, Md........	275.00
		——— 6,385.00

REAL ESTATE NOTES

Secured by First Deeds of Trust:

Michael G. Daoud, 6½ Pct., due May 28, 1928........		3,000.00
James M. Hill, 6½ Pct., due Jan'y 9, 1929 (Guaranteed by Thomas P. Bones and James D. Hobbs)		2,500.00
William A. Hill and Harry Wardman, 6½ Pct., due March 2, 1930		2,500.00
A. Joseph Howar, 6½ Pct., due March 10, 1928		2,500.00
" " due Jan'y 11, 1929......		2,500.00
Edward J. Kyle, 6½ Pct., due Nov'r 12, 1928 (Guaranteed by Harry Wardman and Thomas P. Bones)		6,000.00
Bryce G. Payne, 6½ Pct., due June 30, 1930 (Guaranteed by Howard M. Etchison).............		2,500.00

Erwin G. Shaffer, 6½ Pct., due Jan'y 29, 1928 (Guar-
          anteed by Howard M. Etchison) 2,500.00
Rose G. Waggaman, 6 Pct., due May 1, 1931......... 2,000.00
Harry Wardman and Thomas P. Bones, 6½ Pct., due
          March 14, 1930 .... 5,000.00
                                                              ———— 31,000.00

                                                              $51,835.00

                    Respectfully submitted,
                              HARRY T. DOMER, *Treasurer.*

                              Baltimore, Md., July 30, 1928.
    We have audited the accounts of the National Lutheran Home for the
Aged for the two years ended June 30, 1928, and we certify that, in our
opinion, the foregoing statements submitted by its Treasurer are correct.
                    LYBRAND, ROSS BROS & MONTGOMERY,
                              Accountants and Auditors.

    The auditor's report on accounts of this Board was accepted.

    The report of the Board of Deaconess work was presented by
the Rev. G. Albert Getty, who introduced the Revs. Charles E.
Hay and E. F. Bachmann.

REPORT OF THE BOARD OF DEACONESS WORK

    The Deaconess work within the United Lutheran Church is making
progress. The two Motherhouses, Baltimore and Philadelphia, now have
171 Sisters, an encouraging number, but altogether insufficient to meet the
many demands made upon your Motherhouses. The interest in the diaconate
is continually spreading and the intelligent and sympathetic attitude towards
the diaconate is most gratifying to your Board and to those who have
dedicated their lives to this calling. The Board is endeavoring to spread
constructive information throughout the Church by means of leaflets, booklets, articles in Church papers and by personal presentations on every occasion available. The Women's Missionary Society of the United Lutheran
Church, its various officers and its Department of Deaconess work, are
furnishing a most effective publicity, and to them we desire to express our
sincere appreciation, Upon their continued sympathetic appeals, reaching
down to every local missionary society and directly to the young women
needed for the diaconate, will to a larger extent depend the growth of our
Motherhouses in the future. At the same time we recognize the Luther

League as an agency of great value in our effort to enlist young women in this ministry of mercy. The recent emphasis on "Life Service" should lead many Luther Leaguers to a serious consideration of the diaconate, especially as it furnishes a remarkable variety of service, an opportunity for the development and use of almost every talent. Many doors are open to the diaconate even now which cannot be entered because of the shortage of Sisters—doors which offer a great extension of the Church's influence.

Dr. Charles E. Sadtler, the veteran member of the Board of Deaconess Work, at the opening of the biennium, after serving as a physician of the Motherhouse for more than thirty years, was called to his eternal home on September 9, 1927. Having reached the constitutional limit of his present term, Dr. E. H. Delk closes with the present convention an uninterrupted term of twenty-nine years on this and the former Board. Both President and Treasurer retire for the same reason and with them a fifth member who has served for eight consecutive years. The Board desires to place on record its appreciation of the long and loyal services rendered.

The Eighteenth Conference of Lutheran Motherhouses in America was held May 16th and 17th at Chicago. All the Motherhouses were represented. The total number of Sisters at present enrolled was reported as 414—a net gain of eighteen within the biennium. Special papers were read by pastors and head sisters and by Dr. G. A. Getty, president of the Board of Deaconess Work of the United Lutheran Church. There was earnest discussion of various problems arising in the prosecution of the work, with emphasis upon the features essential to proper development. The next meeting will be held at the Minneapolis Motherhouse in 1930.

BALTIMORE MOTHERHOUSE

The Baltimore Motherhouse was established directly by the General Synod in 1895, encouraged by the success of the similar institution founded at Philadelphia ten years before. As the latter institution had under its supervision the Lankenau Hospital and kindly offered to furnish the necessary medical experience included in the normal deaconess training, the new Motherhouse naturally devoted its energies primarily to the development of a curriculum adapted to prepare its candidates at the same time for a somewhat wider field of service in the Church.

Course of Training

The regular classroom work covers 862 hours annually. It embraces Bible Study, Old and New Testament History and Geography, the Life of Christ, Catechetics, Ethics, Religions of the World, Life of Luther, Diaconics, Nursing, Weekday Religious Education, Church Music and Personal Work. There are fifteen special lectures by prominent leaders in the various departments of the Church's activity and experienced deaconesses. Much time is devoted to the gaining of practical experience in Sunday schools, parish visiting under supervision of city pastors, observation hours in local benevolent institutions and kindergartens, weekday church schools and Children's Summer Home conducted by the Sisters. There are frequent devotional services in the Motherhouse led by the pastors and by older Sisters.

Consecration Service

Consecration services were held on June 28, 1927, and June 26, 1928, at which after appropriate sermons by Dr. W. C. Schaeffer, Jr., and Dr. J. S. Simon, six probationers, Sisters Hanna Eichhorn, Katherine Schubert, Sara Shuey, Inez Metzger, Catherine Neuhardt and Edna Schmid were consecrated as deaconesses.

Severance of Relation to Motherhouse

Two Sisters have at their own request been released from their relation to the Motherhouse, one on account of physical debility and the other in view of changed conditions in her home.

Location of Sisters

The sixty-five sisters now in connection with the Motherhouse are at present located as follows:

RESIDENT AT MOTHERHOUSE

Sister Sophia Jepson, Head Sister.
Sister Edna Hill, Training Sister.
Sister Carolyn Filler, Kindergarten Teacher.
Sister Bertha Mehring, Household Economics.
Sister Lina Schuehler, Sewing Department.
Sister Katherine Aufhammer, Sewing Department.
Sister Anna Albright, Private Nursing.
Sister May Haltiwanger, Private Nursing.
Sister Mamie Hartman, Private Nursing.
Sister Ethel Rhyne, Private Nursing.
Sister Magdalene Kasewurm, General Assistant.
Sister Sarah Anthony, General Assistant.
Sister Lucy Eyster, unassigned.
Sister Mary Harris, unassigned.
Sister Stella Fattman, completing the course.

SERVING IN CONGREGATIONS AND INSTITUTIONS

Sister Christina Gleichert, First Church, Baltimore, Md.
Sister Lydia Perry, Trinity Church, Canton, O.
Sister Louise Stitzer, Church of the Reformation, Rochester, N. Y.
Sister Louise Moeller, St. John's Church, New York.
Sister Ida Klucker, Tabitha Home, Lincoln, Nebr.
Sister Mildred Bingaman, St. Matthew's Church, Philadelphia, Pa.
Sister Harriet Franklin, Memorial Church, Harrisburg, Pa.
Sister Flora Ohler, Good Shepherd Home, Allentown, Pa.
Sister Mabel Stanley, National Home for Aged, Washington, D. C.

Sister Laura Gilliland, Muhlenberg Mission, Africa.
Sister Eva Witmyer, Lowman Home, White Rock, S. C.
Sister Dorathea Hesse, Franke Home, Charleston, S. C.
Sister Caroline Wagenbach, Good Shepherd Home, Allentown, Pa.
Sister Zora Heckert, Lutheran Girls' Hospice, Baltimore, Md.
Sister Helene Kuechler, Zion Church, Syracuse, N. Y.
Sister Clara Smyre, Christiansted, St. Croix, Virgin Islands.
Sister Christian Jaborg, Inner Mission Society, Baltimore, Md.
Sister Ruth Wagner, First Church, Richmond, Va.
Sister Bessie Engstrom, Trinity Church, Akron, O.
Sister Theodora Schmidt, Church of the Reformation, Baltimore, Md.
Sister Georgia Bushman, Trinity Church, Germantown, Pa.
Sister Anna Friedrich, Zion Church, Sunbury, Pa.
Sister Bertha Schwanewede, Christ Church, Baltimore, Md.
Sister Alma Boarts, Glenwood Avenue Church, Toledo, O.
Sister Pearle Lyerly, Church of the Advent, New York.
Sister Martha Hansen, Lutheran Settlement, Philadelphia.
Sister Amy Baver, St. Luke's Church, Brooklyn, N. Y.
Sister Eleanor Frank, Seventh Street Lutheran Church, Lebanon, Pa,
Sister Zedena Ross, Children's Mission Home, Knoxville, Tenn.
Sister Hanna Eichhorn, St. Paul's Church, Allentown, Pa.
Sister Katherine Schubert, Tressler Orphans' Home, Loysville, Pa.
Sister Meta Fellerman, Gethsemane Church, Philadelphia, Pa.
Sister Inez Metzger, First Church, Albany, N. Y.
Sister Catherine Neuhardt, Trinity Church, Hagerstown, Md.
Sister Edna Schmid, St. John's Church, Brooklyn, N. Y.
Sister Mary Junas, Slavic Mission, New York.
Sister Margaret Lang, St. John's German Church, Reading, Pa.
Sister Ida Steuerwald, First Church, Mansfield, O.
Sister Rose Zemanek, Emanuel Church, Meriden, Conn.
Sister Edith Kohllahn, Salem Church, Bethlehem, Pa.
Sister Madaline Schaefer, Lutheran Church, Waynesboro, Pa.
Sister Myrtle Cutshawl, Trinity Church, Lancaster, Pa.
Sister Geraldine Cutshawl, Grace Church, Lancaster, Pa.
Sister Delphine Dasher, English Church, Pottsville, Pa.
Sister Dorothy Keck, Lutheran Settlement, Philadelphia.
Sister Vernetta Kunkel, St. John's Church, The Bronx, New York City.
Sister Anna Melville, St. Matthew's Church, Hanover, Pa.
Sister Ruth Paris, Church of Our Saviour's Atonement, New York City.
Sister Chloe Sibold, Concordia Church, Buffalo, N. Y.
Sister Marie Stork, St. Peter's Church, Middletown, Pa.

Training for General Christian Work

The Baltimore Motherhouse also offers special instruction and training to earnest young women who do not have the diaconate in view, but desire to prepare themselves for more efficient Christian service. Of the 235 who have taken advantage of these special courses many are now occupying important positions in the church upon their own initiative. The Motherhouse has no responsibility for their direction or support but rejoices in the faithful services which they are rendering. A number of them have become deaconesses.

(The following paragraph was prepared by a committee from the

Deaconess Board with the request that it be published in connection with the Biennial Report. Committee, Revs. E. F. Bachmann, D.D., and W. A. Wade, D.D.)

TWENTY-FIFTH ANNIVERSARY OF THE PASTORATE OF THE REV. CHARLES E. HAY, D.D.

In recognition and appreciation of the fact that January, 1929, will mark the twenty-fifth anniversary of the pastorate of the Rev. Chas. E. Hay, D.D., at the Baltimore Deaconess Motherhouse, the Deaconess Board, in session June 26, 1928, appointed a committee to prepare an item on this significant anniversary for the biennial report. Dr. Hay became the pastor and executive head of the Baltimore Motherhouse January, 1904, and he has filled the office of General Secretary of the Board since 1922. The Motherhouse was founded in 1895, built and maintained by the General Synod, although for ten years previous to that time, it was being talked of and planned. With the merger, it became the property of the United Lutheran Church, and is under the direct control of the Deaconess Board, elected by said body. The present beautiful stone building was dedicated June 10, 1911, by the President of the General Synod, then in session at Washington, D. C. The building and equipment, which are valued at $200,000, have been added during the administration of Dr. Hay, who, during his twenty-five years of faithful service, has presented the cause of the various Synods and congregations of the Church. Besides his splendid service as pastor, Dr. Hay is teacher of Diaconics, Catechetics, Topical Bible Study, Ethics and the Life of Luther, thus training many young women for the diaconate in this country and mission fields, as well as many others who are filling various positions in the church and parish. Gifted with an affable disposition, and at the same time having fine literary training and equipment for such service, he is rendering an invaluable contribution to the Lutheran Church that shall bear fruit during the years to come. Beloved by all members of the Board and all who know him, Dr. Hay occupies a unique position in the Deaconess work. With due recognition of the fine service rendered by those who labored before Dr. Hay's time of service at the Motherhouse, and also that of his co-laborers, credit is due Dr. Hay for much of the growth and development of the work and the Deaconess cause. A committee has been appointed to properly recognize the anniversary in January, 1929.

THE PHILADELPHIA MOTHERHOUSE

Four decades have passed since the Philadelphia Motherhouse of Deaconesses was organized, though the actual ministry of mercy of its Sisters dates back to 1884. On December 6, 1888, the beautiful building, a gift of John D. Lankenau named in memory of his departed wife, Mary J. Drexel, was dedicated and turned over to the Board of Trustees. At the same service Pastor A. Cordes was installed as the first rector and pastor.

The Motherhouse is planning to observe the fortieth anniversary on December 6th and would bring this to the attention of the Church as a date of importance to the entire deaconess work in America. The Philadelphia Motherhouse, being the oldest in this country, trained the first Sisters for the Swedish Motherhouse in Omaha and rendered the same service later for the Baltimore Motherhouse. It furnished the first Training Sister of the newly organized Milwaukee Motherhouse and received for additional training one or more Sisters from the Motherhouses in St. Paul, Chicago and Brush and from a Presbyterian Training School giving also the full course of training to several Sisters of the Evangelical Association. Philadelphia issued the invitation for the organization of the Lutheran Motherhouse Conference of America in 1896, which has contributed much to the unity of spirit and uniformity of principles in the development of the Lutheran diaconate in this country.

More than 200 Sisters have been associated with this Motherhouse during these forty years. The Sisterhood numbers at present eight-one deaconesses and twenty-five probationers, a total of 106 Sisters. Of these, thirty-nine have been in the service twenty-five years or more while exactly one-half, or fifty-three, have entered within the past fifteen years. These figures are proof of the stability of the deaconess work and of its increasing appeal to the young women of our Church.

During the past biennium twelve new Sisters were admitted. This gain is offset by a loss of six, leaving a net gain of six, a number altogether too small in view of the manifold demands made on the Motherhouse by the fields now served and by new fields offered. Doors opened to our deaconesses, even by important secular institutions where Christian service and influence would have been a distinct blessing, could not be entered because of the shortage of Sisters.

The service rendered by the Sisters of the Philadelphia Motherhouse is of great variety. The Motherhouse itself conducts a Home for the Aged with fifty men and women and a Children's Hospital where 2,211 were admitted during the biennium and 5,050 children made 37,161 visits to the dispensary.

At the Lankenau Hospital, where our Sisters are in charge of most of the stations, 8,132 patients were admitted during the past two years and 13,010 adults treated in the dispensary.

The Kensington Dispensary for the Treatment of Tuberculosis, in charge of one of our Sisters, had 449 patients in its care in 1927, and sent 244 children for recuperation to the Preventorium "River Crest," in groups of about twenty-five children from a few weeks to a few months at a time. "River Crest" will increase its capacity almost fourfold this fall when the new buildings are to be dedicated. This will also require more Sisters.

The Tabor Home for children from unfortunate families has seventy-five boys and girls in care of our Sisters, and the Erie Lutheran Home for the Aged has over forty men and women. One of our Sisters is the Executive Secretary of the Inner Mission Society of Berks County, Pa., with headquarters in Reading, where on July 1st a Hospice for Women was opened with a Sister as the housemother.

Sisters of our Motherhouse are engaged in parish work in Zion's, Tabor, and Trinity congregations, Philadelphia; in St. John's, Easton; Trinity, Pottsville; St. Paul's, New York City; Trinity, New Haven, Conn.; and St. John's, Erie, Pa.

By action of the Deaconess Board there are associated with the Philadelphia Motherhouse Sister Emma Francis and Sister Edith Prince, natives of the Virgin Islands and laboring under the direction of the Board of American Missions in the Ebenezer Orphanage, Frederiksted, St. Croix.

A unique place in the life of the Church is filled by the Lankenau School for Girls, for both resident and day pupils, conducted by the Philadelphia Motherhouse. The course is parallel to that of the public school system providing for six grades and a Junior and a Senior High School of three years each. The majority of the faculty are deaconesses and the others are all high-grade teachers with experience. In charge is a deaconess, a graduate of the University of Pennsylvania. Since 1890 this school has rendered an invaluable service to the Church and to hundreds of non-Lutherans who realize the importance of Christian character building while receiving a thorough training fully up to the best educational standards.

The Sisters of the Philadelphia Motherhouse are actually doing twenty-six different kinds of work in connection with their various fields of labor, many of these requiring highly specialized training beyond the two-year course for all probationers. Sisters inclined to nursing are given the full three-year course with State Board examination, making them Registered Nurses. One has been made a licensed pharmacist, another is a qualified assistant, while a third is a Doctor of Pharmacy. Others are given special courses as needed in their work, for it is the aim of the Motherhouse as far as possible to enable every Sister to measure up to the professional standards required by the State or other secular organizations.

Far more important, however, is the spiritual life of the Sisters. Besides the two preaching services on Sundays, Bible study is conducted on two evenings a week by the Directing Sister and one evening is devoted by the pastor to a study of some phase of diaconics. The Sisters have a "quiet hour" for meditation to interrupt the routine of a long and strenuous day, and on four evenings a week the day closes with a brief service in the chapel for the Sisters and others of the large Motherhouse family. This emphasis of their spiritual life is the more important as deaconesses are not held by any special vows and as their work loses its value when no longer done from a spiritual motive.

In view of the great demand for deaconesses by congregations, institutions and missionary organizations, and in view of the exceptional opportunities open to capable and consecrated young women, many of whom are "standing all the day idle," while laborers for the vineyard are so urgently needed, we would appeal to every pastor and to every loyal member of the Church to help enlist young women for Christ's service in the diaconate. There is room for such as have only a modest education but are willing and able to learn, and room for graduates of colleges and professional schools not afraid of work. The Lord needed both Peter, the fisherman, and Paul, the university graduate, and both labored in unity of spirit as humble servants.

The Philadelphia Motherhouse desires to express its sincere gratitude to the United Lutheran Church for the financial support received. On the $5,000 appropriation for our Motherhouse included in the budget of the Board of Deaconess Work, we received $4,000 in 1926 and $4,351.32 in 1927. These amounts helped to reduce but not wipe out the deficits incurred as will be seen from the following summary statement taken from our treasurer's report, a complete copy of which has been filed with the treasurer of the Board of Deaconess Work.

1926 Receipts	$80,469.02
Expenses	95,752.29
Overdrawn	15,283.27
Less From United Lutheran Church	4,000.00
Deficit	$11,283.27
1927 Receipts	$86,858.48
Expenses	101,563.80
Overdrawn	14,705.32
From U. L. C.	4,351.32
Deficit	$10,354.00

These deficits were furthermore reduced by $5,000 each year from the income of our annual Donation Day. While the Motherhouse hopes by strict economy and increased income to make a more favorable showing in the near future, heavy repairs on the Motherhouse building valued at over a million dollars, will be a severe drain on our treasury no less than the high wages for our employees and nurses and the high cost of food-stuffs and materials.

In this connection it may be of interest to state that the Philadelphia Motherhouse is also listed as a congregation of the Ministerium of Pennsylvania and as such has regularly met its apportionments, and that the Sisters' Missionary Society always meets its obligations in full. The $1,262 apportioned for the Ministerial Pension Fund last February was oversubscribed. The Motherhouse raising $1,517.00 in cash and subscriptions.

God Whose guidance and blessing were so evident in our work during the past biennium, will also in due time provide the means to carry it on and to develop it still more, so that in ever increasing measure it will be a medium of blessing to His Church.

Respectfully submitted,
E. F. BACHMANN, *Pastor.*

RESOLUTIONS SUGGESTED BY THE BOARD

1. That we recognize the deaconess calling as a most helpful agency in the upbuilding of the kingdom of Christ and in the practical application of the merciful spirit of the Gospel.

2. That we rejoice in the present widespread interest in religious education, which greatly enlarges the sphere of appropriate deaconess activity.

3. That we approve the admission to the training courses of our Motherhouses of capable young women other than prospective deaconesses, who may desire special preparation for Christian service.

4. That we call special attention to the peculiar advantages of the Motherhouse system for the training of capable young women for efficient life service in the diaconate.

5. That we regard the intelligent co-operation of the pastors of our congregations as essential to the adequate development of this important work and urge the prayerful interest of the Church at large in the securing of a larger number of candidates.

Respectfully submitted,
G. ALBERT GETTY.
CHARLES E. HAY.

TREASURER'S REPORT

For the Two Years Ended June 30, 1928, and 1927
BALANCE SHEET, June 30, 1928
ASSETS:

Cash: The Baltimore Trust Company, Exchange		
Bank Office	$4,295.20	
Hopkins Place Savings Bank	9,656.07	
Maryland Trust Company	124.19	
Held by Rev. Charles E. Hay	800.00	
		$14,875.46

Real estate, buildings, etc., at book values:
Motherhouse, North and Thomas Avenues,
Baltimore, Md. $200,000.00
Properties at 1901 and 1905 Thomas Avenue,
Baltimore, Md. 17,497.00
Ground rents 24,591.66
Lorraine Park Cemetery burial lot 600.00
————————— 242,688.66

$257,564.12

FUNDS:

New Building Fund $19,057.73
Endowment funds 6,128.19
Annuity funds 20,300.00
General Fund 212,078.20
————————— $257,564.12

BALANCE SHEET, June 30, 1927

ASSETS:

Cash: The Baltimore Trust Company, Exchange
Bank Office $441.65
Hopkins Place Savings Bank 8,527.69
Maryland Trust Company 465.98
Held by Rev. Charles E. Hay 800.00
————————— $10,235.32

Real estate, buildings, etc., at book values:
Motherhouse, North and Thomas Avenues,
Baltimore, Md. $200,000.00
Properties at 1901 and 1905 Thomas Avenue,
Baltimore, Md. 16,097.00
Ground rents 23,191.66
Lorraine Park Cemetery Lot 600.00
————————— 239,888.66

$250,123.98

FUNDS:

New building fund $18,582.48
Endowment fund 4,475.06
Annuity funds 20,500.00
General fund 206,566.44
————————— $250,123.98

CASH RECEIPTS AND DISBURSEMENTS
For the Year Ended June 30, 1928
RECEIPTS:

	General Fund	Endow- ment Fund	New Building Fund	Annuity Fund
United Lutheran Church in America	$29,820.00			
United, general and branch synods..	31.03			
Donations	128.83	$581.40	$171.00	
Tuition	4,549.85			
Kindergarten	366.88			
Nursing	684.30			
Stations	7,969.15			
Annuity				$800.00
Bank interest	8.21	71.73	304.25	
Income from investments	1,358.33			
	$44,916.58	$653.13	$475.25	$800.00
Total cash receipts		$46,844.96		

DISBURSEMENTS:

Salaries of superintendent and assistant	$5,000.00
Superintendent's traveling expenses..	122.79
Wages of general and domestic help	4,383.00
Maintenance of motherhouse and cottages	203.83
Miscellaneous expenses of motherhouse and cottages	736.86
Furniture and fixtures purchased ..	500.35
Insurance	221.60
Expenses of other officers and board representatives	595.60
Expenses of grounds	92.50
Household expenses	5,900.00
Personal expenses of sisters	1,856.92
Tuition fees refunded	225.00
Sisters' training fund	75.00
Professional services for sisters	675.95
Sisters' allowances	5,858.85
Sisters' traveling expenses	404.07
Wearing apparel	1,953.42
Lectures and class instructions	664.70
Class and library books	473.55
Printing and stationery	840.50
Office salary and expenses	706.04
Fuel and light	2,286.41
Contribution to Mary J. Drexel Home and Philadelphia Motherhouse of Deaconesses	3,731.38
Sewing room expenses	100.00
Grain, feed and garden supplies	484.29
Auditing	100.00
Annuities paid	1,347.00

	General Fund	Endow-ment Fund	New Building Fund	Annuity Fund
Ground rent purchased	250.00			$1,150.00
New heating system, 1901 Thomas Avenue	1,400.00			
Discounts earned	134.79			
	$41,054.82			$1,150.00

Total cash disbursements $42,204.82
Cash balance, July 1, 1927 .... $10,235.32
Total cash receipts 46,844.96

　　　　　　　　　　　　　　　　　　　　　　　　　57,080.28
Less, total cash disbursements 42,204.82

Cash balance, June 30, 1928 .... $14,875.46

CASH RECEIPTS AND DISBURSEMENTS
For the Year Ended June 30, 1927
RECEIPTS:

	General Fund	Endow-ment Fund	New Building Fund	Annuity Fund
United Lutheran Church in America	$26,670.00			
United, general and branch synods	140.56			
Donations		$113.96	$208.05	
Tuition	4,230.69			
Kindergarten	229.91			
Nursing	504.07			
Stations	6,388.07			
Legacy			209.20	
Annuity				$10,000.00
Bank interest	122.55	59.83	276.15	
Proceeds of bond called			1,000.00	
Income from investments	925.05		25.00	
	$39,210.90	$173.79	$1,718.40	$10,000.00

Total cash receipts $51,103.09

DISBURSEMENTS:

	General Fund
Salaries of superintendent and assistant	$5,000.00
Superintendent's traveling ex-penses	139.29
Wages of general and domestic help	4,255.00
Maintenance of motherhouse and cottages	1,788.82
Miscellaneous e x p e n s e s of motherhouse and cottages ..	1,311.67

	General Fund	Endowment Fund	New Building Fund	Annuity Fund
Furniture and fixtures purchased	263.45			
Insurance	114.00			
Expenses of other officers and board representatives	638.24			
Expenses of grounds	207.33			
Household expenses	6,100.00			
Personal expenses of sisters ...	1,348.32			
Sisters' training fund	100.00			
Professional services for sisters	629.68			
Sisters' allowances	7,632.30			
Sisters' traveling expenses	140.78			
Wearing apparel	2,161.53			
Lectures and class instruction..	763.30			
Class and library books	503.71			
Printing and stationery	964.64			
Office salary and expenses	381.69			
Fuel and light	2,332.25			
Contribution to Mary J. Drexel H o m e and Philadelphia Motherhouse of Deaconesses	3,351.32			
Sewing room expenses	150.00			
Grain, feed and garden supplies	311.44			
Auditing	135.00			
Annuities paid	1,407.00			
Ground rent purchased				$12,933.33
Discounts earned	181.66			
	$41,949.10			$12,933.33

Total cash disbursements	$54,882.43
Cash balance, July 1, 1926	$14,014.66
Total cash receipts	51,103.09
	65,117.75
Less, Total cash disbursements	54,882.43
Cash balance, June 30, 1927	$10,235.32

Respectfully submitted,

FREDERICK J. SINGLEY, *Treasurer.*

Baltimore, Md., July 30, 1928.

We have audited the accounts of the Board of Deaconess Work of the United Lutheran Church in America for the two years ended June 30, 1928, and we certify that, in our opinion, the foregoing statements submitted by its Treasurer are correct.

LYBRAND. ROSS BROS. & MONTGOMERY,
Accountants and Auditors.

MEMORANDUM

The Treasurer reported that the income from the Annuity Fund is now in excess of the annual payments. That the annual payments now aggregate $1,347—which on January 1, 1929, will be increased to $1,395.

That the principal of the Annuity Fund is invested in the following ground rents, all of which yield six per cent on the investment, free of taxes:

$120.00 on 2002 E. 30th St.
78.00 on 3007 Wayne Ave.
90.00 on 2430 Liberty Heights Ave.
60.00 on 5301 Midwood Ave.
75.00 on 338 N. Hilton St.
65.00 on 247 N. Payson St.
84.00 on 3810 Plateau Ave.
43.50 on 819 S. Ellwood Ave.
80.00 on 2019 W. North Ave.
90.00 on 5018 Wakefield Road.
90.00 on 5022 Wakefield Road.
90.00 on 5020 Wakefield Road.
72.00 on 38 S. Calverton Road.
84.00 on 40 S. Calverton Road.
90.00 on 3903 Woodbine Ave.
90.00 on 46 Prospect Ave.
90.00 on 53 Prospect Ave.
84.00 on 20 Prospect Ave.

The annual income of which aggregates $1,475.50.

The memorandum was received and ordered to be printed in connection with the Treasurer's Report.

Resolutions 1 to 5 were adopted.

The auditor's report on accounts of the Board of Deaconess Work was accepted.

Mr. Harry Hodges presented the report of the Board of Ministerial Pensions and Relief.

THE REPORT OF THE BOARD OF MINISTERIAL PENSIONS AND RELIEF

The past biennium has been one of great activity in preparing for and conducting the Pension Endowment Campaign.

Dr. Miller

Just prior to the advent of the Campaign, the Board suffered a great loss in the untimely death of its consecrated and efficient Executive Secretary, the Rev. Edgar Grim Miller, D.D., who labored both in season and out of season, with heart, mind and hand for the cause so dear to him.

The following resolution enacted by the Board voices its appreciation of the man and his work:

"MEMORIAL TO DOCTOR EDGAR GRIM MILLER

"God's ways are not our ways—He moves in a mysterious way His wonders to perform!

"On Monday, July 18th, there passed from this world and entered into the joy of his Lord, Dr. Edgar Grim Miller. Taken from us just at a time when his unselfish work for his Brethren in the Gospel through the Pension Board had reached its peak of usefulness, we fellow members and co-laborers on the Board of Ministerial Pensions and Relief, bow in grief and sorrow at what seems to us, his untimely call, from the Heavenly Father, to lay down his most efficient and helpful work! We humans cannot comprehend the ways of our loving Heavenly Father, but as Christian men we realize our times are in His hands and that He doeth all things well.

"Edgar Grim Miller was an outstanding Christian man—forceful, yet gentle, a tower of strength amongst his Brethren. His one aim and ambition in life was to make the United Lutheran Church Pension system a strong, virile force for good to his fellow ministers of the Gospel and a blessed Relief for their families. Dr. Miller had a great heart, full of kindness, coupled with justice and no appeal for aid ever came to his desk which did not receive his careful personal, heartfelt attention and sympathetic action.

"He had travelled far and wide, telling the needs of the Pension Board with all the zeal and fire at his command. He planned early and late, day in and day out, giving all his great powers and time in the interests of our work, namely, the Relief of the Servants of God in the ministry of the Word!

"To our minds, this constant, zealous, nerve-trying strain proved too much for his strength so that he lay down his life for the cause he loved.

"It will be hard indeed to fill his place as Executive Secretary—but the loving service must go on, so we look for guidance from the Father of us all Who has called Edgar Grim Miller from his strenuous work here below to a rest with the Saints above! Therefore, with hearts full of thankfulness that God had given to us this wise, good friend to be our guide and Christian companion, we sumbit in all humility to His Divine Wisdom and pray that He will deal gently and lovingly with his dear wife and her fine family.

"We desire that a copy of this Memorial be handed to Dr. Miller's widow and family, and that it also be sent to our Church paper, *The Lutheran*. with the request that it be inserted in an early issue, that all may know of the worth and esteem in which Dr. Miller was help by his fellow members of

THE BOARD OF MINISTERIAL PENSIONS AND RELIEF
OF THE UNITED LUTHERAN CHURCH IN AMERICA."

The Board placed Dr. Miller among the Campaign memorials.

Mr. Hagan

In the crisis, the indefatigable treasurer, Mr. Peter P. Hagan, hearing the call, "Moses, my servant, is dead; now, therefore, arise," took upon himself the duties of Secretary and Campaign Chairman, and with a fine disregard for personal interests literally threw himself into the Campaign, which accounts in a large measure for its success.

Mr. Myers

Just prior to the inauguration of the Campaign, Mr. Henry E. Passavant, the President, found it necessary on account of ill health, to withdraw from the Board.

Mr. Paul F. Myers, of Washington, D. C., was elected his successor.

Although new to the work, Mr. Myers applied himself forcefully to the preparations for and the conduct of the Campaign.

The Church owes a lasting debt of gratitude to Messrs. Hagan and Myers.

Mr. Hodges

While the Board had assigned the Campaign direction to the efficient firm of Ward, Wells, Dreshman and Gates, the death of Dr. Miller made a vacancy in the organization of one with a comprehensive knowledge of the Church, a requisite in a campaign. Because of his knowledge gained through ten years of service as Executive Secretary of the Luther League of America, Mr. Harry Hodges was drafted to become a part of the Campaign Organization.

At the close of the Campaign, the Board unanimously elected Mr. Hodges to succeed Dr. Miller as its Executive Secretary.

The Campaign

The Campaign for Ministerial Pensions is an epoch in the United Lutheran Church. Never in its history has a general cause received such whole-hearted endorsement and co-operation and been crowned with such glorious success.

Several truths were demonstrated:

The Church has and will give the money for a cause in which it has a vital interest.

The Church can accomplish any task with whole-hearted co-operation.

The hold the ministry has on the hearts of the people.

The unequal advance of ministers' salaries with the advanced price of commodities.

The fallacy of the pastor attempting to be the guardian of the mind and purse of his parishoners.

The thorough knowledge of a cause brings an adequate response from the people.

There are a number of items in connection with the Campaign which the Church should take cognizance of:

In large campaigns, it is the rule to secure 25 per cent. of the amount sought, in large gifts prior to the campaign proper. But $150,000 was given in large gifts in our Campaign, including the $50,000 gift from the Board of Publication. The balance was the gift of the people making up the membership of the United Lutheran Church in America.

The cost of the Campaign was less than three per cent. This is unique.

The Boards and Auxiliary Organizations gave the services of their Secretaries as Regional Directors and speakers willingly and graciously. The Synodical and Conference officials also did heroic service. The Board of Pensions herewith records its high appreciation.

Mr. C. H. Dreshman and his staff gave time and energy far beyond the contract agreements, putting heart as well as mind into the work.

The Lutheran Bureau, which conducted the publicity, was in constant touch with the Associated Press and our office files are eloquent to the fact that America knew that we were conducting a Campaign.

A vote of appreciation to all has been passed by the Board. The Campaign was not a matter of the Board, however, but of the Church, and *a vote of thanks* is its prerogative.

But first, let us thank God, who put into the hearts of His people, the urge to give back to Him, four million dollars of the money which He had intrusted to their keeping for the care of His aged servants and their families.

At the time of the writing of this report (August 1, 1928) the amount subscribed is $4,176,135, and the amount paid $820,000.

The tabulation by Synods is as follows:

Quotas and Subscriptions by Synods

Synod	Quota	Subscribed
Pennsylvania Ministerium	$ 844,446	$ 849,220
New York Ministerium	367,056	311,091
Pittsburgh	301,038	341,509
Ohio	273,306	345,000
West Penna.	209,388	191,023
East Penna.	202,992	285,364
Maryland	184,302	222,487
Susquehanna	160,416	128,626
New York	142,524	113,719
Illinois	136,866	172,903
N. Y. & N. E.	135,336	235,367
Allegheny	128,706	140,563
Northwest	102,540	114,200
North Carolina	99,858	82,712
Canada	84,726	45,604
South Carolina	82,212	55,028
Virginia	65,868	67,939
German Nebraska	53,220	26,953
Michigan	52,770	54,169
Indiana	51,156	48,492
Nebraska	49,410	54,842
Wartburg	46,590	27,600
Slovak Zion	32,478	1,710
Kansas	31,368	35,160
Iowa	30,012	26,500
Manitoba	29,748	3,000 (Incomplete)
California	28,938	31,924
West Virginia	21,480	28,273
Georgia	20,400	27,535
Texas	18,096	11,810
Pacific	12,372	19,116
Rocky Mountain	8,880	12,968
Nova Scotia	7,458	7,902
Mississippi	2,214	3,225
Porto Rico		2.601
Publication Board		50,000
	$4,017,850	$4,176,135

The following memorials have been entered in the permanent records of the Board:

Rev. Charles S. Albert, D.D.
Rev. Luther E. Albert, D.D.
Rev. J. G. Amschler
Major Enos R. Artman
Mrs. Emma M. Aumont
Rev. John Bachman, D.D., LL.D.
Mrs. Adam H. Bartel
Mr. George C. Baum
Mrs. Maria Louisa Baum
Rev. William Miller Baum, D.D.
Mrs. Wilhemina Bein
Mrs. Fredericka M. Bohney
Rev. William S. Bowman
Louisa Holbrook Buch
Robert George Chisolm
Peder Christensen
Emily E. A. Corpening
John Eli Corpening
Rev. M. S. Cressman, D.D.
Rev. Theodore R. Crouse
Rev. Hugo Erdman
Abraham Ernst
Rev. Andrew S. Fichthorn, D.D.
Hon. Robert H. Foerderer
Rev. William Keller Frick, D.D.
Rev. H. C. Garvic
Rev. G. H. Gerberding, D.D., LL.D.
Rev. David M. Gilbert, D.D.
Rev. Paul Glasow
Rev. George Goettmann, D.D.
Kate Brown Haag
Rev. S. T. Hallman, D.D.
The Harter Family
Rev. Charles A. Hay, D.D.
Dr. Lewis Hay
Mrs. Elsie Heid
Percy Aage Heide
Rev. Theophilus Heilig, D.D.
Rev. A. M. Heilman, D.D.
Rev. Lee M. Heilman, D.D.
Maria A. Heischmann
Rev. C. Theodore Heischmann
Rev. Socrates Henkel, D.D.
Anna Sohl Henrich
John W. Henrich
William Henrich
Rev. G. Hinterleitner, D.D.
Rev. A. Homrighaus, D.D.
Rev. Ed. Trail Horn, D.D., LL.D.
Charles and Elizabeth Humbert
Rev. Jerome Case Jackson
Mrs. Elizabeth C. Justi
Rev. A. Arthur King
Rev. John Krechting, D.D.

Henry Kull
Mr. and Mrs. Warren S. Lee
James and Betty Seville Lees
Rev. D. S. Lentz
Rev. George Lochman, D.D.
Flora E. Lukens
Rev. E. L. Lybrand
Rev. H. L. McMurray
August G. Mayer
Mrs. Columbia Victory Miller
Rev. Edgar Grim Miller, D.D.
William J. Miller
Rev. George S. Murphy, D.D.
Amanda E. Myers
Rev. Fred. William Oswald
Rev. W. A. Passavant, D.D
Rev. M. L. Pence
Rev. Philip Pfatteicher
Rev. Johann George Pfuhl
Rev. Henry Reumann
William G. Riter
Mrs. Caroline F. Rumpp
Rev. William Rusmiselle
Rev. Jonathan Sarver, D.D.
William J. Schich
Fred S. Schmidt
Rev. John G. Schmucker, D.D.
Anna R. Schulte
Rev. Joseph A. Seiss, D.D., LL.D.
Rev. J. Luther Sibole
Rev. L. L. Smith. D.D.
Rev. and Mrs. G. F. Snyder
Rev. Adolph Spaeth, D.D., LL.D.
Mrs. Augusta C. Stafford
The B. T. Steiner Family
Rev. J. P. Stirewalt, D.D.
Rev. Charles M. Stock, D.D.
Rev. Joel Swartz
Mrs. Margaret Mae Swope
Stephen Thomas
Rev. Daniel D. Trexler
Mrs. Amelia Manns Turkel
Rev. J. H. Umbenhen, Ph.D.
Jules C. Veil
Frederick and Augusta Vogel
Henry Von Glahn
Charles W. Wattles
Rev. Carl Weiss
Jacob Wingard
William R. Yeager
John Ziegler
The Deceased Pastors of Trinity
    Church of Canton, Ohio.

Statistics

Since our last report the folowing deductions and additions have been made in our roll:

Deductions—Ministers, 62; Widows, 39; Children, 26.

Additions—Ministers, 56; Widows, 93; Children, 59.

The roll by Synods is as follows:

Pension Roll by Synods—June 30, 1928

Synod	Retired	Disabled	Widows	Children	Daughters	Pension	Relief
Alleghany	6	0	11	0	0	$ 4,000	$ 620
California	7	2	6	1	0	3,950	500
Canada	9	1	12	2	0	5,500	410
East Penna.	8	1	34	8	1	10,100	760
Georgia	1	1	6	5	1	2,250	240
Ger. Nebraska	6	1	13	10	0	5,200	330
Illinois	4	2	19	8	2	6,400	370
Indiana	3	1	4	2	0	2,100	150
Iowa	2	0	2	0	0	1,000	50
Kansas	5	0	9	0	0	3,300	280
Manitoba	2	4	4	4	0	2,800	460
Maryland	5	0	32†	2	1	8,300	440
Michigan	3	0	13	2	0	3,600	130
Mississippi	2	0	0	0	0	600	
Nebraska	3	0	7	3	0	2,450	160
New York Min.	8	2	23	1	1	7,850	800
N. Y. & N. E.	3	0	8	2	0	2,600	130
N. Y. Synod	12	0	29	7	0	9,750	1,400
North Carolina	7	1	23	5	0	7,250	760
Northwest	4	0	4†	1	0	2,150	80
Nova Scotia	0	0	0	0	0		
Ohio	18	1	35	10	0	13,200	1,220
Pacific	0	0	3	0	0	600	
Min. of Penna.	13	7*	54	11	0	17,350	1,052
Pittsburgh	12	3**	36	11	0	12,250	900
Rocky Mountain	5	0	0	0	0	1,500	150
Slovak Zion	0	0	0	0	0		
South Carolina	1	0	18	4	0	4,100	500
Susquehanna	9	0	15	1	0	5,750	280
Texas	0	0	3	0	0	600	80
Virginia	8	1	15	5	0	5,950	330
Wartburg	5	0	3	0	0	2,100	200
West Penna	9	0	27	14	0	8,800	690
West Virginia	0	0	2	0	0	400	
Total (1928)	180	28	470	119	6	$163,750	$13,472
Total (1926)	189	21	424	99	5	$153,750	$14,290

Notes:

* Includes a missionary.

† Includes widow receiving $25 per month through special agreement.

Annuity Bonds and Bequests

The attention of the Church is called to the fact that the Board issues Annuity Bonds at a liberal rate of interest and pastors and attorneys are asked to call attention to their parishoners to these bonds and to suggest the Board of Ministerial Pensions and Relief as an institution worthy of remembrances in their wills.

Board Actions

The consideration of the increasing of pensions will not be entered into for one year.

The Board will not undertake group insurance and suggests that where it is desired Synods make provision for it.

The Campaign Endowment Fund to be invested in liquid assets.

The same apportionment granted during the last biennium be asked for the coming biennium.

Vacancies

During the past biennium the following vacancies were caused in the Board by death and resignation:

Rev. M. L. Zweizig, D.D.—by resignation.
G. L. Cromer, LL.D.—by resignation.
J. B. Franke—by death.
Henry E. Passavant—by resignation.

With the approval of the Executive Board, the following persons were elected to fill the vacancies thus caused:

O. A. Sardeson, Chicago, Ill., to succeed Dr. Zweizig.
J. L. Fisher, Salisbury, N. C., to succeed Dr. Cromer.
Paul F. Myers, Washington, D. C., to succeed Mr. Passavant.
A. F. Sittloh, Richmond, Ind., to succeed Mr. Franke.

At this convention the terms of the following members expire:

Rev Luther DeYoe, D.D., Philadelphia, Pa. Ineligible for re-election.
Mr. J. H. Brandt, Philadelphia, Pa. Ineligible for re-election.
Mr. O. A. Sardeson, Chicago, Ill. Eligible for re-election.
Mr. E. J. Young, Wadsworth, Ohio. Ineligible for re-election.
Mr. J. L. Fisher, Salisbury, N. C. Eligible for re-election.

The Board places in nomination the following:

Rev. Otto Kleine, Philadelphia, Pa.
Mr. A. Raymond Bard, Reading, Pa.
Mr. O. A. Sardeson, Chicago, Ill.
Mr. J. L. Fisher, Salisbury, N. C.
Judge Henry H. Harter, Canton, Ohio.

Recommendations

1. That the same apportionment be granted the Board for the coming biennium as granted for the past biennium.

2. That the Synods be requested to appoint continuation committees, consisting of one layman from each conference with the Conference President as an advisory member, to secure the full synodical quota both in subscriptions and payments.

3. That the following be adopted as the expression of the United Lutheran Church in relation to the 1928 Campaign for a Pension Endowment Fund:

The Board of Ministerial Pensions and Relief interprets the response of the churches to the appeal for a Four Million Dollar Endowment Fund as more than an approval of the need of more adequate pensions for retired and disabled ministers, ministers' widows and dependent children. It was indeed most emphatically such an approval. The sentiments voiced throughout the church during the period in which the appeal was organized, the alacrity with which thousands of representatives of congregations volunteered to work for the Fund and the more than 200,000 generous subscriptions of the membership of the churches bear witness of an almost universal desire to remove economic anxieties from the pastors.

It is, furthermore, our sincere conviction (1) that the Board's project—a more adequate pension fund for those in whose interest it has been established and empowered—has received from the church such unmistakable authorization as to confirm beyond any possible questioning the wisdom of its policy in carrying through its special campaign. The Board is thereby made grateful both for the approval of its policy and for the confidence placed in its ability to perform the work entrusted to it.

(2) We deem ourselves obligated to testify to the Church in convention assembled, correlative convictions reached by us through the campaign. Our communion of believers, in responding so promptly and generously to the proposition laid before them bore witness to the valuation in which they hold the word and sacraments as administered through the pastoral office. In this period of ecclesiastical unrest and of wide-spread indifference to the divinely established agencies of salvation, the Church should be confirmed in confidence in its simple plan of organization and its pastors should accept with complete sincerity the testimony of the people concerning their stewardship of spiritual things. The community of believers has once more registered their high estimate of the office filled by the Christian minister.

Incidental in the campaign, but of vast consequence, is the self revelation it has brought to the United Lutheran Church of its hitherto unrealized possibilities of achievement on a great and impressive scale. Doubts, heretofore paralyzing to initiative, of the Church's ability to plan and successfully execute comprehensive enterprises commensurate with its opportunities, have been resolved. It has been a vision of its latent resources and of the possibility of mobilizing and combining them for the service of God and the world.

(3) We further regard the campaign and its results as proof that divine favor permeates the life of the United Lutheran Church. From the general organization through the Synods into conferences and congregations there was united action. Prayer and fellowship, plan and realization, zeal and patience, unity and individuality have made themselves evident. With humble sincerity, God's guidance was sought. The results show our Lord's intimate confidence far higher than the material products of the work done. Without divine blessing, nothing would have been accomplished. With divine blessing all things are possible.

Under such circumstances the Church in convention assembled can do nothing less than register its gratitude to God and its thankful recognition of the co-operation of officials, of ministers, of congregations and of individuals in the successful campaign for the Four Million Dollar Endowment Fund for Ministerial Pensions.

The Treasurer's report follows:

> HARRY HODGES, *Executive Secretary.*
> PAUL F. MYERS,
> PETER P. HAGAN.

TREASURER'S REPORT OF THE BOARD OF MINISTERIAL PENSIONS AND RELIEF

Philadelphia, July 25, 1928.

We have audited the accounts of the Treasurer of the Board of Ministerial Pensions and Relief of the United Lutheran Church in America for the two years ended June 30, 1928, and we certify that, in our opinion, the annexed statements:

Balance Sheet, June 30, 1928
Statement of Receipts and Disbursements for the Year ended June 30, 1927
Statement of Receipts and Disbursements for the Year ended June 30, 1928
Investments, June 30, 1928

are in accordance with the books of account and are correct.

> LYBRAND, ROSS BROS. & MONTGOMERY,
> *Accountants and Auditors.*

BALANCE SHEET, June 30, 1928

ASSETS

Cash in banks and on hand		$849,241.50
Investments, at ledger values:		
U. S. Liberty Loan Bonds	$ 10,554.12	
Other Bonds	121,946.53	
Mortgages	4,300.00	
		136,800.65
Real Estate, at ledger values:		
Sime's Farm, Wheatland Co., Montana	1.00	
40 Acres, Geneva Township, Midland Co., Mich..	1.00	
		2.00
Office Furniture and Fixtures		1,504.23
		$987,548.38

LIABILITIES

Annuities:		
Pension Endowment Fund	$ 55,750.00	
Relief Endowment Fund	23,350.00	
		$ 79,100.00

Funds:

Pension Endowment	774,217.94
Relief Endowment	73,621.37
Pension General	61,101.95
Relief General	492.88

908,448.38

$987,548.38

STATEMENT OF RECEIPTS AND DISBURSEMENTS
For the Year Ended June 30, 1927

RECEIPTS	Pension Endowment Fund	Pension General Fund	Relief Endowment Fund	Relief General Fund
United Lutheran Church		$149,225.00		
United, General and Branch Synods		6,540.00		
Women's Missionary Society.		5,000.00		
Bequests	$ 1,115.83	1,356.77		$ 930.00
Donations	165,00	4,244.48	$ 486.00	10,733.55
Interest:				
On Bank Balances	853.42	996.32	283.56	144.90
On Bills and Accounts Receivable	90.00		59.62	
On Mortgages	191.28			
On Investments	4,072.00		4,805.00	
Donations under Annuity Plan	2,700.00			
Collections on Mortgages	3,500.00			
Sale of Real Estate			20.00	
Investments Matured or Sold.	13,000.00			
Advances on Montana Property refunded, 16 Pct., with interest	25.18			
	$25,712.71	$167,363.27	$5,654.18	$11,808.45

DISBURSEMENTS				
Pensions and Relief:				
Retired Ministers		$ 55,816.72		$ 6,769.00
Disabled Ministers		6,737.61		150.00
Widows and Mothers of Ministers		86,715.95		9,790.00
Children of Ministers		5,046.24		
Annuity Interest		3,129.55		1,920.16
Salary of Executive Secretary		3,600.00		
Salary of Office Secretary		1,325.00		
Traveling Expenses of Executive Secretary		339.35		

	Pension Endowment Fund	Pension General Fund	Relief Endowment Fund	Relief General Fund
Expenses of Treasurer and other Board Members..		958.97		
Printing and Stationery		1,148.10		
Office Supplies and Expenses.		717.40		
Rental of Office		712.50		
Auditing		350.00		
Advertising		501.02		
General Expenses ....$	3.00	191.42	$ 58.65	
Campaign Expenses		4,183.97		
Investments Purchased	3,500.00			
	$3,503.00	$171,473.80	$58.65	$18,629.16

RECONCILEMENT OF CASH

	Pension Endowment Fund	Pension General Fund	Relief Endowment Fund	Relief General Fund
Balances, July 1, 1926	$30,751.70	$ 42,936.54	$ 9,853.02	$ 5,236.09
Cash Receipts for the period.	25,712.71	167,363.27	5,654.18	11,808.45
	56,464.41	210,299.81	15,507.20	17,044.54
Disbursements, as above.....	3,503.00	171,473.80	58.65	18,629.16
	52,961.41	38,826.01	15,448.55	1,584.62
Transfers between Funds as of June 30, 1927	5,231.88	5,231.88	5,148.18	5 148.18
	$47,729.53	$ 44.057.89	$10,300.37	$ 3,563.56

Balance, June 30, 1927..... $105,651.35

For the Year Ended June 30, 1928

RECEIPTS	Pension Endowment Fund	Pension General Fund	Relief Endowment Fund	Relief General Fund
Campaign Endowment Fund	$813,000.99			
United Lutheran Church....		$166,850.00		
United, General and Branch Synods		1,560.11		
Women's Missionary Society.		5,000.00		
Bequests	200.00	4,503.71		
Donations	34.00	1,459.08		$ 8,727.31
Interest:				
On Bank Balances	2,122.55	32.73	$ 565.95	141.24
On Investments	3,449.74		4,541.24	
Donations under Annuity Plan	11,400.00		500.00	
Investments Matured or Sold	1,050.00		21,000.00	
Advances on Montana Property refunded, 16 Pct. with interest	85.57			
	$831,342.85	$179,405.63	$26,607.19	$ 8,868.55

	Pension Endowment Fund	Pension General Fund	Relief Endowment Fund	Relief General Fund
DISBURSEMENTS				
Pensions and Relief:				
Retired Ministers		$ 53,579.18		$ 6,819.50
Disabled Ministers		7,951.88		125.00
Widows and Mothers of Ministers		91,620.71		9,335.85
Children of Ministers		5,499.33		
Annuity Interest		3,480.60		1,751.83
Salary of Executive Secty...		2,100.00		
Salary of Office Secretary..		1,715.00		
Expenses of Treasurer and other Board Members		839.33		
Printing and Stationery......		260.42		
Office Supplies and Expenses		494.59		
Rental of Office		765.00		
Auditing		350.00		
Advertising		530.05		
General Expenses		166.50		
Campaign Expenses $115,163.80				
Equipment Purchased		85.50		
	$115,163.80	$169,438.09		$18,032.18
RECONCILEMENT OF CASH				
Balances, July 1, 1927 ......$ 47,729.53		$ 44,057.89	$10,300.37	$ 3,563.56
Cash Receipts for the period 831,342.85		179,405.63	26,607.19	8,868.55
	879,072.38	223,463.52	36,907.56	12,432.11
Disbursements, as above.... 115,163.80		169,438.09		18,032.18
	763,908.58	54,025.43	36,907.56	5,600.07
Transfers between Funds as of June 30, 1928 .... 5,572.29		5,572.29	5,107.19	5 107.19
	$758,336.29	$ 59,597.72	$31,800.37	$ 492.88

Balance, June 30, 1928 ... $849,241.50

INVESTMENTS, June 30, 1928

	Ledger Values		
	Pension Endowment Fund	Relief Endowment Fund	Totals
U. S. Government Obligations:			
$11,000 U. S. Fourth Liberty Loan 4¼s.$10,554.12			
			$ 10,554.12
Other Bonds:			
$ 5,000 Bell Telephone Co. of Penna. 5s, 1960 ....$ 5,041.25			
5,000 Central District Telephone Co. 5s, 1943		$ 4,875.00	

		Ledger Values		
		Pension Endowment Fund	Relief Endowment Fund	Totals
1,000	Charleston Consolidated Ry., Gas & Electric Co. 5s, 1999 ..		1,000.00	
6,000	Chicago, Indianapolis & Louisville 5s, 1966		6,000.00	
1,000	Des Moines City Railway Co. 5s, 1936		950.00	
2,000	Erie R. R. Equip. Tr. "GG" 5½s, 1933	2,000.00		
500	Fort Spring, Green Brier Co., W. Va., 5s, 1936		500.00	
5,000	Georgia Light, Power & Ry. Co. 5s, 1941		4,645.00	
1,000	Howard Gas & Coal Co. 6s, 1937		1,000.00	
5,000	Lehigh Valley R. R. Co. 5s, 2003	5,110.00		
1,000	Maryland Elec. Ry. Co. 6½s, 1957, "A"	1,000.00		
1,000	Minnesota Power & Light Co. 6s, 1950		1,000.00	
1,000	Newberry College 6s, 1929	1,000.00		
1,000	Pacific Telephone & Telegraph Co. 5s, 1937		1,000.00	
1,000	Penna. R. R. Co. Cons. 4s, 1948.	1,000.00		
5,000	Penna. R. R. Co. Genl. 4½s, 1965	5,000.00		
1,000	Penna. R. R. Co. 10-year 7s, 1930	1,000.00		
5,000	Phila. Electric Co. 5s, 1960....	4,990.28		
25,000	Phila. Electric Power Co. 5½s, 1972	15,150.00	10,100.00	
25,500	Phila. Rapid Transit 6s, 1944...	10,500.00	15,000.00	
5,000	Pittsburgh, Cincinnati & St. Louis 5s, 1975	4,985.00		
1,000	Southern Railway Co., St. Louis Div., 4s, 1951		1,000.00	
1,000	Spencer, Roane Co., W. Va., 5s, 1946		1,000.00	
2,000	Tennessee Power Co. 5s, 1962..		1,600.00	
1,000	United Railway & Electric Co. of Baltimore 5s, 1936		1,000.00	
5,000	Virginia Power Co. 5s, 1942....		4,500.00	
10,000	Walnut St. Trust Bldg. 6s, 1932.		10,000.00	
		$56,776.53	$65,170.00	
				121,946.53

Mortgages:

218 Maple Ave., Springfield Gardens, L. I., N. Y. ....$	3,500.00		
Participating Trust Certificate, Property Park County, Montana, 6 Pct..	800.00		
	$ 4,300.00		4,300.00
Total Investments ....$	71,630.65	$65,170.00	$136,800.65

PETER P. HAGAN, *Treasurer.*

The Chair ruled that resolution No. 1 was covered by the Budget. Resolutions 2 and 3 were adopted.

The auditor's report on accounts of the Board was accepted.

On motion the President was granted the privilege of using his own judgment in deciding the order in which unfinished business and the business remaining should be brought up.

The Convention resumed consideration of the report of the Committee on Common Service Book.

The President stated that the memorial from the Synod of Ohio concerning arrangement of words and music had been covered. (See Minutes Fifth Meeting, Morning Session—Secretary.)

The Secretary read the memorial from the Pittsburgh Synod (See Item 2 of the report of the Committee on Memorials from Constituent Synods) concerning a fuller index of hymns. On motion this memorial was referred to the Common Service Book Committee.

The Rev. A. Steimle reported that the Committee appointed to take into consideration the extent to which the survey of educational institutions shall be made public unanimously agreed that the procedure of distribution be in accordance with the statement in the report of the Board. The report was accepted.

The Secretary submitted the report of the Commissioners to the National Lutheran Council and presented the Rev. J. A. Morehead, Executive Director of the Council, and also Revs. Isaac Cannaday and John Aberly.

REPORT OF THE COMMISSIONERS TO THE NATIONAL LUTHERAN COUNCIL

Your Commissioners have the honor to submit their report of the work of the National Lutheran Council for the past biennium of the United Lutheran Church in America:

It is believed that the National Lutheran Council with God's blessing has made gradual but definite progress in the several departments of its work during the past two years. This general Lutheran agency has taken steps to impress its true character upon the consciousness of the Church by the codification of its governing Rules and Regulations. The regular work has been placed on a more solid basis for effective action. A common Lutheran front has in considerable part been established before the government, in the consciousness of the general public, and in relation to other branches of the Christian Church. Some definite lines of common service, whose real importance and value are not fully apparent on the surface, have been discovered and are being faithfully cultivated. The ecumenical Lutheran consciousness, including a true conception of the place and mission of the Evangelical Lutheran Church within Christendom has been developed in a marked degree both at home and abroad during the past ten years of the Council's existence. In all these cheering manifestations of the life and service of the Evangelical Lutheran Churches of this country and the world, the National Lutheran Council has had its part.

The Commissioners of the Lutheran Church Bodies officially participating in the agency of the Council are as follows:

COMMISSIONERS OF PARTICIPATING CHURCH BODIES

United Lutheran Church:

The Rev. Charles M. Jacobs, D.D.
The Rev. J. A. W. Haas, D.D., LL.D.
The Rev. Charles J. Smith, D.D.
The Rev. P. W. Koller, D.D.
The Rev. C. A. Freed, D.D.
The Rev. M. G. G. Scherer, D.D.
Hon. E. F. Eilert
Mr. G. F. Greiner

Norwegian Lutheran Church:

The Rev. J. A. Aasgaard, D.D.
The Rev. L. W. Boe, D.D., LL.D
The Rev. J. A. O. Stub, D.D.

Augustana Synod:

The Rev. G. A. Brandelle, D.D., LL.D.
The Rev. Peter Peterson, D.D.

Joint Synod of Ohio:

The Rev. C. C. Hein, D.D.
The Rev. E. Poppen

United Danish Church:

The Rev. N. C. Carlsen

Lutheran Free Church:

The Rev. H. J. Urdahl

Icelandic Synod:

The Rev. K. K. Olafson

Besides these Lutheran Church Bodies which have regularly supported the agency of the Council, the Finnish Ev. Luth. Church (Suomi Synod), Buffalo Synod, Danish Lutheran Church, Jehovah Conference, Eielsen Synod, Lutheran Brethren, and the Finnish Apostolic Church, have shared in the emergency work of World Service. These facts illustrate the extent of Lutheran co-operation in merciful work through the agency of the Council.

MEETINGS AND ORGANIZATION

Two regular meetings were held, both in Chicago, in January of the years 1927 and 1928.

At the annual meeting in 1927, the following officers, who were re-elected a year later, were chosen:

The Rev. G. A. Brandelle, D.D., LL.D., President
The Rev. C. C. Hein, D.D., Vice-President.
The Rev. N. C. Carlsen, Secretary.
Hon. E. F. Eilert, Treasurer.

AMENDMENTS OF REGULATIONS GOVERNING THE COUNCIL

The revised statement of the Preamble, Regulations and Standing Resolutions governing the National Lutheran Council, presented for adoption at the Richmond Convention, were approved by all participating Lutheran Church Bodies, with the suggestion of two minor changes. The Ev. Luth. Joint Synod of Ohio proposed that Item 2 of Article II, Division A, be amended to read: "To represent 'Lutheran interests before'"; the United Lutheran Church at its Richmond Convention requested the addition of the following Standing Resolution: "Any surplus remaining out of the contributions of any Body after deducting such Body's apportionment of expenditures, as provided for in Article XIV, shall, upon the dissolution or termination of the Council, be returned to the treasury of such Body."

At its annual meeting in January, 1927, the Council adopted these changes and recommended them to participating Church Bodies. All Bodies meeting since these amendments have been recommended have approved them.

REGULAR WORK

The cause of World Service, designed to meet a great emergency, has occupied the foreground in the activities of the National Lutheran Council since the World War. This was doubtless wise because of the greatness of the task to be accomplished and because of the necessity of concentrating the interest of the Church upon the essential work of rescuing starving people and preserving endangered activities and institutions of the Church. With a view to meeting efficiently this call to a merciful work of enormous proportions, the National Lutheran Council and its regular work at home have been kept modestly in the background. Under the circumstances, it is perhaps not surprising that many seem to have forgotten that the Council has a permanent mission of service for the Lutheran Church at large in North America. The Council is now facing the task of effectively serving the Church at home. This general Lutheran agency was not merely a temporary organization for war-time service, like the National Lutheran Commission for Soldiers' and Sailors' Welfare, but was launched in 1918 to extend and complete the noble work so well begun by the National Lutheran Commission and to care on a permanent basis for the general or common interests of all Lutheran Church Bodies in North America. During the ten years of its existence, the Council has had a regular program for the service of Lutheranism in general in the United States and Canada, whose execution has been proceeding quietly but steadily. The value and importance of the establishment and maintenance of such a general Lutheran agency has been amply demonstrated.

In this connection, the careful study of the Rules and Regulations governing the National Lutheran Council as set out in full on pages 28 and 29 of the Lutheran World Almanac and Encyclopedia for 1928 is suggested. The purposes of the National Lutheran Council as set out in these Regulations are essentially the same as those adopted at the time of its organization in 1918. Full information concerning the Council's program of regular work at home and of emergency work abroad may be found on pages 35 to 39 of the Lutheran World Almanac for 1926 and on pages 28 to 30 of the Lutheran World Almanac for 1928.

But what has the National Lutheran Council accomplished in the field of its regular work in North America during the past fiscal year?

Representation.—Through its Executive Director, the Council has regularly represented the interests of the Lutheran Church at large in relation to many ecclesiastical, philanthropic, economic, and other movements or organizations. Particularly important and valuable has been the service of the Council in working in co-operation with and through the American Committee on the Rights of Religious Minorities for the improvement of the condition of these minorities, including the Lutheran ones, in the countries of Eastern and Southeastern Europe. A deputation was sent by the American Committee on the Rights of Religious Minorities to Rumania for direct investigation of the actual condition of religious minorities in that country. Helpful contact was had both with the people of the religious minorities and with the government of the country. The American Committee has interested itself in the publication and circulation of a book entitled "Rumania Ten Years After," which embodies the documented report of its deputation. The sbustance of this book has had wide publicity in the press. It is believed that the public opinion aroused by the spread of accurate information relative to the condition of certain religious groups in Rumania cannot but influence the Rumanian Government toward greater care in carrying out the provisions of the treaties for the protection of the rights of religious minorities in that country. Approximately 400,000 Lutherans, including those of the Magyar and German churches, are directly and seriously involved in the conditions for whose relief the American Committee is striving.

In relation to governments in North America, the National Lutheran Council has given through its Statistical Department during the past fiscal year a vast amount of service, having value both to all Lutheran Church Bodies in the United States and to the Government itself, in co-operating with the Census Department with a view to securing complete and accurate facts for the 1926 Census of Religious Bodies. The time and labor of the personnel of the Council was freely given to the Census Department, but some extra costs for material, etc., was paid by this department of the Government, so much was the service rendered appreciated.

By organizing and publishing after careful research the principles and facts pertaining to the National Origins Clause of the Immigration Law, it can be justly claimed that the National Lutheran Council helped to bring about the delay for another year of the enforcement of this law, which leaves the immigration quotas from Lutheran countries the same as heretofore.

Perhaps the most significant achievement during the past year was that of securing through the process of prolonged negotiation a more favorably strategic position for the Lutheran group of Christians in this country. From time immemorial, Lutherans have lost position and influence in America because of their divisions. They have been classified in the government records, not as one group of Christians essentially one in faith, but as twenty or more independent denominations. While the organic divisions of Lutherans can be explained historically, nevertheless, it remains true that they are not altogether without blame in the matter of divisions and consequent possible inefficiency. But the Lutherans of the United States are essentially one in the faith and in its confession—the essence of true inner unity and the only safe foundation for organic union. From this point of view, the National Lutheran Council since its organization has labored through its publicity, statistical and representation services for the establishment in the public mind of the conception that the Lutherans of all Church Bodies and Synods are essentially one group or denomination of Christians. As the result of long negotiation, this conception has been recognized by the Census Bureau in its forthcoming Reports of Census of Religious Bodies for the year 1926. The heading of the section covering the Church of the Reformation will not be "Lutheran Bodies" as hitherto, but simply *Lutherans*. The entire section about the *Lutherans* will begin with a general statement setting forth the countries from which the forefathers of the Lutheran citizenship of this country came, their early history, their common doctrinal basis, church polity, etc. This will be followed by a general but distinctive statement and the statistical facts in regular order, covering each particular Lutheran Church Body or Synod in the United States. Thus a far more favorable strategic position has been won for the Evangelical Lutheran Church in the authoritative documents of the Government, which will influence the views and writing of all.

Statistical and Reference Library Service.—The statistical and reference library service has been regularly conducted during the past year. To the regular personnel, consisting of Dr. G. L. Kieffer, Dr. O. M. Norlie, a stenographer and a clerk, was added special assistants during the period of the production of the manuscript for the Lutheran World Almanac. Because of the absence of Dr. Kieffer on sick leave during the summer of 1927, the Rev. Prof. A. R. Wentz, Ph.D., D.D., was secured as substitute as a member of the Editorial Committee for three months' full-time service for the preparation of the manuscript for the fifth edition of the Lutheran World Almanac and Encyclopedia. He did most acceptable service. The records covering the current facts concerning the Lutheran Church in the United States and Canada have been kept up-to-date. Hundreds of inquiries for information have been answered. Articles for encyclopedias have been written. But the single work of most importance accomplished by this department during the past year was the production of the Lutheran World Almanac and Encyclopedia for 1928. This book is recognized as an authoritative Lutheran reference book both in this country and in Europe.

Publicity.—The service of the National Lutheran Council in the field of Lutheran publicity can only be truly measured if one compares the present frequency with which items of Lutheran news appear in the columns of newspapers throughout the entire country with that which existed at the time of its organization about ten years ago. The Publicity Department of the Council (known as News Bureau or Lutheran Bureau) is furnished with files, typewriters, multigraph, mimeograph and addressograph machines and other necessary equipment for the conduct of a national church news agency. The personnel consists of six persons, including Mr. W. P. Elson, Publicity Secretary, who give their full-time to this branch of the work.

The News Bureau of the Council has adopted specific lines of activity:

A. A News Bulletin of six pages, containing the freshest and most important items of Lutheran news occurring in America and throughout the world, is sent each week to the editors of the seventy or more Lutheran periodicals in the United States and Canada and to a limited list of newsworkers. This same weekly church paper, *News Bulletin,* is also sent to the editors of the general religious press. This weekly service to the church press is supplemented by *News Bulletin Specials,* carrying articles on important topics.

B. Whenever Lutheran news of importance is received relative to the work of the Church in any Church Body or Synod in this country or elsewhere in the world, if it has news value for the secular press, it is sent out in Bulletins for mail release to the leading dailies of the United States and Canada, or is furnished to the headquarters in New York of the wire services of North America, such as the Associated Press, the United Press, etc. Ninety-four general news stories were mailed to lists of from 884 to 1,400 daily newspapers in the United States and Canada, and 176 items of news value only in certain sections were sent to lists of newspapers from five in number to 700. Thirty-nine news articles were translated and sent to German-language newspapers, averaging about 140 in number, and one release was translated and mailed to 155 Swedish-language papers. Eight professional wire and news agencies and individual news-papers received a total of 256 stories, and the same group received 166 "news tips," delivered in person, by mail, messenger, telegraph, or tele-phone. "News tips" consist largely of brief advance notices of coming events of importance in all parts of the country which are important for spot coverage, accomplished through the local reporters, in each instance, of the wire agencies concerned. None of the material sent to the public press has failed to appear in print. In fact, the steady supply of news material to the public press is welcomed and encouragingly used through-out the United States and Canada. On the other hand, the News Bureau has experienced greater difficulty in obtaining adequate and prompt reports of news events than in the acceptance of its material by the editors. The condition of the maintenance of a completely effective national church news agency, which needs now to be emphasized, is the regular and prompt transmission of news facts through the Council's Publicity Bureau by the executives, boards, committees, and individual news agencies of the Luth-eran Church Bodies in America.

C. The Council offers the services of its News Bureau free for con-vention publicity to all participating Church Bodies and many of them avail themselves of this opportunity. Many are using their agency for convention press service.

D. The Council offers the services of its News Bureau free for year-around special publicity to participating Bodies, in co-operation with their several individual Bureaus or Committees on Publicity. An increasing number of Lutheran Church Bodies are availing themselves of this oppor-tunity to utilize the contacts and influence of this national Lutheran agency in making their own publicity service more universal and effective.

But the main function of the Council in the dissemination of Lutheran news is to promote more effective knowledge of the message and achieve-ments of the Lutheran Church among all the people by the promotion of general church publicity. It is conservatively estimated on the basis of the reports of several clipping agencies that the News Bureau of the Na-tional Lutheran Council has secured at least 50,000 inserts of items of

Lutheran news in the newspapers of the United States and Canada during the past year.

BUDGET FOR THE MAINTENANCE OF THE AGENCY OF THE COUNCIL

For the maintenance of the Council with its Executive and Business Offices, its Publicity Bureau and Reference and Statistical Departments, including a personnel of fourteen, the National Lutheran Council recommends an annual budget of $33,896.66, apportioned as follows:

United Lutheran Church ....$	18,488.87
Norwegian Lutheran Church	6,066.89
Augustana Synod	4,678.36
Joint Synod of Ohio	3,466.44
United Danish Church	374.82
Lutheran Free Church	700.87
Icelandic Synod	120.41
Total ....$	33,896.66

The amount paid on its quota by the United Lutheran Church in the year 1927 was $17,335.18; amount contributed on the 1928 quota up to August 1st is $11,049.02.

EMERGENCY WORK OR WORLD SERVICE

The summary of the World Service activities of the Council to date are given for the information of the Church.

The cash receipts of all the Appeals for World Service from the beginning to August 1st, 1928, are as follows:

United Lutheran Church $2,027,630.07
Norwegian Lutheran Church	592,879.27
Augustana Synod	355,602.67
Joint Synod of Ohio	582,825.03
United Danish Church	44,988.86
Lutheran Free Church	30,051.97
Icelandic Synod	3,136.70
Iowa Synod	86,623.40
Buffalo Synod	14,789.74
Immanuel Synod	208.06
Jehovah Conference	2,663.01
Eielsen Synod	1,354.54
Lutheran Brethren	807.97
Danish Synod	13,099.04
Suomi Synod	5,934.86
Finnish National Church	1,942.95
Finnish Apostolic Church	485.42
Synodical Conference	2,552.69
Independent	7,093.22
Lutheran Student Association	2,210.99
Private and Individual Sources	2,350.00
Unknown	250,925.15
Christmas Seals	12,896.09
	$4,043,051.70

The cash receipts for World Service during the past biennium up to August 1st, 1928, are as follows:

United Lutheran Church ....$	54,799.77
Norwegian Lutheran Church	7,204.42
Augustana Synod	9,739.43
Joint Synod of Ohio	5,097.01
United Danish Church	513.77
Lutheran Free Church	1,946.27
Iowa Synod	5.00
Buffalo Synod	123.72
Jehovah Conference	232.50
Eielsen Synod	171.08
Danish Synod	5.80
Icelandic Synod	150.00
Suomi Synod	218.69
Independent	3.00
Lutheran Student Association	2,210.99
Private and Other Individual Sources.............................	2,350.00
Unknown	2,351.78
	$87,123.23

The expenditures for relief and reconstruction from August 1st, 1926, to August 1st, 1928, are as follows:

Russia ....$	37,757.13	
Germany	7,593.31	
Poland	3,746.00	
Austria	4,515.30	
Roumania	3,311.00	
Czecho-Slovakia	1,719.01	
Jugoslavia	1,720.83	
Lithuania	800.00	
France	2,295.35	
Bulgaria	50.55	
Hungary	1,521.47	
Latvia	3,000.00	
Spain	56.00	
Switzerland	540.00	
Clothing Transportation	59.10	
Mississippi Flood	250.00	
		$68,935.05
For Foreign Mission Relief:		
China ....$	14,905.42	
India	44,441.71	
Africa	13,895.50	
		73,242.63
		$142,177.68

WORLD SERVICE PROGRAM FOR 1928

At its annual meeting in January, 1928, the National Lutheran Council adopted a specific World Service program for the current year. For its execution, the raising of the sum of $100,000 was recommended and has been approved by participating Lutheran Church Bodies.

In the good providence of God, the Evangelical Lutheran Churches in many countries of Europe affected by the World War have in large part, if not entirely, regained ability to maintain themselves and their own work. But some are called upon to endure such hard conditions that continued life without further help from their brethren in other lands is quite impossible. Hence it is unquestionably true that very important unfinished tasks of Lutheran World Service still challenge the interest of American Lutherans. Unless these definite undertakings are resolutely completed, the good already accomplished will prove in large part to have been unavailing. Therefore, having before it all available information, the National Lutheran Council decided at its last annual meeting in January to raise during the year 1928 the sum of $100,000 for the continuation of the program of Lutheran World Service. The share of the United Lutheran Church is $52,410. Of this amount, on August 1st, 1928, the Council has received $10,250.72. It is of the utmost importance that the share falling to the United Lutheran Church be raised in order that vital interests of the Church may not suffer.

The appeal thus made to the Church is based upon careful estimates of amounts needed for specific purposes, in continuance of work that the Council is already doing. The estimates are as follows:

For relief and reconstruction in Europe:
Russia $35,000.00
Other countries (twelve in all)... 33,000.00
Student relief 10,000.00

    Total for Europe... $78,000.00
For Foreign Missions:
Africa ....$ 5,222.00
China 3,477.34
India 25,200.00
                                                  $33,899.34

    Grand total $111,899.34

In submitting this estimate, along with the appeal, attention is called to two additional facts. The first is that the Lutheran churches in Europe are already beginning to contribute funds for the objects designated. These contributions are made through the Executive Committee of the World Convention. It is estimated that in 1928 they will amount to approximately $15,000.

The second fact is that the Council has adopted a definite policy of reduction in Foreign Mission appropriations. At its annual meeting in 1927 the Council adopted a recommendation of the Foreign Missions Conference to the effect that such appropriations should not be continued for longer than three years, and that reductions should be made at the rate of 33 1-3 per cent per year, beginning with 1927. It has not been possible to enforce this rule rigidly, but the missions that are now beneficiaries of the Council have been informed that they cannot expect continuance of aid after January 1, 1930.

QUADRICENTENNIALS IN 1929 AND 1930

The Council calls the attention of the Church to the important anniversaries that will fall in the years 1929 and 1930. The year 1929 will be the four hundredth anniversary of Luther's Catechisms and and of the Second Diet of Spires, where the name Protestant was first given to the Lutherans of Germany. The following year will be the four hundredth anniversary of the Augsburg Confession. It is important that all of these anniversaries shall be fittingly celebrated by the Lutherans of America, and the Council offers its services to all the participating bodies for the planning and carrying out of a nation-wide program for these celebrations, with especial emphasis on the year 1930. It has already determined to carry on a campaign of publicity in 1929 and to maintain a Speakers' Bureau for the convenience of local committees during that year. A special committee has been appointed to suggest plans for a proper celebration of 1930. In these, as in all other things, the Council is the servant of the bodies that have created and maintained it.

THE FUTURE OF THE COUNCIL

The National Lutheran Council has its face to the future. At its next meeting, the tenth anniversary of the organization of this general Lutheran agency will be suitably celebrated by reviewing the service it has rendered to the Lutheran Church Bodies of America and of the world. A special committee is considering the practicability of enlarging its program of work for the service of the Lutheran Church at large in the United States and Canada. The cause of wider Lutheran understanding and co-operation as represented by the agency of the Council is commended by your Commissioners to the abiding interest and loyal support of all forward-looking Lutherans in the United States and Canada.

As information, it should be stated that the headquarters of the Council was transferred, May 1, 1927, from 437 5th Avenue to 39 E. 35th Street, New York.

RECOMMENDATIONS

Your Commissioners offer the following general recommendations:

1. That the United Lutheran Church's share of the budget for the maintenance of the agency of the Council be assumed and that arrangements be made for its full payment.
2. That the 1928 World Service Appeal for $100,000 be approved and that Constituent Synods, their pastors and congregations, be urged to contribute at least their proportionate part of $52,410 falling to the share of the United Lutheran Church.

3. That the United Lutheran Church approve the recommendations of the Council relative to the Quadricentennial Celebrations of Luther's Catechisms, the Diet of Spires, the Augsburg Confession, etc., in the years 1929 and 1930, and heartily commend the participation in joint plans for their suitable celebration.

Respectfully submitted,
CHARLES M. JACOBS,
For the Commissioners.

REPORT OF THE NATIONAL LUTHERAN COUNCIL ON SPECIAL PUBLICITY SERVICE RENDERED TO THE UNITED LUTHERAN CHURCH

Pursuant to a renewed agreement with the United Lutheran Church through its Executive Board, the News Bureau of the National Lutheran Council has continued during the past biennium the previously arranged plan for supplying newspapers throughout the United States and Canada with year-round publicity concerning the Church and its various agencies and constituent synods. The office personnel and equipment have been utilized in supplying selected items of news directly to daily and weekly newspapers and to professional news agencies which re-transmit news stories to the daily press. Because the facilities for publicity of the agency of the Council are available for the free use of the United Lutheran Church, as of all other participating Lutheran Church Bodies, this entire individual news service for the particular benefit of the United Lutheran Church has been conducted for two years at a total extra cost for special personnel, postage, material and the like of $5,099.20.

The volume of this service is significant. During the twenty-one months from the close of the Richmond Convention to August 1, 1928, 108 news articles of varying sectional importance were supplied to local lists of dailies and weeklies ranging from 5 to 349 in number. Twenty-eight general news stories concerning the work of the Church were sent to lists of from 1,153 to 1,368 dailies throughout the United States and Canada, and seventeen articles were translated and sent to 145 German newspapers. During the twenty-one months, 113 news stories were released to seven wire and news agencies, and 119 "news tips" by telephone, telegraph, messenger and mail were delivered to wire and news agencies, photo news services and individual selected newspapers. Five releases of special significance were supplied to Lutheran editors and the general religious press, and four special letters accompanying or concerning matters of news interest were sent to lists of pastors ranging from 200 to 2,854.

The above listing includes special service which has been given to the Pension Campaign, the College Survey, various constituent synods, and conventions of United Lutheran Church groups. Publicity for the Erie

Convention of the Church is not included in this listing, since the work has for the most part been done subsequent to August 1st, and was by no means complete when this report was tabulated.

The publicity handled from August 1 to November 1, 1926, which period includes the Richmond Convention of the Church, was as follows: 40 articles of secular importance to local lists ranging from 35 to 603 in number; 48 general news stories to national lists, numbering from 884 to 1,250; 11 articles translated for German-language dailies; 48 news stories to wire agencies; 34 "news tips" to wire and photo agencies and individual newspapers; one letter sent to 2,045 pastors, enclosing a news story and newspaper pictures in mat form; and 36 photographs of news personages or events supplied to various newspapers.

The honest effort is made to supply the newspapers with legitimate news of the Church properly prepared and carefully edited so as to reach the editor's desk in the most nearly acceptable form. Through a sense of news values, facts are frequently uncovered which should by all means be given to the public but which the participants consider not of sufficient newspaper interest. Likewise, in the office of the Bureau, a vast quantity of material is considered and rejected because it lacks the general appeal which it must have before newspapers will publish it. It is a process of evaluating news, weeding out certain material and amplifying other. Accuracy, completeness, and the selection of significant and interesting facts are carefully cultivated and jealously guarded. A guarantee of authenticity is signed at the end of each news article for the protection of newspaper editors, rewrite-men, and reporters.

The success with which the efforts of the News Bureau have met reveals first, the will of the church to make known the important things it is doing; second, the sheer news value of any movement or act which concerns hundreds of thousands of church people; and third, a most receptive attitude on the part of newspapers in general, whose editors are ever ready to use real news whenever it comes to their attention and never ready to print articles for mere propaganda purpose.

As the editor of the small town daily or weekly is always on the alert for items of personal interest concerning the goings and comings of the citizens and is grateful to those of his subscribers who "turn reporter" long enough to telephone such items to him so the editor of any newspaper which concerns itself with events of general importance is receptive to genuine news supplied him from whatever authentic source. That some few are wary of what they term "free hand-outs" is due solely to the misuse which commercial concerns have made of publicity channels, Many dollar-seeking concerns without high ethical standards have attempted to abuse press privileges through coercive or subtle methods to induce newspapers to publish without charge in news columns that which rightly comes under the head of paid advertising. The newspaper editor is hard to find who does not resent such questionable methods on the part of unscrupulous business concerns, and who, conversely, does not welcome news and human interest stories concerning the associations and agencies established not for profit but for the welfare of humanity. Into this classification fall naturally the churches and all their works of mercy, including hospitals, homes for the aged orphanages, and the like. The church has need for news-covering and news-disseminating agencies. It has need for friendly, cordial relationships with those men who are devoting their lives to the great profession of journalism. It has no need whatever for press agents or press agentry.

The sole aims of the News Bureau of the National Lutheran Council in its publicity service to the United Lutheran Church are to further the growing spirit of friendly co-operation which already exists between the press and the Lutheran Church; to provide the newspapers in all parts of the United States and Canada with a reliable source of live and interesting church news, put into their hands while it is news, thereby presenting to newspaper readers a more complete picture of current life than can be secured from the featuring of politics, business, sports, and amusements alone; to see that those events within the Church which have news value are made known to the general public, particularly in so far as they present to newspaper readers a true picture of the high aims and noble purposes of the church; and to serve that true religion may function more fully through the public press in the promotion of true culture, idealism and civilization.

The systematic improvement of the publicity service of the United Lutheran Church may be effected by certain definite measures, to wit:

1. The creation of an efficient publicity committee in every community to supply church news to the local press and to report matters of wider interest to general news agencies;

2. The maintenance of a news bureau by every constituent synod, helpfully articulated with the national Lutheran agency for publicity, for intensive work within its own jurisdiction and for the communication and distribution of news in co-operation with the Council;

3. The even more regular and prompt reportng of news material to the News Bureau of the National Lutheran Council by boards, committees, auxiliary organizations, constituent synods and their news agencies.

Respectfully submitted,
J. A. MOREHEAD, Executive Director.

Resolution No. 1 of the Commissioners' Report was referred to the Finance Committee of the Executive Board. Resolutions 2 and 3 were adopted.

The Convention adjourned with prayer by the Rev. W. I. Guss.

Afternoon Session

Tuesday, October 16, 2.00 o'clock.

Devotions were conducted by the Rev. E. E. Stauffer.

The President called the Convention to order.

Moved and carried, That a vote of thanks be given to the Erie Trust Company for their services in cashing check for transportation.

The Rev. H. Offermann, Chairman of the Committee of Reference and Counsel, presented the following resolution, submitted by the Rev. Paul E. Scherer, and recommended that it be referred to the Executive Board for action:

Whereas, It has been the constant desire of the United Lutheran Church that the separated bodies of Lutherans in America should advance toward an ever larger and more complete expression of the inner unity of their faith, and

Whereas, The United Lutheran Church has declared, "In the case of those Church Bodies calling themselves Evangelical Lutheran, and subscribing the Confessions which have always been regarded as the standards of Evangelical Lutheran doctrine, The United Lutheran Church in America recognizes no doctrinal reasons against complete co-operation and organic union with such bodies,"

Therefore, be it Resolved, That the Executive Board be instructed to appoint a commission of not less than four and not more than six members, to be composed of an equal number of laymen and clergymen, to be known as the Commission on Lutheran Church Unity, which shall have the duty of actively representing the United Lutheran Church in the promotion of Lutheran unification in America; and shall act under the supervision of the Executive Board.

The resolution was so referred.

The Chairman of the Committee also submitted the following resolution offered by Mr. W. H. Stackel:

Resolved, That the Executive Board be requested to prepare and submit to the several Boards of the Church issuing annuity bonds, a two-fold annuity plan, the one of which shall obligate the Board to a fixed amount of interest at a rate approximating the interest earned, and the other to the rates now prevailing and which graduate according to the age of the annuitant.

The resolution was referred to the Executive Board.

The Committee presented the following resolution offered and supported by the Rev. Edwin Heyl Delk:

The United Lutheran Church in America in Convention assembled at Erie, Pa., hereby declares its profound gratitude to Almighty God for the steady advance which is being made towards the realization of a perpetual peace among the nations of the earth. We believe that the material losses of war, the fears engendered, the consequent hatreds and the immeasurable suffering and sorrow resultant from international conflicts make war a devastating calamity for both the victor and vanquished. The voice of ancient prophets, Christian publicists and the Prince of Peace give us assurance of the possibility of abolishing war as a means of settling international disputes. Our Church rejoices in that prospect and declares her faith in the coming of that glad day of perpetual peace and world-wide brotherhood in Jesus Christ.

Resolved, That a copy of this resolution be sent to the President of the United States, the Secretary of State, and the Chairman of the Foreign Relations Committee.

The resolution was referred to the Committee on Moral and Social Welfare.

The Chairman of the Committee introduced the Rev. George W. Brown, Secretary of the American Bible Society. After Dr. Brown's address the Secretary presented the report of the Representative in the Advisory Board of the American Bible Society.

REPORT OF REPRESENTATIVE IN THE ADVISORY BOARD OF THE AMERICAN BIBLE SOCIETY

Your representative in the Advisory Board of the American Bible Society begs leave to submit his fifth biennial report.

The Advisory Board is composed of delegated representatives from twenty-nine Protestant bodies in the United States. Three of these are Lutheran; namely, the Augustana Synod, the United Norwegian, and the United Lutheran Church in America. The Board meets annually at the Bible House, Astor Place, New York City, to consider the recommendations of the secretaries and the treasurer of the Society and to submit its findings to the Board of Managers, with whom it is invited to sit throughout their consideration. Your representative was present at the meetings of the Advisory Board in December, 1926 and 1927.

The American Bible Society which is rounding out the one hundred thirteenth year of its service, is one of the pillars of our American Christianity and one of the great missionary organizations of the world. Its sole object is "to encourage a wider circulation of the Holy Scriptures without note or comment." Its work is three-fold: Translation, publication, distribution. So important has the work of translation become that the senior general secretary, the Rev. Dr. William I. Haven, has been made secretary in charge of versions.

It is the chief business of the American Bible Society to provide annually several millions of volumes of the Scriptures in not less than one hundred and fifty languages and dialects and in sixteen languages and systems of raised type for the blind.

Although the Bible or some part of it has been translated into more than eight hundred languages and dialects much work remains to be done. We have recently learned that in Africa alone there are over eight hundred known languages and dialects. Of these only two hundred and forty-three have any part of the Bible in the spoken language of the people.

Written language is the key to the experience of mankind. In scores of cases the spoken language of a tribe has for the first time been put into writing by the translation of the Bible.

Translation work through the coming year will be done by the Society in two of the American Indian dialects, in Central America, in South, East and Central Africa. Revision in some of the Philippine dialects will also be undertaken. Much of this work is done by the Society as the accredited agency of the leading Protestant churches of this country, thus furnishing the missions with the Scriptures in the spoken language of the people.

5,622,000 copies of the Scriptures, consisting of whole Bibles, Testaments and portions of the Gospel will be needed for distribution next year, in addition to the Scriptures already on hand.

In war-torn China the Bible is asked for as never before. A new Bible House is being built in Peking. Peru is open for the distribution of the Bible. Bibles cannot be sent into Russia but the Society has given plates to Russian Christians from which an edition of 25,000 copies was published. The Bible, for the first time since the Reformation is to be published in France by a secular publishing house, due largely to donations from the American Bible Society.

More than 65,000 copies of the Scriptures were sent, free, to the sufferers in the Mississippi flood. So many requests for Bibles with family record pages were received from these people, that a special edition has been published, to be distributed also without cost.

The budget of the Society for 1928 is $1,345,426. The Society from the beginning has been supported by voluntary contributions. These come in the form of trusts and legacies, the benevolences of the churches, and individual gifts. The Advisory Council was much impressed with the opportunity of the Society and the stubborn limitation of the Society's income. After prolonged discussion and prayer the following resolution, offered by Bishop Darlington of the Protestant Episcopal Church, and seconded by Bishop Denny of the Methodist Episcopal Church, South, was adopted:

Whereas, The Bible is the basis of all Christian work: and Whereas, We believe that all the churches should make official appropriations to the American Bible Society for the wider distribution of the Bible, hailing this opportunity with readiness, knowing that such support is really the strongest aid to their own endeavors in home and foreign lands, and

Whereas, The budget of the American Bible Society for 1928, unanimously approved by the Advisory Council does not begin to cover the opportunity open to the Society, but we cannot suggest that the Society should so enlarge its work as to cumber itself with debt; and

Whereas, We believe that the time has come to set before those who constitute a chief source of income the providential possibilities before the Society, and its present financial status, therefore,

Be it Resolved, That the Board of Managers of the American Bible Society be asked to appeal to the churches of Christ in America for largely increased gifts toward the wider distribution of the Scriptures;

That this appeal be sent out in the name of the Advisory Council in annual session;

That a copy be sent to every representative of the churches in this council, and to all the church press.

Your representative recommends:

That the United Lutheran Church continue its representation in the Advisory Board.

Respectfully submitted,

HERBERT C. ALLEMAN,

Representative of the U. L. C.

The recommendation was adopted.

With the approval of the Committee of Reference and Counsel, the Rev. R. D. Clare presented the following resolution which was adopted:

Whereas, the Church's power and influence in the great centers of population depend upon the statesmanlike leadership of the pastors and congregations now faithfully doing a work not only of local but of nation-wide significance, under the changing conditions of the twentieth century, therefore

Be it Resolved, That the United Lutheran Church in Convention assembled recommend that her churches located in great metropolitan centers should give most serious consideration to the matter of co-ordinating their work by means of larger co-operation, merger, or whatever other method local conditions seem to warrant, in order that in all such centers the highest interests of the Church and of the Kingdom may be effectively promoted.

The Rev. J. F. Ohl presented the report of the Committee on Church Music.

REPORT OF THE COMMITTEE ON CHURCH MUSIC

It is beginning to be felt that many people in the churches have for some reason or reasons lost the sense of worship. To such an extent is this true that other communions, besides our own, now have their committees on church music, charged with the duty of finding a remedy for this condition. The Protestant Episcopal Church has had a Joint Commission on Church Music since 1919, the Presbyterian Church its Commission on Music and Worship since 1925, and the Methodist Episcopal Church, North, its Commission on Music since 1924, reconstituted as the Commission on Worship and Music, effective since May, 1928. All three deplore the fact that worship in many places is not what it should be and make suggestions for its improvement.

In what does worship consist? Is it something external that finds its expression in vestments, processionals, recessionals, and the like? Or is it the outpouring in prayer, praise and thanksgiving of a heart that feels its need, a heart that has tasted God's goodness and mercy, a heart full of gratitude for all of God's gifts, especially for the blessings of redemption? Such a heart will find its fitting medium of expression in the forms of devotion and hymns that have through the ages been the Church's treasures. But amid the cares, and riches, and pleasures of this life not all hearts are thus attuned with the result that words mean little to many. Indeed, there are those to whom the music seems to be the chief thing, and among such the remark has even been made that the words are of no account. But the mere singing of notes is not worship. When Paul said that he wished to sing with the spirit, and *with the understanding* also (I Cor. 14: 15), he certainly had in mind the words and what the words expressed and conveyed. Hence, to worship in spirit and in truth, the words, not only of the hymns but of the entire service, must be given the first attention. The organist must realize what they say that he may properly interpret them in his playing. The choir must have a true appreciation of their contents that it may sing them with due reverence. And the congregation must penetrate into their meaning that its worship may become the real expression of the heart and not a mere formal performance on notes. Possibly, the loss of the sense of worship on the part of the congregation may in a great measure be traced to the failure of many Sunday schools to teach the growing youth how to worship. Hence the question:

WHAT DOES YOUR SUNDAY SCHOOL SING

The Committee offers no apology for again referring to this subject. A survey recently made in our largest synod disclosed the fact that in a considerable number of schools books of the "cheap" hymn and tune variety are still in use; and what is true in this synod the committee knows to be true in other synods. Books of this kind find their way into our schools on the false assumption that children delight only in rollicking rhythms, and that hence there must be a radical difference between hymns and tunes for children and those for adults. But God is not worshiped in jig, and ragtime and jazz. There is neither prayer, praise, nor thanksgiving in teaching children to sing in syncopated measure, "Bright-*en* the cor-*ner* where you are;" or such sentimental slush as "Somewhere, Somewhere, Beautiful Isle of Somewhere, Land of the true, where we live life anew,— Beautiful Isle of Somewhere;" or doggerel like this: "When Jesus makes up His jewels, That nothing from Him can sever, Oh, that I may be chosen to shine in glory forever. He'll gather them sometime, He'll gather them sometime, He'll gather them sometime, The purified spirits sometime." Yet it is just as much the Church's duty to teach children how to worship as it is to teach them what to believe. To the latter unusual attention is given these days. There is a profusion of lessons and lesson helps for both scholars and teachers; and to prepare the latter for their work many teachers' training schools and classes have come into existence. But how much serious attention do Sunday schools give to the devotional side of their work? To what extent are the children taught to express their faith in a well-ordered service, and in genuine hymns and worthy tunes? Is time ever taken to explain the Sunday school or Church service, or to teach the children the meaning of some choice hymn or hymns, many of which should be committed to memory?

We hear much these days about the irreverence of the young, and their unwillingness to come to the services of God's house. But when, as children in the Sunday school, they were taught to sing meaningless rhymes to tunes that remind of the jazz band and set the feet going, is it any wonder that they did not catch the spirit of genuine devotion, and that at a later period they find no pleasure in the sober services of the sanctuary!

What can be done with the children of the Sunday school has in the last year been strikingly demonstrated in Trinity Church, Lancaster, Pa., the Rev. Dr. McIntosh, pastor. The organist, Mr. Harry A. Sykes, taught them to sing the Church service and some of the best hymns and tunes in the Common Service Book. Once a month the school assembles with the adult congregation at the morning service, and joins in the singing. The congregational singing on these Sundays is unexcelled, and so much pleasure does their participation give the children that on the intervening Sundays they come to church in increasing numbers,—a clear proof that when children are taught in the Sunday school what they ought to sing, their devotional life will develop in the right direction, and in later years they will not feel like strangers when they come into the house of God. Therefore, in loyalty to the children and the Church, Sunday schools should use the Church's publications.

SCHOOLS OF CHURCH MUSIC

Though the Committee has done so before it must again direct attention to the subject of connecting departments of church music with our theological seminaries. The need of such schools, in which organists, choir directors, and men preparing for the ministry, can be trained in church music, is increasingly felt in other communions. In the Committee's last report mention was made of the fact that Northwestern University, at Evanston, Ill., a Methodist institution, had received a gift of $100,000 to establish a course in church music in connection with its present School of Music. And now the announcement is made that this fall Union Theological Seminary in New York will open "a school of sacred music to train choirmasters, organists and other leaders in the ministry of music, and teachers of sacred music in schools and colleges." The announcement says further that "it seems desirable that those who are. to lead in church music should be educated in fellowship with men preparing for the Christian ministry, and to some extent in the same classrooms." In this kind of work we Lutherans, with our great traditions and rich heritage, have hardly made a beginning, unless it be in some of the Scandinavian institutions of the middle west. Something is done, of course, in our colleges and seminaries. At Mt. Airy, Dr. Reed includes Church Music in his department, lectures on the history of Church Music and on the Music of the Liturgy and the Hymnal, besides giving attention to the practical training of the students in the proper musical rendering of the services and hymns in the Common Service Book. During the biennium, Mr. Seibert and Mr. Marks of the Committee lectured respectively at Wagner College and Muhlenberg College. The School of Music at Wittenberg College is constantly doing a great deal of practical work. Here the students of the Hamma Divinity School can also take advantage of the instruction offered by the School of Music under the capable direction of Professor Bach. Within the past year Dr. Bach delivered a series of twelve lectures before the students of the Divinity School. In the School of Music very particular attention is given to the training of organists, and a number of former students now occupy positions in Lutheran and other churches. The several choruses and glee clubs also make a study of choral music, and, as a united body, on occasions render sacred works of the masters. Should the present plans for the further development of the School of Music come to full fruition, the Church may yet get at Wittenberg a center of training in church music such as the Committee not only desires there, but in connection with our institutions elsewhere. The Commissions of the Protestant Episcopal and of the Presbyterian Church both stress the need of providing courses in church music in theological seminaries. In all our seminaries we are very careful to guard the faith, but how to express the faith in proper acts of devotion seems to receive only minor attention. Who will be the first in the U. L. C. to establish a department of church music in one of our seminaries?

As bearing indirectly on this subject, Mr. Seibert makes the following observations: "Congregations should encourage their organists to study. Many times the salary of an organist does not warrant an expenditure for lessons. Salaries should be provided to enable the organist to take lessons. The Church receives the direct benefit through a higher state of efficiency on the part of the entire musical organization. The Lutheran organist should read the current musical papers. The organist should use every opportunity to hear good music. He should profit by a close association with his contemporaries in other denominations. Nothing is gained and much is lost by isolating oneself professionally. A low standard of music exists in many Lutheran churches, not because of a lack of familiarity with Lutheran church music or inferiority of programs, but because of conditions which make it impossible to render the music in finished style. The Lutheran Church is rich in its heritage as regards music. No church can boast of such traditions. But these two elements will not by themselves make our music what all of us want it to be. There must be a concerted effort on the part of pastors, congregations, and organists to see that the music is given the proper preparation and that the organist or director has the proper musical equipment and background."

CONVOCATION

Although the Committee is always ready to hold Convocations it regrets to say that during the past biennium it received only one invitation to do so. This came from Baltimore. Locally sponsored by the Ministers' Association, under the leadership of Drs. J. E. Byers and William A. Wade, a very successful and largely attended Convocation was held in Grace Church, February 22, 1927. Two papers, one on "The Church Services and their Music," and the other on "The Music of the Congregational Hymn," were the features of the two-day sessions, and in the evening there was a full Choral Vesper Service based on the Church Year. A large chorus choir, under the direction of Mr. J. W. Scott, with Miss Edith Menkel at the organ, rendered the musical numbers at all the sessions. Besides the local interest manifested, it was very gratifying to the committee to find a goodly representation of the faculty and students of the Gettysburg Theological Seminary in attendance.

But even if the committee was not given the opportunity to hold other Convocations individual members were active in other ways. The chairman and secretary lectured at the Summer Schools of the North Carolina, South Carolina, Georgia, Virginia and Michigan Synods, using the Common Service Book as the basis; Dr. Reed on various occasions spoke to congregations and other groups on the Common Service Book and demonstrated its proper use; Pastor Lantz delivered a series of addresses before a large assembly of Sunday school teachers at Reading, Pa.; Pastor Trabert continued his work of promoting church music on the Pacific coast; and numerous organ recitals were given by professional members of the Committee, especially by Mr. Seibert. All these efforts have no doubt contributed to the understanding of our services, and the improvement of our music.

Three Suggestions

1. Pastors could do much to improve congregational singing by now and then devoting a Sunday evening to hymn singing, prefacing each hymn and its tune with a brief history and analysis of the hymn, and giving such information about the tune as may be available. Unfamiliar tunes should be well prepared by the choir, and after their first use should soon be repeated. Thus congregations can in a short time come to know numerous tunes to which they may now be strangers. In preparing for services of this kind pastors will find the following books helpful:

JOHN JULIAN: *Dictionary of Hymnology,* New York, Scribners.

JAMES T. LIGHTWOOD: *Hymn Tunes and Their Story,* London, Charles H. Kelley.

PETER C. LUTKIN: *Music in the Church,* Milwaukee, Young Churchman Co.

EDWARD DICKINSON: *Music in the History of the Western Church,* New York, Scribners.

2. Families should also make liberal use of the Common Service Book and the Parish School Hymnal in the home. Many families today have one or more members who can play, and an hour or two a week spent around the piano or organ in rehearsing hymns and tunes would be most profitable and aid greatly in promoting congregational singing.

3. To correct the slovenly manner in which the liturgy, service music, hymns and tunes are often rendered at synodical meetings, synods, wherever possible, should appoint a person or persons having the needed knowledge and understanding to make provision for the proper use of the Church's liturgy and music. Every effort should be made to have the services at conventions of synods and conferences representative. They should be liturgically correct and musically adequate. Only if this is the case can

they accomplish their purpose devotionally and be helpful as object lessons to pastors and congregations with little or no training along these lines.

A LOSS

We record with sorrow the death of the Rev. George C. F. Haas, D.D., a valued member of the Committee since its appointment in 1918. Dr. Haas was well and favorably known as a student of hymnology and church music, and was the composer of a number of hymn tunes that are now in use.

The Committee,

J. F. OHL, *Chairman.*

GOMER C. REES, *Secretary.*

The Rev. Luther D. Reed presented the report of the Committee on Church Architecture.

REPORT OF THE COMMITTEE ON CHURCH ARCHITECTURE

Thirty-six meetings of the Committee, attended chiefly by the local members, were held during the biennium. At the organization meeting Dr. Ohl was elected chairman, and Dr. Reed secretary.

With deep regret the Committee reports the death of two of its professional members, George Croll Baum, of Philadelphia, and J. A. Dempwolf, of York, Pa. Mr. Baum was for ten years an active and exceedingly useful member of the Committee, which is deeply sensible of the loss which it has sustained in his death. Many churches, and the fine institutional buildings designed by him for his alma mater, Gettysburg College, and at Roanoke, Va., etc., will long remind the Church not only of his professional ability but of his singularly noble Christian character.

Eighty-seven sets of plans were reviewed by the Committee and reports rendered. These plans came from thirty-three States and Canada. Following is a summary of the opinions given.

PLANS APPROVED AND COMMENDED

The First Church, Albany, N. Y., the Rev. Dr. C. E. Frontz, pastor, Delano and Aldrich, N. Y., architects. The Committee congratulated the congregation upon securing competent architectural service for their important problem, and gave its judgment upon points particularly requested, viz., arrangements for a highly departmentalized school and the matter of architectural style. It expressed the opinion that a congregation whose history reaches into the Colonial period may well consider building in the early American style. It suggested, in the interest of churchly association and feeling, the possible use of a spire instead of a cupola, and a restudy of the arrangement shown for the choir and chancel.

Church of the Nativity, Hampden Heights, Reading, Pa., Ritcher and Eiler. Reading, architects. Plans cordially approved with important suggestions as to wider chancel, proportion of the window openings, etc.

The Church at Durham, N. C., the Rev. J. L. Thornburg, pastor, Northrup and O'Brien, Winston-Salem, N. C., architects. Plans approved and commended for the use of ground and the general proportion and design of the building. Certain minor suggestions were made.

Ebenezer Church, Columbia, S. C., the Rev. P. D. Brown, pastor, Thomas, Martin and Kirkpatrick, Philadelphia, architects. The plans, which call for a Gothic building with an admirable arrangement of the chancel, sacristy, baptistery, etc., in relation to a fine nave, were heartily commended.

Immanuel Church Philadelphia, the Rev. Armin G. Weng, pastor, Thomas, Martin and Kirpatrick, Philadelphia, architects. Plans reviewed by the officers and commended.

Church of the Atonement, Syracuse, N. Y., Frederick R. Lear, architect. Plans which were approved and commended call for a group with the parish house as the first unit. Suggestions as to a more churchly interior in the future church were given.

Christ Church, Upper Darby, Pa., Norman Hulme, Philadelphia, architect. Plans approved and commended, with minor suggestions with references to chancel details and window design in the Sunday school building.

Block plan for a group of buildings and plans for a parish house for the Church of the Ascension, Snyder, N. Y., James W. Kideney, Buffalo, architect, approved and commended.

The First Lutheran Church, Norfolk, Va., the Rev. L. W. Strickler, pastor, C. J. Calrow, Norfolk, architect. Plans approved and commended as a well-planned group with an attractive and churchly effect. Certain minor suggestions were given.

PLANS APPROVED

Kensington Avenue Church, Buffalo, N. Y., C. F. Obenhack, Niagara Falls, architect. Plans approved with minor suggestions concerning architectural details and the organ chamber.

St. Paul's Fourth Church, Spokane, Wash., Mackay and Woodroofe, architects. Plans approved with suggestions concerning lengthening the building to gain better proportion, and restudy of the chancel.

Mt. Lebanon, Pittsburgh, Pa., O. M. Topp, architect. Plans approved, though the Committee recorded its judgment that the unusual design is not as well adapted to church work as a more conventional type would be. Suggestions were also given concerning chancel and choir arrangement.

Luther Memorial, Detroit, Mich., Byron Mills, architect. Completed plans approved with the exception of chancel arrangements.

Plans for a temporary church at Amon Heights, N. J., prepared by Mr. Schnabel, were approved with suggestions concerning the floor plan and numerous details in the chancel.

Sketches for a parish building for the Church of the Resurrection, Irondequoit, N. Y., J. F. Stobel, architect, approved with important reservations as to the wisdom of erecting this type of building and as to whether the best possible use of the lot was made. Suggestions concerning the building itself, and the chancel were also given.

St. John's Church, Monrovia, Calif., Quintin and Kerr, Alhambra, Calif., architects, Frank O. Eager, Monrovia, associate architect. Plans cordially approved with minor suggestions.

Trinity Church, Long Beach, Calif., Quintin and Kerr, Alhambra, Calif., architects. Plans approved with suggestions for chancel and organ details, and for location of the font.

Preliminary sketches for a simple chapel of oak and native stone at Andrews, N. C., A. C. Messerschmidt, Richmond, Va., architect, approved with minor suggestions.

Plans for enlarging the Church of the Atonement, Racine, Wis., Hugo C. Haeuser, Milwaukee, architect, approved with various suggestions, the Committee appreciating the difficulty of the problem confronting the architect.

Trinity Church, Runnemede, N. J., J. Herbert Rodey, Collingswood, architect. Plans approved, except that the congregation was advised against building a basement Sunday school.

Of two plans for Calvary Church, West Chester, Pa., by Norman Hulme, Philadelphia, architect, one was approved with minor suggestions.

Plans for Temple Church, Delaware Gardens, N. J., Sundt, Wenner and Stewart, architects, approved.

Plans for Calvary Church, Louisville, Ky., Saunders and Wenedell, Louisville, architects, approved in general with suggestions for lengthening the nave.

Church of the Resurrection, St. Albans, L. I., Cherry and Matz, New York, architects. Plans approved with an expression of regret that no more ground was available to prevent crowding when the group is completed.

Plans for proposed rebuilding of St. John's Church, Anderson, Ind., A. Honeywell, Indianapolis, architect, approved in general with important recommendations concerning chancel and choir arrangements, etc.

St. John's Church, Great Falls, Mont., Bird and Van Tegligen, architects. Plans approved with important suggestions concerning the proportions of the building, depth of the chancel, entrance hall, window designs, etc.

Plans for the first unit of the Sunday school building for the Church of the Advocate, West Lawn, Reading, Ritcher and Eiler, Reading, architects, approved with suggestions concerning improvement in proportions, size of window openings, etc.

Plans for a new plant for the Church of the Redeemer, Queens Village, L. I., George Alexander, Brooklyn, architect, approved with suggestions concerning entrances to the parish building, improvements in the chancel arrangement and seating arrangements in the gallery.

Zion Church, Greensburg, Pa., J. C. Fulton and Son, Uniontown, architects. Plans approved with suggestions that the tower be redesigned so as to be given greater importance and impressiveness, or else that it be eliminated entirely. Other minor suggestions were also made.

Plans for the remodeling of a dwelling for temporary use by the Church of the Saviour, Jamaica, N. Y., Louis Allmendinger, architect, approved as a temporary measure.

Plans for extensive alterations to Emmanuel Church, Souderton, Pa., O. M. Talley, Telford, architect, cordially approved.

Plans for Honterus (Siebenberger) Church, at Gary, Ind., Iver-Viehe-Naess and Co., Chicago, architects, approved with certain suggestions, though the Committee regretted that, because of cost, it was not possible to secure a more attractive building.

Preliminary plans for Pentecost Church, Milwaukee, H. C. Haeuser, architect, approved as to exterior elevations. Suggestions concerning the interior, particularly the chancel and choir arrangements, were given. Revised plans received important suggestions concerning relation of the two units in the plan, proportion and other fundamental features. Later revisions approved.

Revised plans for Trinity Church, Kingsport, Tenn., and Grace Church, Boone, N. C., H. C. Messerschmidt, Richmond, Va., architect, approved.

Final floor plans and elevations for the Church of St. John the Baptist (Slovak), Camden, N. J., the office of George C. Baum, Philadelphia, architect, approved.

Trinity Church, Denver, Col. (Barnitz Memorial), Huntington Architecture Company, R. O. Perry, associate. Plans approved as a satisfactory solution of a difficult problem. Suggestions concerning wider chancel and additional exits were given.

St. John's (Siebenberger Church), Farrell, Pa., O. M. Topp, Pittsburgh, architect. Plans approved with suggestions concerning chancel details, stairways, etc.

Trinity Church, Clairton, Pa., O. M. Topp, Pittsburgh, architect. Plans approved with suggestions concerning treatment of elevations as well as location of choir and organ.

St. Paul's Church, Lansdowne, Carl B. Berger, Philadelphia, architect.

Suggestions were given for restudy, particularly in the arrangement of the chancel, the treatment of tower, vestibule, etc. Revised plans approved with minor suggestions.

Church of Our Redeemer, Baltimore, J. Freund, Baltimore, architect. Plans approved with minor suggestions.

Preliminary drawings for the Church of the Incarnation, Washington, D. C., Ritcher and Eiler, Reading, architects, approved, the Committee expressing regret at the unfortunate proportion of the nave, due to the limitations of the lot. The addition of another bay to the nave was urged.

St. Stephen's Church, Chicago, Elmer T. Behrens, Chicago, architect. Plans approved, with suggestions concerning treatment of roof lines and windows on the side elevations, stairways and organ location.

Trinity Church, Niles, Ohio, Zenk and Campbell, Youngstown, Ohio architects. Plans approved with important suggestions concerning fundamental features of design and details of arrangement.

Christ Church Beaver Falls, Pa., J. E. Martsolf, New Brighton, architect. Plans approved with minor suggestions arising from topographical conditions.

Floor plans for a simple stucco building for Daytona Beach, Fla., Espedahl and Espedahl, architects, approved with suggestions concerning treatment of the elevations with the possible use of the Spanish mission style, etc.

Epiphany Church, Pittsburgh, Pa., John Lewis Beatty, architect. Plans approved with suggestions for restudy of the front elevation, treatment of the basement windows and the organ space.

Alternate plans for the completion of Luther Memorial Church, Philadelphia, Norman Hulme, architect, were considered. The Committee advised the adoption of the one which would develop the original clerestory plan.

Plans for the proposed group of buildings for St. John's Church, Westville, N. J., prepared by Messrs. Emmert and Early, of George C. Baum's office, Philadelphia, approved with the suggestion that the church and the parish building would both gain if the parsonage would not be built on the same plot.

St. John's Church, Brooklyn, Baltimore, Md., Alfred Cookman Leach, Baltimore, architect. Plans approved with suggestions concerning design of tower and main entrance and interior trusses.

Plans for Sunday school building for Calvary Church, Laureldale, Pa., Schull and Richardson, architects, approved, with suggestions as to exterior elevations. Attention was also called to defects in the floor plan of the future church buiding.

St. Luke's Church, Saxonburg, Pa., Arthur N. Steinmark, Pittsburgh, architect. Plans reviewed by the officers of the Committee and approved.

Augsburg Church, Detroit, Mich., S. H. Spier, architect. Block plans, floor plan and perspective drawing approved with minor suggestions concerning material and details of design.

PLANS NOT APPROVED

Christ Church, Little Neck, L. I., George W. Reynolds, Freeport, N. Y., architect. Plans for a chapel not approved as deficient in architectural and churchly character.

Calvary Church, Natrona Heights, Pa., P. R. L. Hogener, New Kensington, Pa., architect. The mission was cautioned in the matter of expense, as the plans called for a clerestory type of building with tower. Suggestions were also given for redesigning the chancel, A new set of plans by O. M. Topp, Pittsburgh, architect, was approved with minor suggestions.

St. John's Church, Monrovia, Calif., Frank O. Eager, Monrovia, architect. Revised plans not approved as deficient in churchly design. The congregation was advised to secure the services of an architect whose experience in church work would assure them of a satisfactory building. Plans subsequently prepared by Quintin and Kerr, Alhambra, Calif., were cordially approved.

Plans for a portable chapel by the American Portable House Company, Seattle, for St. Paul's Church, Teaneck, N. J., were not approved, the Committee's judgment being that a portable building is only suitable as a temporary structure. Other plans by Thomas Dunn, and sketches by H. E. Tingen, New York, architects, were not regarded as satisfactory. Plans subsequently prepared by Cherry and Matz, New York, were cordially approved, but the congregation was not able to build from these because of expense. The Committee's approval was finally given to an adaptation of a stock plan, which provides a simple frame building of a temporary nature.

Sketch for proposed hall for Calvary Community Church, Bronx, N. Y., not approved as not prepared by a qualified architect.

Holy Trinity Church, Kingsport, Tenn., and Grace Church, Boone, N. C., H. C. Messerschmidt, Richmond, Va., architect. Sketches not approved as being incomplete, showing a confusion of styles, and inadequate chancel arrangements. Revised plans were cordially approved with minor suggestions.

Bethany Church, Baltimore, Md., John Freund, Baltimore, architect. Plans not approved as faulty in floor plan and in elevation. The Committee recommended a restudy.

Plans for temporary mission chapel at Wilkinsburg Manor, Pa., O. M. Topp, Pittsburgh, architect, not approved, the Committee expressing the judgment that the architect, whom it knows to be thoroughly competent, had been given an impossible problem. A square building with the Sunday school on one side of the auditorium and opening into it, cannot receive churchly treatment. A restudy was advised.

Plans for a Parish Hall for Calvary Church, Pelham Park, Bronx, N. Y., Joseph L. Kling, Bronx, architect, not approved, as deficient in architectural and churchly character.

Plans for Trinity Church, Kalamazoo, Mich., A. H. Ellwood and Son, Elkhart, Ind., architects, not approved as deficient in floor plan and exterior design. The congregation was urged not to employ frame construction with brick veneer for a building of this importance, but to build solid masonry walls. Revised plans later submitted, were approved.

Plans for the first unit of Bethany Church, Toledo, Ohio, R. C. Gotwald, Springfield, architect, were criticized unfavorably with respect to proportions, choir and organ provision, etc. Revised plans were also not deemed satisfactory in point of architectural and ecclesiastical character.

Plans for school and parish building, Wellesley, Ont., W. H. E. Schmalz, architect, were considered and a suggestion made that the building be redesigned along simpler lines, so as to get better results for the money expended.

Christ Church, Bywood, Philadelphia, Norman Hulme, Philadelphia, architect. Plans for a church were returned with request that they be tradictory. A conference was subsequently held with the mission superintendent, the pastor and representatives of the architect, and the Committee recommended the purchase of a new site or the retention of fiften feet in their present holdings in order to provide an adequate chancel.

Plans for the parish house of the Church of the Atonement, Syracuse, N. Y., Gustave Giersberg, designer, not approved as not indicating an adequate study of the plot, and as not providing a churchly building.

St. John's Church, Hollywood, Fla., D. Anderson Dickey, Hollywood, architect. Plans not approved as incomplete and in various respects conrestudied in order to secure greater harmony of style and an improvement in plan and exterior elevations.

Preliminary sketches for St. Luke's Church, Bloomington, Minn., returned as inadequate and incomplete. Subsequent unsigned plans were returned with the recommendation that the congregation employ an architect qualified in church design.

Plans for the First Church, Nashville, Tenn., Asmus and Clark, architects, approved so far as general proportions of the church and Sunday school building were concerned, but a restudy was requested with reference to chancel design and exterior elevations.

Plans for a chapel at Somer's Point, N. J., Norman Hulme, Philadelphia, architect, not approved, the Committee suggesting a treatment more in conformity with Mr. Hulme's design for Calvary Church, West Chester. Revised plans were subsequently approved.

Fragmentary plans for a church building, the name of congregation and place not indicated, Daniel Dickey, Hollywood, Fla., architect, were reviewed and suggestions given as to improvement in the design.

Plans for the First Hungarian Church, Akron, Ohio, N. P. Lauer, Akron, architect, not approved as deficient in ecclesiastical design. Various suggestions were given.

Plans for a new building for girls at Bethesda Home, Meadville, Pa., were returned as inadequate, having evidently been prepared by one without even elementary architectural knowledge.

Plans for the first unit of a building for the Church of the Incarnation, Columbia, S. C., Lafaye and Lafaye, Columbia, architects, were not approved because of great confusion of style, though fairly satisfactory in some other respects. A restudy was requested, and revised plans were regarded as considerably improved.

Plans for Grace Church, Phoenix, Ariz., V. L. Wallingford, architect, were returned for restudy because of unsatisfactory proportion and design, particularly in the window openings and other details. Revised plans were approved.

Unsigned plans for Central Church, Mason City, Ia., were returned with the advice that an architect familiar with church design and the requirements of a liturgical church, be secured. Later plans by J. S. Bartley, Waterloo, Ia., architect, were considered with appreciation of the study that had been made, particularly of engineering problems, and of a fine perspective drawing. The floor plans were not approved, however, as not in agreement with the perspective, and as lacking simplicity and churchly feeling.

Floor plans for St. Matthew's Church, Welland, Ont., were approved with the exception of a diagonal main entrance and the elevations, which showed a confusion of domestic and nondescript features. A new set of plans by Norman A. Kearns, architect, was later approved.

Plans for the Second Church, Schenectady, N. Y., N. W. Krause, builder, were not approved as deficient in architectural and churchly quality. Other plans for a simple frame building, prepared by Cherry and Matz, were approved with suggestions concerning chancel arrangement.

Plans for the mission at Willmette, Ill., Chester Stack, architect, were not approved as deficient in proportion, design and chancel arrangement. Feeling that the expenditure of $85,000 for a building of this character would be most unwise, the Committee suggested a restudy with possible help of an associate architect familiar with good church design.

Plans for a church plant for St. Luke's Church, Park Ridge, Ill., were considered, and while the grouping in general was approved, further study of details was advised.

Plans for a chapel for Trinity mission, Clark's Summit, Pa., were returned with the suggestion that an architect qualified by training and experience to design a churchly edifice be secured.

OTHER OPINIONS RENDERED

The counsel of the Committee was sought in a number of other projects, some of which were of unusual importance.

In response to a request from the Rev. John H. Harms, D.D., president of the Board of the Lutheran Woman's College, Washington, D. C., for suggestions as to the best method of procedure in securing plans for its proposed group of buildings, the Committee submitted recommendations.

Plans for the Church of the Redeemer, Brooklyn, N. Y., prepared by the Goodhue Associates, N. Y., architects, were considered. The Committee expressed its high appreciation of the drawings which indicate a building of unusual and attractive character, fine in line and proportion. The Committee expressed its regret at the limitations imposed upon the architects by the congregation, which insisted upon the use of circular pews taken from the former church, and upon a location for the choir facing the congregation. The congregation was urged to leave the architects, who are capable of producing results of the highest order, free to design a building of real distinction which would meet with unqualified approval and be a model and inspiration for others. Suggestions were also given concerning different arrangement of the chancel and the choir if the general plan was not modified.

The Rev. W. Otterbein, pastor of North Austin Church, Chicago, met with the Committee to discuss plans for enlarging their present church building, or otherwise providing for the rapidly growing congregation which now numbers 1,900. Plans for enlarging by Iver-Viehe-Naess and Co., Chicago, architects, which provides for doubling the seating, but proposed two chancels with an altar in each, with a pulpit platform between the chancels, were not regarded favorably, and the Committee advised against their adoption. The Committee suggested three propositions: First, that the congregation consider dividing and building an entirely new church for part of its membership; second, that the present building be remodeled as a parish house and a new church building erected adjacent; third, that the present building be torn down and a larger building erected with its axis at right angles to the present edifice. The congregation was also urged to prepare a block plan of the property and adjacent ground as the first step in any new work.

The judgment of the Committee was requested upon plans for a new church building for St. Luke's Church, Reading, the Rev. W. A. Fluck, pastor, Ritcher and Eiler, Reading, architects. The plans called for a large Gothic building seating approximately 1,200, to be built on an almost square lot immediately adjoining the present church building, which is to be remodeled for Sunday school and parish work. The Committee suggested a restudy, believing that the proportions of the almost square building proposed would not lend themselves to good treatment in the Gothic style. The exterior suggests a building with aisles and clerestory, but the absence of supporting columns within suggests a hall-type of interior rather than a churchly effect. The close proximity of the new building to the old was also felt to be a disadvantage to both in respect to light and air and exterior grouping. The possibility of using both lots for the erection of a new building of better proportions, and at right angles to the present church, was suggested for consideration.

The Rev. Henry L. Gerstmyer, with members of his church council, and Mr. John Freund, architect, of Baltimore, conferred with the Committee concerning plans for Bethany Church, Baltimore, Md. The congregation was advised to purchase additional ground so as to secure a building of different proportions if possible, or to redesign the building in another style.

CONFERENCES AND CORRESPONDENCE

The chairman and the secretary personally held a number of conferences with pastors, and architects. The secretary, upon invitation, visited a dozen or more different places to meet building committees and discuss plans. An extensive correspondence was conducted with pastors, architects and others in twenty-eight States and Canada; the chairman reporting letters from ninety-two persons and the secretary letters from 161 persons.

The Rev. George H. Schnur, D.D., counselled with a number of pastors and building committees in the Pittsburgh Synod, and lectured on "Church Architecture" to the student body of Hamma Divinity School. The Rev. E. A. Trabert performed a similar service in conferring with representatives of congregations on the Pacific Coast and advising them concerning building programs.

The secretary and Prof. Krauss represented the Committee at a meeting of executives of the Bureaus of Architecture of the different churches with the Committee of the Home Missions Council, in Chicago, October 5 and 6, 1927. Eleven church agencies were represented and about forty architects were in attendance. The general tendency toward churchly types of building and the emphasis upon parish buildings, adapted particularly to the work of religious education, were pronounced features of the conference.

ANALYSIS OF REPORTS RENDERED

Eighty-seven sets of plans were reviewed by the Committee and constructive criticisms given. Fifty-four plans were approved and nine of these received special commendation. Twenty-nine plans were not approved. Counsel as to fundamental considerations was given in four other cases.

A conservative estimate by the secretary of the Committee indicates that the cost represented by these plans exceeds $4,500,000. It is probable that building projects representing an equal amount were initiated by congregations and institutions which did not consult the Committee. The contemplated expenditure of this large sum of nearly $10,000,000 during the biennium, suggests the question as to whether the Church is receiving full architectural and churchly values for the investments made. The experience of the Committee indicates that it is not.

The fifty-four plans approved represent approximately three-fourths of the total expenditure proposed. But only nine of these were regarded as of sufficient excellence to merit special commendation. The twenty-nine plans not approved represent more than $1,000,000 in estimated cost, and were for the most part for mission congregations. As a rule, these plans were quite deficient not only in churchly character, but in qualities of good architectural design and construction. Many of them were not prepared by professionally trained architects familiar with present-day standards, but by draftsmen or builders whose services had been sought in the interest of a false economy. The best interests of the local congregation and of the Church at large cannot be served by the erection in any community of church buildings whose crude proportions, unchurchly arrangement and poor construction express lack of knowledge, poor taste and deficiency in church consciousness.

The large number of plans approved but not commended should also be noted. These represent approximately $2,000,000 in estimated cost, more than twice the amount of the plans commended. In other words, if all the plans submitted were executed, the Church would receive utterly unsatisfactory values for twenty-five per cent, passable values for fifty per cent, and really good values for only twenty-five per cent of its money expended. This would be regarded as most unsatisfactory in any other sphere, and the Church should so regard it in the matter of its Church Architecture.

The difficulty is not primarily a question of money. Most frequently it is a question of architectural service. The most important question which confronts those intending to build is the choice of an architect. The Committee cannot urge too strongly the fundamental importance of securing architects whose training and experience have been of the highest order, and whose gifts and sympathies also qualify them to do church work of superior excellence. A congregation with $100,000 to spend, for example, can secure a church building of charm and distinction if it employs the right architect. Another congregation may spend an equal amount and secure a building of equal size, but one utterly commonplace and unimpressive if a less able man be employed.

The fact is not generally appreciated that the number of thoroughly equipped architects capable of producing church work of distinction, while constantly increasing throughout the country, is still very limited. Our largest cities, with dozens of practicing architects, often have but one or two each, qualified to do church work of excellence. Sometimes, indeed, there are none such. Our schools of architecture, fine as many of them are, frequently give but slight attention to this special field. Architects themselves are usually, and quite naturally, absorbed in the mass of general work which crowds their offices,—commercial, domestic, industrial, institutional and civic projects of all sorts. Only an unusual type of man, with rather rare sympathies and gifts, is attracted by the less remunerative and much more difficult work represented in the distinctively ecclesiastical field.

The first mistake of our congregations, therefore, generally arises from lack of information or of poor judgment which keeps them from securing the highest type of architectural service. Real improvement will only come when mission superintendents and congregations realize the necessity of securing qualified architects even for the simplest mission buildings, and when all our pastors and congregations realize the importance of securing only the ablest architects, with ample experience in church work, for their particular problems.

The second mistake is often that of hampering the architect by impossible conditions or insufficient funds. A lot that is too small, or that is poorly proportioned, can make the erection of a really good building impossible. Frequently too much in the way of size or capacity is demanded for the money provided. Often the funds are barely sufficient for the plainest type of building of the cheapest materials, and even the ablest architect is prevented from securing effective treatment of masses or interesting detail. Our people, who are constantly spending increasing amounts for comfortable homes, food, clothing, automobiles, amusements and travel, must come forward with larger offerings for the Lord's work also if we are to have worthy and beautiful church buildings.

There must be a more general recognition of the vastly higher standards now prevailing in Church Architecture. National prosperity and increased church activity, combined with the general advance in standards of living and a heightened appreciation of the beautiful and the churchly, have raised these standards enormously in the past decade or two. Our congregations must realize not only the inadequacy of present commonplace, unattractive and unchurchly buildings, but if they plan to build they must meet new requirements in special fields, e. g., religious education, as well as higher standards of quality and taste in general. The ablest architects in the land cannot produce creditable work under impossible conditions. They must have adequate ground, sufficient funds, and a certain freedom if they are to achieve success.

The innermost strength of the Church is not in brick and stone, but adequate and attractive church buildings are exceedingly important factors in enabling the Church to do its best work and exert its widest possible influence, and the Church must be willing to pay for the value it hopes to receive.

Courses in Church Architecture in Our Seminaries

Because of the great importance of the subject in the devotional and practical life of the Church, and because of the spiritual as well as the financial values involved, the Committee urges the desirability of having all our Theological Seminaries make provision for instruction of our future ministers in at least the fundamentals of good church building. So far as the Committee knows, but one of our Seminaries regularly gives a prescribed course of any extent in the history of church architecture and its practical problems, with lantern illustrations, collateral readings, study of plans, and visits to representative buildings.

The Committee would also bring to the attention of Synods and Conferences the desirability of placing the subject of Church Architecture upon the programs, with someone well qualified to present the topic.

Publications

"Practical Suggestions for Building Committees." The Committee reprinted this pamphlet and distributed hundreds of copies.

"Church Principles in Church Architecture." This is a twenty-page pamphlet prepared by the Secretary, Dr. Reed, and now in its third printing.

"Space Requirements for Church Organs." This is a valuable statement prepared by the Chairman, Dr. Ohl, in collaboration with representatives of one of the large organ building companies.

"Architectural Leaflets." This is a series of attractive four-page folders. Each number contains cuts of successful church buildings of modest size and cost, with descriptive write-up. Four such leaflets have already been published, and the Committee hopes that the illustrations and descriptions will be suggestive not only to pastors and building committees, but to architects as well, particularly in acquainting them with the liturgical requirements of the Lutheran Church.

A Bureau of Architecture Proposed

The Committee on Church Architecture is the Church's agency for bringing the ideals and the experience of the whole Church to bear helpfully upon the building problems of local congregations. The Committee is constantly ready to advise pastors and committees on projects within its field so far as physical conditions permit. It will suggest names of capable architects in different sections; from them the local congregation may make a final choice. It meets frequently to review plans and submit constructive criticisms and suggestions. Its literature is available free of cost for all who desire it.

It would seem that these activities represent about all that it is possible for the Committee to undertake under its present plan of organization.

There are many other things which would be of great service to the Church if they could be inaugurated and effectively pushed. To develop and supervise them would require the entire time of a capable man, the establishment of an office, and the employment of at least one or more assistants.

The Committee has given considerable attention to the work of the Architectural Bureaus of other churches. Some of these are thoroughly organized with a director, a consulting architect, and a staff of a dozen or more. They are maintained partly by appropriations from the respective church bodies, and partly by fees from the congregations assisted. They render a great deal of service gratis, such as consultation, reviewing plans, dissemination of literature, etc., much as our Committee has been doing. They are able, however, to offer constructive and practical assistance which we cannot attempt.

Thus they send capable representatives to advise with pastors and building committees on the field. They also undertake the actual preparation of preliminary plans, and even of working drawings, at moderate cost for those who desire this. Particularly in the case of mission congregations their work is most helpful. Frequently without cost to the mission, they give it the benefit of expert opinion on the important questions arising out of local conditions in the formative stages of mission development. They are also often able to make preliminary studies and give suggestions of great value to independent congregations and to local architects who actually design the buildings, the cost of this service being deducted, by consent of the architects, from the regular fees paid them by the congregations. Altogether these agencies are elevating the standards of church building in their respective communions immeasurably.

Your Committee is convinced that the United Lutheran Church should take steps looking toward the establishment of a Bureau of Architecture to continue and further develop the work of its present Committee on Architecture.

We therefore recommend:

1. That the Committee on Church Architecture be authorized to make a thorough study of the advisability of creating a Bureau of Architecture and, if such a Bureau be decided upon, to present plans to the Executive Board for the establishment of the same January 1, 1930.

2. That the Executive Board be authorized to act upon the report of the Committee, and, if it approve the same, to put the new arrangement into effect as of January 1, 1930, and to finance the work of the Bureau by an appropriation not exceeding $8,500 per year for the first biennium.

Respectfully submitted,

LUTHER D. REED, *Secretary.*
J. F. OHL, *Chairman.*

The recommendations of the Committee were adopted.

The Rev. George H. Schnur presented the report of the Statistical and Church Year Book Committee and introduced the Rev. George Linn Kieffer, Statistical Secretary, who addressed the Convention.

REPORT OF THE STATISTICAL AND CHURCH YEAR BOOK COMMITTEE

STATISTICAL SECRETARIES OF THE CONSTITUENT SYNODS

THE BIENNIAL STATISTICAL CONFERENCE

The Statistical and Church Year Book Committee of the United Lutheran Church in America, during the biennium 1927-28, throughout all of their work have had the co-operation of the Statistical Secretaries of the Constituent Synods of the United Lutheran Church in America.

At the Conference of the Statistical Secretaries of the United Lutheran Church, held, at the time of the United Lutheran Church Convention, in Richmond, October 23, 1926, representatives from twenty-three synods were present.

At this Conference the following subjects were discussed: Systems of Parish Records, Report of the State of the Church Blank, local congregational auxiliary blanks, the Standard Assembly Sheet, the Standard Parochial Report Blank, problems of the different synods, such as found in the New York Ministerium, in the Ohio Synod, the Alleghany Synod, Nebraska Synod, Wartburg Synod, and the Synod of the Northwest. In general these problems were non-reporting congregations; under reporting of membership (one pastor reporting only half of the membership he reported in his parish paper); over emphasis of "Otherwise Losses"; the difference between the benevolence as reported by the pastor and the benevolence as reported by the synodical treasurer, and the problem of different fiscal years. Even two additional rubrics for the Standard Parochial Blank were suggested by the Conference of Statistical Secretaries at Richmond, namely, the "Largest Communion" and the "Average Attendance."

The Conference had the privilege of seeing the original Joshua Kocherthal record of baptisms, marriages, deaths, etc.; the record of the West Camp Church, 1709-1729, the translation of which has since appeared in the "Lutheran Quarterly," beginning January, 1927.

Each member present at the Conference received a copy of Dr. Carroll's statistics of the churches for the year 1925 as well as his article summarizing the religious statistics covering the period of twenty-five years, 1900-1925.

The Chairman of the Committee, Dr. George H. Schnur, explained the use of the "Parish Register" and Mr. H. E. Pugh, a member of the Statistical and Church Year Book Committee, presented the proposed simplified Standard Parochial Blank which was adopted by the Conference of Statistical Secretaries.

The use of the Standard Assembly Sheet and the system of Standard Record Cards by the Statistical Secretaries was explained by the Statistical Secretary, Rev. G. L. Kieffer, at which time he also emphasized the necessity of the use of the Standard Parish Register, and the method of classifying the congregations as to urban and rural according to the standards of the U. S. Bureau of Census. He also explained the method of taking the 1926 Religious Census and urged the help of the Statistical Secretaries in bringing out the co-operation of all of the pastors of the United Lutheran Church in America.

A motion was passed by the Conference requesting the Statistical and Church Year Book Committee of the United Lutheran Church to confer with the United Lutheran Church officers in order to arrange for a more suitable time for the biennial Statistical Conference at the next United Lutheran Church Convention at Erie, Pa., in order that more time and opportunity would be given for the benefit of the Statistical Secretaries of the Constituent Synods of the United Lutheran Church in America.

Among the men who attended the Statistical Conference who were not statistical secretaries during the biennium, 1925-26, were, from the Pennsylvania Ministerium, Rev. Roy L. Winters; from New York Ministerium, Secretaries Rev. F. R. Noeldeke and Rev. H. C. Freimuth and the Rev. H. B. Dickert; from the West Pennsylvania Synod, the treasurer, Rev. E. C. Ruby, D.D.; from the Georgia Synod, Treasurer Dr. R. L. Gnann; California Synod, Dr. Jesse W. Ball, Ph.D.; from the Northwest Synod, Rev. C. C. Roth; from the Pacific Synod, Mr. H. H. Petershagen.

The following constituent synods were represented by their statistical secretaries: Pennsylvania Ministerium, West Pennsylvania, Virginia, New York, Ohio, East Pennsylvania, Alleghany, Pittsburgh, Illinois, Texas, Susquehanna, Synod of Central Pennsylvania, Iowa, Michigan, Canada, Kansas, Nebraska, New York and New England, and West Virginia. The statistical secretaries of the following synods were not present: New York Ministerium, North Carolina, Maryland (on account of illness), South Carolina, Indiana, Mississippi, Wartburg, German Nebraska, California, Rocky Mountain, Northwest, Manitoba, Pacific, Nova Scotia, Slovak Zion, although some of these synods were represented by other men.

Another such Conference has been arranged to be held at the time of the United Lutheran Church Convention at Erie, Pennsylvania. Announcement of place and time will be made later.

These Conferences, which have now been held at the time of the Buffalo, Chicago, and Richmond Conventions, have proven most valuable. The fullest conformity to the standards have naturally resulted in the synods that were represented at these conferences.

LIST OF STATISTICAL SECRETARIES

The following served as Statistical Secretaries of the Constituent Synods of the United Lutheran Church in America, during the biennium, 1927-28:

	1927	1928
Ministerium of Pa.	Rev. Ira F. Frankenfield	Rev. Ira F. Frankenfield
Ministerium of N. Y.	Rev. B. Mehrtens	Rev. Geo. R. F. Tamke
United Synod of N. C.	Rev. E. H. Kohn, Ph.D.	Rev. E. H. Kohn, Ph.D.
Synod of Maryland	Rev. W. G. Minnick	Rev. W. G. Minnick
Synod of S. Carolina	Rev. H. S. Petrea	Rev. H. S. Petrea
Synod of West Pa.	Rev. D. S. Martin	Rev. D. S. Martin
Synod of Virginia	Mr. Harry E. Pugh, 105 Lancaster Rd., Richmond, Va.	Mr. Harry E. Pugh
Synod of N. Y.	Rev. A. L. Dillenbeck	Rev. A. L. Dillenbeck
Synod of Ohio	Mr. Armor W. Ulrici, 3747 Elsmere Ave., Cincinnati, Ohio	Mr. Armor W. Ulrici
East Pa. Synod	Rev. J. D. Krout	Rev. J. D. Krout
Alleghany Synod	Rev. C. P. Bastian	Rev. C. P. Bastian
Pittsburgh Synod	Rev. Geo. H. Schnur	Rev. Geo. H. Schnur
Indiana Synod	Mr. H. D. C. Loemker, 2151 Emerson Ave., Louisville, Ky.	Mr. H. D. C. Loemker
Illinois Synod	Mr. Frederick Sachse, 1523 Edgewater Ave., Chicago, Ill.	Mr. Frederick Sachse
Texas Synod	Rev. Paul C. Kuehner	Rev. F. F. Eberhardt
Susquehanna Synod of Central Pa.	Rev. C. S. Bottiger	Rev. C. S. Bottiger
Mississippi Synod	Rev. E. K. Counts	Rev. E. K. Counts
Synod of Iowa	Rev. Leland H. Lesher	Rev. Leland H. Lesher
Michigan Synod	Rev. Alvah K. Jones	Rev. Alvah K. Jones
Synod of Georgia	Rev. E. B. Keisler	Mr. W. B. Clarke, Blun Bldg., Savannah, Ga. Mr. D. E. Wilson, 324 W. Shadowlawn Ave., Atlanta, Ga.
Synod of Canada	Rev. O. Stockmann	Rev. O. Stockmann
Synod of Kansas	Rev. A. L. Groseclose	Rev. A. L. Groseclose
Synod of Nebraska	Rev. J. C. Hershey	Rev. J. C. Hershey
Wartburg Synod	Rev. H. R. Pontow	Rev. H. R. Pontow
German Nebraska Synod.	Rev. P. Waldschmidt	Rev. P. Waldschmidt
Synod of California	Rev. John E. Hoick	Rev. John E. Hoick
Rocky Mt. Synod	Rev. C L. Ramme	Rev. C. L. Ramme
Synod of the Northwest.	Rev. L. F. Gruber	Rev. D. E. Bosserman
Manitoba Synod	Rev. G. A. Heimann	Rev. G. A. Heimann
Pacific Synod	Rev. F. T. Lucas	Rev. F. T. Lucas
N. Y. and N. E.	Rev. Clarence L. Braun.	Rev. Clarence L. Braun
Nova Scotia Synod	Rev. G. P. Endy	Rev. G. P. Endy
Synod of West Virginia	Rev. C. E. Butler	Rev. C. E. Butler
Slovak "Zion" Synod	Rev. Andrew Balaska	Rev. Andrew B. Svasko

Granted time brings some changes, yet changes in the personnel in this specialized field, when such changes can be avoided, must be regretted as the statistical work requires a certain bent of mind and should carry with it preparation in the way of technical study and experience of years. Perhaps not sufficient emphasis has been placed upon these requirements.

PRINTED MINUTES: PROGRESS IN UNIFORMITY AND STANDARDIZATION

The latest Minutes available, 1928 (1927), of the thirty-four constituent synods of the United Lutheran Church showed a remarkable progress in uniformity and the meeting of the requirements of standardization. Most of the synods having forty-one congregations met the standard of forty-one lines to the page. A few are below and thus increase their number of pages; and a number exceed the forty-one lines and thus decrease their number of pages.

With the exception of Manitoba and Slovak Zion, who do not use the Standard Parochial Blank in their Minutes, all but two synods, Texas and Alleghany, print totals for their entire synod. Again excepting Manitoba and Slovak Zion, all of the synods but seven, New York Ministerium, North Carolina, Alleghany, Texas, Wartburg, Northwest, and Nova Scotia, insert comparisons with previous years, in their tables. Again excepting Manitoba and Slovak Zion, all of the synods but five have their tables printed with the rubrics covering but two pages. Indiana uses three pages, Texas three, and Wartburg four. The Wartburg Synod prints the rubrics across the narrow width of the page and not lengthwise. Nova Scotia and the New York Ministerium use inserts. All the rest of the synods with the exception of the two that do not conform, Manitoba and Slovak Zion, print their rubrics lengthwise across the page. Two synods use inserts, namely, Nova Scotia and the New York Ministerium, printing their Parochial Report on a large separate sheet and pasting the sheet into the minutes. Two of the synods use a form smaller than six by nine for the printing of their minutes. These are Kansas and Nova Scotia. One of the synods, German Nebraska, uses a form larger than six by nine. There has been marked progress in the size of the minutes and all of the synods now have printed minutes. However, too much paper is used for the printing of the minutes; the margins are too large with the consequent increase in the number of pages, waste of postage, and cost of printing. A table showing the uniformity in size and printing of the Minutes of the Constituent Synods of the United Lutheran Church has been prepared for use at this Convention, especially to be presented at the meeting of the Statistical Secretaries.

STATISTICAL AND CHURCH YEAR BOOK COMMITTEE

ORGANIZATION AND MEETINGS

Your Committee held two meetings during the biennium—April 20, 1927, and May 2, 1928. The first meeting was held in the room of Rev. G. L. Kieffer, at the Hospital for Ruptured and Crippled, East 42nd Street, and in the office of the United Lutheran Church, 437 Fifth Avenue, both in New York City. The second meeting was held in the Chapel of the Lutheran Church House, 39 East 35th Street, New York, N. Y.

At the first meeting, Rev. George H. Schnur, D.D., was elected Chairman of the Committee and Rev. G. L. Kieffer was elected Secretary and Treasurer.

At the 1927 meeting the Rev. George H. Schnur was elected Editor of the 1928 United Lutheran Church Year Book and at the 1928 meeting the Rev. George H. Schnur was elected Editor of the 1929 United Lutheran Church Year Book.

The Rev. W. M. Kopenhaver has been unable to attend the meeting of the Committee on account of illness. The prayers of all are extended to God in behalf of this faithful servant of the church in his affliction.

HELPING THE STATISTICAL SECRETARIES

Various Statistical Secretaries have been helped with their individual problems. In addition, there has been released to all of the Statistical Secretaries a letter advising them of the publication of various statistical books, especially that of Rev. Herman C. Weber, entitled "Presbyterian Statistics Through One Hundred Years—1826 to 1926—Tabulated, Visualized, and Interpreted."

Annually the Religious Statistics of Dr. H. K. Carroll, as printed in the *Christian Hearld*, the Benevolence Statistics of the United Stewardship Council, and the review article of the "Lutherans" as prepared for the Encyclopedias by Rev. G. L. Kieffer, has been sent to all of the Statistical Secretaries and many Lutheran leaders.

TOOLS PROVIDED FOR THE STATISTICAL SECRETARIES

The Standard Assembly Sheet and the Standard Parochial Blank have both been revised and reprinted. The revisions in each case being in harmony with the recommendations of the Statistical Conference of the Statistical Secretaries held at Richmond, Va. Additional revisions which have grown out of the experience of various Statistical Secretaries, have already been proposed and considered and some of them adopted by the Statistical and Church Year Book Committee of the United Lutheran Church and will be incorporated in the next printing of the Blanks.

Again the various Constituent Synods' attention is called to a system of seven Parish Record Cards which enable the Statistical Secretaries to keep a ten-year record for each congregation of (1) Pastor (s); (2) Officers; (3) Membership; (4) Organizations; (5) Value of Church Property; (6) Finances; (7) Extra ruled blank cards. Every Constituent Synod should provide these cards for their Statistical Secretaries. This is an item to which the Statistical Secretaries of the Constituent Synods should give immediate attention. A permanent card file record for every congregation within the bounds of their synod should be built. This will prove eventually of inestimable value to the Budget Committee, State of the Church Committee, etc., of the Constituent Synods as every congregation's record and ability in every phase of work can be ascertained at a glance.

TOOLS FOR PASTORS

The *Parish Register,* which appeared under the editorship of Dr. George H. Schnur, Chairman of the Statistical and Church Year Book Committee, at the close of the last biennium, has been received with universal satisfaction. Your Committee feels it inadvisable to grant the request for a cheaper edition of the *Register* in that this alone can be attained by the use of wood pulp paper instead of linen paper, and cheaper material in binding, etc., which are not permanent in quality. Besides the reduction in price that would be attained would not warrant the sacrifice in quality which alone makes a record permanent.

The Annual Congregational Blanks for the gathering of the annual congregational statistics as well as the statistics needed by the pastor for the proper use of the Standard Parochial Blank, are in the hands of the printer and proofs should be at hand at the time of the Erie Convention. They are (1) Blank for Congregational Schools; (2) Blank for Congregational Societies and Organizations; (3) Blank for the Report of the Church Council and Board of Trustees. These Blanks have had the approval of the Conference of Statistical Secretaries at Richmond and have been revised and re-revised by the Statistical and Church Year Book Committee and have been examined and approved by the Executive Secretaries of the various Boards and General Organizations of the United Lutheran Church.

The Monthly Congregational Blanks providing a system of reports to be used by the church councils in their monthly meetings, are also in the process of final preparation. Proofs of these should also be available for the Erie Convention. They are Blanks for (1) the report of the Pastor; (2) the report of the financial secretaries; (3) the report of the congregational treasurers: (a) Current and unusual expenses, (b) Benevolence; (4) the report of committees and boards. The use of such Blanks is also approved and recommended by the Conference of the Statistical Secretaries as held at Richmond, Va., and is urgently requested by the Statistical and Church Year Book Committee.

It is only by the introduction of standard and efficient methods that the greatest value of the work of any organization can be found. Your Committee has worked now almost ten years in preparing this system of Standard Blanks. It has not been an easy task but the result has already won the commendation and approval of experts in church efficiency, such as Dr. Arthur Swift of the Religious Work Department of Union Theological Seminary, Columbia University; Dr. H. K. Carroll, American church statistician, and others. These Blanks represent ten years of progress, experience, and research, and have been released only as the church has felt the need and desire for them. The entire system has been built around the Standard Parochial Report Blank. Orderliness and method used in the proper way make for spirituality.

THE EVERY MEMBER AND HOUSE TO HOUSE CANVASS

The Lutheran Laymen's Movement for Stewardship annually provides the necessary Blanks for the Every Member Canvass for finances. With the approval of the Conference of Statistical Secretaries at Richmond, Va., the Statistical and Church Year Book Committee have provided a Blank to be used in the house to house visitation or canvass for church membership. The Statistical and Church Year Book Committee urges the use of this Blank in all visitation campaigns, whether initiated by the local congregations or by others, and co-operated in by the congregation.

THE YEAR BOOK OF THE UNITED LUTHERAN CHURCH

Your Committee at both of its meetings in 1927 and 1928 passed upon and approved the contents of the United Lutheran Church Year Book for 1928 and 1929, both issues of which appeared under the editorship of Rev. George H. Schnur, D.D. The statistical material, the alphabetical directory, and geographical directory, excepting the allocation of the pastors to their congregations in large cities, were provided by the Statistical Secretary of the United Lutheran Church in America, Rev. G. L. Kieffer. The Statistical and Church Year Book Committee assumes responsibility for the contents of the United Lutheran Church Year Book.

RELEASES THROUGH THE NATIONAL LUTHERAN COUNCIL

The Statistical Secretary of the United Lutheran Church in America supplied the United Lutheran Church statistics to the National Lutheran Council for the *Lutheran World Almanac* for 1927-28, for the Council's annual releases through Dr. H. K. Carroll for his articles on religious denominations in the United States as published in the *Christian Herald*, 1927 and 1928; to Dr. H. S. Myers of the United Stewardship Council for the benevolence statistics, 1927-1928; to the editors of the *Americana*, the *International Year Book* in the articles on "The Lutherans"; to the editors of the *World Almanac*, the *Brooklyn Eagle Almanac*, and the *Long Island Almanac*, etc., and to the National Lutheran Council for such additional releases as have been made on Lutheran statistics.

INCOMPLETE PAROCHIAL STATISTICAL REPORTS

Two of the Constituent Synods of the United Lutheran Church, namely, Manitoba and Slovak Zion, have not conformed in using the Standard Parochial Blank and the Standard Assembly Sheets. Their statistics are therefore incomplete and their rubrics are few. These synods should conform at once.

All Statistical Secretaries of Constituent Synods should strike totals of their Parochial Reports and make comparisons with previous years. These comparisons and totals should be printed at the end of the Parochial Reports. No efficient Statistical Secretary will strike totals when not all of the congregations have reported the most essential rubrics on membership, church valuation, etc. Before striking totals the Statistical Secretaries must insert previous reports. This, however, is no excuse for non-reporting congregations. Every congregation should deem it a privilege and an honor to make a full report, using the Standard Parochial Blank. In doing so, they cannot help but feel that they are, even though perhaps small, a part of the larger unit and units—the Constituent Synod, the United Lutheran Church, the Lutherans of America and of the World.

JUGGLING OF COMMUNING MEMBERSHIP

It must be admitted that the shifting of the apportionment from the Confirmed Membership to the Communing (or communicant, as defined) has brought with it a consequent juggling and trimming of the membership as reported under this rubric. This has been summarily recognized by a number of Constituent Synods as shown in the printed Minutes of these synods. Summary penalties for inaccurate reports have already been established in these synods.

As the pastor is responsible for the proper, accurate, and honest Parochial Report, the Statistical and Church Year Book Committee hardly knows what comment should be made on this state of affairs, especially since it concerns the actual record of those who participated at least once a year in the Sacrament of Holy Communion. A summary of the actual situation is submitted under "Statistics Supplied to the Treasurer of the United Lutheran Church."

STATISTICS SUPPLIED TO THE TREASURER OF THE UNITED LUTHERAN CHURCH

The Statistical Secretary has supplied the Treasurer, Dr. E. Clarence Miller, with two tables: one for 1926 and one for 1927, showing the communing (or communicant as defined) membership of each of the Constituent Synods as well as a grand total of the United Lutheran Church in the United States and Canada. The total communing membership as reported to Dr. Miller for 1927 was 676,437, and as published in the 1928 United Lutheran Church Year Book, it was 669,698. From one report to the next later report, therefore, increases were shown in communing members for the Ministerium of Pennsylvania, the Synod of Virginia, the Synod of Ohio, the Synod of Iowa, Pittsburgh Synod, Indiana Synod, Illinois Synod, Michigan Synod, Synod of Georgia, Synod of Canada, Synod of Kansas, Synod of California, Rocky Mountain Synod, Manitoba Synod, Pacific Synod, Nova Scotia Synod, Slovak Zion Synod. Decreases were shown for the following synods: Synod of Maryland, South Carolina, Texas, Susquehanna, Synod of Central Pennsylvania, Mississippi Synod, Wartburg Synod, German Nebraska Synod, West Virginia. No increase or decrease was shown for the following: Ministerium of New York, North Carolina, West Pennsylvania, New York, East Pennsylvania, Nebraska, Northwest, New York and New England. The New York Ministerium pled for more time and later joined the group showing a decrease.

The report as finally submitted to Dr. Miller showed the following non-synodical communing membership in the United Lutheran Church: Ministerium of New York, 3,355; Maryland, 20; New York Synod, 910; Pittsburgh, 1,222; Texas, 296; German Nebraska, 3,075; Pacific, 25; Slovak Zion did not report, making a total of 8,845 of non-synodical communing membership reported.

End of Fiscal Year

At the time of the writing of this report all of the Constituent Synods of the United Lutheran Church excepting German Nebraska, Indiana, Mississippi, and Ohio have conformed to the standard in ending their fiscal years on December 31st, the end of the calendar year. Psychologically the human mind is set for ending even church affairs and reports with the calendar year. Your Committee raises the question, whether, for the sake of efficiency, all boards, committees, synods, churches, etc., should not conform and capitalize this human trait. It is hardly necessary to comment that it is only possible to secure uniform statistics and that it is only possible to make true comparisons where the same period of time is involved. The Statistical and Church Year Book Committee believes that all fiscal years should correspond to the calendar year.

Blank for the Report on the State of the Church

This important Blank has been available for some time for the use of Constituent Synods by their officers, State of the Church Committees, etc. It is to be hoped that the Constituent Synods will avail themselves of this Blank and that uniformity in reports will be thereby arrived at.

Urban and Rural Congregations

The new State of the Church Blank provides rubrics for the reporting of the fact whether a congregation is urban or rural according to the U. S. Census Bureau standard of over 2,500 population being urban and under 2,500 population being rural. The statistics for the United Lutheran Church as of 1926 are thus given in the report of the 1926 U. S. Religious Census.

U. S. Census of Religious Bodies—1926—United Lutheran Church in America

First of importance to be presented is that of the. U. S. Census of Religious Bodies of 1926 as pertaining to the United Lutheran Church in America. Since the formation of the United Lutheran Church in 1918 a card file for congregations has been kept in the office of the Statistical Secretary of the United Lutheran Church. From year to year as the Minutes of the Constituent Synods appear, the list of congregations has been checked against this card file. The Bureau of Census, Department of Commerce, Washington, D. C., had a girl make copies of these cards and this file was then checked against the file of the returns in the Census of Religious Bodies, 1916, as kept in the Bureau of Census, Department of Commerce, Washington, D. C. Many differences between the two files came to the surface. These differences were sent by the Bureau of Census to the Statistical Secretary, who in turn got in touch with Statistical Secretaries, neighboring pastors, and pastors endeavoring to clear up all of the differences. Continuous reports were made to the Bureau of Census, Department of Commerce, Washington, D. C. This was the first stage of the work.

The second stage was the sending out of the schedules according to the final card file. These schedules were accompanied with a letter from your Statistical Secretary who was designated as the Lutheran representative of the Bureau of Census, Department of Commerce, Washington, D. C., and also accompanied by a letter from the Director of the Bureau of Census, Dr. W. M. Steuart.

The third stage of the census was the gathering of the returns. The first report submitted by the Bureau of Census to your Statistical Secretary showed a list of 69 United Lutheran Church Congregations who had failed to file their returns. A second list showed 29, a third list, 7, and a final list one congregation—vacant. This schedule was finally secured through the efforts of the Statistical Secretary of the New York Synod, Rev. A. L. Dillenbeck, D.D., Rev. George R. Swartz, President of the Hartwick Conference of the New York Synod, and a Mr. Schell, a lawyer member of the congregation in question, Gallupville, N. Y. But before the Gallupville report was signed the Bureau of Census released a preliminary press report showing 3,649 of the United Lutheran Churches in America in 1926 as compared with 3,559 churches in 1916; total baptized membership, 1,213,944, as compared with 996,910 in 1916 (according to the 1917 Year Book, U. S. only). As to confirmed membership, 865,588 were reported over 13 years of age in 1926, as compared with 763,596 in 1916. 1,527 congregations were located in urban territory and 2,122 in rural territory. Of the total baptized membership, 1,213,944, 816,555 were in urban churches and 397,389 in rural churches. 1,512 urban churches reported expenditures of $16,220,477, and 2,064 rural churches reported $4,942,254. The value of church property reported by 1,468 urban churches was $90,084,919, and that reported by 2,047 rural churches was $24,440,122.

The total expenditures for 1926, as reported by 3,576 churches, amounted to $21,162,701, including $17,509,100 for current expenses and improvements, $3,640,988 for benevolences, missions, etc., and $12,613, not classified. The total expenditures reported by 3,485 churches in 1916 were $7,929,663. The value of church edifices (including furniture and equipment), as reported by 3,515 churches for 1926, was $114,525,048, which may be compared with $48,498,217 reported by 3,465 churches in 1916.

Sunday schools were reported by 3,415 churches of this organization in 1926, with 62,184 officers and teachers and 619,781 scholars. The number of officers and teachers in the Sunday schools as reported for 1916 was 57,947, and the number of scholars, 578,238.

STATISTICS FOR THE U. L. C. IN A. BY STATES

State	No. of Churches		Membership		Expenditures: 1926		Value of Church Edifices: 1926	
	1926	1916	1926	1916	Churches Reporting	Amount	Churches Reporting	Amount
Total	3,649	3,559	1,213,944	763,596	3,576	$21,162,701	3,515	$114,525,048
Urban	1,527		816,555		1,512	16,220,447	1,468	90,084,919
Rural	2,122		397,389		2,064	4,942,254	2,047	24,440,129
New England:								
Massachusetts ...	6	4	1,827	1,168	6	24,354	6	151,000
Connecticut	26	26	11,393	7,996	24	180,188	23	1,067,500
Middle Atlantic:								
New York	296	279	147,452	90,917	291	3,115,087	278	17,056,081
New Jersey	111	93	43,443	26,243	109	614,467	99	3,886,500
Pennsylvania	1,443	1,464	551,202	361,346	1,433	8,635,153	1,422	48,325,334
East North Central:								
Ohio	302	317	84,531	61,577	299	1,596,706	298	9,827,100
Indiana	118	126	21,833	14,169	117	386,038	115	2,483,175
Illinois	159	145	55,242	28,974	158	1,137,696	155	5,293,055
Michigan	31	17	8,242	4,312	27	198,350	27	1,145,200
Wisconsin	49	33	23,331	7,282	48	360,034	43	2,488,090
W. North Central:								
Minnesota	30	23	15,476	5,807	30	349,991	28	1,258,000
Iowa	41	36	14,602	7,457	41	216,963	41	1,015,210
Missouri	19	17	3,950	2,375	18	155,830	16	616,650
North Dakota ...	11	5	2,361	713	11	24,291	7	108,100
South Dakota ...	4	3	499	456	4	4,759	3	15,000
Nebraska	122	132	32,489	18,206	122	434,232	121	1,843,396
Kansas	45	52	9,103	6,780	44	191,146	44	846,600
South Atlantic:								
Delaware	3	3	1,203	1,045	3	40,097	3	199,000

STATISTICS FOR THE U. L. C. IN A. BY STATES

State	No. of Churches		Membership		Expenditures: 1926		Value of Church Edifices: 1926	
	1926	1916	1926	1916	Churches Reporting	Amount	Churches Reporting	Amount
Maryland	135	126	52,693	33,555	134	824,650	130	4,235,450
District of Columbia	14	12	5,106	3,416	14	135,408	13	1,844,000
Virginia	147	160	19,252	15,271	137	258,422	140	1,424,550
West Virginia	43	42	7,993	5,983	35	252,792	40	1,034,600
North Carolina	165	154	34,682	19,450	156	715,651	156	2,372,879
South Carolina	110	103	25,756	14,788	107	311,473	108	1,451,150
Georgia	26	26	5,759	3,739	22	109,541	24	520,000
Florida	9	4	1,567	555	9	87,706	6	309,000
E. South Central:								
Kentucky	19	18	4,881	3,845	19	134,864	19	607,978
Tennessee	27	34	3,248	2,808	25	39,540	26	518,400
Mississippi	13	10	880	567	12	9,222	12	42,400
W. South Central:								
Oklahoma	5	5	976	636	5	19,987	5	122,400
Texas	28	12	5,917	1,682	26	46,301	23	138,000
Mountain:								
Montana	4	1	550	179	4	13,763		(**)
Colorado	18	16	2,535	1,700	17	186,903	16	334,100
Pacific:								
Washington	17	13	2,791	985	16	77,992	15	205,300
Oregon	10	9	1,312	891	10	21,870	10	140,500
California	37	29	8,778	5,865	37	203,996	35	1,403,450
Other States*	6	10	1,089	858	6	47,238	8	195,900

* States having less than 3 churches (or less than 3 churches reporting value of edifices).

** Included in amount for "Other States."

Note: Similar statements have been issued for 138 Religious Bodies, including 14 Lutheran Bodies, and others will be given out as soon as the figures are available.

The history statement of the United Lutheran Church has been written by a member of the Committee, Rev. M. G. G. Scherer, D.D. This statement with a fuller report will appear in the bulletin on the Lutherans covering all General Lutheran Church Bodies, and the full statistics will appear in the two volumes on the "Census of Religious Bodies, 1926." The Statistical and Church Year Book Committee and the Statistical Secretary of the United Lutheran Church commend all who co-operated in this Census.

SHALL THE 1930 U. S. CENSUS CONTAIN THE QUESTION CONCERNING RELIGIOUS AFFILIATION OF MEMBERS

In harmony with the action of the Statistical and Church Year Book Committee and with the United Lutheran Church (see Buffalo minutes, page 333; Chicago minutes, page 455; Richmond minutes, page 444) the Statistical Secretary of the United Lutheran Church is at work with the American Lutheran Statistical Association in attempting to bring about the placing of the question, "What is your church affiliation or preference?" as one of the questions on the schedule for the 1930 regular decennial census of the United States population. To this end the Statistical Secretary, as an officer of the American Lutheran Statistical Association, met with Dr. W. M. Steuart, Director of the Bureau of Census, Department of Commerce, and with other officers of the American Lutheran Statistical Association, and by appointment, with Congressman Rev. O. J. Kvale. The question is being considered by the Director along with about fifty other questions that are appealing for placement on the 1930 Census Schedule. Congressman Kvale has manifested much interest in the proposition and in all probability will have a bill introduced in both House and Senate amending the 1930 Census Enabling Law so as to place the question on the schedule. This will bring about the much desired religious census of population similar to that of Canada, the European countries, excepting Great Britain, and all the rest of the world. It will in all probability reveal a Lutheran population of from 18 to 20 million. To this extent, of course, it will reveal to Lutherans and non-Lutherans to what extent the Lutheran Church has assimilated in its membership the Lutheran population, and even though some people will not tell the truth and to that extent the report will be only comparative, nevertheless, in revealing the work which lies before our Lutheran Church it should prove the greatest home mission incentive that has ever come to the attention of our Lutheran Church in America.

THE UNITED STEWARDSHIP COUNCIL STATISTICS—1927

The Statistical Secretary of the United Lutheran Church, through the National Lutheran Council, reported membership, benevolence gifts, congregational expenses, as well as the per capita gifts for benevolence, congregational expenses, and total expenses for the United Lutheran Church

and other General Lutheran Church Bodies to the United Stewardship
Council. Their report for 1927 places the United Lutheran Church eighteenth, with a per capita for benevolence of $3.63. It is the lowest of the
three groups: Lutheran, Other Synods; Lutheran Synodical Conference, and
United Lutheran Church, according to the nomenclature and grouping. The
highest per capita in the entire report is the United Presbyterian—$11.65.
The highest Lutheran is "Lutheran, Other Synods," not including Synodical
Conference and the United Lutheran Church, $4.20—the Synodical Con-
ference, $3.94. The United Lutheran Church's entire report as given in
the United Stewardship Council report is as follows: "18—United Lutheran,
Per Capita Gifts: Budget Benevolences, $3.63; Congregational Expenses,
$20.62; All Purposes, $24.25. Total Gifts for Budget Benevolences,
$3,290,966; Total Gifts for Congregational Expenses, $18,728,678; Total
Gifts for all Purposes, $22,019,644; Membership in U. S. and Canada,
908,190."

H. K. Carroll's Statistics

The Statistical Secretary of the United Lutheran Church, through the
National Lutheran Council, reported to Dr. H. K. Carroll, the statistics
for the United Lutheran Church and other General Lutheran Church
Bodies. They were released by him in the April 14, 1928, issue of the
Christian Herald. Your Statistical Secretary required signed statements
by Statistical Secretaries of the Constituent Synods, and as a result of the
check-up made by these men the United Lutheran Church reports 2,944
ministers, 3,679 congregations, 1,285,048 baptized members, 890,671 confirmed members; and the total for all Lutherans was 10,727 ministers,
15,448 congregations, 4,032,156 baptized members, 2,656,158 confirmed
members. This gave the United Lutheran Church a decrease of 83
ministers, 3 churches, and an increase of 30,038 members and all Lutherans
a decrease of 68 ministers, and a decrease of 101 churches, but an increase
of 67,879 confirmed members. This was the third largest increase reported
by any group, being exceeded by the Roman Catholics and the Methodists,
the Lutherans, however, being first in per capita increase. The Lutherans
again regained third place among the Protestants, being exceeded only
by the Methodists and the Baptists in confirmed or communicant members.

Annual Review of the Work of the Lutherans—1927

The Statistical Secretary of the United Lutheran Church in America,
through the National Lutheran Council reported an analytical study of
the work of the United Lutheran Church in 1927 giving not only the
United Lutheran Church statistics but also a report and evaluation of the
outstanding events in the United Lutheran Church in 1927. This report
was submitted to the Lutheran press and encyclopedias, such as the
"Americana," "American Year Book," the "International Encyclopedias,"
etc.

In this general article with the heading "Lutherans—1927," one of the statistical items told the number of Lutheran congregations of different size as follows:

Lutheran Congregations (All General Bodies)	U.L.C. Congregations	Baptized Membership
1	1	5,000 to 6,000
2	1	4,000 to 5,000
10	6	3,000 to 4,000
65	23	2,000 to 3,000
127	54	1,500 to 2,000
43	16	1,400 to 1,500
40	17	1,300 to 1,400
74	34	1,200 to 1,300
58	24	1,100 to 1,200
120	45	1,000 to 1,100
540	221	

Out of the total table the United Lutheran Church in America has 221 congregations with a baptized membership between 1,000 to 6,000.

STATISTICAL HANDBOOK OF THE UNITED LUTHERAN CHURCH

The lack of complete uniformity in the Statistical Reports of the Constituent Synods and in the printing of the Minutes of the Constituent Synods have made the production of the Statistical Handbook of the United Lutheran Church, during the last biennium, impossible. Two synods, Manitoba and Slovak Zion, still do not use the Standard Parochial Blank. The 1927 Nova Scotia and the 1927 New York Ministerium use insert sheets for the printing of statistical reports. The Wartburg Synod printed the rubrics across the narrow part of the page, requiring many extra pages for the printing of their statistics. Still other synods use more than two pages in printing the rubrics lengthwise across the page. It is to be hoped that these synods will conform in the printing of the 1928 and 1929 minutes and thus make it possible in 1929, after ten years of statistical work of the United Lutheran Church, to produce the Statistical Handbook. The Statistical and Church Year Book Committee desires to produce this Handbook in 1929 and will do so if all of the Constituent Synods will co-operate.

The type for the pages for the Parochial Reports of the Constituent Synods for 1929 should be kept intact for use by the Statistical and Church Year Book Committee of the United Lutheran Church in the production of the Statistical Handbook of the United Lutheran Church.

CO-OPERATION WITH THEOLOGICAL SEMINARIES OF THE UNITED LUTHERAN CHURCH

The Statistical Secretary of the United Lutheran Church has provided Standard Parochial Blanks, Standard State of the Church Blanks, to the professors of practical theology of a number of the Theological Seminaries of the United Lutheran Church in order that the members of the classes in practical theology might receive copies of these Blanks.

The Statistical Secretary of the United Lutheran Church also addressed the Senior Class of the Gettysburg Lutheran Theological Seminary during their visit to New York City, at the Lutheran Church House, at which time the statistical work of the United Lutheran Church was explained as well as each pastor's part therein.

Four Page Folder for Pastors

With the completion of the system of Standard Report Blanks such a folder explaining the use of these Blanks will prove of real value to the pastors and will be provided for the Statistical Secretaries of the Constituent Synods to mail with the Standard Parochial Blanks for the year, 1929.

Four Page Folder of Instruction for Statistical Secretaries

With but few changes in the personnel of Statistical Secretaries the Statistical and Church Year Book Committee and the Statistical Secretary of the United Lutheran Church have been able to give the necessary instruction to the new men by letter. Here also an instruction folder, built around the system of Standard Report Blanks, will prove of value and will be available at the beginning of the year, 1929.

Expenses

The expenses of the Statistical and Church Year Book Committee have been met by the Treasurer of the United Lutheran Church in America, the amount being recorded in the Treasurer's report.

Charts and Graphs

The Chairman of the Statistical and Church Year Book Committee and Statistical Secretary of the United Lutheran Church beg permission to present such charts and graphs as they may deem advisable at the time of the Convention, which may or may not be desired as part of the minutes.

Parochial Statistics of the United Lutheran Church—1926-1927

The table showing totals for the Parochial Statistics of the Constituent Synods as well as for the United Lutheran Church for the years 1926 and 1927 are herewith appended; also a table of comparative statistics covering the last seven years, covering the nine years—1919 to 1927.

It is, however, to be regretted that some of the Statistical Secretaries of the Constituent Synods failed to submit their separate Parochial Reports or copies of their minutes, including the statistics for 1927, in time to be included in the bulletin. These statistics will be available for the minutes of this Convention as well as complete comparative tables.

Recommendations

1.   That the Constituent Synods be requested in the printing of their minutes, to make the page after the title page a calendar page, indicating the special days and dates of the United Lutheran Church and the special days and dates of the Constituent Synod, and also a table showing the use of the Budget Benevolence Dollar of the United Lutheran Church and one showing the use of the Budget Benevolence Dollar of the Constituent Synod, or a table showing a combination of both.

2.   That we request the Constituent Synods to urge their congregations to use the "Parish Register" prepared by your Committee for use in congregations of the United Lutheran Church.

3.   That we request the Constituent Synods to secure sufficient number of the sets of the Standard Parish Record cards for Statistical Secretaries, so that the Statistical Secretaries of the Constituent Synods can complete a card file of all of the congregations of their synod.

4.   That we request the Constituent Synods to make use of the State of the Church Blank now ready in final form, as provided by the Statistical Committee of the United Lutheran Church in America.

5.   That we request the Constituent Synods to introduce into the congregations of the United Lutheran Church in America, the standard auxiliary congregational blanks for monthly and annual reports and such other blanks as the Statistical Committee in conference with the Statistical Secretaries of the Constituent Synods of the United Lutheran Church may be able to provide in order that accurate and uniform statistics of the United Lutheran Church in America may become possible.

6.   That we request all Constituent Synods to use the Standard Parochial Blanks and Standard Assembly Sheets not in modified, but in complete form, thereby conforming their practice to the standard of the United Lutheran Church.

7.   That all Constituent Synods of the United Lutheran Church be again requested to have their minutes printed in uniform size and style; and, to have their Parochial Statistics printed lengthwise on the page and not crosswise on a vertical page, using only two pages for all the rubrics, and using approximately forty-one lines to the page; all Parochial Statistics to contain a summary in which a total is given for the synod for the year, together with a total for the preceding year; also, a comparative statement under "Increase" and "Decrease" on all rubrics.

8.   That the Constituent Synods be requested to hold the type for the pages of their Parochial Statistics in their Minutes of 1929 for the use of the Statistical and Church Year Book Committee of the United Lutheran Church in the production of the Statistical Handbook of the United Lutheran Church in 1929.

9.   That the Constituent Synods be again requested to make provision for their Statistical Secretaries at future conventions of the United Lutheran

Church in order that they may attend the Conference of Statistical Secretaries which will meet at the time of the Convention.

10. We request that the fiscal years of all congregational organizations, congregations, Constituent Synods of the United Lutheran Church, be made concurrent with the calendar year ending December 31st each year, and that all published reports and statistics be of the date December 31st of the previous year, thereby aiding the effort for accurate and uniform statistics in the United Lutheran Church.

11. That we express to the U. S. Bureau of Census, Washington, D. C., and especially to Director Dr. W. M. Steuart, and Dr. T. J. Murphy, Special Agent in charge of the 1926 Religious Census, the appreciation of the United Lutheran Church for their hearty and sympathetic co-operation in the taking of the U. S. Religious Census of the United Lutheran Church in America.

Respectfully submitted,

Statistical and Church Year Book Committee.

GEORGE H. SCHNUR, Chairman,
GEORGE LINN KIEFFER, Secretary-Treasurer,
M. G. G. SCHERER,
C. W. CASSELL,
C. J. ROCKEY,
M. G. L. RIETZ,
J. D. KROUT,
H. E. PUGH.

REPORT OF THE STATISTICAL SECRETARY OF THE UNITED LUTHERAN CHURCH IN AMERICA

The report of the Statistical Secretary of the United Lutheran Church in America is in part embodied in the report of the Statistical and Church Year Book Committee.

Attention is respectfully called to a part of the Committee report concerning a submission of charts and graphs.

The Statistical Secretary of the United Lutheran Church has had the fullest co-operation of the Statistical Secretaries of the Constituent Synods. Many have been the requests that have had to be made, and the responses usually have been prompt.

Efforts looking forward to unification and conformity in carrying forth the work and in presenting the statistical material in the minutes of the Constituent Synods must be noted. This is especially true of the New York Ministerium under the leadership of the President, Rev. Herman Brezing, and the Statistical Secretary, Rev. Geo. R. F. Tamke. They deserve the commendation of the Statistical and Church Year Book Committee, which they already have by special action, and also the commendation of the United Lutheran Church. The noble efforts of other Statistical Secretaries in having their reports in the minutes of their Constituent Synods conform to standard placement, arrangement, and size, are also commended especially in this report, by having their minutes pointed out as conforming.

The salary of the Statistical Secretary during the biennium was $600 per annum.

Respectfully submitted,

G. L. KIEFFER, *Statistical Secretary.*

THE REPORT OF THE EDITOR OF THE "UNITED LUTHERAN CHURCH YEAR BOOK"

The report of the editor of the "United Lutheran Church Year Book" is embodied in the report of the Statistical and Church Year Book Committee.

Respectfully submitted,

GEORGE H. SCHNUR, *Editor of the 1927 and 1928 Year Book.*

PAROCHIAL REPORT OF THE UNITED LUTHERAN CHURCH IN AMERICA (1926)
United States and Canada

INDEX NUMBER	SYNOD (1)	When Organized (2)	Pastors (3)	Parishes (4)	Congregations (5)	Membership — Baptized (6)	Membership — Confirmed (7)	Membership — Communing (8)	Accessions Children — Baptism (9)	Accessions Children — Otherwise (10)	Accessions Adult — Baptism (11)	Accessions Adult — Confirmation (12)	Accessions Adult — Certificate (13)	Accessions Adult — Otherwise (14)	Losses Children — Death (15)	Losses Children — Otherwise (16)	Losses Adult — Death (17)	Losses Adult — Certificate (18)	Losses Adult — Otherwise (19)
1	Ministerium of Pa.	Aug. 15, 1748	443	373	588	278,356	190,854	140,005	7,571	3,164	531	912	2,998	2,264	501	3,087	2,985	1,968	3,744
2	Ministerium of New York	Oct. 23, 1786	165	142	147	96,717	70,853	52,654	2,387	1,228	139	1,997	436	1,235	112	483	808	246	573
3	United Synod of N. C.	May 2, 1803	106	83	160	33,664	24,055	18,517	955	321	116	781	737	87	35	172	244	506	89
4	Synod of Maryland	Oct. 11, 1820	127	102	139	62,544	46,169	31,560	1,865	413	239	1,580	695	798	100	398	637	312	1,078
5	Synod of S. Carolina	Jan. 14, 1824	57	65	109	25,906	19,103	13,601	546	235	74	518	501	54	28	137	183	655	52
6	Synod of W. Penna.	Sept. 5, 1825	109	69	159	55,386	41,027	35,408	1,309	305	326	1,323	802	345	82	197	651	255	1,060
7	Synod of Virginia	Aug. 16, 1829	88	86	159	22,481	17,773	11,531	397	189	279	452	373	212	19	73	208	397	192
8	Synod of New York	Oct. 26, 1830	160	146	159	56,159	36,895	36,895	1,467	1,384	625	1,271	565	1,632	88	701	863	1,035	1,043
9	Synod of Ohio	Nov. 7, 1836	222	195	283	79,395	56,105	47,688	2,184	908	338	1,922	1,376	1,463	132	557	371	758	2,427
10	East Pennsylvania Synod	May 2, 1842	160	160	160	65,858	47,463	33,988	1,560	430	236	1,432	1,302	698	72	390	618	461	1,251
11	Allegheny Synod	Sept. 9, 1842	76	73	151	39,828	29,721	21,624	1,038	221	349	2,789	506	246	74	442	371	1,452	855
12	Pittsburgh Synod	Jan. 15, 1845	268	220	312	111,848	76,410	51,001	3,046	1,466	123	2,769	1,851	1,701	209	1,350	944	144	1,926
13	Indiana Synod	Oct. 28, 1848	61	63	75	15,025	11,515	8,768	324	115	322	368	226	165	11	78	33	376	281
14	Illinois Synod	Sept. 8, 1851	142	118	138	43,636	28,422	23,426	1,390	1,270	12	1,522	649	1,512	85	847	315	23	1,508
15	Texas Synod	Nov. 10, 1851	18	17	30	5,943	3,731	3,138	142	68	219	172	76	66	11	26	33	512	81
16	Susquehanna Synod of C. Pa.	Feb. 21, 1855	99	82	165	49,557	37,539	26,695	1,048	240	8	1,011	692	445	88	138	556	4	493
17	Mississippi Synod	July 25, 1855	9	5	9	855	694	256	10	…	112	8	147	…	…	7	4	112	1
18	Synod of Iowa	Sept. 3, 1855	32	32	32	11,478	7,000	5,369	391	342	170	339	147	424	12	81	71	145	212
19	Michigan Synod	Oct. 27, 1860	63	59	83	18,873	13,725	9,015	436	279	36	322	348	445	25	315	176	60	310
20	Synod of Georgia	July 20, 1860	25	30	44	7,474	5,818	3,643	134	100	36	168	259	36	3	18	47	137	33
21	Synod of Canada	July 21, 1861	60	62	92	28,454	19,084	15,070	643	225	78	638	76	342	52	160	223	124	334
22	Synod of Kansas	Nov. 5, 1868	43	35	42	8,883	5,818	4,945	209	166	15	190	230	97	18	241	71	25	879
23	Synod of Nebraska	Sept. 1, 1871	46	44	53	16,950	11,389	7,930	131	21	39	11	39	37	2	44	21	41	178
24	Wartburg Synod	… 1875	53	47	57	18,830	12,260	9,145	542	201	429	429	38	480	43	145	125	42	235
25	German Nebraska Synod	July 24, 1890	85	79	91	8,696	12,980	9,575	474	26	24	417	51	151	26	78	117	87	84
26	Synod of California	April 6, 1891	66	37	37	8,084	5,033	5,032	258	242	24	223	251	222	2	138	55	57	266
27	Rocky Mountain Synod	May 22, 1891	24	19	19	3,047	1,752	1,528	137	102	…	72	122	230	7	72	71	…	180
28	Synod of the Northwest	Sept. 16, 1891	91	74	84	43,208	27,828	21,516	1,510	1,950	270	1,700	360	2,660	58	924	165	347	1,488
29	Manitoba Synod	July 26, 1897	41	34	54	10,693	5,825	4,013	472	…	…	334	105	242	…	…	98	66	283
30	Pacific Synod	Sept. 26, 1901	36	32	31	4,739	2,730	2,107	156	242	23	131	911	1,374	16	269	35	479	1,253
31	N. Y. and N. Eng. Synod	Sept. 23, 1903	99	78	78	33,182	24,770	24,770	1,304	1,664	109	1,456	19	15	53	579	289	15	27
32	Nova Scotia Synod	July 10, 1903	18	8	8	6,060	3,019	1,272	155	…	4	78	116	100	6	2	34	74	465
33	Synod of West Virginia	April 17, 1912	28	37	37	6,269	4,124	3,452	173	46	23	100	…	…	6	636	63	4	…
34	Slovak "Zion" Synod	June 10, 1919	23	28	50	10,825	7,161	5,413	198	…	1	3	…	…	1	4	43	…	…
35	Total for U. S. and Canada		3,127	2,706	3,576	1,315,620	916,858	677,287	34,562	17,573	5,178	25,451	16,866	19,781	1,983	12,789	11,758	11,467	22,831
36	Total Outside U. S. and Canada		125		1,840	139,925	59,502	49,049	334	178	2	15,950	196	59	2	6	21	39	
37	U. L. C. World Total		3,252	2,706	5,416	1,555,545	976,420	726,336	34,896	17,751	5,180	41,401	17,063	19,840	1,985	12,795	11,779	11,506	22,831

PAROCHIAL REPORT OF THE UNITED LUTHERAN CHURCH IN AMERICA (1925)—(Continued)

Index No.	Church Papers: No. Sub. to Official Papers	No. S. S. Papers Distribute	No. Sub. to Other Ch. Papers	Church Schools — Sunday: Number	Officers and Teachers	Scholars	Home Dept.	Cradle Roll	Weekday: Number	Teachers	Scholars	Catechumens	Students: Ministry	Deaconess	In Lutheran Institutions	In Non-Luth. Institutions	Church Societies — Men's: Number	Members	Women's: Number	Members	Young P.: Number	Members	Financial — Church Edifices	Parsonages	School and Parish Houses
	20	21	22	23	24	25	26	27	28	29	30	31	32	33	34	35	36	37	38	39	40	41	42	43	44
1	8,238	7,262	6,141	583	11,488	115,657	5,379	12,695	85	529	7,536	8,251	104	20	305	1,139	206	9,783	674	34,006	548	24,044	18,061,236	2,373,598	1,412,250
2	1,600	4,704	1,288	141	2,521	22,437	398	3,081	34	98	1,792	1,202	39	3	54	163	26	6,091	196	13,598	179	7,889	5,721,775	1,035,925	327,700
3	2,865	4,888	1,552	130	1,785	21,138	2,084	3,078	46	251	4,131	2,726	33	2	225	235	38	1,125	134	3,754	169	5,303	2,095,139	350,052	71,000
4	2,450	5,975	2,075	142	3,443	33,708	2,434	4,175	32	106	1,058	2,388	33	1	68	446	62	3,126	209	11,184	192	8,105	5,138,310	738,650	269,300
5	1,713	1,854	882	107	1,295	13,386	631	883	38	220	3,363	1,941	28		214	192	28	1,131	131	3,920	135	4,209	1,162,750	240,640	91,000
6	1,756	5,049	858	160	3,621	42,981	1,492	3,563	18	95	1,282	3,598	39	3	159	247	20	796	213	9,920	173	7,381	3,695,150	547,100	225,500
7	2,072	2,815	1,458	130	1,496	14,181	1,131	1,335	17	77	882	581	11	4	83	139	75	2,965	113	3,884	115	4,042	1,637,850	384,092	87,800
8	2,990	7,947	586	126	2,271	18,440	1,600	2,806	35	65	829	1,654	36	5	65	188	24	5,814	230	8,661	203	5,340	5,028,075	802,150	271,000
9	3,226	23,359	1,748	276	5,041	51,421	3,971	4,043	21	127	1,661	3,243	59	1	356	675	87	5,085	451	19,934	240	6,547	8,799,000	919,424	434,100
10	2,275	9,700	1,771	156	3,942	38,888	1,445	4,293	26	147	1,644	2,658	63	1	141	384	27	1,297	268	11,647	225	7,998	6,466,798	952,400	342,000
11	2,438	10,337	1,874	132	2,553	24,616	570	2,735	25	159	2,023	1,881	53	2	86	359	118	709	162	5,730	118	4,014	2,980,100	427,430	14,500
12	3,864	22,371	5,313	301	5,348	50,068	3,283	6,815	58	334	4,778	4,417	26	7	224	616	27	3,079	455	16,970	334	10,414	9,065,989	1,285,875	344,235
13	910	4,001	236	70	1,103	8,884	402	860	19	49	580	566	15	6	24	119	23		107	3,329	50	1,306	1,424,125	210,787	37,800
14	2,264	13,798	1,590	134	2,777	26,130	31	2,915	19	131	1,268	1,796	35	5	102	308	69	79	237	8,568	177	5,402	4,431,758	539,750	183,850
15	336	423	26	29	198	1,699	1,942	139	6	19	246	202	3	4	4	15	5	29	25	812	17	614	124,800	40,300	17,750
16	1,093	4,752	1,182	166	3,111	32,002	14	2,737	31	178	2,390	1,908	3	1	103	345	46	2,441	182	6,924	140	4,933	3,887,125	454,600	38,000
17	34	34	23	12	67	376		16	11	26	40	5	2		1	3	2		10	109	6	72	34,000	3,100	
18	443	3,077	137	29	590	4,876	98	795	4	26	282	564	12	2	26	161	9	373	42	2,156	42	1,700	784,450	154,500	9,000
19	666	5,277	456	76	1,186	10,159	213	965	34	84	340	60	10	3	50	181	25	999	112	3,776	63	1,710	2,217,800	199,200	77,000
20	548	847	121	27	359	3,080		274	18	18	95	228	10		16	37	7	213	45	1,345	50	993	687,600	101,600	104,000
21	1,474	2,205	1,082	81	785	6,052	9	874	21	40	531	613	33		57	89	6	322	62	2,744	57	2,023	962,880	198,325	8,200
22	399	4,330	275	39	664	5,134	180	545	12	40	36	314	14		24	169	11	361	82	2,572	42	1,074	1,094,900	179,500	33,000
23	707	1,613	2,923	54	935	7,777	303	1,181	21	21	396	533	10		71	235	11	357	78	2,453	59	1,605	1,209,850	160,250	15,000
24	653	1,560	310	40	460	5,155	34	384	16	21	729	590	9		12	18	1	746	65	2,662	41	1,301	810,000	175,200	48,000
25	781	1,724	147	70	403	4,269	38	235	33	43	235	371	9		38	28	19	8	64	1,753	33	1,206	695,000	223,700	17,000
26	380	917	150	36	405	3,182	88	324	5	10	169	91	5		1	98	11	269	60	1,761	40	832	1,220,750	85,950	3,000
27	226	26	26	14	211	1,442	165	197	3	3	176	181	2			44	6	150	28	667	17	326	357,050	43,000	
28	1,513	6,351	1,061	80	1,583	13,615	164	2,396	57	57	1,212	2,384	41		58	293	46	1,817	126	5,063	134	3,456	3,449,400	310,500	120,600
29				31	141	1,623			54	54	1,709	228	8		16	67	8	176	42	270	34	441	315,700		
30	275	1,272	175	84	287	2,295	50	157	2	2	27		37	5	34	493	60	3,735	135	858	157	612	268,662	67,100	2,000
31	1,644	4,184	2,494	20	1,914	17,844	610	2,929	33	182	2,343	1,648	37		3	50			13	6,790		4,611	4,866,981	440,500	93,000
32	13	130	206	32	149	1,176		102	5	16	280	91	3	8	8	15	10	316	13	472	5	119	189,870	31,000	
33	838	1,922	407	16	447	3,473	158	411		16	970	462	14	13	2				44	1,255	30	730	696,400	122,550	850
34					30	1,097																	311,300	83,000	
35	50,684	167,418	38,573	3,524	62,609	608,261	27,309	65,938	647	3157	45,366	48,272	851	79	2,632	7,555	1,294	59,190	4,830	199,855	3,825	130,552	99,894,373	13,881,748	5,198,535
36	33	126		1,080	1,860	50,817		80	996	1537	32,894	132	118		1	10	1	30	8	185	10	288	2,409,747	50,658	16,400
37	50,717	167,544	38,573	4,604	64,469	659,078	27,309	66,019	1643	4694	78,260	48,404	969	79	2,633	7,565	1,295	59,220	4,838	200,040	3,835	130,840	102,304,120	13,932,406	5,214,935

PAROCHIAL REPORT OF THE UNITED LUTHERAN CHURCH IN AMERICA (1926)—(Continued).

FINANCIAL

INDEX NUMBER	VALUATION OF CHURCH PROPERTY				CONGREGATIONAL EXPENSES			CONGREGATIONAL BENEVOLENCE									SUMMARY	
								APPORTIONED				UNAPPORTIONED						
	45 Endowment	46 Other Property	47 Total Valuation	48 Indebtedness	49 Current	50 Unusual	51 Total	52 Paid	53 Excess	54 Deficit	55 Education	56 Foreign Missions	57 Home Missions	58 Inner Missions	59 Other Benevolence	60 Total Unapportioned Benevolence	61 Total Benevolence	62 Total Expenditures
1	1,002,183	1,157,918	24,007,285	2,340,000	1,488,695	1,272,642	2,761,337	219,605	1,589	93,761	54,001	35,702	13,588	42,330	66,164	211,785	431,390	3,192,727
2	100,708	1,036,200	8,722,308	741,735	510,534	290,640	801,174	69,783	23	7,695	41,064	2,574	1,328	9,667	36,551	91,184	160,967	962,141
3	36,900	140,425	2,693,516	267,874	200,285	371,753	572,038	44,745		103	23,858	10,294	6,242	14,432	15,342	70,168	114,913	686,951
4	88,730	419,156	6,654,146	647,668	481,566	390,684	872,250	35,833	4,433	11,475	9,137	19,572	8,734	33,097	19,036	89,626	193,900	1,066,150
5	11,000	88,607	1,593,997	118,334	133,404	82,700	216,104	101,245	126	13,503	10,263	3,792	2,729	10,666	12,135	59,308	73,797	289,901
6	310,693	342,599	5,121,042	191,437	357,351	258,890	616,241	31,794	394	11,146	8,342	17,885	3,086	18,412	59,308	107,033	160,553	776,794
7	62,409	104,875	2,277,026	137,993	153,062	57,706	211,368	74,513	310	10,509	16,035	6,323	1,538	17,519	7,498	48,913	75,416	286,784
8	172,731	336,142	6,610,098	950,044	475,435	549,263	1,024,698	211,918	3,477	53,105	19,280	23,690	8,797	15,518	15,895	83,180	106,797	1,131,495
9	100,246	368,469	10,621,239	1,222,917	792,689	648,508	1,441,197	123,923	532	36,163	5,766	35,336	8,607	19,455	25,569	94,733	315,464	1,756,661
10	142,847	240,954	6,144,999	1,126,064	595,511	740,649	1,336,160	88,617		29,000	15,938	16,646	3,390	26,481	25,901	116,105	240,028	1,576,188
11	27,990	148,734	1,126,064	300,294	293,322	193,939	487,261	189,793	7,161	7,667	5,938	29,014	13,122	6,790	24,437	56,929	145,946	632,807
12	129,659	578,872	3,598,754	1,645,686	892,973	884,387	1,777,360	32,059		51,071	15,938	2,423	3,655	60,835	38,771	157,680	347,473	2,124,833
13	41,338	129,459	11,404,630	315,544	170,325	70,494	240,819	93,617	527	13,208	3,868	11,458	7,647	5,706	5,556	21,208	53,267	294,086
14	32,791	255,005	5,443,154	1,163,321	453,701	376,023	829,724	87,091	47	3,303	16,026	406	177	14,761	16,771	66,663	160,280	990,004
15	7,000	7,000	1,843,805	28,429	20,939	16,294	37,233	887	53	10,793	204	329	329	4,074	582	5,556	5,443	42,676
16	58,053	79,713	4,517,491	472,722	335,398	335,285	670,683	87,091	3,396	377	20,025	9,822	2,463	4,074	18,641	55,025	142,116	812,799
17		2,000	39,100	4,943	3,476	1,467	4,943	887			85	17	17	256	502	1,389	1,389	6,332
18	8,600	39,660	996,210	226,332	92,819	56,439	149,258	13,465	135	5,499	349	706	543	1,062	4,786	18,251	18,251	167,509
19	6,625	151,550	2,652,175	633,929	172,555	314,263	486,818	29,821	433	10,770	2,103	2,044	724	2,605	12,944	42,765	42,765	529,583
20	10,000	102,200	1,005,400	271,533	63,155	65,907	129,062	9,565		291	1,134	716	249	1,552	22,386	32,151	32,151	161,213
21	29,970	70,575	1,269,950	89,798	137,458	36,698	174,156	31,797	466	31,111	2,238	1,472	433	238	10,008	41,805	41,805	215,961
22	6,250	44,200	1,357,350	244,957	117,040	164,100	281,140	20,715	140	5,729	5,535	1,751	196	3,010	13,891	34,606	34,606	315,746
23	44,200	133,554	1,523,064	131,390	33,562	6,768	40,330	8,174	22	2,445	709	590	190	1,212	4,574	12,748	12,748	53,078
24	4,410	35,400	1,071,700	118,020	91,439	51,530	142,969	9,440	120	3,469		460	978	959	5,645	15,085	15,085	158,054
25	3,100	71,285	1,011,685	52,030	92,269	73,093	165,362	10,947	108	34,416	861	679	476	859	8,029	18,976	18,976	184,338
26	3,800	61,313	1,371,013	234,240	83,568	84,481	168,049	13,582	461	4,863	1,439	2,060	866	1,490	9,337	22,919	22,919	190,968
27		20,745	421,695	167,190	48,071	154,768	202,839	7,453	65	2,319		915	186	489	6,664	14,117	14,117	216,936
28		91,330	3,974,530		328,428	465,494	793,922	56,844			12,949	5,231	1,629	4,284	37,280	94,124	94,124	888,046
29	3,000		315,700		69,266		69,266	7,803							1,559	1,559	9,362	78,628
30		45,300	383,062	114,046	42,156	25,261	67,417	6,368	1,095	375	1,821	387	60	546	1,281	4,095	10,463	77,880
31	149,200	1,003,805	6,553,486	1,066,644	577,190	542,328	1,119,518	100,932		798	12,159	16,253	6,134	13,162	13,362	61,070	162,002	1,281,520
32	1,300	1,300	223,020	16,336	14,188	3,976	18,164	2,293			82	48		40	1,021	1,191	3,484	21,648
33	1,000	81,400	901,350	178,400	59,545	50,866	110,414	10,584		5,370	394	1,380	161	1,574	6,044	16,628	16,628	127,042
34	2,400	52,000	448,700	79,650	61,200	13,717	74,917	10,584	290		394	650	190	190	1,061	1,061	1,061	75,978
35	2,547,863	7,441,745	128,964,264	15,300,109	9,443,178	8,651,013	18,094,191	1,853,225	30,138	460,334	300,820	268,875	100,063	314,697	441,606	1,426,061	3,279,286	21,373,477
36	25,000	51,875	2,553,680	40,000	156,163		156,163								1,079	1,079	1,079	11,465
37	2,572,063	7,493,620	131,517,944	15,340,109	9,599,341	8,651,013	18,250,354	1,853,225	30,138	460,334	300,820	268,875	100,063	314,697	442,685	1,427,140	3,280,365	21,384,942

COMPARATIVE PAROCHIAL REPORT OF THE UNITED LUTHERAN CHURCH IN AMERICA FOR 1919-1920-1921-1922-1923-1924-1925 AND 1926

INDEX NUMBER	YEAR	Pastors	Parishes	Congregations	MEMBERSHIP Baptized	MEMBERSHIP Confirmed	MEMBERSHIP Communing	ACCESSIONS CHILDREN Baptism	ACCESSIONS CHILDREN Otherwise	ACCESSIONS ADULT Baptism	ACCESSIONS ADULT Confirmation	ACCESSIONS ADULT Certificate	ACCESSIONS ADULT Otherwise	LOSSES CHILDREN Death	LOSSES CHILDREN Otherwise	LOSSES Death	LOSSES ADULT Certificate	LOSSES ADULT Otherwise
1	1926	3,127	2,706	3,876	1,315,620	916,858	677,287	34,562	17,573	5,178	25,451	16,866	19,781	1,983	12,789	11,758	11,467	22,831
2	1925	3,011	2,649	3,875	1,276,176	886,840	669,695	35,307	16,658	5,536	31,071	17,366	18,504	2,004	12,335	11,454	12,111	23,935
3	1 Year's Gain	116	57	1	39,444	30,018	7,592		915				1,277		454	304		
4	1 Year's Decrease							745		358	5,620	500		21			644	1,104
5	1926	3,127	2,706	3,876	1,315,620	916,858	677,287	34,562	17,573	5,178	25,451	16,866	19,781	1,983	12,789	11,758	11,467	22,831
6	1924	2,983	2,643	3,829	1,201,401	856,180	645,836	35,138	14,029	5,746	31,020	17,314	18,090	1,982	9,918	11,250	11,887	23,356
7	2 Year's Gain	144	63	47	114,219	60,678	31,451		3,544				1,691	1	2,871	508		
8	2 Years' Decrease							576		568	5,569	448					420	525
9	1926	3,127	2,706	3,876	1,315,620	916,858	677,287	34,562	17,573	5,178	25,451	16,866	19,781	1,983	12,789	11,758	11,467	22,831
10	1923	2,924	2,566	3,812	1,201,401	839,279	633,184	33,387	12,419	4,472	28,188	15,600	16,125	2,244	9,788	11,518	11,016	25,436
11	3 Years' Gain	203	140	64	114,219	77,579	44,103	1,175	5,154	706		1,266	3,656		3,001	240	451	
12	3 Years' Decrease										2,737			261				2,605
13	1926	3,127	2,706	3,876	1,315,620	916,858	677,287	34,562	17,573	5,178	25,451	16,866	19,781	1,983	12,789	11,758	11,467	22,831
14	1922	2,900	2,501	3,732	1,164,550	819,063	621,123	36,016	12,704	5,599	30,954	16,345	16,445	2,334	9,370	11,741	10,934	25,650
15	4 Years' Gain	227	205	144	151,070	97,795	56,164		4,869			523	3,336		3,419	17	533	
16	4 Years' Decrease							1,454		421	5,503			351				2,819
17	1926	3,127	2,706	3,876	1,315,620	916,858	677,287	34,562	17,573	5,178	25,451	16,866	19,781	1,983	12,789	11,758	11,467	22,831
18	1921	2,887	2,492	3,803	1,147,007	801,250	597,708	37,403	11,773	5,302	30,467	16,456	16,500	2,392	8,921	11,051	11,475	25,485
19	5 Years' Gain	240	214	73	168,613	115,608	79,519		5,800			410	3,281		3,868	707		
20	5 Years' Decrease							2,841		124	5,016			409			8	2,654
21	1926	3,127	2,706	3,876	1,315,620	916,858	677,287	34,562	17,573	5,178	25,451	16,866	19,781	1,983	12,789	11,758	11,467	22,831
22	1920	2,812		3,775	1,117,938	791,400	580,018	36,438		4,834	29,380	15,214	14,571			11,554	11,610	26,550
23	6 Years' Gain	315		101	197,682	125,458	97,269			344		1,652	5,210			204		
24	6 Years' Decrease							1,876			3,929						143	3,719
25	1926	3,127	2,706	3,876	1,315,620	916,858	677,287	34,562	17,573	5,178	25,451	16,866	19,781	1,983	12,789	11,758	11,467	22,831
26	1919	2,843		3,473	1,094,153	776,852	474,553	34,785		4,400	27,645	13,915	9,235			14,073	10,664	23,467
27	7 Years' Gain	284		403	221,467	140,276	202,734			778		2,951	10,546				803	
28	7 Years' Decrease							223			2,194					2,315		636

1926 AND 1925 GAINS COMPARED

INDEX NUMBER		Pastors	Parishes	Congregations	Baptized	Confirmed	Communing	Children Baptism	Children Otherwise	Adult Baptism	Confirmation	Adult Certificate	Adult Otherwise	Children Death	Children Otherwise	Death	Adult Certificate	Adult Otherwise
29	1926 Gain	116	57	1	39,444	30,018	7,592	745	915	358	5,620	500	1,277	21	454	304	644	1,104
30	1926 Decrease																	
31	1925 Gain	28	6	46	38,167	30,660	23,859	169	2,629	210	51	52	414	22	2,417	204	224	579
32	1925 Decrease																	
33	1926 Net Gain	88	51	45	277	642	16,267	914	1,714	148	5,671	552	863	43	1,963	100	868	1,683
34	1926 Net Decrease																	

COMPARATIVE PAROCHIAL REPORT OF THE UNITED LUTHERAN CHURCH IN AMERICA FOR 1919-1920-1921-1922-1923-1924-1925 AND 1926—Continued

| INDEX NUMBER | CHURCH PAPERS | | | CHURCH SCHOOLS | | | | | | | | | | | STUDENTS | | CHURCH SOCIETIES | | | | | | FINANCIAL — VALUATION CH'CH PROPERTY | | |
	No. Sub. to Official Papers	No. S. S. Papers Distributed	No. Sub. to Other Ch. Papers	SUNDAY Number	SUNDAY Officers and Teachers	SUNDAY Scholars	SUNDAY Home Dept.	SUNDAY Cradle Roll	WEEKDAY Number	WEEKDAY Teachers	WEEKDAY Scholars	Catechumens	Ministry	Deaconess	In Lutheran Institutions	In Non-Luth. Institutions	MEN'S Number	MEN'S Members	WOMEN'S Number	WOMEN'S Members	YOUNG P. Number	YOUNG P. Members	Church Edifices	Parsonages	School and Parish Houses
1	50,684	167,418	38,573	3,524	62,609	608,261	27,309	65,938	647	3,157	45,366	48,272	851		2,632	7,555	1,294	59,190	4,830	199,855	3,825	130,552	99,894,373	13,881,748	5,198,535
2	50,735	174,407	36,101	3,531	59,940	590,169	28,187	65,706	651	2,704	42,372	49,216	826	90	2,551	6,753	1,211	56,892	4,515	184,475	3,547	122,330	86,288,340	12,532,190	3,919,089
3	51		2,472	7	2,669	18,092	878	232	4	453	2,994	944	25		81	802	83	2,298	315	15,380	278	8,172	13,606,033	1,349,558	1,279,446
4	50,684	167,418	33,573	3,524	62,609	608,261	27,309	65,938	647	3,157	45,366	48,272	851		2,632	7,555	1,294	59,190	4,830	199,855	3,825	130,552	99,894,373	13,881,748	5,198,535
5	50,224	162,037	39,471	3,515	59,205	571,737	28,028	63,853	557	2,051	38,824	49,310	828	68	2,530	5,841	1,213	56,605	4,307	181,449	3,400	10,277	78,525,563	11,619,150	3,136,620
6	460	5,381		9	3,404	36,524		2,085	90	1,106	6,542		11	23	102	1,714	81	2,585	523	18,406	425	10,275	21,368,810	2,262,598	2,061,915
7			898				719					1,038													
8	50,684	167,418	38,573	3,524	62,609	608,261	27,309	65,938	647	3,157	45,366	48,272	851		2,632	7,555	1,294	59,190	4,830	199,855	3,825	130,552	99,894,373	13,881,748	5,198,635
9	47,618	152,731	34,708	3,440	56,863	552,872	27,164	61,995	523	1,638	28,438	45,238	746	67	2,381	5,402	1,137	53,706	4,151	174,535	3,200	115,726	70,971,368	10,415,614	2,463,970
10	3,066	14,687	3,865	84	5,746	55,389	145	3,943	124	1,519	16,928	3,034	5	12	251	2,153	157	5,484	679	25,320	625	14,826	28,923,005	3,466,134	2,734,565
11																									
12	50,684	167,418	38,573	3,524	62,609	608,261	27,309	65,938	647	3,157	45,366	48,272	851		2,632	7,555	1,294	59,190	4,830	199,855	3,825	130,552	99,894,373	13,881,748	5,198,535
13	49,267	144,631	33,867	3,465	55,330	555,510	23,506	59,264	490	1,453	25,149	35,311	717	59	2,015	4,520	1,102	52,525	4,013	173,270	3,132	115,294	65,598,841	9,237,584	1,584,150
14	1,417	22,787	4,706	59	7,279	52,751	1,137	6,674	157	1,704	20,217	12,961	134	20	617	3,035	192		817	26,585	693	15,318	34,295,532	4,644,161	3,614,385
15																									
16	50,684	167,418	38,573	3,524	62,609	608,261	27,309	65,938	647	3,157	45,366	48,272	851		2,632	7,555	1,294	59,190	4,830	199,855	3,825	130,552	99,894,373	13,881,748	5,198,535
17	50,969	118,139	21,454	3,683	54,268	522,691	26,142	52,148	375	954	17,534	34,034	582	85	1,712	4,292	967	47,052	3,618	154,089	2,694	106,842	63,193,694	8,138,433	878,400
18	13,715	49,279	17,119	158	8,341	85,570	1,167	3,790	272	2,203	27,832	14,238	269		920	3,263	327	12,138	1,212	45,766	1,131	23,710	36,700,679	5,743,315	4,320,135
19																									
20	50,684	167,418	38,573	3,524	62,609	608,261	27,309	65,938	647	3,157	45,366	48,272	851		2,632	7,555	1,294	59,190	4,830	199,855	3,825	130,552	99,894,373	13,881,748	5,198,535
21				3,399	52,691	515,815	23,506	46,300	190	326	7,070	44,334	577	46	1,888	4,316	892	39,426	3,547	139,205	2,367	92,822		6,928,456	
22					52,939						38,296														
23				125			3,803	19,638	457	2,831		3,938	274	33	794	3,239	402	19,764	1,283	60,650	1,458	37,730			
24	50,684	167,418	38,573	3,524	62,609	608,261	27,309	65,938	647	3,157	45,366	48,272	851		2,632	7,555	1,294	59,190	4,830	199,855	3,825	130,552	99,894,373	13,881,748	5,198,535
25				3,399	52,524	514,924	19,019	32,228	109	130	4,779	36,689	526	14	233	611	708	32,550	2,811	104,760	2,114	81,746		2,071,193	
26				112	9,085	93,337	8,200	33,710	538	3,027	40,587	11,583	325	65	2,399	6,944	586	26,640	2,019	95,095	1,711	48,806	28,923,005	11,810,555	
27																									
28																									

1926 AND 1925 GAINS COMPARED

INDEX NUMBER	No. Sub. to Official Papers	No. S. S. Papers Distributed	No. Sub. to Other Ch. Papers	SUNDAY Number	SUNDAY Officers and Teachers	SUNDAY Scholars	SUNDAY Home Dept.	SUNDAY Cradle Roll	WEEKDAY Number	WEEKDAY Teachers	WEEKDAY Scholars	Catechumens	Ministry	Deaconess	In Lutheran Institutions	In Non-Luth. Institutions	MEN'S Number	MEN'S Members	WOMEN'S Number	WOMEN'S Members	YOUNG P. Number	YOUNG P. Members	Church Edifices	Parsonages	School and Parish Houses
29			2,472	7	2,669	18,092	878	232	4	453	2,994	944	25	11	81	802	83	2,298	315	15,380	278	8,172	13,606,033	1,349,558	1,279,446
30	51	6,989		7	735		159	1,853	94	653	3,548			22	21	912		287	208	3,026	147	2,103	7,762,777	913,040	788,469
31	511	12,370	16	16		18,432						94													
32		3,370												2	60										
33		5,842												33		110		2,011	107	12,354	131	6,069	5,843,256	436,518	495,977
34	562	19,359	23	23	1,934	340	1,037	1,621	98	200	554	830	27												

COMPARATIVE PAROCHIAL REPORT OF THE UNITED LUTHERAN CHURCH IN AMERICA FOR 1919-1920-1921-1922-1923-1924-1925 AND 1926—Continued

FINANCIAL

Column groupings: **Valuation of Church Property** (Endowment, Other Property, Total Valuation, Indebtedness); **Congregational Expenses** (Current, Unusual, Total); **Congregational Benevolence — Apportioned** (Paid, Excess, Deficit); **Congregational Benevolence — Unapportioned** (Education, Foreign Missions, Home Missions, Inner Missions, Other Benevolence), Total Unapportioned Benevolence; **Summary** (Total Benevolence, Total Expenditures).

Index No.	Endowment	Other Property	Total Valuation	Indebtedness	Current	Unusual	Total	Paid	Excess	Deficit	Education	Foreign Missions	Home Missions	Inner Missions	Other Benevolence	Total Unapp. Benevolence	Total Benevolence	Total Expenditures
1	2,547,863	7,441,745	128,964,264	15,300,109	9,443,178	8,651,013	18,094,191	1,853,225	30,138	460,334	300,820	268,875	100,063	314,697	441,606	1,426,061	3,279,286	21,373,477
2	2,353,469	6,733,780	111,836,808	11,437,989	8,676,760	7,014,663	15,691,423	1,828,761	41,395	458,335	623,116	218,881	110,766	403,638	526,722	1,883,123	3,711,884	19,403,307
3	164,394	707,965	17,107,396	3,842,120	766,418	1,636,350	2,402,768	24,464	11,257	1,999	322,296	49,994	10,703	88,941	85,116	457,062	432,598	1,970,170
4																		
5	2,547,863	7,441,745	128,964,264	15,300,109	9,443,178	8,651,013	18,094,191	1,853,225	30,138	460,334	300,820	268,875	100,063	314,697	441,606	1,426,061	3,279,286	21,373,477
6	2,281,248	5,806,395	101,368,976	9,265,083	8,041,339	6,818,421	14,859,760	1,748,347	44,595	390,112	320,448	256,587	160,597	354,336	672,022	1,763,990	3,512,337	18,372,097
7	266,615	1,635,350	27,595,288	6,035,026	1,401,839	1,832,592	3,234,431	104,878	14,457	70,222	19,628	12,288	60,534	39,639	230,416	337,929	233,051	3,001,380
8																		
9	2,547,863	7,441,745	128,964,264	15,300,109	9,443,178	8,651,013	18,094,191	1,853,225	30,138	460,334	300,820	268,875	100,063	314,697	441,606	1,426,061	3,279,286	21,373,477
10	2,007,027	4,973,232	90,831,211	7,441,246	7,387,503	4,635,721	12,023,314	1,605,290	48,060	378,486	316,056	227,718	86,762	261,050	596,888	1,488,474	3,093,764	15,117,078
11	540,836	2,468,513	38,133,053	7,888,863	2,055,585	4,015,292	6,070,877	247,935	17,922	81,848	15,236	41,157	13,301	53,647	155,282	62,413	185,522	6,256,399
12																		
13	2,547,863	7,441,745	128,964,264	15,300,109	9,443,178	8,651,013	18,094,191	1,853,225	30,138	460,334	300,820	268,875	100,063	314,697	441,606	1,426,061	3,279,286	21,373,477
14	1,851,134	3,701,544	81,973,253	7,047,140	6,816,379	4,009,146	10,825,545	1,513,077	45,328	368,687	292,682	155,599	72,287	233,324	777,002	1,530,894	3,043,971	13,869,516
15	696,729	3,740,201	46,991,011	8,252,969	2,626,779	4,641,867	7,268,646	340,148	15,190	91,647	8,138	113,276	27,776	81,373	335,396	104,833	235,315	7,503,901
16																		
17	2,547,863	7,441,745	128,964,264	15,300,109	9,443,178	8,651,013	18,094,191	1,853,225	30,138	460,334	300,820	268,875	100,063	314,697	441,606	1,426,061	3,279,286	21,373,477
18	1,895,798	2,400,790	76,507,115	6,011,472	6,621,268	3,835,135	10,456,403	1,440,132	62,601	342,307	569,521	140,190	66,369	240,927	884,653	1,901,660	3,341,792	13,798,195
19	652,065	5,040,955	52,457,149	9,288,637	2,821,910	4,815,878	7,637,788	413,093	32,463	118,027	268,701	128,685	33,694	73,770	443,047	475,599	62,506	7,575,282
20																		
21	2,547,863	7,441,745	128,964,264	15,300,109	9,443,178	8,651,013	18,094,191	1,853,225	30,138	460,334	300,820	268,875	100,063	314,697	441,606	1,426,061	3,279,286	21,373,477
22	2,065,974		70,142,813	5,581,845	5,630,943	2,968,750	8,599,693	1,206,115			612,121		36,017	233,909	933,743	1,865,798	3,071,913	11,671,606
23	481,889		58,821,451	9,718,264	3,812,235	5,682,263	9,494,498	647,110			311,305		64,046	80,788	512,137	439,737	207,373	9,701,871
24																		
25	2,547,863	7,441,745	128,964,264	15,300,109	9,443,178	8,651,013	18,094,191	1,853,225	30,138	460,334	300,820	268,875	100,063	314,697	441,606	1,426,061	3,279,286	21,373,477
26	1,032,292		42,383,332	5,581,845	4,984,795	1,916,749	6,901,544	1,344,202					5,459			908,586	2,252,788	9,154,332
27	1,515,571		86,580,932	9,718,264	4,458,383	6,734,264	11,192,647	500,023			300,744		94,604		461,375	517,475	1,026,498	12,219,145
28																		

1926 AND 1925 GAINS COMPARED

Index No.	Endowment	Other Property	Total Valuation	Indebtedness	Current	Unusual	Total	Paid	Excess	Deficit	Education	Foreign Missions	Home Missions	Inner Missions	Other Benevolence	Total Unapp. Benevolence	Total Benevolence	Total Expenditures
29	164,394	707,965	17,107,396	3,842,120	766,418	1,636,350	2,402,768	24,464	11,257	1,999	322,296	49,994	10,703	88,941	85,116	457,062	432,598	1,970,170
30	102,221	927,385	10,487,892	2,192,906	635,421	196,242	831,663	80,414	3,200	68,223	302,668	37,706	49,831	49,302	145,300	119,133	199,547	1,031,210
31	62,173	219,420	6,619,504	1,649,214	130,997	440,108	1,571,105	55,050	8,057	66,224	624,964	87,700	39,128	138,243	60,184	576,195	632,145	938,960

PAROCHIAL REPORT OF THE UNITED LUTHERAN CHURCH IN AMERICA (1926)
Including Statistics Outside Continental United States and Canada.

PAROCHIAL

Index No.	Country	Province	Pastors	When Organized	Congregations	Membership Baptized	Membership Confirmed	Membership Communing	Acc. Children Baptism	Acc. Children Otherwise	Acc. Adult Baptism	Acc. Adult Confirmation	Acc. Adult Certificate	Acc. Adult Otherwise	Losses Children Death	Losses Children Otherwise	Losses Adult Death	Losses Adult Certificate	Losses Adult Otherwise
1	India	Madras	For. 23 Native 39	1843	1,491	129,865	54,178	45,458				15,122							
2	Africa	Liberia	For. 7 Native 0	1860	21	300	194	194				94							
3	Japan	Kyushu-Hondo	For. 15 Native 19	1893	3	2,475	1,094	1,047				200							
4	Argentina	Buenos Aires	For. 2 Native 3	1908	3	495	368	68				76							
5	British Guiana	New Amsterdam	For. 1 Native 3	1915	4	275	200	200				50							
6	China	Shantung	For. 5 Native 0	1897		2,219	955	620	114			210							
7	Porto Rico		ULC 6	1898	11	1,492	710	369	20	47		55	52				17	33	
8	Virgin Islands		Non ULC 1	1666	5	1,961	1,263	677	200			79	50		2		4	6	
9	Harlem, N.Y.C.		ULC 2	1920	2	843	600	460		131	2	64	94	59		6			
10	Total		125		1,540	139,925	59,562	49,049	334	178	2	15,950	196	59	2	6	21	39	
11	U.S. & Canada		3,127		3,876	1,315,620	916,858	677,287	34,562	17,573	5,178	25,451	16,866	19,781	1,983	12,789	11,758	11,467	22,831
12	Grand Total		3,252		5,416	1,555,545	976,420	726,336	34,896	17,751	5,180	41,401	17,062	19,840	1,985	12,795	11,779	11,506	22,831

PAROCHIAL — CHURCH SCHOOLS, STUDENTS, CHURCH SOCIETIES / FINANCIAL

Index No.	Ch. Papers No. Sub. to Official Papers	No. S.S. Papers Distributed	No. Sub. to Other Ch. Papers	Sunday Number	Sunday Officers and Teachers	Sunday Scholars	Sunday Home Dept.	Sunday Cradle Roll	Weekday Number	Weekday Teachers	Weekday Scholars	Catechumens	Ministry	Deaconess	In Lutheran Institutions	In Non-Luth. Institutions	Men's Number	Men's Members	Women's Number	Women's Members	Young P. Number	Young P. Members	Church Edifices	Parsonages	School and Parish Houses
1				982	1,526	44,318			969	1,484	30,000		100										1,000,000		
2				8	25	588			13	26	444												75,000		
3				8	30	2,410					200												700,000		4,800
4				11	46	492			3	4	300												200,000		
5				6	10	350			5														13,700		
6				41	52	150			7	5	642		1		1	4					7	173	185,000	24,175	11,600
7	12	50		18	82	1,598			7	7	900	37	12						2	19	2	75	70,282		
8	15	40		5	65	726				7	276	70	3			6			3	36			112,765	20,483	
9	6	36		1	24	185		80	2		132	25	2		1		1	30	3	130	1	40	53,000		
10	33	126		1,080	1,860	50,817		80	996	1,537	32,894	132	118		1	10	1	30	8	185	10	288	2,409,747	50,658	16,400
11	50,684	167,418	38,573	3,524	62,609	608,261	27,309	65,939	647	3,157	45,366	48,272	851	79	2,632	7,555	1,294	59,190	4,830	199,855	3,825	130,552	99,894,373	13,881,748	5,198,535
12	50,717	167,544	38,573	4,604	64,469	659,078	27,309	66,019	1,643	4,694	78,260	48,404	969	79	2,633	7,565	1,295	59,220	4,838	200,040	3,835	130,840	102,304,120	13,932,406	5,214,935

PAROCHIAL REPORT OF THE UNITED LUTHERAN CHURCH IN AMERICA (1926)
Including Statistics Outside Continental United States and Canada.—(Continued).

FINANCIAL

Index Number	Valuation of Church Property				Congregational Expenses			Congregational Benevolence									Summary	
								Apportioned				Unapportioned						
	Endowment	Other Property	Total Valuation	Indebtedness	Current	Unusual	Total	Paid	Excess	Deficit	Education	Foreign Missions	Home Missions	Inner Missions	Other Benevolence	Total Unapportioned Benevolence	Total Benevolence	Total Expenditures
1			1,000,000		135,000		135,000											
2			75,000															
3			700,000		7,800		7,800											
4			200,000		2,977		2,977											
5	25,000	2,500	52,000															
6			185,000															
7		16,175	110,632		2,129		2,129								683	683	683	2,812
8		29,200	174,048		3,010		3,010											3,010
9		4,000	57,000	40,000	5,247		5,247								396	396	396	5,643
10	25,000	51,875	2,553,680	40,000	156,163		156,163								1,079	1,079	1,079	11,465
11	2,547,063	7,441,745	128,964,264	15,300,109	9,443,178	8,651,013	18,094,191	1,853,225	30,138	460,334	300,820	268,875	100,063	314,697	441,606	1,426,061	3,279,286	21,373,477
12	2,572,063	7,493,620	131,517,944	15,340,109	9,599,341	8,651,013	18,250,354	1,853,225	30,138	460,334	300,820	268,875	100,063	314,697	442,685	1,427,140	3,280,365	21,384,942

COMPARISON OF TOTALS OF ACCESSIONS AND LOSSES, NET VALUATION

COMPARISON OF TOTALS OF ACCESSIONS AND LOSSES

1926 Total accessions 119,411
1925 Total accessions 142,442
1926 Decrease in accessions 23,031
1925 Increase in accessions 21,105
1926 Net decrease in accessions 44,136

1926 Total losses 60,828
1925 Total losses 61,839
1926 Decrease in losses 1,011
1925 Increase in losses 3,446
1926 Net decrease in losses 4,457

1926 Accessions gain over losses..... 58,582
1925 Accessions gain over losses...... 80,603
1926 Loss in accessions gain over losses 22,021
1925 Gain in accessions gain over losses 17,000
1926 Net loss 39,021

NET VALUATION

1926 Total valuation $128,964,264
1926 Total indebtedness 15,300,109
1926 Net valuation 113,664,155
1925 Net valuation 100,398,878
1926 Gain net valuation 13,265,277

1924 Net valuation 92,103.946
1923 Net valuation 83,389,965
1922 Net valuation 74,926,113
1921 Net valuation 70,495,643
1920 Net valuation 64,560.968
1919 Net valuation 37,855,419

PER CAPITAS

	Current Expenses	Unusual Expenses	Total Congregational	Apportionment Benev. Paid	Total Benevolence	Total Expenditures
1926 Per Capita (916,858 cf.m.)........	$10.30	$9.44	$19.73	$2.02	$3.58	$23.31
1925 Per Capita (886,840 cf.m.)........	9.78	7.91	17.69	2.06	4.19	21.88
1926 Gain per capita	.52	1.53	2.04			1.43
1926 Loss per capita				.04	.61	
1924 Per Capita (856,180 cf.m.)........	9.39	7.96	17.36	2.04	4.10	21.46
1925 Gain per capita	.39		.33	.02	.09	.42
1925 Loss per capita		.05				
1923 Per Capita (839,279 cf.m.)........	8.80	5.52	14.33	1.91	3.52	18.00
1922 Per Capita (819,063 cf.m.)........	8.32	4.89	13.21	1.84	3.71	16.93
1921 Per Capita (801,250 cf.m.)........	8.26	4.79	13.05	1.79	4.17	17.22
1920 Per Capita (791,400 cf.m.)........	7.15	3.75	10.90	1.52	3.88	14.78
1919 Per Capita (776,582 cf.m.)........	6.42	2.46	8.88	1.73	2.90	11.78

PAROCHIAL REPORT OF THE UNITED LUTHERAN CHURCH IN AMERICA—1927
United States and Canada

PAROCHIAL

Index Number	SYNOD	When Organized	Pastors	Parishes	Congregations	MEMBERSHIP			ACCESSIONS						LOSSES				
						Baptized	Confirmed	Communing	CHILDREN		ADULT				CHILDREN		ADULT		
									Baptism	Otherwise	Baptism	Confirmation	Certificate	Otherwise	Death	Otherwise	Death	Certificate	Otherwise
1	Ministerium of Pa.	Aug. 15, 1748	443	374	589	280,105	191,155	140,733	7,400	3,174	525	7,090	3,100	2,320	479	2,913	2,983	2,115	5,151
2	Ministerium of New York	Oct. 23, 1786	168	145	145	96,864	67,230	48,049	2,904	1,364	130	2,332	736	1,306	136	767	1,442	410	592
3	United Synod of N. C.	May 2, 1803	103	160	160	34,337	24,370	18,704	1,748	174	96	765	471	86	79	53	238	438	237
4	Synod of Maryland	Oct. 11, 1820	125	101	138	63,754	46,959	31,873	1,748	580	188	1,638	774	792	87	849	650	631	763
5	Synod of S. Carolina	Jan. 14, 1824	60	38	110	26,570	19,372	19,372	593	227	75	673	460	60	23	95	161	342	59
6	Synod of W. Penna.	Sept. 5, 1825	116	92	160	56,973	42,499	34,949	1,718	469	328	1,449	1,126	648	70	474	722	726	658
7	Synod of Virginia	Aug. 10, 1829	87	77	174	22,980	18,356	12,033	336	191	259	421	338	221	30	125	237	257	90
8	Synod of New York	Oct. 26, 1830	180	148	160	57,700	38,287	24,210	1,681	1,201	189	1,348	621	936	89	721	456	454	950
9	Synod of Ohio	Nov. 7, 1836	222	195	233	79,395	53,373	47,688	2,184	908	625	1,922	1,376	872	132	557	868	1,035	2,427
10	East Pennsylvania Synod	May 2, 1842	169	129	158	66,653	48,373	33,816	1,609	639	352	1,604	1,214	559	123	332	630	712	1,218
11	Alleghany Synod	Sept. 9, 1842	77	70	146	40,302	30,240	21,315	921	362	257	903	499	303	28	303	401	486	561
12	Pittsburgh Synod	Jan. 15, 1845	268	220	316	115,144	78,775	52,477	3,195	1,768	415	2,790	1,705	2,230	183	1,445	894	1,225	2,665
13	Indiana Synod	Oct. 28, 1848	61	63	73	15,025	11,515	8,768	324	115	123	368	226	165	11	78	126	144	281
14	Illinois Synod	Sept. 8, 1851	142	118	139	47,014	31,071	26,364	1,662	1,263	415	1,761	902	1,441	89	953	344	427	1,239
15	Texas Synod	Nov. 10, 1851	22	27	30	6,000	3,884	3,017	161	135	17	246	71	179	8	26	53	41	276
16	Susquehanna Synod of C. Pa.	Feb. 21, 1855	102	83	165	51,029	38,128	26,450	1,173	369	249	1,106	798	429	57	922	485	467	667
17	Mississippi Synod	July 25, 1855	9	6	12	855	694	256	10	2	8	11	9		15	233	8	4	1
18	Synod of Iowa	Sept. 3, 1855	32	32	32	13,040	8,248	6,231	472	353	147	514	189	532	21	487	66	140	143
19	Michigan Synod	Oct. 27, 1855	63	59	87	20,195	14,493	9,315	550	395	156	417	585	310			231	212	381
20	Synod of Georgia	July 20, 1860	25	30	44	7,467	5,002	3,685	100	48	20	132	313	207	4	207	45	72	233
21	Synod of Canada	July 21, 1861	90	64	90	28,339	19,009	14,806	627	133	20	508	70	237	34	88	226	114	377
22	Synod of Kansas	Nov. 5, 1868	44	35	43	9,497	6,745	5,060	311	163	85	256	306	633	25	144	101	168	315
23	Synod of Nebraska	Sept. 1, 1871	52	42	52	18,078	12,122	8,252	595	220	167	542	308	248	27	148	88	263	310
24	Wartburg Synod	1875	53	47	57	18,830	12,260	9,145	533	177	47	349	27	417	26	78	125	36	224
25	German Nebraska Synod	July 24, 1890	85	79	91	18,696	12,960	9,575	474	26	24	417	51	151	29	161	117	109	84
26	Synod of California	Apr. 2, 1891	63	38	38	8,523	5,414	4,005	344	221	39	315	263	336	18	78	86	67	366
27	Rocky Mt. Synod	May 6, 1891	24	15	15	3,115	2,341	1,605	114	91	35	101	146	142	7	194	31		103
28	Synod of the Northwest	Sept. 22, 1891	90	76	84	45,158	28,807	21,407	1,388	1,409	222	1,393	373	1,595	56	1,383	190	308	2,085
29	Manitoba Synod	July 16, 1897	41	34	75	11,164	6,156	4,477	460	267	28	371	158	236	13	120	88	60	117
30	Pacific Synod	Sept. 26, 1901	36	32	30	5,119	2,971	2,183	188	1,783	119	172	1,388	1,249	48	851	269	516	1,601
31	N. Y. and N. Eng. Synod	Sept. 23, 1902	106	85	85	53,444	35,123	25,511	1,416			1,535	19		42	42	51	23	30
32	Nova Scotia Synod	July 10, 1903	8	8	31	6,012	2,992	2,183	116	5	14	197	19		12	22	29	23	30
33	Synod of West Virginia	April 17, 1912	17	23	37	6,400	4,200	3,294	192	27	23	156	82		8	27	81	73	135
34	Slovak "Zion" Synod	June 10, 1919	19	21	29	13,848	8,779	4,853	307	5		69	66	6	17	7	148		125
35	Total for U. S. and Canada		3,184	2,699	3,881	1,321,780	933,650	676,496	36,668	18,264	5,397	33,871	18,704	20,012	2,023	14,772	12,677	12,117	24,464
36	Total Outside U. S. and Canada		148		1,631	147,236	62,623	49,132	182	49	2	16,446	134		24	74	63	68	40
37	U. L. C.—World Total		3,332	2,689	5,512	1,469,016	996,273	725,628	36,840	18,313	5,399	50,317	18,838	20,012	2,047	4,846	12,740	12,185	24,504

PAROCHIAL REPORT OF THE UNITED LUTHERAN CHURCH IN AMERICA—1927
Continued

Index Number	CHURCH PAPERS			CHURCH SCHOOLS								Catechumens	STUDENTS				CHURCH SOCIETIES						FINANCIAL		
	No. Sub. to Official Papers	No. S.S. Papers Distributed	No. Sub. to Other Ch. Papers	SUNDAY					WEEKDAY				Ministry	Deaconess	In Lutheran Institutions	In Non-Lutheran Institutions	MEN'S		WOMEN'S		YOUNG P.		VALUATION CHURCH PROPERTY		
				Number	Officers and Teachers	Scholars	Home Dept.	Cradle Roll	Number	Teachers	Scholars						Number	Members	Number	Members	Number	Members	Church Edifices	Parsonages	School and Parish Houses
1	7,869	15,744	5,546	587	11,650	116,248	5,347	12,809	120	707	1,539	6,951	116	17	323	1311	209	10,133	712	35,419	590	23,478	18,861,560	2,360,548	1,767,957
2	1,885	5,036	1,636	161	2,737	24,739	352	4,129	34	102		2,364	37		62	198	120	6,905	249	15,811	226	8,305	7,272,325	1,208,625	1,170,800
3	1,244	2,166	2,576	144	1,895	19,910	89	890	59	52	1,539	2,736	16	7	165	236	32	1,308	129	3,582	161	1,161	2,566,650	376,590	78,048
4	1,834	5,335	2,210	143	3,528	34,301	2,403	4,068	18	131	1,410	2,080	35	4	63	423	50	3,168	227	10,399	196	7,770	5,827,650	735,350	312,700
5	1,185	2,075	1,729	106	1,815	12,961	298	3,190	45	150	3,375	2,288	26	2	230	248	67		137	4,221	147	4,250	1,252,086	239,299	123,000
6	1,801	3,475	1,589	160	1,582	43,131	1,497	1,163	35	292	3,873	3,850	11	3	168	334	29	2,033	235	9,929	181	7,880	3,949,200	562,044	324,000
7	1,572	2,356	2,186	139	2,312	14,802	508	3,249	23	105	2,504	681	26	1	72	157	36	866	151	4,133	110	3,851	1,746,450	396,092	87,800
8	1,320	5,873	915	130	3,765	18,180	982	4,043	35	76	1,321	1,553	26	1	74	219	24	2,896	235	9,035	207	5,486	7,379,636	855,300	383,800
9	3,226	23,589	1,748	276	5,041	51,421	1,600	4,041	35	127	1,661	3,243	59	2	356	675	67	5,814	451	19,934	240	6,547	8,799,000	919,424	434,100
10	2,066	7,965	1,688	156	2,488	41,025	1,277	2,501	43	273	3,222	2,276	54	1	115	509	131	5,167	268	12,281	237	7,483	7,136,913	997,835	415,876
11	1,247	7,719	3,309	126	5,504	23,917	3,017	6,655	45	341	4,353	1,631	30	1	85	346	27	1,228	164	5,310	108	3,770	2,963,500	451,232	45,000
12	4,910	20,988	12,472	301	3,097	26,874	570	860	82	433	5,990	4,712	68	4	217	688	131	5,459	503	17,692	367	11,432	9,819,930	1,377,600	320,000
13	910	4,001	236	70	221	8,884	31	122	9	49	580	566	15	1	24	119	23	709	107	3,329	50	1,306	1,424,125	210,787	37,300
14	1,822	13,050	1,452	136	3,148	32,206	1,669	2,747	36	207	191	1,705	37	3	96	424	72	3,493	265	9,338	206	6,360	4,643,548	569,513	173,600
15	225	328	608	28	221	1,776	520	2,980	7	17	2,709	289	41	4	43	18	5	93	29	937	27	698	132,000	46,800	9,750
16	1,128	6,372	1,151	166	3,148	32,206	1,669	2,747	35	233		2,018	35	1	152	389	48	2,585	185	7,216	150	5,283	4,025,300	493,803	114,500
17	34			12	67	376	14	5	5	11	40	5	2	1	1	3				109		72	34,000	3,100	
18	472	3,288	298	31	598	5,527	106	794	5	60	215	859	11	1	33	173	10	403	60	2,256	60	2,155	1,008,950	159,900	8,000
19	524	5,866	633	79	1,280	10,783	197	945	12	22	634	730	10	1	41	55	26	1,048	125	4,521	73	1,724	2,672,872	229,400	103,125
20	614	998	409	30	398	3,272		288	4	28	167	201	5	1	16	34	8	220	57	1,729	44	1,305	63,100	89,700	207,781
21	401	1,564	616	79	811	6,040	7	865	22	20	553	628	26	1	46	56	7	270	55	2,643	57	2,127	1,002,280	198,600	70,925
22	722	2,228	339	42	667	5,511	172	603	10	44	698	412	13	2	23	135	18	504	90	2,642	51	1,206	1,164,900	210,100	34,500
23	639	3,527	2,863	53	935	7,881	80	989	16	53	471	1,155	17	1	83	271	11	312	83	2,566	63	1,578	1,213,886	161,579	16,000
24	781	1,728	308	55	407	4,384	36	313	33	21	729	488	18	1	11	28	13	719	83	2,248	42	1,229	771,000	240,300	50,700
25	389	1,560	147	38	403	4,209	91	235	6	43	127	590	4	1	38	18	13	345	64	1,996	43	1,206	695,900	223,700	17,000
26	1,621	1,109	68	15	456	3,366	155	368	4	54	176	494	5	3	2	39	13	126	64	727	49	926	1,305,768	71,500	47,000
27	1,233	6,340	995	83	240	1,522	91	234	17	39	1,109	101	4	1	51	303	13	1,931	23	5,220	18	329	373,950	38,700	4,500
28				50	1,618	13,312	155	2,246	57	54	1,679	1,681	28	3			49		138	291	149	3,961	3,235,698	301,500	184,154
29					136	1,841				39									17	1,178			327,050		
30	236	1,618	273	31	297	2,493	43	270	3	23	3,432	182	3	2	6	103	10	215	52	7,370	22	489	387,300	70,800	2,000
31	1,343	3,526	1,028	90	2,095	18,239	430	2,740	43	234		1,443	24	7	52	570	67	3,881	150	440	36	716	5,481,619	522,500	283,500
32	11	100	140	15	131	846		124		7	388	160	4	2	3				12	1,198	171	4,656	189,870	31,000	
33	573	1,487	589	30	436	3,357	132	293	6	23	1,370	299	1	1	8	53	10	315	44		5	134	749,040	123,000	2,000
34	70			19	62	1,113	1	26	28	41		32	1	3	1						30	740	470,800	121,500	
35	43,917	162,246	49,825	3,651	64,212	613,863	25,826	65,544	928	4,183	58,491	48,523	761	52	2626	8338	1383	63,146	5,181	208,003	3,986	133,682	108,956,533	14,508,321	6,830,516
36	33	158	24	24	1,863	50,827		99	1,077	1,678	38,567	139	188		1	14	1	36	8	202	10	280	2,436,300	31,000	4,800
37	43,950	162,404	49,825	3,675	66,075	664,690	25,826	65,643	2005	5,861	97,058	48,962	949	52	2627	8352	1384	63,182	5,189	208,205	3,996	133,962	113,392,833	14,629,321	6,835,316

PAROCHIAL REPORT OF THE UNITED LUTHERAN CHURCH IN AMERICA—1927
Concluded

FINANCIAL

Index Number	Valuation of Church Property — Endowment	Other Property	Total Valuation	Indebtedness	Congregational Expenses — Current	Unusual	Total	Congregational Benevolence / Apportioned — Paid	Excess	Deficit	Education	Unapportioned — Foreign Missions	Home Missions	Inner Missions	Other Benevolence	Total Un-Apportioned Benevolence	Summary — Total Benevolence	Total Expenditures
1	1,046,940	1,773,911	25,810,916	3,065,151	1,608,788	1,737,769	3,346,557	361,323	4,254	135,105	44,419	33,373	13,912	67,415	50,078	209,197	570,520	3,917,077
2	147,911	563,920	10,363,581	893,201	572,821	400,332	973,153	102,174	472	101,271	18,936	3,118	1,307	51,386	29,707	104,454	206,628	1,179,781
3	46,242	143,222	3,211,059	360,311	203,087	295,624	499,611	70,080		13,065	6,789	78,013	6,206	14,184	20,851	195,563	265,643	765,254
4	90,855	382,650	7,349,805	798,888	516,196	476,176	992,372	109,646	2,738	13,052	17,228	17,696	11,027	77,818	31,288	134,181	243,827	1,236,199
5	65,000	44,360	1,724,245	133,863	137,739	90,536	228,275	36,097		21,307	9,445	3,475	5,410	11,177	11,024	44,339	80,436	308,711
6	260,316	478,416	5,579,976	336,193	475,881	462,053	937,934	134,120	7,205	21,807	10,415	18,489	5,410	12,534	6,365	75,809	209,929	1,147,863
7	35,409	166,425	2,455,176	69,932	158,612	69,932	228,544	34,257	186	17,886	121,055	6,090	2,582	6,939	9,318	40,934	75,191	303,735
8	183,278	182,478	8,884,492	1,158,008	536,051	424,267	960,318	69,615	619	55,621	16,035	4,148	2,008	9,455	6,365	140,515	210,130	1,170,448
9	100,246	368,469	10,621,239	1,222,917	792,689	648,508	1,441,197	211,918	3,477	36,163	15,013	23,690	8,797	39,659	26,003	103,546	315,464	1,756,661
10	145,967	317,650	9,014,241	1,294,857	674,739	550,409	1,225,198	127,396	632	20,946	16,143	33,142	9,874	69,693	29,473	128,691	256,087	1,481,285
11	36,762	149,083	3,640,577	310,845	319,697	133,165	452,862	87,726	5,281	3,578	17,162	22,414	4,071	12,123	5,556	72,325	160,051	612,913
12	167,862	770,963	12,456,325	1,974,105	964,753	635,748	1,600,501	197,590		40,410	3,868	14,455	20,509	69,481	15,492	199,259	396,849	1,997,350
13	41,338	261,402	1,843,509	315,544	170,325	70,494	240,819	32,059	527	13,209	48,501	2,423	10,380	5,706	802	21,208	53,267	294,086
14	42,706	12,818	5,600,669	30,668	523,637	254,188	777,825	99,845	442	13,139	353	3,655	20,697	209,525	6,228	109,525	209,370	987,195
15	230	120,541	201,598	480,300	25,270	13,683	38,953	4,069	14	377	7,827	1,643	171	93	37,919	502	10,297	49,250
16	54,830	38,210	4,308,974	3,476	349,317	185,443	534,760	95,135	3,008	10,154	85	103	8,072	8,072	256	37,919	13,054	667,814
17	2,000	40,978	39,100	39,100	3,476	1,467	4,943	887	1	85	4,187	8,651	400	1,071	11,726	502	1,389	6,332
18	5,200	65,860	1,220,260	326,960	130,395	63,599	193,994	15,251	522	10,154	643	51	1,195	4,425	4,423	11,003	26,254	200,248
19	8,500	64,574	2,994,875	694,497	196,995	190,813	387,808	40,416		14,102	1,572	922	631	2,091	7,358	17,380	57,796	446,604
20	13,424	66,590	447,939	320,481	75,729	131,669	207,398	11,092	222	581	1,587	3,759	1,042	3,416	17,339	22,891	33,983	241,381
21	27,500	152,647	1,363,879	98,497	136,481	84,024	220,505	31,026		37,012	1,329	847	1,286	2,235	3,190	5,547	36,573	257,078
22	13,450	26,555	1,489,540	228,213	163,537	78,792	242,629	27,983	222	12,050	7,323	1,429	631	690	9,781	10,348	38,331	280,960
23	4,460	71,285	1,548,572	126,648	127,348	46,237	173,585	31,066	387	3,763	1,587	1,127	3,223	2,354	3,190	26,579	37,645	231,230
24	3,100	53,138	1,091,655	143,620	99,673	53,397	153,070	9,025	76	34,416	2,695	3,967	376	859	4,899	4,899	13,924	186,994
25	3,800	26,555	1,011,685	52,030	92,269	93,093	165,362	10,947	108	6,294	2,984	376	784	1,486	3,031	3,031	13,976	184,338
26	2,250	71,285	1,479,656	248,011	106,553	115,633	222,186	14,147	287	1,089	247	679	476	293	3,588	7,906	22,053	244,239
27		53,138	429,950	157,565	43,097	25,769	68,866	5,946	5		575	1,721	864	354	885	2,523	8,469	77,335
28	3,000	12,800	3,801,237		372,404	166,013	538,417	55,020			22,871	864	354	8,916	19,408	58,520	113,540	64,550
29		76,885	327,050	182,814	54,729	20,229	54,729	7,899		1,878		354	281		1,389	1,389	9,821	82,263
30		11,487	471,587	471,587	49,476	478,119	69,705	100,191	10	3,478	1,819	4,261	3,064	865	1,244	4,659	12,558	1,298,546
31	175,290	815,534	7,278,443	1,266,831	654,054	16,285	1,132,173	1,993	1,243		6,891	450	8,810	21,746	14,088	66,112	166,373	17,550
32			222,740	16,285	12,299	2,146	28,584	11,082	203	3,380	114	14,647	190		924	1,112	3,105	136,241
33	128,000	128,000	1,002,640	164,529	68,214	50,123	118,337	938			502	74		2,907	2,097	6,822	17,904	76,420
34	31,500	31,500	632,500	118,150	69,420	4,775	74,195					1,126			1,287	1,287	2,225	
35	2,757,866	7,523,560	140,600,870	17,883,930	10,487,050	8,034,224	18,521,226	2,156,391	31,925	623,483	434,917	320,647	129,359	480,531	515,817	1,881,271	4,087,662	22,558,888
36	25,000	51,500	2,582,600	39,000	163,175		163,175								2,108	2,108	2,108	14,283
37	2,782,866	7,575,060	143,192,470	17,922,930	10,650,176	8,034,224	18,684,401	2,156,391	31,925	623,483	434,917	320,647	129,359	480,531	517,925	1,883,379	4,089,770	23,573,171

COMPARATIVE PAROCHIAL REPORT OF THE UNITED LUTHERAN CHURCH IN AMERICA FOR 1919, 1920, 1921, 1922, 1923, 1924, 1925, 1926, 1927

PAROCHIAL

Index Number	YEAR	Pastors	Parishes	Congregations	MEMBERSHIP			ACCESSIONS						LOSSES					CHURCH PAPERS		
					Baptized	Confirmed	Communing	Children Baptism	Children Otherwise	Adult Baptism	Adult Confirmation	Adult Certificate	Adult Otherwise	Children Death	Children Otherwise	Adult Death	Adult Certificate	Adult Otherwise	No. Sub. to Official Papers	No. S. S. Papers Distributed	No. Sub. to Other Ch. Papers
1	1927	3,184	2,689	3,881	1,321,780	933,650	676,496	36,668	18,264	5,397	33,871	18,704	20,012	2,023	14,772	12,677	12,117	24,464	43,917	162,246	49,825
2	1926	3,127	2,706	3,876	1,315,620	916,858	677,287	34,562	17,573	5,178	25,451	16,866	19,781	1,983	12,789	11,758	11,467	22,831	50,684	167,418	38,573
3	1 Year's Gain	57		5	6,160	16,792		2,106	691	219	8,420	1,838	231	40	1,983	919	650	1,633			11,252
4	1 Year's Decrease		17				791												6,767	5,172	
5	1927	3,184	2,689	3,881	1,321,780	933,650	676,496	36,668	18,264	5,397	33,871	18,704	20,012	2,023	14,772	12,677	12,117	24,464	43,917	162,246	49,825
6	1925	3,011	2,649	3,875	1,276,176	886,840	669,695	35,307	16,658	5,536	31,071	17,366	18,504	2,004	12,335	11,454	12,111	23,935	50,735	174,407	36,101
7	2 Years' Gain	173	40	6	45,604	46,810	6,801	1,361	1,606		2,800	1,338	1,608	19	2,437	1,223	6	529			13,724
8	2 Years' Decrease									139									6,818	12,161	
9	1927	3,184	2,689	3,881	1,321,780	933,650	676,496	36,668	18,264	5,397	33,871	18,704	20,012	2,023	14,772	12,677	12,117	24,464	43,917	162,246	49,825
10	1924	2,983	2,643	3,829	1,238,009	856,180	645,836	35,138	14,029	5,746	31,020	17,314	18,090	1,982	9,918	11,250	11,887	23,356	50,224	162,037	39,471
11	3 Years' Gain	201	46	52	83,771	77,470	30,660	1,530	4,235		2,851	1,390	1,922	41	4,854	1,427	230	1,108		209	10,354
12	3 Years' Decrease									349									6,307		
13	1927	3,184	2,689	3,881	1,321,780	933,650	676,496	36,668	18,264	5,397	33,871	18,704	20,012	2,023	14,772	12,677	12,117	24,464	43,917	162,246	49,825
14	1923	2,924	2,566	3,812	1,201,401	839,279	633,184	33,387	12,419	4,472	28,188	15,600	16,125	2,244	9,788	11,518	11,016	25,430	47,618	152,731	34,708
15	4 Years' Gain	260	123	69	120,379	94,371	43,312	3,281	5,845	925	5,683	3,104	3,887		4,984	1,159	1,101			9,515	15,117
16	4 Years' Decrease													221				972	3,701		
17	1927	3,184	2,689	3,881	1,321,780	933,650	676,496	36,668	18,264	5,397	33,871	18,704	20,012	2,023	14,772	12,677	12,117	24,464	43,917	162,246	49,825
18	1922	2,900	2,501	3,732	1,164,550	819,063	621,123	36,016	12,704	5,599	30,954	16,345	16,445	2,334	9,370	11,741	10,934	25,650	49,267	144,631	33,867
19	5 Years' Gain	284	188	149	157,230	114,587	55,373	652	5,560		2,917	2,359	3,567		5,402	936	1,183			17,615	15,958
20	5 Years' Decrease									202				311				1,186	5,350		
21	1927	3,184	2,689	3,881	1,321,780	933,650	676,496	36,668	18,264	5,397	33,871	18,704	20,012	2,023	14,772	12,677	12,117	24,464	43,917	162,246	49,825
22	1921	2,887	2,492	3,803	1,147,007	801,250	597,768	37,403	11,773	5,302	30,467	16,456	16,500	2,392	8,921	11,051	11,475	23,485	36,969	118,139	21,454
23	6 Years' Gain	297	197	78	174,773	132,400	78,728		6,491	95	3,404	2,248	3,512		5,851	1,626	642	1,021	6,948	44,107	28,371
24	6 Years' Decrease							735						369							
25	1927	3,184	2,689	3,881	1,321,780	933,650	676,496	36,668	18,264	5,397	33,871	18,704	20,012	2,023	14,772	12,677	12,117	24,464	43,917	162,246	49,825
26	1920	2,812		3,775	1,117,938	791,400	580,018	36,438		4,834	29,380	15,214	14,571			11,554	11,610	26,550			
27	7 Years' Gain	372		106	203,842	142,250	96,478	230		563	4,491	3,490	5,441			1,113	507				
28	7 Years' Decrease																	2,086			
29	1927	3,184	2,689	3,881	1,321,780	933,650	676,496	36,668	18,264	5,397	33,871	18,704	20,012	2,023	14,772	12,677	12,117	24,464	43,917	162,246	49,825
30	1919	2,843		3,473	1,094,153	776,582	474,553	34,785		4,400	27,645	13,915	9,235			14,073	10,664	23,467			
31	8 Years' Gain	341		408	227,627	157,068	201,943	1,883		997	6,226	4,789	10,777				1,453	997			
32	8 Years' Decrease															1,404					

COMPARATIVE PAROCHIAL REPORT OF THE UNITED LUTHERAN CHURCH IN AMERICA FOR 1919, 1920, 1921, 1922, 1923, 1924, 1925, 1926, 1927
Continued

Index Number	PAROCHIAL — Church Schools — Sunday					PAROCHIAL — Church Schools — Weekday			Catechumens	Students				Church Societies — Men's		Women's		Young P.		Financial — Valuation Church Property		
	Number	Officers and Teachers	Scholars	Home Dept.	Cradle Roll	Number	Teachers	Scholars		Ministry	Deaconess	In Lutheran Institutions	In Non-Lutheran Institutions	Number	Members	Number	Members	Number	Members	Church Edifices	Parsonages	School and Parish Houses
1	3,651	64,212	613,863	25,826	65,544	928	4,183	58,491	48,823	761	52	2,626	8,338	1,383	63,146	5,181	208,003	3,986	133,682	108,956,533	14,598,321	6,830,516
2	3,524	62,609	608,261	27,309	65,938	647	3,157	45,366	48,272	851	79	2,632	7,555	1,294	59,190	4,830	199,855	3,825	130,552	99,894,373	13,881,748	5,198,535
3	127	1,603	5,602	1,483	394	281	1,026	13,125	551	90	27	6	783	89	3,956	351	8,148	161	3,130	9,062,160	716,573	1,631,981
4																						
5	3,651	64,212	613,863	25,826	65,544	928	4,183	58,491	48,823	761	52	2,626	8,338	1,383	63,146	5,181	208,003	3,986	133,682	108,956,533	14,598,321	6,830,516
6	3,531	59,940	590,169	28,187	65,706	651	2,704	42,372	49,216	826	90	2,551	6,753	1,211	56,892	4,515	184,475	3,547	122,380	86,288,340	12,532,190	3,919,089
7	120	4,272	23,694	2,361	162	277	1,479	16,119	393	65	38	75	1,585	172	6,254	666	23,528	439	11,302	22,668,193	2,066,131	2,911,427
8																						
9	3,651	64,212	613,863	25,826	65,544	928	4,183	58,491	48,823	761	52	2,626	8,338	1,383	63,146	5,181	208,003	3,986	133,682	108,956,533	14,598,321	6,830,516
10	3,515	59,205	571,737	28,028	63,853	557	2,051	38,824	49,310	828	68	2,530	5,841	1,213	56,605	4,307	181,449	3,400	120,277	78,525,563	11,169,150	3,136,620
11	136	5,007	42,126	2,202	1,691	371	2,132	19,667	487	67	16	96	2,497	170	6,541	874	26,554	586	13,405	30,430,970	3,429,171	3,693,896
12																						
13	3,651	64,212	613,863	25,826	65,544	928	4,183	58,491	48,823	761	52	2,626	8,338	1,383	63,146	5,181	208,003	3,986	133,682	108,956,533	14,598,321	6,830,516
14	3,440	56,863	552,872	22,164	61,995	523	1,638	28,438	45,238	746	67	2,381	5,402	1,137	53,706	4,151	174,535	3,200	115,726	70,971,368	10,415,614	2,463,970
15	211	7,349	60,991	3,662	3,549	405	2,545	30,053	3,585	15	15	245	2,936	246	9,440	1,030	33,468	786	17,956	37,985,165	4,182,707	4,366,546
16																						
17	3,651	64,212	613,863	25,826	65,544	928	4,183	58,491	48,823	761	52	2,626	8,338	1,383	63,146	5,181	208,003	3,986	133,682	108,956,533	14,598,321	6,830,516
18	3,465	55,330	555,510	23,206	59,264	490	1,453	25,149	35,311	717	59	2,015	4,520	1,102	52,525	4,013	173,270	3,132	115,234	65,598,841	9,237,584	1,584,150
19	186	8,882	58,353	2,620	6,280	438	2,730	33,342	13,512	44	7	611	3,818	281	10,621	1,168	34,733	854	18,448	43,357,692	5,360,737	5,246,366
20																						
21	3,651	64,212	613,863	25,826	65,544	928	4,183	58,491	48,823	761	52	2,626	8,338	1,383	63,146	5,181	208,003	3,986	133,682	108,956,533	14,598,321	6,830,516
22	3,682	54,208	522,691	26,142	52,148	375	954	17,534	34,034	582	85	1,712	4,292	967	47,052	3,618	154,089	2,694	106,842	63,193,694	8,138,433	873,400
23		9,944	91,172	316	13,396	553	3,229	40,957	14,789	179	33	914	4,046	416	16,094	1,563	53,914	1,292	26,840	45,762,839	6,459,888	5,957,116
24	31																					
25	3,651	64,212	613,863	25,826	65,544	928	4,183	58,491	48,823	761	52	2,626	8,338	1,383	63,146	5,181	208,003	3,986	133,682	108,956,533	14,598,321	6,830,516
26	3,399	52,939	515,815	23,506	46,300	190	326	7,070	34,334	577	46	1,838	4,316	892	39,426	3,547	139,205	2,367	92,822		6,928,456	
27	252	11,273	98,048	2,320	19,244	738	3,857	51,421	14,489	184	6	788	4,022	491	23,720	1,634	68,798	1,619	40,860		7,669,865	
28																						
29	3,651	64,212	613,863	25,826	65,544	928	4,183	58,491	48,823	761	52	2,626	8,338	1,383	63,146	5,181	208,003	3,986	133,682	108,956,533	14,598,321	6,830,516
30	3,412	53,524	514,924	19,019	32,228	109	130	4,779	36,689	526	14	223	611	708	32,550	2,811	104,760	2,114	81,746		2,071,193	
31	239	10,688	98,939	6,807	33,316	819	4,053	53,712	12,134	235	38	2,403	7,727	675	30,596	2,370	103,243	1,872	51,936		12,527,128	
32																						

COMPARATIVE PAROCHIAL REPORT OF THE UNITED LUTHERAN CHURCH IN AMERICA FOR 1919, 1920, 1921, 1922, 1923, 1924, 1925, 1926, 1927
Concluded

FINANCIAL

Index Number	Endowment	Other Property	Total Valuation	Indebtedness	Current	Unusual	Total	Paid	Excess	Deficit	Education	Foreign Missions	Home Missions	Inner Missions	Other Benevolence	Total Un-Apportioned Benevolence	Total Benevolence	Total Expenditures
	VALUATION CHURCH PROPERTY				CONGREGATIONAL EXPENSES			CONGREGATIONAL BENEVOLENCE — APPORTIONED				UNAPPORTIONED					SUMMARY	
1	2,757,866	7,523,560	140,609,870	17,883,930	10,487,001	8,034,224	18,521,226	2,156,391	31,925	623,483	434,917	320,647	129,359	480,531	515,817	1,881,271	4,037,662	22,558,888
2	2,547,063	7,441,745	128,964,264	15,300,109	9,443,178	8,651,013	18,094,191	1,853,225	30,138	460,334	300,820	268,875	100,063	314,697	441,606	1,426,061	3,279,286	21,373,477
3	210,803	81,815	11,645,606	2,583,821	1,043,823		427,125	303,166	1,787	163,149	134,097	51,772	29,296	165,834	74,211	455,210	758,376	1,185,411
4						616,789												
5	2,757,866	7,523,560	140,609,870	17,883,930	10,487,001	8,034,224	18,521,226	2,156,391	31,925	623,483	434,917	320,647	129,359	480,531	515,817	1,881,271	4,037,662	22,558,888
6	2,383,469	6,733,780	111,856,868	11,457,989	8,676,760	7,014,663	15,691,423	1,828,761	41,395	458,335	623,116	218,881	110,766	403,638	526,722	1,883,123	3,711,884	19,403,307
7	374,397	789,780	28,753,002	6,425,941	1,810,241	1,019,561	2,829,803	327,630		165,148		101,766	18,593	76,893				3,155,581
8									9,470		188,199				10,905	1,852	325,778	
9	2,757,866	7,523,560	140,609,870	17,883,930	10,487,001	8,034,224	18,521,226	2,156,391	31,925	623,483	434,917	320,647	129,359	480,531	515,817	1,881,271	4,037,662	22,558,888
10	2,281,248	5,806,395	101,368,976	9,265,083	8,041,339	6,818,421	14,859,760	1,748,347	44,595	390,112	320,448	256,587	160,597	354,336	672,022	1,763,990	3,512,337	18,372,097
11	476,618	1,717,165	39,240,894	8,618,847	2,445,662	1,215,803	3,661,466	408,044		233,371	114,469	64,060		126,195		117,281	525,325	4,186,791
12									12,670				31,238		156,205			
13	2,757,866	7,523,560	140,609,870	17,883,930	10,487,001	8,034,224	18,521,226	2,156,391	31,925	623,483	434,917	320,647	129,359	480,531	515,817	1,881,271	4,037,662	22,558,888
14	2,007,027	4,973,232	90,831,211	7,441,244	7,387,593	4,635,721	12,023,314	1,605,290	48,060	378,486	316,056	227,718	86,762	261,050	596,888	1,488,474	3,093,764	15,117,078
15	750,839	2,550,328	49,778,659	10,442,684	3,099,408	3,398,503	6,497,912	551,101		244,997	118,861	92,929	42,597	219,481		392,797	943,898	7,441,810
16									16,135						81,071			
17	2,757,866	7,523,560	140,609,870	17,883,930	10,487,001	8,034,224	18,521,226	2,156,391	31,925	623,483	434,917	320,647	129,359	480,531	515,817	1,881,271	4,037,662	22,558,888
18	1,851,134	3,701,544	81,973,253	7,047,140	6,816,399	8,009,146	10,825,645	1,513,077	45,328	368,687	292,682	155,599	72,287	233,324	777,002	1,530,894	3,043,971	13,869,516
19	906,732	3,822,016	58,636,617	10,836,790	3,670,602	25,078	7,695,681	643,314		254,796	142,235	165,048	57,072	247,207		350,357	993,691	8,689,372
20									13,403						261,185			
21	2,757,866	7,523,560	140,609,870	17,883,930	10,487,001	8,034,224	18,521,226	2,156,391	31,925	623,483	434,917	320,647	129,359	480,531	515,817	1,881,271	4,037,662	22,558,888
22	1,895,798	2,400,790	76,507,115	6,011,472	6,621,268	3,835,135	10,456,403	1,440,132	62,601	342,307	569,521	140,190	66,369	240,927	884,653	1,901,660	3,341,792	13,798,195
23	862,068	5,122,770	64,102,755	11,872,458	3,865,733	4,199,089	8,064,823	716,259		281,176		180,457	62,990	239,604			695,870	8,760,693
24									30,676		134,604				368,836	20,389		
25	2,757,866	7,523,560	140,609,870	17,883,930	10,487,001	8,034,224	18,521,226	2,156,391	31,925	623,483	434,917	320,647	129,359	480,531	515,817	1,881,271	4,037,662	22,558,888
26	2,065,974		70,142,813	5,581,845	5,630,943	2,968,750	8,599,693	1,206,115			612,129		36,017	233,909	983,743	1,865,798	3,071,913	11,671,606
27	691,892		70,467,057	12,302,085	5,856,058	5,065,074	9,921,523	950,276					93,342	246,622		15,473	965,749	10,887,284
28											177,212				467,926			
29	2,757,866	7,523,560	140,609,870	17,883,930	10,487,001	8,034,224	18,521,226	2,156,391	31,925	623,483	434,917	320,647	129,359	480,531	515,817	1,881,271	4,037,662	22,558,888
30	1,032,292		42,383,332	4,527,913	4,984,795	1,916,749	6,911,544	1,344,202			76		5,459	480,461	902,981	908,586	2,252,788	9,154,332
31	1,725,574		98,226,538	13,356,017	5,496,206	6,117,475	11,609,682	812,189			434,841		123,900	70		972,685	1,784,874	13,404,556
32															387,164			

PAROCHIAL REPORT OF THE UNITED L UTHERAN CHURCH IN AMERICA—1927
1927 and 1926 Gains Compared

PAROCHIAL

Index Number					MEMBERSHIP				ACCESSIONS						LOSSES						CHURCH PAPERS		
									CHILDREN		ADULT				CHILDREN		ADULT						
		Pastors	Parishes	Congregations	Baptized	Confirmed	Communing		Baptism	Otherwise	Confirmation	Certificate	Otherwise		Death	Otherwise	Death	Certificate	Otherwise		No. Sub. to Official Papers	No. S.S. Papers Distributed	No. Sub. to Other Ch. Papers
1	1927 Gain	57	17	5	6,160	16,792	791		2,106	691	8,420	1,838	231		40	1,983	919	650	1,633		6,767	5,172	11,252
2	1927 Decrease																						
3	1926 Gain	116	57	1	39,444	30,018	7,592		745	915	5,620	500	1,227		21	454	304	644	1,104		51	6,989	2,472
4	1926 Decrease																						
5	1927 Net Gain			4	33,284	13,226	8,383		2,851	224	14,040	2,338	996		61	1,529	615	1,294	2,737		6,716	1,817	8,780
6	1927 Net Decrease.	59	74																				

PAROCHIAL

Index Number		CHURCH SCHOOLS								Catechumens	STUDENTS				CHURCH SOCIETIES					
		SUNDAY					WEEKDAY								MEN'S		WOMEN'S		YOUNG P.	
		Officers and Teachers	Scholars	Home Dept.	Cradle Roll	Number	Number	Teachers	Scholars		Ministry	Deaconess	In Lutheran Institutions	In Non-Lutheran Institutions	Number	Members	Number	Members	Number	Members
1		1,603	5,602	1,483	394	127	281	1,026	13,125	551	90	27	6	783	89	3,956	351	8,148	161	3,130
2																				
3		2,669	18,092	878	232	7	4	453	2,994	944	25	11	81	802	83	2,298	315	15,380	278	8,172
4																				
5		1,066	12,490	605	626	134	285	573	10,131	1,495	115	16	87	19	6	1,658	36	7,232	117	5,042
6																				

FINANCIAL

Index Number		VALUATION CHURCH PROPERTY		
		Church Edifices	Parsonages	School and Parish Houses
1		9,062,160	716,573	1,631,981
2				
3		13,606,033	1,349,558	1,229,446
4				
5		4,543,873	632,985	402,535
6				

FINANCIAL

Index Number	VALUATION CHURCH PROPERTY				CONGREGATIONAL EXPENSES			APPORTIONED			CONGREGATIONAL BENEVOLENCE UNAPPORTIONED						SUMMARY	
	Endowment	Other Property	Total Valuation	Indebtedness	Current	Unusual	Total	Paid	Excess	Deficit	Education	Foreign Missions	Home Missions	Inner Missions	Other Benevolence	Total Un-apportioned Benevolence	Total Benevolence	Total Expenditures
1	210,803	81,815	11,645,606	2,558,821	1,043,823	616,789	427,125	303,166	1,787	163,149	134,097	51,772	29,296	165,834	74,211	455,216	758,336	1,185,411
2																		
3	164,394	707,965	17,107,396	3,842,120	766,418	1,636,350	2,402,768	24,464	11,257	1,999	322,296	49,994	10,703	88,941	85,116	457,062	432,598	1,970,170
4																		
5	6,400	626,150	5,461,790	1,258,299	277,405	2,253,139	1,975,643	278,702	13,044	161,150	456,393	1,778	39,999	254,775	159,327	912,278	1,190,934	784,759
6																		

PAROCHIAL REPORT OF THE UNITED LUTHERAN CHURCH IN AMERICA—1927
Including Statistics Outside Continental United States and Canada

PAROCHIAL

Index Number	Country	Province	When Organized	Pastors	Congregations	MEMBERSHIP Baptized	MEMBERSHIP Confirmed	MEMBERSHIP Communing	ACCESSIONS CHILDREN Baptism	ACCESSIONS CHILDREN Otherwise	ACCESSIONS ADULT Baptism	ACCESSIONS ADULT Confirmation	ACCESSIONS ADULT Certificate	LOSSES CHILDREN Death	LOSSES CHILDREN Otherwise	LOSSES ADULT Death	LOSSES ADULT Certificate	LOSSES ADULT Otherwise	FINANCIAL Church Edifices	FINANCIAL Parsonages	FINANCIAL School and Parish Houses
1	India	Madras	1842	For. 28 Native51	1,491	136,555	57,324	45,458				14,961							1,116,600		
2	Africa	Liberia	1860	For. 11 Native 0	45	300	200	150				30							75,000		
3	Japan	Kyushu-Hondo	1893	For. 14 Native20	25	2,500	1,000	1,047				1,000							600,000		
4	Argentina	Buenos Aires	1908	For. 2 Native 3	10	664	500					40							208,000		
5	British Guiana	New Amsterdam	1915	For. 2 Native 0	7	300	200	200				30							13,700		
6	China	Shantung	1897	For. 2 Native 0	35	2,390	1,237	620	87	21		245	35	17					185,000		
7	Porto Rico		1898	U.L.C.6	11	1,582	737	410	34			60	10	4	28	27	41		71,000	6,000	
8	Virgin Islands		1666	U.L.C.2 Other 1	5	1,982	759	701	61	28		62	89	3	31	23		40	113,000	25,000	4,800
9	Harlem, N.Y.		1920	U.L.C.2	2	963	666	478			2	18			15	13	27		54,000		
10	Total Outside U.S. & Canada			148	1,631	147,236	62,623	49,132	182	49	2	16,446	134	24	74	63	68	40	2,436,300	31,000	4,800
11	U.S. and Canada			3,184	3,881	1,321,780	933,650	676,496	36,668	18,264	5,357	33,871	18,704	2,023	4,772	12,677	12,117	24,464	108,956,533	14,598,321	6,839,516
12	Grand Total			3,332	5,512	1,469,016	996,273	725,628	36,840	18,313	5,359	50,317	18,838	2,047	4,846	12,740	12,185	24,504	111,392,833	14,629,321	6,835,316

PAROCHIAL

Index Number	CHURCH SOCIETIES YOUNG P. Members	CHURCH SOCIETIES YOUNG P. Members	CHURCH SOCIETIES WOMEN'S Members	CHURCH SOCIETIES WOMEN'S Number	CHURCH SOCIETIES MEN'S Members	CHURCH SOCIETIES MEN'S Number	STUDENTS In Non-Lutheran Institutions	STUDENTS In Lutheran Institutions	STUDENTS Deaconess	STUDENTS Ministry	Catechumens	CHURCH SCHOOLS WEEKDAY Scholars	CHURCH SCHOOLS WEEKDAY Teachers	CHURCH SCHOOLS WEEKDAY Number	Cradle Roll	Home Dept.	CHURCH SCHOOLS SUNDAY Scholars	CHURCH SCHOOLS SUNDAY Officers and Teachers	CHURCH SCHOOLS SUNDAY Number	CHURCH PAPERS No. Sub. to Other Ch. Papers	CHURCH PAPERS No. S. S. Papers Distributed	CHURCH PAPERS No. Sub. to Official Papers
1										172		33,464	1,500	995			45,857	1,526				
2										8		500		8			500	25				
3												700	30				800	30				
4										2		1,560	40	11			536	46				
5										1		250		6			250	10				
6			20	2			6			1	48	1,669	41	41			300	52			62	13
7		7	41	3			8	1		4	60	301	52	5			1,617	83	18		45	15
8	181	1	141	3	36	1					31	123	8	2	99		730	65	5		51	5
9	68												7				237	26	1			
	31																					
10	280	10	202	8	36	1	14	1		188	139	38,567	1,678	1077	99		50,827	1,863	24	158	158	33
11	133,682	3,986	208,003	5,181	63,146	1383	8338	2626	52	761	48,823	58,491	4,183	928	65,544	25,826	613,863	64,212	3,651	49,825	162,246	43,917
12	133,967	3,996	208,205	5,189	63,182	1384	8352	2627	52	949	48,962	97,058	5,861	2005	65,643	25,826	664,690	66,075	3,675	49,825	162,404	43,950

PAROCHIAL REPORT OF THE UNITED LUTHERAN CHURCH IN AMERICA—1927
Including Statistics Outside Continental United States and Canada—Continued

FINANCIAL

Index Number	Valuation Church Property				Congregational Expenses			Congregational Benevolence										Summary	
	Endowment	Other Property	Total Valuation	Indebtedness	Current	Unusual	Total	Apportioned			Education	Unapportioned				Total Un-Apportioned Benevolence	Total Benevolence	Total Expenditures
								Paid	Excess	Deficit		Foreign Missions	Home Missions	Inner Missions	Other Benevolence			
1			1,116,600		138,000		138,000												
2			75,000		0		0												
3		2,500	600,000		8,000		8,000												
4			208,000		3,000		3,000												
5	25,000		52,000		0		0												
6			185,000		2,000		2,000												
7		16,000	112,000		2,987		2,987									781	781	781	3,768
8		30,000	176,000		3,808		3,808									927	927	927	4,735
9		3,000	58,000	39,000	5,380		5,380									400	400	400	5,780
10	25,000	51,500	2,582,600	39,000	163,175		163,175									2,108	2,108	2,018	14,283
11	2,757,866	7,523,560	140,609,870	17,883,930	10,487,001	8,034,224	18,684,401	2,156,391	31,925	623,483	434,917	320,647	129,359	480,531	515,817	1,818,271	4,037,662	22,558,888
12	2,782,866	7,575,060	143,192,470	17,922,930	10,650,176	8,034,224	18,521,226	2,156,391	31,925	623,483	434,917	320,647	129,359	480,531	517,925	1,863,379	4,039,770	22,573,171

COMPARISON OF TOTALS OF ACCESSIONS AND LOSSES, NET VALUATION AND PER CAPITAS

COMPARISON OF TOTALS OF ACCESSIONS AND LOSSES

1927 Total accessions 132,916	1927 Total losses 66,053
1926 Total accessions 119,411	1926 Total losses 60,828
1927 Increase in accessions 13,505	1927 Increase in losses.......................... 5,225
1926 Decrease in accessions 23,031	1926 Decrease in losses 1,011
1927 Net increase in accessions........ 36,536	1927 Net increase in losses 6,236

1927 Accessions gain over losses 66,863
1926 Accessions gain over losses 58,583
1927 Gain in accessions gain over losses... 8,280
1926 Loss in accessions gain over losses... 22,021
1927 Net gain 30,301

COMPARISON OF NET VALUATION

1927 Total valuation $140,609,870	1924 Net valuation $92,103,946
1927 Total indebtedness 17,883,930	1923 Net valuation 83,389,965
1927 Net valuation 122,725,940	1922 Net valuation 74,926,113
1926 Net valuation 113,664,155	1921 Net valuation 70,495,643
1927 Gain net valuation.............. 9,061,785	1920 Net valuation 64,560,968
1925 Net valuation 100,398,878	1919 Net valuation 37,855,419

PER CAPITAS

	Current Expenses	Unusual Expenses	Total Congregational	Apportionment Benev. Paid	Total Benevolence	Total Expenditures
1927 Per capita ....(933,650 cf.m.)	$11.23	$8.60	$19.84	$2.31	$4.32	$24.16
1926 Per capita ....(916,858 cf.m.)	10.30	9.44	19.73	2.02	3.58	23.31
1927 Gain per capita	.93		.11	.29	.74	.85
1927 Loss per capita		.84				
1925 Per capita ....(886,840 cf.m.)	9.78	7.91	17.69	2.06	4.19	21.88
1926 Gain per capita	.52	1.53	2.04			1.43
1926 Loss per capita				.04	.61	
1924 Per capita ....(856,180 cf.m.)	9.39	7.96	17.36	2.04	4.10	21.46
1923 Per capita ....(839,279 cf.m.)	8.80	5.52	14.33	1.91	3.52	18.00
1922 Per capita ....(819,063 cf.m.)	8.32	4.89	13.21	1.84	3.71	16.93
1921 Per capita ....(801,250 cf.m.)	8.26	4.79	13.05	1.79	4.17	17.22
1920 Per capita ....(791,400 cf.m.)	7.15	3.75	10.90	1.52	3.88	14.78
1919 Per capita ....(776,582 cf.m.)	6.42	2.46	8.88	1.73	2.90	11.78

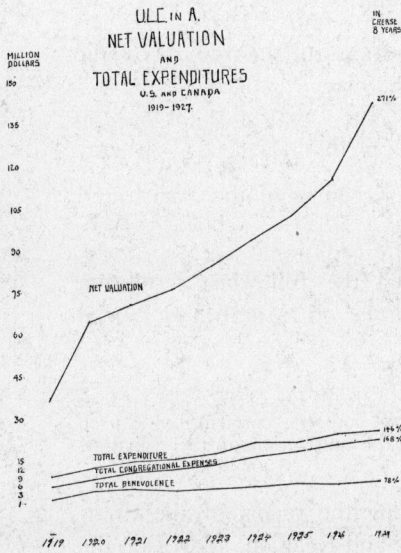

U.L.C. IN A.
NET VALUATION
AND
TOTAL EXPENDITURES
U.S. AND CANADA
1919–1927.

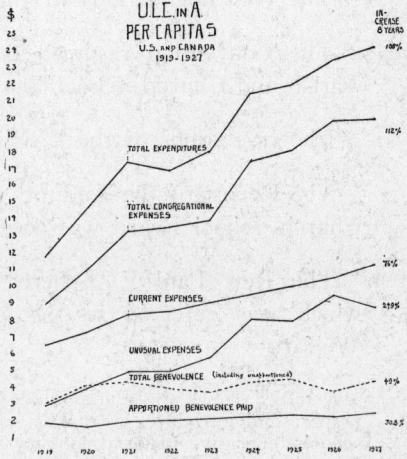

U.L.C. IN A.
PER CAPITAS
U.S. AND CANADA
1919–1927.

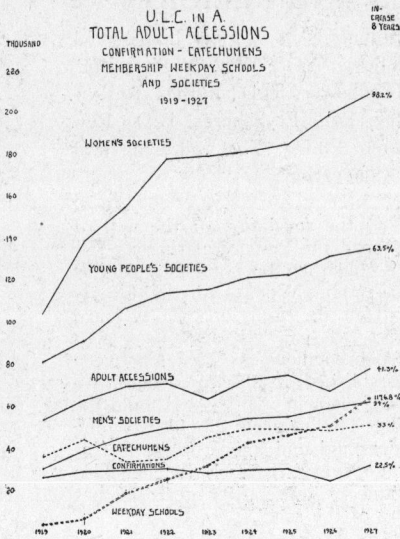

U.L.C. IN A.
TOTAL ADULT ACCESSIONS
CONFIRMATION – CATECHUMENS
MEMBERSHIP WEEKDAY SCHOOLS
AND SOCIETIES
1919–1927

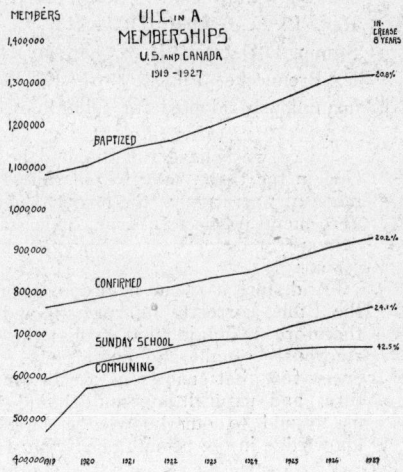

U.L.C. IN A.
MEMBERSHIPS
U.S. AND CANADA
1919–1927

The recommendations of the Committee were adopted.

The Convention resumed consideration of the report of the Parish and Church School Board.

The resolutions of the Board were adopted.

The Report of the Auditors of the accounts of the Parish and Church School Board was accepted.

The Rev. Paul E. Scherer offered the following resolution which was referred to the Committee on Moral and Social Welfare:

Resolved, That the Parish and Church School Board be requested to prepare and introduce, as rapidly as possible, into the curricula of church schools, educative material looking toward the cultivation of the Spirit of Peace among the nations.

Dr. Wm. J. Showalter, in presenting the report of the Commission on the Relationship of Science and Religion, addressed the Convention.

REPORT OF COMMISSION ON THE RELATION-SHIP BETWEEN SCIENCE AND RELIGION

The Commission was convened in Washington, D. C., on January 13, 1928; all the members were present as follows: Dr. Wm. J. Showalter, Rev. L. F. Gruber, D.D., Rev. S. G. Hefelbower, D.D., Ph.D., Rev. J. Stump, D.D., Rev. L. S. Keyser, D.D., Rev. Paul E. Scherer, D.D., Rev. E. Brennecke, Ph.D., Prof. K. F. Bascomb Ph.D. The following was unanimously adopted for submission to the Convention:

"Since we believe the Bible to be primarily the revelation of the will of God in the realm of spiritual things, and regard the laws of nature as His mode of operation in the physical world, we hold that there must be perfect agreement between a true understanding of His Word and the clearly demonstrated facts of science as derived from the study of the physical cosmos.

"And since it is our firm conviction that such harmony does exist between the Bible, correctly interpreted, and the established results of science, we therefore maintain that truth, the essential element of both, should be rigorously sought and confidently followed. The Church should welcome every fact that enables us the better to understand and interpret the Scriptures and natural law and should encourage every research that enables us to add to our knowledge of nature and to our power to use that knowledge in the promotion of the well being of the race.

"On the other hand, recognizing the fact that the established truths of modern science may legitimately be understood to make definite and positive contributions to religious thought, we deplore any unwarranted exploitation of science in the interest of a mechanistic and deterministic view of the universe which leaves no room for God and spiritual values."

Respectfully submitted for the Commission,

PAUL SCHERER, *Secretary.*

Dr. Showalter was followed in the discussion by the Revs. Offermann, Mackensen, Gruber, Wentz, Mattes, Paul E. Scherer, Hon. F. M. Riter and the Secretary.

Moved and carried, to amend the first line of paragraph one so that it shall read as follows: "Since we believe that the Bible is primarily the record of the revelation," etc.

Moved and carried, to amend the fourth line of paragrph one by striking out the words "a true understanding of His Word," and substituting "the Word of God rightly understood."

The report as amended was accepted as a valuable statement of opinion which we heartily commend.

The report of the Commission on Relationship between Science and Religion as amended follows:

"Since we believe that the Bible is primarily the record of the revelation of the will of God in the realm of spiritual things, and regard the laws of nature as His mode of operation in the physical world, we hold that there must be perfect agreement between the Word of God rightly understood and the clearly demonstrated facts of science as derived from the study of the physical cosmos.

"And since it is our firm conviction that such harmony does exist between the Bible, correctly interpreted, and the established results of science, we therefore maintain that truth, the essential element of both, should be rigorously sought and confidently followed. The Church should welcome every fact that enables us the better to understand and interpret the Scriptures and natural law and should encourage every research that enables us to add to our knowledge of nature and to our power to use that knowledge in the promotion of the well being of the race.

"On the other hand, recognizing the fact that the established truths of modern science may legitimately be understood to make definite and positive contributions to religious thought, we deplore any unwarranted exploitation of science in the interest of a mechanistic and deterministic view of the universe which leaves no room for God and spiritual values."

The Rev. E. E. Fischer presented the report of the Committee on Moral and Social Welfare.

REPORT OF THE COMMITTEE ON MORAL AND SOCIAL WELFARE

The Committee met on February 10, 1927, for the purpose of organizing and outlining its work for the biennium. The organization was effected with the election of Dr. E. E. Fischer as chairman and Dr. E. C. Dinwiddie as secretary. One subsequent meeting was held, on May 18, 1928, for the consideration of this report.

The original purpose of the Committee was to discuss a number of subjects on which it thought it expedient that our Church express an opinion. But in the course of its work it discovered that this would require more space than was justifiable. It has therefore confined itself to the discussion of the two important subjects of the Family and Marriage, including in the latter the question of Divorce, on which it was specifically instructed to deliver an opinion.

Before entering upon these discussions, however, the Committee desires to present a resolution of a general character on the Church's relation to the great social and moral questions of the day. In the opinion of the Committee, the Church's task is neither fulfilled nor its opportunity met in this respect when it has simply passed resolutions at its conventions. There is need of definite instruction on these questions. Especially are our young people in need of guidance to help them in forming right Christian attitudes. The wide dissemination of radical ideas, especially on questions like Marriage and the Family, is bound in time to affect even our Christian groups unless opposed by systematic instruction from the Christian point of view.

The following resolution is therefore proposed for consideration and adoption:

"In view of the obligation resting upon the Church to enlighten and stimulate the Christian conscience with respect to the Christian way of life; the Committee on Moral and Social Welfare hereby respectfully requests the United Lutheran Church, in convention assembled, to instruct the Parish and Church School Board, and to encourage other educational agencies of the Church, to take opportunity wherever possible to point out the application of Christian truth and principles to the social and moral problems of the day."

I. THE FAMILY

The seriousness of the situation with respect to the family in the United States is not yet fully appreciated by the people as a whole. The divorce rate continues to rise; homes continue to be disrupted, and family discipline as a consequence is being steadily undermined. Yet little of a constructive nature is being done to counteract the evil. Occasionally one hears a voice of protest raised, but more than protest is required to overcome the influence of the radical ideas which are being so widely disseminated at the present day. There is needed a new conscience, together with a vigorous educational propaganda under conservative auspices, if the present trend is to be stayed, and the family preserved on a firm and truly rational foundation.

It is not the purpose of this report to analyze in detail all the factors which are tending to undermine the family. The purpose is rather to point out in a constructive way the principles which, from the viewpoint of the Church, must form the basis of any educational program which has as its end the preservation of the family. Perhaps it is true, as is often claimed at the present day, that the modern family needs to be adjusted to the changed situation which has arisen with a new economic and social order. But these adjustments must be kept within a certain limit. There are principles underlying the family which are basic to its integrity and stability as an institution, and no adjustments can be sanctioned which would in any way violate these principles.

1. Among these principles the first to be held in view is that the family as an institution belongs by divine appointment to the natural order and constitutes an indispensable factor in the orderly governance of the life of mankind. Nothing in the way of adjustment therefore which would tend to weaken the family tie should be countenanced.

On the surface this principle appears self-evident, and yet it is being violated so frequently as to make its emphatic reassertion necessary. Its import is that the family and not the individual is the unit of social organization, and only what is conducive to a stable family life is conducive to the good order of society as a whole. The tendency in large circles at the present day is to exalt the right of the individual to happiness, even at the expense of the family. But any tendency which subordinates the family to a selfish individualism is bound to work harm. The family is the great training school in social living. Within its intimate circle the individual learns the meaning of obedience, reverence, altruism, self-control and the other virtues which are basic to the good order of society. Whatever strikes at the family, therefore, strikes at the foundation upon which the nation and civilization itself must rest, and needs to be strenuously opposed.

2. The second principle is that parenthood is not only a great privilege, but also a great responsibility, involving obligations which cannot be neglected without serious consequences. Children have a right to the time, labor and sacrifice which their proper nurture and training demand, and any social arrangement which is inclined to lead to their neglect needs to be condemned.

There is a growing tendency at the present day to justify the claim of womanhood to the right of supplementing the vocation of motherhood with some other vocation in life. Mothers in increasing numbers are engaging in some remunerative employment or following careers which necessitate their absence from the home for the greater part of the day. In some instances it is maintained that economic pressure makes it compulsory for the wife to add to the family income; in others, that the wife and mother has equal right with the husband and father to make her contribution to the larger work of the world.

Whether the present trend represents a temporary phenomenon of our social life or a permanent change of attitude the future alone can reveal. Under any circumstances, however, it cannot be viewed otherwise than with serious misgivings. The question is not one of woman's capacity to earn, or ability to make worthy contributions to the life of the world. This is freely granted. It is a question of the dignity, worth and primary obligation of motherhood. Where the mother's continued absence from the home involves the neglect of children during the most formative period of their lives, no accomplishment in other fields can atone for the harm which is done. This must remain the conviction of the Church and constitute a part of the instruction which she is to impart to Christian young womanhood.

3. The third principle is that the true unity of the family can be maintained only by a process of mutual self-impartation, which seeks the good of the family as a whole, while at the same time safeguarding the integrity and worth of each individual member.

Much of the difficulty which the modern family is experiencing is caused by an undue self-assertion on the part of one or another member, leading to a clashing of wills, and so disturbing the peace and harmony of the home. In the close, intimate association which family life involves it is imperative that there be patience, a mutual forebearance, a spirit of service and of reconciliation, if the unity of the family is to be preserved. This is especially true in view of the dignity and worth which we have now come to attach to the individual personality. Wives are no longer inclined to submit without limit to the tyranny of despotic husbands, nor are husbands willing to endure the wilfullness or neglect of inconsiderate wives. Divorce is too easily obtained and other methods of self-support too easily found to make necessary the continuance of a marriage relationship which has become distasteful to either party.

But the remedy should not be sought in divorce. This is the fallacy of our modern thinking. The remedy should be sought in the cultivation of those ideals which will make each intent upon pleasing the other. The modern family has by no means outgrown the need of idealism. As a matter of fact, any effort to establish the family upon a sane and stable foundation which finds no place for love and the virtues which spring out of love is bound to prove futile. This is especially true in view of the democratization which has overtaken the family and which has made the need of a spiritual bond more imperative than ever.

4. The fourth principle is that true religion is essential to the maintenance of a real home.

After all, it is *religion* which imparts a true idealism to family life, roots love in the will, thus binding the various members into a harmonious whole and establishing the unity of the family upon a substantial foundation. Perhaps the growth of individualism is unavoidable. But for that very reason it is essential that religion be allowed to contribute its part to the solution of the problem which the modern family is facing. No other factor is so important. Without the will to preserve the bond it is futile to expect a stable family life, and *religion* alone is able to create the will.

To this conviction the Church should testify without hesitation or fear of contradiction. Upon this conviction she should build her program. However loud the voices which are preaching radical doctrines with respect to the family at the present day, the Church must not lose confidence in her own message and methods of solution. Rather is it incumbent upon her to testify the more boldly to what she deems essential in view of the strength of the opposition which she must face.

Therefore, the Committee presents the following resolutions:

We reaffirm our conviction:
That the family is a divine institution and that the orderly governance of the life of mankind is directly dependent upon the preservation of *its* integrity and stability.

That, in view of *the unique relation* in which parents and children stand to one another, any social arrangement which tends to separate children from their parents arbitrarily or unnecessarily is opposed to the common good and needs to be condemned.

That the unity and stability of the family can be maintained most effectively through the cultivation of a mutual good will which will constrain each member to seek the good of all and not a merely selfish happiness.

That genuine good will between the members of a family can best be cultivated through the power of *true religion*.

Therefore, be it resolved,

1. That pastors be urged to testify clearly and emphatically to the value and necessity of religion in order that the family as an institution may be maintained against the forces which are tending to undermine it at the present day.

2. That, inasmuch as the example and precept of godly parents is of far greater potency than any reform or prohibitive measures which may be proposed or attempted to combat the divorce and other evils which threaten the family, Christian parents be exhorted to make the home the true nursery and training school of Christian living.

3. That the Church seek in every way to assist parents in the discharge of this duty, by encouraging the practice of family worship and by in-

troducing into the curricula of its schools such material as will help to inculcate Christian ideals of marriage and family life in the youth.

II. MARRIAGE AND DIVORCE

(This portion of the report is based upon material gathered by a sub-committee of which the Rev. J. Henry Harms, D.D., was chairman.)

The instability of the modern family is clearly revealed in the mounting divorce rate. At present the rate in the United States is about one divorce to every seven marriages. (In Canada it is one to 109.) This fact is in itself startling, but it does not fully indicate the gravity of the situation. What is even more threatening is the fact that great numbers at the present day, including some of the teachers of our youth, have ceased to regard divorce as in any way an evil. On the contrary, it is now accepted in large circles as a necessary and salutary expedient of modern life, affording a convenient means of escape when the continuance in the marriage relationship has ceased for any reason to be desirable.

It is this attitude which bodes ill for the future and renders it exceedingly difficult to cope with the situation in a large way. Marriage and divorce, so far as their legal aspects are concerned, are controlled and regulated by the State. Without stricter marriage and divorce laws it is futile to expect a general improvement in the situation. And yet public opinion in its present state seems unwilling or unprepared to alter the existing laws in favor of a stricter code.

But whatever may be the situation from the legislative point of view, there are Christian convictions on the subject of marriage which are binding on the Christian conscience and which the Church must maintain. It is true that when a minister performs a marriage he acts as an official of the State, and is amenable to the laws of the State according to which he performs the marriage. But this does not exempt him from his Christian obligation. Unless he is convinced that he can sanction a marriage from the Christian point of view, he should have the courage to refuse to perform it. This applies not only to cases in which one or both parties may be divorced persons, but to all cases where the blessing of God cannot be invoked with a good conscience. The rite of Christian marriage constitutes one of the services of the Church, and it is always with this idea in mind that the minister of the Gospel should perform it. As long as there is laxity in this respect, it will be impossible for the Church to testify as it should to the sanctity of the marriage bond.

There is another duty devolving upon the Church; namely, to safeguard its own membership against the pernicious influence of the low standards which now prevail so generally. Happy marriages are still the rule and not the exception among Christians; but there is little reason to expect that this condition will continue unless the Church seeks deliberately and aggressively to overcome the effects of the modern trend. Without a system of education, which is not only intent upon pointing out the evils of the present situation, but aims to inculcate right standards, the future of even our Christian youth is problematical. Protest is necessary but more is required. Our youth must be taught the positive obligations of marriage from the Christian point of view. Without education there is no guarantee that the rising Christian generation will remain unaffected.

The Meaning of Marriage

With respect to the meaning and purpose of marriage the Christian teaching is explicit. Marriage performs a twofold function. In the first place, it is the divinely appointed way for the establishment and maintenance of the family. This factor has already been dealt with in another section of this report and need not be enlarged upon. Its significance here is to point out the value which marriage has for society as a whole, and the reason why it needs to be protected against the capriciousness of individualism. Only upon the basis of a stable marriage relationship can the family prosper and accomplish its indispensable task. And in the second place, marriage is intended by God to assist the individual to realize the highest ends of being, not only from the temporal, but also from the spiritual point of view. In a very real sense it is one of life's great schools. The discipline which it involves and the opportunities which it offers can be made to develop character according to the will of God. But the fulfillment of this purpose also demands a rigid form of marriage. To esteem the relationship lightly is not only to miss its spiritual blessings but to deprive life of one of its most helpful forms of discipline.

The idea of marriage as divinely instituted involves, therefore, by its every nature the principles of monogamy and indissolubility. Where it is regarded as only a temporary union, having as its end the attainment of a merely selfish happiness and so to be formed and broken at will, its true purpose is frustrated. Only a life-long union between one man and one woman, involving complete self-impartation, is compatible with social as well as with individual well being. Any other view of marriage as an institution would not only be contrary to the will of God but a distinct menace to the social order.

For the Christian marriage has still another significance. It is a type of the mystical union of Christ with His Bride the Church. Husbands are to love their wives as Christ loved the Church and gave Himself for it, and wives are to submit themselves to their own husbands as unto the Lord. Where marriage is thus consummated "in the Lord," the oneness of husband and wife will be established upon a firm spiritual foundation. Together they will become heirs of the grace of God. All carnal and purely human considerations will fall into the background and the union will be maintained in perfect freedom. This constitutes the unique characteristic of a Christian marriage, and should be made prominent in any effort to instruct the young with respect to the meaning and obligations of the marriage estate.

Divorce

On the question of divorce the teaching of the Church is not uniform. Not only is there a divergence of opinion between Protestants and Romanists, but Protestants themselves are not of one mind on the subject. Among the latter there is general agreement on the question of adultery as a justifiable cause for divorce. The statement of our Lord in Matt. 5 : 32, and repeated in 19 : 9, is regarded as final on this subject. But on the question of desertion there is no unanimity, one group maintaining that when it is "malicious," it may be regarded as a justifiable cause, another refusing to recognize it as a justifiable cause under any circumstances.

Until recently this difference was accepted as a fact and each group was content to conform its practice to its conscientious convictions. Of late, however, there has appeared a tendency on the part of some whose churches recognize the validity of divorce for desertion to question the propriety of this attitude. The large increase in the number of divorces granted each year for desertion, and especially the abuse to which this cause is being subjected in modern divorce proceedings, have raised the question of the moral right of the Church to sanction the remarriage of any persons divorced for desertion. This fact, together with the situation itself, makes it expedient that the whole matter be re-examined in the light of the Scriptures and of modern conditions. The following statement is therefore submitted for consideration to the United Lutheran Church.

Divorce for Desertion

The passage upon which the Scriptural justification for divorce for the cause of desertion is grounded is I Cor. 7 : 15, where Paul writes, "But if the unbelieving depart, let him depart. A brother or a sister is not under bondage in such cases; but God has called us to peace." The context is as follows: Paul has been answering a series of questions which had been submitted to him by the Corinthian congregation. Among these evidently was one which inquired what attitude the believer should take toward the marriage relationship in the case of mixed marriages, that is, where the other party was a heathen or a Jew; and more especially, what his attitude should be in those instances in which the other party to a mixed marriage deserted.

The first question Paul answers by asserting that mixed marriages are binding. Religious differences in themselves do not constitute a justifiable cause for divorce. "If any brother hath a wife that believeth not, and she be pleased to dwell with him, let him not put her away. And the woman that hath an husband that believeth not, and if he be pleased to dwell with her, let her not put him away."—I Cor. 7 : 12, 13. The question at issue here, it should be noted, was not one simply of separation but of actual divorce. This is indicated by the apostle's use in both clauses of the verb "aphienai"—to put away—which was one of the technical words to signify divorce. In these instances, therefore, divorce was not to be thought of.

The second question, concerning the attitude of the believer when the unbeliever deserted, Paul answers by declaring that "a brother or a sister is not under bondage in such cases." The apostle is evidently drawing a contrast. In the former cases, where the believer was not deserted, he maintains that he continued to be under bondage. In the latter case, where the unbeliever deserted, the brother or sister was no longer under bondage.

It is the meaning of this expression "not under bondage," therefore, which is the crucial question. The interpretation which has been given to it by those who have found in it a justification for divorce has been "not under bondage to the marriage relation." This was the meaning which Luther, Calvin and Zwingli gave to it, which has since been followed by the majority of Lutheran and Reformed dogmaticians and exegetes, and which has been widely accepted among Protestant Christians. When so interpreted its import is that the marriage bond is effectually severed by desertion, enabling the deserted one to secure a legal divorce, and permitting him, when so divorced, to marry again without violating any Christian principles. Over against this view is the view of those who maintain that the expression justifies separation but carries with it no right of remarriage.

The objections which are now being offered to the former interpretation are in the main three. It is maintained, in the first place, that it reads too much into the words *"ou dedoulotai"*—is not under bondage. All that the apostle meant to imply, it is argued, was that the brother or sister, in such cases was not bound to continue to live with the deserting one or to continue to seek reconciliation. It should be noted, however, that the cases of which the apostle was speaking were cases where the separation had already been put into force. There could have been no question of the believer living any longer with the deserter or of seeking reconciliation with him. The latter had gone with the avowed purpose of never returning. Had the slightest hope of reconciliation remained we may rest assured that the apostle would not have released the believer from the obligation of pursuing it. His advice then would have been for such a one to remain unmarried or to become reconciled. But here it is simply "let him depart. A brother or a sister is not under bondage in such cases." An inference therefore is that he wanted the brother or sister to know that the marriage had been dissolved and that the believer was no more bound by it. Of the right to remarry nothing is said. This follows only if it is assumed that it is actual divorce which the apostle had in mind.

This interpretation appears to be substantiated by the literal meaning of *"ou dedoulotai"*—"is not bound like a slave." A slave's status remained unchanged, however outward circumstances changed. Even the death of his master did not essentially change his status: he remained a slave. But Paul contends that the Christian did not bear this relation to the marriage covenant—he was not bound to it like a slave. The desertion changed his status. Just as death freed the surviving party and opened the way for another marriage—Romans 7 : 2—so desertion freed the deserted one, and likewise opened the way for another marriage.

One fact ought not to be lost sight of in the whole discussion; namely, that the desertion must be final and complete. This probably was in the apostle's mind when he added the warning, "But God has called us to peace." It is true, the peace to which he referred was the inner peace—not even marital infelicity was to rob the Christian of that, for to that he had been called by God. But this inner peace could be morally maintained only where every effort had been made to maintain the outward peace. In other words, nothing humanly possible should be left undone to prevent the desertion, or, if this occurred, to bring about a reconciliation. Only after these efforts failed was the marriage to be considered dissolved. The Church, at any rate, has felt the necessity of safeguarding itself in this particular by so interpreting the mind of the apostle. It has insisted that desertion must be "malicious" in order to be a justifiable cause for divorce, and that only those who have been deserted in this way can be married again with the sanction of the Church. In every other instance it has insisted upon separation without the right of remarriage.

The second objection is that, in interpreting the meaning of Paul's words as sanctioning divorce for desertion, the apostle is made to teach a doctrine which is contrary to a specific teaching of our Lord. Our Lord permitted divorce for the one reason of adultery. By permitting divorce for the additional reason of desertion Paul, it is held, would be guilty of modifying our Lord's teaching in an essential particular, and this would destroy the unity of the Scriptures.

That Paul knew what he was doing is evident from the fact that he does not claim to have a command of Christ on which to ground his advice with respect to mixed marriages. He introduces this advice with the words, "But to the rest speak I, not the Lord." His meaning is not that on this subject he cannot speak as an inspired apostle. He knows himself to have "the Spirit of God," as he claims at the close of the chapter, even when he is speaking by permission and not by commandment. What he means is that he had no specific word of Christ with which to answer the question which had been raised. For the answer to this question he had to draw on the mind of Christ as that mind had been formed within him by the Holy Spirit.

There is something in this very attitude which should make us pause. Had Paul desired to impress upon those who had been deserted nothing more than the necessity of living separately, he would not have been at a loss for a specific command of Christ. Then Christ's words which apparently make adultery the only justifiable cause for divorce and so permit remarriage under no other circumstances would have been literally applicable. But evidently Paul did not regard these words as applicable to the circumstances under discussion. Jesus had answered the question, "Is it lawful for a man to put away his wife for every cause?" It was a question which involved the interpretation of the Jewish law on divorce. According to Moses, divorce was permitted the husband if he discovered some uncleanness in his wife. Did this mean that a man could put his wife away on the slightest pretext, as some claimed, or only for adultery, as others claimed? Jesus answered that a man had no right to put away his wife for every cause. The "uncleanness" must be adultery in order to justify divorce with the right to remarry.

It should be noticed, however, that Jesus did not answer the specific question which had been asked Him until He had called attention to the fact that the law of Moses, however interpreted, did not represent the original will of God. What the law of Moses permitted with respect to divorce was a condescension to a sinful humanity because of the hardness of man's heart. According to the will of God marriage was to be regarded as indissoluble. So it was established by the Creation narrative which antedated the Mosaic legislation and which Jesus reaffirmed as embodying the original will of God. Even though adultery therefore could be regarded as severing the marriage bond, thus permitting divorce, the divorce itself should not be regarded as in accordance with God's will. It might be inescapable, but only because of man's sinfulness. This is the natural inference from Jesus' argument in Matt. 19:3-9, and justifies the attitude which condemns all divorce as contrary to the will of God, demanding that even the "innocent" party to a divorce give evidence of suitable repentance before he be married again with the sanction of the Church.

Paul, in answering the question which had been proposed to him, follows the method of his Lord. He first makes sure that the will of God as reaffirmed by Christ is understood. Marriage according to the will of God is to be regarded as indissoluble: husbands are not to put away their wives and wives are not to depart from their husbands.—I Cor. 7:10, 11. This is the will of God and therefore constitutes the ideal in His Kingdom; and it is according to this ideal that marriages between Christians are to be maintained. Should circumstances arise which would make separation expedient, there is to be no remarriage. In the Kingdom of God reconciliation is in order and nothing should be done to hinder it.

Having said this, Paul proceeds to answer the specific question which had been asked him concerning the status of mixed marriages after the unbeliever had deserted. His verdict is that a brother or a sister is not under bondage in such cases. It appears that even as adultery severs the bond, so does desertion when it is complete and final. In the latter case no less than in the former, man by the hardness of his heart makes the fulfillment of the will of God impossible. Crime, sickness, cruelty, incompatibility of temper may make temporary separation expedient or necessary, but none of these causes in itself destroys the possibility of reconciliation. In the complex life of the early Church these causes were no less operative than they are today. But there is nothing in the New Testament even to hint that they were regarded as justifiable causes for divorce. But malicious desertion differs from 'hese. It destroys the essence of the marriage relationship.

Whether or not Paul altered in an essential way the teaching of Christ depends on whether we regard the saying in Matt. 19:9 as exhaustive legislation on the subject of divorce, which Christ intended to be binding upon the Church for all time, or merely as an answer to a specific question which had been asked Him, and therefore only as an illustration of the way in which His teaching with respect to the indissolubility of marriage would have to be applied in a sinful world. If it is legislation then it represents a unique divergence from Jesus' ordinary way of teaching; for nowhere else does He legislate. His method is always to lay down the principles of His Kingdom and then to allow men to make the necessary applications as circumstances arise.

Indeed, so fixed is this method of teaching that many scholars have come to regard the clause, "saving for the cause of fornication" as an interpolation. The original saying of Jesus, they maintain, is found in Mark 10:11 (Cf. Luke 16:18) where marriage is declared to be indissoluble without any modifying clause whatsoever. What we have in Matthew is an attempt on the part of the evangelist, not without some justification, to apply Jesus' original saying to actual circumstances.

But be that as it may, Paul apparently knew Jesus' saying on divorce only as it is found in Mark.

In the seventh chapter of I Corinthians no mention is made anywhere of any excepting clause. The apostle knows only the principle of an indissoluble marriage as embodying the mind of Christ. The application of this principle to the peculiar circumstances which Christianity met in the heathen world had to be worked out, as was the case with other principles. This Paul does in the case of desertion. He simply carries forward the application of the principle which Christ had laid down to the circumstances as they arose in the early Church. A similar task awaits the Church of this as of every age. The problem today is to determine what constitutes desertion, not merely from the legal, but from the spiritual point of view. When may it be said that one has utterly forsaken the marriage bond to which he had been a party?

The third objection is the practical one that, by admitting desertion as a justifiable cause for divorce, the Church is found in the position of fostering the very laxity which it ought so much to deplore and combat. That this cause is being notoriously abused at the present day is patent to every one. But the wisdom, to say nothing of the right, of the Church of barring it entirely must be seriously questioned. Adultery as a justifiable cause for divorce may also be, and is, abused. But the way in which to combat the abuse is not by refusing to recognize the effects of adultery upon the marriage relation. Those who are guilty of the crime and remain unrepentant should be punished. The State for its part should be more zealous in enforcing the law which makes adultery a punishable offence; while the Church should be more conscientious in the way in which it carries out the rule not to sanction the remarriage of the guilty party to a divorce under any circumstances.

The abuse of the cause of desertion should be remedied in a similar way. To refuse to recognize the effects of malicious desertion upon the marriage relation would be mistaken zeal. The Church can and should protect itself by requiring a stricter adherence on the part of both clergy and laity to the principles which govern its attitude toward the remarriage of those who have been divorced for desertion. How this can best be done remains to be determined. To demand that the officiating pastor guide his conduct by what the divorce papers set forth will not suffice. With the present lax conscience on divorce it often occurs that the guilty party, especially if it is the wife, is permitted to secure the divorce, while the innocent party, out of a perverted sense of honor or of sportsmanship, will take the blame and legal guilt. Perhaps the safest course to pursue is to investigate, so far as is possible, each individual case, and by personal conference to determine where the guilt lies, and above all whether the divorced person who desires to remarry truly understands the meaning of the rite and the serious obligations which it involves. It is in this direction probably that the Church's effort to reform must move, for along this line abundant opportunity will be found, not only to testify to the Christian ideal of marriage, but also to oppose the present abuse without surrendering an essential principle.

These are the reasons why the Committee hesitates to suggest any change in the traditional attitude of the Lutheran Church on the question of the Scriptural grounds for divorce. While it believes that the convictions of those who hold to only one ground for divorce should be respected and that the Church should do nothing to coerce their consciences in the matter, it feels that it would be neither wise nor expedient to abandon a doctrine or practice which has the authority of the Word of God, simply because of the abuse to which it may be subjected by the world. What the United Lutheran Church is now asked to do is to endorse as a Church substantially what the former General Synod declared to be its position at its meeting in 1907 and what the former General Council declared to be its position at its meeting in 1903, and what is declared to be the teaching of the Scriptures in the Lutheran Commentary—Matthew, by C. F. Schaeffer; Mark, by J. A. W. Haas; and I Corinthians, by H. E. Jacobs.

Statement on Marriage and Divorce

1. The United Lutheran Church, in accordance with the teaching of the Scriptures, holds that marriage is a holy estate, ordained of God, and to be held in honor by all. It deeply deplores the increasing disregard of the sanctity of the marriage tie, and solemnly protests against all teaching and practice which violate this sanctity and are therefore contrary to the revealed will of God.

2. It urges its pastors to instruct their people regularly and systematically in the meaning and responsibilities of marriage; to seek to maintain among them a Christian conscience on divorce; to be ready, whenever conditions demand it and opportunity offers, to bring the gospel of reconciliation to bear upon those who may be in serious danger of estrangement; and in general to minister through Word and Sacrament to that growth in grace which is the only effectual safeguard against the moral laxity of the times.

3. While it is indispensable that a pastor in performing a marriage comply with every civil requirement, we maintain that he is also accountable to God, and that he therefore not only has the right, but should feel constrained, to refuse to perform any marriage which so far as he has had the opportunity of discovering after earnest endeavor to ascertain the facts, is not in accordance with the divine requirements. The rite of Christian marriage is a service of the Church and its distinctively religious character when performed by a minister of the Church should never be subordinated to other considerations.

4. With respect to divorce we hold that marriage according to the will of God is indissoluble and is normally terminated only by the death of either party. When it is otherwise dissolved the will of God is frustrated. In general, therefore, all divorce is to be condemned and, whenever possible, avoided.

5. A majority of the dogmaticians of the Lutheran Church in the past have taught that the marriage bond is effectually dissolved by the sins of adultery and malicious desertion, and that, when a divorce has been legally granted for either of these causes, the innocent party is free to marry again. This position we now reaffirm, without, however, attempting to coerce the consciences of those who believe that the Scriptures teach that there is but one sufficient cause for divorce; namely, adultery.

6. With respect to the remarriage of divorced persons, the United Lutheran Church recommends to its constituent synods that they insist that their pastors abide by the rule that only the innocent party to a divorce which has been granted on scriptural grounds can be remarried under the auspices of the Lutheran Church during the lifetime of the other party, and then not until the expiration of a year after the divorce shall have been granted.

7. The matter of retaining within, or admitting to, the membership of the Church persons who have been divorced on other than scriptural

grounds and who have remarried during the lifetime of the former husband or wife falls under the rule of discipline provided for by the constitution of the congregation. In all such instances pastors and church councils are exhorted to proceed with care and true spiritual wisdom, having proper regard for the Church's purity and honor, but also mindful of her mission to minister the means of grace so that sinners may be converted, restored and saved.

For the Committee,

E. E. FISCHER, Chairman.

The resolution concerning "the application of Christian truth and principles to the social and moral problems of the day" and instructing the Parish and Church School Board in regard thereto, was adopted.

The resolutions under I, 4, were adopted.

On motion to adopt the resolutions appended to the "Statement on Marriage and Divorce," the Rev. N. Willison, with the concurrence of the Committee, offered the following substitute for Item 5:

It is evident that Christ regarded adultery as a just ground for divorce. Therefore when a divorce has been legally granted on this ground the innocent party is free to marry again. As to whether St. Paul regarded malicious desertion as virtual adultery and therefore as a second just ground for divorce the Church has not held a unanimous view. When the state grants a divorce on this ground a pastor must be guided by the regulations of his own synod and of his own conscience as to whether the innocent party may be remarried with the sanction of the Church.

Besides Dr. Fischer and Dr. Willison, the following participated in the discussion: the Rev. H. Offermann, Judge Henry Harter, the Rev. K. Klinger and the Rev. A. R. Wentz.

It was moved and carried, That the report, together with the amendment suggested, be referred back to the Committee on Moral and Social Welfare to report at the next convention of the United Lutheran Church and that a special order be arranged for the consideration of the report.

The Rev. Marion J. Kline presented the report of the Committee on President's Report.

REPORT OF THE COMMITTEE ON THE REPORT OF THE PRESIDENT

The report of the President records certain appointments of a special character which he made in his official position. These appointments become part of the official Minutes of this Convention by the reception of his report. Hence requires no action.

The report makes most appreciative reference to the long and faithful services of the Rev. George W. Sandt, D.D., LL.D., as the Editor of *The Lutheran* and records the reception of his resignation on Luther's Birthday, 1927.

Your Committee learns with deep appreciation that the Committee on Church Papers has proposed fitting recognition of the influential and invaluable services of Dr. Sandt and hence makes no additional recommendation on this item of the report. But the Committee desires to make record of the gracious reference to it by the President in his official report.

The report gives the official ruling of the President as to the time when those elected to membership on Boards and Committees shall take office. Your Committee recommends that the ruling be approved.

The report includes brief—but very significant—statistical information concerning the development and growth of the Church during the first decade of her history.

Your Committee recommends that the thanksgiving of the church, in convention assembled, for the blessing of our Lord upon her work, be voiced in prayer by President Knubel, upon the adoption of this report.

Over two-thirds of the report deals with the fundamental subject of what has been fittingly designated as "The Undone Task of the Church." It stresses the need for the ministry of mercy. President Knubel calls our attention to the fact that in his biennial reports he has frequently referred to the classification of the work of the Church as evangelistic, educational and merciful.

The first two of these spheres of the activities of the Church have already been given consideration and action has been taken. We have set ourselves prayerfully and earnestly to the task of bringing our congregations to a recognition of their responsibility thereto.

This present report, in a convincing and compelling way, summons the Church to a recognition of her duty and privilege, and to a consecration of our pastors and congregations to this ministry of mercy.

Your Committee recommends that this Convention respond to this inspirational summons of our President with the following action:

1. That all pastors of our Church stress the obligation and the privilege of serving love, in Christ's Name and for His sake.

2. That Synodical Presidents, with their Executive Committees, formulate and recommend to their congregations, definite and specific ways in

which this may be made practical and effective in the life and activities of our congregations.

Your Committee recommends that the Church in convention assembled heartily express her appreciation of the efficient and devoted service of President Knubel in the discharge of the duties and responsibilities of his office during this first decade of her life, and that we assure him of our unfailing and earnest prayers to Christ, our Lord and Master, in his behalf.

Respectfully submitted for the Committee,

MARION JUSTUS KLINE.

The report was adopted.

The Rev. J. A. Morehead presented orally the report of the Executive Committee of the Lutheran World Convention. The report was received and Dr. Morehead was granted the privilege of submitting it to the Secretary in writing for inclusion in the Minutes.

REPORT OF THE EXECUTIVE COMMITTEE FOR CONTINUATION WORK OF THE LUTHERAN WORLD CONVENTION

INTRODUCTORY STATEMENT

During the eventful years since the First Lutheran World Convention at Eisenach in 1923, the Executive Committee appointed on that historic occasion has had the responsibility of the careful study of existing Lutheran Churches throughout the world, of the enlistment of their interest in the ecumenical Lutheran movement, and of making preparations for the Second Lutheran World Convention. Through the unifying power of the truth of the Gospel by the gracious working of the Holy Spirit, it is true that considerable progress had been made before 1914 both in Europe and America toward conscious inner unity and its expression in free associations or practical agencies and even in organic unions. Moreover, many barriers were cleared away by the World War and the succeeding work of Christian love and mercy for fellow Lutherans in distress, who were taught in the school of adversity to discover and know each other. Thus on the basis of the past, by the unifying power of the truth, and in the gracious providence of God, came the consummation of the First Lutheran World Convention at Eisenach.

The Magnitude of the Task.—To the appreciation of the magnitude of the task confronting the series of Lutheran World Conventions, arrangements for one of which have been placed in the hands of the Executive Committee, a true historical perspective is necessary. More than four hundred years ago, when the truth of the Gospel was obscured by the "commandments of men," including many false teachings and practices, God raised up His servant, Martin Luther and the other reformers to liberate the truth and to republish the original essential message of Christianity that the Word of God might have free course. In marvelous ways since the Reformation, the restored full message of the pure Gospel has been glorified throughout the world. In many lands among many peoples, the fruitage of the preaching of the Word and the right administration of the Sacraments has become manifest in the development of Evangelical Lutheran Churches. Partly by the necessity of isolation, partly through the exercise of private judgment and the right of free development on the basis of the truth, both the political background and individuality have profoundly influenced the growth of the new-born Evangelical Lutheran Churches in the various countries of the world. Thus came into being the present situation of these Churches throughout the earth, involving diversity in organization, divergence even in some details of doctrine or their expression, isolation, misunderstanding, ignorance of one another, prejudice and nationalistic divisions or separation from each other. Through the influences of nationalism and individualism, this diversity has at times appeared to be so great as to obscure the inner essential unity in the faith of the Gospel as witnessed by the historic confessions of the Evangelical Lutheran Church. The present task of World Lutheranism is to discover the actually existing inner unity in the faith and to promote its conscious and true development among Christians of the Lutheran tradition, name and confession. Under the actual conditions prevailing, intelligent devotion to this great cause presupposes on the part of its servants the possession of something of the divine patience, confidence in the power of the truth and humble reliance upon God's gracious working. Surely the development of genuine Lutheran unity in world terms claims the unstinted devotion of all who share in the heritage of the conservative Protestant reformation. The support of the more conservative Synods is important to maintain a true balance.

American Responsibility for Christian Unity.—The modern movements looking to Christian unity have naturally and properly quickened the consciences of Lutherans in regard to the question as to the way and manner in which they may be enabled to make a substantial contribution to the fulfillment of the Saviour's prayer that they may all be one. It is the conviction of the Committee that the Lutheran Churches of the world can make their best contribution to the unity of the Chrisian Church (a) by laboring for inner unity in the truth among the Lutheran groups throughout the world and (b) by making a faithful testimony to the full truth of the Gospel as God has given it unto them to apprehend it, to experience it, and to confess it through the heritage from the fathers. Because the Lutheran Churches of the world comprise almost fifty per cent of Protestantism, they have even from the statistical point of view a tremendous responsibility for the unity of Protestantism in the truth and for the unity of the Christian Church at large. From the viewpoint of its conservative stand for positive Christianity, of its possession of the full truth of the Gospel centering in Jesus Christ as the world's divine Saviour, the Church of the Reformation has an even greater responsibility to witness to the truth and so to further Lutheran unity and the ultimate unity of the Christian Church in the world.

In this world adventure (after four hundred years) in Lutheran unity in world terms, the Executive Committee has been especially thankful to meet a responsive spirit among the majority of the Lutheran Church Bodies in the United States and Canada. While we are grateful to God for the ready support of the Lutheran World Convention movement received in this country, it is not unnatural but under the circumstances is rather to be expected. The Lutheranism of America is free from many of the complications in relation to the state and to nationalism which have developed through the centuries in the Old World. The faith and confession of the Churches are at once the source of their origin and the principle of their development and forms. Moreover, the Lutheran Church Bodies of North America in general and the United Lutheran Church in particular are cross sections of World Lutheranism, in that their members have been derived from immigrations from all Lutheran countries of the Old World. These Lutherans of many races, languages and nationalities, holding to the one faith of the Gospel revealed in the Holy Scriptures and witnessed by the historic confessions of the Church, have demonstrated the fact that Lutherans of diverse racial and national origin can live and work together happily in the service of Christ and His Church. It is the privilege of American Lutheranism to establish the contention that what can be done in continental terms for true Lutheran unity and co-operation can also be done in world terms.

MEETINGS

During the past biennium, two annual meetings of the Executive Committee were held, one at Budapest, Hungary, in October, 1927, and one at Copenhagen, Denmark, in June, 1928. Each of these meetings continued for about ten days.

THE DUAL PRINCIPLE OF ORGANIZATION AND THE PROBLEM OF FINANCE

The operations of the Executive Committee have been rendered difficult by the dual principle underlying the organization of the First Lutheran World Convention at Eisenach, although no other form seemed possible in 1923. It will be remembered that the membership of the Eisenach Conference was composed (a) of the official delegates appointed by participating Church Bodies in America and (b) of individuals selected by the Joint Committee on Arrangements from the Lutheran Churches of Europe. Therefore, when it came to securing the necessary funds both for the operating expenses of the Executive Committee and for its recommended programs of relief and reconstruction, it was comparatively simple to appeal to the Lutheran Church Bodies in America and their established agency for World Service, but it was quite unreasonable to expect the Lutheran churchmen of Europe, individually appointed by a general committee, to become responsible for Europe's share of the financing of the Lutheran World Convention movement. Hence your Committee was confronted at the beginning with an intensely difficult practical problem. For the discharge of the responsibilities committed to it by the First Lutheran World Convention, pursuant to the approval of participating Churches, the Executive Committee has found no other way in the formative stage of the movement than to build patiently and carefully by the method of recommendation and appeal upon the foundations which had been laid at Eisenach and in the life of the Church. In America, the participating Lutheran Church Bodies have been requested under a more or less definite budget to contribute in proportion to their confirmed membership to the operating expenses of the Committee and also to support approved relief programs through their agency for this purpose of the National Lutheran Council; in Europe, the informal representatives of the Churches at the First Lutheran World Convention, especially the members of the Large Committee in co-operation with the members of the Executive Committee, have been asked to secure contributions both for operating expenses and for the programs of Lutheran relief. Through the personal influence of these representative Lutherans in Europe, the Lutheran Free Churches in Germany and some Lutheran Landeskirchen in Germany and other lands have been interested in making contributions to the treasuries both for operating expenses and for relief. Ecumenical Lutheran groups, relief organizations, and Churches, such as the *Allgmeine Ev. Luth. Konferenz,* the *Lutherischer Bund,* the *Gustav Adolf Verein* of Sweden, the Danish Relief Committee, and the Churches themselves in the smaller countries of Europe have been invited to co-operate actively, and are responding gradually and more generously as the years go by to the call for the support of the Committee's work and to the need of their suffering brethren, particularly in Russia and in other countries where there are weak or minority Churches.

American Lutheranism has in general had the advantage in organization and in available wealth since the World War for these forms of international Lutheran co-operation. But the outlook is that, with better organization and the recovery of normal economic strength, the Lutheran Churches of Europe will share proportionately and largely in whatever practical operations future Lutheran World Conventions may project and approve.

FINANCIAL REPORTS AND BUDGETS
1.—*Committee Operating Expenses.*
Partial Report for Period from June 1, 1926, to July 10, 1928.
Receipts

June 1, 1926, Balance on hand $1,208.35
Special Gifts 520.00

America:
United Lutheran Church	$2,405.68	
Norwegian Lutheran Church	1,205.60	
Augustana Synod	866.93	
Joint Synod of Ohio		4,478.21

Europe:
Czechoslovakia	30.00	
Denmark	160.80	
Germany	101.20	
Sweden	160.80	452.80

$6,659.36

Expenditures

Traveling expenses of members of Executive Committee	$2,040.74	
Deputation work in connection with Budapest meeting of Executive Committee	1,885.39	
Office expenses in New York and Copenhagen (postage, secretary, stationery, etc.)	396.14	
News Exchange Bulletin	199.28	
Exchange	15.19	4,536.74

Balance		$2,122.62
Balance in New York	$1,495.49	
Balance in Copenhagen	648.19	approximate

$2,143.68

(Rate of exchange figured at $26.80 for 100 Danish crowns.)

It is merely a matter of justice to call your attention to the fact that very substantial contributions, which do not appear in the foregoing satements, but which have greatly reduced the amount of the operating expenses of the Committee, were made to cover the expenses of the meetings of the Committee at Copenhagen, Gothenburg, Hague-Amsterdam, Dresden, Budapest and Warsaw, by the entertaining Churches.

BUDGET FOR THE YEAR 1929

At its recent meeting at Copenhagen, the Executive Committee recommended that the sum of $6,000 in addition to the amounts due on the budget of other years be asked for the year 1929, half to be assigned to Europe and the other half to American Churches participating. This sum has been distributed to provide for the following items of an annual budget to finance the operations of the Executive Committee to be flexibly administered as follows:

1. Expenses of the Executive Committee, including traveling expenses of members, office expenses and incidentals........$2,500.00
2. Deputation work of members of the Committee in various countries 1,000.00
3. International Lutheran News Exchange, printing, etc.... 1,000.00

4. Expenses of preparation for the Lutheran World Convention
   in Copenhagen in 1929 .... 1,000.00
5. Office expenses and contingent fund 500.00

                                                              $6,000.00

The recommended apportionment of the amount of $3,000 among partici-
pating American bodies together with balance due for other years, is as
follows:

United Lutheran Church
  Balance due 1928 ....$1,702.84
Apportionment 1929 .... 1,702.84

                                                              $3,405.68

Norwegian Lutheran Church
  Apportionment 1929 ....   602.65

Joint Synod of Ohio
  Balance due 1926-28 .... 947.79
  Apportionment 1929 .... 315.93

                                                              $1,263.72

Augustana Synod
  Apportionment 1929 .... 433.31

                                                              $5,705.36

It is hoped that the United Lutheran Church will approve this flexible
budget and accept its share of $1,702.84.

   2. *Receipts for Lutheran Relief and Conservation July* 15, 1926 to
                        June 15, 1928.

Europe
  Czechoslovakia ....$ 45.31
  Denmark (Danish Relief Committee) 6,413.46
  France (Paris Synod) 19.60
  Germany (A. E. L. K., Lutherischer Bund, Landes-
    kirschen, etc.) 932.06
  Holland 10.02
  Hungary 347.94
  Jugoslavia 381.49
  Latvia 190.22
  Lithuania 33.50
  Norway 128.83
  Poland .:......................................   797.53
  Sweden (Gustav Adolf Verein) 284.00

                                                              $9,583.96

America:
  National Lutheran Council 71,808.07

                                                             $81,392.03

                        Disbursements
Austria $4,856.45
Belgium 422.63
Czechoslovakia 1,974.60
Esthonia 142.84
France 3,666.91

```
Germany  .............................................  7,436.23
Hungary  .............................................  1,578.60
Jugoslavia  ..........................................  2,527.28
Latvia  ..............................................  3,182.24
Lithuania  ...........................................    300.00
Poland  ..............................................  5,433.08
Rumania  .............................................  3,540.75
Russia  ..............................................45,902.42
Spain  ...............................................    388.00
Switzerland  .........................................     40.00
```

$81,392.03

(Rate of exchange figured at $26.80 for 100 Danish crowns.)

Program of Relief and Reconstruction Recommended for 1929

As the Minutes of the Richmond Convention and the Report of the Executive Board at the present Convention indicate, the contribution of the share of the United Lutheran Church in America for the program of Lutheran relief and reconstruction recommended by the Executive Committee was referred to the National Lutheran Council. Although available funds were insufficient to do all that was necessary to execute the complete program, the Lutherans of America through the Council were the strongest supporters of this important program of World Lutheranism, as the foregoing statement shows.

The Executive Committee of the Lutheran World Convention recommends that the sum of $100,000 be raised during the year 1929 (a) for Russian relief, (b) for the aid of the weak and minority churches of western and southeastern Europe, and (c) for the aid of students for the ministry. Of this amount of $100,000, it is proposed that one-third be raised by the Lutheran Churches of Europe and two-thirds by the Lutheran Church Bodies of North America. It is recommended that according to its good pleasure the United Lutheran Church, as at its last Convention, favorably refer this entire matter so far as it is concerned to the National Lutheran Council for action.

Preparations for the Second Lutheran World Convention

1. The Executive Committee for Continuation Work has taken very seriously its assigned task of making adequate preparations for a Second Lutheran World Convention. Not the mere arrangement of a program but the preparation of the mind of the Churches representing a Lutheran population of more than sixty millions was and is the major task. That Lutherans throughout the earth receive accurate knowledge of their Church as a whole—its strengths and weaknesses, its failures and achievements, its condition and problems, its opportunities of reciprocal service, and its great mission with consequent growth in love and sense of common responsibility was necessary to create *the will to hold* a Second Lutheran World Convention.

In the prosecution of its work, the Committee has held annual meetings, but always in different countries. In connection with these meetings, members of the Committee have done systematic deputation work, *i. e.,* have visited the Lutherans in countries adjacent to the place of meeting each year for sympathetic conference about local problems, for public meetings at which the conservative principles of Lutheranism were presented, the condition and strength of the Lutheran Churches in all countries of the world were described, and the plans for a Second Lutheran World Convention were outlined. An international Lutheran News Bulletin, which is sent periodically to the editors of the Lutheran Church papers throughout the world, has also been established. An Editorial Committee charged with the responsibility of the preparation and publication of a Handbook of World Lutheranism before the next Convention is at work. Dr. A. R. Wentz of this body is the American member.

2. *An advance in the matter of representation.*

(a) The following American Lutheran Church Bodies have decided to send delegates: United Lutheran Church, Norwegian Lutheran Church, Augustana Synod, Joint Synod of Ohio, Lutheran Free Church, United Danish Church, Danish Lutheran Church and the Icelandic Synod. The Iowa Synod has decided to send a friendly visitor.

(b) It will be remembered that the following brief but positive doctrinal statement was adopted at the First Lutheran World Convention at Eisenach in 1923:

"The Lutheran World Convention acknowledges the Holy Scriptures of the Old and New Testaments as the only source of the infallible norm of church doctrine and practice, and sees in the Confessions of the Lutheran Church, especially in the Unaltered Augsburg Confession and Luther's Small Catechism, a pure exposition of the Word of God."

(c) The information having been received during the past year that some Church Bodies in Europe would welcome an invitation to send official delegates, the Committee decided to invite any Evangelical Lutheran Church so disposed, if in agreement with the foregoing basal doctrinal statement, to name and recommend for approval to the Executive Committee the proper number of official delegates for its representation at Copenhagen. It is highly probable, therefore, that an encouraging number of free and territorial Evangelical Lutheran Churches in Central Europe will send regular delegates to the Copenhagen Convention next year.

3. The following program of subjects was decided upon by the Executive Committee at its 1928 meeting in June at Copenhagen:

"The Origin and Significance of Luther's Large and Small Catechism."
"The Duty of the Present Generation to Transmit through Education its Heritage of Faith to the Next Generation."
"The Faith and the Confession of the Church in the Light of Marburg and Augsburg."

"The Distinctive Contribution of Lutheranism to Christendom."
"How Should We Strive for an Inner Awakening of our Church?"
"The Lutheran Conception of the Relation between Christianity and the World."
"The Lutheran Church and the Social Crisis."
"How May the Inner Unity among the Lutheran Churches be Furthered?"
"Report of the Executive Committee with suggestions for the future organization of the World Convention."
"Helping Our Needy Brethren in the Faith (Diaspora, etc.)."
"The Chief Problems for Lutheran Missionary Work that arise from the Present Situation."

Ample opportunity will be given for the discussion of the themes by the delegates or regular participants in the Second Lutheran World Convention. One-half day during the Convention will be set apart for meetings of Lutheran college and university professors, immigrant workers, inner mission specialists, foreign mission representatives, editors of Lutheran Church papers, Lutheran relief workers, Lutheran women, students, or others interested in special church activities who may on their own initiative desire to arrange for brief sectional conferences. Daily devotions and frequent public services will be offered throughout the entire Convention. One-fourth of the speakers will be appointed from Germany, one-fourth from the Scandinavian countries, one-fourth from America and one-fourth from the Lutheran Churches in the other countries of Europe and Asia, as well as the young churches in non-Christian lands.

THE GROWTH OF THE CONSCIOUSNESS AND MANIFESTATION OF LUTHERAN SOLIDARITY

During recent years, the Lutheran Churches of Norway, Sweden, Denmark, Finland and the Baltic Republics have begun the practice of holding annual conferences for the furtherance of good understanding and for the consideration of common problems in the North-European center of Lutheranism. The Free Lutheran Churches of Germany have formed a general association, the *Ev. Luth. Landeskirchen* of that country have established a "Bishop's Conference," and both the *Lutherischer Bund* and the *Allegemeine Ev. Luth. Konferenz,* particularly the latter at its great Congress for Lutheran Unification at Hamburg during the current year, have done much to strengthen the confessional Lutheran consciousness in the birth-land of the Reformation. The widely scattered and racially diverse Lutheran constituency of Russia, under the severest and most difficult conditions, have been enabled to organize one general Evangelical Lutheran Church in that country, as has also been done in Rumania and in Jugoslavia. Evidences of the presence of the ecumenical Lutheran spirit in other countries of Europe are manifest, even if they have not as yet found consummation in tangible forms of organization. Several small Lutheran Synods or groups in Australia have formed the United Evangelical Lutheran Church in that country. The accomplished or prospective merger of nine Ev. Luth. Church Bodies or Synods in America into three larger Church Bodies in the United States and Canada are too well known to require more than a reference. These and other manifestations of growth in inner unity and its expression in organized forms are encouraging evidences of the growth of the spirit of pan-Lutheranism which gives hopeful promise of the future of World Lutheranism.

The Executive Committee records with satisfaction the growing tendency of Lutherans participating in general Christian movements to seek a common ground in their own faith for testimony and service. Notable examples are the two private meetings of Lutherans during the Conference on Faith and Order at Lausanne, which not only furthered acquaintance and understanding among the Lutherans there present, but enabled them to make a significant contribution to the course of events at that important gathering of Christians. In like manner, at the recent Jerusalem Conference of the International Missionary Council, where the restatement of the Christian message to the heathen world was attempted, Lutherans in attendance conferred. In order that the Church of the Reformation make faithfully its legitimate contribution to Christendom and to the world, the importance of such free and informal conferences among Lutherans having part in general movements of the Christian Church can scarcely be over-emphasized.

CONCLUSION

In this labor of love, the members of the Executive Committee have ever recognized the fact that the Lutheran World Convention movement is essentially spiritual in character. It looks to the discovery of existing inner unity, to its development, to the alignment of those who are truly one in the faith. It stands frankly for conservative Lutheranism, for positive Christianity. Whether one thinks of Stockholm or Lausanne, it becomes increasingly clear that our most hopeful outlook for making an essential contribution to ultimate Christian unity lies along the way of the mobilization of the forces of the Church through the Lutheran World Convention movement. On the same way lies also the best prospect of increasing loyalty to the heritage of the Reformation and increasing usefulness in the advancement of Christ's kingdom on the earth. Without interference with the autonomy of any existing Church, it is possible on the basis of the common faith in the use of the simplest means and methods to become the servants of all. Thank God, there has been Lutheran understanding and co-operation on the foreign mission field, for migrating and dispersed peoples, for brethren in distress after war and famine, and for the strengthening of the weak places. But, after the high endeavor of Christian brotherly love to rescue and rebuild in the wake of the Great War, shall the Lutheran Churches of the world retire to their own political boundaries and individual concerns? Or shall the ecumenical Lutheran spirit grow and Lutheran co-operation in world terms continue? These are some of the issues to be decided at Copenhagen.

Respectfully submitted,

For the Executive Committee,

JOHN A. MOREHEAD, *Chairman.*

The Rev. J. F. Lambert read the report of the Necrologist as follows:

NECROLOGY REPORT

The deaths of 109 ministers, twenty laymen and eight laywomen are noted in this report.

A summary of the ministers deceased during the first decennium of the United Lutheran Church may interest many.

Biennia	Total	Pastors	Officials	Educators	Titled	Authors	Retired	Aver. Age
1	74	37	3	4	24	13	25	66 plus
2	89	39	6	2	25	19	38	68 plus
3	98	40	4	2	21	16	49	68 plus
4	106	42	6	7	31	22	50	69 plus
5	109	49	7	2	30	8	51	68 plus
	476	207	26	17	131	78	213	67 **plus**

Minister's Name	Synod	Birthplace	Date	Ordination	Place of Death	Date	Age	Yrs. of Service	Burial Place
Aikens, Charles T., D.D.	Sq	Siglerville, Pa.	Dec. 14,	1862...1888	Selinsgrove, Pa.	June 21, 1927	64	6—7—39	Selinsgrove, Pa.
Amschler, John G.	Pg	Limmersdorf, Ger	Aug. 28,	1860...1883	Natrona, Pa.	June 9, 1927	66	9—11—44	Natrona, Pa.
Atkins, Paul A.	Va				Harrisonburg, Va.	July 13, 1927			
Bartholomew, Amos H.	Pg	Annapolis, O.	Sep. 21,	1841...1869	Los Angeles, Calif.	Feb. 21, 1927	85	5—0—53	Greensburg, Pa.
Bell, Ezra K., D.D., LL.D.	Md	Leitersburg, Md.	Nov. 14,	1853...1879	Baltimore, Md.	Sept. 3, 1927	73	9—29—48	Baltimore, Md.
Bergstresser, Frederich L., D.D.	Sq.	Selinsgrove, Pa.	Apr. 4,	1860...1887	Harrisburg, Pa.	June 9, 1928	68	2—5—24	Harrisburg, Pa.
Bergstresser, Ralph H., D.D.	WP	Lykens, Pa.	Jan. 2,	1882...1906	Baltimore, Md.	May 1, 1927	45	3—29—21	Hanover, Pa.
Bodine, John V.	NY	Catawissa, Pa.	Oct. 20,	1842...1879	Tallmans, N. Y.	Oct. 25, 1927	85	0—5—15	Catawissa, Pa.
Boyer, Matthew G., D.D.	Il	Markelsburg, Pa.	Mar. 10,	1839...1867	Upper Darby, Pa.	Sept. 19, 1927	88	6—10—55	Markelsburg, Pa.
Cochel, George Z.	EP	nr. Greenford, O.	Nov. 23,	1840...1872	Lucas, O.	Mar. 27, 1927	86	4—42	Wooster, O.
Cook, Herman C.	PM	Altenwald, Pa.	July 16,	1845...1869	Wilmington, Del.	Feb. 23, 1927	81	7—7—53	West Chester, Pa.
Cooper, Charles J., D.D.	Md	Lanark, Pa.	Apr. 1,	1847...1870	Allentown, Pa.	July 14, 1927	80	3—13—54	Allentown, Pa.
Derr, Samuel J.	NM	nr. Middletown, Md.	Sep. 6,	1855...1886	Hempstead, Md.	Aug. 9, 1927	71	1—2—30	Hempstead, Md.
Dewald, Harry E.	Il	Alsace	Dec. 19,	1849...1872	New Brunswick, N.J.	Mar. 17, 1927	77	2—8—55	New Brunswick, N. J.
Dickey, Harry E.	PM	nr. Richmond, Ind.	Apr. 8,	1885...1914	Repalle, India	Oct. 2, 1926	41	5—24—12	Guntur, India
Doerr, Frederick	PM	Lancaster, Pa.	Sep. 20,	1864...1895	Wilmington, Del.	Nov. 23, 1926	62	2—3—31	Lancaster, Pa.
Druckenmiller, George D.	Il	Hereford, Pa.	Feb. 26,	1864...1897	Tamaqua, Pa.	Feb. 8, 1928	64	2—31	Zionsville, Pa.
Dunlap, G. W., D.D., Ph.D.	Il	York, Pa.	Dec. 8,	1853...1873	Green Cove Sprgs., Florida	Jan. 30, 1928	77	1—22	York, Pa.
Durst, Robert R.	Pg	Greenville, Pa.	Sep. 20,	1855...1882	Harrisburg, Pa.	Mar. 5, 1928	72	5—28—42	McKees Rocks, Pa.
Dutton, William A.	SC	nr. Rural Retreat, Va.	Apr. 16,	1859...1897	Columbia, S. C.	Aug. 15, 1926	67	3—29—24	Columbia, S. C.
Epting, Monroe J., D.D.	Ga	Newberry Co., S. C.	Sep. 29,	1860...1888	Savannah, Ga.	July 13, 1926	66	9—15—39	Savannah, Ga.
Eyster, Charles M.	Md	Thomasville, Pa.	Dec. 21,	1857...1884	Baltimore, Md.	July 13, 1926	68	6—22—42	Baltimore, Md.
Fake, Byron E., D.D.	NY	Frey's Bush, N. Y.	June 5,	1854...1882	Clifton Sprgs., N. Y.	July 27, 1927	73	1—22—45	Fort Plain, N. Y.
Fastnacht, Abram G., D.D.	WP	Ephrata, Pa.	Nov. 14,	1845...1873	York, Pa.	Aug. 11, 1927	81	7—18—43	York, Pa.
Fleck, Lindley N.	Al	Sinking Valley, Pa.	Apr. 29,	1850...1884	Woodland, Pa.	Sept. 9, 1927	76	9—3	Sinking Valley, Pa.
Frehrer, Jacob	O	Switzerland	July 10,	1844...1897	San Antonio, Tex.	Mar. 28, 1926	82	4—19	Victoria, Tex.
Garland D. Frank, D.D.	GN	Perry Co., Pa.	May 1,	1859...1891	Dayton, O.	June 9, 1928	63	7—29—23	Gettysburg, Pa.
Gensichen, Frederick	Sq	Pommerania, Ger.	Oct. 16,	1853...1884	Pappillion, Nebr.	Apr. 10, 1927	68	1—13—43	Leigh, Nebr.
Gephart, Calvin F.	NW	Milheim, Pa.	Aug. 21,	1847...1890	Lewistown, Pa.	Mar. 27, 1927	73	5—24—36	Lewistown, Pa.
Gerberding, G. H., D.D., LL.D.	Pg	Pittsburgh, Pa.	Aug. 14,	1863...1876	Hickory, N. C.	Sept. 20, 1926	79	1—16—51	Minneapolis, Minn.
Glatzert, Paul J. C.	GN	Niederschleswig, Ger.	June 29,	1867...1890	Johnsonburg, Pa.	Sept. 30, 1926	63	1—16—36	Johnsonburg, Pa.
Grauenhorst, Louis F. T.	Al	Guetzlaffehagen, Ger.	Oct. 4,	1840...1893	Lincoln, Nebr.	Jan. 29, 1926	50	2—21—33	Lincoln, Nebr.
Gross, George D.	PM	Lancaster Co., Pa.	Sep. 29,	1860...1880	Johnstown, Pa.	Jan. 28, 1928	86	3—29—35	Roaring Springs, Pa.
Grossman, Moses	NM	nr. Lititz, Pa.	May 5,	1854...1893	Conyngham, Pa.	Sept. 29, 1927	67	3—29—35	Conyngham, Pa.
Haas, George C. F., D.D.		Philadelphia, Pa.			Grymes Hill, S. I., N. Y.		73	4—24—47	Middlevillage, L. I.
Haberland, Michael E.	Il	Guelph, Can.	Sep. 29,	1868...1901	Chicago, Ill.	Jan. 27, 1927	58	3—28—26	Chicago, Ill.
Hafer, Robert A.	NY	Philadelphia, Pa.	Dec. 23,	1852...1879	Jersey City, N. J.	June 16, 1927	74	5—23—31	Weehawken, N. J.
Hale, Henry F.	PM	Philadelphia, Pa.	May 28,	1876...1901	Overbrook, Pa.	Apr. 28, 1927	50	11—26	Philadelphia, Pa.

Minister's Name	Synod	Birthplace	Date	Ordination	Place of Death	Date	Age	Yrs. of Service	Burial Place
Hallman, Samuel T., D.D.	SC	Lexington Co., S. C.	Sep. 3, 1844	1868	Spartanburg, S. C.	Mar. 8, 1927	82—6—5	59	Spartanburg, S. C.
Hartman, A. Stewart, D.D.	WP	Adams Co., Pa.	Dec. 19, 1845	1871	Baltimore, Md.	Apr. 2, 1928	82—3—13	57	Chambersburg, Pa.
Heilig, Theophilus, D.D.	PM	Center Square, Pa.	July 31, 1837	1862	Philadelphia, Pa.	Jan. 25, 1927	89—5—25	52	Stroudsburg, Pa.
Henning, Max C.	NY	Siebenberg, Ger.	May 4, 1851	1891	R. D. No. 3, Boonville, N. Y.	Jan. 18, 1928	76—8—14		Boonville, N. Y.
Henry, Luther	EP	Blain, Pa.	Apr. 18, 1877	1905	Harrisburg, Pa.	June 13, 1927	50—1—25	19	Harrisburg, Pa.
Herbster, Samuel K.	Pg	Stony Creek, Pa.	Mar. 28, 1851	1878	Greensburg, Pa.	May 30, 1928	77—2—2	48	Greensburg, Pa.
Hesson, Andrew J.	Il	Littlestown, Pa.	Jan. 24, 1839	1868	Chicago, Ill	Mar. 26, 1928	89—2—2	40	Chicago, Ill.
Hoffman, J. L., D.D.	Md		1865	1891	Baltimore, Md.	May 19, 1928	63		
Horst, Heinrich	NY	Ulrichstein, Ger.	Dec. 30, 1867	1923	Gelsenkucken, Ger.	Dec. 29, 1925	57—11—29		Gelsenkucken, Ger.
Howard, Frank J.	O	Willimantic, Conn.	July 26, 1867	1904	Holgate, O.	July 24, 1927	59—11—28	23	Millersburg, O.
Hufford, James A., D.D.	Va	Wytheville, Va.	Sep. 27, 1862	1888	Kingsport, Tenn.	Feb. 12, 1927	64—6—17	39	Wytheville, Va.
Hufford, Rufus W., D.D.	EP	nr. Bucyrus, O.	1847	1876	Reading, Pa.	Nov. 14, 1926	79—1—15		Reading, Pa.
Jackson, Jerome C.	Md	Racine, Wis.	Nov. 27, 1896	1921	Gettysburg, Pa.	Mar. 21, 1927	30—3—17	6	Gettysburg, Pa.
Johnston, E. S.	Al	Belleville, Pa.	Apr. 9, 1834	1861	Elk Lick, Pa.	July 21, 1926	92—3—12	55	Elk Lick, Pa.
Jubelt, Paul F.	NM	Schlessig-Holstein, Germany	1868	1888	Brooklyn, N. Y.	Jan. 4, 1928	60	40	Brooklyn, N. Y.
Junge, William T.	NM	Barkow-Mechlenburg, Germany	May 29, 1872	1895	New York, N. Y.	Sept. 1, 1926	54—3—2	31	Rochester, N. Y.
Keister, Thurston O.	Va	Strasburg, Va.	May 16, 1860	1886	Edinburg, Va.	Jan. 12, 1928	67—7—26	41	Edinburg, Va.
Kern, Isaac H.	PM	Bowmansville, Pa.	Aug. 23, 1881	1908	Mahanoy City, Pa.	Feb. 29, 1928	46—6—6	20	Mohnton, Pa.
Kerschner, Charles A.	O	Kutztown, Pa.	Dec. 31, 1860	1895	Allentown, Pa.	Apr. 5, 1928	67—3—5	33	Allentown, O.
Kiefer, Simon P.	O	Smithville, O.	Aug. 10, 1847	1874	Wooster, O.	May 9, 1926	79—0—9		Wooster, O.
Klein, Frederick W.	NM	Mainz, Germany	Aug. 10, 1856	1882	Bridgeport, Conn.	Aug. 28, 1927	70—0—18	45	Owatorma, Minn.
Kleine, Paul B. W. A.	Cn	Ohra-Niederfeld, Germany	Oct. 22, 1870	1891	Milverton, Can.	June 20, 1927	56—7—28	36	Waterloo, Can.
Koehle, John	Cn	Galicia, Aus.	Jan. 22, 1900	1925	Chalk River, Can.	Oct. 2, 1926			Waterloo, Can.
Kramlich, William W.	PM	Kutztown, Pa.	1866	1891	Danville, Pa.	Jan. 22, 1926	61—10—7	36	Kutztown, Pa.
Krause, Alfred B. P.	NM	Polzin, Pommern, Germany	1866		New York, N. Y.	Nov. 29, 1927			Kutztown, Pa.
Krider, Isaac, D.D.	Al	Gatesburg, Pa.	Apr. 25, 1855	1888	New York, N. Y.	Oct. 7, 1926	71—5—12	38	Staten Island, N. Y.
Kuhns, Samuel W.	Va	Clarion Co., Pa.	Apr. 22, 1846	1875	Altoona, Pa.	Feb. 18, 1928	81—9—26	41	Duncansville, Pa.
Larrick, Charles U.	O	nr. Pleasant City, O.	Jan. 10, 1848	1874	Springfield, O.	Feb. 6, 1928	80—0—26	48	Emlonton, Pa.
Lawrence, David W.	NY	Gallatin, N. Y.	Feb. 2, 1846	1874	Stuyvesant, N. Y.	Jan. 26, 1928	81—11—24		Stuyvesant, N. Y.
Manges, Edmond	WP	Somerset Co., Pa.	Jan. 23, 1842	1873	York, Pa.	June 13, 1926	84—6—28		York, Pa.
Mathias, Henry J.	Cf	Lexington Co., S. C.	Oct. 25, 1842	1898	San Bernardino, Cal.	May 23, 1927	84—7—16	29	San Bernardino, Cal.
Mayser, Frederick P., D.D.	PM	Wuertemberg, Ger.	Feb. 12, 1843	1868	Philadelphia, Pa.	June 13, 1928	85—4—1	60	Lancaster, Pa.
Michler, Arthur T.	PM	Easton, Pa.	1881	1901	Philadelphia, Pa.	Apr. 13, 1927	46—1—24	17	Slatington, Pa.
Millar, G. William	PM	Hunterstown, Pa.	May 21, 1867	1902	Annville, Pa.	May 21, 1928	60—8—28	26	Annville, Pa.
Miller, Edgar G., D.D.	EP	Philadelphia, Pa.	July 8, 1865	1888	Philadelphia, Pa.	July 13, 1927	62—0—5	39	Philadelphia, Pa.

Minister's Name	Synod	Birthplace	Date	Ordination	Place of Death	Date	Age	Yrs. of Service	Burial Place
Miller, Patrick H., D.D.	Md	nr. Salem, Va.	June 12, 1849	1875	Baltimore, Md.	Nov. 26, 1927	78	5—14	Baltimore, Md.
Minnich, Michael R.	PM	Schellsburg, Pa.	Nov. 14, 1846	1873	Philadelphia, Pa.	Nov. 3, 1928	81	1—19—55	Philadelphia, Pa.
Mueller, Franz J.	Pf	Bingen, Ger.	Sept. 3, 1857	1889	Bothel, Wash.	Dec. 27, 1926	69	3—24	Seattle, Wash.
Nelson, George W.	SC	Brooklyn, N. Y.	Apr. 21, 1894	1921	Summerville, S. C.	Oct. 14, 1926	32	5—22—5	Charleston, S. C.
Neumaerker, Richard W., D.D.	GN	Sprottau, Ger.	Nov. 6, 1844	1870	Columbus, Neb.	Mar. 30, 1928	83	4—24—55	Columbus, Nebr.
Rankin, George L., D.D.	Pg	Westmoreland Co., Pa.	Aug. 29, 1851	1881	Wilkinsburg, Pa.	Jan. 28, 1928	76	4—27—47	Greenville, Pa.
Reighard, John C.	Sq	Cessna, Pa.	Oct. 19, 1853	1891	Gettysburg, Pa.	July 23, 1927	68	9—4—32	Gettysburg, Pa.
Reller, Herman C.	Pg	Miltonsburg, O.	Mar. 29, 1862	1893	Pittsburgh, Pa.	Feb. 9, 1927	64	10—10	Pittsburgh, Pa.
Rembe, Heinrich	Cn	Eisleben, Ger.	Feb. 24, 1858	1888	Hamilton, Can.	Feb. 2, 1927	69	0—8—39	Hamilton, Can.
Remensnyder, J. B., D.D., LL.D.	NY	Staunton, Va.	Feb. 24, 1841	1865	New York, N. Y.	Jan. 2, 1927	85	10—8—62	New York, N. Y.
Reuman, Henry	NM	Gross Offenseth, Germany	Oct. 6, 1857	1886	Collinsville, Conn.	Jan. 19, 1928	70	3—13—42	Pleasant Valley, N. Y.
Rudisill, Andrew J., D.D.	Al	Gettysburg, Pa.	Dec. 25, 1867	1896	Altoona, Pa.	Apr. 18, 1927	59	3—23—31	Huntingdon, Pa.
Runge, Gustav F. K.	Mn	Wunschow, Ger.	Sept. 8, 1874	1896	Oliver, Can.	Apr. 1, 1927	52	7—23	Edmonton, Can.
Rupley, Daniel E., D.D.	EP	Lancaster, Pa.	June 20, 1849	1878	Philadelphia, Pa.	Apr. 1, 1927	77	10—23—48	Philadelphia, Pa.
Rutherford, William L., D.D.	Cf	Bainbridge, Pa.	Jan. 8, 1863	1892	Galt, Calif.	Feb. 10, 1928	66	10—20—34	Sacramento, Calif.
Schantz, Elmer E.	EP	Geryville, Pa.	Sept. 16, 1861	1895	Schaefferstown, Pa.	Dec. 2, 1926	65	3—5—31	Schaefferstown, Pa.
Seel, Henry A.	Pg	Etna, Pa.	Jan. 29, 1886	1921	Etna, Pa.	Nov. 17, 1927	41	9—18—6	Etna, Pa.
Selner, Wilson	Al	Bucks Co., Pa.	Sept. 24, 1847	1875	Luthersburg, Pa.	Sept. 19, 1927	79	6—13—51	Luthersburg, Pa.
Shanor, Henry K.	Pg	Butler, Pa.	Mar. 9, 1853	1891	Sewickley, Pa.	Oct. 19, 1927	74	7—10—45	Butler, Pa.
Shealy, Jefferson D.	SC	nr. Leesville, S. C.	Feb. 22, 1862	1891	Leesville, S. C.	Oct. 3, 1926	64	7—17—35	nr. Leesville, S. C.
Sherman, Eugene F.	NY	Pottsville, Pa.	Aug. 30, 1855	1888	Glen Gardner, N. J.	Feb. 21, 1927	71	5—21	Spruce Run, N. J.
Sommer, Alfred J.	RM	Kappel, Switzerland	July 14, 1877	1909	Denver, Colo.	June 8, 1928	50	10—24—19	Charles City, Ia.
Spieckerman, August	GN	Barmen, Ger.	Mar. 16, 1875	1902	Bloomfield, Nebr.	Mar. 5, 1927	51	11—22—25	Roek Port, Mo.
Stacy, Curtis G.	O	Hillsville, Pa.	May 9, 1871	1900	Springfield, O.	June 30, 1927	54	1—14—18	Springfield, O.
Stolz, Karl R.	Pg	Strehlen, Ger.	Nov. 21, 1874	1905	Beaver Falls, Pa.	May 29, 1928	53	6—20—23	Beaver Falls, Pa.
Stupp, Solomon B.	O	Berks Co., Pa.	Feb. 28, 1857	1883	West Liberty, O.	Apr. 3, 1928	71	1—12—39	West Liberty, O.
Summers, Howard C.	O	Springfield, O.	Nov. 24, 1881	1907	Cleveland, O.	Sept. 9, 1927	45	9—10—20	Cleveland, O.
Tapper, Andrew E. H.	PM	Lancaster, Pa.	Feb. 27, 1895	1921	Philadelphia, Pa.	July 4, 1927	32	4—13—6	Lancaster, Pa.
Tiemann, Christian F.	Cn	Wuertemberg, Ger.	Sept. 13, 1845	1872	Kitchener, Can.	Mar. 27, 1928	75	6—4—44	Steelton, Pa.
Veit, Frederick W., D.D.	Md	nr. Newry, Pa.	May 14, 1844	1876	Newry, Pa.	Jan. 13, 1927	81	10—27—55	Sebastopol, Can.
Weaver, Francis H.	PM	Bernville, Pa.	Mar. 9, 1863	1888	Boyertown, Pa.	Apr. 14, 1928	83	10—24	Alington, Va.
Weber, Adam M.	O	nr. Marshallville, O.	Mar. 27, 1890	1918	Uniontown, O.	July 14, 1926	63	3—14—38	Bernville, Pa.
Weygandt, Jay B.	Md	Burksfork, Va.	Jan. 27, 1848	1877	Takoma Park, D. C.	July 9, 1928	30	—28—10	nr. Marshallville, O.
Willis, James	Pg	Plumsteadville, Pa.	Sept. 25, 1853	1885	Uniontown, Pa.	Feb. 7, 1927	79	6—26—44	Washington, D. C.
Wismer, Isaac K.	NY	Gardersville, N. Y.	Apr. 12, 1839	1871	San Jose, Calif.	Apr. 1, 1928	74	5—1—37	Uniontown, Pa.
Yost, Theodore J.	Cf	New Jerusalem, Pa.	May 2, 1876	1906	Myerstown, Pa.	Oct. 12, 1927	88	6—11	New York, N. Y.
Young, Silas W. E.	PM	Salisbury, Pa.	May 24, 1847	1879	Washington, D. C.	Oct. 5, 1926	50	5—2—20	San Jose, Cal.
Yutzy, Jacob, D.D.	Cf	Hamburg, Pa.	Oct. 17, 1857	1881	Wyomissing, Pa.	June 13, 1927	80	—19	Dryville, Pa.
Zweizig, Martin L., D.D.	PM				Indiana, Pa.	Mar. 22, 1927	69	5—41	Selinsgrove, Pa.

Minister's Name	Synod	Birthplace	Date	Ordination	Place of Death	Date	Age	Yrs. of Service	Burial Place
Laymen									
Baum, George C.	EP	York, Pa.	July 15, 1872		Philadelphia, Pa.	Nov. 16, 1926	54	4— 1	Reading, Pa.
Breidenbaugh, Prof. Edw. S., Sc.D.	EP	Newville, Pa.	Jan. 13, 1849		Gettysburg, Pa.	Sept. 5, 1926	77	7—22	Gettysburg, Pa.
Campbell, Edmond E.	EP	Waynesboro, Pa.	Jan. 21, 1859		Mechanicsburg, Pa.	Aug. 4, 1926	67	6-13	Mechanicsburg, Pa.
Chiquoine, Alexander D.	EP	Philadelphia, Pa.	Sept. 3, 1865		Moore, Pa.	Feb. 21, 1927	61	5-18	Mifflinburg, Pa.
Doub, William W.	Md	Myresville, Md.	Apr. 18, 1865		Baltimore, Md.	Apr. 2, 1927	61	9-14	Middletown, Md.
Efird, Daniel F.	SC	Pine Ridge, S. C.	Jan. 25, 1861		Lexington, S. C.	Aug. 19, 1927	66	6-24	nr. Lexington, S. C.
Franke, J. B.	Mh				Fort Wayne, Ind.	Jan. 5, 1927			Fort Wayne, Ind.
Hines, Henry C.	Md	Baltimore, Md.	Nov. 5, 1852		Baltimore, Md.	July 17, 1927	74	8-12	Baltimore, Md.
Horton, William T.	Sq	Belleville, Pa.	Feb. 19, 1861		Selinsgrove, Pa.	May 10, 1927	66	2-21	Selinsgrove, Pa.
Muncke, Ernest C.	NM	Wasungen Thuringia.	Mar. 9, 1856		Hempstead, N. Y.	Feb. 1, 1928	61	10-22	Hempstead, N. Y.
Nielson, Carl H., M.D.	Ia	Westo, Ia.	Apr. 24, 1887		Liberia, Africa	Jan. 29, 1928	40	9-5	Liberia, Africa
Pflaum, Christian	PM	Philadelphia, Pa.	July 14, 1855		Philadelphia, Pa.	Nov. 16, 1926	68	4-2	Philadelphia, Pa.
Roehrs, John F. T.	NM	Hamburg, Ger.	Dec. 17, 1848		Bronx, N. Y.	Apr. 28, 1928	79	4-11	New York, N.Y.
Sadler, Charles E., M.D.	Md	Shippensburg, Pa.	Oct. 2, 1851		Baltimore, Md.	Sept. 9, 1927	75	11-7	Baltimore, Md.
Schlegelmilch, George E., Esq.	PM	Philadelphia, Pa.	June 6, 1862		Philadelphia, Pa.	June 9, 1927	65	3	Philadelphia, Pa.
Steeble, Louis W.	PM	Philadelphia, Pa.	Dec. 12, 1871		Trenton, N. J.	Jan. 30, 1927	55	1-29	Barmouth, Pa.
Stifel, Charles F.	Pg	Wheeling, W. Va.	Apr. 12, 1847		Pittsburgh, Pa.	May 21, 1927	80	1-9	Pittsburgh, Pa.
Swink, Hon. Louis M.	NC	Salisbury, N. C.	Oct. 6, 1872		Washington, D. C.	May 18, 1927	54	7-12	Winston-Salem, N. C.
Thorstenberg, Prof. Edward, Ph.D.	Pf	Assaria, Kan.	June 26, 1873		Eugene, Ore.	Apr. 8, 1928	54	9-13	Eugene, Ore.
Woll, Peter, Jr.	PM	Philadelphia, Pa.	May 29, 1862		Philadelphia, Pa.	Mar. 12, 1927	63	9-13	Philadelphia, Pa.
Laywomen									
Beaver, Vella M.	Pg	Greenville, Pa.	May 10, 1855		Pittsburgh, Pa.	Apr. 29, 1927	71	11-19	Greenville, Pa.
Cronk, Katherine Scherer	Va	Marion, Va.	July 14, 1877		Philadelphia, Pa.	Mar. 12, 1927	49	7-28	Richmond, Va.
Dimm, Martha E.	Sq				Selinsgrove, Pa.	May 1, 1927			Selinsgrove, Pa.
Mantz, Martha	EP	Indiana, Pa.	Aug. 21, 1841		Lincoln, Nebr.	Feb. 17, 1928			At.hison, Kan.
Monroe, Harriet E.	Md	Indiana, Pa.	Aug. 21, 1842		Washington, D. C.	July 19, 1927	84	10-25	Waterloo, Can.
Neudoerfer, Anna Rohrer	Cn	Eden, Pa.	Jan. 1, 1887		Waterloo, Can.	Oct. 19, 1927	40	9-17	Nevada, Ia.
Simmons, A. Letta	Il	Decorah, Ia.	May 14, 1877		Nevada, Ia.	Mar. 31, 1928	50	10-17	Nevada, Ia.
Smith, Salome M.	O		May 13, 1858		nr. Lancaster, O.	Oct. 15, 1926	68	5— 2	nr. Lancaster, O.

Respectfully submitted,

JAMES F. LAMBERT, *Necrologist.*

The Convention was led in prayer by the Rev. J. E. Byers while the Convention stood.

The Rev. H. Offermann presented the report of the Committee on German Interests.

REPORT OF THE COMMITTEE ON GERMAN INTERESTS

When the United Lutheran Church called this committee into existence four years ago at Chicago, its action was based upon the conviction, that the interests of the entire Church as well as the needs of its large German constituency, spread over the entire length and breadth of the Church, demanded the organization of a central agency to coordinate and foster the various German interests of the United Lutheran Church. The work of this committee during the past two bienniums has succeeded only in part in gaining general recognition on the part of Boards and agencies of the Church. Its influence, however, is growing. There is no question that the United Lutheran Church in all its parts is thoroughly and sincerely sympathetic to this important sector of its life. A closer understanding between the various German groups and a fuller appreciation of the possibilities of its German fields by the Church will eventually lead to a greater usefulness of this committee. The trend toward such developments is apparent even now. It will finally bring about a harmonization of interests and a cooperation in all branches of the Church's activities which will shed rich blessings upon the entire United Lutheran Church.

The committee met on December 29, 1926; May 4, 1927; February 1, 1928; April 26, 1928. All meetings were held in Philadelphia. Prof. Henry Offermann, D.D., was elected chairman. Pastor F. O. Evers served as secretary.

After the sanction of the Executive Board of the United Lutheran Church had been duly obtained, the Committee called and prepared the program for the Fifth General German Conference of the United Lutheran Church. For the first time in the history of our body a general meeting, representing this United Lutheran Church in America, was convened upon Canadian soil. From the historic field of the Canada Synod urgent invitations had been sent and were gladly accepted. The Conference met in stately St. Matthew's Church at Kitchener, Ont., Rev. John Schmieder, pastor, on October 5 and 6, 1927. All sections of the German portions of the Church were represented with the exception of the remote fields of Texas and German Nebraska. Over one hundred delegates constituted the conferences, among whom a representative number of laymen was found. The officers of the

Conference were: Rev. Reinhold Tappert, D.D., president; Rev. J. A. W. Kirsch, vice-president; Rev. H. Hansen, secretary; Mr. William Moennig, treasurer. The opening service, followed by the observance of the Lord's Supper, was made especially impressive through the sermon of the president, Dr. R. Tappert. The attention of the Conference centered around questions of general importance and mutual interest. The German Home Mission work, the care of German immigrants, provisions for the education of a bi-lingual ministry, publications in the German language,—all these important phases of German church life received the serious consideration which they deserve. Emphasis was laid upon an increasing readiness to support the financial program of the Church. The campaign for the Pension Fund found hearty endorsement, likewise the continued service of the National Lutheran Council in ministering to the suffering Lutherans abroad. All resolutions of the Conference were duly submitted to and reviewed by this committee. The influence of this harmonious convention upon the constituency of the Canada Synod in all its parts will make itself felt for many years to come.

Outstanding resolutions of the Conference, as reviewed and endorsed by this committee and forwarded for action to the respective agencies, are as follows:

1. Concerning missionary opportunities in the Canadian Northwest:

"The Fifth General German Conference calls attention to the large and increasing immigration of German Lutherans into the Canadian West, a fact which singles out this field as the most promising and important one for Home Mission work on our continent; it urges the Boards of the Church to assist the Manitoba Synod in securing men and means in adequate measure for this great work of the U. L. C. A."

This resolution was forwarded with the committee's recommendation to the Board of American Missions and the Board of Education for their favorable consideration.

2. Every Member Canvass. Discussion at the Conference brought forth a strong demand for literature in the German language in connection with the annual visitation of the membership of our congregations. More and more these visitations are becoming an institution also in our German congregations. In order to foster their endeavors, your Committee felt that attention should be called to the need of continually providing pamphlets and descriptive literature in German. The Committee also expressed its gratification over the action of the Conference in stressing the necessity of systematic giving and the general introduction of the Duplex Envelope System.

3. "Lutherischer Herold." The election of an assistant editorial committee was ratified. It consists of Pastors Otto Kleine, Siegmund von Bosse, Julius Hoeppner.

4. Concerning the need of providing an adequate German-English minis-

try, the Conference adopted a set of resolutions, which were heartily approved by your Committee:

A. A consistently strong immigration of German Lutherans into the United States and Canada once more challenges the Church to provide an adequate ministerial supply of German-preaching pastors.

B. Our American congregations should furnish far more sons of German families for the bi-lingual service of the Church and should hold them in this service.

C. Our theological seminaries should give increased attention to the education of such students and should provide instruction in German Homiletics and Catechetics.

Our colleges should lay greater emphasis upon a thorough education in the German language, knowledge of which must be considered indispensable for every Lutheran theologian.

D. We state with regret that our American congregations do not give us young men in sufficient numbers who are qualified for this service; further that such students do not receive the special training in our institutions which they require; and that this important missionary work of the Church in the bi-lingual ministry does not attract our present theological youth.

E. It is, therefore, necessary for the United Lutheran Church to secure and train ministers for this service from Germany, alongside of those trained in our American institutions. Such students should have the opportunity to acquaint themselves, if possible at one designated institution, with the language of the country, the history and life of our American Lutheran Church and with general conditions. Special courses adapted to their peculiar needs are recommended .

At various times during the biennium the Committee was called upon to confer with the Board of Education on the question of providing for the passage and support of graduates from our Breklum-Kropp Seminary in Germany who are granted a two years' additional training course in some American seminary.

To the Board of Inner Missions the Committee suggested the publication and distribution of a Church-Guide for immigrants and the publication of special pamphlets concerning our Lutheran churches in large metropolitan centers.

To the Board of Publication the Committee suggested the establishment of a well-equipped department of German devotional literature in connection with our Publication House at Philadelphia.

A sub-committee for a revision of the German form of Occasional Services had been appointed by the Committee on Common Service Book and met with a similar committee appointed by this committee on December 27, 1927, at Philadelphia. The vacancy on this committee created by the death of Dr. George C. F. Haas was filled by the appointment of the Rev. Siegmund von Bosse. Dr. Strodach and Pastor Otto Kleine were designated a special committee to work out and submit a desirable form of the Occasional Services.

The official German weekly of the United Lutheran Church, "Lutherischer Herold," and the annual year book, "Der Lutherische Kalender," received due attention on the part of the committee.

A model constitution for the use of German congregations of the United Lutheran Church was prepared by the committee and submitted for approval to the Executive Board.

Pastor Theodore Posselt was delegated as visitor to the 1927 Convention of the German Nebraska Synod. The committee intends to gain closer contacts with the German synods in the West by such visitations. Dr. Ernst A. Tappert was in attendance as a guest at the sessions of the Allgemeine Lutherische Konferenz, held in Marburg, Germany, in September, 1927.

The task which your committee is facing is by no means an easy one. Into its sphere of thought and operation practically every activity of the United Lutheran Church is brought. It is to serve as a mediator to work for a better understanding of German issues and needs. It offers itself as a clearing house for any and all agencies of the Church wherever their work touches upon questions affecting the German portion of the Church. It stands in need of the sympathy and the intercession of the entire Church, if it is to accomplish its great and important mission.

H. Offermann, *Chairman.*
F. O. Evers, *Secretary.*

The Rev. Wm. Freas presented the report of the Committee on Army and Navy work.

REPORT OF THE COMMITTEE ON ARMY AND NAVY WORK

Your Committee, appointed after the Richmond Convention, was organized by a mail vote of the members of the Committee. The following were elected as officers and Executive Committee:

Rev. C. D. Trexler, Chairman; Rev. Wm. Freas, D.D., Secretary and Treasurer; Mr. Charles H. Dahmer. Rev. S. T. Nicholas, D. D., was elected as Washington representative.

Members of this Committee were appointed separately as members of the General Committee on Army and Navy Chaplains of the Federal Council. This Committee held frequent meetings, a few of them combined with conferences of special interest. At these meetings one or more of the Committee were present. Among the Conferences was one called by Secretary of War, Dwight F. Davis, where the intensification of the program for moral and religious instruction and guidance was the item of chief importance. Your Committee has held no meeting during the biennium, the work being done through the Executive Committee.

I. REGULAR CHAPLAINS

The Lutheran Church has six Chaplains in the Army. Of these, three are members of the United Lutheran Church in America. In the Navy we have two Chaplains, one of them a member of the United Lutheran Church in America. One application for Army Chaplaincy is in our hands at this time. The Lutheran Church is given a quota of eight Chaplains. As vacancies occur, the effort to secure pastors for such vacancies will be made. During the biennium, one application for Naval Chaplaincy was presented to your Committee and approved by it. The Navy Department felt it necessary to refuse the application, due to a slight physical disability. It was made clear that this was the only cause for failure to appoint.

Our Chaplains remain to a large degree out of touch with the Church. In two instances this was caused by foreign service. In the other instances, the posts of the men were situated where little contact with the Church was possible.

Many Synods and the government make no provision for payment of expenses of Chaplains in attending. their Synodical meetings. Unless the Synod cares to bear this expense, the Chaplains must attend at their own expense, or remain away. Distance from place of Synod meeting often makes the expense of attending prohibitive.

Vacancies in the Chaplaincy occur from time to time. If we can be ready to supply a candidate when the vacancy occurs, we would have the preference. It is difficult, however, to ask a man to wait such an opportunity with the uncertainty affecting his work as a regular pastor.

The standards for Chaplaincy are being raised. The Departments are reluctant to take anything but our best men. The Church also has a pride in being well represented in this service. The position of Chaplains is being slowly bettered, but inequalities between this and other branches of the military service still continue.

II. RESERVE CHAPLAINS

During the biennium, your Committee has investigated and approved for appointment to the Reserve Chaplains' Corps eleven men. Of this number, seven are members of the United Lutheran Church in America. The total of Lutheran Reserve Chaplains under appointment is now seventy-one; thirty-seven of this number are of our branch of the Lutheran Church.

III. GENERAL MATTERS

Chaplain J. A. St. Clair still is busy at Maywood, Ill., Hospital. He is inadequately supported. The Norwegian Lutheran Church, from the fund returned to it by the National Lutheran Commission for Soliders and Sailors Welfare, has contributed towards his support. His salary has been supplemented by funds secured by a few interested laymen in the Middle West and the Ministerial Association of Chicago. Your Committee has been making efforts to increase the interest in his work,

An item of unusual interest to the Church is the retirement of Col. Axton as Chief of Chaplains. Chaplain Axton has been most gracious in his relations with your Committee and it is with keen regret that we realize the necessity of his retirement . He has been succeeded by Col. Easterbrook, who has already shown a delightful spirit in our relations. Upon his retirement, Chaplain Axton was appropriately honored, in which your Committee had a part.

Requests for the medals issued by the National Lutheran Commission still come to us. These are being supplied as asked for. Inquiries for the Army and Navy Service Book have been frequent. Such requests come particularly from Reserve Corps Chaplains, although some individuals make such requests. Unfortunately, they can no longer be supplied.

A few names of Lutheran soldiers and sailors have been received. To them have been sent copies of a former series of the "Message for the Day," supplied by the Inner Mission Board.

Local pastors still continue to serve at certain posts where no Chaplains are assigned. For many of these points nothing can be done, as they are far removed from any of our congregations.

Respectfully submitted,

Wm. Freas, *Secretary.*

Charles D. Trexler, *Chairman,*

The Rev. Paul E. Scherer presented the report of the Committee on Conference with the Y. M. C. A.

REPORT OF THE COMMITTEE ON THE YOUNG MEN'S CHRISTIAN ASSOCIATION

Since the Convention at Richmond two meetings of the General Counselling Commission of the Churches have been held in New York City, November 18, 1926, and November 3, 1927. Twenty-one churches were represented on the Commission, nineteen having appointed standing committees. The meeting in November, 1926, was devoted largely to a discussion of the data arrived at in the study of Church and Association relations in the two hundred cities of from 5,000 to 25,000 population. A report of this study as it touched upon the relations of our own communion with the Y. M. C. A. was made by your committee at the last Convention. Complete information with accompanying graphs is available through the committee. Only one item in detail can be included in this statement. In two hundred cities it was discovered that the 540 Association Secretaries either belong to local churches or are in process of transfer, and hold 823 service positions in addition to their professional activities. This was brought out in order to throw light on the attitude of the leaders of the organized Y. M. C. A. toward the churches. It was suggested that all such material in the hands of commissioners be sent upon request to professors in theological seminaries who might wish to make use of it in connection with their lectures on modern Church and Inter-Church Movements. Meanwhile presentations of policy and program have been made by Association Secretaries before a number of national church bodies, some of which have passed resolutions favorable to the further development of co-operative relations. In local fields there has been actual co-operation in Evangelism, in the development of weekday religious instruction, in the promotion of recreational groups, and in Christian Citizenship Training Programs. Local, regional, and state conferences between Church and Association leaders have been encouraged wherever and whenever the churches have desired them.

The meeting in November, 1927, concerned itself chiefly with the subject of existing co-operation between the Church and Y. M. C. A. in the field of recreational activity. In brief, it was shown that the 186 city associations responding gave definite co-operation with 3,327 local churches, with 131,453 different boys and men, women and girls, participating. The use of the Y. M. C. A, equipment by church groups under church name and leadership seemed to be rapidly increasing, though an astonishing number of churches were providing their own gymnasiums. One hundred and sixteen associations reported that 186 physical directors were office holders in their own churches, occupying 239 working positions, aside from their specific activities as secretaries of the association. One of the greatest difficulties encountered was in the attempt to evaluate the results of this co-operation in the development of social and religious attitudes, though a considerable number of associations reported improvement in Church and Bible School attendance, in social attitudes and in citizenship, in many cases giving evidence. Local churches were urged to acquaint themselves with what the association has to offer in leadership, equipment and program.

Your Committee has no recommendations to offer, except that wherever further information is desired application be made through the chairman. Articles with regard to the Commission's work will continue to appear in *The Lutheran* from time to time.

Respectfully submitted,
PAUL E. SCHERER, *For the Committee.*

The Secretary presented the report of the Committee on Transportation.

REPORT OF COMMITTEE ON TRANS-PORTATION

This Committee has functioned in the usual way throughout the biennium. The Rev. John M. Bramkamp, D.D., of Chicago, has rendered very efficient service in the capacity of Western Secretary of Transportation. The Chairman of the Committee and the Secretary of the United Lutheran Church have performed similar services for the eastern lines of railway.

The usual concessions have been secured from the several Passenger Associations whereby reduced rates, under the Certificate Plan, have been made available for those attending this Convention. Mr. Harvey C. Miller, who has served as a committee on validation of Certificates since the organization of the United Lutheran Church, has also kindly undertaken that service for the present Convention.

Respectfully submitted,
HARVEY C. MILLER, *Chairman.*
M. G. G. SCHERER, *Secretary.*

The following resolution was adopted:

Resolved, That our Committee on Transportation, especially its officers, be authorized to represent the United Lutheran Church in America in all arrangements with the railroads in accordance with the regulations of the Interstate Commerce Commission, and to certify to those for whom free transportation may be asked.

The Rev. Luther D. Reed asked the privilege of filing the report of the Archivist. The privilege was granted; the report to be printed in the Minutes.

REPORT OF THE ARCHIVIST

The Archivist reports the receipt of the official correspondence of the President and Secretary of the United Lutheran Church for the years 1922-1924;

Also the necrology reports, 1920-1926;

Also miscellaneous minutes of Synod and historical and other souvenir programs of various congregations.

In addition a large number of obituary notices of ministers and prominent laymen have been clipped from the church papers, mounted and arranged.

Respectfully submitted,
LUTHER D. REED, *Archivist.*

The Rev. John F. Fedders presented the report of the Committee on Leave of Absence.

REPORT OF THE COMMITTEE ON LEAVE OF ABSENCE

Your Committee rejoices in the attendance of 270 clerical and 239 lay delegates out of a possible attendance of 271 clerical and 269 lay delegates elected to this Convention.

Eighteen delegations report 100 per cent attendance. The Synod of West Virginia and the Texas Synod report all delegates present at all sessions. The presence of two delegates from our Church in the Andhra country, India, is a source of special rejoicing.

Upon recommendation of the chairmen of synodical delegations we recommend that the following be excused for absence:

Synod of New York: Rev. R. J. Van Deusen, Rev. H. H. Wahl, Mr. F. E. Oberlander, Mr. H. K. Hess, Rev. A. S. Hardy, D.D., Rev. L. H. Grandy, Mr. A. Hayner, Mr. A. S. Larson, Rev. C. P. Jensen, Dr. H. C. Yeckel, Rev. A. L. Dillenbeck, Rev. E. J. Flanders.

Wartburg Synod: Mr. A. J. Ruppel.

Illinois Synod: Mr. C. J. Driever, Mr. C. W. Howe.

Rocky Mountain Synod: Mr. A. E. Johnson.

Iowa Synod: Mr. John L. Berger.

Indiana Synod: Rev. J. C. Waltz, Rev. J. Earl Spaid.

Michigan Synod: Mr. J. E. Landenberger, Mr. C. W. Kantz.

Nebraska Synod: Mr. Karl E. Vogel, Rev. O. D. Baltzly, D.D.

Pittsburgh Synod: Rev. M. R. Kunkelman, Mr. J. A. Hill

Nova Scotia Synod: Mr. Douglas Conrad.

South Carolina Synod: Mr. W. A. Rast, Prof. S. J. Derrick, Prof. J. C. Kinard.

North Carolina Synod: Hon. B. B. Miller, Prof. H. L. Mock, Hon. A. L. Starr.

Northwest Synod: Mr. J. K. Jensen, Mr. J. W. Jouno, Mr. F. W. Peschau, Rev. A. A. Zinck, D.D.

Allegheny Synod: Rev. F. S. Schultz, Mr. C. L. Shaver, Dr. G. G. Harman, Mr. C. R. Bossler, Mr. Harry Shaffer.

West Pennsylvania Synod: Mr. G. W. Hafer.

Synod of Virginia: Mr. F. B. Walters, Mr. J. S. Dix.

Ministerium of New York: Rev. C. Betz, Mr. L. Henrich.

Ministerium of Pennsylvania: Hon. Claude T. Reno, Rev. H. E. Jacobs, D.D., Rev. C. M. Jacobs, D.D.; Mr. J. F. Henninger, Mr. R. H. Schatz, Rev. W. A. Fluck, Rev. H. F. Miller, Rev. J. H. Harms, D.D.

German Synod of Nebraska: Rev. F. Bahr, D.D.

Respectfully submitted,
JOHN F. FEDDERS, <i>Chairman.</i>
WILLIAM C. DRACH, <i>Secretary.</i>

The recommendation of the Committee was adopted.

The Rev. A. R. Wentz presented the Minutes of the Lutheran Historical Society.

MINUTES OF THE LUTHERAN HISTORICAL SOCIETY

Erie, Pa., October 16, 1928.

The Society was called to order by President Manhart.

The Rev. W. A. Wade was appointed Secretary pro tem.

The report of Professor A. R. Wentz, the Curator, was read and adopted, as follows:

The work of the Curator during the past biennium has been mostly routine. No special projects have been undertaken. The collection of materials has continued to grow normally and during the biennium has been consulted by many students of our Lutheran history. The work of gathering, binding, and cataloging the files of materials has gone on apace.

The report of the Treasurer, Mr. J. E. Musselman, was presented and adopted, showing a balance of $197.93 to meet the needs of the next biennium.

The amendments to the Constitution of the Society, proposed at the meeting in Richmond, October 22, 1926 (see Minutes of the U. L. C. A. for 1926, page 643), were adopted, making the Society an auxiliary of the United Lutheran Church alone.

The following officers were elected:

President—Rev. Prof. F. P. Manhart, D.D., LL.D.

Vice-Presidents—Mr. H. M. M. Richards, Litt.D.; Rev. W. J. Finck, D.D.

Curator—Rev. Prof. A. R. Wentz, Ph.D., D.D.

Secretary—Rev. Prof. H. C. Alleman, D.D

Treasurer—Mr. J. Elmer Musselman.

Extra Members of the Executive Committee—Rev. Pres. G. Morris Smith and Rev. Prof. H. D. Hoover, Ph.D., D.D., S.T.D.

The minutes were read and approved.

WILLIAM A. WADE, *Secretary pro tem.*

The Secretary presented the report of the Lutheran Church Book and Literature Society.

REPORT OF LUTHERAN CHURCH BOOK AND LITERATURE SOCIETY

For the Year 1927

Since its institution the Society has furnished, free of cost to the recipients, the following:

The Church Book and the Common Service Book

To 156 mission congregations in the United States, Canada, and the West Indies	4,405 copies
To 15 institutions	320 copies
Total copies so furnished	4,725

The Sunday School Book

To 60 mission congregations or Sunday schools	2,004 copies
To one institution	50 copies
Total copies so furnished	2,054

The Lutheran

To free libraries in Philadelphia, New York City, Brooklyn and elsewhere, 500 yearly subscriptions.

To a limited extent the Society has also furnished where needed Catechisms, Tracts, the Army and Navy Service Book and miscellaneous books.

During 1927 the service of the Society was limited on account of lack of funds, and we were able to respond to only two applications as follows:

Camp Miller, Delaware Water Gap, 50 copies Common Service Book.
Northwest College, Watertown, Wis., one copy Common Service Book.

During 1927 we furnished 38 yearly subscriptions to *The Lutheran* to free libraries.

M. L. HOLLOWAY, *Secretary.*

The Secretary read the recommendation concerning the reception of the Florida Synod (Executive Board's Report, III, B, 5). The recommendation was adopted by a rising vote.

Moved and carried, to authorize the Executive Board to arrange for the printing of the Minutes.

Moved and carried, That the Executive Board have power to approve the Minutes of Tuesday's sessions.

After prayer by the Rev. A. B. Leamer, the Convention was closed at 6:10 P. M. with the Order for the Closing of Synods.

M. G. G. SCHERER, *Secretary.*

LIST OF BOARDS AND ELECTIVE COMMITTEES

1. Executive Board.
2. Commission of Adjudication.
3. Board of Foreign Missions.
4. Board of American Missions.
5. Board of Northwestern Missions.
6. Immigrants Mission Board.
7. West Indies Mission, Board.
8. Board of Education.
9. Inner Mission Board.
10. Board of Publication.
11. Board of Ministerial Pensions and Relief.
12. Parish and Church School Board.
13. Board of Deaconess Work.
14. National Lutheran Home for the Aged.
15. Committee on Church Papers.
16. Executive Committee of the Laymen's Movement.

LIST OF STANDING COMMITTEES, COMMISSIONS, ETC.

1. Statistical and Church Year Book Committee.
2. Committee on Common Service Book.
3. Committee on Church Music.
4. Committee on German Interests.
5. Committee on Lutheran Brotherhoods.
6. Committee on Women's Work.
7. Committee on Associations of Young People.
8. Committee on Army and Navy Work.
9. Committee on Moral and Social Welfare.
10. Committee on Evangelism.
11. Committee on Church Architecture.
12. Committee on Publicity.
13. Committee on Transportation.
14. Necrologist.
15. Archivist.
16. Such other Standing Committees as may be provided for from time to time.

SPECIAL COMMITTEES

1. Committee to Conduct the opening and Closing Services of Each Session.
2. Committee on Leave of Absence.
3. Committee on Proceedings of District Synods.
4. Committee of Reference and Counsel.
5. Committee to Nominate Executive Committee of Laymen's Movement.
6. Committee to Nominate Members of Boards.
7. Committee to Nominate Members of Executive Board and all Elective Commissions or Committees.
8. Committee of Tellers.

BOARDS AND ELECTIVE COMMITTEES
EXECUTIVE BOARD

President—Rev. F. H. Knubel, D.D., L.L.D., 39 East Thirty-fifth Street, New York City.

Secretary—Rev. M. G. G. Scherer, D.D., 39 East Thirty-fifth Street, New York City.

Treasurer—E. Clarence Miller, LL.D., 1508 Walnut Street, Philadelphia, Pa.

Term Expires 1932

Rev. A. C. R. Keiter; Rev. Charles D. Trexler; Rev. A. R. Wentz, D.D., Ph.D.; Hon. Wm. E. Hirt; Hon. John F. Kramer; George E. Neff, Esq.

Term Expires 1930

Rev. Ellis B. Burgess, D.D.; Rev. W. H. Greever, D.D.; Rev. A. H. Smith, D.D.; Mr. John Greiner, Jr; B. B. Miller, Esq.; Mr. W. H. Stackel.

COMMISSION OF ADJUDICATION

President—Rev. H. E. Jacobs, D.D., LL.D., S.T.D., 7301 Germantown Avenue, Mt. Airy, Philadelphia, Pa.

Vice-President—Rev. Luther Kuhlman, D.D., 106 Carlisle Street, Gettysburg, Pa.

Secretary—Rev. R. E. Tulloss, Ph.D., D.D., Wittenberg College, Springfield, Ohio.

Clerk—Hon. E. K. Strong, Columbia City, Ind.

Term Expires 1934

Rev. George Gebert, D.D.; Rev. A. G. Voigt, D.D. LL.D.; Hon. E. K. Strong.

Term Expires 1932

Rev Luther Kuhlman, D.D.; Rev. W. F. Rangeler, D.D.; Hon. C. M. Efird, LL.D.

Term Expires 1930

Rev. H. E. Jacobs, D.D., LL.D., S.T.D.; Rev. R. E. Tulloss, Ph.D., D.D.; Hon. H. W. Harter.

BOARD OF FOREIGN MISSIONS

President—Rev. C. T. Benze, D.D., 7304 Boyer Street, Mt. Airy, Philadelphia, Pa.

Vice-President—Rev. J. E. Byers, D.D., 2900 Guilford Avenue, Baltimore, Md.

Executive Secretary—Rev. Paul W. Koller, D.D., 18 East Mt. Vernon Place, Baltimore, Md.

Recording Secretary—Rev. George Drach, D.D., 18 E. Mt. Vernon Place, Baltimore, Md.

Treasurer—Mr. Geo. R. Weitzel, York, Pa.

General Secretaries in Charge of Departments of Work—Rev. George Drach, D.D., Literature, India and Japan; Rev. L. B. Wolf, D.D., Home Base, China and South America; Rev. M. Edwin Thomas, D.D., Special Gifts and Africa.

Term Expires 1934

Rev. H. C. Brillhart, D.D.; Rev. J. E. Byers, D.D.; Rev. G. A. Greiss, D.D.; Rev. E. R. Jaxheimer; Mr. A. Y. Leech, Jr.; Paul Van Reed Miller, Esq.; Mr. W. A. Rast.

Term Expires 1932

Rev. Charles A. Dennig; Rev. S. W. Herman, D.D.; Rev. J. T. Huddle, D.D.; Rev. J. L. Sieber, D.D.; Mr. Martin H. Buehler; Mr. Charles H. Dahmer; Mr. William H. Menges.

Term Expires 1930

Rev C. T. Benze, D.D.; Rev. R. C. G. Bielinski; Rev. G. Albert Getty, D.D.; Rev. J. L Morgan, D.D.; Rev. H. W. Snyder, D.D.; Prof. C. W. Foss; Mr. James M. Snyder.

Co-operating Members—Rev. L. G. Abrahamson, D.D.; Rev. G. A. Brandelle, D.D.; Rev. V. W. Bondo; Rev. E. R. Anderson.

Advisory Members—Mrs. S. R. Kepner; Mrs. J. W. Richards.

BOARD OF AMERICAN MISSIONS

President—Rev. J. B. Markward, D.D., 914 N. Fountain Avenue, Springfield, Ohio.

Vice-President—Rev. H. W. A. Hanson, D.D., LL.D., Gettysburg, Pa.

Secretary—Mr. Grant Hultberg, 1228 Spruce Street, Philadelphia, Pa.

Treasurer—Rev. Zenan M. Corbe, D.D., 39 East Thirty-fifth Street, New York City.

Executive Secretary—Rev. F. F. Fry, D.D., 39 East Thirty-fifth Street, New York City.

Divisional Secretary of English Missions—Rev. J. F. Seibert, D.D., 860 Cass Street, Chicago, Ill.

General Superintendents, Division of English Missions—Rev. Geo. H. Hillermann, D.D., 2505 Woolsey Street, Berkeley, Calif.; Rev. A. D. R. Hancher, D.D., 139 E. Monroe Street, Jacksonville, Fla.; Rev. I. Chantry Hoffman, D.D., 319 E. Walnut Lane, Philadelphia, Pa.

General Superintendents, Division of Linguistic Interests—Rev. Paul Ludwig, 860 Cass Street, Chicago, Ill. (German); Rev. A. L. Ramer, Ph.D., 30 S. Jefferson Street, Allentown, Pa. (Slovak-Hungarian); Rev. V. Koivumaki, 232 E. Conan Street, Ely, Minn. (Finnish).

Departmental Secretary of Church Extension and Finance—Rev. Zenan M. Corbe, D.D., 39 East Thirty-fifth Street, New York City.

Term Expires 1934

Rev. A. E. Bell, D.D.; Rev. C. A. Freed, D.D.; Rev. G. K.

Rubrecht, D.D.; Rev. J. C. Seegers, D.D.; Mr. A. H. Durboraw; Mr. Wm. Eck; Mr. S. F. Telleen.

Term Expires 1932

Rev. F. O. Evers; Rev. J. M. Francis, D.D.; Rev. George Gebert, D.D.; Rev. L. H. Larimer, D.D.; Mr. W. E. Black; Mr. W. L. Glatfelter; Mr. H. F. Heuer.

Term Expires 1930

Rev. G. A. Benze, D.D.; Rev. H. W. A. Hanson, D.D.; LL.D.; Rev. J. B Markward, D.D.; Rev. J. Maurer, D.D.; Mr. A. Raymond Bard; Mr. Grant Hultberg; Mr. H. L. Snyder.

Advisory Members—Miss Flora Prince; Mrs. P. M. Rossman.
Representatives on Divisional Committees—Mrs. T. W. Kretschmann; Miss Flora Prince; Mrs. P. M. Rossman.

BOARD OF NORTHWESTERN MISSIONS
Term Expires 1934

Rev. A. E. Bell, D.D.; Rev. C. A. Freed, D.D.; Rev. G. K. Rubrecht, D.D.; Rev. J. C. Seegers, D.D.; Mr. A. H. Durboraw; Mr. Wm. Eck; Mr. S. F. Teleen.

Term Expires 1932

Rev. S. G. R. von Bosse; Rev. F. O. Evers; Rev. M. Koolen, D.D.; Rev. G. H. Michelmann; Mr. Henry S. Albers, Sr; Mr. Aug. Becker; Mr. W. L. Glatfelter.

Term Expires 1930

Rev. G. A. Benze, D.D.; Rev. Emil C. J. Kraeling; Rev. J. B. Markward, D.D.; Rev. J. Maurer, D.D.; Rev. H. D. E. Siebott; Mr. Grant Hultberg; Mr. Carl Hausmann.

IMMIGRANTS MISSION BOARD
Term Expires 1934

Rev. A. E. Bell, D.D.; Rev. C. A. Freed, D.D.; Mr. Wm. Eck; Mr. S. F. Telleen

Term Expires 1932

Rev S. N. Carpenter, D.D.; Rev. George H. Rhodes; Mr. Frank L. Fox; Mr. Jacob Umlauf.

Term Expires 1930

Rev. W. H. Rehrig, Ph.D.; Rev. F. E. Jensen; Mr. S. E. Long; Mr. H. E. Young.

WEST INDIES MISSION BOARD

President—Rev H. W. A. Hanson, D.D., LL.D.
Secretary—Mr. H. F. Heuer.

Term Expires 1934

Rev. A. E. Bell, D.D.; Rev. C. A. Freed, D.D.; Rev. G. K. Rubrecht, D.D.; Rev. J. C. Seegers, D.D.; Mr. A. H. Durboraw; Mr. Wm. Eck; Mr. S. F. Telleen.

Term Expires 1932

Rev. J. A. Eckstrom, B.D.; Rev. F. O. Evers; Rev. H. T. Weiskotten, Ph.D.; Rev. J. A. Weyl; Mr James Gear; Mr. W. L. Glatfelter; Mr. I. Searless Runyon.

Term Expires 1930

Rev. F. H. Bosch; Rev. H. W. A. Hanson, D.D., LL.D; Rev. J. B. Markward, D.D.; Rev. J. H. Meyer, D.D.; Mr. H. F. Heuer; Mr. Grant Hultberg; Mr. H. L. Snyder.

BOARD OF EDUCATION

President—Rev. A. Steimle, D.D.; 174 West Ninety-third Street, New York City.

Vice-President—Prof. Hugo C. M. Wendel, Ph.D., University Heights, New York University, New York City.

Recording Secretary—Rev. W. M. Horn, D.D., 111 Oak Avenue, Ithaca, N. Y.

Treasurer—Mr. John M. Snyder, Elkins Park, Pa.

Secretaries—

College: Rev. C. S. Bauslin, D.D., 212 Evangelical Building, Harrisburg, Pa.

University Students: Rev. C. P. Harry, 210 W. Fornance Street, Norristown, Pa.

Women Students: Miss Mary E. Markley, Litt.D.; Miss Mildred Winston, 39 East Thirty-fifth Street, New York City.

Term Expires 1934

Rev. E. C. Herman, D.D.; Rev. A. J. Holl, D.D.; Rev. Wm. M. Horn, D.D.; Rev. A. A. Zinck, D.D., S.T.D.; Mrs. Adelaide Burge; W. J. Showalter, Sc.D.; Hon. Charles Steele.

Term Expires 1932

Rev. Charles R. Bowers, D.D.; Rev. G. M. Diffenderfer, D.D.; Rev. Paul H. Krauss; Prof. Hugo C. M. Wendel, Ph.D.; Mr. J. H. Dingle; Mr. C. J. Driever; Ralph D. Owen, Ph.D.

Term Expires 1930

Rev. R. D. Clare, D.D.; Rev. William F. Hoppe, D.D.; Rev. E. P. Pfatteicher, D.D., Ph.D.; Rev A. Steimle, D.D.; Prof. R. S. Saby, Ph.D.; Mr. J. L. Clark; Glenn M. Cummings, Esq.

Avisory Members—From Women's Missionary Society: Mrs. W. F. Morehead, Miss Jennie M. Strevig. From Augustana Synod: Rev. George M. Stephenson, Ph.D.

INNER MISSION BOARD

President—Rev. E. F. Bachman, D.D., 2100 South College Avenue, Philadelphia, Pa.

Vice-President—Rev. F. B. Clausen, 281 Prospect Avenue, Brooklyn, N. Y.

Executive Secretary and Treasurer—Rev. William Freas, D.D., 39 East Thirty-fifth Street, New York City.

Secretary for Immigrant Work—Rev. E. A. Sievert, 218 Seventh Avenue, New York City.

Term Expires 1934

Rev. F. B. Clausen, Rev. J. F. Fedders, D.D.; Rev. j. S. Schantz; Mr. A. H. Durboraw; W. J. Showalter, Sc.D.

Term Expires 1932

Rev. H. Brueckner, D.D.; Rev. S. E. Greenawalt, D.D.; Rev. J. J. Scherer, Jr., D.D.; Mr. Robert F Bowe; Harry C Hoffman, M.D.

Term Expires 1930

Rev. E. F. Bachmann, D.D.; Rev. W. H. Bruce Carney, D.D.; Rev. Walter Krumwiede; Mr. James Gear; Mr. G. B. Morehead.

BOARD OF PUBLICATION

President—Hon. E. F. Eilert, C.S.D., 318 West Thirty-ninth Street, New York City.

Vice-President—Rev. C. M. Jacobs, D.D., 7335 Germantown Avenue, Philadelphia, Pa.

Secretary—Rev. N. R. Melhorn, D.D., Litt.D., 1228 Spruce Street, Philadelphia, Pa.

Treasurer—Mr. John M. Snyder, Elkins Park, Pa.

Business Manager—Mr. Grant Hultberg, 1228 Spruce Street, Philadelphia, Pa.

Term Expires 1934

Rev. H. C. Alleman, D.D.; Rev. A. H. Holthusen, Ph.D.; Rev. G. W. Nicely, D.D.; Mr. Croll Keller; Mr. J. C. Lynch; Mr. Otto W. Osterlund; Mr. D. F. Yost.

Term Expires 1932

Rev. Henry Anstadt, D.D.; Rev. Stanley Billheimer, D.D.; Rev. John W. Horine, D.D.; Rev. C. M. Jacobs, D.D.; Charles Baum, M.D.; Mr. John M. Snyder; Mr. M. P. Moller, Jr.

Term Expires 1930

Rev. F. P. Manhart, D.D.; Rev. N. R. Melhorn, D.D., Litt.D.; Rev. C. F. Steck, D.D; Mr Kenneth Baker; Mr. George D. Boschen; F. Wm. Capplemann, Esq.; Hon. E. F. Eilert, C.S.D.

BOARD OF MINISTERIAL PENSIONS AND RELIEF

President—Mr. Paul F. Myers, E. Melrose Street, Chevy Chase, Md.

Vice-President—Rev. M. H. Valentine, D.D., Gettysburg, Pa.

Executive Secretary—Mr. Harry Hodges, 1228 Spruce Street, Philadelphia, Pa.

Treasurer—Mr. Peter P. Hagan, Kensington Avenue and Butler Street, Philadelphia, Pa.

Term Expires 1934

Rev. Otto Kleine; Mr. A. Raymond Bard; Mr. J. L. Fisher; Hon. Henry W. Harter; Mr. M. P. Moller, Sr.

Term Expires 1932

Mr. Peter P. Hagan; Mr. J. Elsie Miller; Mr. Paul F. Myers; Mr. William F. Schneider; Mr. A. F. Sittloh.

Term Expires 1930

Rev. C. L. Miller, D.D.; Rev. Ross H. Stover, D.D.; Rev. M. H. Valentine, D.D.; Mr. George P. Tustin; Mr. J. Harvey Wattles. *Advisory Members*—Mrs. J. G. Traver; Mrs. L. K. Sanford.

PARISH AND CHURCH SCHOOL BOARD

President—Rev. F. M. Urich, D.D., 2336 South Eighteenth Street, Philadelphia, Pa.

Vice-President — Rev. F. R. Knubel, 1225 Park Avenue, Rochester, N. Y.

Secretary—Rev. William L. Hunton, Ph.D., D.D., 1228 Spruce Street, Philadelphia, Pa.

Treasurer—George M. Jones, Esq., 52 North Fourth Street, Reading, Pa.

Field Secretaries—Rev. D. Burt Smith, D.D., 210 East Durham Street, Philadelphia, Pa.; Rev. Charles H. B. Lewis, D.D., 748 Military Avenue, Fremont, Nebr.; Rev. S. White Rhyne, Box 171, Charlotte, N. C.

Term Expires 1934

Rev. P. D. Brown, D.D.; Rev. A. J. Turkle, D.D.; Rev. F. M. Urich, D.D.; Mr. Grant Hultberg

Term Expires 1932

Rev J. D. M. Brown, Litt.D.; Rev. M. Hadwin Fischer, Ph.D., Th.D.; Rev. F. R. Knubel; George M. Jones, Esq.

Term Expires 1930

Rev. William L. Hunton, Ph.D., D.D.; Rev. T. B. Birch, Ph.D., D.D.; Rev. Charles F. Dapp, Ph.D.; Prof. Gilbert P. Voigt.

BOARD OF DEACONESS WORK

President—Rev. William A. Wade, D.D., 505 Harwood Avenue, Baltimore, Md.

Vice-President—Rev. J. F. Ohl, D.D., Mus.D., 826 South St. Bernard Street, Philadelphia, Pa.

Secretary—Rev. Charles E. Hay, D.D., 2500 West North Avenue, Baltimore, Md.

Treasurer—Mr. Pearre E. Crowl, Greenway Apartments, Thirty-fourth and Charles Streets, Baltimore, Md.

Term Expires 1934

Rev. Earl J. Bowman; Rev. U. S. G. Rupp, D.D.; Rev. W. C. Schaeffer, Jr., D.D.; Prof. J. C. Kinard; Mr. Frederick H. Wefer.

Term Expires 1932

Rev. George N. Lauffer, D.D.; Rev. William A. Wade, D.D.; Mr. Pearre E. Crowl; Mr. I. Searles Runyon; Edgar W. Young, Esq.

Term Expires 1930

Rev. E. F. Bachmann, D.D.; Rev. J. F. Crigler, D.D.; Rev. J. F. Ohl, D.D., Mus.D; Hon J. D. Cappelmann; Mr. F. C. Hassold.

Advisory Members—Sister Julia Megner; Mrs. W. P. M. Braun; Mrs. James P. Reese.

NATIONAL LUTHERAN HOME FOR THE AGED

President—Rev. John Weidley, D.D., 233 Second Street, S. E. Washington, D. C.

Vice-President—Rev. J. E. Harms, D.D., Hagerstown, Md.

Recording Secretary—Rev. Richard Schmidt, D.D., 308 Buchanan Street, N. W., Washington, D. C.

Corresponding Secretary—Mr. William H. Finckel, 918 F Street, N. W., Washington, D. C.

Treasurer—Harry T. Domer, Litt.D., 727 Fifteenth Street, N. W., Washington, D. C.

Rev. Henry Anstadt, D.D.; Rev. O. F. Blackwelder; Rev. J. L. Frantz; Rev. J. E. Harms, D.D.; Rev. John T. Huddle, D.D.; Rev. Richard Schmidt, D.D.; Rev. H. E. Snyder; Rev. F. R. Wagner, D.D.; Rev. John Weidley, D.D.; Mr. L. Russell Alden; W. K. Butler, M.D.; Mr. F. E. Cunningham; Harry T. Domer, Litt.D.; Mr William H. Finckel; Mr. John H. Jones; Mr. F. W. Kakel; Mr. Harry L. Snyder.

COMMITTEE ON CHURCH PAPERS

Chairman—Rev. H. F. Offermann, D.D., 7206 Boyer Street, Mt. Airy, Philadelphia, Pa.

Secretary—Rev. E. P. Pfatteicher, D.D., Ph.D., 1228 Spruce Street, Philadelphia, Pa.

Term Expires 1934

Rev. W. H. Greever, D.D.; Rev. J. A. Leas, D.D.; Rev. H. F. Offermann, D.D.

Term Expires 1932

Rev. Henry Anstadt, D.D.; Rev. E. P. Pfatteicher, D.D., Ph.D.; Mr. I. Searles Runyon.

Term Expires 1930

Rev. John Aberly, D.D.; Rev. C. E. Gardner, D.D.; Wm. J. Showalter, Sc.D.

EXECUTIVE COMMITTEE OF THE LAYMEN'S MOVEMENT

Chairman—Mr. J. L. Clark, Ashland, Ohio.

Vice-Chairman—Mr. E. J. Young, Wadsworth, Ohio.

General Secretary—Mr. Arthur P. Black, Our Home Life Building, Washington, D. C.

Associate Secretaries—Mr. C. W. Herman Hess, 604½ Spruce Street, New Castle, Pa.; Mr. George L. Rinkliff, 222 West Euclid Avenue, Springfield, Ohio.

Mr. J. L. Clark; Mr. C. J. Driever; Mr. W. L. Glatfelter; Mr. Peter P. Hagan; E. Clarence Miller, LL.D.; Mr. Harvey C. Miller; Mr. P. A. Myers; W. J. Showalter, ScD.; Mr. E. J. Young.

STANDING COMMITTEES

Statistical and Church Year Book Committee

Rev. G. H. Schnur, D.D. (Convener), 709 East Eleventh Street, Erie, Pa.; Rev. G. L. Kieffer, D.D., Litt.D., 39 East Thirty-fifth Street, New York City, N. Y.; Rev. M. G. L. Rietz, D.D.; Rev. C. W. Cassell; Rev. J. D. Krout; Rev. C. J. Rockey, D.D.; Mr. Harry E. Pugh; Mr. W. Chester Hill; also Secretary of the United Lutheran Church in America (ex-officio).

Committee on Common Service Book

Rev. L. D. Reed, D.D.(Convener), 7204 Boyer Street, Mt. Airy, Philadelphia, Pa.; Rev. H. E. Jacobs, D.D., LL.D., S.T.D.; Rev. Rev. J. F. Ohl, Mus.D., D.D.; Rev. J. C. Mattes, D.D.; Rev. A. Steimle, D.D.; Rev. P. Z. Strodach, D.D.; Rev. M. G. G. Scherer, D.D.; Rev. M. L. Stirewalt, D.D.; Rev. E. E. Fischer, D.D.; Rev. C. W. Leitzell, D.D.; Rev. R. M. Smith, Ph.D., D.D.; Rev. W. E. Fischer, D.D.; Rev. G. A. Getty, D.D.; Rev. Paul J. Hoh; Rev. H. D. Hoover, D.D., Ph.D., S.T.D.

Committee on Church Music

Rev. J. F. Ohl, Mus.D., D.D. (Convener) 826 South St. Bernard Street, Philadelphia, Pa.; Rev. L. D. Reed, D.D.; Rev. H. K. Lantz; Rev. G. C. Rees, D.D.; Rev. E. F. Krauss, D.D.; Rev. E. A. Trabert; Rev. C. T. Benze, D.D.; Rev. J. D. Brown, Litt.D.; Mr. William Benbow; Mr. Harry A. Sykes; Mr. Ralph P. Lewars; Mr. Harold K. Marks; Mr. Henry F. Seibert; Prof. Frederick Lewis Bach, Mus.D.; Mr. Carl F. Pfatteicher, Ph.D.; Mr. Rob Roy Peery.

Committee on German Interests

Rev. H. Offermann, D.D. (Convener), 7206 Boyer Street, Mt. Airy, Philadelphia, Pa.; Rev. G. A. Benze, D.D.; Rev. J. L. Neve, D.D., D.Th.; Rev. F. E. Oberlander, D.D.; Rev. F. H. Bosch; Rev. F. O. Evers; Rev. J. A. Weyl; Rev. T. O. Posselt; Rev. S. G. R. von Bosse; Rev. E. A. Tappert, D.D.; Rev. O. Kleine; Rev. J. Reble; Rev. H. B. Stock, D.D.; Rev. P. Kirsch.

Corresponding Members—The Presidents of the German Nebraska, Manitoba, Texas and Wartburg Synods.

Committee on Lutheran Brotherhoods

Rev. D. A. Davy, D.D. (Covener), 5402 Magnolia Avenue, Chicago, Ill.; Hon. John L. Zimmerman, LL.D.; Rev. W. C. Schaeffer, D.D.; Rev. J. E. Heindel, D.D.; Mr. H. A. Kingsbury; Mr. G. Dalton Myers; Mr. Rodney T. Martinsen; Mr. G. M. Jones; Mr. William J. Bauerle; Mr. H. E. Isenhour; Mr. A. E. Albright; Mr. W. A. Hiltabidle; Mr. William B. Ahlgren; Mr. C. Obenhack; Mr. H. G. Walter.

Committee on Women's Work

Rev. A. H. Smith, D.D. (Convener), 259 Sandusky Street, Ashland, Ohio; Rev. F. A. Kahler, D.D.; Rev. W. H. Shepfer, D.D.; Rev. M. J. Bieber, D.D.; Rev. D. A. Davy, D.D.; Rev. S. J. McDowell, D.D.; Rev. D. Bruce Young.

Committee on Associations of Young People

Rev. H. C. Roehner, D.D. (Convener), 30 S. Mulberry Street, Mansfield, Ohio; Rev. L. H. Lesher, Rev. Oscar Blackwelder, D.D.; Rev. John Schmieder, Rev. U. E. Apple, D.D.; Mr. Ross E. Smith; Mrs. S. T. Peterson; Miss Eva Peeler; Rev. L. M. Kuhns, D.D., Litt.D.

Committee on Army and Navy Work

Rev. Charles D. Trexler (Convener), 7420 Fourth Avenue, Brooklyn, N. Y.; Rev. Wm. Freas, D.D.; Rev. P. F. Bloomhardt, Ph.D.; Rev. R. H. Gearhart; Rev. J. F. Fedders, D.D.; Rev. G. M. Diffenderfer, D.D.; Rev. Emil W. Weber; Mr. C. H. Dahmer; Mr. W. A. G. Lape.

Committee on Moral and Social Welfare

Rev. E. E. Fischer, D.D. (Convener), 7300 Boyer Street, Philadelphia, Pa.; Rev. L. S. Keyser, D.D.; Rev. E. C. Dinwiddie, D.D.; Rev. G. E. Hipsley, D.D.; Rev. J. H. Harms, D.D.; Rev. P. H. Heisey, Ph.D.; Rev. H. W. Tope, D.D.; Rev. W. H. Greever, D.D.; Rev. N. Willison, Litt.D.; Rev. W. A. Sadtler, Ph.D., D.D.

Corresponding Member.—Rev. G. Dorn.

Committee on Evangelism

Rev. J. C. Seegers, D.D. (Convener), 7301 Germantown Avenue, Philadelphia, Pa.; Rev. F. Wolford, D.D.; Rev. A. Pohlman, D.D., M.D.; Rev. P. W. Roth; Rev. E. A. Tappert, D.D.; Rev. John F. Crigler, D.D.; Rev. C. J. Rockey, D.D.; Rev. S. D. Daugherty, D.D.; Rev. Paul J. Hoh; Rev. W. C. Davis, D.D.; Mr. F. Stussy, Jr.

Committee on Church Architecture

Rev. J. F. Ohl, Mus.D., D.D. (Convener), 826 South St. Bernard Street, Philadelphia, Pa.; Rev. L. D. Reed, D.D.; Rev. E. F.

Krauss, D.D.; Rev. E. A. Trabert; Rev. G. H. Schnur, D.D.; Rev. H. S. Kidd; Rev. J. L. Deaton, Jr; Prof. Warren P. Laird, Sc.D.; Mr. Charles Z. Klauder; Mr. A. A. Ritcher; Mr. Albert F. Schenck; Mr. J. Horace Frank; Mr. Luther M. Leisenring; Mr. Charles Obenhack; Mr. Chas. A. Scheuringer.

Committee on Publicity

Rev. H. R. Gold (Convener), 282 Clove Road, New Rochelle, N. Y.; Rev. W. L. Hunton, Ph.D., D.D.; Rev. C. K. Fegley; Rev. M. L. Canup, D.D.; Rev. W. H. Greever, D.D.; Rev. C. L. Fry, D.D.; Rev. A. E. Wagner, D.D., Ph.D.; Rev. W. H. Stutts, D.D,; Rev. E. H. Delk, D.D.; Rev. H. Moehling, Jr.; Mr. William Showalter; Mr. Jesse R. Hildebrand.

Committee on Transportation

Mr. Harvey C. Miller (Convener), 319 Commercial Trust Building, Philadelphia, Pa.; Hon. E. F. Eilert, C.S.D.; Mr. W. H. Hager; Rev. J. M. Bramkamp, D.D., 860 Cass Street, Chicago, Ill., and the Secretary of the United Lutheran Church in America (ex-officio).

Necrologist

Rev. James F. Lambert, D.D., 415 Howertown Avenue, Catasauqua, Pa.

Archivist

Rev. L. D. Reed, D.D., 7204 Boyer Street, Mt. Airy, Philadelphia, Pa.

Statistical Secretary

Rev. G. L. Kieffer, D.D., Litt.D., 39 East Thirty-fifth Street, New York City, N. Y.

Commissioners to the National Lutheran Council

Rev. C. M. Jacobs, D.D. (Convener), 7335 Germantown Avenue, Mt. Airy, Philadelphia, Pa.; Rev. J. A. W. Haas, D.D., LL.D.; Rev. P. W. Koller, D.D.; Rev. C. A. Freed, D.D.; Rev. M. G. G. Scherer, D.D.; Rev. L. W. Steckel, D.D ; Hon. E. F. Eilert, C.S.D.; G. F. Greiner, Esq.

Representatives on the Advisory Committee of the American Bible Society

Rev. H. C. Alleman, D.D., Gettysburg, Pa.

Consultative Representatives to Commissions of the Federal Council of Churches

Administrative Committee—Rev. G. U. Wenner, D.D., LL.D., L.H.D., 355 East Nineteenth Street, New York City, N. Y.; Rev. A. Steimle, D.D.

Washington Committee—Rev. Wm. Freas, D.D., 39 East Thirty-fiifth Street, New York City, N. Y.; Rev. G. M. Diffenderfer, D.D.; Rev. Emil W. Weber.

Commission on International Justice and Good Will—Rev. E. P. Pfatteicher, Ph.D., D.D., 1228 Spruce Street, Philadelphia, Pa.; Rev. E. H. Delk, D.D.; Rev. L. B. Wolf, D.D.

Committee on Mercy and Relief—Rev. F. H. Knubel, D.D., LL.D., 39 East Thirty-fifth Street, New York City, N. Y.; Rev. A. J. Traver.

Committee on Conference with Y. M. C. A.

Rev. P. E. Scherer, D.D. (Chairman), 3 West Sixty-fifth Street, New York City, N. Y.; Mr. W. H. Hager; Robbin B. Wolf, Esq.

COMMITTEE TO PREPARE A STATEMENT CONCERNING RELATIONS OF CHURCH AND STATE

Rev. C. M. Jacobs, D.D., 7335 Germantown Avenue, Mt. Airy, Philadelphia, Pa.; Rev. J. A. W. Haas, D.D., LL.D.; Rev. A. R. Wentz, Ph.D., D.D.; Rev. F. K. Fretz, D.D.

COMMISSION TO STUDY AND REPORT ON THEOLOGICAL EDUCATION IN THE UNITED LUTHERAN CHURCH IN AMERICA

(To be appointed by the Executive Board.)

SPECIAL COMMISSION OF FIFTEEN CONCERNING BUDGET

(To act with Finance Committee of the Executive Board.)
Mr. Peter P. Hagan, 1103 Prospect Avenue, Melrose Park, Pa.;

Mr. Wm. H. Hager; Hon. E. F. Eilert, C.S.D.; Mr. Grant Hult-
berg; Mr. J. L. Clark; Mr. E. J. Young; Mr W. L. Glatfelter;
Hon. J. L. Zimmerman, LL.D.; Rev. E. P. Pfatteicher, Ph.D.,
D.D.; Rev. E. B. Burgess, D.D.; Rev. H. Brezing; Mr. Arthur P.
Black; Mr. Harvey C. Miller; Mr. Charles Steele; Mr. Horace
W. Bikle.

COMMISSION ON WORLD CONFERENCE ON FAITH AND ORDER

Rev. M. G. G. Scherer, D.D., 39 East Thirty-fifth Street, New
York City, N. Y.; Rev. A. Steimle, D.D.; Rev. W. H. Greever,
D.D.; Rev. Holmes Dysinger, D.D., LL.D.; Rev. John Aberly,
D.D.

COMMITTEE ON LUTHERAN CHURCH UNITY

(To be appointed by the Executive Board.)

COMMITTEE OF SEVEN ON INVESTMENT OF ENDOWMENTS

(To be appointed by the Executive Board.)

SPECIAL SOCIETIES

Historical Society of the Evangelical Lutheran Church in the United States of America

President—Rev. Prof. F. P. Manhart, D.D., LL.D.

Vice-Presidents—Mr. H. M. M. Richards, Litt.D.; Rev. W. J.
Finck, D.D.

Curator—Rev. Prof. A. R. Wentz, Ph.D., D.D.

Secretary—Rev. Prof. H. C. Alleman, D.D.

Treasurer—Mr. J. Elmer Musselman.

Extra Members of Executive Committee—Rev. Pres. G. Morris
Smith and Rev. Prof. H. D. Hoover, D.D., Ph.D., S.T.D.

Lutheran Church Book and Literary Society

Corresponding Secretary—Rev. J. S. Schantz.

Recording Secretary—Mr. M. L. Holloway.

Treasurer—Mr. C. F. Hassold.

INDEX